The
Creative Writing
Guide

POETRY,
LITERARY NONFICTION,
FICTION, AND DRAMA

Candace Schaefer
Rick Diamond
Tyler Junior College

 LONGMAN

An imprint of Addison Wesley Longman, Inc.

New York • Reading, Massachusetts • Menlo Park, California • Harlow, England
Don Mills, Ontario • Sydney • Mexico City • Madrid • Amsterdam

Senior Editor: Lisa Moore
Associate Editor: Lynn Huddon
Text Design: David Munger/DTC
Cover Design: Kay Petronio
Photo Researcher: Julie Tesser
Electronic Page Makeup: Karen Milholland/DTC
Printer and Binder: RR Donnelley & Sons Company
Cover Printer: The Lehigh Press, Inc.

For permission to use copyrighted material, grateful acknowledgment is made to the copyright holders on pages 429–430, which are hereby made part of the copyright page.

Library of Congress Cataloging-in-Publication Data

Schaefer, Candace.
    The creative writing guide : poetry, literary nonfiction, fiction,
and drama / Candace Schaefer, Rick Diamond.
       p.   cm.
    Includes bibliographical references (p.) and index.
    ISBN 0-321-01123-6
    1. Authorship.   2. Creative writing.   I. Diamond, Rick.
II. Title.
PN145.S26   1998
808'.02--dc21   97-41812
                                         CIP

Please visit our website at http://longman.awl.com

ISBN 0-321-01123-6

12345678910—DOC—00999897

To Erich, for your encouragement and devotion. You never complained, not once—even when I typed right through the Super Bowl party that we hosted. And to Zachary and Mary Beth, for your love and enthusiasm for life. You inspire me.

—C. S.

To Leslie, my soul-mate, who has supported me in the long process of writing this book and who never tires of hearing me rant about my latest great idea or project; and to my children, Alex and Caitlin, who were patient and gracious while Dad typed for hours on end. You are my joy.

—R. D.

CONTENTS

2. TECHNIQUES, GENRES, AND THE CRAFT OF WRITING   61

PREFACE

It has occurred to us that people have varying expectations regarding any activity, any class, any skill. And this is certainly true in a creative writing class. Some students want to write the Great American Novel. Some students want an easy class that doesn't require any math. Some students want to "find themselves." Some students have written whole novels, and some have only dreamed of writing anything at all. We like to have our students go around the room at the beginning of the first class session and introduce themselves by saying what they write and why they're in the class. It helps us all discover why we're on the writing journey.

One student began class some years ago by announcing, "I'm Bob. I like to read a lot. I've written seventeen pornographic novels, but I want to branch out—I was thinking I might want to write children's stories."

Well, all the instructor can say at that point is, "Let's get started."

As we have encouraged our student writers to think about why they are undertaking the journey of writing, we have learned about their needs. And the great majority of creative writing students we have worked with need a general-purpose text that helps them to think about their own creative process and introduces them to the major literary genres as they write.

For years we pirated exercises from peers and used different textbooks with varying success. Most of all we had to invent most of what worked in our classes and what best helped our students understand the writing process. Out of those years of effort this book has emerged. We have attempted to address student and aspiring writers' needs as they move along the writing path: (1) learning about writing as a means of discovery and expression, (2) studying and practicing literary genres with specifics and craft and exercises to explain and understand the genres, and (3) learning to revise and edit writing in order to share and publish it.

We hope that anyone interested in writing can find some practical help in this text—exercises to start the thinking and writing processes; information about how to put together a story, a poem, a scene, a memoir; and guidelines and advice about how to complete and polish one's writing. We think it's important for writers to explore the issue of what writing is *about*, what it feels like to be a writer and what "the writing life" can be. We try to present a balance between practical, nuts-and-bolts exercises and advice on the one hand, and literary theory and craft on the other. In this way, *The Creative Writing Guide* can meet the needs of writers coming from many different backgrounds, with different expectations, and with different skills and interests.

The Book's Structure

First, although the text is divided into three main parts, these parts don't necessarily correspond to the way the writing process actually works for a given writer. As any writer knows—or will discover—writing is often a confusing, organic, unorganized process of exploration. Writing is a process that has many components and works in many different ways and on many levels, sometimes all at once. A story may percolate in a writer's head for a year, a decade; it may jump forth all in one night's writing session; parts of it may be edited, revised, and completed in a few days, and other parts may take years to polish and rethink until the writer is satisfied.

However, it is often helpful when learning or working with a complex process to break it down into some of its parts and analyze and practice them. The overall sense of the organic creative experience must also be informed and guided by the use of technical tools and craft. We have taught in many different contexts—public and private universities and community colleges, community workshops, corporate seminars, prison classes, and elementary and high schools. And in all of those environments, it is consistently true that student writers do better when writing is seen as made up of understandable, manageable parts which can be studied, read about, practiced, and critiqued.

And, still, as much as we students and teachers of writing may try to analyze and define the process of writing, like any creative thing, it is sometimes simply a mystery. This text acknowledges and celebrates that wonderful magic which is part of the creative endeavor, and so presents both the mystery and the fundamentals.

Part 1—**Writing and Writing Practice**—is about the process of writing creatively, from the most basic beginnings of putting words on paper, to learning the disciplines and tools that will help the writer know writing as both self-discovery and as a disciplined approach to creative expression and exploration.

Part 2—**Techniques, Genres, and the Craft of Writing**—deals with specific literary genres—poetry, literary nonfiction, fiction, and drama—and the terms, definitions, approaches, and considerations the writer needs to know in order to produce work in these genres. We include examples of each genre within each chapter, as well as provide a short collection of works in each genre for readers to consider as representative of different writers' work. We also provide a detailed listing of resources available on the Internet for each genre.

We do *not* presume to cover every kind of writing in the major genres presented. Quite the contrary. Using the three major genres of poetry, fiction, and drama and the emerging genre of literary nonfiction is simply one way to present different kinds of writing. It also serves to introduce the basic components of literature to student writers who come from different cultural contexts, age and lifestyle groups, and levels and styles of academic preparation.

The book explains that the lines between genres are at best blurry; given the experimental work done in literature in the past century, the reader is especially encouraged to think freely and to be willing to learn more about the different ways to express his thoughts in writing. This text attempts to present both traditionally accepted and newly emerging literary forms, genres, theory, and craft. Thus instructor and student can work together to discover what the writer needs in order to grow and learn.

Part 3 — **Revising, Publishing, and the Business of Writing** — is a discussion of some larger questions about writing once a writer begins to complete and publish or share his work. Chapter 14 discusses ways to revise and edit, and ways to rethink a work in order to see it anew and be sure one has accomplished one's objective in writing it. Since many writers are interested in finding out how to publish their work, chapter 15 deals with editing and fine-tuning manuscripts, as well as formats for submitting manuscripts to editors and publishers.

Each chapter opens with **Writing to Warm Up**, exercises designed to spark thinking about the themes and work the chapter will introduce. Throughout each chapter are many exercises, labeled **Writing for Ideas and Practice**, designed to practice the ideas discussed in the chapter. Some of these exercises might be appropriate for sharing with another writer, a small group of fellow writers, or a whole class; other exercises may be better if written only for the writer himself. We don't propose that students do every one of the exercises in each chapter. Rather, we have included many different kinds of exercises, each kind intended to practice a certain concept or skill.

Writing on Your Own appears after the conclusion of each chapter, and provides exercises, prompts, and assignments that require longer responses from students, as a kind of overall summing up of the ideas and information in the chapter. These exercises are designed to produce major pieces of writing, so that in completing each chapter, the reader can put to practice the concepts and skills at hand.

Finally, **Writing to Revise** exercises follow the Writing on Your Own assignments. These exercises provide lessons about how to look at, rethink, and rework the writing the student has produced in each chapter. While revision is dealt with in detail in chapter 15, these revision exercises along the way emphasize revision as part of the entire writing process.

The text concludes with an appendix of 365 journal prompts, a device for encouraging writers to practice their craft and to stay on the writing journey, every day of the year; a list of books and resources the writer may find helpful; and a glossary of literary terms and their definitions.

Alva Johnson said, "Colleges are good at punctuation marks, but not good at what to put between them." Johnson is suggesting that no class, no teacher, and probably no one anywhere can *make anyone* a writer. Numerous writing theorists have admitted that the whole process of making someone become a better writer is partly craft and theory, and partly relative to the individual writer. There are certainly many ways in which a course can offer specific tips, tools, and directions in order to assist student writers on their journeys. But, ultimately, the journey belongs to the student. This text is only a beginning.

So, *bon voyage* and *buena suerte*. May yours be a long and fruitful journey.

Acknowledgments

There are many people who were instrumental in helping us complete this project. Although simple words do not seem adequate, they are all we can offer, since we spent our advance months ago.

We would like to thank Lisa Moore, whose vision made this book possible in the first place and who has seen it through from the start. Lynn Huddon devoted many long hours to making this book the best that it could be. She is the proverbial one in a million and we offer her our eternal gratitude. Thanks also to David Munger for his suggestions and comments.

During the writing of this text, our Tyler Junior College family cheered us on, and we extend our special gratitude to the English faculty, Noamie Byrum, Sheri Hoenshell, and Dr. Linda Watkins. A special word of thanks to our students, who inspire us every day to try to be the teachers that they deserve. Their contributions to this book are priceless. Thanks from Rick to the staff, friends, and prayer partners at Pollard United Methodist Church for their support, and to the Rakes, the Severns, and Charlie and Shirley Teague.

Thanks to all the reviewers whose astute comments helped shape the text throughout our revisions. They include: Mailin Barlow, Valencia Community College; Barry Bauska, University of Puget Sound; Patricia Clark, Grand Valley State University; Bill Clemente, Peru State College; Judith Cohen, Lesley College; Robin Davidson, Houston Community College; Elizabeth Davis, University of California, Davis; Christine Hammond, Howard University; Kendra Kopelke, University of Baltimore; Greg Luthi, Johnson County Community College; Eric Nelson, Georgia State University; Laura Scott, George Mason University; Alan Soldofsky, San Jose State University; Sue Standing, Wheaton College; and Susan Weinberg, Appalachian State University.

—C. S., R. D.

Part One

❖ ❖ ❖ ❖ ❖
❖ ❖ ❖
❖

WRITING AND
WRITING PRACTICE

1

Writing as a Journey

All writers have one thing in common: a need to create an alternate world.

— *John Fowles*

Writing to Warm Up

1. What is creative writing? How does it differ from other kinds of writing you can think of?
2. a. List all the types of writing you can think of.
   b. How many have you done? Which ones do you like to do, and which ones do you avoid?
3. Why would anyone want to be a writer? What is the point of writing? Is it to communicate? If so, why not just use the phone? Is there something about writing creatively that makes it different from all other forms of communication?
4. What is scariest about writing?
5. What is most exciting about writing?

The writer is on a journey. It is a journey of self-discovery, of expression, of creating, of deciding. It is a journey which often results in uncertainty and prompts more questions than it answers. But it is a journey which is worth the risk. John Gardner said in *On Becoming a Novelist* that "the true artist is one who doesn't quit. Novel-writing is not so much a profession as a *yoga*, or way, an alternative to ordinary life-in-the-world."

It is not always the easiest path to take, however. As a writer, you have a paradoxical job to perform. You must face not only your own fears and inhibitions, but also the fact that very often society does not want people to be open with their feelings and ideas. But you also have the opportunity to share your feelings with the world, your ideas, your dreams, your secrets.

WHY I AM A WRITER

As you begin a creative writing course and/or begin a journey as a creative writer, you might want to ask yourself a crucial and often overlooked question: "Why am I a writer?"

Notice that this question is really, "Why do I *want to be* a writer?" True, if you've just begun to think about doing some writing, you aren't really a writer—not in the same sense as someone who has been dedicated to the craft of writing for years, to studying the great writers or the most contemporary of writers or the smallest intricacies of poetry. Lots of people are interested in writing, and lots of people say things like "I sure have thought for years about writing some of this down." It's safe to say that those people aren't writers, specifically for one reason: they don't write.

But to *pursue* writing—because you feel called to it, drawn to it, because you feel that you must do it—to write, to collect little snippets of ideas on scraps of paper, to find yourself scrawling notes about poems or stories or scenes during meetings at work, to study writers you like and to want to do what they do—well, that is much more rare, and it indicates that the Muses may have chosen you.

That is to say, there are those people who feel drawn to write, who feel the need to use writing and creation as a way to order their experiences or the voices in their heads. In the ancient Greek world, when poets began a work they prayed to the Muses, the goddesses of poetry and creation. The poets believed that the gods were speaking through them, using them to order the world and speak to it. Similarly, in Chaucer's late medieval Europe, poets were sometimes called "makers," in the same way that God was called "Maker." A maker was someone who took raw, seemingly chaotic experiences and ideas, and gave them the form and shape and meaning that can come about in art.

So, if you're involved in the process of exploring your experience and your soul and your world through writing, then to some extent, even if it's only a beginning, you are a writer, whether you're a published writer or not. What is the role that writing plays in your life—and what do you want your writing to do? We're not talking yet about things like genre considerations.

Although it's certainly acceptable if you're thinking of something in a certain form already. One of the things the book will discuss is that there really isn't, sometimes, a sequential process in writing; rather, it's often organic; it grows on its own. So if you've already got the final scene of a play in your head, don't dismiss it just because you haven't brainstormed or outlined the play's structure yet.

Deciding what poetic form to give a certain piece will come much later.* It's an important question, but not nearly as important as your sense of why you are taking a writing class or reading this book. Maybe you've never thought about why you want to write, or what you expect to happen with your writing.

After all, different writers have different reasons for writing. Nick Bantock was pulling junk mail from his P.O. box one morning and saw a neighbor with a sky-blue envelope covered with foreign stamps, and thought, "Ooh, I want one of them." He explains, "Then it dawned on me that if you can't get the letters you want, you have to write them yourself." So he created the *Griffin & Sabine* books, fictional correspondence with lavish illustrations and text. Dori Sanders worked in many jobs in her native South Carolina and always scribbled notes about "my observations and things people say—I just can't help myself." Her notes became the novels *Clover* and *Her Own Place*, best-sellers which deal with the farm life of her childhood. Kate Wheeler went to college, received a master's degree in creative writing, and then had to choose between "going to write in New York City or taking care of my mother until she died of breast cancer." She chose to stay, and then became a Buddhist nun briefly, and published an award-winning collection of short stories, *Not Where I Came From*. Thinking about why you want to write may help you get started.

One story relates that a student approached a poet and said, *I want to be a writer*, and the poet asked, *Well, do you like sentences?* The student, like the rich young ruler in the Gospel story, turned away in dismay. But the poet's point was this: to be a writer is to love the things you're working with —words, sentences, sounds, rhymes, rhythm, images.

But is it more than that? Is being a writer about having something to say? About sharing your insight with the world? About changing the way people see something, or sharing with them your experience, real or imagined, in such a way that it makes them see their own experience anew?

What do you think the role of *your* writing will be? Do you want your writing to make a great deal of people happy? Or do you not care who reads your work, as long as you say what you need to say? Are you writing for a specific market, and therefore are you going to have to tailor your work to the tastes of that market? Or do you want to write for yourself? As Kurt Vonnegut, Jr., has said, "Every successful creative person creates with an audience of one in mind."

It is probably way too early to tell who your final audience will be, but it's not a bad thing to think about as you go along. The journey you are on as a writer will unfold many possibilities for your work and your art, so be watching to see what happens. It may be that you'll discover it as you go.

The writer writes because it is a necessity, a calling. In many ways, serious writers are like the Old Testament prophets who dedicated themselves to the task of recalling people to known but ignored truths.

— *Flannery O'Connor*

Writing for Ideas and Practice 1-1

As you imagine your own writing,

1. Whom do you see reading it?
2. What do you see as the result of their reading or their response as they read?
3. What do you hope people will feel, think, decide, experience by reading your work?
4. What will readers feel, think, decide, experience by reading your work one hundred years from now? Five hundred years from now? Five thousand years from now?
5. Draw this scale and then place a mark for yourself on it where appropriate:

I Am a Writer Because:

1	5	10
I want to explore my feelings	I want to learn about the writing craft	I want to publish and make money

Classify yourself with a number. Are you a one? A five? Maybe a ten? Or perhaps you are many different numbers at once, with different motivations for taking a creative writing course and writing creatively. Or perhaps you are something in between — "I'm sort of a four, because I'm reading this book to learn about how to write the short stories I'm interested in, but it's not so much to make money as to discover things about myself and my feelings." Share your answers with other student writers.

6. What is your ultimate goal as a writer?

   - Are you interested in writing because you read about some authors who made it big after a successful first novel, so this is a way to escape your humdrum job?
   - Have you always been a writer, doodling and writing poems as a way to organize your experience?
   - Are you just interested in knowing more about writing, whether or not it turns into something profitable?
   - Are your goals some combination of many things? What are they?

   Write your answer down in your notebook or journal, and date it.[1] You may be surprised at your answer when you look back at it months or years from now.

7. What is writing for, in general? What is the purpose of literature, of art, of music, of poetry, of a short story, of a play? What would you like your part in that overall purpose to be?
8. If there were a publishing company on the phone right now, offering you seventy thousand dollars for your next release no matter what it was, what would you write for them? Why?
9. Why, then, are you taking this creative writing course or reading this creative writing textbook? What is your aim in doing this work?

---

1 We discuss some techniques for keeping a journal in chapter 2.

First of all, don't judge anyone else's answers. There are no wrong answers in creative writing, only dishonest answers. It may be that the writer feels a certain way about writing now, and as he progresses, his answer will change. That has certainly happened to many creative people. And bear this in mind as well: if one person says she wants to write in order to create an autobiographical series of sketches about her childhood during the Depression to pass along to her grandchildren, and another person says he wants to write because he is trying to come up with song lyrics that reflect his rage and indignation at the injustices in modern society, those two people may not be as far removed from one another's purposes as you might think. Both are attempting to take their experiences and feelings and translate them into a tangible form—either to think it out themselves, or to share with others, or both. That's what writing is. All of us have many reasons for wanting to write, some of which we're not even aware of.

This is the kind of discussion—this sharing about why we write—that can help beginning writers. Writers or even "closet writers" often feel out of place in the world of "regular" people who are not burdened or gifted by the desire to create literature. So it can be very comforting to hear that other writers aren't sure of what they are doing either, or that there are many ways in which to be a writer, or see that there are other beginning writers who are finding their way and have even had some successes.

It also helps to think about what you want your writing to be. This does not mean that you have no room to renegotiate. Rick has worked off and on for years with his own writing and its direction. As he puts it, "Partly that's because there are many different things in which I'm interested. I like children's literature; I like poetry; I like theological and philosophical essays; I like feature stories in magazines; I love short stories and wrote my master's thesis on the twentieth-century American short story; I like history; I like art and cartooning and drawing. So which should I do? I have written and created and published in each of these areas, and while it can be very exciting to try different things, sometimes the question arises, What am I doing? If I'm not just concentrating in one area, does that mean I'm not sufficiently dedicated to it?" Some writers would say yes; others would vehemently disagree.

Don't be discouraged. Keep experimenting. But as you experiment, keep thinking about what, deep down, you want to do with your writing and why—not in terms of what genre you want to work in or where you want to publish, but in terms of what your own writing means to you and what you want it to be about.

Writing for Ideas and Practice 1-2

1. Write a prayer to your imaginary Muse or Inspiration; what do you want him/her/it to do with you and your writing?

2. Make a plan, right now, for what you want to write. Make a list of the things you'd like to create and explore with your writing—for the next six months, one year, five years, ten years. It might include the kinds of writing you want to do, or the subjects you want to cover. It might list what you want to have published.

As you acquire and use the writing tools in this book, you will focus on expressing your experience, real or imagined, in ways that communicate that experience in concrete terms, to your readers. One of the ways to write honestly is to be clear about why you're writing and what you're writing—it's okay if you're not sure, as long as you keep your focus in mind, even in the back of your mind. Then, as you learn about the different genres of writing, as you discover what you're about, this focus can help you choose what type of writing you want to do.

All writing is a form of prayer.

— *John Keats*

All art is a kind of confession, more or less oblique. All artists, if they are to survive, are forced, at last, to tell the whole story; to vomit the anguish up.

— *James Baldwin*

THE NEED TO EXPRESS ONESELF

Writing for Ideas and Practice 1-3

1. Are children less inhibited than adults? Why or why not?
2. What causes people to become restrained in expressing their feelings?
3. Is this process of learning not to express emotions healthy? Why or why not?
4. Write a paragraph describing a rainbow. Now write the paragraph you might have written when you were six.

Why don't you get up on the table right now and sing us a song? Come on! Everybody, up on the tables, and let's all sing "Old MacDonald Had a Farm" and dance a little jig. No? Why not?

Poet, essayist, critic, and translator Robert Bly has said that poetry is about telling the truth. He suggests that by the time we graduate from high school, we are professional liars. That is, he says, we lie automatically, no matter what anybody asks us. If they ask how we're doing, we say, "Fine."

Bly recalls that his own childhood on a farm up in Minnesota was anything but fine; his father was an alcoholic. Bly goes on to say that he went off to college and learned more sophisticated language, but no more about telling the truth, until finally, after graduate school back east, he returned to the farm and began to try to let what he calls "one honest thought, one honest feeling" come to him. Sometimes, he says, he would sit by a tree for hours until finally the thought would come to him, "Wow, that's a beautiful tree." And from there, an honest thought, he could begin to tell the truth about his own experiences, feelings, memories, opinions, and so on.[2]

William Blake, Romantic poet, visionary, and artist, shows this loss of innocence and spark and creativity in this poem:

    ### The Garden of Love

I went to the Garden of Love
And saw what I never had seen
A chapel was built in the midst
Where I used to play on the green

And the gates of this chapel were shut   5
And "Thou Shalt Not" writ over the door
And priests in black gowns were walking their rounds
And binding with briars my joys and desires.

Writing for Ideas and Practice 1-4

1. What is Blake suggesting when the speaker of the poem contrasts the green where he used to play and the chapel which now stands?
2. What is suggested by the chapel, the priests, and the phrase "Thou Shalt Not"?
3. What is Blake suggesting with the phrase "binding with briars my joys and desires"?
4. What is involved in the process of losing one's innocence? Do you see the process as positive, negative, or some mixture of both? Why?

Young children are by nature honest. When Candace's son was young, if he had done something wrong, he would lead her by the finger to the scene of the crime. Rick's daughter, a five-year-old, loves to dance in the mall. She loves to sing in the mall. If she finds out she's going to the cookie store, she jumps up and down with glee and giggles and sings and skips all the

---

2 This experience is discussed in the Bill Moyers video, "Where the Soul Lives," a part of the video series *The Power of the Word.*

way down the mall to the cookie place. In front of everyone. If they don't have her favorite kind of cookie, she will weep sadly and sit on the floor and feel genuinely terrible. And she isn't afraid to cry or laugh in front of other people.

Lots of kids are like this, but grown-ups sometimes seem to have forgotten or suppressed this spontaneous urge to express ourselves. As children are exposed to the adult world, they lose their untamed, asocial honesty. And with the loss of honesty comes the loss of a part of their creative spirit. They learn to hold back once they learn "the rules" of social conformity. Many young parents remark that one of the first words their toddlers learn is not "Mama" or "Daddy" but "NO!" As in Blake's poem, we want to return to "the Garden of Love" where all is innocence and goodness and trust, but as we grow up, the "gates of the chapel [are] shut"—we learn that we must grow up, become adults, even though in the adult world we aren't allowed, often, to express ourselves, because the authorities around and above us "bind with briars [our] joys and desires."

William Wordsworth, another Romantic poet, observed over and over in his poetry that children possess a kind of natural intelligence and even wisdom which society drums out of them. Consider this passage from his "Ode: Intimations of Immortality":

Shades of the prison house begin to close
    upon the growing boy. . . .

    The homely Nurse doth all she can
To make her Foster Child, her Inmate, Man,
    Forget the glories he hath known . . .

The rules which govern us, Wordsworth is saying, become a prison, and we forget "the glories" which we knew as children. Any deviation from the norm is suspect in every social system, and opens one to ridicule. Think of all the ways our peers punish us when we are different.

Writing for Ideas and Practice 1-5

1. List five specific cruel or hurtful things other kids said to you when you were growing up. Now, write a short poem or a page of dialogue that uses these five words or phrases.
2. What kinds of hard lessons did you learn at the hands of other kids when you were growing up?
3. What do you think the effect of those sorts of experiences has been on your sense of yourself, your ability to express your ideas, and your interpersonal relationships? Your writing?

Both of us, when we began teaching years ago, abandoned the use of red pens to mark students' papers. Why? Because so many students had had so many *terrible* experiences in school with teachers' vivid red ink reminders of their blunders and errors, that we found our students much more able to actually pay attention to what we had written if it wasn't written in red. Think of all the things your teachers told you to do *differently*—or not to do at all. Candace's high school English teacher told her that she needed some sort of psychological help, based on an analysis of her handwriting and a short story Candace had written (in which she killed off the main character at the end). Our experiences in school and in growing up terrify us into becoming blocked and uncreative.

It's true, then, what Bly says, that we all become professional liars—or that we all lose touch with what is within us, and that as writers we must work to find ways to get in touch with it and express it truthfully. On the one hand, writers are supposed to be like anyone else, normal adults functioning in society; but on the other hand, writers have this urge somehow to express that which lies hidden, that which perhaps has never been expressed or even thought about. On the one hand, the writer wants to communicate what he or she has found; on the other hand, the reader may not understand or appreciate what the artist thinks, feels, sees, creates, sings.

This dilemma can be very scary. Sometimes the writer sits down to write, and it happens that the more she thinks about her own experience, her own beliefs, her own past, her own perceived limitations or problems, the less able she is to write. She thinks, *This is ridiculous,* or, *This is crazy, people will think I'm nuts,* or, *Nobody will understand a thing I'm saying,* or, *My mother told me I should have been a lawyer.*

These blocks to our creativity can be quite intimidating. Writers for centuries have had to grapple with the blank page—the huge opportunity, and huge burden, of writing, of creating something out of nothing.

When you began your college studies, you had to take something like Writing 101 or Freshman Composition, an introductory writing class that wasn't supposed to be about creative writing, but about the basic skill of written communication you would need in order to do well in your classes, English and otherwise. The class might have been easy for you, but it's a hard class for most students. Why? Because of what Bly says—that when you complete high school, you're an accomplished liar, lying automatically, and then you go to English class and the teacher assigns you to write five hundred words about your deepest inner thoughts or about some observation you have made in regard to some subject of interest.

When students in Writing 101 are asked by their instructor to write an essay about a significant experience in their lives, what happens? They may react in one or more of the following ways:

a) They sit and stare at a blank piece of paper for weeks.
b) They come to the instructor and complain, "I don't know what to write about."

c) They write one sentence, decide that idea is stupid, crumple up the piece of paper, write another sentence on a new piece of paper, decide the new idea is even stupider, crumple it up, write another sentence—and continue this sequence for fifty-three sheets of paper until finally just giving up and writing something mediocre because it is two o'clock in the morning and they are trapped because the essay is due the next day at 8:00 A.M.

d) They do all of the above, in which case, they probably hate what they turn in, but it is too late, and they just turn it in and hope for the best.

Why is it so hard to write about a significant experience in one's life? You can do it—you've had incredibly significant experiences—summers with your grandparents, the time you got lost, that crazy first date with the boy you loved all of your junior year, that one weekend at church camp, the night your parents (or your children) told you about their impending divorce, your trip to New York or Yosemite or Prague or Disneyland, the death of someone you loved, the birth of your children. So why can't most students write about any of those things? Why, when faced with an assignment, do so many of us freeze up and find we have nothing to say?

Almost everyone who writes has to face that same ailment we all suffer from, writers or not: the Inner Censor that says, *You aren't allowed to express your feelings or your ideas—you'll be ridiculed and misunderstood, you'll be hurt.*

So why won't anybody get up on the table and sing "Old MacDonald" for the class? Because we're afraid? Of *course* we're afraid! People will think you're crazy if you get up in front of everyone and tell them your innermost thoughts or express your deepest feelings—or even the feelings of the moment.* We all adopt our own stances and speech patterns appropriate for every context. Adults can have one stance and pattern when they are in the office, another when they are at church, another when they are in their backyards with friends, another when they are at the ball game, another when they are at the bank. Americans are an awfully talkative bunch of people, and yet wary of people who talk deeper than surface level. One of our students, Henrik, a Danish exchangee, remarked how odd it was that everyone in America kept asking him, "How are you?" He remarked, "They ask me how I am, but they don't wait for me to tell them. I guess they don't want to know. I think I will tell them next time that I am feeling crappy, and see how it goes with them." Henrik's right. We don't want to know.

But—you're a writer, and you have got to tell your story, even if no one acts as if he wants to hear it. How do you deal with that?

> There are those people, of course, who will in fact get up on the table and sing; very often, we look at those people and relegate them to being "band nerds" or "free spirits" or "flower children" and dismiss them. Writers are caught in this same dilemma: some writers are extroverts who love to talk and write and read their writing and share themselves; others, however, are quiet, reclusive, even closed to human interaction. Either type can make a great writer.

Writing for Ideas and Practice 1-6

1. What negative things do you think of when you do something wrong or when you're about to do something you're afraid to do—what tapes play in your head, what things do you think of just beforehand or just afterward?

2. What tools do you use to silence those voices of guilt and embarrassment, or those voices of warning and ridicule? Do you whisper positive affirmations to yourself? Do you laugh? Do you go on and ignore them? Write a letter to those voices of guilt and embarrassment, of warning and ridicule. What to you want to say to them? "Dear Inner Censor, . . ."

3. Are you someone who completes things, or someone who leaves things undone? Does this pattern continue in your writing as well?

4. Are you someone who procrastinates, or someone who jumps in and attacks? Does this pattern continue in your writing as well?

5. Write about a time when you had trouble expressing yourself. What was the situation? Was it writing for a class? Was it dancing for the family at Christmas? Was it telling your spouse your feelings? What did that feel like? Record as many specific details about the experience as possible.

Sometimes, writers don't seem to quite fit in with the rest of society. Ernest Hemingway, traumatized and disillusioned by his experiences as a young man during World War I, left his wealthy suburban home outside Chicago and wandered across Europe. T. S. Eliot left his home in Missouri and ended up in the world of post-Victorian England. Emily Dickinson all but became a hermit in her parents' house in Amherst, Massachusetts, preferring to "stay at home" rather than compromise in order to assimilate into Puritan New England society. Walt Whitman, homosexual, passionate in his desire to reform and speak to nineteenth-century America, traveled from job to job and place to place, sharing his poetry and his vision for the world — only later in life was he admired for his genius. James Baldwin worked for years during the Civil Rights Movement of the 1960s to change society, eventually settling in France where he felt he could be free of the repression of his homeland.

The writer not only attempts to live out her own experience, but to make sense of it, and does so through her art. And this, it seems, is not something everyone on the planet does. As one of our students wrote, "Nobody in my family seems too worried about all those voices I keep hearing, but I can't get them out of my head unless I write about them." This student wasn't schizophrenic; he was honestly someone who needed to write in order to express himself and make sense of his experience.

Does this mean that artists and writers are the only rebels, the only people with ideas that run counter to the mainstream? Of course not. But it does mean that writers, who see things other people do not, as a result are very often ostracized or misunderstood. And they are often unwilling to conform to mainstream society's values and viewpoints.

Does this mean that artists, in order to be truly visionary and gifted with something worth saying, are *necessarily* odd or unsociable or misfits?

Absolutely not. For all of the rebellious writers, one can also list writers and artists who seem to fit in perfectly with the outward norms and appearances of the society around them. William Carlos Williams was a physician. Wallace Stevens was an insurance executive. Shakespeare was a theater owner and manager. But it is nevertheless true that writers by definition are involved in a process which by its very nature makes them *different*, in a way, from other people. Picasso said, "I paint what I think, not what I see." His point is not merely about non-representational art; he is suggesting that the artist sees beyond the surface of things, and that the courageous artist is the one who will work to uncover or communicate that deeper reality. The writer's journey is a journey of discovery which requires an openness to things within, a willingness to try to see into the unknown which others don't yet see.

NOT KNOWING

Part of the journey of writing is to discover. And that's part of the joy of writing as well. It is also part of the incredibly hard work of writing. After all, the writer is going somewhere no one else has gone, and trailblazing is hard work, uncertain, a struggle with underbrush and vines and quicksand. But it is also exhilarating.

Nobel Prize-winning author William Faulkner once said that all of his books were failures and that he loved them nevertheless. If one were to begin with that premise in mind about one's own writing, wouldn't it be easier to begin? If everything you write is going to be less than you want it to be and yet, at the same time, reveal new and amazing things to you and to the world, what could be better than that? Poet W. S. Merwin has said that a student asked the poet John Berryman in a poetry writing class how the student writer is to know if he is on the right track; Berryman replied, "You don't. You can never know. If you have to know, don't write." Richard Hugo has written, "Knowing can be a limiting thing." In his book *The Triggering Town*, he adds,

 One mark of a beginning writer is his impulse to push language around to make it accommodate what he has already conceived to be the truth, or, in some cases, what he has already conceived to be the form. Even Auden, clever enough at times to make music conform to the truth, was fond of quoting the woman in the Forster novel who said something like, "How do I know what I think until I see what I've said.". . . .

You don't know what the subject is, and the moment you run out of things to say about Autumn Rain start talking about something else. In fact, it's a good idea to talk about something else before you run out of things to say about Autumn Rain.

Don't be afraid to jump ahead. . . . when you are writing you must assume that the next thing you put down belongs not for reasons of logic, good sense, or narrative development, but because you put it there.

Actor James Caan has explained that in filming one scene in the movie *The Godfather*, he was particularly stumped about how to portray his character's tense relationship with his father, Marlon Brando's Don Corleone. Caan said that after a night of problematic filming, the next morning he woke up and just began to act like a boor, rude, a juvenile delinquent—"like Don Rickles." He didn't know why, but when he arrived at the set, he started handing people money, teasing them, threatening them, harassing them, and then carried that mood into filming. The scene worked beautifully. He had discovered something within that allowed him to express the emotions needed.

Not knowing means that the writer can be open, that the journey can be not so much about arriving at a finished product, but about discovering as one goes along. This is not to say that having goals for one's writing is bad. The first part of this chapter suggested that the writer should begin and then continue to think about his goals as a writer, both in terms of what he accomplishes by writing, and of what he hopes to write and publish and for whom.

But it is an important part of your journey as a writer to continue to be open, to experiment, to be willing to say and write and think things that are not necessarily assigned or safe or anticipated, and to be open to what *might* happen in your writing, without necessarily knowing. E. B. White likened the writer to a hunter, sitting in a blind, waiting, trying to stay awake.

BEING OPEN

One of the important things I learned in making watercolors was not to worry, not to care too much.

— *Henry Miller*

Think about writing you've done in the past, writing that you enjoyed. Perhaps it was for school, or for your own amusement or enjoyment. Think about those moments in which you were able to draw or paint or sculpt or sing or dance or write without inhibitions, without worries. Perhaps you felt that you had something significant to say, or perhaps you just liked writing out your thoughts and feelings. So you wrote and wrote and wrote, and it just flowed out and it was wonderful and you loved expressing yourself.

In classrooms, families, offices, factories full of people afraid to express themselves, the writer finds a way to open up and write. She lets her ideas and feelings and opinions flow onto the page. How can this happen? It is certainly mysterious; as John Gardner says, "Every writer knows there is something mysterious about the ability, on any given day, to write." And that mysterious thing happens to the writer.

What often happens is that that writer, whether in Freshman Composition or in church or in letters or in love notes or in journals or in Creative Writing class, doesn't even know what's going on. We have had students so many times come up and tell us as they are turning in their essays, "I don't know how I did it—it just came to me! I guess the topic just triggered something in me, but I had a lot to say. I had a lot more to say than I thought I had!"

How does this happen? It might happen when one is completely relaxed and free, just sitting down to write without worries or deadlines. On the other hand, of course, a student writer might be given an assignment that requires her to use a specific form of poem, sometimes even providing some of the words she is to use. Strangely, this type of assignment is often very liberating as well, for it forces the writer to concentrate on form rather than on substance, message. The writer spends time listening to the rhythm, counting syllables, looking for rhymes. The ideas come when the writer is concentrating on something else. That is part of the process of discovery.

The writer is discovering her own feelings, her own ideas, her own experience, her own fears, her own dreams. Sometimes it's an easy process, sometimes it's difficult. But it's always a process of finding out something, and that something can be anything.

We have had many student writers, young and old, who as a result of our classes on creative writing learned a great deal about who they were and what they were about. Sometimes that learning was painful; other times it was delightful; sometimes it was both. Most often, the writing process just led to more writing, more discovery, more awareness, and then more writing again. That's the idea.

So a great deal of your journey of discovery will be punctuated by happy accidents, glimpses of the private, the visionary, the pretend, which become a part of your art. Graeme Base, Australian author and illustrator, says, "I don't know that you can dictate what makes a good book. It's like trying to write music to a math formula. It excludes the idea of entertainment, imagination, a sense of fun or pure nonsense." The artist Sark suggests, "Most creativity is playing. Some of my best results came from 'mistakes.'" Theodore Geisel—Dr. Seuss—would often discover ideas for his books by accident. Once, he was sketching an elephant on tracing paper, and the piece of paper ended up on top of a drawing of a tree; that gave him the idea of Horton, the elephant hatching an egg in a nest. During a phone conversation he was absently doodling; when he got off the phone, he found that he had drawn a moose with animals in its antlers; the book that resulted was *Thidwick, the Big-Hearted Moose*. Perhaps someone else's impulse would have been to dismiss the doodles as nonsense, but Dr. Seuss saw them as inspiration. Chris Van Allsburg, children's book author and illustrator, explains that with his book *The Polar Express*, "I had a vision of a train standing still in a forest. Steam was coming off the train. It was cold. I don't know why that vision came, but once it did I began asking myself questions about it, and the story revealed itself." About the sketches his book-writing career began with, he says, "They were odd little sketches—I don't know where they came from." So your long journey into the world of creativity requires you to be both open-minded and open-hearted.

Writing for Ideas and Practice 1-7

1. Have you ever had the experience of just writing and not worrying about what you would say or how it would go? How did it feel?
2. Have you ever had the experience of writing about a specific topic and finding nothing to say, even though you have plenty of ideas about it?
3. Is it better to know exactly what you're trying to express or explore, or just follow along while you find out what you're writing?
4. Have you ever found yourself writing and not writing what you thought you were going to write—you ended up writing something else? Describe that experience.
5. Write a short story about an experience you have had in learning about your own creative process—either how it worked well, or how it was thwarted, or both.

If you're writing to be brilliant or make money or impress people with your use of the language, then good luck. You can probably do any of those things. If, however, you're writing because, as Erica Jong said, there is "a burning coal in your gut," you'll write, and while it may be only for you, your writing will be good and meaningful. That's writing as therapy, as journey, as a true record of life.

And, we say, be on that journey. Name yourself a writer, as of today. Writing teacher, poet, and novelist Natalie Goldberg advises her students in her book *Wild Mind: Living the Writer's Life,*

 Every morning as soon as you wake up and each night before you go to sleep, say to yourself, simply and clearly, "I am a writer." It doesn't matter if you believe it. Just plant that seed. . . . Go ahead. Say it: "I am a writer." Practice saying it when people ask you what you do. You might feel like a complete fool. That is okay. Step forward and say it anyway.

One student we know took this so to heart that she quit a job she had which was taking all her energy and time, and began working for a dairy. "If I work at the dairy," she said, "all I have to think about all day long is cows—and then I'm ready to do what I really do when I get home: write. It percolates in me all day long and when I get home, I'm ready to be a writer!"

A thought, though, about the issue of the ultimate purpose of your writing: one student, Brent, wrote this advice to himself and his classmates and instructor:

 If you are waiting to write a book that will change the world for the better then you have given yourself one of the lamest excuses ever not to write anything at all. . . . Write because writing is what you do and don't allow such preconceived notions to get in the way of fulfilling your potential. Be an uncut block of wood, and let what happens happen. Let the wind take what you write wherever it needs to take it. But remember that if you weigh it down with too much crap then the wind cannot even pick it up, much less carry it into perpetuity.

It is difficult to find that balance—between saying something significant, and just saying something, period. Writing teachers and authors say that to expect yourself to dredge up the deepest truths in the world and be profound is ridiculous and impossible—and yet they also say that the writer must strive somehow to tell the truth in her writing. You're expected on the one hand to make sense and say something meaningful, and on the other hand, to remain open and able to detect the slightest hint of the most silly and seemingly unconnected idea or detail. It's a delicate balance, but one worth working toward.

And remember: this is *your* writing. Don't be afraid to write for fear of what people will say. Keep writing.

Writing on Your Own

1. What are you/have you been most afraid of or what have you found most difficult about writing? Are you afraid of grammar? Spelling? That someone else will read your writing and find out your secrets? That someone else will read your writing, period? That you will be graded by a teacher or judged by a peer?
2. What is the worst thing that will happen if you keep writing?
3. What is the worst thing that will happen if you stop writing?
4. Answer, in a two-hundred-word (or so) essay, why you write. OR—Write a mission statement for yourself as a writer: *This Is Why I am a Writer* or *What I Am About as a Writer!* Make it short; too long, and you get into a discussion rather than a simple statement. One or two sentences will do.
5. Write a short poem, story, scene, or sketch that you have wanted to write for a while. Once you have finished writing it, ask yourself,
   - Why did I want to write that?
   - What happened as a result of my writing that?
   - Whom would I like to have read this writing? Why?
6. Make a list of goals for your writing; if you can, add dates to it, so that you can think about how much or what kind of writing you would like to have done by a certain time in the future.

When you become literate then you have to go on this journey of recreating yourself by pulling in all the roots that are dangling. Somehow weeding all of this extraordinary emotional mosaic, so that when you speak you carry your own voice, not the voice of someone else.

— *poet Jimmy Santiago Baca*

2

Writing Habits

If I write well, it is because I have a chair in which it is impossible to get comfortable.

— *Goethe*

Writing to Warm Up

1. What kind of writing space do you imagine a great writer using? Is it an old roll-top wooden desk with papers sticking out everywhere? Or is it a studio with high ceilings and wooden beams? Or is it a typewriter on a crate in the basement? Perhaps a couch with books piled on the floor and a laptop sitting open and ready?
2. What kind of writing space do you have?
3. What kind of writing space would you like to have?
4. Is it necessary to sit down (or stand) in one's studio in order to write? What are some other appropriate writing poses? Lying down? Sitting in a cafe? Keep going; list at least ten other places or stances for writing.
5. List five ways in which one's writing space is not even about physical space, as much as about personal space and time, or about how one orders one's life.

THE WRITING SPACE

Space can mean a physical space you use when you write, or it can mean a space in time you reserve for your writing. For now, *consider* physical space and its components in the writing process.

August 1, 1983. I am in the cellar now with my typewriter and piles of papers, etc., driven like a rat to this lightless airless corner and have not been at all in a good mood.

— *Carolyn Chute*

James Dickey called his office "The Cave of Making"

Erle Stanley Gardner's reconstructed study

What kind of place — in physical space as well as in time, and even in one's attitude toward approaching the act of writing — is best for writing? The question may seem trivial, but it isn't. Having a space or a group of spaces a writer goes to in order to write can have a huge effect on her ability to write, the kind of writing she does, and the attitude she has when she is there. Here are some student responses to the above question:

Student Writing

I like to go to my room to write. I still live with my parents, and it's the room I've lived in since I was five. It's got all my things in it, and when I'm there, I feel safe and like I can say anything and it'll be okay. I don't like anyone to come in when I'm writing, though, so I put my "Stay Out" sign on the door, curl up on my bed with all my stuffed animals and my stereo on, and I can write.

Student Writing

I choose the lake. When I'm away from my kids, my husband, my chores, my to-do list—then I'm a better person, and I can concentrate. There are no distractions at our lake lot. We have a trailer there, and I go out one or two mornings a week after the kids are at school and write in total silence. Well, I hear the birds, and the fish splashing in our cove. It's heaven.

Student Writing

I can't write in the dorm. I can't write in the library — too many people saying hi. I can't write in the study hall—it's too depressing. So I go sit in my car in South Parking Lot and spread my stuff around in the seats and write by streetlight. It's a place I can be myself and usually nobody bugs me.

It would be wonderful if we all had a huge studio with pictures on the wall, a fireplace, bookshelves and a huge couch and a gigantic wooden desk to write on. Byron and Shelley traveled through Europe, staying in estates and abandoned old castles and homes near picturesque Swiss lakes while they wrote their beautiful poems. The Brownings traveled through Italy, composing love lyrics in villas above charming town squares. Norman Rockwell had a beautiful old New England barn he had converted into a painting studio. Unfortunately, the best most of us can manage is a corner of a room, if that. But if that corner is your corner, mark it as your territory and use that place for your writing with regularity and with authority. Claim it and use it. One Faulkner anecdote says that he had a room in his house, the walls of which he would whitewash when he had finished one work. He would then begin to make notes on the walls about the people who would appear in his next work, mapping out their relationships, family trees, and so forth.

Writing for Ideas and Practice 2-1

1. Would your ideal writing space be cluttered or neat? Would you stack papers and spread out books all over the place, or would you organize everything neatly and put

it away in file cabinets and drawers? Would you cover the walls with art and ideas and notes, or leave them pristine, clean, bare?

2. Bring to class three artifacts from your writing space and share with the class why those things are a part of your writing space.

I've always written in bed, longhand, with a clipboard against my knees. I could not even compose on a typewriter.

— *Frank Conroy*

Cartoonist Jim Benton liked to draw on the floor when he was a kid; his mother used paper and pencils to pacify him when he was a toddler; she eventually gave him one of the walls of the kitchen so he could draw with grease pencils. He would dig paper out of a trash can behind a print shop. As an adult, he has a studio made from "an otherwise useless garage" at his home, which looks like "someone broke a piñata." Says Benton, "I like to draw on the floor. It's still the best place to read the Sunday funnies."

Joyce Saenz-Harris writes that J. California Cooper "writes her stories in bed, in longhand, usually in the early-morning hours. She says she is 'a bed-crazy person,' and that writing by hand 'is the only way I can get these people (the characters' voices) to come.'" Then she "transfers her work to a computer, to be printed out in manuscript form. 'I don't know how to write,' she says disarmingly. 'I just do it.'"

Think about how you like to use the space where you write.

And it doesn't have to be your own studio or house. It may be that you can find a space that you don't own. Natalie Goldberg has a chapter in *Writing Down the Bones* called "Writing in Restaurants" which has some great suggestions. Here is an excerpt:

 When you select a cafe to write in, you must establish a relationship. Go hungry so you will want to eat. . . . I want the people in the restaurant to know I appreciate the time and space they are giving me. Also, if you are taking up a table for a few hours, leave more than the ordinary tip. . . . Do not show up at lunch or dinner when they are the most crowded. Go at the end of rush hour when the waitress will be glad to see you, because she is very tired and knows you won't order a lot and don't expect fast service. . . . But why go to all this bother? Why not just stay home and write? It is a trick I use. It's good to change the scenery from time to time, and at home there is the telephone, the refrigerator, the dishes to be washed, a shower to be taken, the letter carrier to greet. It's good to get away.

If writing in a cafe doesn't appeal to you, then where else would you like to write? Some writers we've talked to have suggested setting aside a small amount of money for many months until they can afford to rent a tiny space somewhere—a cubbyhole in the back of a warehouse, a small part of an unused office space. They find that paying for a space creates the need to go and use that space, and they develop discipline in using it. For many years, John Cheever used to ride the elevator down like all the other business executives in his New York City apartment house at eight o'clock in the morning, only when they left the building to go to their offices, he would go to the basement where he had a table and a typewriter to work. In later years, when he had moved into a bedroom community north of the city, he would board the commuter train just like the other businessmen first thing in the morning, ride into the city, and write at a rented office he had there. He said the discipline of going to the place where he wrote gave his life routine and regularity which he would not otherwise have had.

A park, a bench near a crowded corner, the backyard — all of these make good places to write, if the writer isn't easily distracted by noise, other people, interruptions. And that raises another question—what will you surround yourself with in your writing space, both physically and in terms of people and noises?

Within Your Writing Space: Music, Silence, or Talk?

Henry David Thoreau went into Walden Woods and built himself a cabin to live in. While there, away from distractions and able to concentrate on his own thoughts and the natural world around him, he composed amazing observations about himself, nature, and society. But is it necessary to leave the company of people in order to write? It would certainly seem that writing is a solitary business.

In comparing the writer's life to that of the trappers of old, Ron Hansen says: "Even if you are employed at a university, there's that same sense of rootlessness, of getting away from a regular job and a forty-hour week in order to work longer and lonelier in the wilderness. And in two years or more, you come back with your pelts, and if you've been lucky you are crazed with riches for a little while, and then you go back to the woods again." J. California Cooper lived for some years in solitude and near anonymity in Marshall, a small town in rural East Texas, in "an idiosyncratic, inconspicuous but densely textured sanctum of her own devising. Here, she has her pair of goldfinches and her two cats: one neurotically shy to the point of invisibility, one aggressively sociable. She also has eight chickens, all named, who provide her with fresh eggs to eat and give away. She surrounds herself with shelves of books and music, with hanging plants, manuscripts and works of art in progress."

The components of one's environment matter. Frederick Franck has said, "A non-creative environment is one that constantly bombards us, I said, overloads our switchboard with noise, with agitation and with visual stimuli. Once we can detach ourselves from all these distractions, find a way of 'inscape' of 'centering,' the same environment becomes creative again." Some writers prefer to play music while they write; others require silence. Children's book author and illustrator Maurice Sendak has noted that when he is drawing, he plays music in his studio, but when he is writing the stories, he has to have complete silence.

Do you study best with music on, or in silence? Do you read best with music on, or in silence, or with people talking? Some of our students say they prefer to read and write with music on, but it must be music they know well, so they're not aware of the words, or music with no words, such as classical music. One of our students told us, "listening to music is the only way I can keep the front part of my brain busy while I think."

Most writers agree that writing is best done without the intrusion of other people—except, in the case of writing in a cafe, the occasional visit from a waitress. In the cafe, one has the extra distractions of people talking and perhaps music playing; for some, that environment is helpful, and for others, it's annoying. One student noted, "I put the phone under a pillow while I'm working. That way, I sort of know it's there, and I can sort of hear it ringing, so I'm sort of still connected to the rest of the world, but I get this cool sense of power by not answering it."

Raymond Carver observed that before he was successful enough to write full-time, "I figured if I could squeeze in an hour or two a day for myself, after job and family, that was more than good enough. That was heaven itself. . . . But sometimes, for one reason or another, I couldn't get the hour . . . my kids were in full cry then . . . and they were eating me alive." Writers with families and children have an especially difficult job. But juggling children and jobs and schedules can produce a discipline of its own. James Baldwin noted, "I start work when everyone has gone to bed. I've had to do that ever since I was young—I had to wait until the kids were asleep. And then I was working at various jobs during the day. I've always had to write at night. But now that I'm established I do it because I'm alone at night." And don't despair; poet Lucille Clifton says that she published her first collection when her children were ages seven, five, four, three, two, and one—so, she says, "a lot of things are possible that people don't think are possible."

Writing for Ideas and Practice 2-2

1. Do you prefer to write when someone else is around, or in solitude? Do you like to play music when you read or write, or do you prefer silence?
2. Write for fifteen minutes in total silence.
3. Write for fifteen minutes while some background noise is going — the television, or voices in a restaurant you're in, or perhaps the sounds in someplace unusual.
4. Write while listening to different kinds of music — classical, soul, rock 'n' roll, jazz, world music, 50's doo-wop.

5. Now read what you wrote for questions 2–4. Note any differences in content and structure. Were there any circumstances that you felt had an adverse effect on your writing? Were there any that you felt had a positive effect?

It would seem that everyone writes best under his own best conditions, according to his lifestyle, preferences, the demands on his time, and so on. For instance, Candace used to write anywhere. She could write on the back of a Dairy Queen hamburger wrapper and on the backs of bank deposit slips while driving sixty miles an hour down an L.A. freeway listening to a Dodgers game blaring over the radio. Lines of poetry would come to her on her morning run because of the natural rhythm of her breath and the sound of shoes against the blacktop road. She had to hurry home before she forgot the words. She would make a mad dash for a pen as she burst through the door, scribbling lines on the palm of her hand. That worked just fine, until one summer she became obsessed with writing utensils and other tools. She bought a fountain pen and an artist's pad and designated a certain time every day to write. And she became hopelessly blocked. She wasn't comfortable knowing that she had defined when she could write and when she could not. Whatever came out when she had her fountain pen was writing. However, when she had been writing on scraps, she hadn't had to worry whether they were any good, because she could throw them away if she didn't like them later. Often, they turned into stories and poems, but she knew she didn't *have* to make anything of them. So she threw away the artist's pad and the fancy pen dried out, and she hasn't been blocked since.

One's writing space, therefore, is a very personal thing, one which you will want to tailor and continually refine—but don't make it something it's not.

Time Space — Routines, Schedules, Approaches

Perhaps physical space is less important than one's state of mind, or one's attitude or approach toward the act of writing.

Writing for Ideas and Practice 2-3

1. What sorts of routines do you think published writers have? Do they work leisurely, do they work endlessly? What sort of routine would you like to have, if your full-time job were to write?
2. Find one writer you really like and do some research to see whether he or she relied more on inspiration to write, or used a writing schedule, or some combination of both.

Annie Dillard warns, "It is almost prurient, this daydreaming about the writing life, as if there were such a thing, or as if, if there were, you could call it living. Recently a newspaper photographer chewed me out for not writing at a typewriter in a book-lined study. He knew how a writer worked, even if I didn't." She then adds, as if to note the normality of her life in spite of her being a writer, "I work mornings only. I go out to lunch. Afternoons I play with the baby, walk with my husband, or shovel mail."

It is true that aspiring writers and writers' fans are intensely curious about the routines that writers use in their writing. Fans are always curious about celebrities. But with writers, it is as if there is a secret formula out there, and if one adopts it, then one becomes a writer. The irony is that with writing, there is probably less a set formula or approach than with any other profession. As we noted above, writers have many different jobs and routines. It may be helpful for you as a student writer to think about how you will schedule your writing time, and how, in time, that schedule may grow and develop.

The main thing to remember regarding this subject is that if you want to be a writer, you must write. It's up to you to find your own place, your own schedule, your own media. Bernard Malamud says that "You write by sitting down and writing. There's no particular time or place—you suit yourself, your nature. How one works, assuming he's disciplined, doesn't matter. If he or she is not disciplined, no sympathetic magic will help." Fran Lebowitz said the following in an interview in 1993 in *Harper's Magazine*, regarding a ten-year writer's block she went through:

I sulked. Sulking is a big effort. So is not writing. I only realized that when I did start writing. When I started getting real work done, I realized how much easier it is to write than not to write. Not writing is probably the most exhausting profession I've ever encountered. It takes it out of you. It's very psychically wearing not to write—I mean if you're supposed to be writing.

Writing for Ideas and Practice 2-4

1. Respond to this quote by William Stafford: "When I write, I like to have an interval before me when I am not likely to be interrupted. For me, this means usually the early morning, before others are awake. I get pen and paper, take a glance out the window (often it is dark out there), and wait. It is like fishing. But I do not wait very long, for there is always a nibble—and this is where receptivity comes in. To get started, I will accept anything that occurs to me. Something always occurs, of course, to any of us. We can't keep from thinking."
2. Do you prefer to write, read, and study in long, uninterrupted sessions, or do you prefer to take breaks? Why?
3. What do you know about your own learning and working style, and how do you think that predisposition or those habits affect your writing?

Getting Started and Your Routine

Writing is easy. All you do is stare at a blank sheet of paper until drops of blood form on your forehead.

— Gaene Fowler

Later in this chapter, we will discuss the need for the writer to break through certain blocks to creativity, and suggest prompts and exercises to defeat the Inner Censor which prohibits one from freely expressing one's ideas, thoughts, feelings, imagination. Part of that process can be built into your writing routine. Some writers begin their writing sessions with various techniques for initiating the writing process. For instance, someone might begin by writing a letter, by writing in his journal, by reading, or by doing certain warm-up exercises much the same way an athlete warms up before a competition or race.

Breaking into the creative mode may be nothing more than the act of beginning to write. And, as practicing writers know, beginning the writing process is often slow, but once the process starts, it is almost always self-generating—the more you write, the more you have to say.

Here is what some writers have said about their own methods of beginning the writing and creative process:

Annie Dillard has noted, "At first I revved up for *Pilgrim at Tinker Creek* by copying the whole book out every day in longhand." Tom Robbins, a writer of fanciful novels, says, "My biological alarm wakes me daily at precisely 8:30 A.M., whereupon I switch on the radio to an all-news station, refusing to get out of bed until I've heard an announcer mention the number 'twenty-three.' It's extremely rare when I'm not up by 9:00, although a few times I've had to lie in the sack past noon. Being punched in, so to speak, by the universe allows each day to begin on an extraordinary note."

And Edward Albee adds, "There's a time to go to the typewriter. It's like a dog—the way a dog before it craps wanders around in circles—a piece of earth, an area of grass, circles it for a long time before it squats. It's like that—figuratively circling the typewriter getting ready to write, and then finally one sits down. I think I sit down to the typewriter when it's time to sit down to the typewriter."

Writing for Ideas and Practice 2-5

1. What do you to do to get your own writing process started? Write a paragraph that describes your work habits.
2. What thoughts run through your head when you sit down to write? Why?

As one writes, one discovers one's schedule as much as one creates it. Like anything else—marriage, a new job, a new class—you simply have to have done the thing for a while before you know how it works best and what is going to happen. And every process changes, over time. The only way to learn how to write is to write.

Brilliant students sometimes have terrible study habits, because they have not had to develop good habits along the way. So, many of our brightest students have made only mediocre progress in their writing—because they didn't turn in enough work. They say they are writers, but many of them don't write. Then again, you may be one of those tortured artists, like Dostoyevsky, who gambled his money away, or Edgar Allan Poe, who drank his money away; both sometimes had to write entire books within days of a publisher's deadline in order not to go to debtor's prison, or lose their jobs, or both. It's safe to say they had pretty terrible *study habits,* but they *wrote brilliantly.* You'll have to figure your own process out as you go. A victory for a writer is very often simply to put words on paper. A good rule of thumb, then, is to continue to think about what you want to achieve with your writing work, in a creative writing class or on your own, and work toward those goals, setting up schedules that help you build good habits and discipline.

DEFEATING THE CENSOR

In chapter 1, we discussed the difficulty of dealing with the blocks that arise along the writer's journey. We suggested then that the writer should stay "open," willing to think about and write about any number of ideas or feelings that may arise. But beyond the general advice to remain open and to see one's writing as a journey, some specific techniques for responding when one is blocked may be helpful.

What if you're totally blocked—you can't write, you have nothing to say, you have no ideas, you're frustrated and stymied and stuck and you're convinced that everything you've written is trash? What can you do to deal with such a problem?

First of all, being blocked is not an end. This is merely another part of the journey. The writer's job is to be in the path of discovery—and there will be roadblocks. But there are ways to go through and around those blocks. As the obstetrics nurses often tell the expectant mothers suffering from huge abdomens and swollen feet, "pregnancy is not a chronic condition." That is, it *will end,* one way or the other. And so will a writer's block, given the writer's resolve and some helpful tools.

There are all sorts of quick ways to put words on paper. Students in English classes in high school and college do things like brainstorming, freewriting, looping, and so on. These tried-and-true techniques have been helpful to countless students in the past. So if you have some of those techniques you already like to use, you should continue. And when they are applied specifically to creative writing, they have new possibilities and can be used in focused ways to begin the writing process and bring out ideas, observations, memories, and emotions that can be excellent material for your writing.

In this textbook, we're calling exercises and prompts like this "diving boards." They are like diving boards, in that the writing process is very much like diving into water: one is not exactly sure sometimes what is down there; it may be dark, it may be cold. Even in the most controlled swimming pool experience, to dive off the board still involves an element of faith, of leaping out into the air. And a diving board, unlike the steps in the shallow end, doesn't allow you to creep in slowly. Sometimes the best way to unblock yourself is simply to jump in.

Writing for Ideas and Practice 2-6

1. What kind of exercises have you had to do in school to get your writing process started? Have teachers assigned you tasks like brainstorming, outlining, and so forth? Which ones have worked best for you? Which ones do you still use, on your own?
2. Design a tool for unblocking or jump-starting the creative process. Try it out on yourself. Try it out on a classmate. See if it works.

Relaxed Writing: Diving Board #1

Many writing teachers talk about journaling, freewriting, and other devices with which writers can put words on paper casually and even nonsensically as a way to defeat one's Inner Censor. An excellent technique for getting started, even when you don't have anything to say or you're blocked or feeling stupid or lazy, is sitting down at your desk and throwing words on the page, in no order, and with no specific focus or intent other than to defeat the blank page which is both your opportunity and your enemy.

Give yourself some boundaries or goals: you might want to write leisurely and see what you come up with in, say, twenty minutes, or you might set the goal that you are going to keep writing until you fill three pages. You may even say you'll write until you find at least five topics or lines or paragraphs you like — but then, sometimes that approach can be counterproductive. The point is not to write something profound or even good; the point is just to put words on paper. Just put words on paper, no matter how stupid or illogical or incongruent. You can make something out of them later. After all, when a potter sits down to throw a pot or a vase or a bowl, she doesn't start off with anything except mud. Sometimes we're afraid to start with mud; we think we have to be so brilliant, so profound—and then we end up writing nothing because we're afraid we're not brilliant or profound enough. One student wrote,

I'm one of those creative people, not one of those detail people. Which means that I'm really a perfectionist, and the idea that I might not measure up to my own twisted ideal of what I *ought* to be doing makes me afraid deep inside to do *anything*. So even though I come across flip and cool and laid back, I'm really a control freak, afraid I can't take care of the details after all. And so I don't do much creating, because what if what I create really bites and everyone knows I'm a fraud? It'll be just like third grade again, me reading my poem to the class and them laughing at me. So the point is, don't call on me, please, to read my poems aloud in class. I may seem relaxed, but I'm not. I'm terrified.

Maybe we're afraid of what we might or might not say or reveal or discover. Maybe we're afraid we'll be graded for grammar or content. But when you're just diving in, there's no one here watching or grading—just you. Which, of course, is part of why it's scary. If you've been not writing all this time and blaming it on the mean teacher or parent or peer who stunted your creativity, *now*, they're not here to blame. The Censor protests, *Yeah, but what if the writing you've finally given yourself permission to create isn't any good? What then?* The answer, of course, is to bulldoze over the Censor with sheets full of words. Keep telling yourself just to put the words on the paper and keep going.

Your Inner Censor, however, may go nuts. It may scream, protest, throw fits, insist that you stop, that you check your spelling, that you not say that horrible thing you just said, that you apologize, that what you're writing is dumb. Writing freely like this will be torture, perhaps. But when you begin exercising for the first time, when your muscles protest, do you stop exercising? Of course not. You keep faithful to your exercise routine, and in time, those muscles not only put up with your working them, they begin to beg for you to exercise. They learn to be strong and work because you've trained them to. Expressing yourself may be new to you, but it is something you can do with practice. And yes, it's not natural to write all this crazy stuff on paper. It seems dumb. Well, it *is* dumb. Great. That's the idea. As Natalie Goldberg says in *Writing Down the Bones*, "First thoughts have tremendous energy. It is the way the mind first flashes on something. The internal censor usually squelches them. So we live in the realm of second and third thoughts, thoughts on thought, twice and three times removed from the direct connection of the first fresh flash." We want to get to first thoughts here.

When you do this sort of free, relaxed writing, do the following:

- never worry about how much you're writing or how much of it you can use;
- don't count the words;
- don't pay any attention to grammar, spelling, syntax;
- never worry that what you are writing isn't good.

Kit Reed has said, "All writers begin by writing garbage. It's how the human mind works—we have to impose order on chaos. Later you can make it make sense. You're going to have to write a lot of crap before you write anything good, so you might as well get started." So get started.

Writing for Ideas and Practice 2-7

1. Write freely in response to any one of the following prompts for a full two pages:
   a. Dogs
   b. Spring
   c. Anxiety
   d. If only
   e. The bell tower
   f. Grass
   g. Lunch

2. Then, when you have written a certain amount, look back at it and do a few things.

    One, get up and take a break. Walk off. Eat something. Smoke. Whatever you do to relax. It's okay to take breaks; it's necessary. Sometimes writers go into a white-hot stream of writing that can last for hours or even days, and that's great. But you probably shouldn't plan on that being your normal pattern, or you'll go crazy. Instead, pace yourself. This isn't a sprint; it's a marathon. You may have to do a lot of writing over a long time before you find what you are looking for; it may be that you weren't looking for anything specific at all, and you're just exploring, in which case, getting there isn't the point anyway.

    Two, read it. This may be painful or it may be funny. You may cringe at the grammar, the mistakes, the dumb stuff you thought of, whatever. The Censor will be *tsk*ing now, shaking its head, muttering to you, "I *told* you so, but you wouldn't slow down and listen to *me.* And this is all the *thanks I get* for being here to guide you for all these years! Remember what happened in seventh grade when you didn't listen to me and all the kids laughed at recess? I'm always right! Don't do this to yourself!" The Censor has a lot invested in keeping this sort of uncontrolled, free communication in check. After all, as we've talked about, the whole point of the Censor is to make us able to fit in to "society" and be normal.

    But the beauty is, as a writer, you're already breaking a lot of society's rules, so go for it. Just write. No one is looking. So defeat the Censor. Keep writing. And read it—see, it's not so bad. Natalie Goldberg says of this moment, "You must be a great warrior when you contact first thoughts and write from them. Especially at the beginning you may feel great emotions and energy that will sweep you away, but you don't stop writing. You continue to use your pen and record the details of your life and penetrate into the heart of them."

    Three, underline or circle or star anything you have written that you like a lot or that you think is interesting or that makes you uncomfortable or that you think would make a good story, article, poem, novel, scene, whatever.

    This does not mean that you're being profound or deep yet. All this means is that you're planting seeds for the next exercise, the next level. Notice the next step:

Four, pick one of the ideas, sentences, phrases, details—even just a word—that you like or dislike, or just notice from what you have written.

Start another page; put this new thing you've gleaned on the top of that page, and use that as a prompt for the next thing you're writing. For instance, say you wrote in response to the prompt "dogs," and toward the end of your two pages, you wrote:

> Lucy is such a ridiculous jerk, such a hag, she's amazing, I cant stand her her mother either, she's driving me crazy and that dog dog that ridiculous cocker spaniel she keeps talking about she loves so much—to much—anyway I don't want to talk about her any more lets talk about some other kind of dog . . .

Now, to anyone else, this may not be particularly important or significant, but it occurs to you as you reread this writing selection that your relationship with Lucy, your friend from work, may have something in it worth writing about. So on the next page, you could write "Lucy" at the top—and then use that as a diving board to the next ideas.

This process is great because it does nothing except make it okay to put junk on paper. And that's what writers need—to put words on paper. Or, as Joe Bob Briggs[1] has advised to young writers, "Write every day, write every day, write every day. That is all I know." And this free writing is a way to get started.

Now, try a related diving board exercise, in which the only difference is *time*. In this exercise, add a couple of further restrictions just to make it interesting.

First, don't just set a time limit and then write whatever. Instead, set a time limit—a timer is definitely best here, because you won't have a moment to look up at the clock or your watch—and then *write without stopping, without lifting the pen from the paper, without looking back at anything you have written, for the entire time.*

This drives our students crazy. We tell them, "Okay, we're going to write for five minutes, and just write until I tell you to stop." And five minutes doesn't sound like much. But then, when they get going, they're rolling along, and get tired, and sneak a quick peek at their watches, and *it's only been two minutes!* So after a few more minutes, they *ahem*, they clear their throats, they shake their writing hands to get the blood flowing.

What then? Basically, the same guidelines apply that apply to Diving Board #1. You still go back and look at what you've written (after a break) and see if there are any interesting ideas in there. And then you just keep writing some more.

---

1 The World's Only Drive-In Movie Critic, and the alter ego of award-winning writer John Bloom.

Tricking the Censor: Diving Board #2

The techniques described in Diving Board #1 are good if you haven't a notion of where you are going with your writing. It's excellent for journal writing, or writing because you write at 8:00 P.M. every night no matter what. But most writers have ideas, or at least vague notions, tugging at them constantly. The difficulty is that these notions are sometimes just edgy feelings, shadows of ideas that won't take seed on their own. For those times, you might find that you need to release your idea in order to regain it. This exercise is akin to the *Eureka!* or *Aha!* moment of discovery.

When you have a vision or feeling but can't articulate it, take up a mindless physical task. It doesn't have to be strenuous, but it helps if it is repetitive. A sport that requires concentration such as soccer or even golf won't work. Walking at dusk, pulling weeds, brushing your dog — all of these tasks allow your mind to relax. Let go of your idea and involve yourself in the rhythm of what you are doing. Mindless, repetitive physical activity can distract your conscious mind, your left brain, while your right brain, the unconscious, creative mind, is able to sort out what it thinks or feels about the issue you're working on in your writing.

Many times the words will come to you if you stop trying to force them out. It is as if the words want to be written, but they must come out on their own. When they do emerge, they come from the inside, not the outside.

If a seed germinates, if an idea grows from just a line or a phrase, then you have a beginning. If you are shooting hoops or mowing the yard and a good thought comes, stop what you are doing and write down what comes to you, even if it's just on a scrap of paper. You can nurture it during your regular writing session, but write down what comes to you immediately. Write it on the palm of your hand, on a napkin, anywhere. You can't wait — once you come back into the house and feed the dog and answer the telephone, it will be too late.

So—if you've been blocked or confused or frustrated about an idea that just wouldn't work, take a break and think about something else, and then it will come to you. This writing technique does count on the Muse being around, something you can't always count on if you write at the same time every day no matter what, but you will find that once you begin cultivating ideas in this way, more ideas will come, both all day and during your scheduled writing time. Don't only write during the times when you sit down to write. The more you write, the more you will begin to listen to your relaxed mind, to what Natalie Goldberg calls your "wild mind." And the more you listen, the more you will hear.

Playing and Nurturing: Diving Board #3

Julia Cameron has published a workbook, *The Artist's Way: A Spiritual Path to Higher Creativity*. Cameron's approach involves journaling and other writing tools, including setting a weekly "date" — that is, a time to do something one enjoys purely for its own, creativity-inspiring sake. Each week's chapter title begins with the phrase "Recovering Your Sense of"—and there are many parts of the self she encourages her reader to recover: identity, abundance, possibility, strength, faith. In her approach, when we are able to connect with these important parts of ourselves which we have often lost along the way, we are able to be creative and expressive.*

The diving board at work here is the practice of spending time with your creative side, the part of you that craves attention and play and demands to be listened to. Many people spend all day long working, running errands, dealing with stress, and struggling—and then expect to sit down at the word processor for fifteen minutes and suddenly be creative and open and expressive. While it is very possible for stress to produce great creative work, writers very often find that unless they indulge their creativity, they are unable to call it at will to do their bidding.

San Francisco artist/writer Sark has an approach even more fanciful than Cameron's; she recommends writing while lying in bed, taking naps, playing, dancing, cutting up paper and making designs, and so on. Her thesis is that "repression is poison to creativity. The longer you repress it, the more stuffed down it becomes."

Here are some suggestions about how to play with your own creative drives and feelings in a way that nurtures and encourages them:

- Wear a funny or strange hat all afternoon one day a week around the house.
- Do something frivolous and even foolish on a regular basis—once a week, perhaps.
- Find a writer you like and find a passage you like by that author; copy it, word for word, twice. Do not change anything, not even punctuation.
- Find something you've written that you're not quite sure about or even that you're pretty proud of. Get a copy of this piece of writing, take it outside, and burn it. (If you're really brave or in need of a serious jolt, burn the only copy.)
- Buy yourself something—flowers, candy, a new CD—for no good reason.
- Find something you've written that you like or that you're proud of, and copy it by hand, word for word, without editing or changing anything, even punctuation.
- Pretend you're someone else; adopt a pseudonym, a persona, even another personality. Now write as if you were that person—but don't include anything in your writing that you, the real you, would write about.
- Write in the bathtub.
- Write outside.

Cameron continually challenges the participant to evaluate the level to which he or she is a "blocked creative" person, and to deal with that blocked creativity in ways that allow one's creativity to emerge.

JOURNALS AND OTHER RECORDING DEVICES

Thinking is the activity I love best, and writing to me is simply thinking through my fingers.

— *Isaac Asimov*

Journaling is one of the best ways writers can record their thoughts, ideas, impressions, and questions. It's also a great way to gather other people's ideas, through things you read, magazine articles you like, drawings that stimulate your writing process, and so forth. And, like the diving board exercises above, it's often an invaluable tool, not only because it is a record of one's life and thoughts, but also because it is a way for the writer to put words on paper as a means of defeating the blank page.* Many famous writers have used journal writing to help their creative processes and later have had those journals published. John Steinbeck, for instance, wrote *The Journal of a Novel* as he was writing *East of Eden*. Often, ideas come when a writer is recording in her journal on an unrelated topic. The mind works all the time, the unconscious often storing ideas and making connections while the conscious is doing other things. And both writers and non-writers who keep regular journals attest to the process's ability to help order their thoughts; they become addicted to the routine of journal writing; over time the discipline is a force that helps their minds make sense. May Sarton has noted, "What the journal does is make you see what is really happening to you, and to some extent, in my case, I think it's actually made me do certain things on a certain day because of the journals."

The appendix "Writing Every Day: 365 Journal Prompts" at the end of the text may be of help to you in finding ideas to write about in your journal.

Julia Cameron, in *The Artist's Way*, suggests keeping what she calls "morning pages." She explains:

Put simply, the morning pages are three pages of longhand writing, strictly stream-of-consciousness. "Oh, god, another morning. I have NOTHING to say. I need to wash the curtains. Did I get my laundry done yesterday? Blah, blah, blah . . ." They might also, more ingloriously, be called *brain drain,* since that is one of their main functions. . . . These morning meanderings are not meant to be *art.* Or even *writing.* . . . All that angry, whiny, petty stuff that you write down in the morning stands between you and your creativity. Worrying about the job, the laundry, the funny knock in the car, the weird look in your lover's eye—this stuff eddies through our subconsciousness and muddies our days. Get it on the page.

Do you see her approach? It is a means by which the writer simply puts words on paper—and thereby creates a space in which the mind can be free to create. The enemy of any journal writing, of course, is not so much the Censor within but the endless string of daily life details that keep the writer from writing. So a good habit to develop is that of keeping a journal. And journal keeping doesn't have to be a perfectly regular habit; some writers prefer to write in their journals or sketchbooks only when they have an idea. One artist we know keeps a journal when something extraordinary is happening—his family is on a vacation, or there is a sickness, or they are moving from one house to another.

Writing for Ideas and Practice 2-8

1. Write at a regular time, every day, in a journal for fifteen minutes or until you fill three pages.
2. Turn your paper to the side and write until you fill five sideways pages.
3. Get some big paper—poster-size, or butcher-paper rolled out in big sheets you cut off—and lay on the floor or on a table. Write until you fill a huge piece of paper.
4. Write for a few days without paying any attention to margins.
5. Get a tiny notebook, small enough to fit in your pocket. Write in it for a few days.
6. Do not speak any words aloud for one whole day; instead, write everything you want to say.
7. Evaluate each of the above techniques you used. Which ones opened up your writing and thinking process?

Another tool you can use for generating ideas and for helping your process along is to keep an **idea file** or "morgue." This idea file can be anything—your journal, of course, in which you not only write but also insert notes, pictures, magazine and newspaper articles, letters, and so forth. You may want to use a folder, a crate, a file drawer—one writer we know gathers her idea file into bundles, wraps them in brown paper, and ties the bundles with string. Idea files can be helpful because they are not only records of what a writer has been thinking about and reading, but also they can be used for reference.

Some argument exists as to whether to keep one's writing or not. Some writers believe in getting rid of old manuscripts and drafts. Eudora Welty has said that every time she begins a new draft, she discards the previous one—as a way to begin afresh. Ernest Hemingway, on the other hand, like Annie Dillard (see her quote on page 26) would copy out his entire manuscript up to the point where he had previously stopped writing, and then begin from there. Some writers keep all their writings, even every rough draft or snippet of paper. After Hawthorne died, those going through his papers discovered all sorts of notes and ideas for stories and novels he had not yet written. Over a career of many years, the files of such a writer could get pretty huge! And the issue of how to keep manuscripts and other writing files safe is an issue to consider; Ralph Ellison was working on his second novel when his house burned, and the manuscripts along with it. The novel was never finished. It is said that the very private J. D. Salinger has a fire-proof, cinder-block studio in which he does his work and stores it, safe from harm—and intruders.

Between keeping one's idea files and one's drafts and manuscripts, the writer can create a very helpful tool for going back, refreshing one's mind about thoughts and observations from years past, and revisiting past experiences and interests. But not every writer prefers to keep such material. Arguments still continue about the actual canon of Shakespeare's work, because he kept his scripts private so that other theater companies couldn't pirate his plays — and then, according to some scholars, destroyed all the copies. So perhaps if, in five hundred years, you want the scholars studying your work to have your authoritative version of your writing, you should be sure to leave it in a safe place.

Writing for Ideas and Practice 2-9

1. Do you prefer to store your school papers, family records, old manuscripts, and letters, or not? Why?
2. In your writing space, do you have a place for storing your work? If you could design your ideal writing space, what facilities would it have for storing your work, if any?
3. Start an idea file or morgue, separate from your journal. Then, later, look in it, and ask yourself, what is in it? Why?

Reading

One last tool you can use to help ideas and the writing process is to think about what you are putting into your mind and heart, not in terms of art or music, but in terms of *what you read.*

It is widely accepted by writers and teachers of writing and literature that what one reads has a huge impact upon what one thinks about, as well as upon one's thinking processes and abilities. Nabokov's advice to readers is, "Fondle the details." And there is a sense that if one reads good things, one will find stimulation and ideas to help the writing and thinking process. Annie Dillard says to be careful what you read, for that is what you will write.

For centuries, thinking people have been trading "reading lists" — lists of books they recommend to others to read. Were you ever given a reading list in school? Did you want to read the books on it? Why or why not? Thomas Jefferson compiled a reading list for "A Virginia Gentleman" for a younger friend of his; the curators of the museum at Jefferson's Monticello home have gathered copies of the books on that reading list, and the breadth of subject matter and depth of thought represented in those books is a testament to the greatness of Jefferson's mind.

It is interesting, of course, to analyze your own reading habits, as a kind of record of what you put into your system. Like a diet, a reading plan can be a conscious effort to introduce only certain things into your thinking process. And the list shouldn't be confined to reading only; in contemporary society, we put many different kinds of information into our heads every day —radio, television, video, computer games and interactions, billboards, mail, movies, and so forth. So perhaps you might want to think about all the information you ingest, and what its effect may be on your writing.

Ray Bradbury has said,

 If you stuff yourself full of poems, essays, plays, stories, novels, films, comic strips, magazines, music, you automatically explode every morning like Old Faithful. I have never had a dry spell in my life, mainly because I feed myself well, to the point of bursting. I wake early and hear my morning voices leaping around in my head like jumping beans. I get out of bed to trap them before they escape.

So use your reading material as your writing material as well. Specifically, your job as a writer is to take your experience, your memories, your feelings, and use those in your writing. So what you read will certainly be a part of your writing as well.

Writing for Ideas and Practice 2-10

1. Keep track of everything you read in a day—everything, including advertisements, if possible. If that's too much, keep track of everything you read in one hour. What makes up the greatest part of those materials? What do you think the effect of that is on your thinking and writing process?

2. Create a reading list for yourself based on what you would like to read, not on an image you would like to project or on someone else's expectations for you. Then, share your reading list, if you like, with other readers.

3. Create a plan for what kinds of stimuli you want your brain to have, to last perhaps one week. Include a variety of materials and then note in your journal what effects those materials had on your feelings and thoughts.

4. What do you automatically turn on when entering the house or the car—the radio? The television? The computer? The answering machine? Track your own listening and viewing habits and see what effect you think they have on your thinking and writing process.

5. What books and authors are your absolute favorites? Which ones have made a difference in the way you think, what you value, what you remember? Make a list and share it with someone else.

6. Collect words and phrases from your reading for a span of time—a day, perhaps. Write a poem, a letter, or a story, the words and phrases of which come from your reading.

PERSISTENCE AND HABITS

A great part of courage is the courage of having done the thing before.

— *Ralph Waldo Emerson*

Practice is the best of all instructors.

— *Publius Syrus*

A final component in the routines and approaches to writing you might consider is the habit of persistence. John Gardner said, "It is the sheer act of writing, more than anything else, that makes a writer." So the habits you develop, which cause or enable you to write, are not merely matters of routine, but investments in becoming a writer. Former Mississippi firefighter Larry Brown writes,

I have chosen this thing to do, away from my family, the doors closed, characters who form in my head and move to the paper, black symbols on a white sheet, no more than that. It may seem senseless to anybody else, but I know there is a purpose to my work: the spending of years at the typewriter writing until I become better than I am now, until I can publish a book, until I can see that book in a library or a bookstore.

I love this thing, even if it does not love me back.

Perhaps a final thought about your writing habits may be to say that it is imperative that you be committed not simply to writing, but to thinking about your writing habits and your writing outcomes. As chapter 1 suggested that you think and write about your goals for your writing, this chapter has presented various questions for you to consider about your work habits and the environments in which you write or wish to write. As you write, you will continue to discover your habits all along the journey.

Chapter 3 will deal with tools the writer uses to capture details—both objective details dealing with tangible and factual data, and subjective details regarding feelings, memories, and ideas. All of this work leads you farther into your own writing, consciously and deliberately, toward what you want your writing to be. But remember, too, that the only real way to understand yourself as a writer is to write.

Some final thoughts on persistence and the work and habits of writing: Anne Hamilton has noted, "If you write 1,000 words a day—that's only 4 typewritten pages—in three months, you'll have 90,000 words, a book!" So perhaps the goal isn't so far off after all. Dorothy Allison has said of this urge to write, this persistent and unyielding commitment to pursue writing, that it is the commitment to "get it down, to tell it again, to make sense of something—by god just once—to be real in the world, without lies or evasions or sweet-talking nonsense. . . . [My writing is] my deep abiding desire to live fleshed and strengthened on the page, a way to tell the truth as a kind of magic not cheapened or distorted by a need to please any damn body at all." Keep writing, and you'll find your writing life.

Writing on Your Own

1. Look back at the list you wrote in response to the Writing on Your Own exercise # 6 in chapter 1 about what kinds of things you would like to write. Pick one. Create a piece of writing that you may have wanted to do for a while—a poem, a short story, a scene, an article, an autobiographical sketch, a song lyric. (Use one of the journal prompts in the back of the book if you need ideas.) Make it something short—this is just an exercise, not a Pulitzer Prize winner (maybe).

2. a. List the steps you used in creating the work—did you sit down and write the entire thing, start to finish? Did you employ a schedule? A deadline? How much did you rely on inspiration? Did you revise? How much? How effective was the revision process? When, if ever, did you move from enthusiasm about the work to being tired of it? What starts and stops did you encounter along the way? How did they impact your writing process?

   b. Specifically, what environments, in terms of space, noise, and surroundings, did you use while writing? What effects did those environments have on your writing?

   c. Analyze your own writing process: how successful is it in producing good work?

3. Write a story, poem, scene, or memoir that no one can read—because it is too private to share with anyone. Write the unspeakable. The instructor doesn't even have to read it. Once it's done, and you've said what you really wanted to say or explored something scary or hard to face, take all the notes and drafts and pages outside, and burn them. You may substitute throwing them in the trash if you prefer. (Or, you may really like what you've written, and decide to keep it after all!)

Writing to Revise

1. Pick a piece of writing you have produced recently. Make a list of everything you can think of regarding the writing habits that influenced your writing it—what music were you listening to, where you wrote it, what you had been reading, what time of day it was and what routine you kept when you wrote it, and so forth.

2. Rewrite the piece, and surrounding the time or times in which you write the revision, change as many of the writing habits as you can. How did changing those factors influence your re-seeing of the piece?

3

WRITING WITH DETAIL

Writing to Warm Up

1. Is it better to write about what you know personally in your own experience, or to write about things that are far removed from your own experience and which you imagine?
2. Are you comfortable writing about things in your past? Why or why not?
3. How good a scientist are you—that is, how good are you at observing, recording detail, making notes about the details around you?

This chapter will encourage you to acquire and practice the skill of gathering specific, sensory details which will make any writing you do—poetry, memoir, drama, fiction—more powerful. We'll also discuss a number of places from which to gather those details: from specific sensory details found in one's immediate environment, from one's memory, and from one's imagination.

John Gardner said, about the writer's task:

 The unconscious is smart. Writers have this brilliance in them as surely as do trout fisherman and mountain climbers. The trick is to bring it out, get it down. . . . the writer who sets down exactly what he sees and feels, carefully revising time after time until he fully believes it, noticing when what he's saying is mere rhetoric or derivative vision, noticing when what he's said is not noble or impressive but silly—that writer, insofar as the world is just, will outlast Gibraltar.

— *from* On Becoming a Novelist

One of the most important jobs a writer has is to capture details. There are two ways to describe anything: with generalizations, and with specifics. The specifics may be sensory details gathered by the five senses, or they may be explicit objective details such as size, shape, color. Either way, details make one's writing more powerful than if the writing were simply a string of generalizations. This is not to say that general, large-scale statements are not appropriate in good writing; it is practically impossible to write about anything without making at least some overall observations. However, good writing, like any good art, is at least as concerned with the specific detail as with the general.

Look at a great work of art, or music, or film, or literature. Great artists are able to include specific, palpable, measurable, even common details in their work—and in so doing, perhaps paradoxically, they make their work universal. To describe a tree in such detail that any reader understands what one is describing is to show that tree to that reader, and so to make the tree a part of the reader's experience by having him see it in his mind's eye.

Is it enough simply to describe a tree? Or should the writer say something profound about the tree and its significance to the work of literature in which it appears? We argue that it is best to begin with the descriptive details, before anything else. Garrison Keillor has said that he would much prefer to read or write three hundred well-chosen words about geese than a thousand words making generalizations about America or love. That is, it matters much more for the author to depict what is authentic and specific, so that it resonates with truth, rather than to write about a general idea or impression. An excellent way to infuse one's writing with what is true is to include many, many specific details which ground the work in a specific context—physically, emotionally. Those details can come from many places. They can be found in the writer's everyday experiences; they can be found in the writer's memories of past experiences; they can be found in the writer's imagination, fusing the details of daily reality with the creative process in order to forge something new. Regardless of where she gets her details, the writer is obligated to find the details that best serve her work of art—and the more specific those details are, the better.

Too often, student writers—and, for that matter, published authors—choose the easy, the general, and the *lazy* word. Imagine that you are in any town, and you want to understand that town. If you drive through quickly, taking short glances around, you will get a sense of the city, its layout, its major features. But you will never know a city, a neighborhood, a street, until you walk through it. If you have ever walked a long distance in a town or city you thought you knew, you have found that there were details—small flowers in the sidewalk cracks, horses' smells in hidden pastures, little shops behind a corner—that you had never noticed before. But once you've walked down that street, it will always be alive afterward. The writer's job is to slow down, notice the details, record them. It is said that James Joyce sometimes labored for days over one sentence, working to make sure that sentence contained exactly the right words, the right nuances, the right subtleties. William S. Burroughs wrote, in *Naked Lunch*, "There is only one thing a writer can write about: what is in front of his senses at the moment of writing. . . . I am a recording instrument." The writer must learn to collect and capture details, and then those details can become something more than themselves.

Think about a little boy in front of a classroom of first graders. He stands with his hands behind his back, holding—something. And he begins to talk, "Um, I, um, I have, um, I have something I brought and I brought it, and it's squiggly—it's green, I think, and it has some purple or something on it too, I think, and it's wet and slimy 'cause I just took it out of the jar I had it in, and it's got these long leg things, and it's got these little bump dealies all over it, and it's sort of moving, and I think its mouth is opening, and I've had it since last Wednesday when we went to the creek behind my apartments, and it's really cute—"

The rest of the class of six-year-olds will by now have become nearly uncontrollable. And understandably so. Why? Because they want to *see the thing itself!* They don't want to hear generalizations or imprecise details—they want to see the frog, to touch it, to smell it.

And a good writer knows that his job is to show the frog.

A way to show the reader the real thing, the frog, is to include many, many specific, sensory details. In the following paragraphs you will see ways to find details in the tangible world of the senses in order to make your writing authentic and powerful.

USING THE FIVE SENSES

Believe it or not, just observing what's around you can lead to some of the most profound writing experiences you can have. And whatever comes out of that observation process—whether it's the background for a scene or the surroundings you use in a poem, or it's just a simple detail that has meaning for you—slowing down enough and focusing enough really to notice and study your surroundings is invariably a valuable investment of your time and effort.

Don't think that you have to go to someplace profound or picturesque—the ruins of Tintern Abbey on the Wye River in the Lake District in England, or the pyramids of Egypt, or the howling winds of a storm on the South Pacific have made great settings for great works, but so have kitchens and cafes and bedrooms and offices and suburban driveways and cabins by ponds and city streets and city walls. Consider a few examples, excerpts from writing by great writers past and present, and notice the use of specific, concrete details representing each of the five senses.

The early lilacs became part of this child,
And grass and white and red morning-glories, and white and red clover, and the
    song of the phoebe-bird,
And the Third-month lamb and the sow's pink-faint litter, and the mare's foal and the
    cow's calf,
And the noisy brood of the barnyard or by the mire of the pond-side,
And the fish suspending themselves so curiously below there, and the beautiful
    curious liquid,
And the water-plants with their graceful flat heads
                       — *Walt Whitman, from "There Was a Child Went Forth"*

Whitman's description includes colors, such as those of the flowers; sounds, such as the birds' songs and the barnyard's noises; images of fish suspended and the shapes of the water plants. A catalog of details like this one creates a vivid picture for the reader. Alice Walker contributes another example of sensory detail to create a powerful feeling for the reader:

The house was more dilapidated than when I was last there, barely a shack, but it was overgrown with yellow roses which my family had planted many years ago. The air was heavy and sweet and very peaceful. I felt strange walking through the gate and up the old rickety steps. But the strangeness left me as I caught sight of the long white beard I loved so well flowing down the thin body over the familiar quilt coverlet. Mr. Sweet!

His eyes were closed tight and his hands, crossed over his stomach, were thin and delicate, no longer scratchy. I remembered how always before I had run and jumped up on him just anywhere; now I knew he would not be able to support my weight. I looked around at my parents, and was surprised to see that my father and mother also looked old and frail. My father, his own hair very gray, leaned over the quietly sleeping old man, who, incidentally, smelled still of wine and tobacco . . .
                       — *from "To Hell With Dying"*

Walker uses the details describing Mr. Sweet's house—the smells of the air, the old steps, the flowers—and then uses the same affectionate, familiar kinds of descriptors to characterize Mr. Sweet himself. Those particular details in this passage make the scene vivid, real, immediate: his long white beard, his blanket, his body's shape and condition, his hair, his smell. If Walker had chosen simply to generalize and say "Mr. Sweet was the dearest man in the world to me—I always loved coming to see him," she would certainly cheat the reader and the story by making it less concrete. In the following poem, Wilfred Owen uses specific sensory detail for yet another effect:

If in some smothering dreams you too could pace
Behind the wagon that we flung him in,
And watch the white eyes writhing in his face,
His hanging face, like a devil's sick of sin;   20
If you could hear, at every jolt, the blood
Come gargling from the froth-corrupted lungs,
Obscene as cancer, bitter as the cud
Of vile, incurable sores on innocent tongues —

— *from "Dulce Et Decorum Est"*

Owen uses very specific details to create a horrible, wrenching portrayal of a battle during World War I. Students often find this poem difficult to read, not because it is hard to understand but because it is hard to *take* — it so powerfully describes a hideous and repulsive scene. Seeing the soldiers flinging the dying man into the wagon, watching him gasp for air, and hearing him choke and gargle up blood, make the scene one that cannot be ignored. And that is Owen's intent. The poem as a whole argues that propagandists who present war as a glorious, noble effort are liars — for war, from the soldier's perspective, is anything but glorious. But for Owen to state his point without the specific descriptors wouldn't be as effective.

Writing for Ideas and Practice 3-1

1. Choose one of the above passages and list what was being described with specific sensory detail — smells, sights, sounds, tastes, temperatures, textures.
2. Which of the passages is most descriptive, in terms of the details included?
3. Which of the passages creates the strongest image in your mind or feeling in you?

All of these writers are using everyday details, of sight, sound, smell, taste, and touch, not just to record the experience, the place and time, in the work, but also to make those places and times real for the reader. And so can you. Here's one way to do it:

Begin with something small. Challenge yourself to capture all of its detail — all of it. A dentist friend who is also an excellent artist skilled at photo-realistic drawings was asked by an art student, "How do you get the picture to look so real?" His answer was deceptively simple: "I draw exactly what I see." If you have ever tried to capture in a drawing or in words something to the exact detail, you know how terribly difficult a job that is. So, start with something small. Don't try to describe the entire crowd at a Super Bowl game, or even the entire contents of a Thanksgiving dinner table; rather, begin with something small, specific, limited in scope.

Writing for Ideas and Practice 3-2

1. Find an object, an ordinary object you have with you all the time—a pencil, a pen, a comb, a key, a spoon. Now, while studying that object visually and with your other senses, write 250 words describing it. Do not include any information about how you feel about that object or what you associate with it; you may only describe its physical characteristics.

2. This is a group project.
   a. Gather enough rocks so that everyone in the group can have one. Make sure each rock is different.
   b. Have someone separately mark each of the rocks with a number or code so that the rocks can be identified later.
   c. Pass out the rocks, with each person writing down (in a secret place) the identifying number or code of the rock he has been assigned.
   d. Each person should write a description of his rock on a separate sheet, using every possible sensory detail—measurements, color, texture, smell, taste, weight, shape, and so forth.
   e. When each person is done, he should take the rocks and the descriptions to a side or front desk or table, and stack the rocks together and the sheets together.
   f. When everyone is done, all in the group may come up and get a description, and then try to pick out the rock that fits the description. There will be confusion.
   g. Have anyone who is absolutely convinced that he has the correct rock matching the description read the description aloud; then, the person who wrote the description should verify whether it is, in fact, the correct description.
   h. Continue the process until all rocks are correctly identified. There will be many rocks that don't fit the first description chosen, but don't worry. The point is that most of us are not used to being precise in our word choice and use of descriptors, and this is a good way to learn.

We are still focusing on finding the details the writer finds around her, rather than those within her memories or imagination. Yes, the memory and the imagination can provide excellent details, as the second half of this chapter will explore. But it is very important to learn to be specific. The details you sense in your immediate surroundings form the basis for tangible details in your writing. Often, writers resort to generalizations because gathering the specific sensory details seems more difficult than writing more general statements. But a string of generalizations or cliches is ineffective in communicating a true experience, whereas a string of specific details, even with no additional comment by the author, can make an incredibly powerful impression. Consider many imagistic and haiku poems, for example, which often seem to have no comment by the writer, but which communicate powerfully.*

These forms of poetry will be discussed in the next four chapters.

Writing for Ideas and Practice 3-3

1. Go outside. This works fine wherever you are. Have someone call out one of the five senses every ten minutes: "Sight" and ten minutes go by, and then "Smell," and so on. (You can time yourself, but if you're paying attention to your watch, you'll be distracted; it might be better to set a timer, so you won't worry about the time so much.) Record every single detail related to that sense you can in that ten-minute period.

   Here is a student example:

   I hear a/c running.
   see gray sidewalk poured concrete, with the lines made by sweaty men 15 years ago and cracks in the side of the step in front of me
   all silver-gray, not shiny posts as what do you call them railings
   My eyes are sort of beeping, throbbing—this has been a long day
   I hear a very loud bird repeating its song
   and another, too? yes—they're marking territory or mating, same thing
   I feel the warmth of this stony concrete ramp in front of me against my stomach and knee and thigh
   my right heel is lifted, my feet ache
   I've been on my feet all day
   I still hear the steady, reliable, methodical hum of the a/c—I look over and see
   the bird's song-call-whistle, wheet, wheet, wheeeet, is repeating and echoing around me
   the a/c unit inside the science building and a brown burnt umber screen of slats of metal blocks it flows from the outside
   the bricks are pink and orange and brown and beige and ugly
   no, the building is ugly, its shape
   the white trim, the columns
   I smell the cool breeze, it cools the sweat on my arms

2. Describe the room you are in. Describe it in every detail possible. But confine your description to only two hundred words. Then, write again, this time choosing even more specific words and images as a way to make the next two-hundred-word description even more powerful and compact. Keep repeating this exercise until your description simply cannot be any more tight or specific, until no words are wasted. Don't worry about complete sentences.

3. Do the same exercise as #2 above, only this time describe your own face while looking in a mirror.

4. Test your memory for details; look at a picture or a scene for thirty seconds, and then without looking, write down every detail you can remember, with as much specificity as possible. Then, return to the picture or scene and check to see how many details you captured, and how many you missed.

These exercises all give the writer ways to uncover, notice, and record specific sensory detail. The importance of this skill, though elementary, cannot be overstated. Nonfiction writer Diane Ackerman has lamented that many nature writers aren't concerned enough about "getting the facts right"—rather, they select only some sensory detail and then make generalizations based on those few data. Don't make that mistake. Let the details show the reader what you are trying to say—and a great place to gather those details is all around you.

Once you have begun to acquire the skill of capturing specific, physical, sensory detail, it is time to practice another means of finding details: using the same processes to capture specific sensory detail from one's imagination, from one's memory, and from one's emotions. The memory and the imagination are full of powerful details—sights, smells, colors, characters, light, sound.

Finding Specific Details in the Imagination and Memory

To a certain extent, all writing is personal. That is to say, all writing reflects the perspective of its author, even perhaps the most seemingly impersonal and objective list of details. As we saw in the earlier exercises about comparing descriptions of rooms and rocks, no two people collect the same two lists of details about the same experience or object; each list shows what an individual sees or thinks. So everything a writer writes, to some extent, is in a way *about that writer*. It is very appropriate, then, for the writer to learn to find the details in his imagination and memory—and to use those details as specifically as possible.

Writing for Ideas and Practice 3-4

1. Cut out thirty nouns and verbs from a newspaper, a magazine, or some other source. Then, put all the nouns into a hat or a bowl, and put all the verbs into another hat or bowl. Draw out one noun and one verb, and write for ten minutes about what those two words suggest to you when they are combined. Here is an example:

Pillow   Fill

I hate full pillows. The kind that make my head tilt up, out of bed. Fluffy ones, full of feathers or down or styrofoamy plastic stuff, all lumpy and supposedly soft, they aren't soft. They make my neck hurt. I can't get comfortable. I twist my rear and my legs and feet for hours, all night trying to settle in further.

I have no idea how to fill a pillow. I have no idea what a pillow might fill. I guess I'm reminded of the Princess and the Pea story, where the Princess can't sleep because she is so dainty that she can detect or whatever a pea underneath all those mattresses. I know if I sleep better, my wife is less grumpy.

2. Write in response to the following prompts for five minutes each. This time, don't try to record sensory details; instead, write down impressions and thoughts.
   - window
   - darkness
   - a car
   - a bag of sugar
   - baby

   Now, go back and underline all of the specific physical and sensory details you recorded.

3. This time, do the same exercise as #2 above, except using these prompts that are less impersonal, more emotionally and imaginatively driven in nature, but still be prepared to underline specific and sensory details afterward:
   - love
   - betrayal
   - sickness
   - ambition

4. Was it more difficult to write with specific details when responding to physical objects as prompts, as in the first set, or with more personal, emotional prompts, as in the second set? Why?

We have already talked about some of the ways that writers trick themselves into writing, through use of certain habits, physical writing spaces, and surroundings. Remember that Robert Bly says that the reason writers must tell the truth is because most people lie automatically all day long. This means that many people "check out" emotionally and even mentally; they stop paying attention to their feelings and their environments, the details within and around them. But writers try to be sensitive to their environments and to their feelings and memories; they learn to pay attention to small details and notice the things other people often don't see.

As we discussed in chapter 1, some people find it very difficult to write about details in their memories. When you are writing about your past, or responding to events in your past or in your private life, then the subject matter has become personal. However, as we've said, one of the objectives of the writing journey is for the writer to have the option to deal with his feelings, his past, his present, by writing about what he has experienced and felt, even if it may be blocked or hidden or painful.

All of us have experiences and ideas worth writing about in some way or another. So, as you think about your purpose as a writer and why you want to write, you also need to think about what your own experience can tell you about your thinking process, your emotions, and the things which you alone can contribute to the world of ideas through your writing.

Does this mean that the only source for meaningful writing material is one's own experience? Absolutely not. The writer strives to invent a new reality, not to record "what happened." Creative writing is not journalism — it is imagination and language, invention and exploration, forms and rhythms and images. But it is possible and even desirable for the writer to find a way to get in touch with some basic, fundamental details about herself in order to secure a basis of details from which to work. Often, we human beings have difficulty separating our sense of what is happening to us and around us from how we feel. But collecting some specific data about your past, your family, your experiences, can create a kind of database which you can then consider in an impersonal, detached way as a source for information and material. You may be able to "back off" from the details in your memories and experiences enough to see them through writing, perhaps almost objectively—in which case you can use those details in a different way than if they were still tied up to feelings and memories.

Writing for Ideas and Practice 3-5

1. In about two hundred and fifty words, define yourself for someone who does not know you well or at all. Who are you? What are you about? What is important to you, what is scary for you, what do you love, what are some of your basic characteristics? Remember, this is to be a fairly detached, non-emotional description, as if you were an objective observer.

2. Quickly write down everything you can fit in fifty words about any three of the following people in your life; don't censor any idea or memory you have, just record the sensory details you remember about them.
   a. Grandmother
   b. Father
   c. Ninth grade teacher
   d. Best friend
   e. Boss
   f. Enemy

3. Pick one of these figures, and, as fast as you can and with no censoring, record every specific detail you can about that person; fill three pages. Here's an example written by a student in one of our classes:

> Granny she played poker for money and wheezed and coughed and stumbled through her house if my grandfather hadn't been killed, I wouldn't be here — my mother might have just been a spunky little farmer's daughter and she might've felt more like staying home and less like going off and running away from home and getting married . . . my grandmother—wrinkles a sad face, even though she smiled a lot and tried to look serene, a sad face, she got tired and sad and couldn't go on after a while, two dead husbands and a bad track record;

the smell of cigarettes in her LTD; rum and Cokes and watching Johnny Carson; she regretted a lot; she never knew what it was like to step outside her tiny world, and she didn't understand her children or grandchildren but it didn't matter they kept coming back to her, coming home, I wonder what she thought of my father . . .

4. Fill out this inventory of your past as fully and completely as possible, with no censoring or whitewashing the details you remember. Is it possible simply to record "just the facts"? Probably not. We all see things through our own imaginative and emotional filters. And yet, in beginning, it is important to record specific details as closely as possible to the way they actually occurred, so that you can use them.

My childhood:
- I loved:
- I hated:
- My best friend:
- Something I lost:
- Something I learned:
- Something I needed:

My high school:
- I loved:
- I hated:
- My best friend:
- Something I lost:
- Something I learned:
- Something I needed:

Summer holidays:
- Who was there:
- What we did:
- What I felt:
- What I wanted and didn't get:
- What I got and didn't want:
- What I remember most vividly:

Winter holidays:
- Who was there:
- What we did:
- What I felt:
- What I wanted and didn't get:
- What I got and didn't want:
- What I remember most vividly:

My family:
- I regret:
- I wished for:
- I never got:
- I always wanted:
- I dearly loved:
- I miss:

We are working on ways to uncover, notice, and use the sensory, descriptive, specific details which are part of every scene worth writing about, even the most potentially vague, general ideas from the imagination or the memory. The writer can go to the fleeting thought, the scrap of an idea, the scarce recollection, and with the imagination, can and must find all sorts of concrete, vivid ways to communicate those ideas to the reader. You are learning to do just that.

Writing for Ideas and Practice 3-6

1. Respond quickly—in bursts of short ideas freewritten in response to each of the following prompts:
   a. I think
   b. I hate
   c. I wish
   d. I learned
   e. I love
   f. I regret
2. Gather three or four photographs or drawings from various sources (but the fewer advertisements, the better—it will work more powerfully if you use a book of art, of photographs, or a history book). Pick one photograph at a time; look at the photograph, and then record:
   a. all of the specific, non-emotional details you can in one minute, those that describe the photograph simply based on what anyone looking at the photograph would see or be able to surmise;
   b. all of the specific personal, imaginative details you can in one minute, those details one can't find in looking, but which you the writer find in your imagination as you look at the person(s) and/or scenes in the work.

Using Specific Details in Your Writing

Consider a thought about the issue of finding personal details in one's memories and impressions and feelings: ironically, your specific memories, rather than giving you material for your writing, can get in the way of your writing, because you're too tied to your memories to allow your imagination to do the work to let your story or poem or play emerge. Nietzsche said, "We have art in order not to die of the truth." If real life made sense, why would we need art at all? Why would we need art to help us organize and make sense of our experience? So using an actual memory may be helpful, but it may be detrimental as well.

Richard Hugo in *The Triggering Town* says to *forget* all those specific memories, and write pretending you are someone or something else. He suggests that when writing, you can pretend your poem takes place in any setting. It is even good to deliberately change the actual details of memory and experience. Then, you can use not necessarily the details that occurred, but those that are most appropriate for the subject you are imaginatively exploring with your writing. Certainly, you will use specific detail. Some of it may be from memory. Some of it may be from imagination. Some of it may be from present experience and observation, which we practiced in the first part of this chapter. But the artist's job is to pick and choose among those specific, sensory details, both real and imagined, to create a new kind of reality through his writing.

Russian acting theorist and teacher Konstantin Stanislavsky advocated studying "affective memory," one's deepest memories which correspond to the situation facing one's character, in order to help an actor to get in touch with the character he was performing. Lee Strasberg applied Stanislavsky's ideas and developed "the Method" school of acting, which he taught at the Actors Studio. His rival, however, the great acting coach Stella Adler, argued that what is best is to connect to one's imagination, not one's past. "The conscious mind will limit your acting and cripple you," she argued. "Your creative imagination will not."

Perhaps the truth lies in neither of these extremes. It is possible for the writer somehow to do both—to connect the things in her memory with the things in her imagination, and in that fusion to create something altogether new and true. Creative writing, in fact, is a mixture of memory, experience, and imagination. The ideal progression might be to get in touch with your own feelings and memories, along with the details you see and you remember, and to concurrently imagine and create alternate worlds in your own writing.

We don't know how much of Shakespeare's own life experience went into the situations in his plays; we do know, however, that Shakespeare presents powerful emotions and experiences in his plays which correspond to universal human experiences, translatable into different languages, contexts, and cultures, and still "true" for all. All good writing has an authenticity that comes from being *true*. This doesn't mean the events in them actually happened; the events usually didn't happen, though sometimes writers can take their own experiences or those of others and use them for the basic material from which to create a story, a poem, a play. When a piece of writing is true, it honestly reflects the heart, the mind, the idea, the emotions it is trying to share with the reader. And you *know* when something is true, and when it is fake or cheap or formulaic. The measure of the "right" details to include is not whether they actually occurred or exist, but whether they serve the work of art's overall purpose or progression, in order to make the work "true." And if it is true for enough people, it can become great writing. It is for this reason that Jean Cocteau said, "The poet is a liar who always speaks the truth," and Anatole France said, "To know is nothing at all; to imagine is everything."

Robert Frost's poem "Home Burial," for instance, is a poem that rings true for many readers. It depicts a husband and wife grieving over the death of a small child, and whose body the husband has just buried in the old family cemetery out back. This excerpt comes just as the wife has realized she can see the graveyard out her window. Read this part of the poem and see if it rings true for you:

"Don't, don't, don't, don't," she cried.

She withdrew shrinking from beneath his arm
That rested on the banister, and slid downstairs;
And turned on him with such a daunting look,   35
He said twice over before he knew himself:
"Can't a man speak of his own child he's lost?"

"Not you! Oh, where's my hat? Oh, I don't need it!
I must get out of here. I must get air.
I don't know rightly whether any man can."   40

"Amy! Don't go to someone else this time.
Listen to me. I won't come down the stairs."
He sat and fixed his chin between his fists.
"There's something I should like to ask you, dear."

"You don't know how to ask it."   45
                                          "Help me, then."
Her fingers moved the latch for all reply.

Frost tells the truth in this poem. It isn't a pleasant subject, but it is a reflection of a real human experience, whether this incident or one like it actually happened in Frost's life. That's not the point; Frost connected to a
truth of human experience, and wrote about it with specific details and
truthful emotions in a way that communicates the experience powerfully.

Rick was using this poem in a creative writing class as an example of
how character can be communicated through dialogue and suggestion rather
than direct explanation. Two students took turns reading the parts, and it
was going along well, everyone looking down and making notes as they read,
when an older man in the back of the room got up and walked toward Rick.
As Rick describes it, "I looked up, and it was one of my best students, a fellow named Mike; he had tears in his eyes, and as he passed me, he murmured, 'Can't go on—I'll wait in the hall on this one—too close to memory.'
Now, had this man had to bury his own child? Or was the strained dialogue
and interaction between the husband and wife too pointed, too painful for
him to read? I never found out, but the poem had hit home."

Natalie Goldberg advises her students that if they begin to cry while
they write, just keep crying and keep writing. Write through the tears.
Maybe that might have helped Mike. But the point is that we are to tell the
truth, no matter what, if we are to get to the heart of what the artist within
us is trying to express—and the specific details we use make the heart of
the thing real, tangible, visible.

For instance, notice the unflinching detail and human emotion in this
passage from *The Iliad*:

> So, when he had spoken, glorious Hector reached out to his baby,
> who shrank back to his beautifully dressed nurse's breast,
> screaming, terrified at the sight of his great father,
> afraid of the helmet's shining bronze and the horse-hair crest,
> which the boy thought were nodding at him from above.
> And at that, his loving father laughed aloud; his mother did, too;
> and great Hector took off his helmet, smiling,
> and put the beautiful war dressing on the ground. He reached
> again for his dear son, and tumbled him in his strong arms, and
> kissed the boy, and, closing his eyes, said a prayer to the gods:
> "Father Zeus and all you gods, I ask that this son of mine
> be granted greatness by you, and be a great ruler over his people—
> become as strong as I am, and someday rule over our city of Troy,
> and someday let them all say, 'He is an even better man than his father,'
> when he walks in from fighting and defeating his enemies,
> bringing home the bloody, glorious trophies of war, making his family proud."

The scene depicts a man leaving his family to go to war, an emotional scene. What is especially poignant about this passage is that Hector is the doomed hero, the man who, in defending his city and his family, will die; and the young boy he holds in his arms will die at the hands of the Greeks, thrown from the top of the city walls. Homer here focuses on a tiny, almost insignificant detail, a warrior pausing to embrace his son before going out to battle. But it isn't at all insignificant; instead, it tells us everything about Hector. We see him smiling and laughing at his son amidst the thick of battle and almost certain defeat; we see him praying to the gods not for his own glory but for his son's; we see his splendor as a warrior and a prince, but also his sensitivity as a man. That's our job as writers: to know what we're writing about, and to tell it as clearly and as honestly as possible with specific details. It doesn't have to be overt; sometimes writers get to the truth seemingly indirectly, through the back door—but they are still giving us the truth.

Literature is full of these great and minor scenes which tell the truth —big ones, from *The Iliad* or some other great work, and little ones, tucked away in quiet moments where only the most attentive reader will discover them. The greatest writers are great not because they do great things with form or language or style, but because their writing is full of this unflinching, truthful depiction of experience. Shakespeare, it has been said, is great partly because he has no "perfect" characters—all of his characters, no matter how noble, have complex personalities with flaws and weaknesses. Sometimes the best modern heroes are also tinged with the details that reveal the truth of real human experience; when Bruce Willis played the lead in the first *Die Hard* movie, one of his aims, he said, was to portray a reluctant hero who was "terrified—I mean, the guy's up against a whole squad of bad guys and he's alone and barefoot; I just had to make him scared—I know I would be"—so that, in contrast to the traditional superhero, James Bond or Batman or a John Wayne character, what audiences saw in the details of Willis's portrayal, his hands shaking as he loaded his gun and his face flinching as he had to run barefoot across shattered glass, was a very human and truthful way to present the character.

Writing for Ideas and Practice 3-7

1. You are a child in a crowded room filled with adults and no one will listen to you. Record the scene and the child's feelings with as many specific, sensory details and as few generalizations as possible.
2. Now, you are a lonely woman on the verge of suicide whose daughter is dying of cancer and who hears the footsteps of her abusive husband on the porch while it is raining. Record the scene and the woman's feelings with as many specific, sensory details and as few generalizations as you can.
3. Look at a great work of art such as a painting or a sculpture depicting a person or group of persons. (Seeing the work in person is best if you can manage it; if not, a print in a book or a slide will do; a photocopy will not.) How does the scene in the picture or the sculpture make you feel? Imagine you are a character in the picture or the figure in the sculpture; what does the character feel, think, say? Why? Be very, very specific and descriptive.

Your job as a writer, then, is to capture details from many sources—both the most impersonal from your observations, and the personal, connected to emotions, memories, imagination; both immediately about you, and within your thoughts and memories. Those details, when specific and sensory, make good writing powerful and real. Knowing which details to use is delicate and exhilarating and often frustrating. It is also the stuff of good writing.

Writing on Your Own

1. Conjure up a memory. It doesn't have to be anything profound or traumatic, though it can be if you wish. It can be from the recent or distant past. Think about that memory for a moment, and then do the following exercises in freewriting style, in response to the memory:
   a. Describe it in every detail you can—every sensory and specific detail—so that it is grounded in concrete detail as well as emotional overtone.
   b. Record every feeling, thought, association you have with the memory—all the personal, emotional, imaginative details you can find in your memory or in your present feelings about this memory event.

    c. Imagine that you are an outsider and describe the scene as if you were watching it but not one of the people or things involved in it. Which of the details would you record?

    d. Imagine that you are someone in the memory, but you are not yourself as it happened to you; describe it now, with both impersonal, sensory detail and personal, emotional, imaginative detail, related from the point of view of the other person.

    e. Give an account of what happened, but as yourself in the present—not as you were when you were involved at the time. What will the difference in perspective bring you to see?

    f. Take the material you have generated and change its form, turning it into a poem, a scene in a play, a short story, or an autobiographical sketch.

2. Perform the same exercise as above, only this time the scene you are describing is not a memory of something you experienced in the past, but an imaginary scene which you have invented. There will probably be both elements of memory and purely imagined elements in your writing as you create the fictional scene. But be sure that the scene contains many, many specific details and sensory images to make it concrete, vivid, and powerful.

3. Pick any short poem or very short story you like, and do the following in response to it:

    a. List all of the sensory descriptors and details in the work, those that simply give it its specific context and setting.

    b. List all of the personal, emotional, imaginative descriptive words and details in the work, those that describe not the sensory detail of the setting but those that describe and communicate the feelings and imaginative elements in the work.

    c. Write about why the author chose the balance between impersonal, sensory details and personal, emotional, imaginative details in the work, and what effect that mixture has on your reading of it.

Writing to Revise

1. Find any one part of a piece you have written recently which you feel doesn't contain genuine, truthful communication of experience and emotion. It may be only a few lines from a poem, or one paragraph from a short story. Make a list of the things you find lacking in the excerpt—"Mary shouldn't react to her mother that way, she's too angry," perhaps, or "The character might need to be less certain of his actions here —I'm not sure." Once you have identified the excerpt, do the following things:

    a. Reread it several times, and mark the specific words or details you think need to be changed or rethought.

    b. Write a number of options for each word or detail you have identified; give yourself many options.

    c. Try as vividly as possible to connect to the actual experience or emotion or idea

being explored in the piece, and be willing to rethink the entire piece if necessary in order to find the truth in it.

d. Pick the option that best would set the piece on the right course, or write a new
option, and rewrite the excerpt—or the entire piece.

A Transition to Part Two

Pick a piece of writing you would like to do, from your idea file or morgue. Think about
what that writing is about, at its heart, and then answer: would I like to write it as a short
story, a poem, a play, or a memoir? Notice that in the next part of the book, we are going
to begin discussing specific literary genres and tools—but those tools are never the point.
The tools serve the overall purpose of the work; the purpose is for you to express your experience, real or imagined, in a way that is true and meaningful. Answer the following
questions:

1. What have you learned so far about your own writing process?
2. Look back at your goals and outlooks on writing you recorded in response to chapter
    1. What have you kept the same attitude about? What have you changed? Why?
3. Now that you've had some practice and spent time thinking about it, what do you
    want to write, and why? What do you *not* want to write, and why not?

Writing in the Information Age: Internet Resources

The proliferation of personal computers has drastically changed the way writers work and conduct business. Nowhere is this fact more apparent than on the Internet. As a writer, you can use the Internet to join writers' groups, use search engines to find information, take writing courses, or even publish your work on the World Wide Web.

There is an abundance of excellent information on the Internet, but the Internet is not like a public or college library, where information is organized in a prescribed fashion and supervised by a qualified librarian. Rather, the Internet is a global network of communication and information, and anyone with access to a server can put a site on or communicate via the Net. Web sites can be commercial, educational, or personal. Therefore, some Internet resources are more helpful and reliable than others, and deciding whether or not you receive accurate information is largely up to you. Nevertheless, you can access an abundance of pertinent and helpful information on writing and other topics of interest without leaving your home.

E-mail Lists

If you have e-mail capabilities, you might want to join an e-mail list for writers or on writing. An e-mail list is an asynchronous discussion group consisting of a group of people who have some common interest. You subscribe to a list by sending an e-mail request to the listserv. Then you receive a copy of each message each individual member of the listserv sends to the group. If you would like to contribute to the discussion, you send a message to the listserv, and a copy of your message goes to each member on the list. There are slight variations in listserv procedures, but the most common way of subscribing to a list is to send an e-mail requesting that you be added to the list. These requests are usually handled electronically, so it is important to follow the procedures you find in the descriptions of the lists. Usually, the instructions ask you to send a message to the listserv (or majordomo) and include the following information in the body of your message:

SUBSCRIBE <NAME OF GROUP> <FIRST NAME LAST NAME>

(Omit the brackets in your message and leave the subject line blank.)

You will receive a confirmation of your subscription, usually within twenty-four hours, as well as an **FAQ** (Frequently Asked Questions) message. DO NOT delete the FAQ, for it will give you directions on posting to the list, unsubscribing to the list, and other important information.

When you join a list, you will begin to receive mail automatically. Be sure to **lurk** (observe) for a short time to get to know the topics being discussed and to familiarize yourself with the type of community you have joined. Joining a list is a bit like coming into the room during the middle of a lengthy conversation, and it takes a little while to gain your bearings. Interrupting the conversation with an inappropriate comment or statement is embarrassing, and some lists are kinder than others to **newbies**, or newcomers. You might get **flamed** (chastised or insulted), although most lists are actually close-knit communities of people who care for one another and encourage the free exchange of information.

A comprehensive list of e-mail lists can be found at **The Liszt Directory of E-mail Discussion Groups** at **http://www.liszt.com**. You can search this list by keyword (poetry, fiction, etc.) and get descriptions and subscription procedures for e-mail groups that fit that category. Some of these lists are high volume, and some of them stay on topic better than others. If you subscribe to a list that you are dissatisfied with, try another list. It might take a couple of attempts before you find the community of writers that you feel comfortable with.

Usenet Newsgroups

The Usenet newsgroup is like an e-mail list in that it is a way for people to communicate with each other on a specific topic. The difference is that Usenet groups in general have a much larger audience. Think of the Usenet newsgroups as giant virtual bulletin boards divided by topic. These newsgroups contain postings of items of interest and can serve as a way of carrying on very public asynchronous conversations. There are discussions and heated debates, requests for information, and invitations to Web sites or events. The concept is at the same time anarchical and hierarchical, and the topics begin with a very general abbreviation, such as rec. (for recreation, hobbies, literature), soc. (for social topics), or misc. (for miscellaneous). The topics then get more specific with each new abbreviation, such as rec.arts for the arts, and rec.arts.books for specific discussions or postings on books. As with any information you find using the Internet, remember that newsgroups are not refereed for accuracy and tend to be more public than e-mail lists, so you should be discriminating in sifting through these postings.

You can access newsgroups through your Web browser, and many Internet services provide separate newsgroup readers. If you find these readers to be inadequate, you can find shareware newsreaders to download from the Internet. If you access the Internet from a university, keep in mind that not all systems administrators subscribe to newsgroups, especially ones in the .alt category. Anyone can set up an .alt newsgroup, and although there are some really good newsgroups in this category, others can be rather bizarre or offensive. You can find a newsgroup for your topic at **The Liszt of Newsgroups at http://www.liszt.com/news/**. You can also use the Web to search for postings on newsgroups. One way to search is to access **The Deja News Search Page** at **http://dejanews.com/** or **Altavista Search Engine** at **http://altavista.digital.com**. Both sites search by keyword, but if you use Altavista, pull the drop-down Search menu and ask the engine to search Usenet newsgroups instead of the Web.

The World Wide Web

Perhaps the part of the Internet that gets the most publicity and traffic is the World Wide Web. The World Wide Web is a treasure chest of information for writers. Using a Web browser such as Netscape Navigator or Microsoft Internet Explorer, you can find information about the craft of writing, read Web-published literature from Shakespeare to Spam haiku, or shop for software products that will aid you with the writing process.

You can search for information on the World Wide Web in two ways. One is to type in the exact address of the Web site you want to visit, and the other is to use a search engine to search for sites by topic. Think of the search in this way: If you want to send a letter to someone, and you know the address, all you have to do is address the letter and put it in the mail. In surfing the Net, the **URL** (Uniform Resource Locator) is the address, and you type in this address in the **Location** or **URL** box of your Web browser.

On the other hand, if you know what you are looking for but don't have a specific address to find the information, then you will want to search the Net with a search engine, or a search index, just as you would look in the phone book to find someone's address. Type in a topic, and the search engine or index looks for Web sites that match the keywords you have entered. Although Web addresses and sites change frequently, here are the URLs of a few search engines and indexes you might find helpful:

Yahoo	http://www.yahoo.com/
Lycos	http://www.lycos.com/
Webcrawler	http://www.webcrawler.com/
Altavista	http://altavista.digital.com/
Hotbot	http://hotbot.com/
Metasearch	http://metasearch.com/

Your search results will be displayed as a list of titles which are underlined. These are hyperlinks, and a click of the mouse on a hyperlink will transport you to that Web site. You can then maneuver back and forth until you find what you are looking for. Follow the links into cyberspace until you get lost and then work your way back home. Some of our best discoveries on the Net came from wandering aimlessly through cyberspace.

There are numerous resources for writers on the Web, including online writing courses, writing tips, articles on writing and literature, and works of literature on the Internet. Some of these include classics and public domain works that you download through gopher and FTP sites,[1] and some of them have been designed specifically for publication on the World Wide Web. They have been coded into **HTML** (HyperText Markup Language—the language of the Web), and although some of the literature is converted to Web format from the printed page, others are published exlusively as Web documents, either in electronic magazines and journals or as part of someone's personal home page. Whatever the source, these documents are designed to be read on the Web, and many of them integrate hyperlinks as part of the text itself, forming a new subgenre of literature, hypertext literature. If you have access to a server and have a good HTML editing program or know a little HTML coding, you can enter the realm of Web publishing. You won't get rich or win the Pulitzer, but it is one way of going global with your work.

Once you start exploring the Internet, you will find multitudes of places to visit, some designed for edification, and some just for fun. The information you find in Web sites, just like in other Internet resources, is not necessarily monitored, so always check the accuracy of the information you receive, but there are many wonderful and helpful resources out in cyberspace, so it is worth a look. Happy surfing!

---

1 Gopher and FTP sites can be accessed through most WWW browsers.

Part Two

❖ ❖ ❖ ❖
❖ ❖ ❖
❖

Techniques, Genres, and the Craft of Writing

THE VISION OF POETRY

The previous chapter focused on capturing detail in your mind's eye and recreating that detail in your writing. This chapter expands on how to capture detail in your work by looking not only at objective and subjective detail, but by also examining figurative language and showing you how using figurative language can help you add detail and texture to your writing. Although this chapter is primarily concerned with poetry, you will find figurative language in all writing genres.

Writing to Warm Up

Read the following prose passage several times.

> The faded purse loops from the back arm of the wheelchair, hanging onto dignity, its pea-green exterior worn from being gripped and hugged for thirty years. The gold clasp is too difficult for knotted hands to open, but the purse is now just an ornament anyway, or a security blanket, for it has not seen the outside of the nursing home in many years. Once this majestic purse hung on a proud arm, filled with hair combs, lemon drops wrapped in tissues, and a pocketbook with extra nickels for the children when they smiled and said "Please." Now the purse is empty, for no children come to this too-warm place that smells like stale sheets and stringy hair.

1. Now take out the connectors and all of the words you feel are superfluous and arrange the remaining words on the page any way you wish.

2. Compare your version with other students'. What is the difference in content and style in your selection from the original?
3. What does examining the language in the passage by rearranging it tell you about the language? About the ideas in the passage?

DEFINING POETRY

Visualize a story or scene you have written. In your mind's eye, the scene plays like a movie. You see action, even if the story only moves psychologically. A character moves, grows, changes, and you react to the movement. However, this chapter is not concerned with relating a scene in a linear way. Rather, your intent will be to create a single slide or series of slides to project to your reader. These slides can be shown alone or in a series—they can even tell a story—but they aren't as concerned with linear time or vision as narration usually is. For example, although the ballad tells a story, most ballads are more concerned with telling a story that derives its meaning from feeling rather than from plot, and you might find gaps in the story line and implausible story lines.

We speak here of poetry, but the word *poetry* conjures up preconceived notions about what a poem should be, usually based on definitions in the glossaries of literature books. Many beginning writers ponder technique—stanzaic form, rhyme, meter, scansion—and before they know it they are so overwhelmed by form that they risk losing sight of the essence of the poem. Craft and technique are important, of course, but technique should complement and underscore the idea, not supersede or detract from it.

Without relying on technical or dictionary definitions, write your own definition of poetry, and try to be as subjective and personal as possible. When you have finished, read your definition aloud. Does it qualify for the glossary of a literature book? Or does it capture the "taut truth" and lead "where Beauty stands and waits," to use the words of Lawrence Ferlinghetti?

We asked some of our students for their definitions of poetry, and here are some of their responses:

Poetry is . . .

- "a condensed microcosm of life as we humans try to interpret it"
- "a tribute to man's existence"
- "inscribed emotions"
- "a puzzle; you must put the pieces together to understand the picture"

Okay, you think, *but those are students' definitions. What about "real" poets?* Students *are* "real" poets, but let's look at how some established and anthologized poets define poetry:

- Walt Whitman thought of the poet as a prophet, and said, "Let me not dare . . . to attempt the definition of poetry."
- Robert Frost, in "The Figure a Poem Makes," stated that poetry "begins in delight, it inclines to the impulse, it assumes direction with the first line laid down, it runs a course of lucky events, and ends in a clarification of life."
- E. B. White said that a "true poem contains a seed of wonder: but a bad poem, egg-fashion, stinks." He also said, "Poetry is intensity, and nothing is intense for long."

Many poets have addressed this topic in their poetry, including recent Nobel Prize winner Wislawa Szymborska:

 Some Like Poetry

Some—
that means not all.
Not even the majority of all but the minority.
Not counting school, where one must,
and poets themselves,   5
there will be perhaps two in a thousand.

Like—
but one also likes chicken-noodle soup,
one likes compliments and the color blue,
one likes an old scarf,   10
one likes to prove one's point,
one likes to pet a dog.

Poetry—
but what sort of thing is poetry?
More than one shaky answer   15
has been given to this question.
But I do not know and do not know and clutch on to it
as to a saving bannister.

So who has the right answer? What *is* poetry? And if poetry eludes definition, how can you learn how to write it? One of the most wonderful things about writing poetry is that you can follow established patterns or defy definition. The writer can invent, reinvent, regenerate, mystify, and communicate—all in the same poem.

Imagery

Poets, whether they use traditional forms or create their own form, must create their own vision from darkness, meaning out of meaninglessness. Writing poetry is paradoxical in nature. The genre can free the writer from all of the restrictions that are a part of scene-based writing, and yet being given that freedom does not make writing poetry "easier." As a poet, you are faced with overwhelming choices. You can choose, for instance, to dispense with traditional poetic form, as E. E. Cummings did, and create your own light from chaos:

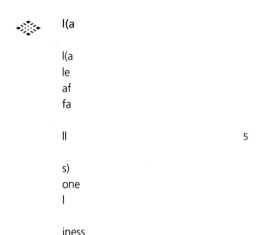

l(a

l(a
le
af
fa

ll   5

s)
one
l

iness

In this poem Cummings challenges his reader to rise above assumptions of what a poem should be. In fact, he plants a kind of dynamite in the words themselves, scattering them down the page. Is this an act of anarchy? Or is it nonsensical? Look at the poem and see how carefully it is constructed. In the text of the poem, a leaf falls, one leaf, alone—loneliness is created not only in the words but also in the way the letters are arranged on the page. In this poem, as in many of his poems, Cummings asks us to open ourselves to the possibility that language can be used in many different ways, and yet the poem still communicates an idea and a feeling.

If the poet dispenses with tradition, then, his challenge, whether his style is complex or simple, is to create light, not just to make what is dark even darker. The Irish poet W. B. Yeats said, "Hammer your thoughts into unity." Your form, then, follows your thoughts.

Of course, it is your prerogative to follow a traditional form, but sometimes a beginning poet risks drowning in form, picture lost, vision obscured. He says, "Now I am going to write a pantoum about my girlfriend." He stares at the whiteness of the blank page, and as he writes, he scratches out all he has written. The form masters the poet; the poet becomes a puppet. This is not to say that deciding to write a poem using a specific form is wrong. Later in this text you will be asked to practice different poetic forms, and many times you will discover your ideas as you practice form. For now, though, our focus is on discovering ideas in a different way.

Later, we will examine some of the well-known traditional forms and practice them, and knowledge and practice will aid you in polishing technique as well as in discovering new ideas. As you become more comfortable with the traditional forms, you might find that you enjoy the challenge of constraint, that in form you find freedom. For now, however, remember this: *Poetry moves from inside.* Let your vision emerge first; then decide on a form that best expresses that vision.

Writing for Ideas and Practice 4-1

1. Go back to Writing for Ideas and Practice 3-3. That exercise asked you to go outside and gather details using your five senses. Repeat that exercise now, and this time, instead of gathering everything you can, focus your attention on something small; find something that you wouldn't have noticed while standing. Search for the tiny, the minute. In no more than ten words, capture it — its appearance and its essence. Choose your words carefully, and arrange those words on the page in any way you wish. Read your word picture aloud. How does it sound?

2. This exercise is the same as the previous one, but now, find a partner. Each of you should write your own description of the same object. Again, you may arrange your words in any order on the page. Share your word pictures with each other. Are they the same? Different? How? Why?

3. List the five greatest simple things in life. Think simple; be specific: a hot bubble bath, a great meal, salt water fishing. Choose one of the items on your list and paint a word picture of it. In your description, show us the joy that exists in it. Share your pictures with others.

4. This exercise is similar to an earlier exercise, but this time, choose a passage describing someone in an example of prose you like—a story, a novel, an article—and boil it down by taking out all the connectors, the articles like "the" and "an," and the phrases and sentences in which the author is telling instead of showing. Then, look at what you have left. Rearrange it on the page, and there you have the makings of a poem.

The preceding exercises are designed to provoke thought regarding two important considerations about poetry:

- Poetry is prose in concentrated form; careful **diction** (word choice) is of paramount importance.
- Pictures speak louder than words. Show your readers what you want them to see and feel by relating **images**, or word pictures.

Although many poets use specific images as a *part* of the whole poem, some poetic movements have stressed that the singular image *is* the whole poem. The Japanese haiku poets and, later, the Imagist poets wrote poems that focus on creating *one image* that evokes *one feeling*. In this kind of poem, the poet must capture that essence of what she is trying to communicate, and communicate that essence directly. For example, consider the following poems written by the haiku master Basho:

Winter rain—
the field stubble
  has blackened.

Summer grass—
all that's left
  of warriors' dreams.

Both of these poems, like many haiku poems, focus on a particular season. The seasons indicate progression of time or age as well as mood. The image is created in the first part of the poem, and the conclusion or insight comes in the second part of the poem or is implied, as in "Winter Rain."

Each poem is a statement or embodiment of one image which suggests one primary emotion or draws one significant conclusion, though it may not be easy to find in one quick reading. This poetic form relies solely upon **imagery**, or word pictures, to communicate its feeling.

At the beginning of the twentieth century, the Imagist movement, founded by Ezra Pound and later led by H. D. (Hilda Doolittle), was greatly influenced by Japanese haiku poets such as Basho. These poets also used imagery as the singular force of a poem, but they did not necessarily adhere to the Haiku form. They composed in free verse and advocated using musical phrasing as a rhythmic basis rather than adhering to a strict form such as the syllabic structure of the haiku masters.

Poets such as William Carlos Williams and Carl Sandburg created poems that use words in a way similar to how the Impressionist painters used color—to create images that communicate not just what something looks like, but how to perceive it, to *feel* it, as well. Here is a poem by Carl Sandburg which is a good example of using an image as the singular force of a poem.

 Fog

The fog comes
on little cat feet.
It sits looking
over harbor and city
on silent haunches   5
and then moves on.

What is this poem about? An important philosophical insight? An obscure theme? Anyone who reads more into the poem than just what it says will be missing a delight: the poem is about *fog*. It centers around a single image, the fog coming in like a cat. But instead of just saying, "it was foggy yesterday and the fog reminded me of a cat, the way it curled around my block," the poem communicates the essence of that experience with one simple image which creates a feeling.

Here's another example which centers upon one image. Read this poem by William Carlos Williams, then close your eyes and *feel* it.

This Is Just to Say

I have eaten
the plums
that were in
the icebox
and which   5
you were probably
saving
for breakfast

Forgive me
they were delicious   10
so sweet
and so cold

Can you *experience* the poem when you read it? See it; taste it; *be there*. You might even want to draw or color the images that you see in the poem to experience them even more fully. Now look at the poem again. Try to experience what the poem is saying beyond the sweet, cold plums. What is the speaker's attitude? Is he really remorseful, asking for forgiveness, or is he being playful? The poem also indicates a relationship between two people. Can you draw any conclusions about the relationship between them from the text of the poem? The poem is concentrated—a few words say a great deal, and not just about plums, either.

Of course, not all poets write short poems which contain only one visual image. Most poets, though, use some type of imagery in their poems. Although the following poem is longer than a haiku or imagist poem, it also uses one dominant image as its center. In this poem Galway Kinnell takes great care in choosing words that make the reader experience the delight of blackberry eating, then equates that experience with writing poetry:

    Blackberry Eating

I love to go out in late September
among the fat, overripe, icy, black blackberries
to eat blackberries for breakfast,
the stalks very prickly, a penalty
they earn for knowing the black art   5
of blackberry-making; and as I stand among them
lifting the stalks to my mouth, the ripest berries
fall almost unbidden to my tongue,
as words sometimes do, certain peculiar words
like *strengths* or *squinched*,   10
many-lettered, one-syllabled lumps,
which I squeeze, squinch open, and splurge well
in the silent, startled, icy, black language
of blackberry-eating in late September.

Kinnell uses the word *black* seven times in the poem. Why? What is the similarity between composing poems and blackberry eating? By focusing on an image or a specific action, the poet stays true to the idea that initiated this chapter: most poetry is not *intentionally* obscure, but is based on the reality of the poet's experience and imagination, expressed primarily through images. Chapter 3 prompted you to use your senses to capture concrete, specific detail in your writing, and expressing what you *see* in your poems can help you communicate those abstract ideas and feelings that are sometimes difficult to articulate in new ways.

Although most poetry employs imagery, the majority of poets do not use one single image to communicate an idea; instead, they combine images in their poems. Some of these images are more esoteric than others and are more difficult to either understand or to experience. The poet brings to the blank page all that he is, all that he knows, and all that he imagines; therefore, not all poetry is understandable to all readers at a glance. The poet T. S. Eliot, for example, combines images coupled with complex allusions or references to create a portrait of an unsure, middle-aged man in "The Love Song of J. Alfred Prufrock." The first three stanzas show how seemingly antithetical images are joined:

Let us go then, you and I,
When the evening is spread out against the sky
Like a patient etherized upon a table;
Let us go, through certain half-deserted streets,
The muttering retreats   5
Of restless nights in one-night cheap hotels
And sawdust restaurants with oyster-shells:
Streets that follow like a tedious argument
Of insidious intent
To lead you to an overwhelming question . . .   10
Oh, do not ask, 'What is it?'
Let us go and make our visit.

In the room the women come and go
Talking of Michelangelo.

The yellow fog that rubs its back upon the window-panes,   15
The yellow smoke that rubs its muzzle on the window-panes,
Licked its tongue into the corners of the evening,
Lingered upon the pools that stand in drains,
Let fall upon its back the soot that falls from chimneys,
Slipped by the terrace, made a sudden leap,   20
And seeing that it was a soft October night,
Curled once about the house, and fell asleep.

Count how many different pictures or images Eliot presents in these first three stanzas. What time of day is it, and how is it described? What do the streets look like? What kinds of places are found on these streets? What animal is the yellow fog being compared to?

Writing for Ideas and Practice 4-2

1. Think of a special moment in your life. Now think of something concrete that you associate with that moment. It could be a wedding ring, a baseball glove, or the vinyl upholstery of the back seat of your car. It could be anything, but it must be yours. Describe the experience by using the concrete image as a focal point. Make the reader see and feel at the same time.
2. In "This Is Just to Say," William Carlos Williams uses the image of the plum as a starting point for his poem. Create a piece in which you use food to tell about yourself or someone else. Use any aspect of food as the image you hook onto, whether it be a food item, food preparation, or eating.[1]

Here is a student sample response to this exercise in which the speaker contrasts himself and his wife by using food as a focal point:

Celery in the blender,
chopped fine and chopped again.
Mix in olives, cabbage, carrots,
lots of pepper in the blend.
Crunch! Crunch! Crunch!   5
(My wife hates the *Crunch*.)
"Want me to eat this somewhere?"
"No dear, that's OK,
it's not bothering me," she'll say.
I won't hear for another day   10
how she hated the
Crunch! Crunch! Crunch!
She likes sweet and smooth and creamy,
ice cream, stuff like that.
I like crunchy, nuts and chips,   15
not baked, but fried in fat.
But ice cream's OK too.
Vanilla with chips mixed in.
Crunch! Crunch! Crunch!
There's that *Crunch* again.   20

---

1 For a short story that uses food in the same way this exercise asks you to do, see Dorothy Allison's story "Lesbian Appetites" in her collection *Trash*.

Crunch until the silence sounds
with quiet in the end.

— *David Birkman*

You can also find inspiration and images in works of art as well as from things you see around you. The association between poetry and art, with its abundance of and reliance on visual imagery, is so great that many poets have generated poems based on their interpretation of a visual work of art. This poem by William Carlos Williams brings the painting to life by describing the scene, and also by capturing the motion of the dancers through his use of rhyme and rhythm.

The Dance

In Breughel's great picture, The Kermess,
the dancers go round, they go round and
around, the squeal and the blare and the
tweedle of bagpipes, a bugle and fiddles
tipping their bellies (round as the thick-   5
sided glasses whose wash they impound)
their hips and their bellies off balance
to turn them. Kicking and rolling about
the Fair Grounds, swinging their butts, those
shanks must be sound to bear up under such   10
rollicking measures, prance and they dance
in Breughel's great picture, The Kermess.

The Carnival (The Kermess), by Pieter Breughel

Writing for Ideas and Practice 4-3

1. In chapter 3, you looked at art in order to think about how what you saw made you feel, and to practice gathering details. Now, go to an art museum or to an art book again, but this time, write a short word picture in response to the painting. Create the visual image without editorializing. Let your words show the feeling that the work of art created in you.
2. Look through your old family photos. Choose a photograph that evokes some kind of feeling in you, although the photograph need not include you; recreate the photograph in words.

We have looked at what these poets do; now let's look at how they do it. How is it that you can show the reader your vision, like paint on a canvas, and evoke an emotional response from the reader? If poetry is "inscribed emotion," then how do you get there?

Whether you wish to follow the pattern of the Imagists and the haiku poets, or use visual imagery in longer poems, you must still keep carving the excess off your words. Making careful choices about diction and having an understanding of connotation are crucial. You must understand what language can and cannot do for you. Respect words and be sensitive to them. Use the right word, the word that connects you to your poem. Richard Hugo says that "you are after those words you can own and ways of putting them in phrases and lines that are yours by right of obsessive musical deed."

What do you do to make certain words yours? As a poet, many times you will find yourself deliberating over your word choices. Always make sure, therefore, that you have access to a good dictionary and a thesaurus that you feel comfortable using. Don't be so mechanical that you choose words artificially, because they sound "poetic," but consider the possibility of using words which are not already in your working vocabulary. This process, of course, takes time to master.

Most important of all, have fun, and ignore the negative voices that might try to undermine your efforts. When you are *overly* concerned about others' opinions of your work (as well as the negative voices that dwell within you), eventually you will end up looking over everyone else's shoulder, comparing your work to theirs. Don't measure your ability by looking at the work of your *peers*; look inside yourself and find that satisfaction within.

Using a dictionary or thesaurus to choose words for your poem is working backwards, but you will want to expand your word palette. How precise can you be in your word choice? Your words should ooze or burst or whisper with feeling and meaning. Attention to diction will help you take control of your writing, whether you are writing poetry, narration, or dialogue.

Writing for Ideas and Practice 4-4

1. Look up the following color words in a thesaurus. List at least four synonyms for each word. For each synonym, write one thing that that color word makes you think of. Do this quickly — it should be your first reaction, not a logical response. For the word "chestnut" (a synonym of brown), you might think of "horse." Someone else might think of "a winter fireplace."
   a. Brown　　　b. Black　　　c. Yellow
2. On your own, list all the synonyms you can think of for these words:
   a. Home　　　b. See　　　c. Sad
3. For this exercise, divide into groups of three. Each group member picks seven unfamiliar words from the dictionary: seven nouns, seven verbs, and seven adverbs, respectively. Write these words and their definitions down on a piece of paper. Using at least fifteen of the words on the list (plus connectors, if necessary), each group member writes his own poem.

FIGURATIVE LANGUAGE

In addition to being sensitive to individual word choice, many poets employ figurative language to create mental images. According to Holman's *Handbook to Literature*, figurative language is an "intentional departure from the normal order, construction, or meaning of words in order to gain strength and freshness of expression, to create a pictorial effect . . . or to discover and illustrate similarities in otherwise dissimilar things." Of course, the use of figurative language is certainly not the sole domain of the poet, but since poetry is "intensity," according to E. B. White, one will perhaps find figurative language most frequently in this genre. Precise diction will communicate an image or idea to a reader on the water's surface; figurative language allows the poet to submerge and catch the reader in the undercurrent. Or, as W. S. Merwin says, "The poet doesn't just listen—he *hears*. He doesn't just look at the thing —he *sees*. And that's what poetry can do for us, too."

Some figurative language is easily understood at a glance. On the other hand, some figurative language is ambiguous and highly subjective, but this is perhaps because the poet relies on the shared experience and common understanding between reader and writer. In "The Love Song of J. Alfred Prufrock," Eliot uses a biblical reference in lines 81–83, referring to the death of John the Baptist. Herod had put John the Baptist into prison because he had told Herod that it was not lawful for him to have his brother's wife, Herodias. At her mother's request, Herodias's daughter asked that John the Baptist's head be brought on a platter to her. Herod complied. Prufrock describes himself:

But though I have wept and fasted, wept and prayed,
Though I have seen my head (grown slightly bald) brought in upon a platter,
I am no prophet—and here's no great matter;
I have seen the moment of my greatness flicker,
And I have seen the eternal Footman hold my coat, and snicker,   85
And in short, I was afraid.

The allusion is important in showing the reader how Prufrock sees himself. He feels that he has suffered and has been persecuted, but he says that he is not a prophet, like John the Baptist, and not courageous, and when faced with death ("the eternal Footman") he "was afraid."

Eliot continues to use references to literature and history to illustrate Prufrock's view of himself. This time Prufrock contrasts himself with Shakespeare's character Hamlet in lines 111–119:

No! I am not Prince Hamlet, nor was meant to be;
Am an attendant lord, one that will do
To swell a progress, start a scene or two,
Advise the prince; no doubt, an easy tool,
Deferential, glad to be of use,   115
Politic, cautious, and meticulous;
Full of high sentence, but a bit obtuse;
At times, indeed, almost ridiculous—
Almost, at times, the Fool.

In this stanza, Prufrock says that he could not be a hero, such as Hamlet, in life. A secondary role is what he is destined for, and the character he describes himself to be is similar to Polonius, Ophelia's father in *Hamlet*.

Readers can appreciate the poem even if they don't understand the references, but an immediate association, especially here as Prufrock contrasts himself with those who are of heroic character, certainly enhances the reading of the text. As a writer, you are free to use these tools if they add another dimension to your poems, but they are not to be used merely as tricks. They will be most effective if you use them honestly.

The Eliot poem demonstrates one kind of figurative language writers use: **allusion**. An allusion is a short reference to a historical or literary figure, event, or work of art. The allusion is the poet's shortcut to communicating meaning, and it can be esoteric and complex (as in James Joyce's *Ulysses*), but it doesn't have to be. The common association provides a code to understanding, an understanding that relies on the undercurrent of the reader's knowledge and experience to facilitate deeper understanding.

If you have ever explored the World Wide Web, you have encountered hyperlinks. A hyperlink is a connection, and as you click your mouse on the link, the computer jumps to another document related to the document you are looking at. Allusions function in a similar fashion. By referring to another work of art, music, or literature, you lead your readers out of your work momentarily (if they recognize your reference), and when their attention returns to your piece, they bring the meaning of the allusion with them, adding another layer of meaning to your text, just as a Net-surfer peruses the link and then backtracks to the main page. Thus, you have many different entrances and exits in your poem, and they can be obvious or obscure, depending on your intent and the depth of your own knowledge.

Some allusions will take your readers less than a second to recognize, and some could send them scurrying to mythology dictionaries or Shakespeare's texts. Your readers' ability to understand your use of allusion will depend on the depth of their knowledge, but your readers will bring their own "link" with them, adding the richness of the allusion to the main text of your poem.

Sometimes *an entire poem* is an allusion; that is, the poem's foundation is based on the reader's familiarity with the reference. Lucille Clifton has written a number of poems which are rooted in well-known biblical and mythological stories. The following poem, "leda 3," alludes to the Greek myth that Zeus visited the maiden Leda in the form of a swan and coupled with her, and that Helen of Troy was born as a result of this coupling. The poem is told in order to reveal Leda's perspective:

leda 3

a personal note (re: visitations)

always pyrotechnics;
stars spinning into phalluses
of light, serpents promising
sweetness, their forked tongues   5
thick and erect, patriarchs of bird
exposing themselves in the air.
this skin is sick with loneliness.
You want what a man wants,
next time come as a man   10
or don't come.

Lucille Clifton is not the only poet who has used this Greek myth as the basis for a poem. W. B. Yeats's "Leda and the Swan" also uses the Greek myth as its foundation. Yeats also refers to Leda's perspective, but the point of view used here is objective third person rather than first person; therefore, the speaker can only postulate on Leda's feelings. Yeats also alludes to the future lives of the progeny of the coupling, Helen and Clytemnestra (although most sources do not attest to Clytemnestra being the daughter of Zeus). Helen is the famous Helen of Troy, thus "The broken wall, the burning tower," and Clytemnestra murdered her husband, Agamemnon, thus "And Agamemnon dead." Here is the complete text of the poem:

Leda and the Swan

A sudden blow: the great wings beating still
Above the staggering girl, her thighs caressed
By the dark webs, her nape caught in his bill,
He holds her helpless breast upon his breast.

How can those terrified vague fingers push   5
The feathered glory from her loosening thighs?
And how can body, laid in that white rush,
But feel the strange heart beating where it lies?

A shudder in the loins engenders there
The broken wall, the burning roof and tower   10
And Agamemnon dead.
                    Being so caught up,
So mastered by the brute blood of the air,
Did she put on his knowledge with his power
Before the indifferent beak could let her drop?

Both poems focus on the character of Leda—What is Leda like in "leda 3"? What is Leda like in "Leda and the Swan"? What is the essential question posed at the end of the poem?

These are just two examples of poems whose textual references form the basis of the poem itself.* Your choices in employing allusion vary, from short references to something that every one of your readers will understand, to obscure and mysterious references that riddle your poem with complexity. Although the work of literature or art you allude to is not yours, your reference to it must fit smoothly within the context of the poem. The most important thing to remember is to use allusion honestly and not as a "sleight-of-word" trick. The intent of allusion is not to display intellectual prowess, and that kind of use of allusion will add superficiality rather than depth and richness. Remember that your main focus should be to write *your* poem and to bring what you have in you to the poem.

When someone asks you to describe something that he or she is totally unfamiliar with, instinctively you will try to equate that object with something that the other person *is* familiar with. When others ask, "What's it like?" you try your best to describe *it* so that they can create a mental picture. The effectiveness of your response, then, is directly related to your ability to paint a word picture. If you were to say, "It's like nothing you've ever seen before," you really haven't come any closer to communication. But equating one thing with another through the use of **similes** and **metaphors** can help your reader "see" what you mean.

The use of "like" or "as" to link and equate two ideas is called a **simile**. Similes are used in poetry, narrative, dialogue, and human conversation in order to communicate through the use of comparison. The following similes come from poems, but you will encounter similes in all forms of human expression:

Streets that follow like a tedious argument
of insidious intent

—*T. S. Eliot, "The Love Song of J. Alfred Prufrock"*

When the evening is spread out against the sky
Like a patient etherized upon a table

—*T. S. Eliot, "The Love Song of J. Alfred Prufrock"*

I wandered lonely as a cloud
That floats on high o'er vales and hills

—*William Wordsworth, "I Wandered Lonely as a Cloud"*

. . . the ripest berries
fall almost unbidden to my tongue,
as words sometimes do

—*Galway Kinnell, "Blackberry Eating"*

Writing for Ideas and Practice 4-5

1. Think of similes we use to describe the everyday things in our lives—weather, bodily functions, emotions—and list ten.
2. Recall a myth or legend. Write a short poem which either alludes to this myth or legend, or use it as the basis for your text.
3. Create a self-portrait using similes. Finish the following sentences as if you were painting a picture—but not realistically: imaginatively, figuratively.
   a. My toes are like . . .
   b. My nose is like . . .
   c. My hair is like . . .
   d. My voice is like . . .
4. In those similes, you compared something concrete to something concrete in order to create a visual image in your reader's mind. Now try something a little more abstract. Construct similes for the following concepts or ideas, equating them with something concrete.
   a. Love is like . . .
   b. Power is like . . .

A **metaphor** is also a comparison, but the writer equates two things. In its simplest form, one would draw the same type of comparison as a simile, only now omitting the "like" or "as." Instead of saying, "Love is like the moon," one might say, "Love *is* the moon." The equation does not have to be realistically logical, but it must be imaginatively logical. To make it so is up to you.

I. A. Richards termed the two parts of the metaphor as the **tenor**, which is the literal component of the metaphor, and the **vehicle**, which is the figurative component of the metaphor. Thus the word "Love" in the phrase "Love is the moon" would be the tenor, and the word "moon" would be the vehicle. The vehicle exists to illuminate the tenor, and exists because it is connected to the tenor. In order to construct a vehicle that is powerful and effective, use specific detail and the senses as discussed in chapter 3.

Note, however, that the tenor does not always come first in the metaphor. The metaphor can have many different forms. In the phrase "the black cave of her brain echoed / silence as she listened to / remember my name," the tenor is "her brain" and the vehicle is "the black cave." The verb is metaphorical as well, for *echoed* continues the comparison of the cave to the brain.

Here are a few examples of metaphors:

He is all pine and I am apple orchard

— *Robert Frost, "Mending Wall"*

the rain is full of ghosts tonight
— *Edna St. Vincent Millay, "What Lips My Lips Have Kissed"*

Gave thee clothing of delight

— *William Blake, "The Lamb"*

My head is a switchboard
where crossed lines crackle.

— *Marge Piercy, "The Secretary Chant"*

Writing for Ideas and Practice 4-6

1. Create another self-portrait, this time using metaphors. Finish the following sentences to create a picture of yourself. Feel free to arrange the tenor and the vehicle in any way you wish. Your vehicle could be a noun which comes after the verb or before a prepositional phrase, or it could be the object of the preposition as well, referring to the tenor. Your verbs could be metaphorical as well.
   a. My mouth . . .
   b. My toes . . .
   c. My ears . . .
   d. My eyes . . .

2.   Identify the tenor and the vehicle in the metaphors listed above.

In using metaphors and similes, you could make one singular comparison and then move to another image or idea. But, as we saw in poems that extend allusions earlier, it is also possible to use the simile or metaphor in extended form, using an entire poem or a section of a poem to equate two ideas. Consider the following poem by Lawrence Ferlinghetti. Does a singular comparison link all of its disparate ideas?

Constantly Risking Absurdity

Constantly risking absurdity
                            and death
            whenever he performs
                        above the heads
                                    of his audience
        the poet like an acrobat
                        climbs on rime
                            to a high wire of his own making
        and balancing on eyebeams
                        above a sea of faces
            paces his way
                        to the other side of day
        performing entrechats
                        and sleight-of-foot tricks
        and other high theatrics
                        and all without mistaking
            any thing
                        for what it may not be

        For he's the super realist
                        who must perforce perceive
            taut truth
                        before the taking of each stance or step
        in his supposed advance
                        toward that still higher perch
        where Beauty stands and waits
                        with gravity
                        to start her death-defying leap

        And he
            a little charleychaplin man
                        who may or may not catch
            her fair eternal form
                        spreadeagled in the empty air
        of existence

Line 6 begins the simile. Notice that the audience (reader) is watching him. He is trying to capture Beauty (personification) in his poem, which he may or may not do. What is apparent in this poem is the vulnerability of the poet. He is not handsome and strong; he is comic and sad, like Charlie Chaplin. It is the poem which is Beauty. The poet can only hope to catch her as she leaps through the "empty air of existence."

When a poem uses one metaphor throughout the poem, it is referred to as a **conceit**. What is the overall equation (tenor + vehicle) in the following poem?

The Secretary Chant

My hips are a desk.
From my ears hang
chains of paper clips.
Rubber bands form my hair.
My breasts are wells of mimeograph ink.   5
My feet bear casters.
Buzz. Click.
My head is a badly organized file.
My head is a switchboard
where crossed lines crackle.   10
Press my fingers
and in my eyes appear
credit and debit.
Zing. Tinkle.
My navel is a reject button.   15
From my mouth issue canceled reams.
Swollen, heavy, rectangular
I am about to be delivered
of a baby
Xerox machine.   20
File me under W
because I wonce
was
a woman.

— *Marge Piercy*

You will probably employ other types of metaphorical language in your poetry. A special kind of metaphor is **synecdoche**, in which a writer uses a part of something to stand for the whole. Many times we tell someone to lend us *a hand*, but what we really mean is that we want them to help us (probably with more than just one hand).

Metonymy is closely associated with synecdoche, but it occurs when something closely *related* to the thing being named is used instead. If one "bows to the throne," he's actually bowing to the king, who is associated with the throne.

The following poem by Seamus Heaney employs both synecdoche and metonymy in the second stanza:

Docker

There, in the corner, staring at his drink.
The cap juts like a gantry's crossbeam,
Cowling plated forehead and sledgehead jaw.
Speech is clamped in the lips' vice.

That fist would drop a hammer on a Catholic —   5
Oh yes, that kind of thing could start again;
The only Roman collar he tolerates
Smiles all round his sleek pint of porter.

Mosaic imperatives bang home like rivets;
God is a foreman with certain definite views   10
Who orders life in shifts of work and leisure.
A factory horn will blare the Resurrection.

He sits, strong and blunt as a Celtic cross,
Clearly used to silence and an armchair:
Tonight the wife and children will be quiet   15
At slammed door and smoker's cough in the hall.

In line 5 the speaker states, "That *fist* would drop a hammer on a Catholic—." The fist is a part of the docker and acts as synecdoche. Focusing on the fist amplifies the action, and the closed fist emphasizes the docker's anger. Metonymy is used in line 7 as the priesthood or, to make an even broader application, the Catholic Church, is represented by the reference to the *Roman collar* that priests wear as part of their clerical garb. He uses an article of clothing associated with priests to refer to the priesthood. Heaney depicts the small and concrete in order to suggest the large and abstract.

In "Docker," as in many of Heaney's poems, the well-chosen details make the abstract concepts he communicates clearer and more vivid. Use synecdoche and metonymy to zoom in on what you want the reader to focus on in your image. Sometimes a part is more important than the whole. Using synecdoche and metonymy can help you restrict your readers' peripheral vision, so they look just at what you want them to see.

Yet another type of metaphorical language is **apostrophe**, where the speaker directly addresses someone or something not present in the poem. In a dramatic monologue the speaker addresses someone who does not speak but is present in the poem. For example, in Robert Browning's "My Last Duchess" (p. 149), the speaker is speaking to someone actually present in the room. But in apostrophe, it is obvious to the reader that the speaker talks to someone who is not there or something that is not present.

Allen Ginsberg addresses Walt Whitman in his poem "A Supermarket in California," and although it is clear that Whitman is *not* in the supermarket, the reference makes us think of Whitman's time period and attitudes and how America has changed so drastically in the past hundred years. In "Death Be Not Proud," John Donne uses apostrophe to address death as a tangible, palpable enemy whose great force must be overcome. The victory over death that Donne describes is therefore more powerful, more significant than it would be over a mere earthly opponent.

 Death Be Not Proud

Death be not proud, though some have called thee
Mighty and dreadful, for thou art not so;
For those whom thou think'st thou dost overthrow
Die not, poor death, nor yet canst thou kill me.
From rest and sleep, which but thy pictures be,   5
Much pleasure, then from thee much more must flow,
And soonest our best men with thee do go,
Rest of their bones, and soul's delivery.
Thou art slave to fate, chance, kings, and desperate men,
And dost with poison, war, and sickness dwell,   10
And poppy, or charms can make us sleep as well,
And better than thy stroke; why swell'st thou then?
One short sleep past, we wake eternally,
And death shall be no more; death, thou shalt die.

In "Death Be Not Proud" Donne talks directly to death, saying that he is powerless over man, for man will die to death and then gain eternal life. Instead, Donne says, "death, thou shalt die." A special type of metaphorical comparison, sometimes used in conjunction with apostrophe, is **personification**. In personification the poet attributes one or more human qualities to inanimate objects or ideas, as in the line "the wooden beams ached with the sadness of that room." Personification and apostrophe accentuate the intimacy of the poem, bringing the poem closer to the reader because they connect *things* to the human experience.

Even as we discuss these terms in order to clarify or define them, if you have a natural affinity for language you probably already employ metaphorical language in your poetry. Identifying whether a line contains apostrophe, personification, or both might not be as important as making sure that your use of the language adds to the richness of the poem and is intentionally consistent if you want your metaphors to connect, or intentionally inconsistent if you are turning in a different direction in the poem.

Using figurative language is an important tool to use to add texture to your work, but you must take care to ensure that the vision of your poem grows out of the idea rather than being superimposed on it. If your comparisons are original and serve the overall purpose of the poem, they will add a dimension of possibility to your writing.

Although the poet has a rich language heritage to draw from, much figurative language is so overused that although the phrases still relate a picture, we no longer think of the picture in its relation to the idea. These phrases are called **cliches**, and although good authors sometimes use them in **dialogue** or narration to create character, in poetry it is more than likely your intent to create a fresh vision in your reader's mind. The best writing communicates in an extraordinary way. The cliche communicates the familiar in a less than ordinary way and short circuits rather than encourages thought.

Writing for Ideas and Practice 4-7

1. List ten cliches as quickly as you can. You will find that there are regional differences in your collective repertoire here. We'll help you get started: "He's as busy as a bee"; "She's as fat as a hog."
2. Now rewrite any five of your cliches, so that the comparisons are vivid and original.
3. Write a nature poem, in which you use apostrophe, personification, or both.

When you compare, you equate one thing to another, so that the vehicle is restricted to its association with the tenor. A **symbol**, on the other hand, exists in and of itself in a poem, but *at the same time* it suggests something greater and thereby transcends itself. In other words, in addition to its function as a concrete object in the poem, it also represents something abstract.

Human beings inherently think symbolically. For example, children know how to use a stick as a pretend gun or how to pretend they are superheroes by tying a towel around their necks to symbolize a cape. Society introduces us to its more formal conventional symbols at a very early age. Even though our capacity for abstract thought is limited when we are young, we understand that the flag paraded before the class as we say the Pledge of Allegiance represents the concept of *country*, and that our concept of country is not just terrain but ideology as well.

Certain symbols are termed **conventional symbols** because they have one universal interpretation. For example, the figure of a heart is used to symbolize love, or a Star of David symbolizes the Jewish faith. In your writing you can use conventional symbols and retool them so that they symbolize something different, perhaps even the antithesis of their conventional interpretation — but to get beyond the accepted meaning of the conventional symbol is difficult.

As humans, we also have **personal symbols**, those things which mean much to us because of the meaning we associate with them. A very dear friend of Candace's always bought Vienna Fingers cookies because she knew Candace's daughter loved them. Her daughter was in diapers at that time, but now, whenever she sees those cookies in the store, she mentions our friend. Candace could use those cookies as a literary symbol in a poem or story, but the symbol is so subjective and personal that it would be difficult to be perceived by readers. Symbols like these are so subjective that it might be difficult to use them as they are.

That does not mean that you can't use a personal symbol in a poem, but to do so you'll need to turn it inside out so that it can be interpreted, making it a **literary symbol**. (Interpretations of the symbol, however, still might vary from reader to reader.) A literary symbol is probably the middle ground between the conventional and personal symbol. It isn't so common that its representation is obvious, but it isn't so subjective that it is a symbol which will never have meaning beyond the author's personal association. Multiple interpretations will coexist, and ambiguity is acceptable.

In our classes, we don't allow students to "defend" their poems. As others in the class or group comment on the poem, the student writer has a tendency to want to tell the group whether they "got it" or not. As instructors, we encourage our students to let go of their poems and let the poems speak for themselves. In *How Does a Poem Mean?* John Ciardi and Miller Williams use an extended simile to explain this concept:

. . . a symbol is like a rock dropped into a pool; it sends out ripples in all directions, and the ripples are in motion. Who can say where the last ripple disappears? One may have a sense that he at least knows approximately the center point of all those ripples, the point at which the stone struck the water. Yet even then he has trouble marking it precisely. How does one make a mark on water? . . . One is never done with it: every time he looks he sees something new, and it changes even as he watches.

A symbol, then, can take many paths. As poets, we throw a rock into the water and create ripples. The reader follows the ripples.

So how do symbols operate within a poem? In Robert Frost's poem "Mending Wall," the speaker and his neighbor are repairing the wall that divides their property. The wall is just what it is: a physical barrier that defines property lines. Throughout the poem, the narrator questions the need for such a dividing line:

He is all pine and I am apple orchard.
My apple trees will never get across
And eat the cones under his pines, I tell him.

The neighbor's only reply is that "Good fences make good neighbors." The wall is a real object in the poem. But perhaps it also suggests meaning beyond the wall's simple function. Look at the last section of the poem:

"Something there is that doesn't love a wall,   35
That wants it down." I could say "Elves" to him.
But it's not elves exactly, and I'd rather
He said it for himself. I see him there
Bringing a stone grasped firmly by the top
In each hand, like an old-stone savage armed.   40
He moves in darkness as it seems to me,
Not of woods only and the shade of trees.
He will not go behind his father's saying,
And he likes having thought of it so well
He says again, "Good fences make good neighbors."   45

Frost's wall separates two fields, to be sure, and yet at the same time it's a division between people, a barrier of safety, a delineation of who is who and what is whose. The literal and the figurative exist simultaneously. In dealing with symbols, then, follow the ripples where they take you and realize that each ripple is different and yet the same.

Writing for Ideas and Practice 4-8

1. Choose one of the following concrete objects and create a short poem which uses that object as a symbol and also suggests larger meaning:
   a. A tree
   b. A door
   c. A leaf
   d. A river
   e. A mayonnaise jar
   f. Ivy
   g. The sun or the moon

   There is no need to be profound here. This is just an exercise to make sure you know what a symbol is. Later you can write poems with symbols in them, and you can be as mystical or esoteric as you want to be. Here are two student examples:

   ### The Leaf

   In the downward spiral
   of the cool breeze,
   the leaf fluttered to the ground.

   — Carla L. McGaughey

   ### Pines and Dogwoods

   'Tis the season to be a pine
   with an unfaltering disposition—
   existing unchanged,

simple but strong.
Living life of green,   5
death of brown —
one of many mascots
for the month of
ends and
beginnings;   10
love
sacrifice and
joy.
I wish the soul
were made of pine.   15
Alas, it is a dogwood.
Our colors change
with the leaves.
Green springs forth
dreams   20
that anger, fear
love and passion,
turn red.
Yellow emerges
gathering sadness,   25
gaining wisdom.
Brown is brittle —
crumbling
scattering the
feelings that can't be held   30
forever.
I wish the soul were
made of pine.
But we are all
deciduous.   35

— *Adam Carroll*

In capturing vision in poetry, you will want to open yourself up to experience. In his article "Modern Japanese Haiku," Lucien Stryk quotes the master poet Basho: "Learn about a pine tree from a pine tree, and about a bamboo stalk from a bamboo stalk." A. R. Ammons says that poetry "stands not as an isolated esoteric activity but as a formal and substantive essentializing of all action." And E. E. Cummings probably says it best in his foreword to his *Poems 1923–1954*:

 . . . my theory of technique, if I have one, is very far from original; nor is it complicated. I can express it in fifteen words, by quoting The Eternal Question And Immortal

Answer of burlesk, viz., "Would you hit a woman with a child?—No, I'd hit her with a brick." Like the burlesk comedian, I am abnormally fond of that precision which creates movement.

Use your words to capture life and action in your poems. Go forth and see, smell, taste, and touch; then, write it down.

Writing on Your Own

1. Write a series of short poems all on the same topic. The poems should utilize visual poetic techniques and demonstrate your understanding of how to infuse poems with visual images.
2. In her book *Writing Down the Bones,* Natalie Goldberg talks about setting up a poetry booth at a local school carnival. We had a poetry booth at our college last semester to help collect canned food for a local charity. We charged one can of food for a poem written on the spot by one of our Creative Writing students. Gather a group and set up a "poetry booth" of your own. Don't worry too much about quality. This exercise gives you the chance to let your spontaneity foster your creativity, and you will learn to let go of your poems.

Writing to Revise

Choose a poem (two if they are short) that you have written in response to one of the Writing for Ideas and Practice exercises in this chapter. Write another version of the poem, replacing at least five words of your poem with synonyms. Consult a thesaurus if necessary. Now look at both versions. How has the poem changed? Now rewrite it again, incorporating only the changes that you think are effective.

5

THE SOUND OF POETRY

Writing to Warm Up

Read the following poem by Joy Harjo *aloud:*

I Give You Back

I release you, my beautiful and terrible
fear. I release you. You were my beloved
and hated twin, but now, I don't know you
as myself. I release you with all the
pain I would know at the death of   5
my daughters.

You are not my blood anymore.

I give you back to the white soldiers
who burned down my home, beheaded my children,
raped and sodomized my brothers and sisters.   10
I give you back to those who stole the
food from our plates when we were starving.

I release you, fear, because you hold
these scenes in front of me and I was born
with eyes that can never close.   15

I release you, fear, so you can no longer
keep me naked and frozen in the winter,
or smothered under blankets in the summer.

I release you
I release you   20
I release you
I release you

I am not afraid to be angry.
I am not afraid to rejoice.
I am not afraid to be black.   25
I am not afraid to be white.
I am not afraid to be hungry.
I am not afraid to be full.
I am not afraid to be hated.
I am not afraid to be loved,   30
to be loved, to be loved, fear.

Oh, you have choked me, but I gave you the leash.
You have gutted me but I gave you the knife.
You have devoured me, but I laid myself across the fire.
You held my mother down and raped her,   35
          but I gave you the heated thing.

I take myself back, fear.
You are not my shadow any longer.
I won't hold you in my hands.
You can't live in my eyes, my ears, my voice   40
my belly, or in my heart my heart
my heart   my heart

But come here, fear
I am alive and you are so afraid
          of dying.

1. As you read the poem aloud, what did you notice about the construction of the poem?
2. Is the speaker referring to the present here? Is she speaking of her immediate life? If not, what is she referring to?
3. The speaker uses the second person (you) here to create a mirror image. Is the speaker looking at herself and what is inside her? To most of us, fear is "terrible" and "hated," but we don't often call it "beloved." Have you ever seen your fear as something to be treasured?

4. What does this poem say about fear? Is the speaker victorious over fear? How does the poet use *sound* to communicate the theme or subject of the poem?

MUSIC IN POETRY

The previous chapters looked at how writers communicate a visual image or picture in the reader's mind. Much poetry, however, depends on sound to convey feeling or image. Just as a musician who writes a song knows what sounds can be made with each note or combination of notes, a poet knows or discovers what sounds his words will make, and what effect those sounds may have on the reader. Although lyrics are often studied as examples of poetry, the main difference between song lyrics and poetry is that lyrics use music to aid expression. The melodies accompanying the words enhance the sounds of the words themselves and are essential in creating mood. Minor chords tend to produce a sad-sounding song, even if the lyrics are upbeat. Some poets even choose poetic forms that suggest melody, such as a blues poem or a literary ballad.

Not all poems, however, are written in a form that automatically creates sound. No matter the form, the words themselves will echo and sing in the readers' ears, for poetry is as much an oral tradition as it is a written one. Information transmitted in poetic form, specifically a poetic form that employs regular rhyme and rhythm, is easier to remember. Many cultures used poetry as the medium by which history and culture were transmitted from generation to generation, especially if the printed word was inaccessible or non-existent. So, even in modern culture, poetry uses sound and rhythm to reach past the *information* centers in our heads into the hidden, unconscious parts of us. From nursery rhymes to the Psalms, sometimes we don't just memorize poems—we absorb them.

And poets employ this powerful device of sound and musical forms. For instance, although the blues began exclusively as a musical form, poets have used this structure as a purely poetic form as well. As the poet Michael S. Harper says, "There's a whole tradition of blues poems most Americans don't seem to know. It's seen as a music idiom, but it's a literary idiom." But even if the music is merely implied by the form, the blues sound and feel is always apparent, as in the following blues poem by Langston Hughes:

 Young Gal's Blues

I'm gonna walk to the graveyard
'Hind ma friend Miss Cora Lee.
Gonna walk to the graveyard

'Hind ma dear friend Cora Lee
Cause when I'm dead some   5
Body'll have to walk behind me.

I'm goin' to the po' house
To see ma old Aunt Clew.
Goin' to the po' house
To see ma old Aunt Clew.   10
When I'm old an' ugly
I'll want to see somebody, too.

The po' house is lonely
An' the grave is cold.
O, the po' house is lonely,   15
The graveyard grave is cold.
But I'd rather be dead than
To be ugly an' old.

When love is gone what
Can a young gal do?   20
When love is gone, O,
What can a young gal do?
Keep on a-lovin' me, daddy,
Cause I don't want to be blue.

Even though Hughes's poem is not accompanied by music, the blues progression is implied because of his choice of form and the content of his
verses. This poem could be sung as well as recited. The first two lines state
the situation and are repeated in lines three and four. The last two lines of
the stanza comment or draw a conclusion about the first two lines. The
young speaker looks at those around her who are aging and dying, and she
anticipates growing old and lonely herself. In the last stanza, she pleads
with her lover to keep loving her so that she won't be lonely herself. Look
at the use of nonstandard English here. How do you know when nonstandard English will work or when it will appear that you are being artificial? You might find that you have the same dilemma with dialect. The
reader must accept what you are doing, and the poem must speak for itself;
you can't speak for it.

　　The contemporary poet Sandra McPherson also uses the blues form
by imitating the rhythmic pattern and repetition of the first and second
lines, but deviating from the pattern in stanza three. The poem is an example of the blues used purely in a poetic form, for the structure is literary rather than musical in nature. Yet, just as in Hughes's poem, the blues
sound communicates something about the feeling of the poem. In this
poem the speaker is the mother of a troubled daughter:

Bad Mother Blues

When you were arrested, child, and I had to take your pocketknife
When you were booked and I had to confiscate your pocketknife
It had blood on it from where you'd tried to take your life

It was the night before Thanksgiving, all the family coming over
The night before Thanksgiving, all the family coming over   5
We had to hide your porno magazine and put your handcuffs undercover

Each naked man looked at you, said, Baby who do you think you are
Each man looked straight down on you, like a waiting astronomer's star
Solely, disgustedly, each wagged his luster

I've decided to throw horror down the well and wish on it   10
Decided I'll throw horror down the well and wish on it
And up from the water will shine my sweet girl in her baby bonnet

A thief will blind you with his flashlight
                    but a daughter be your bouquet
    A thief will blind you with his flashlight   15
                    but a daughter be your bouquet
    When the thief's your daughter you turn your eyes the other way

I'm going into the sunflower field where all of them are facing me
I'm going into the sunflower field so all of them are facing me
Going to go behind the sunflowers, feel all the sun that I can't see   20

In the first stanza the rhythm follows a typical blues form, but the diction
is more elevated than a traditional blues poem or song. "Confiscate" is not
only a fairly sophisticated term (although the speaker may be using law en-
forcement terms), but it is also a difficult word to sing — try it. The third
stanza deviates from the typical blues form. We will discuss the particulars
of rhythm in the next chapter, but notice that the dactylic foot ($' \cup \cup$) is
used here to slow the rhythm. The last line of the stanza doesn't rhyme (although it is a slant rhyme) and it is much shorter than the others. Is this
irregularity a weakness or a strength?

In these poems the form creates the sound. In the next chapter we will
discuss form at length, but for now, just think of the music you can suggest with your sounds, and begin to think *out loud*, to think with your ears
as well as your mind.

Writing for Ideas and Practice 5-1

1. Write a poem that captures the particular sounds of your words. For example, while
   walking through the woods, you could write . . .

The pines whisper softly as the
breeze shuffles and scatters
the crisp brown leaves.

2. Write a poem that could be set to music. This could be a blues poem, a pop chorus, a hymn, or even a song for jumping rope.

You may have noticed that poetry readings are presently experiencing a new growth in popularity. Poets of late are finding that they are not only invited to colleges and universities, but are in demand at bookstores, cafes, parks, and other places. Growing in popularity are cowboy poetry gatherings, and many poets emphasize performance as an essential part of their art. Two examples are David Mura, a poet who is also an adept performance artist, using body gestures and movement to enhance his reading,[1] and Hal Sirowitz, whose understated, humorous performance style of his "Mother Said" poems has made him popular on the New York poetry "slam" circuits. Here is one of those poems:

 Broken Glass

Make sure you don't break another glass,
Mother said, while you're drinking your milk.
When Moses broke the Ten Commandments,
not only did he have to climb the mountain again
to get new ones, but God punished him   5
by making him wait before he could visit
the Promised Land. And maybe I should let you
drink only out of paper cups, & make you wait
until you own your own home to use glass.
You should be thankful that I'm a lot nicer than God.   10

SOUND DEVICES

Ultimately, the magic must come from the reader's hearing the melodies of the words themselves. But how is it possible to create music from pure words? First of all, poets need to be sensitive to the words they hear, the sounds the words make. Think of words that *sound* ugly or beautiful to you. Combining consonants and vowels in a certain way can communicate feeling separate from the words' literal denotation or even textual connotation.

The following is a stanza from "Me Gustas Cuando Callas" ("I Like for You to Be Still") by the Chilean poet Pablo Neruda. Look at the Spanish words without worrying about understanding the language or translating

1 You can see Mura perform in the Bill Moyers video series *The Language of Life.*

it. Read it aloud or have someone read it to you, so you can close your eyes and feel as you listen.

Como todas las cosas están llenas de mi alma
emerges de las cosas, llena del alma mía.
Mariposa de sueño, te pareces a mi alma,
y te pareces a la palabra meloncolía.

Now, having heard the sounds, look at the poem again. Notice the repetition of the *ia* combined with the *m* and *l* sound along with the playful reversal of the same words and sounds in the last word of each line: "mi alma"(1), "alma mía"(2), "a mi alma"(3), and "melancolía"(4). It is easier to see the repetition of sounds and words and notice what the words look like when you don't know what the text says. Note, for instance, the meaning of the words, as seen in W. S. Merwin's translation of that stanza:

As all things are filled with my soul
you emerge from the things, filled with my soul.
You are like my soul, a butterfly of dream,
and you are like the word Melancholy.

Although the translation conveys the same information, it is difficult for a translator to capture the same magic of the original words themselves and still be true to the textual intent, because the sound of the words is integral to the way a poem communicates. The Russian poet Yevgeny Yevtushenko has pointed out the difficulty he has writing poetry in English or translating from Russian to English, because in Russian the verb endings can be manipulated for sound and rhyme. To exemplify this, for American audiences, he recites some of his poems in Russian without translating them so that his English-speaking audience can feel the beauty of the language just by listening, without having to find the literal meaning of the poem.

Sound doesn't necessarily exist separate from meaning, however. Sometimes sound is *equated* with its meaning. Words that suggest their meanings by the sounds they make, like *chunk* or *sleazy*, are **mimetic**, and words that imitate their meaning by the sounds they make, such as *swish* and *zip*, are **onomatopoetic**. Almost all words ultimately originated from sound, specifically, onomatopoetically or mimetically, and ultimately, language evolves. Sound *is* meaning in many cases.

Writing for Ideas and Practice 5-2

1. Examine vowels and consonants by writing them down and pronouncing them individually. If a letter has more than one sound, utter all of the sounds that it can make.

The letter *g* could be hard, as in *gag;* or it could be soft, as in *lavage;* or it could mimic the letter *j*, as in *generous.* Now combine consonants and vowels in twos and threes, but don't try to construct words. Feel the way your tongue taps your teeth and the way your mouth moves to make vowels. You might want to do this individually, though it can be fun if a group does this exercise together.

2. In a group, generate a list of words that sound ugly or beautiful or silly to you. Ignore the dictionary definitions of the words; just focus on sound. Start with these words and then make your own list:

     flabbergasted   lugubrious   puny

3. List five words that are either onomatopoetic or mimetic. Throw them away, because everyone has already thought of those. Now list five more and share your answers.

Devices such as onomatopoeia and mimesis are not the only tools a poet has to create music in the reader's ear. The way a poet combines consonant and vowel sounds in the lines and stanzas also contributes to the feeling the reader gets as she reads a poem. **Alliteration**, the repetition of the initial consonant sound in two or more words in a line or phrase, is the most obvious way poets combine consonants. Alliteration can add **dissonance** (harsh sounds) to a poem; it can imitate sound; or it can be overused for comic effect. Read the following lines from Percy Bysshe Shelley's "Ozymandias" aloud and listen for alliteration as well as other elements of sound:

 Ozymandias

I met a traveller from an antique land
who said: Two vast and trunkless legs of *st*one
*St*and in the desert. Near them, on the sand,
Half sunk, a shattered visage lies, whose frown,
And wrinkled lip, and sneer of *c*old *c*ommand,   5
Tell that its sculptor well those passions read
Which yet survive, stamped on these lifeless things,
The hand that mocked them, and the heart that fed;
And on the pedestal these words appear:
"My name is Ozymandias, *k*ing of *k*ings: 10
Look on my works, ye Mighty, and despair!"
Nothing beside remains. Round the decay
Of that colossal wreck, *b*oundless and *b*are
The *l*one and *l*evel sands stretch far away.

This poem examines ruins of the stone statue of a tyrant king, Ozymandias, and time and nature's disintegration of the earthly replica of him. On the pedestal of the stone, Ozymandias's words call to all to look to him and his greatness and "despair." Yet this statue is in ruins, and there is nothing left and little powerful about this "colossal wreck" that stands in the desert. Shelley uses alliteration when he describes the king, when he quotes the king, and when he comments on the ultimate destruction of Ozymandias as well as the destruction of his replica. These repeated consonant sounds communicate the harshness of the tyrant as well as ending with the ultimate barrenness of tyranny, as in the line "The lone and level sands stretch far away."

Repetition can also be used to create pleasant and harmonious sounds, as in the Pablo Neruda poem found earlier in this chapter. Poet Wole Soyinka repeats long vowel sounds in stanza two of "Black Singer" to suggest the sound of the singer's voice:

    Black Singer

(for Marge, New York)

Cold wreath of vine, darkly
Coiled about the night; echoes deep within
Bled veins of autumn

A votive vase, her throat
Poured many souls as one; how dark   5
The wine became the night.

Fleshed from out disjointed, out from
The sidewalk hurt of sirens, a darkling
Pool of wine shivers

In light shrapnels, and do you ask   10
How *is* the wine tonight? Dark, lady
Dark in token of the deeper wounds

Full again of promises
Of the deep and silent wounds
Of cruel phases of the darksome wine   15

Song, O Voice, is lonely envoy
Night a runnel for the wine's indifferent flow.*

In addition to sound, Soyinka uses a metaphor which links the singer's voice (the tenor of the metaphor) with wine (the vehicle of the metaphor).

As you think about using alliteration, even as you make deliberate choices about including it, try to infuse alliteration naturally into the poem in a way that doesn't call undue attention to its use. Too much alliteration tends to either irritate or to amuse readers, as in limericks or children's poems. This is fine if that is your intent, but be aware of what effect your use of these techniques will have on a reader.

You might also examine **assonance**, the repetition of vowel sounds, as seen in the poem "Black Singer." In the second line of the second stanza, the long *i* is repeated in the words *wine* and *night*. A writer could also construct her vowels to **ascend**, moving from low, rich-sounding *o*'s and *u*'s to short *i*'s and long *e*'s, or moving the other way to **descend**. For instance, in the following poem, the vowel sounds ascend in each full sentence, beginning with long *o* sounds and ending with *a* and *e* sounds.

Momma

Momma moans;
Folds on folds of
Flesh upon bone
Rest inert in her chair.
Powder blue eyes   5
Imprisoned in a
Mind scattered by time,
Are looking through me
To despair.

— *Candace Schaefer*

The poem imitates the elderly mother's moaning sound with its words. In so doing, it uses vowel sounds to convey through sound the feeling the speaker is experiencing.

In the next poem, Gerard Manley Hopkins uses elements of sound to underscore meaning.

God's Grandeur

The world is charged with the grandeur of God.
    It will flame out, like shining from shook foil;
    It gathers to a greatness, like the ooze of oil
Crushed. Why do men then now not reck his rod?
Generations have trod, have trod, have trod;   5
    And all is seared with trade; bleared, smeared with toil;
    And wears man's smudge and shares man's smell: the soil
Is bare now, nor can foot feel, being shod.
And for all this, nature is never spent;
    There lives the dearest freshness deep down things;   10
And though the last lights off the black West went
    Oh, morning, at the brown brink eastward, springs—
Because the Holy Ghost over the bent
    World broods with warm breast and with ah! bright wings.

Hopkins uses the elements of sound to convey the inevitable, overwhelming power of God. He uses an ascending vowel pattern in line 12, beginning with the long *o* sound in "Oh" and moving up to shorter vowel sounds, ending with the short *i* in "springs." Alliteration is used in the poem as well to emphasize the victorious and swift motion of the rising sun as the *b* sound is repeated in "brown brink."

As a consideration of form, notice how the problem is introduced in the octave and resolved in the sestet. Man has destroyed the natural world again and again, yet God is victorious and the natural world survives, for the Holy Ghost "broods" over the world and cares for it. (Chapter 7 will discuss poetic forms and their uses.)

Writing for Ideas and Practice 5-3

1. Write a four-line stanza employing alliteration.
2. Write a four-line stanza employing an ascending vowel pattern (moving from long to short vowels) or descending vowel patterns (moving from short to long vowels).

RHYME

Another element of sound we have utilized in the poems we have examined is **rhyme**, two or more words with the same sound. Rhyme is an element in many poems and is an essential part of some poetic forms, including the sonnet (as exemplified by the Hopkins poem). And although **end rhyme** (rhyme that comes at the end of a line of poetry) tends to be the most obvious rhyme pattern, it is only one of many possible choices the poet might make in using rhyme. How the poet uses rhyme depends on what ideas she wants to emphasize in her poem and what tone or feeling she wants her poem to communicate.

One of our students was told by an editor that rhyming poetry is no longer "in fashion" and that journals do not print rhyming poetry. The student was frustrated by this statement, since she utilizes end rhyme. While it might be true that some literary journals are not, for the most part, accepting "rhyming" poetry, we told the student that many types of journals and magazines are being published, each one with its own needs. Some accept end rhyme, and some do not. Perhaps what many editors react negatively to is writers who strain and twist a poem so hard to make it rhyme that the poem breaks or bends, negating any power it may have had.

Examine the use of rhyme in the following stanza:

What is a flower if not a friend?
What nature to me may mean will never end.

To be at one with beauty is all, to me,
For I see God at work in every rock and flow'r and tree.

The poem's insistence on ending each two lines with rhyme has made the word choice and rhythms awkward and forced. End-rhyme poetry dominated the poetry of the past, and many amateur writers submit poetry that imitates that end-rhyme pattern. Editors often reject these poems, not because they do not want to publish poems with end rhymes, but because this kind of poery is often done badly. (Some experimental and non-rhyming poetry is bad, too.)

The solution is to write good poetry. Then, whether one's poems employ end rhyme will be unimportant; all that will matter is whether the poem uses all the tools—sound, image, rhythm, form—to serve the poem well. A poet shouldn't *make* a word rhyme for rhyme alone but should be sensitive to the natural meaning and sound of the word. (Chapter 6 discusses how punctuation can mitigate or accentuate end rhyme.)

More importantly, end rhyme is not a standard requirement for determining whether a group of words is a valid "poem" or not. Some poetic forms, such as the sonnet, dictate a specific rhyme scheme or pattern. Overall, however, like any other poetic device, rhyme is a tool that a writer can use for effect and to alter tone, and it can be used in many different forms. End rhyme is just one of many choices.

To analyze end-rhyme schemes, readers assign a letter to the end word in each line. If the end word in the next line rhymes with the line before, that end word, representing that line, is assigned the same letter. If it does not, it is assigned the next letter in the alphabet. The reader then proceeds in this manner throughout the poem, assigning a specific letter to each end sound in the poem.

In his poem "Does It Matter?" Sigfried Sassoon uses regular end rhyme (an abbca pattern—that is, the two *a* lines rhyme, the two *b* lines rhyme, and the *c* line doesn't) along with a rhetorical question in order to communicate a feeling of bitterness. It is significant that the seemingly light tone suggested by the rhyme pattern lends irony to the piece.

 Does It Matter?

Does it matter?—losing your legs? . . .	a
For people will always be kind,	b
And you need not show that you mind	b
When the others come in after hunting	c
To gobble their muffins and eggs.	a 5

Does it matter?—losing your sight? . . .
There's such splendid work for the blind;
And people will always be kind,

As you sit on the terrace remembering
And turning your face to the light.   10

Do they matter?—those dreams from the pit? . . .
You can drink and forget and be glad,
and people won't say that you're mad;
For they know you've fought for your country
And no one will worry a bit.   15

In this poem, the regular rhythm and end rhyme reflect the patronizing and cavalier attitudes those on the home front have towards those soldiers who have returned from World War I. The poem has a sing-song quality to it, a pleasing or light air to it, yet the text is anything but pleasant. The incongruity of the content and the rhythm/rhyme scheme strengthens the bitter and angry tone of the poem. A lot of poetry written by British soldiers during World War I displays this same tone, or at least a negative attitude about war and graphic description about the horrors of war. You might want to look at a group of poems written during a particular period or movement, or dealing with a common theme, and see if there are similarities in how related poems use rhyme or rhythm or sound or form.

If you're thinking about rhyme for your poem, don't just consider end rhyme. You could also utilize **beginning rhyme**, rhyme which occurs in the first syllable of the line, or **internal rhyme**, rhyme which occurs within a line or lines. The **true rhyme** is determined by the correlation of sound in the accented syllables of the words and the syllables which follow them, for example, *wood* and *good*, or *heated* and *seated*. **Eye rhyme** can be found in words that look as if they rhyme on paper but when pronounced aloud do not, for example as in *cough* and *though*.

This is also called **consonance**, although sometimes the term consonance is also used to refer to the repetition of consonant sounds.

Instead of true rhyme, you might experiment with **slant rhyme**. Slant rhyme is rhyme that is slightly imperfect, usually in the vowel sounds, such as the words *body* and *bloody*.* It is used by many poets intentionally, although differences in dialect and changes in the language will affect the reading of a poem for rhyme. What appears to be a slant rhyme might have been a perfect rhyme in the dialect of the poet. A good example of the use of slant rhyme is the poem "Strange Meeting" by Wilfred Owen.

 Strange Meeting

It seemed that out of battle I escaped
Down some profound dull tunnel, long since scooped
Through granites which titanic wars had groined.
Yet also there encumbered sleepers groaned,
Too fast in thought or death to be bestirred.   5
Then, as I probed them, one sprang up, and stared

With piteous recognition in fixed eyes,
Lifting distressful hands as if to bless.
And by his smile, I knew that sullen hall;
By his dead smile I knew we stood in Hell.   10
With a thousand pains that vision's face was grained;
Yet no blood reached there from the upper ground,
And no guns thumped, or down the flues made moan.
"Strange friend," I said, "here is no cause to mourn."
"None," said the other, "save the undone years,   15
The hopelessness. Whatever hope is yours,
Was my life also; I went hunting wild
After the wildest beauty in the world,
Which lies not calm in eyes, or braided hair,
But mocks the steady running of the hour,   20
And if it grieves, grieves richlier than here.
For by my glee might many men have laughed,
And of my weeping something had been left,
Which must die now. I mean the truth untold,
The pity of war, the pity war distilled.   25
Now men will go content with what we spoiled,
Or, discontent, boil bloody, and be spilled.
They will be swift with swiftness of the tigress,
None will break ranks, though nations trek from progress.
Courage was mine, and I had mystery,   30
Wisdom was mine, and I had mastery;
To miss the march of this retreating world
Into vain citadels that are not walled.
Then when much blood had clogged their chariot wheels
I would go up and wash them from sweet wells,   35
Even with truths that lie too deep for taint.
I would have poured my spirit without stint
But not through wounds; not on the cess of war.
Foreheads of men have bled where no wounds were.
I am the enemy you killed, my friend.   40
I knew you in this dark; for so you frowned
Yesterday through me as you jabbed and killed.
I parried; but my hands were loath and cold.
Let us sleep now. . . ."

Owen uses **consonance** in each couplet. In **masculine rhyme**, the rhymed syllable is the last syllable as well as a stressed syllable, as in all but four lines of the poem. In lines 28–29, the rhyme falls on the unstressed syllable. When the words end in unstressed syllables, poets usually rhyme both syllables in each word, which is called **feminine rhyme**, but in lines 28–29, Owen only rhymes the unstressed syllable. This might be because the rhyme in the last syllable is exact (-ess). In lines 30–31, Owen uses another type of rhyme, **triple rhyme**, for all three syllables rhyme. Usually triple rhyme has a comic effect, but in this poem the tone is serious.

There are other ways to rhyme words, so experiment with rhyme, but the main thing to remember in dealing with rhyme and sound in general is to realize that you want to guide your reader to meaning, not only through content but also through technique. You want to call attention to something in your poem, and you can do that through manipulating the sounds of your words for the greatest possible effect.

Writing for Ideas and Practice 5-4

In a group, look at the following rough draft. Examine sound in the poem. Discuss what you like and exactly what you would change about the sound of the poem. Using the devices this chapter has discussed, revise the stanza as a group.

The woods whisper, and I follow where
Pines lie like quilts in canopies overhead.
Dried pine needles are pickup sticks underfoot.
Unsure, I descend down the green, for the
Whisper is dark, and I walk alone.

SYNTAX

Yet another way of creating sound in a poem is by altering word order, or **syntax**. If you want to draw focus to an idea, or if you want to turn yourself and your reader upside down, switch the logical, grammatical, *ordinary* order of your words to create something completely different. This syntax switch will make your reader slow down, and in some cases make him stop to focus on making sense of the text. How far do you want to go with this technique? Do you want just a slight twist, a bit of irony? Or do you want your poem to be a puzzle? It depends on what you want your reader to focus on, and how elusive you want to be.

E. E. Cummings's use of unusual word order sometimes makes his readers feel as if they are in a maze. However, Cummings's deliberately different syntax is used not to confuse, but to challenge the reader, and then to lead the reader to find a new meaning which the usual words in usual order could never have conveyed. Here is an example:

Spring is like a perhaps hand

Spring is like a perhaps hand
(which comes carefully
out of Nowhere)arranging
a window,into which people look(while
people stare   5
arranging and changing placing
carefully there a strange
thing and a known thing here)and

changing everything carefully

spring is like a perhaps   10
Hand in a window
(carefully to
and fro moving New and
Old things,while
people stare carefully   15
moving a perhaps
fraction of flower here placing
an inch of air there)and

without breaking anything.

Pay close attention to the punctuation and visual word placement in the poem, which can be as important as the words themselves. Cummings rearranges words to attract our attention to ideas. Remember, you want to guide your reader to meaning not only through content but also through technique, including rhyme and sound. This is not to say you must be simplistic, but make sure you know what you want to accomplish as you manipulate sound.

Writing on Your Own

Think of a place from your past, present, or even from your dreams that you find yourself visualizing again and again. Write a poem about this place. Write two drafts. In the first, be free with your ideas. How do you feel about this place? Paint the place on paper, using words that communicate feeling as well as meaning.

Try to use words that have vivid, powerful sounds. Are there any sounds associated with this place? Does the wind blow? If so, is it the devil wind that whistles hot from the north – Santa Ana winds, scattering dust into an evil red haze? Or is it the blue norther that groans as it blows across the black dirt of barren winter fields?

In the second draft, which should be written after the poem has cooled a little, revise for vision and sound. Let your knowledge of craft guide your instinct here. Try different words and sounds to see what works best. Look in the mirror for a reflection, and be as objective as possible without losing heart. The mirror and lights are harsh, revealing things about yourself that you would rather not see. It may be necessary to write many subdrafts. That's good. Scratch out a word and substitute another, then another, then another. Rewrite a line many times until it sounds right. Keep at it until you feel a sense of completion.

Writing to Revise

Look at two or three short poems you wrote in response to the exercises in this chapter, and revise them by making at least two syntax changes to each one. You may add and delete words as you see fit as you make those changes. Now read each poem. Which version do you like better? How did the syntax alterations change the content and structure of the poem?

6

The Rhythm of Poetry

Writing to Warm Up

1. What do you envision when you think of a waltz?
2. Read the following poem by Theodore Roethke *aloud:*

My Papa's Waltz

The whiskey on your breath
Could make a small boy dizzy;
But I hung on like death:
Such waltzing was not easy.

We romped until the pans   5
Slid from the kitchen shelf;
My mother's countenance
Could not unfrown itself.

The hand that held my wrist
Was battered on one knuckle;   10
At every step you missed
My right ear scraped a buckle.

You beat time on my head
With a palm caked hard by dirt,
Then waltzed me off to bed   15
Still clinging to your shirt.

3. How does the rhythm of this poem echo a waltz rhythm? Is the content of the poem consistent or incongruous with your picture of what a waltz is or should be?
4. What does the rhythmic pattern and the sound of the poem communicate about the poem's subject?

Chapter 5 examined sound as an element of poetry to explore in constructing a poem. Another element, closely related to sound, is **rhythm** — the movement of sound and silence in a poem. All language has rhythm, spoken or not. Whether or not you intend to write a poem that is to be read aloud, the rhythm of the words and lines reinforce meaning and emotion in the poem. Therefore, movement is something you will want to examine and consider in your writing.

CADENCE

Rhythm is is a result of **cadence,** or the natural sound pattern created by the spoken word. The most obvious analogy is that the rhythm or meter of the poem is like the drumbeat of a song. One taps a foot to the beat of the music or claps in time. Cadence is the heartbeat of the rhythm. Think also of instruments that establish rhythm and sound at the same time. A rhythm guitarist creates sound with one hand as she fingers the chords and strokes the strings with the other hand in a rhythmical pattern, fast or slow, in time with the music. In this way sound and rhythm are created simultaneously, not separately. When you write a poem, you create sound and rhythm as one. This text has presented sound first and now is dealing with rhythm separately, just as if you were to learn to play the guitar, you would try to learn the chord configurations (sound) and then experiment with strokes until you could play a song as a unified whole.

Sometimes cadence is associated with poetry, since in poems cadence is a result of the imposition of a metrical pattern. However, everyday conversation also has a cadence. Some poets use the cadence of natural speech patterns as the rhythm line of their poetry. Walt Whitman utilized the speech patterns of conversation in his poems and is the originator of **free verse** in America. Poets who write in free verse do not use strict metrical patterns to determine units of measure. One way they measure rhythm is through lines and paragraphs. In this kind of poem, ideas are not connected by rhyme or specific meter, but by utilizing a wide range of figures of speech (schemes and tropes) to unify the ideas presented in the poem. Whitman was influenced in part by the Psalms and songs in the Bible. In the following excerpt from the Song of Solomon, simile, metaphor and **anaphora**, the repetition of the initial word in a series of lines, provide unity:

 Song of Songs (Song of Sol. 7:1–6)

How beautiful your sandaled feet, O prince's daughter!
Your graceful legs are like jewels, the work of a craftsman's hands.
Your navel is a rounded goblet that never lacks blended wine.
Your waist is a mound of wheat encircled by lilies.
Your breasts are like two fawns, twins of a gazelle.
Your neck is like an ivory tower.
Your eyes are the pools of Heshbon by the gate of Bath Rabbim.
Your nose is like the tower of Lebanon looking toward Damascus.
Your head crowns you like Mount Carmel.
Your hair is like royal tapestry; the king is held captive by its tresses.
How beautiful you are and how pleasing, O love, with your delights!

METER

The Song of Solomon uses the cadence of speech combined with figures of speech to create a sort of musical phrasing. Some forms of poetry, however, are written to fit a specific meter, an established pattern of rhythm in a poem. English metrical verse is called **accentual-syllabic verse** because the units are measured by the number of accents as well as the number of syllables in each line, although all poems are not measured this way.

Writing for Ideas and Practice 6-1

1. a. Write five lines of poetry about anything, quickly.
   b. Read the lines aloud. Listen to the rhythm in the lines. Read them aloud again and again.
   c. Have someone else read them aloud. Note whether the rhythm was different when someone else read the lines. Now have another person read the lines aloud.
2. Gather five examples of language from any five sources—newspapers, cereal boxes, billboards, advertisements. Record the samples as lines, as if they were poetry. Read them aloud. What rhythms do you hear?

In examining a poem for meter, mark these accented and unaccented syllables, looking for patterns and breaks in those patterns. Look at the following line:

I wished upon the evening star.

What words or syllables do you emphasize or say louder than the others? Mark above those words or syllables with a ´. Now mark the rest of the words or syllables with a ˘. Is this what you marked?

˘ ´ ˘ ´ ˘ ´ ˘ ´
I wished upon the evening star.

This process is called **scansion**, a way of examining a poem's metrical pattern (and/or rhyme scheme) and deviations from the pattern. Think of scansion as ear training, a skill that is just as important for the poet to master as it is for the musician. After you sensitize yourself to rhythm and meter, you will become more adept, and you will be better able to analyze your own poems. Writer Fran Lebowitz has said that she spends a great deal of time counting syllables, and you will find that many other professional writers and poets spend their time doing the same thing. Even if you are not writing a poem that follows a strict metrical form, you will still want to familiarize yourself with the units of measure used in a poem. You might be returning to a certain rhythm again and again without realizing it.

    The basic unit of measure is called the **foot**, a combination of stressed and/or unstressed syllables. In an obvious pun, a foot is the beat of the rhythm, the beat when one taps the foot in time. These feet are repeated and/or combined with other feet within a line of poetry, and this line length is also measured. The names of the metrical feet and their patterns are as follows:

Iambic Foot — one unaccented syllable followed by an accented syllable.

            ˘   ´
    Example: ker-PLOP

Trochaic Foot — one accented syllable followed by an unaccented syllable.

           ´ ˘
    Example: PUMP-kin

Anapestic Foot — two unaccented syllables followed by an accented syllable.

        ˘ ˘ ´
    Example: on-a-TRAIN

Dactylic Foot — an accented syllable followed by two unaccented syllables.

        ´ ˘ ˘
    Example: DES-ti-ny

Amphibrachic Foot — an unaccented syllable followed by an accented syllable followed by an unaccented syllable.

        ˘ ´ ˘
    Example: po-TA-to

The following metrical feet are not as common and therefore are not discussed as often:

Spondaic Foot — two accented syllables. This pattern usually occurs when two stressed monosyllabic words are placed together, for even compound words usually emphasize one syllable over the other.

Example: DÍE, DÍE

Pyrrhic Foot — two unaccented syllables. This pattern is rare, since most English words have an accented syllable.

Example: ŏf thĕ

Monosyllabic Foot — one stressed syllable, an extra stressed syllable in a pattern, possibly called an imperfect foot, but an imperfect foot could be accented or unaccented.

Example:

WHÁT? For the DAWN of the MORNing is BREAKing

As you examine a poem, place accent marks over the accented syllables to see if you can determine a pattern emerging, to see if a certain type of foot is repeated throughout the line. Many times the form will dictate the metrical pattern. Sonnets and blank verse are written in **iambic pentameter.**Pentameter is discussed on p. 111 Indeed, a great deal of English poetry is written using the iambic foot as well, since this meter most naturally fits English speech patterns, although dialectical differences affect pronunciation. Here is Shakespeare's Sonnet #73 scanned for meter. Look for the basic pattern which emerges throughout, and notice how Shakespeare uses iambic pentameter and variations on the pattern:

    ŭ ′ ŭ ′ ŭ   ′ ŭ ′ ŭ ′
That time of year thou mayst in me behold
    ŭ ′ ŭ ′ ŭ ′ ŭ ′ ŭ ′
When yellow leaves, or none, or few, do hang
ŭ ′ ŭ   ′   ŭ   ′ ŭ ′ ŭ ′
Upon those boughs which shake against the cold,
  ′ ′ ŭ ′ ŭ ′ ŭ ŭ ′
Bare ruined choirs, where late the sweet birds sang.
ŭ ′ ŭ ′ ŭ ′ ŭ ′ ŭ ′
In me thou see'st the twilight of such day   5
ŭ ′ ŭ ′ ŭ ′ ŭ ′ ŭ   ′
As after sunset fadeth in the west,
   ŭ ′ ŭ ′ ′ ′ ŭ ′ ŭ ′
Which by and by black night doth take away,
  ′   ′ ŭ ′ ŭ ′ ŭ ′ ŭ ′
Death's second self, that seals up all in rest.

˘ ´ ˘   ´   ˘   ´   ˘ ´ ˘   ´
In me thou see'st the glowing of such fire,
  ˘   ´ ˘   ´ ˘   ´ ˘   ´   ˘ ´
That on the ashes of his youth doth lie,   10
 ´ ˘   ´   ˘   ˘   ´ ˘ ´   ˘ ´
As the deathbed whereon it must expire,
˘   ´   ˘   ´   ˘   ´ ˘   ´   ˘ ´
Consumed with that which it was nourished by.
  ´   ´ ˘   ´   ˘   ´   ˘ ´   ˘   ´
This thou perceiv'st, which makes thy love more strong,
˘ ´   ˘   ´   ˘   ´   ˘ ´   ˘ ´
To love that well which thou must leave ere long.

Notice that although the poem is written in iambic pentameter, the feet are not always divided by words. Sometimes the end of a foot is the same as the end of a word, but sometimes the end of a metrical foot occurs in the middle of a word. This technique softens the sing-song quality of the iambic pentameter. A poet will also deviate from a prescribed pattern to call attention to an idea. For example, in line 7, the poet refers to death as "black night," using a spondaic foot in place of the iambic foot. The use of the spondee here and in other references to death in the poem ("Bare ruined choirs" and "Death's second self") uses rhythm to underscore the harshness of the inevitable death of the speaker.

It is also important to note that some words, although they might not be fully accented, carry more emphasis than a clearly unaccented syllable. If it helps, you could place a half stress mark over those syllables. Scanning is an inexact science, and different scholars have different methods of scanning a poem. Your scan of a poem might differ from another reader's scan, depending on whether you have marked your half-stressed syllables or whether you have a straight scan. Scansion is meant to be a tool for measuring rhythm and candence, not an end to itself.

Although scanning poems for meter may seem mechanical, a straight scan of the poem probably won't be absolutely reflective of an oral reading. Another step you will want to complete in scanning your poems or the poems of others is to read the poem for meaning, perhaps underlining or bracketing those words that you naturally stress to reinforce the meaning of the words in conjunction with one another. This is one of the things actors do as they mark a script, because emphasizing different words as you say them can change the entire meaning of a poem or a passage. For example, notice the difference in meaning between these statements:

"Why are you complaining? I **married** you, didn't I?"
AND
"Why are you complaining? I married **you**, didn't I?"

Once you have discovered a rhythmic pattern, then you can determine

Sources may also call this metrical pattern septameter. the number of feet within the line and label the actual line meter. A line of verse with two feet is called **dimeter**; three feet, **trimeter**; four feet, **tetrameter**; five feet, **pentameter**; six feet, **hexameter**; seven feet, **heptameter**;* and eight feet, **octameter**.

Writing for Ideas and Practice 6-2

1. Try scanning the following lines:

   Peter, Peter pumpkin eater,
   Had a wife and couldn't keep her.
   He put her in a pumpkin shell
   And there he kept her very well.

   What metrical patttern is used in lines 1 and 2? Does the pattern change in lines 3 and 4? How?

2. Shakespeare's plays are written in blank verse (unrhymed iambic pentameter). Look at the following lines from *Macbeth* and note any *obvious* irregularities. Can you see a reason for any of the irregularities?

   MACBETH: She should have died hereafter;
   There would have been a time for such a word.
   Tomorrow, and tomorrow, and tomorrow
   Creeps in this petty pace from day to day
   To the last syllable of recorded time,
   And all our yesterdays have lighted fools
   The way to dusty death. Out, out, brief candle!
   Life's but a walking shadow, a poor player
   That struts and frets his hour upon the stage
   And then is heard no more. It is a tale
   Told by an idiot, full of sound and fury,
   Signifying nothing.

3. Now choose a song you like. Write out the lyrics and scan it for rhythm.

In scanning a poem, it is unusual to find an absolute pattern used throughout. For instance, in scanning a sonnet, (fourteen lines of iambic pentameter), you might find a trochaic or dactylic foot. Let's go back to Hopkins's poem "God's Grandeur,"[1] but this time let's look at how he un-

---

1 "God's Grandeur" is presented in its entirety again later on in the chapter.

derscores content with rhythm and meter. In this poem, the fourth line begins with an accented syllable. Here are the third and fourth lines:

> It gathers to a greatness, like the ooze of oil
> Crushed. Why do men then now not reck his rod?

Does this mean that this poem is inferior, that Hopkins didn't really know how to write in sonnet form? While it is true that you will encounter some poems that you feel are poorly constructed, think about metrical irregularities in another way. What happens when you are reading a poem and something unusual or unexpected occurs? As in Shakespeare's Sonnet #73, many times the poet uses a metrical form as a frame and then uses deviation from the form to call attention to a particular section. The deviation calls attention to itself through its unexpectedness and also alters the pace at which the poem is read, either hurrying or slowing the established metrical pattern. For instance, the more accented syllables (in or out of sequence) a poem has, the slower the poem will read. If you were writing a poem using iambic pentameter and then deviated from this pattern by inserting a spondaic foot (two accented syllables) in each line, the pace of the poem would be slowed, as exemplified in line 6 of "God's Grandeur":

> ᴜ ´ ᴜ ´   ᴜ ´   ´   ´   ᴜ ´
> And all is seared with trade; bleared, smeared with toil.

On the other hand, light verse and children's poems as well as popular songs tend to be quite regular in their metrical structure. Why would this be true? It could be that in poetry like this, the reader wants what he expects, that is, regularity and predictability in structure, comfort and security in content. It also could be that the regular rhythm encourages or enables a reader to read a poem "quickly" or examine it in a cursory fashion. Regular rhythm also makes a poem easier to memorize. Think of the many nursery rhymes you still remember from childhood. They all have a regular sing-song rhythm to them. And one of the reasons Dr. Seuss stands out among all children's verse writers is his mastery of cadence and rhythm as well as his content.

Read the following Dr. Seuss poem aloud:

The Fuddnuddlers

There are so many things
that you really should know.
And that's why I'm bothering
telling you so.
You should know the first names   5
of the Fuddnuddler Brothers
who like to pile each on the heads of the others.
If you start at the top,

there are Bipper and Bud
and Skipper and Jipper   10
and Jeffrey and Jud,
Horatio, Horace and Hendrix and Hud,
and then come Dinwoodie and Dinty and Dud,
also Fitzsimmon and Frederick and Fud,
and Slinkey and Stinkey and Stuart and Stud.   15
And, down at the bottom
is poor little Lud.
But if Lud ever sneezes,
his name will be MUD.

Although the line lengths vary, can you identify the metric foot that is used most often?

STANZAS

Another element of a poem's rhythmic movement is stanza form. A **stanza** is a certain number of lines grouped together, usually forming a pattern throughout the poem, just like the verses in a song. The number of lines you have in your stanzas will partially dictate the pattern of your poem. Here are some of the common stanza forms:

Couplet—a two-line stanza
Tercet—a three-line stanza
Quatrain—a four-line stanza
Cinquain—a five-line stanza
Sestet—a six-line stanza
Septet—a seven-line stanza
Octave—an eight-line stanza

Writing for Ideas and Practice 6-3

Go back to "My Papa's Waltz" and mark the poem for emphasis, underlining words that are emphasized based on content. Have several readers read the poem aloud as the others listen and underline. Now compare notes. Did your answers differ?

In exploring rhythm in your poetry, you might want to look to music as a resource. Although many songs you hear utilize regular rhythms, many poets have used jazz, and, as seen in the previous chapter, blues rhythms as patterns for poems. Poet Sonny Bates uses jazz as the foundation for his poems' rhythms, stating that "You deal with the syllables as notes. . . . You can let it rip and fly. Build the syllables. Yell them out. Make them soft. Extend them. . . . All of a sudden, it becomes something colorful that people can experience." And Michael S. Harper, who also uses jazz rhythms in his poetry and has written poems about jazz musicians, says that poetry and jazz do have many similarities, but points out that different rules govern each.

So how do poets incorporate different, more experimental rhythms into their poetry? In this Michael S. Harper poem, the rhythm provides the undercurrent of the poem, carrying much of the emotion of the poem:

 Nightmare Begins Responsibility

I place these numbed wrists to the pane
watching white uniforms whisk over
him in the tub-kept
prison
fear what they will do in experiment   5
watch my gloved stickshifting gasolined hands
breathe *boxcar-information-please* infirmary tubes
distrusting white-pink mending paperthin
silkened end hairs, distrusting tubes
shrunk in his *trunk-skincapped*   10
shaven head, in thighs
distrusting-white-hands-picking-baboon-light
on this son who will not make his second night
of this wardstrewn intensive airpocket
where his father's asthmatic   15
hymns of *night-train,* train done gone
his mother can only know that he has flown
up into essential calm unseen corridor
going boxscarred home, *mamaborn, sweetsonchild*
gonedowntown into *researchtestingwarehousebatteryacid* 20
mam-son-done-gone/me telling her 'nother
train tonight, no music, no breathstroked
heartbeat in my infinite distrust of them:

and of my distrusting self
white-doctor-who-breathed-for-him-all-night   25
say it for two sons gone,
say nightmare, say it loud
panebreaking heartmadness:
nightmare begins responsibility.

Let's assume that this poem, although it is perhaps most effective when read aloud by Harper himself, is going to be read by someone else aloud or silently. Look at the ways Harper uses typographical formatting to guide the reader to the complex rhythms. He connects words with the hyphen, and he uses italics to emphasize whole words as well as syllables. The power contained in this poem comes from the content of the poem, of course, but notice how the urgent rhythm accentuates the "nightmare." Try scanning this poem, and notice how the jazz rhythms emerge from the text.

Writing for Ideas and Practice 6-4

1. Listen to four different songs or musical compositions, each having distinctly different styles and rhythms. Listen to the music for the rhythm and pace of the music. Write one poetic response to each musical piece which in some way mirrors the rhythm and pace of the song you are listening to.
2. Write a children's poem. The main thing to remember about children's poetry is that although you might incorporate regular rhythm and rhyme in the poem, a rhyme or rhythm that is "stretched" or awkward will still be recognized. It is very difficult to write poetry that is easy to read and remember, yet does not sound strained.

Punctuation

As we have discussed, cadence, or pace, is influenced by the rhythm of the words, but it is also influenced by the amount and kind of punctuation used in a poem. The general rule is that the more punctuation, the slower the poem will read. Of course punctuation isn't the only factor influencing a reader's pace, for we have looked at word placement and syllabic structure as well, but punctuation is an important influence.

When punctuation occurs at the end of a line, it is called an **end-stopped** line. A **run-on** line, also called **enjambment**, occurs if there is no punctuation at the end of the line, or if the idea expressed in one line is continued in the next. Since enjambment urges the reader to move to the next line without pausing, using enjambment can lessen the sing-song effect or a regular end-rhyme pattern. A mark of punctuation that comes within the line itself is called a **caesura**, in its most technical form dividing a foot and/or usually coming near the middle of the line — but neither of these qualifications are restrictive. Caesuras cause the reader to pause or stop in the middle of a line, providing a clear break in thought or slowing the pace of the poem.

Gerard Manley Hopkins was a poet so concerned with sound that he often invented his own syllabic stress, in some poems literally placing accent marks over syllables he wanted emphasized. Let's examine "God's Grandeur" once again. Notice the marking of run-on lines, end-stopped lines, and caesuras, and then read the poem aloud, paying special attention to his "green and red lights."

God's Grandeur

Here is an example of the **end-stopped** line, a line that has a mark of punctuation at the end.

The world is charged with the grandeur of God.*
    It will flame out, like shining from shook foil;
    It gathers to a greatness, like the ooze of oil
Crushed. Why do men then now not reck his rod?
Generations have trod, have trod, have trod;   5
    And all is seared with trade;* bleared, smeared with toil;
    And wears man's smudge and shares man's smell: the soil
Is bare now, nor can foot feel, being shod.
And for all this, nature is never spent;
    There lives the dearest freshness deep down things;   10
And though the last lights off the black West went
    Oh, morning, at the brown brink eastward, springs—

Notice the **enjambment** or **run-on** here. The reader is pushed to the next line.

Because the Holy Ghost over the bent*
    World broods with warm breast and with ah! bright wings.

The **caesura** here slows the pace of the poem. The punctuation determines if the reader slows or stops completely.

Notice that at points Hopkins brings the reader to a complete halt with a period, colon, or exclamation mark, and at other times he slows the pace with commas so that the reader can *hear* what he means. The pacing of the lines reflect the tone and content of the poem. Hopkins's use of commas to separate the words "have trod, have trod, have trod" imitates the motion of slow, plodding movement. In fact, the poem reads fairly slowly at first when the speaker discusses man's attempt to destroy God's creation. Then the pace of the poem moves more quickly toward the end of the poem as Hopkins reveals the inevitable glory and victory of God over all in the new morning. The lack of punctuation in the last two lines accelerates the pace and lifts it upward to the caesura in the last line: "Because the Holy Ghost over the bent / World broods with warm breast and with ah! bright wings."

Sometimes punctuation is limited or omitted altogether. Read aloud the following poem by Mitsuye Yamada:

To the Lady

The one in San Francisco who asked:
Why did the Japanese Americans let
the government put them in
those camps without protest?

Come to think of it I   5
    should've run off to Canada
    should've hijacked a plane to Algeria
    should've pulled myself up from my

bra straps
and kicked'm in the groin   10
should've bombed a bank
should've tried self-immolation
should've holed myself up in a
woodframe house
and let you watch me   15
burn up on the six o'clock news
should've run howling down the street
naked and assaulted you at breakfast
by AP wirephoto
should've screamed bloody murder   20
like Kitty Genovese

Then
YOU would've
come to my aid in shining armor
laid yourself across the railroad track   25
marched on Washington
tatooed a Star of David on your arm
written six million enraged
letters to Congress

But we didn't draw the line   30
anywhere
law and order Executive Order 9066
social order moral order internal order

YOU let'm
I let'm   35
All are punished.

1) What is the speed at which you naturally read this poem? 2) Is there anything that takes the place of punctuation in this poem? 3) What parts slow you down in your reading? 4) And now the *crucial* question: The question the lady asks is so simplistic and short-sighted that the speaker's response is understandably abrupt and sarcastic. How does the pace of the poem reflect the attitude of the speaker or tone of the poem?

In the following poem, notice the way Walt Whitman uses punctuation and line length to group ideas:

When I Heard the Learn'd Astronomer

When I heard the learn'd astronomer,
When the proofs, the figures, were ranged in columns before me,

When I was shown the charts and diagrams, to add, divide, and measure them,
When I sitting heard the astronomer where he lectured with much applause in the
    lecture-room,
How soon unaccountable I became tired and sick,   5
Till rising and gliding out I wander'd off by myself,
In the mystical moist night-air, and from time to time,
Look'd up in perfect silence at the stars.

In this poem Whitman uses **anaphora** (the repetition of a word or words at the beginnings of lines) combined with the progressive extension of the line length in lines 1–4 to show the reader the artificiality of what the astronomer has to *show* the speaker about the stars. Lines 4–8 turn back toward the speaker, the shorter line length reflecting the turn, as he leaves the lecture to go outside and *experience* the "perfect silence" of the stars.

Some poets omit punctuation, like W. S. Merwin, or use it minimally, as seen in Yamada's poem "To the Lady." If you decide not to use punctuation, or if you decide to use it sparsely, perhaps you will have to give even more thought to leading the reader to a correct reading of your poem. You may subscribe to the philosophy that multiple readings are possible and legitimate. In fact, you may encourage it by using deliberate ambiguity, but be sure that is truly what you intend to do. You then might want to consider line length and appropriate spacing (or stanza structure) between passages, realizing that space slows the reader somewhat, and also that word placement on the page will affect a particular reading of your poem, as in "To the Lady."

Writing for Ideas and Practice 6-5

1. The punctuation has been omitted from the following poem. Rewrite this poem two to four times, each time punctuating the poem differently and spacing the words on the page the way you want them to look. Show your poems to a group and read the various revisions. Do different readings produce different contextual results?

   ### Free Flight
   like the phoenix from the ashes she is flying again emerging from inside herself a metamorphosis of strength from agony sun reflecting gold on gold wings blinding eyes with brightness and beauty flying above us all

2. Write four short poems, each one containing a different action or movement. Vary the pace of the poems by experimenting with punctuation, meter, and space. Share your poems with other students.

3. Construct your own poetic form, and then write a poem which follows this model. For example, you could construct a poem which consists of three quatrains of iambic

pentameter, rhyming *abba*. Exchange your form and model poem with others, and have them write a poem based on your model. Be sure to write a poem using your own model before you ask someone else to follow the structure you have invented.

Poetry contains sounds, and those sounds are arranged in rhythm. Being sensitive to rhythm is listening or feeling the rhythm, even if you don't adhere to a specific metrical pattern. Poetry moves, and pacing is determined in part by the placement and combination of accented and unaccented syllables. As a writer you want to realize that you communicate through meter, whether you are conscious of it or not. For now, remember this advice:

 The poem in the head is always perfect. Resistance starts when you try to convert it into language. Language itself is a kind of resistance to the pure flow of self. The solution is to become one's language. You cannot write a poem until you hit upon its rhythm. That rhythm not only belongs to the subject matter, it belongs to your interior world, and the moment they hook up there's a quantum leap of energy.

— *Stanley Kunitz*

Writing on Your Own

Write a long poem with no punctuation and long lines. Then, write the same poem with punctation. Then, write the same poem with punctuation and varying line lengths and stanza breaks.

1. Which version of the poem do you like best, and why?
2. Which version of the poem did you enjoy writing most, and why?
3. Which version of the poem is closest to communicating the feeling and meaning of the poem? Why?

Writing to Revise

Choose two poems that you have written and rewrite each of them three times, each time punctuating the poem differently and experimenting with word placement. You will end up with three different versions of two poems. Have someone read these poems aloud to see if the different versions affect the essential content of the poem.

7

THE FORM OF POETRY

Writing to Warm up

Read the following two poems:

We Real Cool

The pool players
Seven at the golden shovel

We real cool. We
Left school. We

Lurk late. We   5
Strike straight. We

Sing sin. We
Thin gin. We

Jazz June. We
Die soon.   10

What Shall I Give My Children?

What shall I give my children? who are poor,
Who are adjudged the leastwise of the land,
Who are my sweetest lepers, who demand

No velvet and no velvety velour;
But who have begged me for a brisk contour, 5
Crying that they are quasi, contraband
Because unfinished, graven by a hand
Less than angelic, admirable or sure.
My hand is stuffed with mode, design, device.
But I lack access to my proper stone. 10
And plenitude of plan shall not suffice
Nor grief nor love shall be enough alone
To ratify my little halves who bear
Across an autumn freezing everywhere.

Notice how different these two poems are in structure, rhythm, sound, and diction. One poem is a sonnet, and one is written in couplets, but both are written by the same poet: Gwendolyn Brooks.

1. Which do you like better? Which is more successful in fulfilling what it tries to do?
2. Brooks is quoted in *Poets and Writers* magazine as saying that "Poetry is at pains to select." What does she mean by this?
3. Do you feel that you should study recognized poetic forms? Why or why not?
4. Do you like to write poems within a metrical pattern, or to write the lines in varying patterns and rhythms? Why?
5. Ultimately, is a predetermined poetic structure important to you at all? Why or why not?

FREE VERSE

We have discussed many of the independent elements you can use to create poetry; now let's look at putting the elements together into a cohesive package or form. Your poem will have some type of structure, even if it seems to have no shape at all. Many contemporary poets have eschewed metrical patterns and regular rhyme altogether, utilizing **free verse**, a defining term so broad it encompasses the diverse styles of Walt Whitman and E. E. Cummings. Free verse is not measured in metrical feet or syllables, but is created using other patterns, including line patterns, stanza patterns, or even patterns of images. Basically, then, free verse is broader in its scope than specific metrical forms, providing the poet with tremendous freedom, but as Robert Frost warned, "writing free verse is like playing tennis with the net down." Whether you utilize traditional form in your poetry or experiment with free verse, you will still want to employ craft, and to employ craft, you should practice writing using as many different methods as possible.

Free verse is very popular among contemporary poets; however, some poets utilize conventional verse exclusively, and still other poets use a combination of traditional forms and nontraditional forms. Students sometimes gravitate toward free verse as well, but sometimes this isn't a conscious choice at all; rather, it is a choice made out of the desire to communicate an idea, a feeling, truth, without worrying about the poem's form or structure. Other students fit their ideas into four-line stanzas consisting of rhymed iambic pentameter, no matter the idea, not looking at all of their options, or not knowing that they have many options within their grasp.

Even if you choose *never* to use conventional form in your poetry, you might find that experimenting with and learning about form will ultimately increase your sensitivity to language in general, whether you find that you are more comfortable with writing poetry, short stories, or plays. Conrad Aiken said that for practice he wrote one poem in a different form every day to practice technique as a method of training, and he advises those who seek his advice to do the same. John Hollander said that teachers "can teach the *writing* of verse . . . and the *recognition* of true poetry. The rest, writers must teach themselves."

Poems, however, are not meant to be algebraic equations. Explore different forms for different ideas, letting the poem grow organically. You may find that while one idea is best expressed using free verse in the form of a prose poem, another idea is best expressed as a sonnet. In this chapter we will explore the options you have in constructing poems, so that you can make decisions based on what form might best fit your ideas. Although we will not cover *every* known form of poetry, we will introduce you to some of the better-known traditions and ask you to give some of them a try. If you are serious about learning versification in order to learn craft as well as inspiration, you will want to explore further on your own.

Haiku

Earlier in the poetry section of this text, we mentioned imagist poetry as a style of poetry that captures one image that communicates one idea, like a photograph. Imagist poetry is greatly influenced by Japanese haiku poetry. Haiku is usually taught in the grade school curriculum in fourth or fifth grade because it complements the study of syllables, and it provides a nice bulletin board display for parents' night. The form is therefore sometimes seen as being juvenile. Don't believe it—haiku is powerful. Natalie Goldberg said, "Sensation of space is a true test of haiku. No matter how well we learn to write three-line poems, it takes much practice to fill those three lines with an experience of God." Haiku poets such as Issa were poetry teachers, employed for the specific purpose of teaching the art of the Japanese forms. Originally, in late medieval Japan, the **renga** was a form of **linked** poetry, that is, a poetic form that was composed by several different people, used as a court distraction among the elite or as a drinking game among the commoners, but not to be dismissed as merely a pastime for bored courtesans. The form is deeply rooted in Japanese Buddhist belief, and the content of Issa's and Basho's poems reflect that belief.

In the renga, one poet would write the **hokku** (eventually to become the separate form **haiku**), which consisted of three lines, the first containing five syllables, the second containing seven syllables, and the third containing five syllables. The next poet would respond to the hokku with two seven-syllable lines, creating a **tanka**, or a poem consisting of five lines containing a total of thirty-one syllables. Another poet would use the previous two lines and add three more lines, creating a new poem, and then yet another poet would add a couplet to the previous three lines, again creating a new poem. Groups would then continue this pattern, so that in fact it was a social activity, a group poem written under a haiku master, like Basho, Buson, Issa, or Shiki, all considered to be haiku masters in their time. Eventually the hokku became the haiku; and instead of being the basis for the group poem, it was a poem in itself.

The haiku, then, is a poem comprised of three lines and seventeen syllables (divided 5-7-5). However, there are some rules regarding content as well. Conventionally, the haiku's subject is nature, and more specifically the haiku is concerned with a specific seasonal time and place. This doesn't mean that all haikus overtly mention a particular season such as fall or spring, although some of them do. Rather, they intimate a season or a specific temporal mood in their description, and through that description the reader sees nature through a magnifying glass, thus gaining insight. The haiku is not muddled or complicated; it is spare and clean, and the reflection is clear, but not juvenile or simple. While the tanka might have a moral, the haiku speaks for itself, one image, consisting of one slide or one photograph of significance. Here are some haikus:

Year's end,
all corners
  of this floating world, swept.
— *Basho (Trans. by Lucien Stryk)*
	Summer grass—
	all that's left
	  of warriors' dreams.
	— *Basho (Trans. by Robert Hass)*

In a dream
my daughter lifts a melon
  to her soft cheek.
— *Issa (Trans. by Robert Hass)*
	Washing the saucepans—
	the moon glows on her hand
	  in the shallow river.
	— *Issa (Trans. by Robert Hass)*

You might notice that the English translations don't always contain seventeen syllables in the 5-7-5 pattern of the Japanese originals. There are many variations in translations, and each translator is attempting to capture the essence of what is said as well as being true to the wording of the text itself. However, when you write your haiku, you will want to follow the 5-7-5 format discussed above, or be deliberate in your deviation.

Here are some student samples of haiku:

Pecan husks, dry brown
bells swinging in the winter
wind — lonesome today.

Working Woman's Haiku

If I had skipped that
Meeting I could have seen the
Fall leaves change color.

I am preparing
to be lonely. You are to
Leave. Cold winter wind.

Writing for Ideas and Practice 7-1

1. In a group, try some linked poetry. You might make this an ongoing project, kept in one notebook to be passed from person to person. The appointed "haikai" should begin by writing the initial hokku. The first line contains five syllables, the second contains seven syllables, and the third contains five syllables. Then the poem is passed to the next person, who adds the next two lines to create the tanka; the next person then adds three lines to the previous two to make an entirely new poem, and the next person adds a couplet to the previous three lines to make *another* independent poem. The progression then continues in that same three line/two line pattern until your group reaches a predetermined number of verses, which would probably be limited by the amount of time you want to devote to this as well as the number of poets in your group.

2. On your own, write five haikus, and use your surroundings for your subject matter. Try to vary the locations you use as well as the time of day you write. Is there a different mood reflected in the pond at midnight than at midday? In late summer or midwinter?

The poetry of the haiku masters, although Eastern in thought and form, had a tremendous influence on the Imagist poets of the early twentieth century like Ezra Pound and H. D. (Hilda Doolittle). This development isn't surprising, considering that Shiki lived from 1867 to 1902 and is considered to have developed the modern haiku, loosening its restrictions on its form and yet tightening its content. Shiki insisted that the poem speak for itself, naturally, emphasizing that the poem should not be primarily about literal, denotative content, but rather about a feeling, a mood, even an intuition. The Imagists also focused on creating feeling and mood with words, and infused English poetry with the elements of haiku. Look again at the Ezra Pound poem that so exemplifies the influence of haiku on English poetry:

In a Station of the Metro

The apparition of these faces in the crowd;
Petals on a wet, black bough.

Here we have *one* image leading to *one* feeling. As Pound said of this poem, "In a poem of this sort one is trying to record the precise instant when a thing outward and objective transforms itself, or darts into a thing inward and subjective." The intent of this poem is similar to the intent of the traditional haiku, but look at the similarities and differences between this imagist poem and a typical haiku. Haiku poems don't normally have titles, but if this poem were not titled, if the title were in fact the first line, it might look like more like a traditional haiku. In addition, the punch line or surprise line in haiku is usually placed last, especially in Issa's poems. Here it appears that the punch line comes first as the title. Is it a weakness or a strength that the Imagists followed a less structured path, embracing the concept and leaving the rigidity of the form behind?

Using images to convey feelings was not exclusive to the Imagist movement, but it did point poetry in a certain direction; and although the Imagist movement gave way to other movements in poetry, the influence of the Imagists can be felt in much contemporary poetry, even if the poet himself is not intentionally writing an "Imagist" poem. Here are the words of Amiri Baraka in the foreword to Martín Espada's *Rebellion is the Circle of a Lover's Hands*: "Art (created Being) is significant because of the *feelings* (the real life) it can convey. It is the expansiveness of our feelings that are the fuel of evolution. As long as we can feel, we will be alive! When we cannot feel, our 'intellectual process' cannot create, since it is merely rationalized feeling." Now take a look at one of Espada's poems:

 After the Flood in Chinandega
July, 1982

Nicaragua
is a young brown girl
standing in the mud
of a refugee camp,
grinning at the way   5
her green bird
balances himself
on her head

Writing for Ideas and Practice 7-2

1. "After the Flood in Chinandega" is a metaphor—one single metaphor. Can you see anything that reminds you of the imagist poems?

2. Would you want all of your poems to be short imagist poems, or can you see a greater benefit to studying these short forms such as the haiku or imagist poems?

Have you noticed that some of these poems stray from predetermined rules, that word placement on the page can become more individualized, more stylized? These poems are structured with rhythm and sound in mind, of course, but they don't follow preset constructional restraints. Free verse concerns itself with cadence, but some poets place great emphasis on visual presentation. Therefore, in the twentieth century, word placement on the page assumes a significance that most poets had not considered before. It is true that poetry on the page has always had a visual as well as aural dimension. And even as far back as the seventeenth century, poets such as George Herbert experimented with concrete poetry, arranging the words of their poems as pictures on the page. By far, however, the modern poet and reader has more to contend with in this area than ever before. Poet and critic Dana Gioia stated that "it is probably not accidental that the broad-scale development of free verse came from the first generation of writers trained from childhood on the shift-key typewriter introduced in 1878." For example, would this poem, another by E. E. Cummings, be effective in any way if it were read aloud?

    R-P-O-P-H-E-S-S-A-G-R

                              r-p-o-p-h-s-s-a-g-r
                    who
a)s w(e loo)k
upnowgath
          PPEGORHRASS
                              eringint(o-
aThe):l
        eA
          !p:
S   a
              (r
rIvInG   .gRrEaPsPhOs)
                              to
rea(be)rran(com)gi(e)ngly
,grasshopper;

Is a poem a poem if it cannot be read aloud? Cummings uses symbols and letters and word parts to communicate this poem about a grasshopper. Did you know what he was talking about before reading the last line? Is that good or bad? Should poets be less experimental, or do you like what Cummings is doing with (or to) the language?

Not all poets are as experimental as Cummings, and not all of his poetry is impossible to read aloud. As this poem shows, however, the free verse poem is perhaps only limited by one's imagination and definition of what a poem is. Remember that free verse often depends on the arrangement of words on the page, so in your construction of a free verse poem, consider both the aural and visual implications of your words. Some poets use some bits of form, such as irregular stanzaic structure and rhyme which, although irregular, "float" through the poem. The point is that in free verse there are no rules except those you impose on yourself. Is all of this freedom dangerous? When you write in free verse, remember that you *are* working without a net, as Frost said. You might find some way of communicating in verse that no one else has thought of, and then again you might end up with an unintelligible mess. T. S. Eliot once said that "No verse is *libre* [free] for the man who wants to do a good job."

You might consider combining traditional and nontraditional techniques. And you might find that you change styles throughout your writing life. W. S. Merwin wrote formal verse in the 1950s, and without rejecting or invalidating his previous work, began writing free verse in the 1960s, emphasizing oral reading of his works. The point is that you can do whatever you want, but in experimenting you will want to bring everything you know about poetry with you, rather than forgetting everything you know about poetry. A great musician who creates a new type or form or way of producing music takes what he knows of music theory and goes forward into unexplored territory. Not knowing anything about music would mean that eventually, after much experimentation, he would eventually travel in a circle back to the beginning. Study everything and try everything and then determine what works for you.

Writing For Ideas and Practice 7-3

1. Write five poems that you consider to be "Imagist"—short—one image that creates one feeling. Your subject matter can be anything, but the exercise works better if you show something tangible: bread baking in the oven, shorn sheep on a winter's day, the department store on Christmas Eve. Once you have five images (they don't have to be related to each other), connect them into a longer poem. You may add words to connect the images. Play with the order of placement of the images as well. Don't be afraid to be bizarre—think like Picasso here. The following poem is a student response that follows this model:

Combine Graveyard

South bound
drifting back in time
to the graveyard of the dead combine

                    past Shreveport,
                    County becomes   5
                    Parish
                    past Lake Charles
                    to swampy water
                    a place where
                    common sense is   10

              backward thinking.

                    Solid dry
                    dirt becomes
                    deep, wet
                        mud   15
                    cannot walk
                    without sinking.

              Eyesight is dim in thick fog.
                    Trees hang low
                    like green mops   20
                    over sunken logs.
              Write a ballad for the "Kingfish."
                    With chins held high,
                    white men sing—
              "In Louisiana every man is king!"   25

                    The wise bird flies
              high but only the dead
                    come low
                        .   .   .   .

    "Damn, Adam, you'd make a pretty good coon ass you stay here long enough!"
                    says the rice farmer,
                        sharp

                        tough.

                    The new and   50
                        the old
                        tear at
                    the fabric of tradition,

              so I tear off a piece of me

              that I can leave back at the "Lake Arthur Bar,"   55

              feeling a safe happiness in my heart,

and a gray sadness in my mind,

slowly gathering like rust on the
dead combine.

— *Adam Carroll*

2. Write a short poem that is more effective seen on paper than read aloud. Whatever
    your subject is, think about movement and action, bringing that movement and ac-
    tion to the page. Feel free to use symbols and pictures as well as words to communi-
    cate your ideas. Do you work on a computer? Are there possibilities for poetic con-
    struction there? Again you might want to focus on one image or picture, as
    Cummings did in his poem, "R-P-O-P-H-E-S-S-A-G-R."

Traditional Forms

Perhaps right now you don't want to boldly go where no poet has gone before. That's okay; many poets writing today *choose* to utilize conventional
forms to shape their poetry, and although this text will not cover every poetic form ever developed in Western literature, it will examine some of the
more popular forms of poetic convention and tradition.

One form, used from Shakespeare to Milton to Frost, is **blank verse**
— unrhymed iambic pentameter. As we mentioned earlier, iambic pentameter is said to most directly reflect the natural patterns of English
speech. That doesn't necessarily mean that writing it is as easy as writing
prose. Since no rhyme is used to connect phrases, lines, or ideas, the poet
must use punctuation and/or spacing, sometimes grouping ideas into
verse paragraphs, which are determined by content or thought rather
than by metrics. The verse paragraphs provide motion and countermotion.

An example of blank verse is found in Frost's "Mending Wall," presented in its entirety here:

 Mending Wall

Something there is that doesn't love a wall,
That sends the frozen-ground-swell under it,
And spills the upper boulders in the sun;
And makes gaps even two can pass abreast.
The work of hunters is another thing: 5
I have come after them and made repair
Where they have left not one stone on a stone,
But they would have the rabbit out of hiding,
To please the yelping dogs. The gaps I mean,

No one has seen them made or heard them made,   10
But at spring mending-time we find them there.
I let my neighbor know beyond the hill;
And on a day we meet to walk the line
And set the wall between us once again.
We keep the wall between us as we go.   15
To each the boulders that have fallen to each.
And some are loaves and some so nearly balls
We have to use a spell to make them balance:
"Stay where you are until our backs are turned!"
We wear our fingers rough with handling them.   20
Oh, just another kind of outdoor game,
One on a side. It comes to little more:
There where it is we do not need the wall:
He is all pine and I am apple orchard.
My apple trees will never get across   25
And eat the cones under his pines, I tell him.
He only says, "Good fences make good neighbors."
Spring is the mischief in me, and I wonder
If I could put a notion in his head:
"*Why* do they make good neighbors? Isn't it   30
Where there are cows? But here there are no cows.
Before I built a wall I'd ask to know
What I was walling in or walling out,
And to whom I was like to give offense.
Something there is that doesn't love a wall,   35
That wants it down." I could say "Elves" to him,
But it's not elves exactly, and I'd rather
He said It for himself. I see him there
Bringing a stone grasped firmly by the top
In each hand, like an old-stone savage armed.   40
He moves in darkness as it seems to me,
Not of woods only and the shade of trees.
He will not go behind his father's saying,
And he likes having thought of it so well
He says again, "Good fences make good neighbors."   45

What techniques does Frost use to connect the poem since there is no rhyme? Look for caesuras, end-stopped lines, run-on lines, as well as repetition of key elements. Frost writes in all different styles, including the sonnet and rhymed iambic pentameter. What is it about this poem that might be best expressed in blank verse? Why didn't he use the sonnet here? Or stanzas with regular rhyme, as in some of his other poems?

Blank verse is so universal and yet so precise that you will want to practice working in it to some extent, if only to sensitize yourself to the rhythm of iambic pentameter, since it is the fundamental rhythm of many other forms of poetry as well.

Writing for Ideas and Practice 7-4

Think of a difficult decision you must make soon or have made in the past. Perhaps it is a decision regarding the next step in your life, or perhaps a decision you made in the past which has affected who you are or where you are today. Now, imagine a character who could give voice to the decision you have faced. Write a blank verse dramatic monologue, a poem spoken by a character, in which the character contemplates those choices.

Now that we have discussed the basics of form, let's look at some of the prominent poetic forms, developed through the years and utilized in contemporary poetry as well. The two forms we will practice next are both French in origin. The first is the **sestina**, which does not employ rhyme, but achieves unity by repeating end words in the lines according to a strict pattern, and consists of six, six-line stanzas, and a three-line stanza at the end. By numbering the first six lines, we can determine the pattern for the rest of the poem, then we can determine the formula.

The sestina gets a great deal of negative press, most of which it deserves, since its style is rather artificial and thus sometimes seems contrived. There are some really wonderful sestinas, though, and the following sestina is a commentary on the form itself:

 My Confessional Sestina

Let me confess. I'm sick of these sestinas	1
written by youngsters in poetry workshops	2
for the delectation of their fellow students,	3
and then published in little magazines	4
that no one reads, not even the contributors	5
who at least in this omission show some taste.	6
Is this merely a matter of personal taste?	6
I don't think so. Most sestinas	1
are such dull affairs. Just ask the contributors	5
the last time they finished one outside of a workshop,	2
even the poignant one on herpes in that new little magazine	4
edited by their most brilliant fellow student.	3
Let's be honest. It has become a form for students,	3
an exercise to build technique rather than taste	6
and the official entry blank into the little magazines—	4
because despite its reputation, a passable sestina	1
isn't very hard to write, even for kids in workshops	2
who care less about being poets than contributors.	5

Granted nowadays everyone is a contributor.   5
My barber is currently a student   3
in a rigorous correspondence school workshop.   2
At lesson six he can already taste   6
success having just placed his own sestina   1
in a national tonsorial magazine.   4

Who really cares about most little magazines?   4
Eventually not even their own contributors   5
who having published a few preliminary sestinas   1
send their work East to prove they're no longer students.   3
They need to be recognized as the new arbiters of taste   6
so they can teach their own graduate workshops.   2

Where will it end? This grim cycle of workshops   2
churning out poems for little magazines   4
no one honestly finds to their taste?   6
This ever-lengthening column of contributors   5
scavenging the land for more students   3
teaching them to write their boot-camp sestinas?   1

Perhaps there is an afterlife where all contributors   5
have two workshops, a tasteful little magazine, and sexy students   3
who worshipfully memorize their every sestina.   1

— *Dana Gioia*

By numbering the last word in the line, you can determine the pattern for the rest of the poem. Realize that the pattern below is just that, a pattern. You can use it as a model if it helps, but don't be intimidated by the form's intricacy. All we have done is taken the word pattern found in "My Confessional Sestina," numbered the last word in each line, and placed the pattern on the page below. The stanzas are numbered *one* through *seven*, and the word pattern is listed vertically under each stanza number.

One	Two	Three	Four	Five	Six	Seven	
1	6	3	5	4	2	5	*(Words 2, 4,*
2	1	6	3	5	4	3	*and 6 are*
3	5	4	2	1	6	1	*embedded in*
4	2	1	6	3	5		*stanza seven as*
5	4	2	1	6	3		*well.)*
6	3	5	4	2	1		

Yes, this pattern does look like a mathematical equation, and that is what some feel contributes to the artificiality of it, but it does provide some real possibilities, especially when you consider that you are working with the effective use of repetition. If you consider the motion of the poem, you can see the circular movement naturally provided by the form. Of course, the way you punctuate the poem will determine this to some extent, but the possibilities are embedded in the form. Perhaps the best way of approaching this form is to consider a subject, and then think of six key words that would tie the piece together, as Gioia does in his choice of the words *sestina, workshops, students, magazines, contributors,* and *taste.* All of these words refer to key concepts related to his subject. You might think of words that can act as both nouns and verbs to open up some opportunities to use the words in a variety of ways.

In his sestina, Gioia is commenting on much more than the sestina. What does he mean when he says that the students "care less about being poets than contributors"? Is this true? Do you agree with his comments on the sestina? (Perhaps you will want to reserve judgment until you have written one.) More importantly, do you agree with his comments on the state of poetry, or more specifically, his comments on little magazines? Flannery O'Connor was once asked if she thought that universities stifled writers, and her response was that they didn't stifle enough of them. Is this part of Gioia's statement? Or is this poem more an assertion of Andy Warhol's prophetic statement about everyone having his or her fifteen minutes of fame?

Another French form, one that is connected by rhyme instead of repetition, is the **villanelle**. It is intended to be light or pastoral in nature. Like the sestina, it also utilizes repetition, but it uses line repetition rather than word repetition, and it also has a specific rhyme structure. Although the poem is not bucolic, perhaps one of the most powerful villanelles in contemporary poetry is Dylan Thomas's "Do Not Go Gentle into That Good Night":

Do Not Go Gentle into That Good Night

Do not go gentle into that good night,	*a*
Old age should burn and rave at close of day;	*b*
Rage, rage against the dying of the light.	*a*
Though wise men at their end know dark is right,	*a*
Because their words had forked no lightning they	*b*
Do not go gentle into that good night.	*a*
Good men, the last wave by, crying how bright	*a*
Their frail deeds might have danced in a green bay,	*b*
Rage, rage against the dying of the light.	*a*
Wild men who caught and sang the sun in flight,	*a*
And learn, too late, they grieved it on its way,	*b*
Do not go gentle into that good night.	*a*

Grave men, near death, who see with blinding sight	*a*
Blind eyes could blaze like meteors and be gay,	*b*
Rage, rage against the dying of the light.	*a*
And you, my father, there on the sad height,	*a*
Curse, bless, me now with your fierce tears, I pray.	*b*
Do not go gentle into that good night.	*a*
Rage, rage against the dying of the light.	*a*

What is Thomas saying to us about the way we die? Self-help books say that we should progress through the stages and eventually reach a stage where we face and accept death, perhaps as a natural, cyclical process. Thomas seems to dispute this advice. How should we look at death? Accept it or fight it? What is the speaker saying to his father? Does the concept of "death with dignity" factor into this poem at all? Why or why not?

The structure of the poem underscores its content. The villanelle is made up of five tercets and a quatrain, with the following rhyme scheme: *aba/aba/aba/aba/aba/abaa*. There is also a refrain; line 1 is repeated in lines 6, 12, and 18, and line 3 is repeated in lines 9, 15, and 19. This use of repetition through the use of refrain coupled with the *aba* rhyme scheme seems simple at first, and it is easy for the reader to follow. The challenge for the poet is to use the form to increase the poem's power, not diminish it. The repeated lines should therefore carry weight and power so that the repetition of them increases the depth of the poem. The kernel of real meaning, then, is contained in the refrain, and the technical construction of the refrain is tight.

Writing for Ideas and Practice 7-5

1. Using Gioia's sestina as a model, think of something you find ridiculous or absurd. Brainstorm a list of keywords that you associate with it. Choose six words from this list that would best express your thought or idea. Now you can begin to write a sestina. You will want to start with the first stanza, setting your words in order. You do have some freedom in the first stanza, but the arrangements of those words will determine the structure of the rest of the poem, so choose wisely. Now complete the rest of the sestina, following the outline of the form listed earlier.

2. Compile a list of rhyming words that might offer a multitude of logical possibilities in constructing a villanelle, which only has two rhymes. Using a rhyming dictionary here would prove useful, realizing also that slant rhyme might work, depending on your intent. Now construct your refrain, lines that you feel are powerful enough to bear repeating in the poem. These lines will make up lines 1 and 3 and will be re-

peated throughout the poem (see outline of the form). Now complete your villanelle, remembering that sound, especially rhyme and repetition, links the ideas together.

Perhaps of all the poetic forms, the most well-known and most challenging is the **sonnet**. Originally an Italian form made popular by the poet Petrarch in the fourteenth century, the form consists of fourteen lines of iambic pentameter. There are two basic types of sonnets, the Italian or Petrarchan sonnet and the English or Shakespearean sonnet. The **Italian sonnet** consists of two stanzas: an octave, which introduces a problem or situation, and a sestet, which completes the thought or answers the problem introduced in the octave. (These stanzas may or may not be spatially divided.) The rhyme scheme of the Italian sonnet is as follows:

Octave: *abbaabba*
Sestet: *cdecde*   OR   *cdccdc*   OR   *cdedce*

The **English** or **Shakespearean sonnet** is constructed a bit differently. The English sonnet contains three quatrains and a concluding couplet, the couplet summing up the poem, or providing surprise or irony. (Again, the stanzas are not necessarily divided spatially.) The rhyme scheme of the English sonnet follows:

Quatrain one: *abab*
Quatrain two: *cdcd*
Quatrain three: *efef*
Couplet: *gg*

As you can see, the form is highly structured and quite challenging from a technical angle. What is it about this form that has made it "the form of choice" for so many years? As with the imagist poems, although the sonnet might employ more than one image, it deals with one issue, one complete thought, thus the brief fourteen-line form. And it moves; it expresses motion and countermotion in its ideas. The rhyme scheme is structured to provide unity to the poem, yet it doesn't "get in the way" of the poem itself. As a matter of fact, the rhyme scheme is perhaps one of the most challenging aspects of the sonnet form, because rhyme schemes that appear to be stretched or "fake" can really ruin any poem, but a sonnet in particular.

Here are two sonnets, one Italian and one English. Read them aloud for content and form:

ITALIAN/PETRARCHAN SONNET

What Lips My Lips Have Kissed

What lips my lips have kissed, and where, and why,
I have forgotten, and what arms have lain
Under my head till morning; but the rain
Is full of ghosts tonight, that tap and sigh
Upon the glass and listen for reply,   5
And in my heart there stirs a quiet pain
For unremembered lads that not again
Will turn to me at midnight with a cry.
Thus in the winter stands the lonely tree,
Nor knows what birds have vanished one by one,   10
Yet knows its boughs more silent than before:
I cannot say what loves have come and gone,
I only know that summer sang in me
A little while, that in me sings no more.

                    — Edna St. Vincent Millay

Here the speaker is using the seasons to represent a passage in her life, a typical sonnet strategy. What is the speaker mourning in this poem? A particular lover? Or is it that she realizes she is no longer sexually appealing?

ENGLISH/SHAKESPEAREAN SONNET

Sonnet 18

Shall I compare thee to a summer's day?
Thou art more lovely and more temperate.
Rough winds do shake the darling buds of May,
And summer's lease hath all too short a date.
Sometime too hot the eye of heaven shines,   5
And often is his gold complexion dimmed;
And every fair from fair sometimes declines,
By chance, or nature's changing course, untrimmed.
But thy eternal summer shall not fade,
Nor lose possession of that fair thou ow'st;   10
Nor shall death brag thou wand'rest in his shade,
When in eternal lines to time thou grow'st.
    So long as men can breathe or eyes can see,
    So long lives this, and this gives life to thee.

                    — William Shakespeare

The speaker here is ensuring immortality for the subject of this love poem. He uses seasons to signify life, death, and aging, and death is personified (it "brags"). He says that the subject will live forever, or will be forever young, for the speaker has written about her. Nothing can now destroy her youth, for although the seasons change, art remains constant. Did Shakespeare really know that his poem would be read more than four hundred years after it was written? Do you ever think about preserving your own immortality through your writing? How does this poem contrast Millay's poem?

How do you begin to learn such a form? Of course, the best way to learn the sonnet form, or any form for that matter, is to read, study and practice it. You will want to familiarize yourself with poets such as Shakespeare and Petrarch, but you can also find modern poets who utilize the sonnet form.

INFLUENCE AND IMITATION

Once you become familiar with a poet's style, you might use imitation to practice and learn. As writers, we are influenced by what we read. We noted in chapter 3 that Annie Dillard in *The Writing Life* cautions writers to be careful what they read, for that is what they will write. So imitate the poets you read; ultimately it will help you find your own voice. You could also consider responding to a poem or a series of poems. Poet Mark Jarman has written a series of poems entitled "Unholy Sonnets" in response to John Donne's famous "Holy Sonnets." Jarman stated that although he used Donne's sonnets as a model, Donne wrote religious poems in response to deeply rooted "Anglo-Catholic, Christian assumptions widely disseminated and shared in his time." Jarman's intent was to write "devotional poetry against the grain." Therefore, Jarman uses Donne's poetry as a starting point, a jumping off place. Jarman's poems are not meant to be parodies or modern replicas with a one-to-one relationship.

Here is Donne's Holy Sonnet #1:

Thou hast made me, and shall Thy work decay?
Repair me now, for now mine end doth haste;
I run to death, and death meets me as fast,
And all my pleasures are like yesterday.
I dare not move my dim eyes any way,   5
Despair behind, and death before doth cast
Such terror, and my feeble flesh doth waste
By sin in it, which it towards hell doth weigh.
Only Thou art above, and when towards Thee
By Thy leave I can look, I rise again;   10
But our old subtle foe so tempteth me
That not one hour myself I can sustain.
They grace may wing me to prevent his art,
And Thou like adamant draw mine iron heart.

How is Donne's religious faith defined or portrayed here? How would you describe his faith?

Here is Mark Jarman's Unholy Sonnet #1:

Hands folded to construct a church and steeple,
A roof of knuckles, outer walls of skin,
The thumbs as doors, the fingers bent within
To be revealed, wriggling, as "all the people,"
All eight of them, enmeshed, caught by surprise,   5
Turned upward blushing in the sudden light,
The nails like welders' masks, the fit so tight
Among them you can hear their half-choked cries
To be released, to be pried from this mess
They're soldered into somehow — they don't know.   10
But stuck now they are willing to confess,
If that will ease your grip and let them go,
Confess the terror they cannot withstand
Is being locked inside another hand.

Jarman is using the children's game as the point of action in his sonnet here: "Here is the church, here is the steeple; open them up (hands) and see all the people." What does he say about the "people" inside the church? How does this compare and/or contrast with Donne's proclamation of faith? Is Jarman being sacrilegious? Why or why not? Although Jarman uses Donne's "Holy Sonnets" as a model, the basic philosophical concepts differ. That's okay too. You can find your own voice, your own content, as you learn from writers whom you admire, whether you are writing sonnets or some other form. And broaden your scope, for you will find models everywhere.

You can draw from the established canon in your search for poems; however, you can look to folk tradition for poetic models as well. Cowboy poetry is a subgenre specialty that went virtually unrecognized until 1985, when the first Cowboy Poetry Gathering was held in Elko, Nevada. Buck Ramsey, a poet who is well known in the cowboy poetry movement, has not only used the traditional cowboy poetry as a model for his poetry, but has also drawn from a broad range of literature to integrate into his art. Perhaps his best-known poem is "Anthem," which is the prologue to a long narrative poem entitled *As I Rode Out on the Morning*. Although the subject is clearly that of the cowboy's life, Ramsey's form comes from a seemingly unlikely source. He uses the stanzaic form used by Alexander Pushkin in his novel in verse entitled *Eugene Onegin*, which includes a series of fourteen-line stanzas, each rhyming *ababccddeffegg*: Here is a stanza from *Eugene Onegin*:

All Eugene knew is past relating,   *a*
But for one thing he had a bent,   *b*
And I am not exaggerating   *a*
His principal accomplishment;   *b*

From early youth his dedication	c
Was to a single occupation;	c
He knew one torment, one delight	d
Through empty day and idle night:	d
The science of the tender passion	e
That Ovid sang, that brought him here,	f
And closed his turbulent career	f
In such a brief and tragic fashion—	e
Ovid, who here, so far from Rome,	g
Found in the steppes an exile's home.	g

Compare the first stanza from Ramsey's poem:

Anthem

And in the morning I was riding
Out through the breaks of that long plain,
And leather creaking in the quieting
Would sound with trot and trot again.
I lived in time with horse hoof falling;   5
I listened well and heard the calling
The earth, my mother, bade to me,
Though I would still ride wild and free.
And as I flew out on the morning,
Before the bird, before the dawn,   10
I was the poem, I was the song.
My heart would beat the world a warning—
Those horsemen now rode all with me,
And we were good, and we were free.

Ramsey has written a poem that, in essence, is an anthem for cowboys, yet he has not restricted his own reading to the writings of cowboys. Ramsey has said that he is a voracious reader, and his literary background, combined with his experiences as a cowboy, enables him to create a poem that is not just an exercise in imitation, but something totally original, and this is one way new poetry evolves.

You might also find inspiration in tradition folk forms such as the **ballad**. The ballad is a form that developed from narrative folk songs of the British Isles, many of which were recorded in the eighteenth and nineteenth centuries but whose oral traditions go back even farther in history. Traditionally, the ballad is a song that tells some kind of tragic story, usually incorporating dialogue, often dealing with the supernatural, frequently using anomalies of nature to symbolize the tragedy. For example, a ballad might tell of a thorny bush might that grew out of the grave of a young woman who died a tragic and unjust death. Eventually the ballad developed into a recognized poetic form, long an important part of the literary canon in England and America. The ballad poem consists of a number of four-line stanzas rhyming *abcb*, and many examples of the poetic ballad can be found in the literature books as well, from Coleridge's "Rime of the Ancient Mariner" to Edwin Arlington Robinson's "Richard Cory," as well as other poems old and new. Examine the following traditional English ballad:

The Unquiet Grave

The wind doth blow today, my love,
    And a few small drops of rain;
I never had but on true-love,
    In cold grave she was lain.

I'll do as much for my true-love   5
    As any young man may;
I'll sit and mourn all at her grave
    For a twelvemonth and a day.

The twelvemonth and a day being up
    The dead began to speak: 10
"Oh who sits weeping on my grave
    And willl not let me sleep?"

" 'Tis I, my love, sits on your grave
    And will not let you sleep;
For I crave one kiss of your clay-cold lips   15
    And that is all I seek."

"You crave one kiss of my clay-cold lips,
    But my breath smells earthy strong;
If you have one kiss of my clay-cold lips
    Your time will not be long.   20

'Tis down in yonder garden green,
    Love, where we used to walk,
The finest flower that ere was seen
    Is withered to a stalk.

The stalk is withered dry, my love,   25
    So will our hearts decay;
So make yourself content, my love,
    Till God calls you away."

Because of the oral nature of the traditional ballad, the history and accuracy of each ballad is sketchy. There are many versions of this particular ballad, and although it was first recorded in the nineteenth century, it is likely that it originated much earlier. Nevertheless, it follows the traditional ballad form in structure and content.

In Coleridge's "Rime of the Ancient Mariner," an old man stops a young man on his way to a wedding feast to tell him a story. The young man does not want to be detained, but as stanza 4 states, the young man has no choice:

He holds him with his glittering eye—
The Wedding Guest stood still,
And listens like a three years' child:
The Mariner hath his will.

"The Rime of the Ancient Mariner" is a literary ballad, but it has all of the attributes of the traditional ballad. Edwin Arlington Robinson uses the ballad form for his poem "Richard Cory." Read the text of the poem and look for any deviations from the traditional ballad form:

Richard Cory

Whenever Richard Cory went down town,
We people on the pavement looked at him:
He was a gentleman from sole to crown,
Clean favored, and imperially slim.

And he was always quietly arrrayed,   5
And he was always human when he talked;
But still he fluttered pulses when he said,
"Good-morning," and he glittered when he walked.

And he was rich—yes, richer than a king—
And admirably schooled in every grace: 10
In fine, we thought that he was everything
To make us wish we were in his place.

So on we worked, and waited for the light,
And went without the meat, and cursed the bread;
And Richard Cory, one calm summer night,   15
Went home and put a bullet through his head.

In addition to practicing imitation as a way of experimenting with form, you might practice technique and form (while having fun at the same time) by writing parodies. A **parody** is a satirical or humorous imitation of another work, usually a song or poem. Here is a student's parody of the Shakespearean sonnet we examined earlier:

Shall I Compare Thee to a Winter's Day?

Shall I compare thee to a winter's day?
Thou art more distant and more frigid:
Rough words do shake the crying eyes of mine,
And hatred's lease hath all too long a date:
Sometimes too cold the eye of winter burns,   5
And often is your dark reflection marr'd
And every affair from secrecy sometimes declines,
By chance, or strangers' eyes unseen;
But thy eternal winter shall not fade,
Nor lose possession of that cold thou giv'st,   10
And death shall brag I wander'st in his shade,
Before your winter sees the fall,
   So long as you can breathe, or your eyes can see,
   So long lives winter, and this brings death to me.

— *Andy Cooper*

Although this poem is not humorous, it does imitate Sonnet #18, commenting on the "winter" that is brought on by an unfaithful or distant lover. Cooper uses excerpts from the poem, turning the lines so that the theme of this poem is a counterpoint to the original.

To write a good parody, you must know the original thoroughly. Could there be a better way, then, to practice? And you don't just have to write sonnet parodies. Any poem you find potential humor in is fair game, especially those flowery, overstated love poems. Having fun with those poems is a good way to learn form, to find out what you admire or dislike in a poem. This exercise will therefore heighten your awareness as a poet and as a reader. Who knows, you might find that writing parodies is your niche. Although Anthony Hecht is a contemporary poet who has published a great number of poems, he is perhaps best known for his parody of Matthew Arnold's "Dover Beach," called "Dover Bitch." And here is poet Kenneth Koch's parody of William Carlos Williams's "This Is Just to Say," a poem we examine in chapter 4.

First, Williams's original:

This Is Just to Say

I have eaten
the plums
that were in
the ice box
and which   5
you were probably
saving
for breakfast

Forgive me
they were delicious   10
so sweet
and so cold

Variations on a Theme by William Carlos Williams

1
I chopped down the house that you had been saving to live in next summer.
I am sorry, but it was morning, and I had nothing to do
and its wooden beams were so inviting.

2
We laughed at the hollyhocks together
and then I sprayed them with lye.   5
Forgive me. I simply do not know what I am doing.

3
I gave away the money that you had been saving to live on for the next ten years.
The man who asked for it was shabby
and the firm March wind on the porch was so juicy and cold.

4
Last evening we went dancing and I broke your leg.   10
Forgive me. I was clumsy, and
I wanted you here in the wards, where I am the doctor!

— Kenneth Koch

Here Koch refers to the fact that William Carlos Williams was a doctor, and hints that the speaker in the Williams poem and in the parody is insincere in his apology.

Here is a student parody of William Carlos Williams's poetic style:

A patient of mine
Stopped by today
And offered a chicken
In lieu of a pay . . .
So I kicked him downstairs.

— Ace Freeman

In an article on Kenneth Koch in *The American Poetry Review*, David Lehman says that "the best parodies combine homage and critique while striving to transcend their sources." Although that is difficult to accomplish, perhaps that is what you should strive for when you practice imitation and parody. For example, in Koch's poem, Koch parodies Williams, and yet his own voice comes through as well. You are looking at another writer through a window, but while looking out of that window at night, you can't help but see a faint reflection of yourself out of the corner of your eye. Perhaps the strongest poets don't just look for their own reflection in the window, but instead come close enough to the glass to see outside of themselves and embrace the best of what has been written already.

Writing for Ideas and Practice 7-6

1. Look at a group of poems by a particular poet. Get to know the poet's style and recurring themes. It wouldn't hurt to learn a bit of biography as well. (Remember the Williams parody?) Now try your hand at parody. Write a parody of one or more of the poet's poems.

   Here is a student parody of Emily Dickinson's "I Felt a Cleaving in My Mind":

I Felt a Cleaving in My Mind

I felt a Cleaving in my Mind—
As if my Brain had split—
I tried to match it—Seam by Seam—
But could not make them fit.

The thought behind, I strove to join   5
Unto the thought before—
But Sequence ravelled out of Sound
Like Balls—upon a Floor.

— *Emily Dickinson*

A Cleavage in My Mind: A Parody

I felt a cleavage in my mind,
When I slipped with the ax.
Excedrin, Tylenol, and even some glue
Could not append the splintered gray goo.
I felt half a thought   5
Sneak past my splintered skull,
And strove to catch it as it fled,
To put with another, quite futile as I bled.

— *Carla McGaughey*

2. Look through newspapers (old or new) or follow a news story about a tragedy or a person for a period of time. Write a ballad which chronicles the event or the person's

life (or death). Add your imagination to the facts and come up with a really good story. Use the quatrain form and the ballad rhyme scheme *abcb* as your form. If you don't feel particularly solemn, you could tell a humorous story, using hyperbole while following the ballad form.

The best way to learn different forms is to read a wide variety of poems and then practice them: read them aloud, copy them, study them. Try to absorb as much as you can of what has been done by others before you. And then practice to imitate and to originate.

Writing on Your Own

1. Write a sonnet in response to another sonnet. (See Mark Jarman's example earlier in the chapter.) Be sure to use specific details and images, and experiment with rhythm and sound techniques within the restriction of the form.
2. Now it's time to go public. As a class or group, plan a reading or recital of your works. If you can perform on your campus either during the day or in the evening, then do so. If not, call some of the bookstores or coffeehouses in your area. Many of them would be willing to host your group for a reading, and those who already have poetry readings usually have an open-mike night once a week or so. A recent check of the local paper showed eight local poetry spots, all of them with some kind of occasional open-mike spot. Take time to choose your work carefully, and read for each other before you try your work out on a "real" audience. The more you practice reading your work aloud, the more comfortable you will be with your presentation, and you might find that reading your work aloud also facilitates the revision process.

Writing to Revise

Using the poems that you have written in the Writing for Ideas and Practice sections of chapters 4 through 7, begin putting together a portfolio of your work, revising your work as needed. Add more poems to this portfolio, using the daily journal prompts for ideas and experimenting with all of the forms we have discussed in this chapter. Don't forget to continue to experiment with vision and rhythm and sound as you look at form as well.

Internet Resources for Poetry

E-mail List
    Poetry Writing Workshop
    POETRY-W (listserv@psuvm.psu.edu) *An online workshop for poets.*

Usenet Newsgroup
    news:rec.arts.poems   *A newsgroup devoted to poetry of all kinds.*

World Wide Web Resources
    The Ann Arbor Poetry Forum
    http://www.poetryforum.org/   *A listing of literary festivals, a local poetry journal, and other resources.*
    The Electronic Poetry Center
    http://wings.buffalo.edu/epc/   *A site devoted to Web poetry and other resources.*
    The Academy of American Poets
    http://www.poets.org/   *The home page of the Academy. There are poetry displays and essays by and about contemporary poets as well as links to other resources.*
    The United States of Poetry
    http://www.itvs.org/ITVS/programs/USofP/   *A Web site of the PBS television series.*
    AHA! Poetry
    http://www.faximum.com/aha.d/homepage.htm   *A site providing valuable information on writing and reading poetry, with an emphasis on Japanese forms of poetry such as the haiku, tanka, and renga.*
    UbuWeb, Visual and Concrete Poetry
    http://ubuweb.com/vp/   *A well-crafted, artful site devoted to concrete and visual poetry.*
    Glossary of Poetic Terms
    http://shoga.wwa.com/~rgs/glossary.html   *Not the only glossary of poetic terms on the Net, but Robert Shubinski has put together a thorough, user-friendly site with links to other poetry reference sources.*

POETRY TO CONSIDER

Imamu Amiri Baraka

IN MEMORY OF RADIO

Who has ever stopped to think of the divinity of Lamont Cranston?
(Only Jack Kerouac, that I know of: & me.
The rest of you probably had on WCBS and Kate Smith,
Or something equally unattractive.)

What can I say?   5
It is better to have loved and lost
Than to put linoleum in your living rooms?

Am I a sage or something?
Mandrake's hypnotic gesture of the week?
(Remember, I do not have the healing powers of Oral Roberts . . .   10
I cannot, like F. J. Sheen, tell you how to get saved & *rich!*
I cannot even order you to gaschamber satori like Hitler or Goody Knight

& Love is an evil word.
Turn it backwards/see, see what I mean?
An evol word. & besides   15
who understands it?

I certainly wouldn't like to go out on that kind of limb.

Saturday mornings we listened to *Red Lantern* & his undersea folk.
At 11, *Let's Pretend*/& we did/& I, the poet, still do, Thank God!

What was it he used to say (after the transformation, when he was safe   20
& invisible & the unbelievers couldn't throw stones?) "Heh, heh, heh,
Who knows what evil lurks in the hearts of men? The Shadow knows."

O, yes he does
O, yes he does.
An evil word it is,   25
This Love.

Elizabeth Bishop

ONE ART

The art of losing isn't hard to master;
so many things seem filled with the intent
to be lost that their loss is no disaster.

Lose something every day. Accept the fluster
of lost door keys, the hour badly spent.   5
The art of losing isn't hard to master.

Then practice losing farther, losing faster:
places, and names, and where it was you meant
to travel. None of these will bring disaster.

I lost my mother's watch. And look! my last, or   10
next-to-last, of three loved houses went.
The art of losing isn't hard to master.

I lost two cities, lovely ones. And, vaster,
some realms I owned, two rivers, a continent.
I miss them, but it wasn't a disaster.   15

—Even losing you (the joking voice, a gesture
I love) I shan't have lied. It's evident
the art of losing's not too hard to master
though it may look like (*Write it!*) like disaster.

Robert Browning

MY LAST DUCHESS

Ferrara

That's my last duchess painted on the wall,
Looking as if she were alive. I call
That piece a wonder, now: Frà Pandolf's hands
Worked busily a day, and there she stands.
Will't please you sit and look at her? I said   5
"Frà Pandolf" by design, for never read
Strangers like you that pictured countenance,
The depth and passion of its earnest glance,
But to myself they turned (since none puts by
The curtain I have drawn for you, but I)   10
And seemed as they would ask me, if they durst,
How such a glance came there; so, not the first
Are you to turn and ask thus. Sir, 'twas not
Her husband's presence only, called that spot
Of joy into the Duchess' cheek: perhaps   15
Frà Pandolf chanced to say "Her mantle laps
Over my lady's wrist too much," or "Paint
Must never hope to reproduce the faint
Half-flush that dies along her throat": such stuff
Was courtesy, she thought, and cause enough   20
For calling up that spot of joy. She had
A heart—how shall I say?—too soon made glad,
Too easily impressed; she liked whate'er
She looked on, and her looks went everywhere.
Sir, 'twas all one! My favor at her breast,   25
The dropping of the daylight in the West,
The bough of cherries some officious fool
Broke in the orchard for her, the white mule
She rode with round the terrace—all and each
Would draw from her alike the approving speech,   30
Or blush, at least. She thanked men—good! but thanked
Somehow—I know not how—as if she ranked
My gift of a nine-hundred-years-old name
With anybody's gift. Who'd stoop to blame
This sort of trifling? Even had you skill   35
In speech—which I have not—to make your will
Quite clear to such an one, and say, "Just this
Or that in you disgusts me; here you miss,
Or there exceed the mark"—and if she let

Herself be lessoned so, nor plainly set   40
Her wits to yours, forsooth, and made excuse,
—E'en then would be some stooping; and I choose
Never to stoop. Oh sir, she smiled, no doubt,
Whene'er I passed her; but who passed without
Much the same smile? This grew; I gave commands;   45
Then all smiles stopped together. There she stands
As if alive. Will't please you rise? We'll meet
The company below, then. I repeat,
The Count your master's known munificence
Is ample warrant that no just pretense   50
Of mine for dowry will be disallowed;
Though his fair daughter's self, as I avowed
At starting, is my object. Nay, we'll go
Together down, sir. Notice Neptune, though,
Taming a sea-horse, thought a rarity,   55
Which Claus of Innsbruck cast in bronze for me!

James Dickey

On the Hill Below the Lighthouse

Now I can be sure of my sleep;
I have lost the blue sea in my eyelids.
From a place in the mind too deep
For thought, a light like a wind is beginning.
    Now I can be sure of my sleep.   5

When the moon is held strongly within it,
The eye of the mind opens gladly.
Day changes to dark, and is bright,
And miracles trust to the body,
    When the moon is held strongly within it.   10

A woman comes true when I think her.
Her eyes on the window are closing.
She has dressed the stark wood of a chair.
Her form and my body are facing.
    A woman comes true when I think her.   15

Shade swings, and she lies against me.
The lighthouse has opened its brain.

A browed light travels the sea.
Her clothes on the chair spread their wings.
    Shade swings, and she lies against me.   20

Let us lie in returning light,
As a bright arm swoops through the moon.
The sun is dead, thinking of night
Swung round like a thing on a chain.
    Let us lie in returning light.   25

Let us lie where your angel is walking
In shadow, from wall onto wall,
Cast forth from your off-cast clothing
To pace the dim room where we fell.
    Let us lie where your angel is walking,   30

Coming back, coming back, going over.
An arm turns the light world around
The dark. Again we are waiting to hover
In a blaze in the mind like a wind
    Coming back, coming back, going over.   35

    Now I can be sure of my sleep;
    The moon is held strongly within it.
    A woman comes true when I think her.
    Shade swings, and she lies against me.
    Let us lie in returning light,   40
    Let us lie where your angel is walking,
    Coming back, coming back, going over.

Emily Dickinson

THE SPIDER AS AN ARTIST

The Spider as an Artist
Has never been employed —
Though his surpassing Merit
Is freely certified

By every Broom and Bridget   5
Throughout a Christian Land —
Neglected Son of Genius
I take thee by the Hand —

T. S. Eliot

THE LOVE SONG OF
J. ALFRED PRUFROCK

S'io credesse che mia risposta fosse
A persona che mai tornasse al mondo,
Questa fiamma staria senza più scosse.
Ma perciocche giammai di questo fondo
Non tornò vivo alcun, s'i'odo il vero,
Senza tema d'infamia ti rispondo.

Let us go then, you and I,
When the evening is spread out against the sky
Like a patient etherized upon a table;
Let us go, through certain half-deserted streets,
The muttering retreats   5
Of restless nights in one-night cheap hotels
And sawdust restaurants with oyster-shells:
Streets that follow like a tedious argument
Of insidious intent
To lead you to an overwhelming question . . .   10
Oh, do not ask, "What is it?"
Let us go and make our visit.

In the room the women come and go
Talking of Michelangelo.

The yellow fog that rubs its back upon the window-panes,   15
The yellow smoke that rubs its muzzle on the window-panes
Licked its tongue into the corners of the evening,
Lingered upon the pools that stand in drains,
Let fall upon its back the soot that falls from chimneys,
Slipped by the terrace, made a sudden leap,   20
And seeing that it was a soft October night,
Curled once about the house, and fell asleep.

And indeed there will be time
For the yellow smoke that slides along the street,
Rubbing its back upon the window-panes;   25
There will be time, there will be time
To prepare a face to meet the faces that you meet;
There will be time to murder and create,
And time for all the works and days of hands
That lift and drop a question on your plate;   30
Time for you and time for me,

And time yet for a hundred indecisions,
And for a hundred visions and revisions,
Before the taking of a toast and tea.

In the room the women come and go   35
Talking of Michelangelo.

And indeed there will be time
To wonder, "Do I dare?" and, "Do I dare?"
Time to turn back and descend the stair,
With a bald spot in the middle of my hair—   40
(They will say: "How his hair is growing thin!")
My morning coat, my collar mounting firmly to the chin,
My necktie rich and modest, but asserted by a simple pin—
(They will say: "But how his arms and legs are thin!")
Do I dare   45
Disturb the universe?
In a minute there is time
For decisions and revisions which a minute will reverse.

For I have known them all already, known them all:
Have known the evenings, mornings, afternoons,   50
I have measured out my life with coffee spoons;
I know the voices dying with a dying fall
Beneath the music from a farther room.
          So how should I presume?

And I have known the eyes already, known them all—   55
The eyes that fix you in a formulated phrase,
And when I am formulated, sprawling on a pin,
When I am pinned and wriggling on the wall,
Then how should I begin
To spit out all the butt-ends of my days and ways?   60
          And how should I presume?

And I have known the arms already, known them all—
Arms that are braceleted and white and bare
(But in the lamplight, downed with light brown hair!)
Is it perfume from a dress   65
That makes me so digress?
Arms that lie along a table, or wrap about a shawl.
      And should I then presume?
      And how should I begin?

            . . . . .

Shall I say, I have gone at dusk through narrow streets   70
And watched the smoke that rises from the pipes
Of lonely men in shirt-sleeves, leaning out of windows? . . .

I should have been a pair of ragged claws
Scuttling across the floors of silent seas.

. . . . .

And the afternoon, the evening, sleeps so peacefully!   75
Smoothed by long fingers,
Asleep . . . tired . . . or it malingers,
Stretched on the floor, here beside you and me.
Should I, after tea and cakes and ices,
Have the strength to force the moment to its crisis?   80
But though I have wept and fasted, wept and prayed,
Though I have seen my head (grown slightly bald) brought in upon a platter,
I am no prophet—and here's no great matter;
I have seen the moment of my greatness flicker,
And I have seen the eternal Footman hold my coat, and snicker,   85
  And in short, I was afraid.

And would it have been worth it, after all,
After the cups, the marmalade, the tea,
Among the porcelain, among some talk of you and me,
Would it have been worth while,   90
To have bitten off the matter with a smile,
To have squeezed the universe into a ball
To roll it toward some overwhelming question,
To say: "I am Lazarus, come from the dead,
Come back to tell you all, I shall tell you all"—   95
If one, settling a pillow by her head,
  Should say: "That is not what I meant at all.
  That is not it, at all."

And would it have been worth it, after all,
Would it have been worth while,   100
After the sunsets and the dooryards and the sprinkled streets,
After the novels, after the teacups, after the skirts that trail along the floor—
And this, and so much more?—
It is impossible to say just what I mean!
But as if a magic lantern threw the nerves in patterns on a screen: 105
Would it have been worth while
If one, settling a pillow or throwing off a shawl,
And turning toward the window, should say:
  "That is not it at all,
  That is not what I meant, at all."   110

. . . . .

No! I am not Prince Hamlet, nor was meant to be;
Am an attendant lord, one that will do
To swell a progress, start a scene or two,
Advise the prince; no doubt, an easy tool,
Deferential, glad to be of use,   115
Politic, cautious, and meticulous;
Full of high sentence, but a bit obtuse;
At times, indeed, almost ridiculous—
Almost, at times, the Fool.

I grow old . . . I grow old . . .   120
I shall wear the bottoms of my trousers rolled.

Shall I part my hair behind? Do I dare to eat a peach?
I shall wear white flannel trousers, and walk upon the beach.
I have heard the mermaids singing, each to each.

I do not think that they will sing to me.   125

I have seen them riding seaward on the waves
Combing the white hair of the waves blown back
When the wind blows the water white and black.

We have lingered in the chambers of the sea
By sea-girls wreathed with seaweed red and brown   130
Till human voices wake us, and we drown.

Donald Hall

Merle Bascom's .22

"I was twelve when my father gave me this .22
Mossberg carbine—hand-made, with a short octagonal
barrel, stylish as an Indianfighter posing
for a photograph. We ripped up Bokar coffeecans
set into the sandbank by the track—competitive   5
and companionable. He was a good shot, although
his hands already trembled. Or I walked with my friend
Paul who loved airplanes and wanted to be a pilot,
and carried my rifle loosely, pointing it downward;
I aimed at squirrels and missed. Later I shot woodchucks   10
that ate my widowed mother's peas and Kentucky
Wonders when I visited on weekends from college,
or drove up from my Boston suburb, finding the gun
in its closet behind the woodstove. Ten years ago
my mother died; I sold up, and moved here with my work   15
and my second wife, gladly taking my tenancy
in the farmhouse where I intended to live and die.
I used my rifle on another generation
of woodchucks that ate our beans. One autumn an old friend
from college stayed with us after a nervous breakdown: 20
trembling from electroshock, depressed, suicidal.

I wrapped the octagonal Mossberg in a burlap
bag and concealed it under boards in the old grainshed.
In our quiet house he strengthened and stopped shaking.
When he went home I neglected to retrieve my gun,   25
and the next summer woodchucks took over the garden.
I let them. Our lives fitted mountain, creek, and hayfield.
Long days like minnows in the pond quickened and were still.
When I looked up from Plutarch another year had passed.
One Sunday the choir at our church sang Whittier's hymn   30
ending with 'the still small voice of calm.' Idly I thought,
'I must ask them to sing that hymn at my funeral.'
Soon after, I looked for the .22 in the shed,
half expecting it to have vanished, but finding it
wrapped intact where I left it, hardly rusted. I spent   35
a long evening taking it apart and cleaning it;
I thought of my father's hands shaking as he aimed it.
Then I restored the Mossberg to its accustomed place
in the closet behind the stove. At about this time
I learned that my daughter-in-law was two months pregnant: 40
It would be the first grandchild. One day I was walking
alone and imagined a granddaughter visiting:
She loved the old place; she swam in the summer pond with us;
she walked with us in red October; she grew older, she fell
in love with a neighbor, she married. As I daydreamed,   45
suddenly I was seized by a fit of revulsion:
I thought: 'Must I go through all that again? Must I live
another twenty years?' It was as if a body
rose from a hole where I had buried it years ago
while my first marriage was twisting and thrashing to death.   50
One night I was drunk and lost control of my Beetle
off 128 near my ranchhouse. I missed a curve
at seventy miles an hour and careered toward a stone wall.
In a hundredth of a second I knew I would die;
and, as joy fired through my body, I knew something else.   55
But the car slowed itself on rocks and settled to rest.
between an elm and a maple; I sat breathing,
feeling the joy leach out, leaving behind the torment
and terror of my desire. Now I felt this affliction
descend again and metastasize through my body.   60
Today I drove ninety miles, slowly, seatbelt fastened,
to North Andover and Paul's house, where he lives flying
out of Logan for United. I asked him to hide
the firing pin of an octagonal .22.
He nodded and took it from my hands without speaking.   65
I cannot throw it away; it was my father's gift."

John Keats

ODE ON A GRECIAN URN

1
Thou still unravished bride of quietness,
　　Thou foster child of silence and slow time,
Sylvan historian, who canst thus express
　　A flowery tale more sweetly than our rhyme:
What leaf-fringed legend haunts about thy shape　　　　　　5
　　Of deities or mortals, or of both,
　　　　In Tempe or the dales of Arcady?
　　What men or gods are these? What maidens loath?
What mad pursuit? What struggle to escape?
　　　　What pipes and timbrels? What wild ecstasy?　　　　10

2
Heard melodies are sweet, but those unheard
　　Are sweeter; therefore, ye soft pipes, play on;
Not to the sensual ear, but, more endeared,
　　Pipe to the spirit ditties of no tone:
Fair youth, beneath the trees, thou canst not leave　　　　15
　　Thy song, nor ever can those trees be bare;
　　　　Bold Lover, never, never canst thou kiss,
Though winning near the goal—yet, do not grieve;
　　She cannot fade, though thou hast not thy bliss,
　　Forever wilt thou love, and she be fair!　　　　　　　20

3
Ah, happy, happy boughs! that cannot shed
　　Your leaves, nor ever bid the Spring adieu;
And, happy melodist, unwearied,
　　Forever piping songs forever new;
More happy love! more happy, happy love!　　　　　　　25
　　Forever warm and still to be enjoyed,
　　　　Forever panting, and forever young;
All breathing human passion far above,
　　That leaves a heart high-sorrowful and cloyed,
　　　　A burning forehead, and a parching tongue.　　　30

4
Who are these coming to the sacrifice?
　　To what green altar, O mysterious priest,
Lead'st thou that heifer lowing at the skies,
　　And all her silken flanks with garlands dressed?

What little town by river or sea shore,   35
    Or mountain-built with peaceful citadel,
        Is emptied of this folk, this pious morn?
And, little town, thy streets forevermore
    Will silent be; and not a soul to tell
        Why thou art desolate, can e'er return.   40

5
O Attic shape! Fair attitude! with brede
    Of marble men and maidens overwrought,
With forest branches and the trodden weed;
    Thou, silent form, dost tease us out of thought
As doth eternity: Cold Pastoral!   45
    When old age shall this generation waste,
        Thou shalt remain, in midst of other woe
    Than ours, a friend to man, to whom thou say'st,
"Beauty is truth, truth beauty,"—that is all
        Ye know on earth, and all ye need to know.   50

Adrienne Rich

GHAZALS

7/16/68: II
When they mow the fields, I see the world reformed
as if by snow, or fire, or physical desire.

First snow. Death of the city. Ghosts in the air.
Your shade among the shadows, interviewing the mist.

The mail came every day, but letters were missing;   5
by this I knew things were not what they ought to be.

The trees in the long park blurring back
into Olmsted's original dream-work.

The impartial scholar writes me from under house arrest.
I hope you are rotting in hell, Montaigne you bastard.   10

7/23/68
When your sperm enters me, it is altered;
when my thought absorbs yours, a world begins.

If the mind of the teacher is not in love with the mind of the student,
he is simply practicing rape, and deserves at best our pity.

To live outside the law! Or, barely within it,   5
a twig on boiling waters, enclosed inside a bubble

Our words are jammed in an electronic jungle;
sometimes, though, they rise and wheel croaking above the treetoops.

An open window; thick summer night; electric fences trilling.
What are you doing here at the edge of the death-camps, Vivaldi?   10

7/24/68: II
The friend I can trust is the one who will let me have my death.
The rest are actors who want me to stay and further the plot.

At the drive-in movie, above the PanaVision,
beyond the projector beams, you project yourself, great Star.

The eye that used to watch us is dead, but open.   5
Sometimes I still have a sense of being followed.

How long will we be waiting for the police?
How long must I wonder which of my friends would hide me?

Driving at night I feel the Milky Way
streaming above me like the graph of a cry.   10

7/26/68: II
A dead mosquito, flattened against a door;
his image could survive our comings and our goings.

LeRoi! Eldridge! listen to us, we are ghosts
condemned to haunt the cities where you want to be at home.

The white children turn black on the negative.   5
The summer clouds blacken inside the camera-skull.

Every mistake that can be made, we are prepared to make;
anything less would fall short of the reality we're dreaming.

Someone has always been desperate, now it's our turn—
we who were free to weep for Othello and laugh at Caliban.   10

I have learned to smell a *conservateur* a mile away:
they carry illustrated catalogues of all that there is to lose.

Stevie Smith

MOTHER, AMONG THE DUSTBINS

Mother, among the dustbins and the manure
I feel the measure of my humanity, an allure
As of the presence of God. I am sure

In the dustbins, in the manure, in the cat at play,
In the presence of God, in a sure way   5
He moves there. Mother, what do you say?

I too have felt the presence of God in the broom
I hold, in the cobwebs in the room,
But most of all in the silence of the tomb.

Ah! but that thought that informs the hope of our kind   10
Is but an empty thing, what lies behind? —
Naught but the vanity of a protesting mind

That would not die. This is the thought that bounces
Within a conceited head and trounces
Inquiry. Man is most frivolous when he pronounces.   15

Well Mother, I shall continue to think as I do,
And I think you would be wise to do so too,
Can you question the folly of man in the creation of God?
    Who are you?

Diane Wakoski

SESTINA FROM THE HOME GARDENER

These dried-out paint brushes which fell from my lips have been removed
with your departure; they are such minute losses
compared with the light bulb gone from my brain, the sections
of chicken wire from my liver, the precise

silver hammers in my ankles which delicately banged and pointed   5
magnetically to you. Love has become unfamiliar

and plenty of time to tend the paint brushes now. Once unfamiliar
with my processes. Once removed
from that sizzling sun, the ego, to burn my poet shadow to the wall, I
    pointed,
I suppose, only to your own losses   10
which made you hate that 200 pound fish called marriage. Precise
ly, I hate my life, hate its freedom, hate the sections

of fence stripped away, hate the time for endless painting, hate the sections
of my darkened brain that wait for children to snap on the light, the
    unfamiliar
corridors of my heart with strangers running in them, shouting. The
    precise   15
incisions in my hip to extract an image, a dripping pickaxe or palmtree
    removed
and each day my paint brushes get softer and cleaner—better tools, and
    losses
cease to mean loss. Beauty, to each eye, differently pointed.

I admire sign painters and carpenters. I like that black hand pointed
up a drive-way whispering to me, "The Washingtons live in those sections" 20
and I explain autobiographically that George Washington is sympathetic
    to my losses;
His face or name is everywhere. No one is unfamiliar
with the American dollar, and since you've been removed
from my life I can think of nothing else. A precise

replacement for love can't be found. But art and money are precise   25
ly for distraction. The stars popping out of my blood are pointed
nowhere. I have removed
my ankles so that I cannot travel. There are sections
of my brain growing teeth and unfamiliar
hands tie strings through my eyes. But there are losses   30

Of the spirit like vanished bicycle tires and losses
of the body, like the whole bike, every precise
bearing, spoke, gear, even the unfamiliar
handbrakes vanished. I have pointed
myself in every direction, tried sections   35
of every map. It's no use. The real body has been removed.

Removed by the ice tongs. If a puddle remains what losses
can those sections of glacier be? Perhaps a precise
count of drops will substitute the pointed mountain, far away, unfamiliar?

8

WRITING LITERARY NONFICTION

Writing to Warm Up

1. Define "nonfiction." What kinds of writing qualify as nonfiction, and what kinds of writing are clearly not nonfiction? Why?
2. Would you be more interested in writing a story about your life using the actual names and details, or using invented names and details? Why?
3. List four subjects in your world—culture, politics, religion, education, daily routine— you would like to write about and discuss from your point of view. List four things you might want to say or explore about each.

DEFINITIONS

Scan the shelves of your local bookstore. The books are divided into many kinds of writing; some writing is defined by its form, some writing is defined by its subject matter, and some writing is defined by its audience. One category you will encounter which includes multitudes of books, ranging through literally every subject matter and appealing to practically every audience, is **nonfiction**.

How did you define nonfiction? It's hard to define, precisely because its appearance implies that it's not something else – so, what *is* it? Gay

Talese and Barbara Lounsberry argue that "writers of literary nonfiction have always understood that they have the best of all worlds. They can be as artful in language and form as the most ambitious poet, dramatist, or novelist, yet they have the bonus of built-in reader credibility, for the moments they re-present have existed in time." What does the phrase "built-in reader credibility" mean? It means that nonfiction refers to any writing which deals with subjects not invented or imagined by the author, but rather based in or commenting upon the world of events, experiences, and facts—whether the subject be a memory of things past, a discussion of things present, or advice or predictions about things to come. Nonfiction is about real people, real events, real things, the "real world." It is that broad category of writing that can include a book, essay, magazine or newspaper article, philosophical meditation, how-to book, or memoir. A recent scan of the paperback best-sellers in the category of nonfiction included books about:

- The role Irish monks played in maintaining civilization during the collapse of the Roman Empire;
- A poet's memories of her childhood;
- A way for women to better understand their own psychological struggles;
- The need for determination and hope;
- The PGA tour;
- Motherhood;
- A lawsuit against a company accused of being an industrial polluter;
- The history of Gypsies in Europe;
- A woman's near-death experience and its effects upon her.

As you see, nonfiction is indeed a broad category, including all sorts of writing appealing to all sorts of audiences.

Within the category of nonfiction exist books which contain passages of great beauty and art, prose rivaling that of any great novel, and insights into the human condition which plumb the depths of experience and emotion. These books can appear as any type of nonfiction—from memoirs about the past to comments on the most immediate political or social situations, and from the largest observations about culture to the most intimate ruminations about one's own heart. The best of nonfiction can be loosely termed **literary nonfiction**, and as a creative writer, you will want to explore this important and ever-expanding art form. The categorization of some nonfiction as "literary" does not say that other nonfiction is not literary or creative — because "literary nonfiction" isn't so much a distinction about genre as it is an idea about what the writer may be attempting to accomplish through her nonfiction work if it is skillfully written and insightfully composed. Like a work of poetry or fiction or drama, the work of literary nonfiction is intended to express and explore some aspect of the human condition or experience; its specific subject matter is what would be considered nonfiction—that which has actually happened or which exists in reality—and its aim is to examine that reality to its core and to bring some realization to the reader about the writer's understanding of that experience.

Literary nonfiction is not new; its roots go back thousands of years, to the Greek writers who composed artful biographies and histories, to the Christian writers who wrote lives of the saints and spiritual autobiographies, to the travel writers and social commentators of the Middle Ages, and to the forms which have arisen in the past few hundred years, the essay and the article. Some of the great past writers to practice literary nonfiction include Michel de Montaigne, Francis Bacon, Virginia Woolf, Mark Twain, George Orwell, Frederick Douglass, Jonathan Swift, and Ernest Hemingway. Many contemporary writers also write excellent literary nonfiction, as we shall discuss, creating some of the best and most powerful prose literature. Nonfiction is experiencing a new vitality in the last decades of the twentieth century, as new forms of communication and experience call for new and various forms of literary expression. So it is up to you to discover how literary nonfiction can best be used to explore your thoughts, experiences, and feelings.

Memoir and the Story of One's Life

My writing has been about, and was meant to be about, the Texas of my time there. I felt it my job to define and record the Texas culture as I knew it before (and perhaps in the beginning of) transitions toward what it has become, to leave signposts saying to those coming along later, This is how it was then. . . . [And] I have never had much luck keeping myself out of my work.

— *Larry L. King, from* Warning: Writer at Work

We don't see the world as it is . . . we see the world as we are.

— *Ernie Lawson*

Writing for Ideas and Practice 8-1

1. Define "memoir" and "autobiography." Discuss your answers with fellow students.
2. Read the following excerpt from a book-length memoir, William Least Heat Moon's *Blue Highways:*

Beware thoughts that come in the night. They aren't tuned properly; they come in askew, free of sense and restrictions deriving from the most remote of sources. Take the idea of February 17, a day of canceled expectations, the day I learned my job teaching English was finished because of declining enrollment at the college, the day I called my wife from whom I'd been separated for nine months to give her the news, the day she let slip about her "friend" — Rick or Dick or Chick. . . .

That morning, before all the news started hitting the fan, Eddie Short Leaf, who worked a bottomland section of the Missouri River and plowed snow off campus sidewalks, told me if the deep cold didn't break soon the trees would freeze straight through and explode. Indeed.

That night, as I lay wondering whether I would get sleep or explosion, I got the idea instead.

a. List three things you already know that the author will deal with in this memoir.
b. Does this feel like something that actually happened to the author, or is it fiction? How might you know?
c. Think of a time in your own life when you were faced with a situation or feeling similar to the one in Least Heat Moon's opening paragraphs. Write out that memory as clearly as you can recall it. Just tell the story or describe the experience or experiences, including as many sensory details as you can.

One well-known and very important kind of literary nonfiction is the **memoir**. The word "memoir" is of course related to the word "memory," and in relating a story of one's life, one is remembering, and telling the story to the reader. A memoir tells a story about some part of the writer's life, which reflects on themes running through the writer's life.

Not all memoirs—or their longer counterparts, **autobiographies**, which are simply books written to tell as comprehensive an account of the writer's entire life as possible, or of a particular theme running through the writer's life — are written by the rich and famous. Consider Least Heat Moon's memoir, *Blue Highways*, which we quoted above. This was William Least Heat Moon's first book; he wasn't famous; he had nothing sensational or sexy or torrid to report. His book was an understated story of a journey he took through a number of small towns and farms on small highways across America—hardly the stuff of a tell-all tabloid memoir. But, because he wrote well and communicated a truth about his experience during the particular journey he literally and figuratively took, his writing spoke to many people—and the book was a best-seller. No matter your experience, you have a story to tell—in fact, you have many, many stories to tell and observations to recount. We have had scores of creative writing students who started the class with no more than a vague hope in mind—"I want to tell the story of what it was like to grow up during the Vietnam War," or "I have always felt a sense of aloneness in my life, and I want somehow to write it down and understand it." That's the stuff of memoir and autobiography, and to write memoir is to be in the company of many great writers.

The Memoir's Subject

The first issue to consider when one is writing memoir is what to write about. How does one discern what "really matters" in one's memories and the themes running through one's life? After all, if you were to attempt to "write your life story," as many of our students think they want to do, where would you begin?

First, remember that memoir need not try to cover every experience and every detail in a life. It would be impossible to record every detail about even one day in your life. Rather, the writer of memoir attempts to write about his life by examining one detail at a time in order to tell the story, as well as to explore the themes and ideas relative to his story.

Writing for Ideas and Practice 8-2

1. Think of any of the moments in your experience when you have learned a great deal about who you are or how the world works — they need not be huge, life-altering moments; they can be quiet, even small moments, but ones with significance.
2. Record the experience as simply as possible, with as many specific sensory details as possible, so that at the end of the story the reader understands what you learned or experienced.

As you write, you discover your subject; this is true with all writing, and true with memoir as well. What is the memoir's purpose? To tell one's story. But simply to list life details and memories one after another without an overall sense of the *life story* won't suffice. The reader of memoir wants to know the details, and also to know what those details mean to the life overall. Each detail and scene you include, then, should point to issues the memoir is exploring—so that every part of the story tells the story overall. These issues the memoir explores are called **themes**. The themes of the story or memoir are those ideas, patterns, and issues which the memoir keeps returning to and re-examining; they are the subject, as much as the actual details of the story.

Your memoir, then, will tell your life story, and will also communicate what you understand about your story. The details and experiences you choose to include will show this full purpose to your reader. Thomas Merton's wonderful autobiography *The Seven Storey Mountain* begins this way:

 On the last day of January 1915, under the sign of the Water Bearer, in a year of a great war, and down in the shadow of some French mountains on the borders of Spain, I came into the world.

Merton begins his book with his birth, and traces his life story, recounting major and minor events in great detail along the way; however, he doesn't simply catalog "what happened." Instead, he traces major conflicts within and ideas about his life story, using those themes as the bases for the telling of his life. The next sentence introduces one of the major themes of his autobiography, his lifelong struggle to come to terms with his feelings about his relationship with God:

Free by nature, in the image of God, I was nevertheless the prisoner of my own violence and my own selfishness, in the image of the world into which I was born. That world was the picture of Hell, full of men like myself, loving God and yet hating Him; born to love Him, living instead in fear and hopeless self-contradictory hungers.

Merton's book is not a list of or even a telling of the events of his life; rather, it is an examination of his life, in which he tells some of the events in great detail, in order to reconcile and to order his experience and his feelings. Tobias Wolff's *This Boy's Life* recounts his experiences as a young man forced to move about with his wayward mother, enduring his abusive stepfather along the way. The story looks back at the experience and tells it from the viewpoint of the mature narrator, interpreting and explaining the experiences as the story is told. In this way, the story's events come to have meaning not only in themselves, but also in the context of Wolff's life story.

The aim of the nonfiction writer is to explore an idea, a feeling, or an opinion in such a way that the writer shares his own exploration of that idea, feeling, or opinion with the reader. In this regard, memoir and other forms of nonfiction share the same aim — to recount experience of real events and times for the reader. But beyond the memoir the literary nonfiction work is not so much concerned with telling a story as it is with reflecting upon the subject at hand and exploring the writer's viewpoint about that subject. The writer doesn't just tell a story, she focuses on a piece of experience, and in writing about that topic, offers an insight about it.

The term *essay* comes from the French *assai* or "attempt," so that the essay became a kind of attempt by its writer to figure something out, think it through, or mull it over. The essayist writing a memoir may be attempting to explain an idea or feeling, or experience something anew and understand it better, or argue for or against something. It is as if a conversation or debate is taking place, in which the essayist and the reader are engaged, in order to arrive at an understanding of the subject at hand.

Perhaps the point is to find the thing you care about or know well and write about that. Maybe it's the joys and struggles of working as a stay-at-home mom with three children; maybe it's the pain of losing a loved one; maybe it's an amazing thing you have discovered about human nature while serving on a committee in your city. What do you want to *assai*? What do you want to explore, think about, talk about? Write about it.

In "The Best Years of My Life," Betty Rollin writes about her experience with breast cancer. The essayist may take any number of directions in writing about such a subject; she may analyze the effects of cancer on different kinds of patients, or argue for a certain type of funding for cancer research, or list and describe the physical effects of cancer on a woman's body. In this particular essay, however, Rollin is concerned with exploring the person she is and has become as a result of her experience with the illness.

The minute I got cancer, my taste in men improved. It's not that my first husband was a beast. I'm fond of him, but even he would admit he was very hard on me. Maybe I asked for it. Well, once you've been deftly kicked in the pants by God (or whoever distributes breast cancer), you stop wanting kicks from mortals. Everyone who knows the man I married a year ago thinks I'm lucky — even my mother! — and I do, too. But I know it wasn't only luck. It was that cancer made me want someone wonderful.

Rollin takes an issue she knows from her own experience, works through some aspect of it, and shares her ideas about it with the reader. A different essayist might take a different approach to the subject of breast cancer, but that is one of the great strengths of the memoir as a literary form: it affords the writer the power to explore any aspect of an issue in such a way that her ideas about it become shared with the reader.

Writing for Ideas and Practice 8-3

1. Think of a feeling, opinion, or idea you have had rumbling around in your head for a while but which you haven't quite been able to explain or articulate. Write down a phrase or sentence which expresses the subject—"My fear of the dark," "Why I hate classical music," "Strange things happen in me every time I go see my grandmother."
2. Write the fragment or sentence at the center of a piece of paper, and all around the page, in no particular order, write everything you think of when you think about this subject. For example, if you write "My fear of the dark" in the center of the page, in one corner you might write about your fear of the dark when you were a child, and in another corner a thought about the nature of darkness in myth and metaphor, and in another part of the page a few sentences about black cats being bad luck, and off in the margin an account of your own experience with taking the trash out to the pitch-black alley of your back driveway last week and the cat that jumped out and scared you half to death.
3. Look at what you have written; now, group ideas or parts of the subject that seem to be similar or related. Then, put the parts in order—any order. It may be chronological, as in memoir. It may be a progression of what occurs to you when you think about this thing. For example, first, you think of your last visit to Grandmother's house; then, you remember that awful smell of onions and Lysol spray in her kitchen; then, you remember your mother and grandmother fighting about cleanliness; and so on. As you look at what you have written, leave out any ideas or details that don't fit in at this stage of the writing process.

4. Try writing a first draft in which you flesh out these ideas, giving them shape and detail and enough information so that the reader will understand what you're thinking through. Remember that an essay is *an attempt* to think something through, and your first drafts will be discovery drafts in which you encounter more of what you think and feel about this subject.

Susan Sontag has said that she has written essays "to respond to crises" in her life and her obsessions with those crises. When she got cancer, she wrote *Illnesses as Metaphor*, noting later that "needless suffering and death . . . horrifies and enrages me . . . and that's why I wrote" the book. At another point in her life, she had left America for some time; she says that she wrote *Under the Sign of Saturn* in response to her expatriation. When she had written both books, about times in her life during which important things were happening to and within her, she was able then to go on to the next phase in her life. She says, about this urge to write essays about her experiences and feelings, "Having discharged my debts to those obsessions, I feel a tremendous liberation."

What are your subjects, ideas, obsessions? What things interest you, charm you, worry you, anger you, come back to you? These may be the things about which you will write your memoirs.

Writing for Ideas and Practice 8-4

1. What things have you written about in the past? Think about all your past writing, or at least all of your writing within a certain period, and categorize it into two to five subject- or idea-groups. Then, answer: What do you write about? Why?
2. What experiences, ideas, or feelings would you most likely choose to use as subjects of essays to write? Which wouldn't you choose? Try writing a short discussion about a subject you wouldn't necessarily choose first.

Many people have had similar experiences—illnesses, adventures, addictions, love—but no two people will recall those experiences the same way, even if two people share an experience. A lawyer friend says that the one situation he dreads is having to work with more than one eyewitness to a crime—for if only one witness saw "what happened," at least our friend has a clear story to work with, but if three witnesses saw the same thing occur, he must now reconcile how the three stories will invariably differ. What you are trying to do in memoir is not just to tell "what happened," but to explore ideas about your experience, using the details of memory to put flesh on the bones and voices in the mouths of the shades and figures you recall.

What is often important to us as we recall our lives are the conflicts we have experienced and the relationships that have given our lives meaning. The subject of conflict in fiction will be discussed in chapter 10, but for now, define *conflict* as any merging of opposing forces or feelings connected to an experience—the sadness one feels at the death of a relative or friend; the frustration one experiences at seeing hopes dashed; the confusion one senses when expectations and events don't seem to match up. John Updike, for instance, writes about a key conflict in his life, his struggle to deal with his embarrassment about the psoriasis from which he suffered in his early years, in "At War with My Skin," a chapter from his book *Self-Consciousness: Memoirs.*

 . . . I didn't learn to swim, because of my appearance; I stayed away from "The Porgy," the damned pond beyond the poorhouse, and from the public pool in West Reading, and the indoor pool at the Reading "Y," where my father in winter coached the high-school swimming team. To the travails of my freshman year at Harvard was added the humiliation of learning at last to swim, with my spots and my hydrophobia, in a class of quite naked boys. Recently the chunky, mild-spoken man who taught that class over thirty years ago came up to me at a party and pleasantly identified himself; I could scarcely manage politeness, his face so sharply brought back that old suppressed rich mix of chlorine and fear and brave gasping and naked, naked shame.

The everyday, the ordinary, even the private and seemingly mundane details of the writer's life can make the memoir vivid and evocative. Updike's life is full of many experiences and memories, and yet this one detail tells much about who he was as a younger person and who he is as a mature writer looking back at his past. Do not be put off by fears that you have nothing to say; you have much to say. But you must also not be afraid to tackle all or part of your experience for fear of its bigness—as one student commented to us, "I just don't know where to begin!" Anything you remember is important because it is about who you are. Think of the important relationships in your life; what do they say about the themes and overall issues in your life story? Think about the issues of identity and identification you have experienced in your life; what do they say about the themes and overall issues in your life story?

Writing for Ideas and Practice 8-5

1. Think of an experience you have had in which a realization came to you about who you were in relation to other people—your family, your community, your gender, your religion. Briefly tell the story of that experience, and include an explanation of why it brought you to that realization. Be sure to include many specific and sensory details recounting the experience.

2. Briefly list ten memories as quickly as possible. Then, answer the following questions about those memories:
   a.   Are there any common subjects, feelings, or themes among them?
   b.   In what order did the memories in the list appear? Is that significant? Why?
   c.   What sensory data (touch, smell, sight, taste, sound) are associated with these memories?
   d.   What does this exercise tell you about the kinds of things you might want to write about?

As you progress, you discover the themes and overall ideas informing your life story. This process of realization and insight is crucial to memoir. At the heart of memoir is how a person remembers. The story will be composed of details and remembrances of what happened, certainly, but memory is not only selective but also subjective—that is, the memory recalls only selectively, and reshapes experience through the remove of feelings, impressions, the past and the present merging into a new reality. The Updike excerpt above illustrates how powerfully we remember our struggles, and how powerfully those memories still inform who and what we are long after the events have passed. Updike as an adult, now able to treat his "spots" with medicines and maturity, is past those early days, and yet their memory lingers and stands squarely amidst all of his imagination and experiences enough to require a chapter of writing in order to process. Reflection upon what has happened, and what it means, can serve as one of the best and most important bases of memoir.

In the following memoir, Langston Hughes relates an experience from his childhood, and in that retelling, contemplates his understanding of faith, both from the vantage point of the child he was, and the man he has become. Notice that while the memoir tells the story of an actual experience, it accomplishes much more than a simple report of "what happened."

 Salvation

I was saved from sin when I was going on thirteen. But not really saved. It happened like this. There was a big revival at my Auntie Reed's church. Every night for weeks there had been much preaching, singing, praying, and shouting, and some very hardened sinners had been brought to Christ, and the membership of the church had grown by leaps and bounds. Then just before the revival ended, they held a special meeting for children, "to bring the young lambs to the fold." My aunt spoke of it for days ahead. That night I was escorted to the front row and placed on the mourners' bench with all the other young sinners, who had not yet been brought to Jesus.

My aunt told me that when you were saved you saw a light, and something happened to you inside! And Jesus came into your life! And God was with you from then on! She said you could see and hear and feel Jesus in your soul. I believed her. I had heard a great many old people say the same thing and it seemed to me they ought to know. So I sat there calmly in the hot, crowded church, waiting for Jesus to come to me.

The preacher preached a wonderful rhythmical sermon, all moans and shouts and lonely cries and dire pictures of hell, and then he sang a song about the ninety and nine safe in the fold, but one little lamb was left out in the cold. Then he said: "Won't you come? Won't you come to Jesus? Young lambs, won't you come?" And he held out his arms to all us young sinners there on the mourners' bench. And the little girls cried. And some of them jumped up and went to Jesus right away. But most of us just sat there.

A great many old people came and knelt around us and prayed, old women with jet-black faces and braided hair, old men with work-gnarled hands. And the church sang a song about the lower lights are burning, some poor sinners to be saved. And the whole building rocked with prayer and song.

Still I kept waiting to *see* Jesus.

Finally all the young people had gone to the altar and were saved, but one boy and me. He was a rounder's son named Westley. Westley and I were surrounded by sisters and deacons praying. It was very hot in the church, and getting late now. Finally, Westley said to me in a whisper, "God damn! I'm tired o' sitting here. Let's get up and be saved." So he got up and was saved.

Then I was left all alone on the mourners' bench. My aunt came and knelt at my knees and cried, while prayers and songs swirled all around me in the little church. The whole congregation prayed for me alone, in a mighty wail of moans and voices. And I kept waiting serenely for Jesus, waiting, waiting—but he didn't come. I wanted to see him, but nothing happened to me. Nothing! I wanted something to happen to me, but nothing happened.

I heard the songs and the minister saying: "Why don't you come? My dear child, why don't you come to Jesus? Jesus is waiting for you. He wants you. Why don't you come? Sister Reed, what is this child's name?"

"Langston," my aunt sobbed.

"Langston, why don't you come? Why don't you come and be saved? Oh, Lamb of God! Why don't you come?"

Now it was really getting late. I began to be ashamed of myself, holding everything up so long. I began to wonder what God thought about Westley, who certainly hadn't seen Jesus either, but who was now sitting proudly on the platform, swinging his knickerbockered legs and grinning down at me, surrounded by deacons and old women on their knees praying. God had not struck Westley dead for taking his name in vain or for lying in the temple. So I decided that maybe to save further trouble, I'd better lie, too, and say that Jesus had come, and get up and be saved.

So I got up.

Suddenly the whole room broke into a sea of shouting, as they saw me rise. Waves of rejoicing swept the place. Women leaped in the air. My aunt threw her arms around me. The minister took me by the hand and led me to the platform.

When things quieted down, in a hushed silence, punctuated by a few ecstatic "Amens," all the new young lambs were blessed in the name of God. Then joyous singing filled the room.

That night, for the last time in my life but one—for I was a big boy twelve years old—I cried. I cried, in bed alone, and I couldn't stop. I buried my head under the quilts, but my aunt heard me. She woke up and told my uncle I was crying because the Holy Ghost had come into my life, and because I had seen Jesus. But I was really crying because I couldn't bear to tell her that I had lied, that I had deceived everybody in the church, and I hadn't seen Jesus, and that now I didn't believe there was a Jesus any more, since he didn't come to help me.

Writing for Ideas and Practice 8-6

1. What is the overall subject of Hughes's memoir? State in one sentence what you think matters most to the author of the stor
2. What details in the story communicate ughes's attitude toward his subject? List some of the most important details which reveal how he feels looking back at the experience.
3. Look back at the short memoir incident you wrote for Writing for Ideas and Practice 8-2. Write another story about the same experience, but see if in this version you can use the same experience or memory to illustrate a different point or subject.

Hughes's essay focuses on a number of conflicts within the young boy, and between the boy and those around him. He is pressured by his family members, the pastor, the environment, Westley, even the structure of the event itself, to accept something he doesn't understand. He struggles to reconcile disparate elements in what he is experiencing, and finally finds himself unable to make sense of that incongruity except to conclude that "I didn't believe there was a Jesus any more, since he didn't come to help me." So it is a story dealing with many things at once, and one which relates memories and conflicts powerfully.

WHAT TO INCLUDE
AND HOW TO STRUCTURE THE MEMOIR

The writer of the memoir, and especially the writer of autobiography, must not only choose what to write about and how to deal with the conflicts and issues introduced in her story, but also how many of the events and experiences in her life to try to include and explore. As we said earlier, it's impossible to try to relate everything that has happened to you. You should, then, include those events in your life that trace the ideas and themes with which your memoir is concerned. Even in autobiography, the writer can only include pivotal moments in her life; she can't worry that she's forgotten to tell what she made for lunch on September 16, 1987. And as you write, you will discover what parts of the story need to be told. Once you have identified important moments in your life story, you can look back at them and decide what made them important to you.

Consider this example from Native American author N. Scott Momaday's memoir, *The Way to Rainy Mountain*:

> My grandmother had a reverence for the sun, a holy regard that now is all but gone out of mankind. There was a wariness in her, and an ancient awe. She was a Christian in her later years, but she had come a long way about, and she never forgot her birthright. As a child she had been to the Sun Dances; she had taken part in those annual rites, and by then she had learned the restoration of her people. . . .
>
> Now that I can have her only in memory, I see my grandmother in the several postures that were peculiar to her: standing at the wood stove on a winter morning and turning meat in a great iron skillet; sitting at the south window, bent above her beadwork, and afterwards when her vision failed, looking down for a long time into the fold of her hands; going out upon a cane, very slowly as she did when the weight of age came upon her; praying.

Momaday isn't telling his whole life story; he is only describing his grandmother. And yet in describing his grandmother and what her faith and her appearance meant and mean to him, Momaday tells us about who he is and what is important to him—and, in so doing, in some way reveals his whole life and comments upon his whole culture. Small details and experiences can have huge consequences and impacts, and when you choose what to write about, you will want to look for those moments and details that have had an impact.

A technique you might use to decide what to include is to think in terms of *islands of time and experience.* Each major event in your life might be an island, and your life a sailing journey from island to island. Each island contains new developments, new experiences, and what ties them together is your participation in them and their becoming a part of the story, the journey. These islands won't always be the major events, of course—yes, graduation was important, but so was that kiss the week after graduation. Once you have decided upon a series of islands you want to write about, you might collect ideas about each island, say, in a folder or in a separate file in your computer for each island, occurrence, event, or scene. Don't feel you must write from beginning to end. Write about each separate event separately for a while. If they are meant to be part of a single story, the common themes in them will emerge. If not, you can always eliminate some of them from the memoir—or choose just to write about a particular event or feeling on its own.

Writing for Ideas and Practice 8-7

1. Picture your life as a road. Draw a line that traces the road, using twists and turns and stops to indicate seminal experiences, developments, and decisions. Label each of the

stops, twists, or turns. For example, you might note graduations, marriages, births, deaths, moves, or less obvious key moments.

2. On another piece of paper, list the turns, twists, and stops in chronological order, including dates, places, basic details, and names of persons involved.

3. On another piece of paper, make some notes about how you might write all or part of the story and about which events you would want to write about in detail, and which would only be mentioned briefly, or omitted entirely.

4. Try picking just one significant experience and writing the story of that experience with as much detail and insight as possible to make that experience and its repercussions real for you and for your reader.

5. Go back to the notes you made about which parts you would tell in detail and which parts you wouldn't. Pick any three major themes you might trace through your life story — Loss, Betrayal, The Joys of Relationships, Money, What I Learned About My Own Fears, My Father and I, and so on. Now focus on one theme, and revise the list of things you would and would not include or expand upon, according to the theme at hand.

In "Salvation," Hughes uses an **alternating method** to communicate his story. He *reports* certain pieces of information without going into great detail, such as the sentence "Every night for weeks there had been much preaching, singing, praying, and shouting, and some very hardened sinners had been brought to Christ, and the membership of the church had grown by leaps and bounds." Hughes doesn't really describe any of these moments as much as he uses the fairly fast-moving sentence to set up the scene he is about to describe. He then alternates to a *scene*—one of the islands we suggested above—in which he gives much more detailed information such as dialogue, description, and explanation. Notice the slower pace at which the essay moves as it zeroes in on a particular moment:

. . . Then he said: "Won't you come? Won't you come to Jesus? Young lambs, won't you come?" And he held out his arms to all us young sinners there on the mourners' bench. And the little girls cried. And some of them jumped up and went to Jesus right away. But most of us just sat there.

Hughes's overall observations in reporting tell about what is happening or has happened without dwelling on detailed description. The writer uses reporting in this way to convey information that is important to the progression or understanding of the story's structure and events but is not crucial to experience. Time can move quickly in these sections of the memoir; one sentence can move the reader through a day or through several years, and the reader gets a sense of the larger picture of the story, so that reporting connects the moments in which the writer focuses on a particular scene.

The writer then uses scene to focus on a particular moment or impression. You should use scene to show the reader the important or intimate sections of your story. Don't gloss over pivotal moments. Slow down, let the reader linger over them and experience them fully. Although you don't necessarily need to spend six pages describing the wallpaper in your grandmother's house, you will want to use dialogue and detail to bring your reader fully into the experience. Chapter 13 will discuss dialogue more fully, but for now, remember that the reader needs to hear what the people in your story say in those key scenes.

How you pace a long autobiographical memoir will depend on this alternation between overall reporting of the story's components and progression, and the more focused presentation of specific details and scenes within the story. In Jeanne Wakatsuki Houston's *Farewell to Manzanar*, a memoir about her experience during World War II and afterward, Houston uses both reporting and scene to show the reader how a particular part of the story developed. She sets up a scene by first reporting the months prior to it, in the chapter entitled "The Girl of My Dreams":

I was a senior when we moved. In those days, 1951, San Jose was a large town, but not yet a city. Coming from a big high school in southern California gave me some kind of shine, I suppose. It was a chance to start over, and I made the most of it. By the spring of that year, when it came time to elect the annual carnival queen from the graduating seniors, my homeroom chose me.

Here, Houston reports some general developments in the story—her move and her relationship with the new students—as well as some general themes important to the story—the "shine" she had in California, and the smallness of San Jose. She then slows the pace to present a particular scene and those same themes in more detail:

It was pretty clear what the outcome would be, but ballots still had to be cast and counted. The next afternoon I was standing outside my Spanish class when Leonard Rodriguez, who sat next to me, came hurrying down the hall with a revolutionary's fire in his eye. He helped out each day in the administration office. He had just overheard some teachers and a couple of secretaries counting up the votes.

"They're trying to stuff the ballot box," he whispered loudly. "They're fudging on the tally. They're afraid to have a Japanese girl be queen. They've never had one before. They're afraid of what some of the parents will say."

He was pleased he had caught them, and more pleased to be telling this to me, as if some long-held suspicion of conspiracy had finally been confirmed. I shared it with him.

This second excerpt moves much more slowly than the first, paying closer attention to the details of the scene—where the young woman was standing, the young man's name, where he sat in class, where he worked at the school, the exact words he reports and how he had heard them. And because of this detail, this part of the memoir makes very clear the experience and its repercussions, exploring the larger theme of how Jeanne faced the difficulty of being a person of Japanese descent in a largely Caucasian society. As you write your own memoir and autobiography, you will want to describe specific scenes with detail and clarity in order to give your story immediacy and power.

In structuring the alternating scenes and reporting in your memoir or autobiography, you can arrange the events in chronological order or in some other way. Stories can be told in continuous time, moving from the beginning to the end, as Merton's *The Seven Storey Mountain*. It might be, though, that you will want to move back and forth through time. Perhaps you are writing the story of something that happened to you as an adult, but in order to communicate fully the impact it had on you, you must go back and relate a story from your childhood—or from the past of someone in your family, the technique Art Spiegelman uses in *Maus I* and *II*. This technique of moving back and forth in time is called **flashback**. You can move back and forth by combining reporting and scene, using the reporting sections as bridges between scenes, and the scenes to depict the details of the flashbacks, whether the events are in chronological order or not.

Readers are used to flashbacks, and they can follow a story's progression, as long as the writer provides the clues and reporting bridges in order to make the story clear to the reader. A memoir might work as a recollection of a childhood memory, and by setting it up in flashback, the storyteller shows the reader that this is a story meant to be understood not only in terms of what it meant to the boy who experienced it, but also to the man who is remembering it. In *Seven Pillars of Wisdom: A Triumph*, his memoir of the Arab revolt against the Turks during World War I, T. E. Lawrence alternates between describing battles and developments during the campaign, and flashbacks to earlier events and histories which give the reader greater understanding of the present chapter. Annie Dillard, in *Pilgrim at Tinker Creek*, records her experiences and thoughts during a series of months while living in a house near Tinker Creek in a valley in Virginia; throughout the memoir, she includes flashbacks to earlier experiences that year and from years past. Even the beginning of the book is a flashback:

 I used to have a cat, an old fighting tom, who would jump through the open window by my bed in the middle of the night and land on my chest. I'd half-awaken. He'd stick his skull under my nose and purr, stinking of urine and blood. Some nights he kneaded my bare chest with his front paws, powerfully, arching his back, as if sharpening his claws, or pummeling a mother for milk. And some mornings I'd wake in daylight to find my body covered with paw prints in blood; I looked as though I'd been painted with roses. . . .

I still think of that old tomcat, mornings, when I wake. Things are tamer now; I sleep with the window shut.

Dillard uses flashback to make the memoir richer and more complex. You can arrange the events in your memoir or autobiography in whatever way best serves the ideas and feelings you are attempting to bring to the reader.

Remember, too, that the story's structure is only a device by which you explore the story's subject. When you have written enough about the subject and the experience to know what you wish to say about it, your sense of purpose for the piece will inform the choices you make about how to pace the story, what to include, what parts of the story to present in reporting, and what parts to focus on in a scene.

Writing for Ideas and Practice 8-8

1. Reread "Salvation," and note in the margins or on a separate sheet of paper where the reporting sections begin and end. Number the scenes. Note how each scene works separately and with the others to develop the story's sequence and the story's theme.
2. Think of a memory of an experience of loss.
   a. Tell the large details of that story using reporting alone.
   b. Present the story of that experience only by using scene and sensory detail.
   c. Which memoir was longer? Which memoir was easier to write? Which one has more emotional power? What balance do you think will be a good one for you to use in your memoir writing?
3. Write a short memoir in which you recount an experience or realization which took place recently, and in which you include a flashback to an earlier, related experience.
4. Read an autobiography[1] and consider the following questions as you read:
   a. What information is presented as dramatic scene, with dialogue and description?
   b. What information is presented by the narrator without scenes to give details but is only reported?
   c. Does the story move strictly in chronological order? If not, what effect does the alteration of chronology produce in your mind regarding the theme and ideas of the story? How does the writer signal that time shifts have occurred?
   d. What are some of the dominant feelings or ideas the autobiography conveys as it tells its story?

Overall, the rule of thumb for structuring your autobiographical essay is this: use whatever tools are at your disposal to make the story come to life and illustrate its themes clearly. The memoir can use any structure, including narration, to explore its subject. Sometimes the structure you are

---

1 Some wonderful autobiographies and memoirs you may want to look at include: *One Writer's Beginnings* by Eudora Welty; *Growing Up* by Russell Baker; *The Autobiography of Malcolm X* by Malcolm X and Alex Haley; *This Boy's Life* by Tobias Wolff; *An American Childhood* by Annie Dillard; *Silent Dancing: A Remembrance of a Puerto Rican Childhood* by Judith Ortiz Cofer; and *Narrative of the Life of Frederick Douglass, An American Slave* by Frederick Douglass. There are many, many excellent others.

to use will be dictated to you; if you are writing an article on a given subject for a magazine, for instance, the parameters of the magazine's format will in some ways determine how your essay is structured—specifically in terms of length and even subject matter. But within those parameters (and sometimes, for the adventurous writer, just outside those parameters), you are somewhat free to do whatever will make your subject come to life. The article may use narration and stories; it may use descriptive passages full of sensory detail; it may use wild flights of emotion and affect; it may use humor and exaggeration; it may use irony and understatement. The memoir's only concern, ultimately, is the meditation you are creating upon the story of your life, and your feelings and ideas towards it.

Here is a complete essay by Dorien Ross, called "Seeking Home." As you read it, try to think about what it is about—not necessarily what it means, or what it is trying to get you to accept, for an essay may not be arguing anything but merely exploring something. What is the essayist exploring, worrying over, wanting, hoping for, grieving over? And what devices does she use, structurally and thematically, to explore her story?

Seeking Home[2]

You are beginning to succumb to the New York pressure to look a certain way in order to feel a certain way. You are no closer to understanding the mystery of style than you were in high school. You remember a recent conversation with your longtime admired older friend Judith. You cannot deny that one of the reasons you admire Judith is the way she looks. At fifty years old she looks younger than you: slender, groomed, and elegant. She tells you the following story:

It seems that Calvin Klein sent spies to Ralph Lauren in an attempt to discover the secret of his ongoing and remarkable success. He discovers the secret: these clothes simulate the British idea of *home*. Calvin Klein now seeks some idea of what American home style would look like. Not an easy task. But he decides on pioneer-mission style.

This, it seems, is what people are seeking. Seeking home.

You are writing this in an attempt to master your obsession, but understanding has not halted the sense of danger. You know you are in trouble because this is the second morning you have awakened with a list of clothes in your mind that feel crucial to your survival and sense of well-being on the street.

The List

1. sweater $450
2. pants $90
3. long coat $500
4. one good dress $200

2 Reprinted from *Tikkun Magazine, A Bi-Monthly Jewish Critique of Politics, Culture, and Socity.* Subscriptions are $31.00 per year from Tikkun, 26 Fell Street, San Francisco, CA 94102. www.members.aol.com/einsof

You are actually considering spending over $1,000 on clothes. But what's money when we are talking well-being, security, belonging, and home? Spend $5,000 if that's what it will bring you!

Last night's meeting with Susan Hammerstein, a hot literary agent, was warm but disheartening. She basically told you that your writing is beautiful, literary, forceful, but totally unmarketable. Very personal writing she says.

You realize walking home that you are a stylistic outsider. There is too much of you showing through. The clothing list comes to mind. It is relentless. One good dress. One sweater. One long coat. Just like that one across from you on the bus. That's the one. Where did you get it? Pardon me, Miss, where did you get your coat? Bloomingdale's two years ago. And on sale. How fortunate. How smart of you. And your hair, if I may ask? Where was it cut? That's just the way I've always wanted mine to look. The side part just so. The way it falls over the shoulder.

You refrain from asking. Because you would not know where to stop. The next woman getting on the bus has just the right shoes. And the next, the scarf. What about that necklace?

You are relieved to finally get off the bus and walk rapidly, looking at no store windows, to your basement apartment. You close the door behind you and you try to stop the imagery. You light candles. You make tea. You put on Mozart. The list begins to fade.

Later that night a nasty habit returns. In your sleep you walk to the kitchen, take a loaf of bread and bring it back into bed. You begin to stuff handfuls—ripped off—into your mouth. This finally wakes you up. You know this person. This subterranean self. Desperate and helpless. She's been with you a long time. Since your teenage years. She knows nothing of style.

Your brother had style. Your mother also. But alas, you were born without style. You are convinced of this. Last night, before the bread escapade, you actually stood in front of the mirror and held your nose turned up, to see what you would have looked like with the nose job you were destined to have but staunchly refused.

This was a motion that occurred often in your adolescence. Your mother standing behind you in the mirror holding your nose up. First the front view. Then the profile. "Slightly turned up and the bump out . . ."

You didn't buy it. You were insulted. Outraged. It hadn't occurred to you until then that there was anything essentially wrong with your face.

Your uncle was one of the "big two" plastic surgeons on Long Island and you know you heard over and over that we could get a wholesale job. Your grandparents offered to foot the bill and send you to Europe as a reward. Now you understand that they were desperate for you not to look Jewish. They had a hatred for the Semitic face. They brought that hatred over from the old country. From the pine forests of Lithuania.

Uncle Saul Golden will do it wholesale. Everyone in your family except your father and your brother; every cousin, uncle, and aunt had the same nose. Saul Golden's vision of the all-American nose. All over Long Island, in the five towns, this nose appears in markets, synagogues, streets, PTA meetings. Exactly the same. All of them.

You were frightened of Uncle Saul. Not only did he once stick his tongue in your twelve-year-old mouth. In addition, each time you went to that house, that mansion built with old-world nose money, he would show you a picture book of nose choices. You remember the album. Large and glossy pictures of miserable-looking Semitic faces on one side, with the redone versions on the other. He would turn the pages and look at you lustfully.

The other day on the phone, your father made an astonishing joke. He was describing a very ugly person whom a close friend of his married. What was so ugly? you asked, always fascinated by this distinction. Just that really ugly kind of Jewish face, he said. The kind you can't look at. The kind they had posters of in Germany. The kind with the word *Juden* written underneath. Both of you laughed.

Writing for Ideas and Practice 8-9

1. If you began by thinking the essay was about fashion or even life in New York, when did you notice that the essay was about something else? What is the essay's ultimate subject?
2. How does Ross feel about the following issues raised in the memoir:
   a. Her self-image
   b. Her Uncle Saul
   c. Her being Jewish
   d. Her nose
   e. Her sense of fashion
   f. Her "home"—and why do you think the essay is entitled "Seeking Home"?

In a way, the real subject of Ross's essay is the *essayist*—in that the memoir reveals her hopes, her fears, her ideas, her opinions, by telling her story. Any piece of literary nonfiction is the story at hand, but also the writer's ideas and insights about the story.

So, you can include anything at all in your memoir which will help you explore the story. You may write about the leak in your utility room or the dread you feel when you open the mail. You may want to write about the high cost of bananas, or about a favorite book, or about your lunch last Tuesday with your best friend. And while your essay may report what you had for lunch last Tuesday, it will also report what remembering that lunch with your best friend tells you about who you are—and it will tell your reader about who he or she is, as well.

In "Seeking Home," Dorien Ross discusses her subject by exploring her feelings about a number of issues, all of which, when grouped together in the essay, point to one overall feeling the essay communicates: Ross's sense of lost identity and need for acceptance for who she is, flawed and inadequate though she may be perceived to be. The essay deals with experiences and feelings, and attempts to sort them out and to share them with the reader.

Writing for Ideas and Practice 8-10

1. Look back at Ross's essay. How does Ross structure her essay? What devices does she use to explore her subject? List each major thought or issue she deals with in the essay. Describe the progression she makes from idea to idea, and how those ideas relate to or reveal her attitude toward the essay's overall subject.

2. Think of a subject you might like to write about. Then write down at least four different means you might use to explore that subject. It might be that you include a short story about your own experience of this subject, a transcription of a conversation you overheard about the subject, a description of something related to the subject, and a series of arguments presenting different viewpoints regarding the subject.

VOICE

The writer of literary nonfiction has an important concern, besides what to write about or what to use to explore that subject. The writer creates a voice, a persona, a style, that communicates his feelings and ideas. This is of course true for the writer of fiction, the poet, and the dramatist as well, and yet the issue of voice can be especially important in the writing of memoir because the writer of nonfiction is sharing his own story with the reader. The literary nonfiction work presents both the subject at hand and the essayist's mind at work—his thoughts, his opinions, his memories, his experiences.

Writing for Ideas and Practice 8-11

1. Write a brief example of the kinds of words, sentences, and expressions you might imagine someone using in each of the following contexts:
    a.   An attempt to persuade someone in a position of power to change his mind
    b.   A personal meditation on an intense or life-changing experience
    c.   A letter in response to some frustrating loss or injustice
    d.   A reflection on some object or memory of beauty, simplicity, and grace
2. Write two hundred words on any subject about which you have strong feelings. Examine the kinds of words, sentences, and expressions you use. Examine the mood or attitude your writing has communicated. Ask someone else to read the piece, and have him write down what he sees as your attitude toward the subject. Do you see your own writing style as communicating the same way as did your reader? Why or why not? What does this tell you about your voice?

Voice can be described as the personality or the mood of the speaker you hear talking to you as you read the essay or memoir. What is the essayist's attitude toward the subject? What does he know about it? What are his prejudices, his fears, his joys? Voice can be communicated through the essayist's choice of words (Does he use slang? Does he use colloquial terms and phrases? Does he use precise images or generalizations?), and through his sentence style (Are the sentences choppy and fast, like a cab driver's, or slow and long, like a senator's?). Voice also emerges as an overall sense of what the essayist thinks or feels. To find the essayist's voice, you must listen for it—by reading the essay or memoir and encountering the one who is speaking to you. And you must find your own voice as well.

Listen, for example, to the voice in this excerpt:

> A single gentle rain makes the grass many shades greener. So our prospects brighten on the influx of better thoughts. We should be blessed if we lived in the present always, and took advantage of every accident that befell us, like the grass which confesses the influence of the slightest dew that falls on it; and did not spend our time in atoning for the neglect of past opportunities, which we call doing our duty. We loiter in winter while it is already spring. In a pleasant spring morning all men's sins are forgiven. Such a day is a truce to vice.
>
> — *Henry David Thoreau, from* Walden

Notice Thoreau's voice is both distant in its rather formal sentence structure and careful word choice, and yet also warm, inviting. Thoreau includes the reader with himself in the use of the word "we"—and Thoreau calls the reader into the woods with him, to watch the dew and the rain. He includes the reader with him in his meditation on what he wants his own life to be about; phrases such as "We loiter in winter while it is already spring" are at once confessional and a warning, both to himself and to the reader. Yet Thoreau is also formal and careful, arranging his language with precise images and arguments, to suggest the seriousness of his subject matter and his approach to it.

Consider another example of voice:

> At the age of eighty my mother had her last bad fall, and after that her mind wandered free through time. Some days she went to weddings and funerals that had taken place half a century earlier. On others she presided over family dinner cooked on Sunday afternoons for children who were now gray with age. Through all this she lay in bed but moved across time, traveling among the dead decades with a speed and ease beyond the gift of physical science.
>
> — *Russell Baker, from* Growing Up

Baker's voice is, like Thoreau's, conversational and personal. Simply telling the story of one's mother's senility and illness—whether that audience is a reader or a close friend — is very personal in itself. But further, Baker's matter-of-fact and yet soft tone conveys a friendly intimacy with the reader. The voice involves sophisticated sentence structure (such as in the last sentence in the paragraph), and yet that sophistication does not seem formal. Baker seems to want the reader to come along with him as Baker learns about himself by examining his life through the focus, at this point in the memoir, of his aging mother.

Different subjects require different forms and voices. In one essay or even in one part of an essay, a writer may come across as particularly emotional. In Dorien Ross's "Seeking Home," for example, her voice in one section conveys just such emotion ("You didn't buy it. You were insulted. Outraged. It hadn't occurred to you until then that there was anything essentially wrong with your face."). Elsewhere, the voice may come across as distant, controlled, careful, as in another section of Ross's essay ("This, it seems, is what people are seeking. Seeking home.").

What is your voice—or, what voices do you use when you write? Voice allows a sense of the writer and her attitude toward the subject to come through—is the writer mean-spirited, flirtatious, flighty, meditative, angry, in love, hopeful, peaceful? Is yours a memoir about huge matters of the world and society so that you will employ a serious and formal voice, or is it a memoir recounting the tiniest and most personal moments so that you will use intimate, confessional language and images?

Writing for Ideas and Practice 8-12

1. Practice writing in different voices by writing approximately two hundred words about the subject "Work" in any two of the following voices.
   a. Haughty, reserved, aloof, disgusted, above-it-all
   b. Interested, curious, open, willing, young, naive
   c. Knowledgeable, earnest, observant, helpful
   d. Angry, hurt, disappointed, wondering, bitter
2. Look at any piece you have written in the past; analyze the voice you used in the piece. Did it work well with the subject matter at hand? Was your approach appropriate? Would you still use that voice in writing about other subjects or in other formats?
3. Find five published works that have distinct voices, and copy some of the sentences you like best. Get a feel for the rhythm of the sentences and words, and see if you can incorporate some of what you like into your own writing voice.

When the reader reads your work, he will be thinking about your subject, but also, at least at some level, imagining *you*. The voice you use will inform that picture. Seek to discover your voice and style, as well as to construct your style deliberately. It takes work to do this well, but the work is worth the trouble when you succeed. Imitate other writers and then use what you learn from them in your own writing. Experiment. See how different styles of language and word choice fit different subjects and forms.

You would do well to write a long time, and practice, and experiment, and seek the sounds, the rhythms, the moods, and the details which convey what you want the reader to see, hear, and feel in your voice. When Rick was in graduate school, he had a friend who was already an excellent published poet and essayist with a very clear sense of his voice. When Rick would bring him his writing to critique, he would make suggestions about this or that part of the story or essay, but would always end by saying, "And—you need to write more. All the time. Go write more." Rick might protest, "I've written ten drafts of this already!" His friend would simply smile. Rick later comments: "I hated that I still had more learning and writing to do, and yet my friend was right, because for me to discover my own writer's voice has taken years of reading and writing and practicing—and the process continues."

Finally, about the overall purpose of the memoir: some of our students have protested that Hughes isn't completely successful in "Salvation," because the issue isn't resolved at the end. "He doesn't still feel as he did then," they argue, "that was just how he ended up feeling when he was a little kid. Why doesn't he finish it?" Sometimes readers look for a conclusion to a story, to find out how it is wrapped up or "what it means." Yet, the memoir writer can examine an experience or a memory without necessarily finding a conclusion for it. Susan Cheever has written two memoirs, *Home Before Dark* and *Treetops: A Family Memoir*, dealing with her feelings toward her upbringing and how she was influenced by her father, John Cheever. In the books, the younger Cheever explores a number of significant conflicts and themes—the effects of her father's drinking on the family's interaction; the strange feeling she had when she realized that her father was using their family as a basis for some of his short stories; the tension in her parents' marriage and the results that tension brought about in later years in each of the family's three children. Susan Cheever doesn't necessarily *resolve* all of those conflicts and feelings, as much as in writing about them she faces them, sorts them out, rethinks them, examines them —and in so doing, is able to order them and process them within herself, without having "fixed" or resolved them. In fact, writers often say that writing about their experiences and memories validates and celebrates those feelings and ideas—*even the painful or confusing ones*. The aim of the memoir is not to put the experience into a box, but to examine it, to re-order it, to experience it anew, and to share it with the reader so that it becomes a part of the reader's experience as well. Another very powerful example of a memoir which doesn't necessarily resolve all the conflicts it introduces is Art Spiegelman's *Maus I* and *II*, a memoir told in cartoon strip form, in which Spiegelman explores his often difficult relationship with his father, who survived Auschwitz. Spiegelman explores the issues he raises, and works through many of the feelings and conflicts in his story, but to make sense both of the atrocities of the Nazi persecution of the Jews and of the complexities of father-son relationships is an impossible task. Rather, Spiegelman's aim is simply to present the story as powerfully as possible, and to share it with the reader.

Writing for Ideas and Practice 8-13

1. Write a short memory recalling a particularly painful or difficult experience or issue you have struggled with—without resolving the conflicts in the memoir by the end of the story.
2. Share with fellow writers your answer to this question: Was it difficult not to "fix" the problem or conflict introduced in the story? Why or why not?
3. Write a list of at least three other stories or memories you could write about in memoir which would work well without necessarily having a clear resolution at the end.

Memoir is one of the most important kinds of nonfiction; it is popular, just because people want to read other people's life stories. But beyond that, the literary memoir, the memoir or autobiography or diary told with authenticity and power, communicates truths about one's experience in a dynamic and arresting way. Write your life story—and discover that story as you share it with your readers.

The memoir and the many other forms of literary nonfiction, which have become increasingly important in recent years, are found in many media — magazines, newspapers, scholarly journals, speeches, pamphlets, collections, and the Internet. Some literary critics and scholars have been slow to recognize nonfiction as a truly literary form, giving it short shrift because of its often personal approach and its dizzyingly broad range of subjects. Nonetheless, ask anyone who writes literary nonfiction, and he will in all likelihood affirm the artistry needed to choose and arrange the personal, informal, confessional, seemingly lightly cast-off thoughts in an essay or memoir so that the work communicates the very thing the writer intends. Truman Capote, an author known as much for his nonfiction as for his fiction, asserted that "fiction as an art is not any more important than factual, journalistic writing, as a highly developed art. . . . factual writing with all the techniques of fiction—which the journalist would never think of using—is as high an art as, and capable of being a higher art than, modern fiction." Literary nonfiction seems destined to play an increasingly important role in the literature of the future. Some of the best writing to emerge in the last century is in the realm of the essay and the memoir—consider *Pilgrim at Tinker Creek* by Annie Dillard or the essays of E. B. White.

Literary nonfiction, then, is a form which is still emerging, and which you might want to investigate as a corollary to other modes of literary expression. As we said at the beginning of the chapter, the writer of nonfiction has the best of both worlds—imaginative and artful use of language and imagery, as well as the power of writing about what is all around us in our everyday lives and in our past experiences. Like any other important literary form, the essay and the memoir require careful and considerable work and study, and the rewards in reading and writing literary nonfiction are yours to enjoy.

Writing on Your Own

1. Write a memoir about a specific memory, a feeling, or an experience. Use the story or stories you tell in the memoir to illustrate your feelings or attitude.
   a. Communicate your feelings through the details you include, the voice you use, and your combination of presenting the experience or memory and your commentary on the meaning and significance of that experience or memory.
   b. Use flashback or some other variation on chronological order at least once in your memoir.
   c. Utilize a combination of reporting large events and developments, and slower-paced description of scenes.
   d. Utilize a voice which is specific and clearly helpful in relating the story's themes.

Writing to Revise

1. Once you have written your assignment for #1 above, rewrite the memoir with the following guidelines:
   a. Before rewriting it, list what information is presented as scene, and what information is presented as reporting. Evaluate this alternating pattern. Was it appropriate for the memoir's overall effect? Change it as necessary, even if that means cutting parts of the story you really liked.
   b. Rewrite the piece, replacing at least half of the generalizations or reporting you wrote with specific details in example or scene.
   c. Rewrite the piece again, attempting this time to state only once or twice in the entire piece what the piece is about overall. Is the piece stronger for this subtlety?

9

THE HEART OF A STORY:
CHARACTER AND CONFLICT

Writing to Warm Up

1. Write your own definition of a story. What are its parts? What is its purpose?
2. What do you like best about the stories you read? What do you like best about the stories (or a story) you've written?
3. Do you prefer to read stories or poems? Do you think in terms of stories, or poems, or scenes, as in drama? Which is most natural to you when you jot down ideas or compose?

WRITING A STORY

People everywhere write stories, tell stories, and sing stories. One of the most basic parts of creative writing is the telling of stories, in many forms. Kathryn Morton, in her article "The Story-Telling Animal," argues that we all need to tell stories:

 What got people out of the trees was something besides thumbs and gadgets . . . a warp in the simian brain that made us insatiable for patterns—patterns of sequence, of behavior, of feeling—connections, reasons, causes: stories. . . . From the stone-age Tasaday people of the Philippine rain forest to the suburbanites in Scarsdale, narrative is the only art that exists in all human cultures. It is by narrative that we experience our lives. . . . Nothing passes by but the mind grabs it and looks for a way to fit it into a story, or into a variety of possible scripts: He's late—maybe he was in an accident. Maybe he's run off to Tahiti with a blonde. Maybe he stopped on the way here to buy flowers. . . . Feverish for order, our minds seek . . . to make sense out of the greatest mystery we all must face—ourselves.

In other words, we all tell stories all the time. And it's a natural human tendency, one that informs how we live and what we do to order our world. We're all always trying to figure out who we are and what our lives mean, and many people do that by telling stories. The novelist Willa Cather said, "There are only two or three human stories and they go on repeating themselves as fiercely as if they had never happened before."

The product of this basic human drive to tell stories takes many forms. The most obvious and traditional is to write **narration** or **fiction**. A narrative can take many forms. Some are very old, such as the epic verse narrative; some are relatively new, such as the novel and the short story; some are so new they're still very much being developed and explored, such as the screenplay, the short short story, and performance art.

So—what makes a narrative? When you want to write fiction (such as a novel or short story), you may have been thinking about a conflict you've experienced, or a scene you imagined, or an idea you've been playing around with. Writing a story involves taking experience, real or imagined, and shaping it in such a way that the story you tell reveals that experience to you—and to the reader—through a series of events affecting and involving a character or characters. In other words, a story exists in order to explore what will happen when a character or a certain group of characters confront internal and external problems and issues.

Fiction writers, like all writers, aim to express some part of their real or imagined experience; story writers use narrative, just as poets use verse and dramatists use dramatic scenes, but the basic urge and objective is the same. In his essay "What Every Writer Needs," Ernest Hemingway said it this way:

 A writer's problem does not change. He himself changes and the world he lives in changes but his problem remains the same. It is always how to write truly and, having found what is true, to project it in such a way that it becomes a part of the experience of the person who reads it.

So what you're trying to do is to communicate the truth about some kind of experience through the use of a narrative.

Now, why write a *story*, as opposed to writing in some other genre? It may be that you have characters and conflicts between those characters you want to write about, or that your mind works best in sequences of events.

Some writers think in terms of *slides*, "slices of life"—a house, a tree, a moment in time, a single issue or feeling. But the narrative writer thinks in terms more like a *movie*; that is, the narrative writer puts together a series of related pictures in order to express experience. Many factors cause writers to choose to write fiction rather than poetry or essay or drama. Like poetry, fiction must employ vivid images and careful use of words, sounds, and language patterns. Like drama, fiction presents characters in conflict, working through those conflicts. Like nonfiction, fiction involves the writer's exploring someone's feelings or ideas about a given subject.

However, fiction is different, too, from these other genres. The fiction story creates an entirely new reality, existing only on the page and in the mind, not acted out on stage, as in drama. Its characters and actions are imagined and invented, not based on real events and people, as in the memoir. Its main structure is the relating of a series of events, not primarily images, sounds, and language patterns, as in poetry.

So what is a story made of? How do the pictures and characters become arranged and put in order, and how do you know if you're doing it right?

Character

The true artist discovers himself by leaving out a lot. The artist alone sees spirits. But after he has told of their appearing to him, everybody sees them.

— *Goethe*

The most important component in any narrative is going to be the people in it and what they're going through. The people whose story you tell are called **characters**. Without characters, there can be no story. And yet characters are so naturally a part of the story that sometimes we don't notice them—that is, unless a good author entices us into paying attention to them.

But to discover, create, and develop truly good characters takes a lot of practice, or a lot of genius, or even more luck. Edgar Rice Burroughs said, "The only stroke of genius I had as a writer was naming a character Tarzan." Such moments of genius do not completely create a character, however. The writer has to spend enough time with a character to show the reader who that character is and what the character feels, experiences, decides, and how, and why—in a way that makes the reader care how the character moves from point A to point B. This process of invention is a lot tougher than it looks. Good characters don't just happen; they are a deliberate blend of many elements arranged to produce a specific result in the story.

For instance, what do we know about the great American icon, Charlie Brown, from the *Peanuts* comic strip by Charles M. Schulz? In your mind, quickly list five things you know about Charlie Brown. They may be physical details; they may be things you know about his neighborhood or circumstances; they may be things you know about his emotional makeup, or his family, or his habits; they may be things he says or things said to him; they may be things he thinks.

Chances are, you may have included some of the following things on the list:

- he never wins his baseball games
- he has a crazy, funny dog
- he has a friend who carries around a blanket
- he was on a TV show about Christmas
- he has a big round head
- he is depressed a lot
- he has a funny little sister
- he can't fly a kite without it going in a tree
- everyone calls him "blockhead"
- he has a shirt with a zigzag stripe across it
- he lives where it gets cold and snows in the winter
- he gets bad grades in school

That's a fairly comprehensive list of details about Charlie Brown. What does it tell us?

If you grouped all of the *physical details* together, you would know some things about Charlie Brown that tell you some of who he is. And the physical details matter; if he were handsome and tall, with muscles and jet black hair, your sense of him as a character would change immediately. Physical details communicate huge amounts of unspoken information about any character.

For instance, the short fat guy doesn't usually play the leading romantic role in the movies. And although only in stereotypical narrative formulas is the protagonist required to be a handsome man, the physical details the writer assigns a character are chosen because of what they communicate, even if ironically, about the character. In an example of just such an ironic use of physical details about a character, in the movie *Get Shorty*, short, dumpy Danny DeVito plays an egotistical, Oscar-nominated leading man; the contrast between DeVito's appearance and the typical Hollywood hunk is a commentary on the eccentricities and skewed perspective of the movie industry. But on the television series *Taxi*, DeVito was chosen to play the villainous dispatcher partly because his appearance could help to communicate the smallness and even the repulsive nature of his character. You as the writer will need to decide why you want to include certain details about your character based on what effect those details will produce in the reader's perception of the character.

The physical details surrounding a character in his environment are also important. In *Peanuts*, the drawings of suburban houses, skating ponds in winter, the schoolroom, and the living room with the television and the beanbag chair, all set the stage for the things that Charlie Brown will have to deal with. They also reveal to us what is important to him. If a character lives in a wooden shack on the edge of town, we have different information and feelings about that character than we do if that character lives in an opulent mansion on Park Avenue.

Now, consider what we know about Charlie Brown based on what we know about *the characters surrounding* Charlie Brown; his dog, Snoopy, is a carefree, hilariously uninhibited character who serves as a perfect contrast to the worried, tentative Charlie Brown. Likewise, his sensitive, philosophical, blanket-carrying friend Linus serves the function of helping Charlie Brown interpret and understand his feelings and experiences—thus helping the reader understand as well. The fact that the other characters call Charlie Brown "blockhead" tells us something else about him—that he is perceived as a loser, a scapegoat. If he were called by the nickname he dreams of in an early series of *Peanuts* cartoons—"Flash"—we would see him in an entirely different light. If everyone around him were an adult and he were the only child in the comic strip, our perception of him would change. If he had only one friend, a nun or a talk show host or a boa constrictor or a plumber, each of these possibilities would reveal something different about him. As it is, what the characters around him do and say reveals a lot about Charlie Brown.

The things Charlie Brown *does* also tell us about who he is. He pitches for his baseball team, he directs the school play; he is, in fact, a leader. But in all his efforts, he fails, often miserably. He checks his mailbox frequently, waiting for mail that never comes from friends he doesn't have. He feeds and observes his crazy dog, silently commenting on what he thinks normal is—measured by what Snoopy is not. He searches for meaning in life and relationships, which tells us a lot about who he is.

And there are the things he *says* or thinks about. Charlie Brown complains a lot—his famous catch-phrase is "Good grief." He talks to himself a lot about winning the baseball game or having the courage to say hello to "that cute little red-headed girl" whom he's always had a crush on. He goes to the neighborhood psychiatrist, Lucy, and asks her about his problems. He worries about holidays, school, love, his future, being a success, and so on. And we learn about who he is by what he says, to himself and to others.

There are many examples of this same process of character development in other forms of narration than the comic strip. For instance, the American short story writer Flannery O'Connor uses the four methods we listed above—how a character appears, what a character says, what a character does, and how other characters relate to that character—to paint vivid characterizations. Here is an example from "A Good Man Is Hard to Find:"

Bailey didn't look up from his reading so she wheeled around then and faced the children's mother, a young woman in slacks, whose face was as broad and innocent as a cabbage and was tied around with a green head-kerchief that had two points on the top like a rabbit's ears. She was sitting on the sofa, feeding the baby his apricots out of a jar. "The children have been to Florida before," the old lady said. "You all ought to take them somewhere else for a change so they would see different parts of the world and be broad. They never have been to east Tennessee."

The children's mother didn't seem to hear her but the eight-year-old boy, John Wesley, a stocky child with glasses, said, "If you don't want to go to Florida, why dontcha stay at home?" He and the little girl, June Star, were reading the funny papers on the floor.

"She wouldn't stay at home to be queen for a day," June Star said without raising her yellow head.

Notice that the author doesn't say overtly, "This is a pushy old lady; pay attention, she's going to do something nasty," or "These people are a bunch of self-centered brats." The writing is more powerful because the characters are revealed directly to us, as if we are looking at them, listening to them, encountering them ourselves. What do you know about the grandmother, with her "'You all ought to'" speeches? The grandchildren, John Wesley, "stocky . . . with glasses," and June Star with her "yellow head"? The son, Bailey, who won't "look up from his reading," and the "children's mother, a young woman in slacks, whose face was as broad and innocent as a cabbage"? Already, in such a short selection, O'Connor has made the reader begin to form opinions and feelings regarding these characters because of the well-chosen descriptive details.

Character can be created for the reader by the careful choice and use of specific details on your part. You may not find or decide all of the characteristics and actions with which to create each of the characters in your first draft. Just continue to write and to explore, and they'll show up. But even as you let a discovery draft occur, keep thinking ahead: every detail you choose to include means something to the characters and their importance in the story. In the next chapter we'll discuss "dramatic unity," which is the overall sense that the plot and details of your work fit together to create a unified whole—that a story's details aren't selected randomly, but appear not only to develop character but also to advance the story's characters through the issues they must face and resolve in the story. The details in a good story, for instance, suggest themes and issues which will become increasingly important as the story continues. You might want to try reading O'Connor's story, and then going back and seeing the significance of the details in these paragraphs. However, when you write, don't dwell too much on each detail, or you will never develop the story so that it accomplishes its purpose, for you'll be too busy worrying over every tiny word, color, sound, action. Better just to write, and then work on the unity of the details as you go, as we will discuss in chapter 10.

Writing for Ideas and Practice 9-1

1. Read this excerpt from a short story, "Barbie-Q," by Sandra Cisneros.

Yours is the one with mean eyes and a ponytail. Striped swimsuit, stilettos, sunglasses, and gold hoop earrings. Mine is the one with bubble hair. Red swimsuit, stilettos, pearl earrings, and a wire stand. But that's all we can afford, besides one extra outfit apiece. Yours, "Red Flair," sophisticated A-line coatdress with a Jackie Kennedy pillbox hat, white gloves, handbag, and heels included. Mine, "Solo in the Spotlight," evening elegance in black glitter strapless gown with a puffy skirt at the bottom like a mermaid tail, formal-length gloves, pink chiffon scarf, and mike included. From so much dressing and undressing, the black glitter wears off where her titties stick out. This and a dress invented from an old sock when we cut holes here and here and here, the cuff rolled over for the glamorous, fancy-free, off-the-shoulder look.

Every time the same story. Your Barbie is roommates with my Barbie, and my Barbie's boyfriend comes over and your Barbie steals him, okay? Kiss, kiss, kiss. Then the two Barbies fight. You dumbbell! He's mine. Oh no he's not, you stinky! Only Ken's invisible, right? Because we don't have enough money for a stupid-looking boy doll when we'd both rather ask for a new Barbie outfit next Christmas. We have to make do with your mean-eyed Barbie and my bubblehead Barbie and our one outfit apiece not including the sock dress.

Write a brief response to each of these questions, and then share your answers:
a. What do you know about the person speaking?
   1) Family life
   2) Family history
   3) Present circumstances
   4) Attitude toward those circumstances
   5) Desires, hopes, wishes
   6) Fears, problems, needs
   7) Overall impressions you have
b. How do you know these things? What specific details give you the above information?

2. Read the following paragraph from a short story by Katherine Ann Porter called "The Grave," and then be prepared to identify and discuss the same elements you found in exercise 1:

The family cemetery had been a pleasant small neglected garden of tangled rose bushes and ragged cedar trees and cypress, the simple flat stones rising out of uncropped sweet-smelling wild grass. The graves were lying open and empty one burning day when Miranda and her brother Paul, who often went together to hunt rabbits and doves, propped their twenty-two Winchester rifles carefully against the rail fence, climbed over and explored among the graves. She was nine years old and he was twelve.

3. Look at an art book or a book with photographs in it; find any three pictures of individual faces. Now, for each face, make the same list of details about the people in the pictures as in the literary selections in 1 and 2, above.

4. Gather five to seven objects—hats, boxes, pocketknives, spoons, wallets, scarves, buttons, knickknacks, mementos, whatever you can find (they don't have to be your own possessions—in fact, it's better sometimes if they're not yours, and you've just accumulated them or found them or borrowed them or gotten them recently at a swap meet; the whole class can bring their items and all trade them, to shake things up more). Pick one of these things. Think about the person you associate in your imagination with the object. Then, quickly, list a response to the seven questions above about this person.

To review, story writers show the reader a character by:

- describing the character's physical characteristics;
- putting the character in a particular setting—that is, time and place, mood, circumstance;
- revealing information about the character's background, such as family, past, historical information, emotional experiences, habits;
- having the character say things, either to him/herself or to other characters; and
- having the character do things, either on his/her own or in response to other characters and/or events.

You might even want to experiment with the details you're using to develop character by changing the regular, ordinary kinds of details you might normally use. What if, instead of having the hero of your story look like Brad Pitt, you make him look like Danny DeVito? Many times we do or say things we don't expect—and those moments tell us as much about ourselves as our regular routine. Ibsen told the story of writing an early draft of the climactic scene when a scandal was revealed regarding the main character, Nora, in his play *A Doll's House*. Initially, Ibsen wrote the scene so that at a key moment, Nora's husband, Thorvald, says, "Nora, you're ruined"—but in the next draft, Ibsen realized that Thorvald's real concern is not Nora, but himself—and changed the line to, "I'm ruined." The idea is not to include strange details for their own sake; putting a giant mole in the forehead of the beauty queen without tying that detail to the character's development won't serve any purpose. But unusual or unexpected details can help develop a character more fully. Try several different techniques to develop not only your characters' most immediately appropriate characteristics, but also the less obvious details that will help to reveal character.

Writing for Ideas and Practice 9-2

1. Deliberately write a quick character sketch with incongruent and illogical details. Make the character believable even though he/she might not be what the reader expects.

2. Write a short paragraph in which you describe someone in your class, but change just one detail. Then see if a partner can guess what detail has been changed.

A story writer must make very deliberate decisions about what to reveal about each character and why. When we critique students' stories by asking why a particular character is doing some particular thing, it often happens that the student may snarl, *But hey, I don't know why he shot her! He just shot her! I just made it up, that's all! Stop being so picky!* Or maybe the student will just shrug and sheepishly admit, *This is just a first draft; I'm not sure why she left home.* And then some students say, *I wrote it that way because that's how it really happened, and I just changed the names because you had that girl in one of your classes last semester and she doesn't even know I'm writing this story and she'd kill me if she found out you knew she'd done this!* All of these are perfectly normal responses to a careful examination of an early draft. After all, as we said earlier, it takes a while for the author to get to know her/his characters and why they do what they do—just as it takes a while for anyone to get to know anyone. Joyce Carol Oates has said that when she is working on a novel it takes her about six weeks to get to know the characters or for the characters to become real to her. So, the writer must simply keep writing, developing character with care, choosing the details that make the story come to life.

CONFLICT

Other components also add to the working out of a story. Characters aren't the only issue; they are the central focus of the story, but if the characters simply exist in isolation, without decisions to make or things to resolve, the reader won't stay with you long, no matter how many great details you've included about their hair or their childhood homes or their accents.

The real issue here is not just the characters themselves, but the characters and the conflicts they endure and deal with. **Conflict**, along with character, is the central ingredient in any story.

Writing for Ideas and Practice 9-3

1. Quickly answer these questions:
   a. What is conflict?
   b. When have you felt conflict in your life?
   c. How did you resolve conflict? Were you able to resolve it? How did it make you feel? What effects have certain key conflicts had on your life?

2. Now share your answers; here are some students' answers from over the years.
   * Conflict is like a ball peen hammer to the head
   * Conflict for me is my mother
   * I define conflict as that part of life we all have to deal with
   * Conflict is fighting and why we fight—a basic human instinct
   * Conflict is fireworks and bombs and knives and razor blades, and the eyes of the man plotting to use them on you
   * Conflict is the part of the story that makes it worth reading, so I can see how it turns out
3. Read a short story and make lists of all the details the author uses to reveal any one character.

Does conflict sound *bad* to you? People often think of conflict as negative —a fight, or something painful. Sometimes student writers want to stay away from conflict in their stories, exactly for this reason. But here's a rule with which we should begin: *without conflict, you have no story.*

Very often, students will bring us stories that aren't really stories. The writings are memories, or impressions, or imagined incidents. But their stories lack something. For instance, here's a very short example of a story that isn't really a story yet:

I was always the loudest one in the family. Why? I don't know; perhaps I just had a lot to say. But my mother would laugh and say, "Billy, you are so SILLY!" I drove my whole family crazy, even Mom. And at one point, my older brother threatened to kill me. It was a hot summer that year and we were all looking forward to our big trip to Grandma's house. When we got there, it was as if all our troubles melted away.

Why isn't it a story? It has characters, true. And it has conflict, yes—but the conflict isn't resolved or dealt with, only introduced and then abandoned. And stories require that their characters *deal with* conflict, and even *resolve* conflict. Stories are about the reader going through an experience with the character, not merely being told about the character.

So, for the purposes of writing fiction, what is conflict? Conflict is a problem to be worked out, or tension to resolve, facing the main character.

Some exercises follow in which we get a sense of how conflict works with character.

Writing for Ideas and Practice 9-4

1. Pretend you are an ant. What do you do all day? What do you worry about? What do you hope for? What is your family structure like, what's it like in the colony, what's the

queen like—have you ever seen her? Have you ever had something attack you and try to eat you? Have you ever been outside, or are you one of those ants that just carry stuff around in the anthill, feeding the babies? Imagine a scene, in which you, as an ant, face life. Make it short—but be sure to include some element of conflict. What does it feel like to deal with this conflict? (If being an ant doesn't turn you on, pretend you're something else; all that matters is that you invest yourself in a scene, in which a character must deal with the inherent conflicts in life.)

2. Think about a specific memory. It doesn't have to be particularly traumatic or profound; in fact, it's probably better if it isn't. The memory needs to be a trigger, that's all. Go to that memory and describe what's going on. Make stuff up. Lie. Once you start the scene, it doesn't matter whether you're historically accurate or not; what is vastly more important is that you tell the truth about the emotions you find when you get there, and whatever facts, details, names, and so on you find as you write will be fine.

3. Try some freewriting and see if a story comes out of it; many times, it will. A way to do this is to clip a bunch of headlines or just short descriptions out of the newspaper, mix them up in a bag or a hat, and then pick one at random. Write or tape the headline at the top of your page and then just start writing, say, for three or five minutes without stopping. Do not think first; just write. Don't cross anything out. "Police chief refuses audit" or "Rains continue" can conjure up all sorts of conflicts and characters. Just write; you can impose structure and order later.

These exercises are meant to show you that conflict can be found in many different sources; in fact, in the exercises in the section on character, many conflicts already seemed built into the characters themselves. Almost inevitably, where there are people, there will be conflicts.

Writing for Ideas and Practice 9-5

1. Go back to the exercise in which you gathered a group of objects, Writing for Ideas and Practice 9-1.4. In your list of ideas about the person you associated with the object, what conflicts emerge? It may be helpful to restate the questions:
   What do you know about the person speaking?
   a. family life
   b. family history
   c. present circumstances
   d. attitude toward those circumstances
   e. desires, hopes, wishes
   f. fears, problems, worries
   g. overall impressions you have
   In each area, make some notes about the conflicts, both internal and external, you have discovered in your brainstorming about the person you see when you look at the object.

2. The things we read are full of conflict. Read this opening paragraph from a novel:

> He was facing Seventh Avenue, at Times Square. It was past midnight and he had been sitting in the movies, in the top row of the balcony, since two o'clock in the afternoon. Twice he had been awakened by the violent accents of the Italian film, once the usher had awakened him, and twice he had been awakened by caterpillar fingers between his thighs. He was so tired, he had fallen so low, that he scarcely had the energy to be angry; nothing of this belonged to him anymore — *you took the best, so why not take the rest?* — but he had growled in his sleep and bared the white teeth in his dark face and crossed his legs. Then the balcony was nearly empty, the Italian film was approaching a climax; he stumbled down the endless stairs into the street. He was hungry, his mouth felt filthy. He realized too late, as he passed through the doors, that he wanted to urinate. And he was broke. And he had nowhere to go.
>
> — *James Baldwin, from* In Another Country

Now, answer the following questions about the paragraph:
a. What or who is in conflict in this selection?
b. Who is the character and what is he concerned about?
c. What are some specific conflicts the paragraph suggests to you?
d. How do those conflicts remind you of conflicts you've gone through in your own life?

3. Here is a paragraph from a short story; try to list at least three conflicts you can see indicated in the details of this paragraph:

> Mr. Brandish wanted a change. He did not mean at all by this that he wanted to change himself — only his scenery, his pace, and his environment, and that for only a space of eighteen or twenty days. He could leave his office for that long. Brandish was a heavy smoker, and the Surgeon General's report had made him self-conscious about his addiction. It seemed to him that strangers on the street regarded the cigarette in his fingers with disapproval and sometimes with commiseration. This was manifestly absurd, and he needed to get away. He would take a trip. He was divorced at the time, and would go alone.
>
> — *John Cheever, from* "Metamorphoses"

So now perhaps you've discovered where conflict can be found; it's everywhere. Maybe that's why we write stories—to resolve conflicts. Certainly, a large part of literary thought in the Western world has centered on the importance of the resolution of conflict in a story or play.

Some students disagree. "But, I can just have a story about a little boy spending the day with his baby sister, and there doesn't have to be some deep meaningful conflict in that, right?" they ask, and it's true. But if you're writing a piece with no real conflict between or within characters, then the story will have a limited range of possibilities. Only so much can happen before some part of the story suggests conflict of some kind. And the best stories explore all sorts of conflicts—some large, some small.

Something else to consider is that many writers and psychologists argue that everything we write is about *us*, in some way or another, even if we write about fantastic or remote subjects we've supposedly picked out of thin air. These theorists say that everything in our dreams is simply a symbol we use to decode our experience, that the things we dream are us, parts of us, acting out what we're going through.

Writing is a lot like dreaming; in addition to living in everyday reality, we use our imaginations to create an alternative reality which helps us deal with and order that everyday existence. As we discussed in earlier chapters, some students find this thought somewhat disturbing, for they don't want what they write to be about them, just as we don't want a weird or bad dream to come true or to tell us we're strange.

What do you think? You might make a note in your journal or discuss with classmates whether you agree or disagree with the idea that the conflicts you write about will inevitably come from within you or from what you have imagined and/or what you have observed around you. You might also think about how the necessity for dealing with conflict will affect whether you will censor your own writing. Remember, too, that the experiences and issues you choose for your characters will be different from the experiences and issues in your own life, simply because *fiction is invented*.

Why look at the conflicts and feelings in your own life, then, as you write? As we have said, all of us write about the things that are important to us. Many writers use their own experiences as places from which to start writing. But part of the reason for writing fiction is to create what John Gardner called "the fictive dream"—that is, an imaginary world which writer and reader share in creating, in which characters explore and enact conflicts and joys which are separate from—but also reveal—our own. The essayist writes about her own life and ideas, at least in part, but the fiction writer creates a new experience.

Some critics study authors' lives and try to interpret the stories from the perspective of how the author lived. Other schools of thought suggest taking an opposite approach, reading the work as separately from the context as possible, seeking to understand and experience the story solely in connection to the story itself.

You may want to explore this issue for yourself as you create fiction. But know that while many, many fiction writers have included hints of their own experiences in their work, fiction is by nature invented and imaginary. This makes reading and writing fiction especially exciting. What you encounter in a story or novel is a world all its own, to be read and understood on its own terms. History, culture, and context may all inform and surround a story, and yet it exists in a unique place, where the reader and the characters meet. So, though you may mine your own life and memory for ideas and feelings about conflict and characters, don't stop there. Let yourself imagine any manner of character, conflict, event, setting, detail—and weave a thing which is altogether new in the universe—because you made it.

 A pact exists between writer and reader. From the first sentence, the reader should feel the writer at risk—and the reader answers, vulnerable to whatever the language may reveal. This exchange is more intimate, really, than speech or conversation, and quickly enters the luminous realm of dream or memory.

— *Jayne Ann Phillips*

Writing for Ideas and Practice 9-6

1. Childhood is a particularly scary, exciting, eventful time in our lives. Ask yourself a list of questions about your own childhood or past or even present, questions that delve into what scared you or excited you, what you loved or hated, what you dreamed about or suffered under, what you saw and heard and smelled and tasted. This can be a list like:

    When I was in school,
    My favorite food was _____
    The girl I loved most was _____
    My most embarrassing day was _____
    The teacher I remember most fondly was _____
    The thing I felt most angry about was _____

    Very often childhood is full of feelings, ideas, potential stories to tell. Maybe that's where some of your desire or need to tell stories comes from.

2. Try to invent conflict unconnected to your own experience, at least on the surface. List at least four conflicts you can associate or imagine relative to each scene below (but if any one of the situations is similar to a life experience you have known, change the scene so that it is different and the scene you imagine is completely invented):
    a. A sea captain fighting a giant sea creature
    b. A woman spanking her child for torturing the cat
    c. A soldier holding his dying friend in a trench in World War II
    d. A man standing on the edge of a building

3. Here is the first sentence of the short story "Paul's Case" by Willa Cather. Read it and notice the conflicts already present within it:

    It was Paul's afternoon to appear before the faculty of the Pittsburgh High School to account for his various misdemeanors.

    a. What conflicts do you see in this sentence?
    b. Of the conflicts you just listed, which are ones which you can imagine yourself writing about?

c. Write a long paragraph developing those conflicts, using the first sentence as a prompt to begin the paragraph.

As we continue the chapters dealing with narration, we will look at the ways in which authors work out conflicts in their stories. The device authors use to work out conflicts in their stories is called **plot**, and without a clear understanding of how a plot works, you won't be able to get your stories to hold together. But even as the next sections add more information about other components of writing narration, remember: *your story is about the characters in it and the conflicts they must work through.*

You might come up with the conflict first, but the effectiveness of the story is determined by the way the character or characters deal with conflict. Your characters drive the conflict, not the other way around. Every character and conflict will be different; how you create your characters will determine how they deal with conflict and resolve the issues in their paths. Create characters so that each person in your story deals with conflict in a consistent and believable way.

Writing on Your Own

1. Read a short story and make careful lists of all the details the author uses to reveal any one character.
2. Write a short story, following these criteria:
    a. It should be between five hundred and one thousand words in length;
    b. You should only write two drafts;
    c. It must have a character who is working through some personal conflict;
    d. You must use all four methods for revealing character;
    e. The reader must know how the conflict is resolved by the end of the story.
3. Take a conflict from your own experience and write a short story in which your main character deals with that conflict in a way you have not. Perhaps you never told off that irritating teacher. Or perhaps you want your character to use restraint when you did not. Change the details from your own life, though, in writing the story, so that once you are finished writing the story, it is no longer about you and the conflict you experienced, but about the character himself or herself. When you are finished, no one who knows you should know that the story reflects your own experience.

Writing to Revise

1. Revise one of the stories you wrote for Writing on Your Own, this time doing one of the following:
   a. take out one-third of the details you included about the character; OR
   b. add at least thirty-five more details about the character. THEN
   c. examine each detail or group of details about the character—and think about how each detail contributes to the character's development. Be sure the details have a purpose.
2. Take any story you have written and examine the characters. Take any character and list the details the story communicates about that character—physical details, things she says or does, things other characters do or say around her. Then, list the major (and minor, if possible) conflicts the character faces. Write about how well the conflicts are introduced and developed by the details presented. Then, rewrite the story and improve it by changing or adding to any places in the story in which the details are not effective in communicating character as it relates to conflict.

10

The Structure of a Story: Setting and Plot

Writing to Warm Up

Think of any fairy tale, children's story, ghost story, or myth you know. Remember the story in as much detail as you can. Then, respond to these questions:
1. What is the most significant moment in the story? Why?
2. What is each character's role in making the story happen?
3. What is the most important conflict in the story, and how is it dealt with?

What is a story? Why is a story different from other kinds of writing? In chapter 9, we worked on making character and conflict the heart of a story. In this chapter, you will look at another basic element in every story: its structure. We will begin with a discussion of an important element which helps to create a story's direction and to build a story's structure: *setting*. Then, we will examine a central issue for any narrative work, whether it is a very short story or a very long novel: *plot*.

Setting

The artist is born to pick, and choose, and group with science, these elements of nature, that the result may be beautiful.

— *Whistler*

Writing for Ideas and Practice 10-1

1. Imagine that you are in each of the following places. For each place, describe in a brief brainstorming list what visual, spatial, and sensory details you see and experience.

   a. A dark and crowded room
   b. The woods somewhere at sunset
   c. On a cloud
   d. An office building, in the parking garage
   e. A castle

2. Imagine that you are in each of the following years. For each time period, describe in a brief brainstorming list what visual, spatial, and sensory details you see and experience.

   a. 1851
   b. 2999
   c. 1311
   d. 1200 B.C.
   e. 1921

3. Imagine now and make a brainstorming list of what details related to physical locations you might associate with each of the following moods:

   a. Despair
   b. Terror
   c. Loneliness
   d. Loss and grief
   e. Bliss

Looking back at each of the brainstorming lists you wrote, you might analyze and think about a couple of things. There may be threads running through more than one of the lists—these might be themes or patterns the writer in you would like to explore. In any story, you must include details to show your reader where and when the story takes place—and what the mood of the story will be.

These details, gathered together and presented in a different way by every author and in every story, are called setting. **Setting** is the place, time, and mood in which a story takes place. In a good story, setting very often has a great deal to do with what is at the heart of the story.

Garrison Keillor, for instance, has written many stories which take place in a small Minnesota town. Willa Cather wrote stories set on the American plains in the 1800s and early 1900s. Gabriel García Márquez creates mythic, magical regions in South American villages and cities. But for each of these writers and many others, the stories are not just set in these particular times and places; the stories are in a very real way *about* those times and places, almost as much as they are about the characters in the stories.

However, don't decide you're going to write the definitive novel about your neighborhood. The settings of your stories will evolve and grow as your writing grows and you discover your subject matter in what you write about. And remember too that the most important thing in any story is what and how the characters experience and deal with the conflicts and opportunities in the story. Setting is a tool for bringing the story to life and making its conflicts real.

Writing for Ideas and Practice 10-2

"Young Goodman Brown," a short story by Nathaniel Hawthorne, is about all sorts of things and can be read in many different ways. For now, focus only on the setting of the story by reading these excerpts:

> Young Goodman Brown came forth at sunset into the street at Salem village; but put his head back, after crossing the threshold, to exchange a parting kiss with his young wife. And Faith, as the wife was aptly named, thrust her own pretty head into the street, letting the wind play with the pink ribbons of her cap while she called to Goodman Brown.
>
> So they parted; and the young man pursued his way until, being about to turn the corner by the meeting-house, he looked back and saw the head of Faith still peeping after him with a melancholy air, in spite of her pink ribbons.
>
> He had taken a dreary road, darkened by all the gloomiest trees of the forest, which barely stood aside to let the narrow path creep through, and closed immediately behind. It was all as lonely as could be; and there is this peculiarity in such a solitude, that the traveller knows not who may be concealed by the innumerable trunks and the thick boughs overhead; so that with lonely footsteps he may yet be passing through an unseen multitude.

1. List all of the physical details which indicate the *time and place* of the story.
2. Now, list all of the details and descriptors which indicate the overall *mood or feeling* of the story (this is not the theme or the meaning of the story, but rather the basic emotional situation of the story, especially at its beginning).
3. With a partner or a group, make a list together in response to these questions:
   a. When does the story take place? How do you know?
      1) Year or general time period
      2) Season
      3) Time of day
   b. Where does the story take place? How do you know?
      1) General location—country, culture, era
      2) Specific location—physical placement of characters and details
   c. What mood controls or is part of the story? How do you know?
      1) Overall mood—emotion, state
      2) Specific mood—weather, light, temperature, sounds, smells, actions, and words of characters

You may also want to make this list with other stories; "A & P" by John Updike, "Where Are You Going, Where Have You Been?" by Joyce Carol Oates, "Everyday Use" by Alice Walker, "A Very Old Man with Enormous Wings" by Gabriel García Márquez, "Chac-Mool," by Carlos Fuentes, and "Sonny's Blues" by James Baldwin are all good, easy-to-find stories with settings that play significant roles.

In order for the reader to be able to relate to the story, you must identify those details in your story which establish the time, the place, and the overall mood of the story. That does not mean that a story cannot have a minimum of physical descriptors and details; some of the best stories give very little detail to indicate setting. However, even for stories with seemingly few physical or temporal details, the writer chooses specific details to create a setting appropriate for the story. That gives the story a place, both geographically and emotionally or even symbolically, from which to start.

Richard Hugo says that you as the writer must know, at some instinctive level at least, where the story or poem takes place: "Knowing where you are can be a source of creative stability. If you are in Chicago you can go to Rome. If you ain't no place you can't go nowhere." Hugo goes on to explain, "The poem is always in your hometown, but you have a better chance of finding it in another. The reason for that, I believe, is that the stable set of knowns that the poem needs to anchor on is less stable at home than in the town you've just seen for the first time. At home . . . you have complicated emotional responses that defy sorting out. With the strange town, you can assume all knowns are stable, and you owe the details nothing emotionally." However, the author may not *always* know what's there in the story and what isn't; after all, much of great writing is as much subconscious or unconscious as it is planned out and carefully orchestrated. That's one reason we remind you to stay clear about—or at least open to—why you're writing a certain way; it's because the writing process is complex, so you've got to keep your wits about you.

Very often, beginning writers either don't imagine clearly at all, or imagine in too much fuzzy and nonspecific detail, and then they pass those inauthentic details along to the reader. As chapter 3 discussed, using specific detail is essential to any good writing.

Writing for Ideas and Practice 10-3

1. List all the specific physical, sensory details you can about the following places by brainstorming for two minutes each:

   a. Your bedroom

    b.   A beautiful place you have visited

    c.   Your kitchen when you were in high school or a teenager

    d.   The view from your window; pick an age

2. List all the specific physical, sensory details you can about the following events and times by brainstorming for two minutes each. Do not focus so much on what happened, as where and when it happened and what those places in time and space feel like now or felt like then.

    a.   Holidays when you were a child

    b.   The last day of school before summer in fifth or sixth grade

    c.   The Fourth of July

    d.   New Year's

    e.   Your birthday, last year

    f.   This morning's breakfast time

    g.   Your last visit to the doctor or the dentist

Look at what you've written. Are these vivid details? Do you have more than enough to write down? If so, that's because these are real experiences which you can connect to and which elicit a great deal of information and emotion; even if the emotion is not epic, it is *real,* and that's what makes a good setting: the details are tied to the real core of the story and what the story serves to depict.

Writing for Ideas and Practice 10-4

Here is the example we looked at in chapter 9, Katherine Ann Porter's "The Grave." Read the following paragraph and then list the setting details in it:

> The family cemetery had been a pleasant small neglected garden of tangled rose bushes and ragged cedar trees and cypress, the simple flat stones rising out of uncropped sweet-smelling wild grass. The graves were lying open and empty one burning day when Miranda and her brother Paul, who often went together to hunt rabbits and doves, propped their twenty-two Winchester rifles carefully against the rail fence, climbed over and explored among the graves.

Without having read the story, simply make some conjectures as you notice a couple of key details about the setting in this story:

1. What could the significance of a graveyard be?
2. Where is this place? Is it wild, or is it tame? What could that mean to the story?
3. Why might it be significant that this is a "burning day"?
4. What might the details about the foliage here suggest to you?
5. What might the fact that two young children are exploring graves suggest?

There are many levels to examine in such a rich story as "The Grave," but it might be helpful to note just two. One, this is what is called a "coming of age" or "initiation" story. The story concerns a part of Miranda's growing up. That information might be important in thinking about the questions above. Two, the setting of the story sets up a large pattern of living and dead things—the children, the graves; the foliage, the rifles; and so on. That interplay between life and death runs throughout the story and is important to Miranda's initiation experience. So the details in a story's setting can do a great deal to advance the characterizations and the conflicts in the story.

For many students of literature, both readers and writers, the skill of paying attention to the small details in a story is one of the most difficult skills to learn. However, students learn as they go to find all sorts of things they hadn't noticed in a first or even a second reading. Careful reading is always focused on details; as we noted in chapter 3, Vladimir Nabokov commanded all readers, "Fondle the details." It is no accident, for instance, that in Hawthorne's story, the wife's name is Faith, or that the story is set in Salem, Massachusetts—home of the Puritans and their witch trials. Nor is it, as we noted above, an accident that the story starts at sunset. You, too, can enrich your story by creating just the right setting. As you write, you discover details about place and time that you didn't realize existed in the story. Learning how to appreciate detail and how to select details and use them well can separate the mediocre story from the excellent one.

Writing for Ideas and Practice 10-5

1. Imagine a story in which a person faces a crisis involving a betrayal by a close friend. Then, write a few sentences about what you might write for each of the following setting components in such a story:
   a. Time
      1) Era in history
      2) Year
      3) Time of year
      4) Time of day
   b. Physical location
      1) Country or region
      2) City or town
      3) Type of building
      4) Type of room
   c. Mood
      1) Physical details to indicate the emotional overtones of the story
      2) Physical details to indicate the emotional journey of the protagonist, especially when the conflicts arise

Setting, then, forms a framework in which the story operates and unfolds; it gives the reader details about context, so that the story's actions become more concrete, and it gives the story boundaries in which to work. A story taking place in Poland in the 1800s will contain different actions and possibilities than a story taking place in the far future in a colony in outer space. Your choice of details, then, guides the reader and the story.

PLOT

A novel is a prose narrative of some length that has something wrong with it.
— *Randall Jarrell*

I can't allow any of my characters . . . to stop in some halfway position. This doubt-less comes of a Catholic education and a Catholic sense of history—everything works toward its true end or away from it, everything is ultimately saved or lost.
— *Flannery O'Connor*

So far we have talked about some very basic components of any piece of narrative fiction. In chapter 9, we discussed character, and how to build character, and conflict, and how conflict works with character overall. In this chapter, we have worked on setting, and the role it plays in telling the story.

The next element of narration, that which holds it all together, is called **plot**. Plot can be defined as the series of events in the story, chronological or not, which serve to move the story from its beginning through its climax or turning point and to a resolution of its conflicts. Further, plot is also why the story happens, why it moves from beginning to end, why the protagonist learns or grows or becomes something or chooses something. Plot, then, involves *storyline*—the things that happen—and *causality*—why they happen.

Writing for Ideas and Practice 10-6

Begin with this prompt:
She was barefoot when she heard the car door slam and his heavy boots.
1. Now, give yourself exactly fifteen minutes. Write everything you can think of without censoring anything. Do not read the next step until you are finished.
2. Now that you are finished, look at what you've written. In it, find the things that happen in the story. Notice specific actions the characters take or specific things that occur within the story—someone crosses the room, gets in a car, flies away in a hot air balloon, takes out a kitchen knife, seals an envelope.
3. Trace the things that happen in the story. Put them in some coherent order, though it need not be chronological order. If it would help, take out things which don't seem to make the story hold together or make sense. Invent new things you might add to

the story which might make the story flow toward the resolution of the conflicts the characters are facing internally and externally. Make a list of the events that you think might help to tell this story.

As we said in chapter 9, conflicts can be internal, such as a decision about what to do or how to feel; or conflicts can be external, involving some other person or force, such as an enemy or a situation. The central character with whom we identify or on whom we focus in a story is the **protagonist**. The things, characters, forces aligned against the central character, either internal or external, are called **antagonists**.

The protagonist doesn't have to be a "good guy" or perfect; in fact, in many good stories, the protagonist is imperfect and even flawed—Hamlet, or Scarlett O'Hara, or Oedipus in *Oedipus the King,* or Willy Loman in *Death of a Salesman,* or Achilles in *The Iliad,* or Hud in Larry McMurtry's *Horseman, Pass By,* or Jake Barnes in Hemingway's *The Sun Also Rises.* They all have serious personality issues which complicate matters considerably. Yet, of course, we *want* matters complicated; that's why the story interests us. Recently, in fact, even the stereotypical, good-guy heroes of the comic books have been seen as having more complex personalities—Batman in the recent series of movies, Superman in the "Death of Superman" series of comics, as well as a number of other comic series which push the previous boundaries of the genre. And, too, the most compelling heroes aren't all sugar and spice; David, a fascinatingly complex character in the Bible, possesses a deep devotion to God and a brilliant mind, but also a flawed desire for power and an imperfect sense of personal responsibility.

Nevertheless, no matter what the protagonist's struggles or character issues are, the writer must have a clearly identified protagonist or protagonists on whom the reader focuses and on whom all of the story is based. And sometimes it happens that just *defining who the protagonist is* presents problems. In some stories, writers present a series of events, with a character running through each, but the story is not clearly focused on a protagonist's dealing with some central issue or conflict(s). You must write your story so that you and the reader know who the protagonist is and what he or she is about.

It's fine to begin writing a story just to explore, without really knowing what's going on in the characters. In fact, that process of exploration is absolutely necessary. Plot isn't usually pre-packaged—it must be discovered as you write a first or second or even third draft of your story. And in a longer work, such as a novel or a movie screenplay, the writer may introduce more than one protagonist in storylines that all flow together with overlapping characters and events. However, even if you choose to do this, the rules are the same: the protagonist of your story, whether a "good guy" or not, is the person whose progress we follow as he or she moves through the conflicts in the story. By the time you know your characters and why they do what they do, you will be ready to show them to the reader. The reader must have the opportunity to focus on what the protagonist is choosing or learning. Some stories, such as *Lonesome Dove* by Larry McMurtry or *The Robber Bride* by Margaret Atwood contain more than one protagonist, but this fact does not violate our rule about focusing on a clearly defined protagonist. In stories with more than one protagonist, the writer is responsible for developing story lines and conflict developments and resolutions for each protagonist. The events in such stories may overlap, often making a story more complex and satisfying.

In any case, each protagonist must deal with the conflicts you present in your story, and in the course of the story make sure you move the protagonist from one facet of dealing with those conflicts to another.

The point or points at which the protagonist decides how to resolve the story's conflicts, or faces those conflicts, is called the **climax**. This place in the structure of every story is the meeting of forces and events which were caused by the conflicts and decisions and details in the story leading up to the climax. The climax is sometimes called the **turning point** of the story, because it is at this point in the story that the story moves from building conflict to resolving conflict, from introducing what's happening and why, to living out, acting out, the results of the decisions which were connected to the conflicts and rising action of the story.

(The climax is not necessarily the most exciting or violent moment in the story, although it can be. People discussing a movie make a mistake when they talk about the "climactic chase scene"; the chase may have something to do with the climax of the story, but just because a lot of cars go roaring by doesn't mean that the conflicts in the movie are resolved.)

Everything leading up to the climax is called **rising action**; everything that happens as a result of this decision or realization or turning point is called **falling action**. The reasoning here is obvious: the story is *about* the climax. Everything you decide to include in the story—events or details—either leads the protagonist to that moment (or series of moments) or is a result of that moment.

When you ride a roller coaster, as the car slowly leaves the station and pulls up the first long hill, you are already preparing for the drops you are about to make. In a story, everything leading up to the giant dropoff at the top is rising action, being pushed along by conflict and the decisions and characteristics of the protagonist and antagonists. But once the car tops the hill, once the decision has been made, there is no going back—the decision has to be lived out, the ride has to happen, and you have to just hang on and hope for the best. That's how it is with a story: the protagonist makes a series of decisions, and eventually, those decisions result in a climax which is the turning point upon which all the conflicts hinge. Everything in the story relates to that one group of moments—it may be one moment, it may be a series of moments—after which there is no going back. The story's ending *must occur*; it is inevitable. As Max Beerbohm said, in response to someone's lament that there are not enough happy endings in modern literature, "What's all this talk about happy or unhappy endings when it is a question of the *inevitable* ending?"

Then, after the conflicts have subsided, or, to use the roller coaster analogy, it's time to slow down and pull back into the station, your reader may look for what the critics call **resolution**. Another term for this part of the story is **denouement**, the part of the story in which you sum up or explain or bring the conflicts to their conclusion. It doesn't mean that all is well—it may be that all is terrible. It may be that the protagonist has consciously or unconsciously chosen something horrible or destructive or sad. But whatever the conclusion, it must be believable by a careful reader—it's not a surprise, at least not on the second or third reading—the things that you've told the reader make sense because of your carefully constructed plot structure.

In a story, let's say, a man gets up in the morning and feeds his fish. Is this a story? If a story is simply a series of events, as E. M. Forster suggests in *Aspects of the Novel*, then this is a story. But nothing *causative* happens. Of course, something *does happen*—he gets up and feeds his fish. But there's no conflict to be worked through. Something happens, but what we want to know is *why* it happens. Forster says that plot involves the addition of causality.

So consider another alternative: a man lies in his bed one morning and remembers his dead wife. He's all alone and miserable in his seedy little apartment. His life has no meaning without her; she's been dead three months and he doesn't even want to get out of bed. He's just about decided to lie in bed and just starve to death. But then he looks over at the fish tank. In it swim two fish, a male and a female, bright and shining in the slanting light coming in from the window above him as the sun rises. *She loved those fish*, he thinks. *She'd want me to feed them*, he thinks. *At least I have them to remember her by.* So he gets up and feeds the fish.

While this is far from a fully realized or articulate story, it has a definite protagonist, the man, and an antagonist, his grief and sadness, and it presents a clear progression of his dealing with this conflict and a tentative resolution of it. He is in conflict with his own grief and his own desire to stop his pain, the pain of just being alive. He is in literal physical conflict with the process of dying; if he doesn't get up and move about, get food, he will die. And if he doesn't get up, he will be making a choice to die, his way of resolving his conflict with his own pain and sorrow.

Once he has chosen to get up and feed the fish, is he over his grief? No, that process will take time. Will he be okay? We don't really know, but we know that he was able to deal with this particular time in his life and make a decision. In fact, he could have chosen to shoot himself, or to stay in bed and let the fish die too; either way, he makes a decision in response to the conflicts he faces. But if all you have is just a picture of him lying there sad, it's not really a story as much as it's just a moment in a story. That picture may have emotional impact as it presents a single picture of someone in his grief, just as a painting has impact even though it may not tell a story. However, a story does not just present a character's grief; a story presents how that character deals with the grief.

Now it's your turn. Try out some exercises to test your understanding of and ability to deal with the issue of the protagonist and plot.

Writing for Ideas and Practice: 10-7

1. In Writing for Ideas and Practice 9-1.4, you imagined a scene based on an artifact or piece of clothing. Take the person you associated with it and invent a scene in which this person walks around, speaks. Find one simple thing the person must decide or deal with. Not huge — not necessarily a meaning-of-life moment, just little, like whether to sell a calf or whether she was really stealing just because she borrowed those houseshoes and never returned them.

2. Look back at the Writing to Warm Up exercise at the start of this chapter. Take any simple story everybody knows, like Jack and the Beanstalk or Cinderella, one with a definite beginning, middle, and end in which a main character deals with a problem or situation in some way that resolves that issue (unlike Yankee Doodle going to town and calling his feather macaroni, which of itself is just a fragment of a story). Outline it by listing the parts of the story. Study how the small components in it all add up to produce a specific result in the climax and resolution of the conflicts of the story.

3. What would happen if you, like someone who tells jokes badly, retold the story and left some of those basic components out? Retell the story, but forget to include a crucial detail — that Snow White's mother dies when Snow White is just a girl, or that Princess Aurora's parents forgot to invite the evil fairy to the christening — and tell someone else the story or let them read your version of it. Discuss what happens to the story's resolution when the plot detail is left out.

4. Read a newspaper article, one at least two columns long. Does it have a climax? What are some differences between a newspaper article and a short story or novel? What does this tell you about setting up your own narrative writing?

5. Read a short story and find its climax. This can be a story you pick on your own, or a story your instructor assigns you to read. At what point in the story is the protagonist either
   a. Making a decision,
   b. Discovering something about him/herself or the world or both, or
   c. So far along in the development of the events of the story that he/she can't go back to where the story started?

   It may be that the story has more than one turning point, a series of turning points or climaxes. It may be a series of points in the story which work together to move the action from rising to falling, from introduction of conflict to resolution of conflict. This is especially true in a novel, in which the longer format of the work presents a greater opportunity for weaving a number of storylines and conflicts, and so may require not merely one scene as a turning point, but a series of them. (And, as well, a series of details or events to form the resolution of the many conflicts in a story may be necessary.)

Many elements in the story can propel the story towards its climax and resolutions.

First, the conflicts within and outside the protagonist are the engine driving the story forward. The story recounts the protagonist's movement through the conflicts in the story toward a resolution of those conflicts.

Any details that you introduce into the story should move the story toward its climax and resolution, though some details will do so indirectly. For instance, consider a series of descriptive physical and background details showing that the antagonist, Bart, is self-centered and selfish—he likes to kick cats, he hated his schoolmates, he curses incessantly, he cheats in every interaction. These may seem only to be details about his character. However, the moment will come when the protagonist, Sheriff Dan, Bart's brother, must choose between either shooting down the suspected cattle rustlers in cold blood in the dark alleyway, or facing them honestly and giving them a chance to defend themselves in court. Knowing that Bart cares only about his own safety will make the moment more powerful when, on that fateful evening, Dan has the rustlers cornered and must decide how to react while Bart stands behind him whispering, "Kill 'em, Dan—or they'll get you first!" Knowing that he is selfish does not merely enrich Bart as a character; the tension that detail provides drives the story toward the climax, making Dan's climactic choice all the more powerful.

Further, sometimes authors use **foreshadowing** to move the story forward. Foreshadowing is giving hints about what inevitably must happen or be decided, as a way of creating tension and rising conflict, and also weaving the elements in the story together so that they are unified. If, early in the story, the protagonist looks down and notices an axe on the table of his girlfriend's apartment, the reader may feel uneasy and, if only subconsciously, wonder what the axe's presence will mean to the unfolding of the story. Whether the girlfriend turns out to be a serial killer or a weekend forestry worker, the foreshadowing helps move the story even closer to its eventual outcome.

Other characters beside the protagonist and antagonists also can move the story forward. Sometimes extra characters whose function is simply to highlight what the protagonist is experiencing are called **flat characters**. **Round characters**, like protagonists, are three-dimensional, complex, full of possibilities for actions and conflicts. However, the phone operator, the waiter, the policeman, the bystander—these are all characters whom the writer might put in a certain scene for much the same reason that any object might appear. They help the scene become realized for the reader in a way that advances the action.

Note, too, that your stories should not be full of **stock characters**. Stock characters are characters so obvious and predictable that their roles and personalities are nothing but cliches. The kindly old lady, the scheming butler, the nerdy teacher, the brute with a heart of gold—these cliche characters can serve a purpose in advancing the action of your story in that they can provide a plot detail or development that moves the story forward, but we advise you to avoid cliches in your writing, and this pertains especially to character development. Your flat characters need not be stereotypical just because they are not the protagonists of the story. Think of each piece of narrative fiction as someone's story. And in every person's story, some people play major roles and some minor—but those playing minor roles in one person's story play major roles in other stories.

And in fact, the details you choose to include in the story may appear simply to make the story richer overall. Every single detail does not have to be directly related to the plotline, even though, as we said above, in a sense every detail relates to the advancement of the plot at least indirectly. In every story, some characters play simply functional roles (to give street directions, trip the antagonist at the street corner, even serve as contrasts to the main characters), but this is not to say that those playing minor roles may not have interesting characteristics. Readers take great delight in minor characters into which the writer has put much detail to add to the "margins" of the story. Moneypenny in the James Bond stories, Barney Fife on "The Andy Griffith Show," Falstaff in Shakespeare's plays—all of these side characters can enhance the story if the writer makes their actions, appearance, and dialogue vivid and specific, even though their role is still simply to support or contrast the protagonist.

Further, the story need not move from one event to another chronologically—it may use flashback, to slip back and forth from present to past, or it may use **stream of consciousness**. In stream-of-consciousness stories, the protagonist relates her thoughts through interior monologues as she goes through the actions of the story, and those thoughts will not necessarily be sequential or linear. The reader experiences both external action and internal thoughts and feelings about the actions and conflicts in the story.

All of these devices are ways in which you can build your story's plot, moving from introducing characters and conflicts through the protagonist's resolution of those conflicts. But how do you know for sure where the turning point of the story is? If it isn't the chase scene or the bomb exploding, what is it? Well, it certainly *can* be the big event; in Melville's *Moby Dick*, it's the cataclysmic encounter between Ahab and the Whale. The key is to find what's happening in the protagonist: wherever he or she has to deal with the conflict, by making a decision or by going through some change or development, that's going to be tied to the climax of the story. If a story has conflicts, it will have to resolve them, even if it's not a tidy or happy ending. Remember: if a story doesn't have conflicts, it's not a story.

A good way to analyze a story's plot—either your own story or another writer's—is to read the story and then go back and read the story again, paying close attention to the details the author uses to prepare you for what happens in the climax of the story; then, go back and identify the climax of the story. Once you've located that turning point in a story, you know what the story's about.

Here is a short short story which will provide an example of plot development. Read the story, looking for who the protagonist is, what conflicts the protagonist must deal with—and how those conflicts are resolved.

 ### The Appalachian Trail

Today she tells me that it is her ambition to walk the Appalachian Trail, from Maine to Georgia. I ask how far it is. She says, "Some two thousand miles."

"No, no," I reply, "you must mean two hundred, not two thousand."

"I mean two thousand," she says, "more or less, two thousand miles long. I've done some reading, too, about people who've completed the journey. It's amazing."

"Well, you've read the wrong stuff," I say. "You should've read about the ones that didn't make it. Those stories are more important. Why they gave up is probably why you shouldn't be going."

"I don't care about that, I'm going," she says with a determined look. "My mind is made up."

"Let's say you walk, on average, some twenty miles a day. That's twenty into two thousand, right? It goes one hundred times. And so, one hundred equals exactly one hundred years. It'll take you one hundred years!"

"Don't be stupid," she says. "One hundred days, not years."

"Oh, yeah, okay, days," I mumble. I was never good at math. I feel as if someone has suddenly twisted an elastic band around my forehead. I crumple the paper, turn to her and say, "So if it's one hundred days, what is that? How many months?"

"A little over three." She calculates so fast that I agree without thinking. "Fine, but call it four months," I say, "because there's bound to be some delay: weather, shopping for supplies, maybe first-aid treatments. You never know, you have to make allowances."

"All right, I make allowances, four months."

What have I done? It sounds as if all of this nonsense is still in full swing. Say more about the time. "Okay," I say, "so where do we get the time to go? What about my job? What about my responsibilities, your responsibilities too? What about—?"

"What about I send you a postcard when I finish the trip," she says, leaving the room.

I sit there mouthing my pen. I hear her going down the basement steps. Pouting now, I think. Sulking. She knows she's wrong about this one.

"Seen my backpack?" she calls from below. God, she's really going to do it. "Next to mine," I say. "On the shelf beside the freezer."

I am angry with myself. She has had her way, won without even trying. "Take mine down too," I blurt out. "You can't expect to walk the Appalachian Trail all alone." I stare at my feet. "Sorry," I say to them both. "I'm really sorry about all of this."

— *Bruce Eason*

The protagonist, the person telling the story, has a dilemma; the woman is taking a hiking tour—without him. At the beginning of the story, he doesn't understand what she's talking about. So, in the course of the story, he has to deal with his own resistance to her idea about taking this trip. By the end of the story, he must decide whether he will allow her to leave him and go, try to get her not to go, or accept what she wants to do and its ramifications for their relationship. Where is that point in the story? Throughout the story, the protagonist shows his resistance to his companion's trip as she packs to go. As he lists his reasons why she should not go, she barely responds. The story is not about how she feels, but about how he feels about her and about her leaving.

So it's really a story not about the hiking trip, but about his role in their relationship, which the issue of the trip complicates and brings to light. When he says, still hanging onto his resistance, "I hear her going down the basement steps. Pouting now, I think," he is still holding onto his contention that she is wrong to go on this trip, or even perhaps that she is going on this trip as a way to interact with him or give him a message about their relationship. Then, when he figures out that she is not going to give in and stay even though he has told her he wants her to, he says, "She has had her way," and then calls to her to get his backpack. He has by then decided to go with her on her trip, but, more than that, to give in, not to resist her. His resolutely apologizing to his feet indicates that he is not happy about his decision to go along—so this isn't a particularly hopeful resolution of the conflicts in their relationship and within the protagonist. In fact, the conflicts between them may not be resolved at all, but the conflict *in this story*—how he will react to her going on this trip—has been resolved.

One way or the other, the story is about how he faces the conflict between them and within himself. Eason has included details that move the protagonist from his awareness of their relationship at the beginning of the story to his (possibly) new awareness of their relationship—his role in the relationship and who is in control of the relationship—by the end of the story.

If the story isn't carefully constructed, the reader can get lost. But if the story is clearly arranged in a coherent order that presents conflicts and resolves them, then the ending of the story will always be inevitable—it will have **dramatic unity**. What do the terms "inevitable" or "unified" mean? Don't a story's characters have free will? Or doesn't the writer have the freedom to just decide to blow everybody up in a super-surprise ending? Well, good writers try to make conscious choices about what happens in their stories so that the story's plot is consistent with its characterizations and conflicts.

Anton Chekov, the Russian playwright and short story author, is famous for his "zero endings." Many of his stories seem to come to impossibly abrupt conclusions—or perhaps no conclusions; they just end. And yet, it was this same Chekov who gave this warning about his three-act plays: "If a gun is on the wall in Act I, it must be fired in Act III." What he means, in part, is that the things the author chooses to include *matter*. The details contribute to the working out of the plot—they're not just thrown in at random. The author chooses to create character and to advance the plot of the story. And when you become a good reader—and that comes from practice —you begin to notice details that mean something.

In a horror or suspense movie, you know when you hear the scary music that something scary is coming. The movie *Jaws* is a perfect example —when you see the fin far off in the water, five minutes before anyone is eaten, you know it's going to happen. As a writer, your job is similar; if your character is a killer, you somehow have to prepare the reader for somebody to die. We looked earlier at how Flannery O'Connor uses carefully chosen details to create vivid characters in the short story "A Good Man Is Hard to Find." In the opening paragraph, she includes details to set the tone for the story, and to indicate how the story will be resolved:

> The grandmother didn't want to go to Florida. She wanted to visit some of her connections in east Tennessee and she was seizing at every chance to change Bailey's mind. Bailey was the son she lived with, her only boy. He was sitting on the edge of his chair at the table, bent over the orange sports section of the *Journal*. "Now, look here, Bailey," she said, "*see* here, read this," and she stood with one hand on her thin hip and the other rattling the newspaper at his bald head. "Here this fellow that calls himself The Misfit is aloose from the Federal Pen and headed toward Florida and you read here what it says he did to those people. Just you read it. I wouldn't take my children in any direction with a criminal like that aloose in it. I couldn't answer to my conscience if I did."

The tiniest details in this opening paragraph correspond exactly to the entire story's plot. Sure enough, Bailey keeps on ignoring his mother; sure enough, he and the family go towards Florida; sure enough, they meet The Misfit there; sure enough, as the grandmother predicts, The Misfit kills them all. What's amazing, too, are the tiniest little details—the Grandmother stands "rattling" in this opening paragraph; in the end of the story, she is compared to a snake trying to bite The Misfit. No details and no words are wasted in O'Connor's work.

You may respond, *But surely just because someone is scared of the potential threat of a serial killer in the first paragraph of the story, that doesn't mean that everyone in the opening paragraph is going to die by the end of the story!* And that's true. It's not a mathematical formula; Chekov was simply saying that the author of a well-crafted piece of writing picks its details carefully in order to cause a certain inevitability in it—a unity of purpose in everything about the story. That's a tall order, but it can be done, and it's a goal you should work toward. Rick wrote a short story in graduate school for a writing contest; one of the judges was John L'Heureux, the poet and short story writer, who had come to the literary festival at the university. Here's Rick's description of the experience:

> I was fortunate enough to have L'Heureux read my story and then go over it with me in a private session; it was an overly long story with some nice action and beginning character development but no real point, one which I had written at the last minute because my professor had commanded it. However, instead of telling me I was an idiot, L'Heureux very kindly asked as we went through the story, "Now, why

is this detail here?" or, "Why does the character do this in this way? What are you hoping to make happen in the story, or tell us about this character?" It was an eye-opening experience, and one for which I will be eternally grateful. A girl with a much shorter and much clearer story won the contest. A friend said to me, "Man, your story was so much more thick, more complex than hers—I can't believe she won!" To which I replied, "Did you know what her story was about?" "Well, yeah," he admitted. "What was my story about?" I asked, but I knew the answer; *I* hadn't known what my story was about at all—I had just written it once through and hoped for the best.

So, this caveat: do not think that once you begin thinking about a story that all will be well, that it will automatically fall into place and all the plot details will appear and work together. It takes time to develop a storyline and characters that make sense and whose actions and words are related and appropriate for what is happening and being discovered in the story. Don't feel you have to have it all worked out before you can even begin—that won't work. Remember: one thing causes another; one thing builds on another; everything in the story is there for a reason.

Writing for Ideas and Practice 10-8

Here is a story with three possible endings. Pick the ending which you think is inevitable, given the details and plot structure of the beginning of the story. The story is not profound or even good; it is a super-simplified story meant to illustrate the point about rising action and conflict leading inevitably to a clear and precisely chosen resolution.

The scruffy young man with his tousled hair and wrinkled green shirt was sauntering across campus, missing home and kicking the sidewalk. He was thinking of his room and his house and his faraway best friend Louis and his high school sweetheart, when he saw a beautiful woman walking towards the library. Her golden hair shone in the sun like a beacon. She was amazing. So he ditched his Biology lab (which he hated because he didn't know anyone in it—just like all his other classes), and he began to follow her as she walked up the bright sidewalk. Far ahead of him, she would stop briefly as she went, talking to passersby and waving. "She knows everybody on campus," the young man thought to himself. He walked alone, dreaming of her, a halo around her head.

When she arrived at the library, she took the elevator down to the basement floor where the student lounge was located. Ten seconds behind her, the young man took the elevator down and followed her into the lounge. He watched as she talked to a group of Big Men On Campus. She smiled and laughed and talked, confidently patting and hugging the large men around her, who obviously adored her. The young man watching slumped into a chair in a dark corner across the room, frowning.

ENDING A

> Then, the shining young woman suddenly turned away from the men she had been talking to and walked back toward the elevator — and the dark young man. As she passed him, he looked up at her. She didn't see him. And he left an hour later, packed his bags, and took the first bus home.

ENDING B

> Then, the shining young woman turned away from the men she had been talking to and walked back toward the elevator—and the dark young man. As she passed him sitting there, she smiled and stopped. "Hi there, good looking," she said, looking straight into his eyes. He was paralyzed with fear. "I'm Sandy," she said; "Would you take me to the big Sorority Dinner on Saturday?"
>
> He couldn't believe it! "Yes!" he cried. "Yes! You're amazing!" And he got up, took her hand, and walked with her onto the elevator—where they began kissing like mad.

ENDING C

> Then, the shining young woman pulled out a small machine gun. "Hold it right there!" she screamed, and began spraying bullets all over the lounge. "This is for Buffy!"
>
> "No, don't!" the young man shouted, and he leapt over a table and pulled her to the ground, knocking the gun from her hand. She struggled, but it was no use.
>
> The campus police came, later, and awarded him the University's highest honor.

Discuss with your classmates which ending you chose, and then defend your choice with details from the story. Does everyone agree? One of these endings might be plausible; one of them, hopefully, is ridiculous—although it's the kind of thing we see in the movies and TV all the time. And one ending is possible but not likely, given the details of the story.

Practice this kind of careful consideration of what is happening in the story and why it makes the plot work. As Ezra Pound said, "Dichten = condensare"; that's his way of saying to write is to condense, writing is taking the details that matter and composing them in such a way that they make sense in the form or genre you're using. Real life may not be of much help in helping form your story—in fact, as we have discussed, it may be a hindrance. Ivy Compton-Burnett said, "As regards plots I find real life no help at all. Real life seems to have no plots." So it will not always occur that a story just jumps up from your experience or your imagination, fully formed and unified. It might. But it may take a while for you to discover how a story's structure is going to hold together; it may take many drafts and critiques of the story. A detail or element here or there may not seem to fit or have a purpose in advancing the story and the protagonist towards and through the story's climax and resolution. But keep working on the story, and let things emerge as they will. Sometimes a happy accident, a detail that just won't go away, may give you a new sense of what the story is really about. In time the true story, its purpose, and the truly causal relationship between the characters and the events in the story, will emerge.

One has an impulse to bring glad tidings to someone. My sense of literature is a sense of giving, not admonishment. I know almost no pleasure greater than having a piece of fiction draw together disparate incidents so that they relate to one another and confirm that feeling that life itself is a creative process, that one thing is put purposefully upon another, that what is lost in one encounter is replenished in the next, and that we possess some power to make sense of what takes place.

— *John Cheever*

Writing on Your Own

1. Write a short story (five hundred to one thousand words). You might want to consider writing about a person dealing with a problem in a relationship with another person, about a person struggling in a desperate and possibly life-threatening situation, or about a person who is unable to cope with a terrible burden he/she faces. In the story, as we have discussed, include the following elements:
   a. A protagonist;
   b. At least one antagonist, and conflicts;
   c. A turning point/climax;
   d. Resolution of the conflicts introduced in the rising action of the story.
2. Go back and answer the following questions about the story in the exercise above, or about another story you have written:
   a. Who is the protagonist?
   b. Who is the antagonist? Does the story contain more than one? In what ways does the antagonist(s) impede the progress or thwart the efforts and desires of the protagonist?
   c. List all of the other characters in your story, if there are any. Why do these characters appear in the story, and what function do they perform towards propelling the protagonist on to his/her inevitable conclusion, if any?
   d. What was most difficult about making decisions about plot and pacing? What was most helpful about making decisions about plot and pacing? Did those decisions change your sense of the story as you went?
3. Read another student writer's story.
   In that story, locate the following items and make a list of these items, with very brief notes or information for each item:
   a. The protagonist;

b.   The antagonist;

c.   The basic conflicts;

d.   The events which contribute to rising action;

e.   The events which are part of falling action; and

f.   The turning point of the story after which there is no going back for the protagonist.

Do not evaluate the story. If there are any of the items which you feel you cannot locate exactly, give two or three alternatives and then note that you're not sure.

Return the story to its author.

Read what someone else said about the same list of elements in the story you wrote. Did the story communicate clearly? Are the components of its plot structure obvious? Don't worry yet that they may be too obvious; better at the beginning to be a little too obvious, but clear about what you're trying to do, rather than vague because you don't really know what the story's about. And make no mistake: good stories aren't really *about* anything as much as they *show* something *happening in a working out of a character's internal and external struggles.* If a writer says, *But it's a story about love and friendship,* but the plot is convoluted and confused and the protagonist's journey isn't clear, then it's not a story about love and friendship; it's not a story about anything at all.

Writing to Revise

Find a short story you have written before, or use the story you wrote for Writing on Your Own, above. Read the story several times, noticing its structure and how it introduces conflicts, traces them, and resolves them.

a.   Take any one element of the story—a character, an important moment, a conflict, an issue to be dealt with—and change it. Think of how this element, when changed, will change the story; if the protagonist's major stressor was his strained relationship with his father, then make his conflict be with someone else or be about something else with his father.

b.   Rewrite all or part of the story to include this new conflict, replacing any words or images or information in the story that contributed to the construction with that element in it.

c.   Consider how the story changed; did it change for the better? Was it difficult for you to let some of the first story go? Is it important for the story to include certain things in order to remain the same story? Would you be willing to do this kind of revision on a story you're pleased with?

11

The Voice of a Story: Point of View

Writing to Warm Up

1. Describe the voice of one of your parents, your spouse, or another key figure in your life. Be specific: include details about things like tone, pitch, and cadence. What kinds of things does this person often—or always—say? List at least ten things this person says a lot.

2. Quickly, write down a few typical statements which you imagine the following persons might make:
   a. Policeman, 1940s, New York City
   b. Tribal leader, Africa, before Europeans came
   c. Farmer, China, 100 B.C.
   d. Religious hermit, A.D. 349, Egyptian desert
   e. Mother of Roman emperor, A.D. 204

3. Even without the obvious language differences, what are the distinctions between the *types* of things these different people in different contexts say?

A further consideration beyond character, conflict, setting, and plot for the narrative writer is **point of view**. The term *point of view* does not refer to the writer's attitude or opinion toward the subject. Rather, it is a technical device the writer uses: every story is told by a voice, and that voice and the way the author uses it to tell the story make up the story's point of view.

Along with getting a clear sense of the ways in which the story's conflicts work and what those conflicts and the plot and setting devices in the story will show the reader, you'll need to think about who should tell the story and how you want the story told.

The writer can choose from many points of view in telling the story, and each one has certain advantages and certain limitations. The trick is probably not to decide artificially beforehand which one to use and then to tailor an entire novel around the manipulation of that particular point of view, although certainly authors have done so, some to great effect. And certainly you can benefit by practicing certain literary points of view in exercises aimed at learning which point of view is best in which circumstance. But, like any other practice—football drills, drum rudiments—the exercises are only ways to become proficient at the real thing.

Often, writers can get caught up in thinking that the practice is the real thing, that a new trick they've learned or a new voice they've read is that magic thing they've been looking for, the secret that will unlock the scene they've been working on or that will give them the answer to their worries about their voice. But in most cases, experiments with new tricks are merely tricks. Don't be fooled. *Telling the story so that the reader experiences the protagonist's central experience* is the point. The means you use to convey your story and your experience are not the point.

Becoming proficient at the real thing doesn't happen on the first draft. It *certainly* doesn't happen when one sits down and says, "I'm going to write a great novel using the objective point of view." Instead, good writers look at the scene they want to convey, the feelings associated with it, the information they want to give the reader, and then experiment with what kind of voice would suit that arrangement best.

FIRST PERSON

Writing for Ideas and Practice 11-1

1. In a two-hundred-word paragraph, create a scene in which you as an observer describe a man sitting in his easy chair watching television after a long day, when something horrible comes on the news that makes him cry.
2. In a new two-hundred-word paragraph, write the same scene, only this time, tell it imagining that you are the man in the easy chair watching television. Everything the reader experiences must be what he experiences.
3. List five differences between the two paragraphs.

First person involves changing your own voice as a storyteller and injecting *I* into every scene that your narrative contains. As the storyteller, you write as if you were one of the characters in the story. **First person**, then, is that point of view in which the narrator takes on the persona of one of the characters in the story and tells the story as that character, using the terms *I* or *we*.

This point of view is **limited**. You can only include details in the story itself that your character would know. For instance, if you want to tell a story from the viewpoint of a dog, you can't really have the dog understand the complexities of human interaction or understanding—the dog can't read, the dog can't drive a car, the dog, really, can't even understand English, except the most basic commands (unless it's Lassie, and she understands when Timmy explains to her where Mommy is and to go get help before the mine shaft caves in). The temptation exists—as in the example of Lassie—to bend the rules a little. And in some cases bending the rules might help to involve the reader or to heighten things like comic effect or a sense of magic. But the rule generally stands that in a first-person narrative, the narrator must stay that character, or, as is said in acting, you must stay "in character."

First person, both despite and because of this limitation, has great *power*. Why? Because you thrust the reader's imagination into the body, head, experiences, and emotions of the character within the story who tells the story, with all the trappings and accents and flaws and strengths and weaknesses of that character's voice. Charles Dickens's novel *David Copperfield* begins this way: "I am born." Regardless of the limitations of the first person point of view, such an opening is sure to involve the reader.

Writing for Ideas and Practice 11-2

1. Find a piece of literature that is an example of first person. Who tells the story?
2. Find a piece of literature that isn't told in first person. Who tells that story?
3. What are the differences between the two?
4. Read the following selection from "Two Kinds," a story by Amy Tan, and notice what you know about the narrator:

> America was where all my mother's hopes lay. She had come here in 1949 after losing everything in China: her mother and father, her family home, her first husband, and two daughters, twin baby girls. But she never looked back with regret. There were so many ways for things to get better.
>
> We didn't immediately pick the right kind of prodigy. At first my mother thought I could be a Chinese Shirley Temple. We'd watch Shirley's old movies on TV as though they were training films. My mother would poke my arm and say, *"Ni kan."*—You watch. And I would see Shirley tapping her feet, or singing a sailor

song, or pursing her lips into a very round O while saying, "Oh, my goodness."

"*Ni kan,*" said my mother as Shirley's eyes flooded with tears. "You already know how. Don't need talent for crying!"

Soon after my mother got this idea about Shirley Temple, she took me to the beauty training school in the Mission district and put me in the hands of a student who could barely hold the scissors without shaking. Instead of getting big fat curls, I emerged with an uneven mass of crinkly black fuzz. My mother dragged me off to the bathroom and tried to wet down my hair.

"You look like Negro Chinese," she lamented, as if I had done this on purpose.

Answer the following questions about the narrator:
a. What kind of person is this narrator? What are the narrator's assumptions, beliefs, political views, desires, prejudices?
b. What conflict is the narrator dealing with? What does that say about the narrator?
c. What sort of attitude does the narrator have? How do you know?
d. What is this narrator's main interest/objective—at this moment, and in general?
e. How do you imagine the narrator to look? Where does the narrator live?
f. What do you imagine the narrator to be doing now? What will the narrator do in the next part of the story?

Sometimes the narrator's voice can be eccentric; sometimes the character might be slanted, but that's part of the power of first person point of view. For instance, Mark Twain's Huckleberry Finn is a complex, fascinating character, and the book *The Adventures of Huckleberry Finn* is especially powerful partly because Huck himself tells the story. Huck does not simply report the story; he communicates from a specific psychological and philosophical perspective and takes the reader through every experience he undergoes. Here is how he talks:

I never felt easy till the raft was two miles below there and out in the middle of the Mississippi. Then we hung up our signal lantern, and judged that we was free and safe once more. I hadn't had a bite to eat since yesterday, so Jim he got out some corn-dodgers and buttermilk, and pork and cabbage and greens—there ain't nothing in the world so good when it's cooked right—and whilst I eat my supper we talked and had a good time. I was powerful glad to get away from the feuds, and so was Jim to get away from the swamp. We said there warn't no home like a raft, after all. Other places do seem so cramped up and smothery, but a raft don't. You feel mighty free and easy and comfortable on a raft.

Huck's voice is very specific to his character; notice his vocabulary, with its particularities of grammar and region. Further, his talk reflects the things that are important to him, his outlook on the action of the story, his personal hopes and fears, and even the largest themes of the story (life in society which is corrupt versus life on a raft, free of people, in simplicity; the ideal relationship between human beings, based on equality and shared pleasures). Throughout the book, Huck's views on various issues direct the way we readers understand the action, which works well, because Huck is a disarmingly honest character, without any guile or self-interest.

What is the reader to think, though, if the narrator is *wrong*? If the first person point of view is slanted because the narrator is lying, this fact changes how the reader is to know what to think about the action and conflicts in the story. When the writer creates a character who is not to be trusted, this is known as an **unreliable narrator**. A good example is Ring Lardner's story "Haircut," as well as a number of narrators in Edgar Allan Poe's stories. Authors use this device for engaging the reader in the story even further, for the reader cannot merely observe the story as it unfolds — he must *figure out* the narrator and what is happening, which takes effort on the part of the reader and makes the story more involving and interesting.

The "unreliable" narrator, though, must nevertheless be consistent — that is, the author must be sure to explain somehow, even through the narrator, what is going on. Like a judge listening to the conflicting testimonies of two arguing neighbors, the reader must come to an understanding of the conflicts in the story not just as the narrator relates them, but as they are beyond their appearance. William Faulkner's *The Sound and the Fury* has four sections, the first three of which are narrated in turn by three brothers who all see the events of the novel from dramatically different perspectives. This point of view involves the reader in not only observing the action of the story, but seeing it from different first person viewpoints — a highly effective tool.

One of the most famous examples of this highly individual — and therefore powerful — first person narrator is the character who tells the Eudora Welty short story, "Why I Live at the P.O." This is how she starts off the story:

I was getting along fine with Mama, Papa-Daddy and Uncle Rondo until my sister Stella-Rondo just separated from her husband and came back home again. Mr. Whitaker! Of course I went with Mr. Whitaker first, when he first appeared here in China Grove, taking "Pose Yourself" photos, and Stella-Rondo broke us up. Told him I was one-sided. Bigger on one side than the other, which is a deliberate, calculated falsehood: I'm the same. Stella-Rondo is exactly twelve months to the day younger than I am and for that reason she's spoiled.

The reader sees immediately that there are all sorts of conflicts going on in this story — between the narrator, Sister, and Stella-Rondo; between Sister and her parents; between Sister and the town in general. This opening paragraph powerfully draws the reader into the story.

Another way to have a first person narrator tell a story is through some sort of literary setting: the epistolary, or letter-form, style, for instance, in which a character or characters tell the story through a series of letters, such as Alice Walker's *The Color Purple*. There is also the diary or travelogue, in which the character tells the story through his/her personal notes about the events in the story, such as Jonathan Swift's *Gulliver's Travels*.

The narrator doesn't have to be a main character; he or she may be an observer, like Nick Carraway in F. Scott Fitzgerald's *The Great Gatsby*, who watches the main characters and, by virtue of being a participant without being a protagonist, gives the reader a slightly removed perspective. William Faulkner uses such a narrator in the short story "A Rose for Emily," in which a townsperson notes the evolution over decades of the town's awareness that Miss Emily is not what she seems. Louise Erdrich uses such a narrator in "Fleur."

The first-person narrative, then, has some directness and power and the ability to manipulate the story in a number of ways. The first person narrator cannot comment on anything she does not know, so she is limited in what she can and cannot reveal. You'll need to experiment to see whether this approach creates the effect you want, and whether this point of view is appropriate for your story.

THIRD PERSON LIMITED

Closely related to first person but vastly more open to insertions and observations from the author or voice telling the story is **third person limited** point of view. Third person limited is when the narrator limits the action and information the reader receives to that which centers on and/or can be known by only one character in the story. Many, many narratives are told in this way; you can even switch the character you focus on section by section.* The writer chooses to listen in on one character's thoughts, to see things from that character's vantage point in the story. However, the narrator's voice is not that character's voice, as in first person. Instead, the narrator can use any voice—any style of language or structure the writer wishes—but he confines the perspective of the action in the story to that involving just one character.

However, some critics argue that that's a violation of this point of view.

In Hemingway's short story "Indian Camp," the narrator begins by telling the reader that some rowboats have pulled up on a lake shore and some people are getting into them. Then, though, the narrator begins to show the reader more than just the sights and sounds involved; he points our notice to one character in particular, and that character becomes the focus for how we see the story:

The two boats started off in the dark. Nick heard the oarlocks of the other boat quite a way ahead of them in the mist. The Indians rowed with quick choppy strokes. Nick lay back with his father's arms around him. It was cold on the water. The Indian who was rowing them was working very hard, but the other boat moved further ahead in the mist all the time.

"Where are we going, Dad?" Nick asked.

Hemingway takes the bare details of the scene and gives them a particular slant: we see them as if we were in the boat with Nick. We hear what he hears, we see the other boat from his perspective, we feel the cold he feels, we feel his father's arms around him, and we sense his apprehension. Notice that the story is better, more subtle, more powerful because Hemingway doesn't say something like "Nick was really terrified. He had never been across the lake before. It was dark and he huddled against his father for security." All of those things are true, but we aren't *told* them. Instead, by our seeing the story over Nick's shoulder, we are *shown* those things, we feel those things—but it's Hemingway's voice we hear telling us the story, not Nick's.

Joyce Carol Oates's short story "Where Are You Going, Where Have You Been?" is told strictly from the viewpoint of its protagonist, a fifteen-year-old girl named Connie.

It was too hot. She went inside the house and turned on the radio to drown out the quiet. She sat on the edge of her bed, barefoot, and listened for an hour and a half to a program called XYZ Sunday Jamboree, record after record of hard, fast, shrieking songs she sang along with, interspersed by exclamations from "Bobby King": "An' look here you girls at Napoleon's—Son and Charley want you to pay real close attention to this song coming up!"

And Connie paid close attention herself, bathed in a glow of slow-pulsed joy that seemed to rise mysteriously out of the music itself and lay languidly about the airless little room, breathed in and breathed out with each gentle rise and fall of her chest.

After a while she heard a car coming up the drive. She sat up at once, startled because it couldn't be her father so soon. The gravel kept crunching all the way in from the road—the driveway was long—and Connie ran to the window.

The narrator reveals certain details which any observer might notice or report, such as the heat, or the kind of songs on the radio Connie is listening to, or what the disc jockey says, or the sound of the gravel on the driveway. But Oates has chosen to limit the story to Connie's viewpoint without allowing Connie to tell the story herself, so everything that happens is reported as if the reader were looking and listening over Connie's shoulder. The narrator does not say, "a car came up the driveway," but "she heard a car coming up the drive." Further, "The gravel kept crunching *all the way in from the road*"—we are listening from within the house, where Connie is. "It was too hot" is not merely a report of the temperature, it is how Connie feels about the heat. And the third person narrator can say of Connie that she is "bathed in a glow of slow-pulsed joy"—when perhaps Connie herself, were she the first-person narrator, would not be able to articulate such feelings.

In third person limited stories, the author uses her own language patterns to tell the story, but keeps the focus on one character alone. The writer who uses this point of view, then, has the powerful combination of focusing intently upon one character's experiences, thoughts, and actions, and using a style and voice that the character herself might not use or insight that the character might not possess.

Writing for Ideas and Practice 11-3

1. Write a short scene in which appear many characters—perhaps five or so—but only one main character; tell the scene while looking over the shoulder of the protagonist.
2. Now, tell the same story while looking over the shoulder of a character observing the action of the story but not involved directly in it.
3. Look at a scene in any short story you like; make a list of brief notes of what any one character undergoes, sees, smells, thinks, hears, within the space of seven paragraphs.

Objective

We've talked about two points of view which fiction writers often use; now let's look at a third, which is less common but may be one you will want to try. The **objective point of view** is defined as "the fly on the wall" who simply notes what he sees and hears, without intrusion or interpretation. The observer isn't involved in the action of the scene; instead, he's just watching and listening. The objective point of view is characterized by its showing the audience only what the characters look like, say, or do.

Writing for Ideas and Practice 11-4

Write a quick scene for each of the following, recording only observations, sights, and sounds, but no intrusions into thoughts or feelings:
1. A man robbing a liquor store;
2. King Arthur and Queen Guinevere meeting in her bedchamber;
3. An elderly person with a grandchild at the park.

Like the first person and the third person limited, the objective point of view is restricted in what it can say directly to the reader. But it also has great impact, in that it is direct and uncluttered with anyone's—even, in a sense, a narrator's—observations or interpretations. The audience must interpret the actions and words of the characters directly, as opposed to being told by a narrator, or even by a character in the story. It is true that any information provided by any narrator will color how the reader perceives any scene because it is chosen by the narrator/writer, but the objective point of view removes *commentary* by the narrator. Here is an extreme example of intrusive narration:

Suzy felt just awful about slicing her whole family into bits. Her heart beat wildly within her chest as she remembered back to the abuse her mother and father had heaped upon her when she was only a baby. She knew, now, that she had found her revenge. Life is funny that way.

This passage is trite because the narrator has added superfluous and distracting observations as a way to *tell* the reader what to think or what to feel. The objective point of view eliminates this extra interpreter.

Here is an example of the objective point of view from the short story "Hills Like White Elephants" by Ernest Hemingway:

The hills across the valley of the Ebro were long and white. On this side there was no shade and no trees and the station was between two lines of rails in the sun. Close against the side of the station there was the warm shadow of the building and a curtain, made of strings of bamboo beads, hung across the open door into the bar, to keep out flies. The American and the girl with him sat at a table in the shade, outside the building. It was very hot and the express from Barcelona would come in forty minutes. It stopped at this junction for two minutes and went on to Madrid.

"What should we drink?" the girl asked. She had taken off her hat and put it on the table.

"It's pretty hot," the man said.

"Let's drink beer."

Note that in this section of the story, it seems so far that we haven't been told anything about how anybody feels or even what's going on in the scene. Yet even these rudimentary details show us that the story starts in the middle of something: the American and the girl are waiting for a train to come and take them somewhere. Something has already happened in their relationship; as the story unfolds, we see through their dialogue that they are arguing about whether or not to do something. Yet the voice we hear is just giving us the facts that any video camera could record.

Hemingway, who began his career as a reporter for the *Kansas City Star*, was trained in the reporter's code, which is to go and gather the facts and present them without discussion or opinion. He became famous for this sort of voice, which on one level appears to reveal nothing to the reader directly, and yet is very powerful, because the information the reader gets is not cluttered by extra information or interpretation and yet has been chosen and presented by the writer to achieve a particular, powerful effect.

For instance, in the opening we saw above, it may seem that nothing has been revealed to us except some bare facts. However, the entire story is about the couple's argument over whether to have an abortion. They are not married; the American wants to continue their free, unrestricted lifestyle, while the girl somehow wants to keep the man and the baby as well. While it might be tempting to a less accomplished writer to begin the story by explaining these things to the reader, Hemingway instead chooses to show the reader these things in the course of the actions of the story—indirectly, and yet more powerfully than if they had been spelled out.

Notice, too, that there is a kind of remove, a quietness, even, with this point of view. It's usually very distant and subtle. Sometimes it can feel cold. This effect may be good or bad, depending on your aim in telling the story. Raymond Carver uses this approach with powerful results in some of his short stories, which have been called "minimalist" precisely because of his use of this approach and because he only tells the absolutely necessary details. Notice the point of view he uses in these paragraphs from the short story "Popular Mechanics":

Early that day the weather turned and the snow was melting into dirty water. Streaks of it ran down from the little shoulder-high window that faced the backyard. Cars slushed by on the street outside, where it was getting dark. But it was getting dark on the inside too.

He was in the bedroom pushing clothes into a suitcase when she came to the door.

I'm glad you're leaving! I'm glad you're leaving! she said. Do you hear?

He kept on putting his things into the suitcase.

The point of view of this story is so distant and impersonal that it might be easy for the reader to stay removed at first from the emotions and conflicts in the story—and not to be ready for the end of the story and its disturbing conclusion.

Here is another example from "The Blue Hotel," a story by one of the pioneers of this point of view, Stephen Crane:

As the men trooped heavily back into the front room, the two little windows presented views of a turmoiling sea of snow. The huge arms of the wind were making attempts—mighty, circular, futile—to embrace the flakes as they sped. A gatepost like a still man with a blanched face stood aghast amid this profligate fury. In a hearty voice Scully announced the presence of a blizzard. The guests of the blue hotel, lighting their pipes, assented with grunts of lazy masculine contentment.

A great many specific, descriptive, vivid details abound—but no intrusion into the thoughts and feelings of the characters.

Critics will attack a story in which point of view is inconsistent. The reader may resent the writer who attempts the objective point of view and then inserts all sorts of supposedly clever or meaningful explanations throughout the story. Remember: if you're using the objective point of view, your narrator cannot tell the reader any of the characters' thoughts; your narrator cannot overtly explain what's going on in the story; your narrator cannot editorialize in an attempt to be sure the story makes sense.

Remember, too, as the earlier two chapters have discussed, that if the writer doesn't really know what the story's about, neither will the reader. So the objective point of view would be great to practice as a way of figuring out just what exactly the stories you're writing *are* about.

Writing for Ideas and Practice 11-5

1. Read the following paragraph from a romance novel, and then answer the questions below in response to it:

> She burned with passion and anguish; Where was Ronald? Would he come to her? Would she ever see him again? Thoughts swirled in her head, and she nearly swooned. And then, suddenly, he entered the room, the door swinging open, his hair blown about by the tempestuous wind. Her heart beat within her; Would he speak to her? What would she say? And he approached her, arms outstretched . . .

   a. List the details the objective narrator could include.
   b. List the details the objective narrator could not include.
   c. Can a romance novel be told by an objective narrator? Why or why not? What kinds of writing lend themselves to the objective point of view, and which do not?

2. Which of the following excerpts from newspaper articles is objective?
   a. Republicans, responding to threats from the President to override their latest Senate bill, petitioned the public today in a press conference in which Majority Leader Lewis reminded Americans of the "overwhelming need to deal with the budget crisis or else default on the future of all our children."
   b. The Republican majority, angered by the latest attacks by the White House, took their case to a beleaguered and angry American populace today, in a bold attempt to regain the advantage they held before. According to Senator Lewis, "America was bamboozled by the lies of the spending, taxing few." The message addressed an issue overdue for resolution.

3. Consider and then respond to this quote by the writer and teacher John Gardner:

> Whether you're writing about people or dragons, your personal observation of how things happen in the world can turn a dead scene into a vital one. Preliminary good advice might be: write as if you were a movie camera.

How much of your own writing violates this rule? How much obeys it?

4. List or find three stories you like; reread them, paying particular attention to each story's

point of view. For each story, write down why you think the author chose that particular point of view. What advantage did the author gain in choosing that point of view?

OMNISCIENT

A final major point of view to consider is one of the most prevalent, and certainly an immediate choice for many storytellers. The **omniscient** point of view is defined as the narrator of the story having and using access to any information, past or present, stated or silent, enacted or thought, relative to any character in the story he or she tells.

The narrator may include details happening at the present moment in the action of the story; the narrator may also include details which occurred previous to the present action. The narrator may include information about the thoughts and feelings of a character, and may also present the character's outward appearance, actions, and dialogue. The narrator can, essentially, report anything at all, internal or external, past or present —hence the term "omniscient" or all-knowing.

Writing for Ideas and Practice 11-6

1. Read the following excerpt; then, identify every character on whom the narrator focuses attention:

> The girl was watching carefully, her gaze fixed on the man in the corner. She had seen him, somewhere—but where? And why was he so familiar? Her Aunt Maud was one of those people who could remember everything, but Susan had no head for names. And, to her dismay, the man turned. He moved; he saw her. He noticed she was looking at him; *She is so beautiful,* he thought to himself, but didn't change his expression at all. Instead, he walked toward her, without looking directly at her. His friend Cottlestone looked up from the parlor door; his face turned pale; he nearly fainted. "It's the girl from the marketplace!" he hissed to Hedges, who was thinking about the weather.

2. Rewrite the paragraph, focusing on only one character.

The writer of the omniscient point of view must decide which details to include about each character and what is happening in the story, in order to advance the action of the story in the desired direction. Read this paragraph from the short story "The Pupil" by Henry James and note how James reveals information about the characters in the scene:

When Mrs. Moreen bethought herself of this pretext for getting rid of their companion, Pemberton supposed it was precisely to approach the delicate subject of his remuneration. But it had been only to say some things about her son which it was better that a boy of eleven shouldn't catch. They were extravagantly to his advantage, save when she lowered her voice to sigh, tapping her left side familiarly: "And all overclouded by *this,* you know—all at the mercy of a weakness—!" Pemberton gathered that the weakness was in the region of the heart. He had known the poor child was not robust: this was the basis on which he had been invited to treat, through an English lady, an Oxford acquaintance, then at Nice, who happened to know both his needs and those of the amiable American family looking out for something really superior in the way of a resident tutor.

In the paragraph, varied information is gathered from many sources to present to the reader a picture of how Pemberton will become the young boy's tutor. The reader gains insight into Mrs. Moreen's thoughts about why she sent her son out of the room; the reader is given some past history on how the meeting has come about; the reader learns a bit about Pemberton's thinking process; and the reader finds out something about the boy's health condition from the narrator's interpretation of the mother's comment. The omniscient narrator can get information anywhere and use it as it is appropriate.

The omniscient point of view is popular to use partly because it's fun to be omniscient, to tell the story by hopping from character to character, incident to incident, scene to scene, getting inside anyone's head you like. And it is a natural way to tell a story. If you want to tell a story about a group of people, you naturally want to relate details and experiences of importance to all the characters involved. The other points of view we've already talked about, in fact, can seem forced or artificial compared to the omniscient; the omniscient narrator sounds like someone talking, telling a story. And a great many novels and stories, it should come as no surprise, are told from the omniscient point of view. The narrator will move the story's focus from one character to another, one scene to another, even one time period to another. And as long as the story flows along and we don't get too lost, we accept this approach.

As you decide whether to use an omniscient narrator in your storytelling, consider something important. Remember that the major pitfall for writers regarding point of view is *inconsistency.* You must be vigilant about inconsistencies in point of view in any given work, especially longer works. This consistency may take several drafts to acheive. Saul Bellow has noted that he has only a few rules about his own writing, one of which is that he rewrites and revises everything he writes at least ten times. Ten times!

The omniscient point of view often faces the danger of becoming inconsistent. If the writer slides from character to character, listening in on their thoughts, watching things over their shoulders, and commenting on what they're going through, he is very likely to lose track of who's in charge and what the story is about. Like the guy who tells the story all wrong because he can't remember what the point is and includes all sorts of superfluous and distracting details instead of focusing on the few details which will drive the punch-line home, the inconsistent point of view isn't to be trusted.

The omniscient narrator, then, has the great advantage of knowing everything and commenting on everything, and faces the danger of losing focus. The omniscient narrator's focus can become very unclear, and the potential for wandering, sloppy storytelling is always present. It's easy to forget who the real protagonist is, and what the central issues of the story are.

Writing for Ideas and Practice 11-7

1. Write a story in which three characters lament a loss of some sort. In this story, find a way to move from character to character without simply jumping over. Writers use any number of means to tie parts of the story together. They may have a running image or setting detail common to all the characters — a river, a recliner, a handkerchief. Stories may employ a common character reacting to or the focus of all the other characters' thoughts. Or perhaps a plot device moves the reader from character to character.

2. Now, rewrite the scene, interweaving all three characters together — their thoughts, their actions, and an overall sense of how the whole thing works as a unified action.

3. Watch a TV show, perhaps a situation comedy. Take notes as you watch the show: which characters are the focus of the show? Does the show hop from character to character in focus, or does it stay with one character? What specific devices does it use to move from character to character, emphasis to emphasis?

4. Watch a soap opera. Soaps are the most interesting shows in which to track point of view. Actually attempt to write down all the characters who are central to each scene, and especially the ones whose thoughts we hear or see depicted in voice-overs or fantasy or memory sequences. Compare your notes with your classmates'; are the writers and directors of the soap opera you watched consistent in focusing the story?

As a writer, you need to decide along the way of drafting and revising your stories what point of view you will use in presenting the story to the reader. Making informed decisions about the advantages and limitations of each point of view and keeping the point of view within each story consistent will make your stories stronger.

Writing on Your Own

1. Take each of the following basic scenes and write four one-page treatments of it, each one using a different point of view; write each scene in first person, objective, third person limited, and omniscient. The scenes are:

    a. A bird on a sidewalk afraid of a dog on a leash wrapped around a tree — and then the leash snaps;

    b. A man in a crowded taxicab who finds a thousand dollars in the seat;

    c. A child sitting in the back of class raising his/her hand endlessly waiting to be called on, who suddenly realizes he/she doesn't know the answer this time.

2. With another writer, or perhaps just on your own, discuss the advantages and disadvantages of using each of the points of view.

    *   Which do you think is most problematic?
    *   Which is most used in the kinds of stories you write?
    *   Which are you most likely to use?
    *   Which have you started or stopped using lately?
    *   Which are you least likely to use? (It may come to be your favorite.)

Writing to Revise

1. Reread a story you have written and analyze what role your use of point of view played in the writing of the story.

    *   Was it hard to maintain a consistent point of view throughout?
    *   Did you find that as you wrote your drafts, your use of point of view changed?
    *   Did you find point of view considerations a hindrance, or helpful?
    *   Did you like writing in this particular point of view?
    *   Was it difficult?
    *   Was it easy?
    *   Is it a point of view you want to try writing with again? Why?

2. Rewrite a story you have written, changing the point of view. Make notes after you have rewritten the story about what worked well and what did not as you changed each part of the story to fit the new narrator and voice.

Internet Resources for Fiction and Literary Nonfiction

E-mail lists
Creative Writing List
CREWRT-L (listserv@mizzou2.missouri.edu) *A general creative writing list for teachers and students of creative writing — an active group.*

Usenet Discussion Groups
rec.arts.books *General discussion of a wide range of books and literature.*
rec.arts.prose *Specific to prose, but still general in its scope.*
alt.postmodern *Discussions of postmodern literature and writing.*

There are also many newsgroups that focus on fiction genres such as mystery and science fiction. Look at Deja News to see if your interests are represented here.

World Wide Web Sites
Inkspot
http://www.inkspot.com *A comprehensive site providing writers with helpful, practical resources. Also generated from this site is Inklings, an informative biweekly newsletter containing articles on writing and interviews. For more information, send an e-mail message to info@inkspot.com.*
WordSmith's WebBook
http://alfalfapress.com/ws/wswb.html *Articles on writing and links to articles on writing.Includes online resources and a listserv.*
The Eclectic Writer
http://www.eclectics.com/writing/writing.html *Discussions on writing, links to publishers, writers' resources on the Net.*
The Write Page
http://www.writepage.com/index.html *Offers helpful links for writers and advice on writing which focuses on genre.*
Pure Fiction
http://www.purefiction.co.uk/contents.htm *Advice on writing and book reviews. Focuses on mainstream works.*

Narration to Consider

Literary Nonfiction

Frank Conroy

from Stop-Time

Is it the mindlessness of childhood that opens up the world? Today nothing happens in a gas station. I'm eager to leave, to get where I'm going, and the station, like some huge paper cutout, or a Hollywood set, is simply a façade. But at thirteen, sitting with my back against the wall, it was a marvelous place to be. The delicious smell of gasoline, the cars coming and going, the free air hose, the half-heard voices buzzing in the background—these things hung musically in the air, filling me with a sense of well-being. In ten minutes my psyche would be topped up like the tanks of the automobiles.

Downtown the streets were crowded with shoppers. I cut in and out between the slow-moving cars, enjoying my superior mobility. At a red light I took hold of the tailgate of a chicken truck and let it pull me a couple of blocks. Peeling off at the foot of Los Olas Boulevard, I coasted up to the bike rack in front of the Sunset Theater.

It cost nine cents to get in. I bought my ticket, paused in the lobby to select a Powerhouse candy bar, and climbed to the balcony. The theater was almost empty and no one objected when I draped my legs over the seat in front. On the screen was a western, with Randolph Scott as the sheriff. I recognized a cheap process called Trucolor and hissed spontaneously, smiling foolishly at the empty darkness around me afterwards. Except for the gunfights the film was dull and I amused myself finding anachronisms.

The feature was better, an English movie with Ann Todd as a neurotic pianist and James Mason as her teacher. I was sorry when the house lights came on.

Outside, blinking against the sun, I left my bike in the rack and wandered down the street. Something was happening in front of the dime store. I could see a crowd of kids gathered at the doors and a policeman attempting to keep order. I slipped inside behind his back. The place was a madhouse, jammed with hundreds of shrieking children, all pressing toward one of the aisles where some kind of demonstration was going on.

"What's happening?" I asked a kid as I elbowed past.

"It's Ramos and Ricardo," he shouted. "The twins from California."

I pushed my way to the front rank and looked up at the raised platform.

There, under a spotlight, two Oriental gentlemen in natty blue suits were doing some amazing things with yo-yos. Tiny, neat men, no bigger than children, they stared abstractedly off into space while yo-yos flew from their hands, zooming in every direction as if under their own power, leaping out from small fists in arcs, circles, and straight lines. I stared open-mouthed as a yo-yo was thrown down and *stayed down*, spinning at the end of its string a fraction of an inch above the floor.

"Walking the Dog," said the twin, and lowered his yo-yo to the floor. It skipped along beside him for a yard or so and mysteriously returned to his palm.

"The Pendulum," said the other twin, and threw down a yo-yo. "Sleeping," he said, pointing to the toy as it spun at the end of its string. He gathered the line like so much loose spaghetti, making a kind of cat's cradle with his fingers, and gently rocked the spinning yo-yo back and forth through the center. "Watch end of trick closely," he said smiling, and suddenly dropped everything. Instead of the tangled mess we'd all expected the yo-yo wound up safely in his palm.

"Loop-the-Loop." He threw a yo-yo straight ahead. When it returned he didn't catch it, but executed a subtle flick of his wrist and sent it back out again. Five, ten, twenty times. "Two Hands Loop-the-Loop," he said, adding another, alternating so that as one flew away from his right hand the other flew in toward his left.

"Pickpocket," said the other twin, raising the flap of his jacket. He threw the yo-yo between his legs, wrapping the string around his thigh. As he looked out over the crowd the yo-yo dropped, perfectly placed, in his trouser pocket. Laughing, the kids applauded.

I spent the whole afternoon in one spot, watching them, not even moving when they took breaks for fear I'd lose my place. When it was over I spent my last money on a yo-yo, a set of extra strings, and a pamphlet explaining all the tricks, starting from the easiest and working up to the hardest.

Walking back to the bike I was so absorbed a mail truck almost ran me down. I did my first successful trick standing by the rack, a simple but rather spectacular exercise called Around the World. Smiling, I put the yo-yo in my pocket and pulled out the bike. I knew I was going to be good at it.

The common yo-yo is crudely made, with a thick shank between two widely spaced wooden disks. The string is knotted or stapled to the shank. With such an instrument nothing can be done except the simple up-down movement. My yo-yo, on the other hand, was a perfectly balanced construction of hard wood, slightly weighted, flat, with only a sixteenth of an inch between the halves. The string was not attached to the shank, but looped over it in such a way as to allow the wooden part to spin freely on its own axis. The gyroscopic effect thus created kept the yo-yo stable in all attitudes.

I started at the beginning of the book and quickly mastered the novice, in-termediate, and advanced stages, practicing all day every day in the woods across the street from my house. Hour after hour of practice, never moving to the next trick until the one at hand was mastered.

The string was tied to my middle finger, just behind the nail. As I threw—with your palm up, make a fist; throw down your hand, fingers unfolding, as if you were casting grain—a short bit of string would tighten across the sensitive pad of flesh at the tip of my finger. That was the critical area. After a number of weeks I could interpret the condition of the string, the presence of any im-perfections on the shank, but most importantly the exact amount of spin or in-ertial energy left in the yo-yo at any given moment—all from that bit of string on my fingertip. As the throwing motion became more and more natural I found I could make the yo-yo "sleep" for an astonishing length of time—four-teen or fifteen seconds—and still have enough spin left to bring it back to my hand. Gradually the basic moves became reflexes. Sleeping, twirling, swinging, and precise aim. Without thinking, without even looking, I could run through trick after trick involving various combinations of the elemental skills, switch-ing from one to the other in a smooth continuous flow. On particularly good days I would hum a tune under my breath and do it all in time to the music.

Flicking the yo-yo expressed something. The sudden, potentially comic ex-tension of one's arm to twice its length. The precise neatness of it, intrinsically soothing, as if relieving an inner tension too slight to be noticeable, the way a man might hitch up his pants simply to enact a reassuring gesture. It felt good. The comfortable weight in one's hand, the smooth, rapid descent down the string, ending with a barely audible snap as the yo-yo hung balanced, spinning, pregnant with force and the slave of one's fingertip. That it was vaguely mas-turbatory seems inescapable. I doubt that half the pubescent boys in America could have been captured by any other means, as, in the heat of the fad, half of them were. A single Loop-the-Loop might represent, in some mysterious way, the act of masturbation, but to break down the entire repertoire into the three stages of throw, trick, and return representing erection, climax, and de-tumescence seems immoderate.

The greatest pleasure in yo-yoing was an abstract pleasure—watching the dramatization of simple physical laws, and realizing they would never fail if a trick was done correctly. The geometric purity of it! The string wasn't just a string, it was a tool in the enactment of theorems. It was a line, an idea. And the top was an entirely different sort of idea, a gyroscope, capable of storing energy and of interacting with the line. I remember the first time I did a par-ticularly lovely trick, one in which the sleeping yo-yo is swung from right to left while the string is interrupted by an extended index finger. Momentum carries the yo-yo in a circular path around the finger, but instead of completing the arc the yo-yo falls on the taut string between the performer's hands, where it continues to spin in an upright position. My pleasure at that moment was as much from the beauty of the experiment as from pride. Snapping apart my hands I sent the yo-yo into the air above my head, bouncing it off nothing, back into my palm.

I practiced the yo-yo because it pleased me to do so, without the slightest application of will power. It wasn't ambition that drove me, but the nature of yo-yoing. The yo-yo represented my first organized attempt to control the outside world. It fascinated me because I could see my progress in clearly defined stages, and because the intimacy of it, the almost spooky closeness I began to feel with the instrument in my hand, seemed to ensure that nothing irrelevant would interfere. I was, in the language of jazz, "up tight" with my yo-yo, and finally free, in one small area at least, of the paralyzing sloppiness of life in general.

The first significant problem arose in the attempt to do fifty consecutive Loop-the-Loops. After ten or fifteen the yo-yo invariably started to lean and the throws became less clean, resulting in loss of control. I almost skipped the whole thing because fifty seemed excessive. Ten made the point. But there it was, written out in the book. To qualify as an expert you had to do fifty, so fifty I would do.

It took me two days, and I wouldn't have spent a moment more. All those Loop-the-Loops were hard on the strings. Time after time the shank cut them and the yo-yo went sailing off into the air. It was irritating, not only because of the expense (strings were a nickel each, and fabricating your own was unsatisfactory), but because a random element had been introduced. About the only unforeseeable disaster in yo-yoing was to have your string break, and here was a trick designed to do exactly that. Twenty-five would have been enough. If you could do twenty-five clean Loop-the-Loops you could do fifty or a hundred. I supposed they were simply trying to sell strings and went back to the more interesting tricks.

The witty nonsense of Eating Spaghetti, the surprise of The Twirl, the complex neatness of Cannonball, Backwards round the World, or Halfway round the World—I could do them all, without false starts or sloppy endings. I could do every trick in the book. Perfectly.

The day was marked on the kitchen calendar (God Gave Us Bluebell Natural Bottled Gas). I got on my bike and rode into town. Pedaling along the highway I worked out with the yo-yo to break in a new string. The twins were appearing at the dime store.

I could hear the crowd before I turned the corner. Kids were coming on bikes and on foot from every corner of town, rushing down the streets like madmen. Three or four policemen were busy keeping the street clear directly in front of the store, and in a small open space around the doors some of the more adept kids were running through their tricks, showing off to the general audience or stopping to compare notes with their peers. Standing at the edge with my yo-yo safe in my pocket, it didn't take me long to see I had them all covered. A boy in a sailor hat could do some of the harder tricks, but he missed too often to be a serious threat. I went inside.

As Ramos and Ricardo performed I watched their hands carefully, noticing little differences in style and technique. Ricardo was a shade classier, I thought, although Ramos held an edge in the showy two-handed stuff. When they were through we went outside for the contest.

"Everybody in the alley!" Ramos shouted, his head bobbing an inch or two above the others. "Contest starting now in the alley!" A hundred excited children followed the twins into an alley beside the dime store and lined up against the wall.

"Attention all kids!" Ramos yelled, facing us from the middle of the street like a drill sergeant. "To qualify for contest you got to Rock the Cradle. You got to rock yo-yo in cradle four time. Four time! Okay? Three time no good. Okay. Everybody happy?" There were murmurs of disappointment and some of the kids stepped out of line. The rest of us closed ranks. Yo-yos flicked nervously as we waited. "Winner receive grand prize. Special Black Beauty Prize Yo-Yo with Diamonds," said Ramos, gesturing to his brother who smiled and held up the prize, turning it in the air so we could see the four stones set on each side. ("The crowd gasped . . ." I want to write. Of course they didn't. They didn't make a sound, but the impact of the diamond yo-yo was obvious.) We'd never seen anything like it. One imagined how the stones would gleam as it revolved, and how much prettier the tricks would be. The ultimate yo-yo! The only one in town! Who knew what feats were possible with such an instrument? All around me a fierce, nervous resolve was settling into the contestants, suddenly skittish as racehorses.

"Ricardo will show trick with Grand Prize Yo-Yo. Rock the Cradle four time!"

With a perfect, fluid movement Ricardo threw down the yo-yo, gathered the string and leisurely rocked the cradle.

"One!" cried Ramos.

"Two!" the kids joined in.

"Three!" It was really beautiful. He did it so slowly you would have thought he had all the time in the world. I counted seconds under my breath to see how long he made it sleep.

"Four!" said the crowd.

"Thirteen," I said to myself as the yo-yo snapped back into his hand. Thirteen seconds. Excellent time for that particular trick.

"Attention all kids!" Ramos announced. "Contest start now at head of line."

The first boy did a sloppy job of gathering his string but managed to rock the cradle quickly four times.

"Okay." Ramos tapped him on the shoulder and moved to the next boy, who fumbled. "Out." Ricardo followed, doing an occasional Loop-the-Loop with the diamond yo-yo. "Out . . . out . . . okay," said Ramos as he worked down the line.

There was something about the man's inexorable advance that unnerved me. His decisions were fast, and there was no appeal. To my surprise I felt my palms begin to sweat. Closer and closer he came, his voice growing louder, and then suddenly he was standing in front of me. Amazed, I stared at him. It was as if he'd appeared out of thin air.

"What happen boy, you swarrow bubble gum?"

The laughter jolted me out of it. Blushing, I threw down my yo-yo and executed a slow Rock the Cradle, counting the four passes and hesitating a moment at the end so as not to appear rushed.

"Okay." He tapped my shoulder. "Good."

I wiped my hands on my blue jeans and watched him move down the line. "Out . . . out . . . out." He had a large mole on the back of his neck.

Seven boys qualified. Coming back, Ramos called out, "Next trick Backward Round the World! Okay? Go!"

The first two boys missed, but the third was the kid in the sailor hat. Glancing quickly to see that no one was behind him, he hunched up his shoulder, threw, and just barely made the catch. There was some loose string in his hand, but not enough to disqualify him.

Number four missed, as did number five, and it was my turn. I stepped forward, threw the yo-yo almost straight up over my head, and as it began to fall pulled very gently to add some speed. It zipped neatly behind my legs and there was nothing more to do. My head turned to one side, I stood absolutely still and watched the yo-yo come in over my shoulder and slap into my hand. I added a Loop-the-Loop just to show the tightness of the string.

"Did you see that?" I heard someone say.

Number seven missed, so it was between myself and the boy in the sailor hat. His hair was bleached by the sun and combed up over his forehead in a pompadour, held from behind by the white hat. He was a year or two older than me. Blinking his blue eyes nervously, he adjusted the tension of his string.

"Next trick Cannonball! Cannonball! You go first this time," Ramos said to me.

Kids had gathered in a circle around us, those in front quiet and attentive, those in back jumping up and down to get a view. "Move back for room," Ricardo said, pushing them back. "More room, please."

I stepped into the center and paused, looking down at the ground. It was a difficult trick. The yo-yo had to land exactly on the string and there was a chance I'd miss the first time. I knew I wouldn't miss twice. "Can I have one practice?"

Ramos and Ricardo consulted in their mother tongue, and then Ramos held up his hands. "Attention all kids! Each boy have one practice before trick."

The crowd was silent, watching me. I took a deep breath and threw, following the fall of the yo-yo with my eyes, turning slightly, matador-fashion, as it passed me. My finger caught the string, the yo-yo came up and over, and missed. Without pausing I threw again. "Second time," I yelled, so there would be no misunderstanding. The circle had been too big. This time I made it small, sacrificing beauty for security. The yo-yo fell where it belonged and spun for a moment. (A moment I don't rush, my arms widespread, my eyes locked on the spinning toy. The Trick! There it is, brief and magic, right before your eyes! My hands are frozen in the middle of a deaf-and-dumb sentence, holding the whole airy, tenuous statement aloft for everyone to see.) With a quick snap I broke up the trick and made my catch.

Ramos nodded. "Okay. Very good. Now next boy."

Sailor-hat stepped forward, wiping his nose with the back of his hand. He threw once to clear the string.

"One practice," said Ramos.

He nodded.

"C'mon Bobby," someone said. "You can do it."

Bobby threw the yo-yo out to the side, made his move, and missed.

"Damn," he whispered. (He said "dahyum.") The second time he got halfway through the trick before his yo-yo ran out of gas and fell impotently off the string. He picked it up and walked away, winding slowly.

Ramos came over and held my hand in the air. "The winner!" he yelled. "Grand prize Black Beauty Diamond Yo-Yo will now be awarded."

Ricardo stood in front of me. "Take off old yo-yo." I loosened the knot and slipped it off. "Put out hand." I held out my hand and he looped the new string on my finger, just behind the nail, where the mark was. "You like Black Beauty," he said, smiling as he stepped back. "Diamond make pretty colors in the sun."

"Thank you," I said.

"Very good with yo-yo. Later we have contest for whole town. Winner go to Miami for State Championship. Maybe you win. Okay?"

"Okay." I nodded. "Thank you."

A few kids came up to look at Black Beauty. I threw it once or twice to get the feel. It seemed a bit heavier than my old one. Ramos and Ricardo were surrounded as the kids called out their favorite tricks.

"Do Pickpocket! Pickpocket!"

"Do the Double Cannonball!"

"Ramos! Ramos! Do the Turkish Army!"

Smiling, waving their hands to ward off the barrage of requests, the twins worked their way through the crowd toward the mouth of the alley. I watched them moving away and was immediately struck by a wave of fierce and irrational panic. "Wait," I yelled, pushing through after them. "Wait!"

I caught them on the street.

"No more today," Ricardo said, and then paused when he saw it was me. "Okay. The champ. What's wrong? Yo-yo no good?"

"No. It's fine."

"Good. You take care of it."

"I wanted to ask when the contest is. The one where you get to go to Miami."

"Later. After school begins." They began to move away. "We have to go home now."

"Just one more thing," I said, walking after them. "What is the hardest trick you know?"

Ricardo laughed. "Hardest trick killing flies in air."

"No, no. I mean a real trick."

They stopped and looked at me. "There is a very hard trick," Ricardo said. "I don't do it, but Ramos does. Because you won the contest he will show you. But only once, so watch carefully."

We stepped into the lobby of the Sunset Theater. Ramos cleared his string. "Watch," he said, and threw. The trick started out like a Cannonball, and then unexpectedly folded up, opened again, and as I watched breathlessly the entire complex web spun around in the air, propelled by Ramos' two hands making slow circles like a swimmer. The end was like the end of a Cannonball.

"That's beautiful," I said, genuinely awed. "What's it called?"

"The Universe."

"The Universe," I repeated.

"Because it goes around and around," said Ramos, "like the planets."

Anne Moody

FROM COMING OF AGE IN MISSISSIPPI

In mid-September I was back on campus. But didn't very much happen until February when the NAACP held its annual convention in Jackson. They were having a whole lot of interesting speakers: Jackie Robinson, Floyd Patterson, Curt Flood, Margaretta Belafonte, and many others. I wouldn't have missed it for anything. I was so excited that I sent one of the leaflets home to Mama and asked her to come.

Three days later I got a letter from Mama with dried-up tears on it, forbidding me to go to the convention. It went on for more than six pages. She said if I didn't stop that shit she would come to Tougaloo and kill me herself. She told me about the time I last visited her, on Thanksgiving, and she had picked me up at the bus station. She said she picked me up because she was scared some white in my hometown would try to do something to me. She said the sheriff had been by, telling her I was messing around with that NAACP group. She said he told her if I didn't stop it, I could not come back there any more. He said that they didn't need any of those NAACP people messing around in Centreville. She ended the letter by saying that she had burned the leaflet I sent her. "Please don't send any more of that stuff here. I don't want nothing to happen to us here," she said. "If you keep that up, you will never be able to come home again."

I was so damn mad after her letter, I felt like taking the NAACP convention to Centreville. I think I would have, if it had been in my power to do so. The remainder of the week I thought of nothing except going to the convention. I didn't know exactly what to do about it. I didn't want Mama or anyone at home to get hurt because of me.

I had felt something was wrong when I was home. During the four days I was there, Mama had tried to do everything she could to keep me in the house. When I said I was going to see some of my old classmates, she pretended she was sick and said I would have to cook. I knew she was acting strangely, but I hadn't known why. I thought Mama just wanted me to spend most of my time with her, since this was only the second time I had been home since I entered college as a freshman.

Things kept running through my mind after that letter from Mama. My mind was so active, I couldn't sleep at night. I remembered the one time I did leave the house to go to the post office. I had walked past a bunch of white men on the street on my way through town and one said, "Is that the gal goin' to Tougaloo?" He acted kind of mad or something, and I didn't know what was going on. I got a creepy feeling, so I hurried home. When I told Mama about it, she just said, "A lotta people don't like that school." I knew what she meant. Just before I went to Tougaloo, they had housed the Freedom Riders there. The school was being criticized by whites throughout the state.

The night before the convention started, I made up my mind to go, no mat-ter what Mama said. I just wouldn't tell Mama or anyone from home. Then it occurred to me—how did the sheriff or anyone at home know I was working with the NAACP chapter on campus? Somehow they had found out. Now I knew I could never go to Centreville safely again. I kept telling myself that I didn't really care too much about going home, that it was more important to me to go to the convention.

I was there from the very beginning. Jackie Robinson was asked to serve as moderator. This was the first time I had seen him in person. I remembered how when Jackie became the first Negro to play Major League baseball, my un-cles and most of the Negro boys in my hometown started organizing baseball leagues. It did something for them to see a Negro out there playing with all those white players. Jackie was a good moderator, I thought. He kept smiling and joking. People felt relaxed and proud. They appreciated knowing and meeting people of their own race who had done something worth talking about.

When Jackie introduced Floyd Patterson, heavyweight champion of the world, the people applauded for a long, long time. Floyd was kind of shy. He didn't say very much. He didn't have to, just his being there was enough to sat-isfy most of the Negroes who had only seen him on TV. Archie Moore was there too. He wasn't as smooth as Jackie, but he had his way with a crowd. He started telling how he was run out of Mississippi, and the people just cracked up.

I was enjoying the convention so much that I went back for the night ses-sion. Before the night was over, I had gotten autographs from every one of the Negro celebrities.

I had counted on graduating in the spring of 1963, but as it turned out, I couldn't because some of my credits still had to be cleared with Natchez College. A year before, this would have seemed like a terrible disaster, but now I hardly even felt disappointed. I had a good excuse to stay on campus for the summer and work with the Movement, and this was what I really wanted to do. I couldn't go home again anyway, and I couldn't go to New Orleans—I didn't have money enough for bus fare.

During my senior year at Tougaloo, my family hadn't sent me one penny. I had only the small amount of money I had earned at Maple Hill. I couldn't afford to eat at school or live in the dorms, so I had gotten permission to move off campus. I had to prove that I could finish school, even if I had to go hun-gry every day. I knew Raymond and Miss Pearl were just waiting to see me drop out. But something happened to me as I got more and more involved in the Movement. It no longer seemed important to prove anything. I had found something outside myself that gave meaning to my life.

I had become very friendly with my social science professor, John Salter, who was in charge of NAACP activities on campus. All during the year, while the NAACP conducted a boycott of the downtown stores in Jackson, I had been one of Salter's most faithful canvassers and church speakers. During the last week of school, he told me that sit-in demonstrations were about to start in Jackson and that he wanted me to be the spokesman for a team that would sit-in at Woolworth's lunch counter. The two other demonstrators would be classmates of mine, Memphis and Pearlena. Pearlena was a dedicated NAACP worker, but

Memphis had not been very involved in the Movement on campus. It seemed that the organization had had a rough time finding students who were in a position to go to jail. I had nothing to lose one way or the other. Around ten o'-clock the morning of the demonstrations, NAACP headquarters alerted the news services. As a result, the police department was also informed, but neither the policemen nor the newsmen knew exactly where or when the demonstrations would start. They stationed themselves along Capitol Street and waited.

To divert attention from the sit-in at Woolworth's, the picketing started at J. C. Penney's a good fifteen minutes before. The pickets were allowed to walk up and down in front of the store three or four times before they were arrested. At exactly 11 A.M., Pearlena, Memphis, and I entered Woolworth's from the rear entrance. We separated as soon as we stepped into the store, and made small purchases from various counters. Pearlena had given Memphis her watch. He was to let us know when it was 11:14. At 11:14 we were to join him near the lunch counter and at exactly 11:15 we were to take seats at it.

Seconds before 11:15 we were occupying three seats at the previously segregated Woolworth's lunch counter. In the beginning the waitresses seemed to ignore us, as if they really didn't know what was going on. Our waitress walked past us a couple of times before she noticed we had started to write our own orders down and realized we wanted service. She asked us what we wanted. We began to read to her from our order slips. She told us that we would be served at the back counter, which was for Negroes.

"We would like to be served here," I said.

The waitress started to repeat what she had said, then stopped in the middle of the sentence. She turned the lights out behind the counter, and she and the other waitresses almost ran to the back of the store, deserting all their white customers. I guess they thought that violence would start immediately after the whites at the counter realized what was going on. There were five or six other people at the counter. A couple of them just got up and walked away. A girl sitting next to me finished her banana split before leaving. A middle-aged white woman who had not yet been served rose from her seat and came over to us. "I'd like to stay here with you," she said, "but my husband is waiting."

The newsmen came in just as she was leaving. They must have discovered what was going on shortly after some of the people began to leave the store. One of the newsmen ran behind the woman who spoke to us and asked her to identify herself. She refused to give her name, but said she was a native of Vicksburg and a former resident of California. When asked why she had said what she had said to us, she replied, "I am in sympathy with the Negro movement." By this time a crowd of cameramen and reporters had gathered around us taking pictures and asking questions, such as Where were we from? Why did we sit-in? What organization sponsored it? Were we students? From what school? How were we classified?

I told them that we were all students at Tougaloo College, that we were represented by no particular organization, and that we planned to stay there even after the store closed. "All we want is service," was my reply to one of them. After they had finished probing for about twenty minutes, they were almost ready to leave.

At noon, students from a nearby white high school started pouring in to Woolworth's. When they first saw us they were sort of surprised. They didn't know how to react. A few started to heckle and the newsmen became interested again. Then the white students started chanting all kinds of anti-Negro slogans. We were called a little bit of everything. The rest of the seats except the three we were occupying had been roped off to prevent others from sitting down. A couple of the boys took one end of the rope and made it into a hangman's noose. Several attempts were made to put it around our necks. The crowds grew as more students and adults came in for lunch.

We kept our eyes straight forward and did not look at the crowd except for occasional glances to see what was going on. All of a sudden I saw a face I remembered—the drunkard from the bus station sit-in. My eyes lingered on him just long enough for us to recognize each other. Today he was drunk too, so I don't think he remembered where he had seen me before. He took out a knife, opened it, put it in his pocket, and then began to pace the floor. At this point, I told Memphis and Pearlena what was going on. Memphis suggested that we pray. We bowed our heads, and all hell broke loose. A man rushed forward, threw Memphis from his seat, and slapped my face. Then another man who worked in the store threw me against an adjoining counter.

Down on my knees on the floor, I saw Memphis lying near the lunch counter with blood running out of the corners of his mouth. As he tried to protect his face, the man who'd thrown him down kept kicking him against the head. If he had worn hard-soled shoes instead of sneakers, the first kick probably would have killed Memphis. Finally a man dressed in plain clothes identified himself as a police officer and arrested Memphis and his attacker.

Pearlena had been thrown to the floor. She and I got back on our stools after Memphis was arrested. There were some white Tougaloo teachers in the crowd. They asked Pearlena and me if we wanted to leave. They said that things were getting too rough. We didn't know what to do. While we were trying to make up our minds, we were joined by Joan Trumpauer. Now there were three of us and we were integrated. The crowd began to chant, "Communists, Communists, Communists." Some old man in the crowd ordered the students to take us off the stools.

"Which one should I get first?" a big husky boy said.

"That white nigger," the old man said.

The boy lifted Joan from the counter by her waist and carried her out of the store. Simultaneously, I was snatched from my stool by two high school students. I was dragged about thirty feet toward the door by my hair when someone made them turn me loose. As I was getting up off the floor, I saw Joan coming back inside. We started back to the center of the counter to join Pearlena. Lois Chaffee, a white Tougaloo faculty member, was now sitting next to her. So Joan and I just climbed across the rope at the front end of the counter and sat down. There were now four of us, two whites and two Negroes, all women. The mob started smearing us with ketchup, mustard, sugar, pies, and everything on the counter. Soon Joan and I were joined by John Salter, but the moment he sat down he was hit on the jaw with what appeared to be brass knuckles. Blood gushed from his face and someone threw salt into the open wound. Ed King, Tougaloo's chaplain, rushed to him.

At the other end of the counter, Lois and Pearlena were joined by George Raymond, a CORE field worker and a student from Jackson State College. Then a Negro high school boy sat down next to me. The mob took spray paint from the counter and sprayed it on the new demonstrators. The high school student had on a white shirt; the word "nigger" was written on his back with red spray paint.

We sat there for three hours taking a beating when the manager decided to close the store because the mob had begun to go wild with stuff from other counters. He begged and begged everyone to leave. But even after fifteen minutes of begging, no one budged. They would not leave until we did. Then Dr. Beittel, the president of Tougaloo College, came running in. He said he had just heard what was happening.

About ninety policemen were standing outside the store; they had been watching the whole thing through the windows, but had not come in to stop the mob or do anything. President Beittel went outside and asked Captain Ray to come and escort us out. The captain refused, stating the manager had to invite him in before he could enter the premises, so Dr. Beittel himself brought us out. He had told the police that they had better protect us after we were outside the store. When we got outside, the policemen formed a single line that blocked the mob from us. However, they were allowed to throw at us everything they had collected. Within ten minutes, we were picked up by Reverend King in his station wagon and taken to the NAACP headquarters on Lynch Street.

After the sit-in, all I could think of was how sick Mississippi whites were. They believed so much in the segregated Southern way of life, they would kill to preserve it. I sat there in the NAACP office and thought of how many times they had killed when this way of life was threatened. I knew that the killing had just begun. "Many more will die before it is over with," I thought. Before the sit-in, I had always hated the whites in Mississippi. Now I knew it was impossible for me to hate sickness. The whites had a disease, an incurable disease in its final stage. What were our chances against such a disease? I thought of the students, the young Negroes who had just begun to protest, as young interns. When these young interns got older, I thought, they would be the best doctors in the world for social problems.

Before we were taken back to campus, I wanted to get my hair washed. It was stiff with dried mustard, ketchup and sugar. I stopped in at a beauty shop across the street from the NAACP office. I didn't have on any shoes because I had lost them when I was dragged across the floor at Woolworth's. My stockings were sticking to my legs from the mustard that had dried on them. The hairdresser took one look at me and said, "My land, you were in the sit-in, huh?"

"Yes," I answered. "Do you have time to wash my hair and style it?"

"Right away," she said, and she meant right away. There were three other ladies already waiting, but they seemed glad to let me go ahead of them. The hairdresser was real nice. She even took my stockings off and washed my legs while my hair was drying.

There was a mass rally that night at the Pearl Street Church in Jackson, and the place was packed. People were standing two abreast in the aisles. Before the speakers began, all the sit-inners walked out on the stage and were introduced by Medgar Evers. People stood and applauded for what seemed like thirty minutes or more. Medgar told the audience that this was just the beginning of such demonstrations. He asked them to pledge themselves to unite in a massive offensive against segregation in Jackson, and throughout the state. The rally ended with "We Shall Overcome" and sent home hundreds of determined people. It seemed as though Mississippi Negroes were about to get together at last.

Before I demonstrated, I had written Mama. She wrote me back a letter, begging me not to take part in the sit-in. She even sent ten dollars for bus fare to New Orleans. I didn't have one penny, so I kept the money. Mama's letter made me mad. I had to live my life as I saw fit. I had made that decision when I left home. But it hurt to have my family prove to me how scared they were. It hurt me more than anything else—I knew the whites had already started the threats and intimidations. I was the first Negro from my hometown who had openly demonstrated, worked with the NAACP or anything. When Negroes threatened to do anything in Centreville, they were either shot like Samuel O'Quinn or run out of town, like Reverend Dupree.

I didn't answer Mama's letter. Even if I had written one, she wouldn't have received it before she saw the news on TV or heard it on the radio. I waited to hear from her again. And I waited to hear in the news that someone in Centreville had been murdered. If so, I knew it would be a member of my family.

FICTION

Raymond Carver

POPULAR MECHANICS

Early that day the weather turned and the snow was melting into dirty water. Streaks of it ran down from the little shoulder-high window that faced the backyard. Cars slushed by on the street outside, where it was getting dark. But it was getting dark on the inside too.

He was in the bedroom pushing clothes into a suitcase when she came to the door.

I'm glad you're leaving! I'm glad you're leaving! she said. Do you hear?

He kept on putting his things into the suitcase.

Son of a bitch! I'm so glad you're leaving! She began to cry. You can't even look me in the face, can you?

Then she noticed the baby's picture on the bed and picked it up.

He looked at her and she wiped her eyes and stared at him before turning and going back to the living room.

Bring that back, he said.

Just get your things and get out, she said.

He did not answer. He fastened the suitcase, put on his coat, looked around to the bedroom before turning off the light. Then he went out to the living room.

She stood in the doorway of the little kitchen, holding the baby.

I want the baby, he said.

Are you crazy?

No, but I want the baby. I'll get someone to come by for his things.

You're not touching this baby, she said.

The baby had begun to cry and she uncovered the blanket from around his head.

Oh, oh, she said, looking at the baby.

He moved toward her.

For God's sake! she said. She took a step back into the kitchen.

I want the baby.

Get out of here!

She turned and tried to hold the baby over in a corner behind the stove.

But he came up. He reached across the stove and tightened his hands on the baby.

Let go of him, he said.

Get away, get away! she cried.

The baby was red-faced and screaming. In the scuffle they knocked down a flowerpot that hung behind the stove.

He crowded her into the wall then, trying to break her grip. He held on to the baby and pushed with all his weight.

Let go of him, he said.

Don't, she said. You're hurting the baby, she said.

I'm not hurting the baby, he said.

The kitchen window gave no light. In the near-dark he worked on her fisted fingers with one hand and with the other hand he gripped the screaming baby up under an arm near the shoulder.

She felt her fingers being forced open. She felt the baby going from her.

No! she screamed just as her hands came loose.

She would have it, this baby. She grabbed for the baby's other arm. She caught the baby around the wrist and leaned back.

But he would not let go. He felt the baby slipping out of his hands and he pulled back very hard.

In this manner, the issue was decided.

Anton Chekov

Misery

"To Whom Shall I Tell My Grief?"

The twilight of evening. Big flakes of wet snow are whirling lazily about the street lamps, which have just been lighted, and lying in a thin soft layer on roofs, horses' backs, shoulders, caps. Iona Potapov, the sledge-driver, is all white like a ghost. He sits on the box without stirring, bent as double as the living body can be bent. If a regular snowdrift fell on him it seems as though even then he would not think it necessary to shake it off. . . . His little mare is white and motionless too. Her stillness, the angularity of her lines, and the stick-like straightness of her legs make her look like a halfpenny gingerbread horse. She is probably lost in thought. Anyone who has been torn away from the plough, from the familiar gray landscapes, and cast into this slough, full of monstrous lights, of unceasing uproar and hurrying people, is bound to think.

It is a long time since Iona and his nag have budged. They came out of the yard before dinner-time and not a single fare yet. But now the shades of evening are falling on the town. The pale light of the street lamps changes to a vivid color, and the bustle of the street grows noisier.

"Sledge to Vyborgskaya!" Iona hears. "Sledge!"

Iona starts, and through his snow-plastered eyelashes sees an officer in a military overcoat with a hood over his head.

"To Vyborgskaya," repeats the officer. "Are you asleep? To Vyborgskaya!"

In token of assent Iona gives a tug at the reins which sends cakes of snow flying from the horse's back and shoulders. The officer gets into the sledge. The sledge-driver clicks to the horse, cranes his neck like a swan, rises in his seat, and more from habit than necessity brandishes his whip. The mare cranes her neck, too, crooks her stick-like legs, and hesitatingly sets off. . . .

"Where are you shoving, you devil?" Iona immediately hears shouts from the dark mass shifting to and fro before him. "Where the devil are you going? Keep to the r-right!"

"You don't know how to drive! Keep to the right," says the officer angrily.

A coachman driving a carriage swears at him; a pedestrian crossing the road and brushing the horse's nose with his shoulder looks at him angrily and shakes the snow off his sleeve. Iona fidgets on the box as though he were sitting on thorns, jerks his elbows, and turns his eyes about like one possessed, as though he did not know where he was or why he was there.

"What rascals they all are!" says the officer jocosely. "They are simply doing their best to run up against you or fall under the horse's feet. They must be doing it on purpose."

Iona looks at his fare and moves his lips. . . . Apparently he means to say something, but nothing comes out but a sniff.

"What?" inquires the officer.

Iona gives a wry smile, and straining his throat, brings out huskily: "My son . . . , er . . . my son died this week, sir."

"H'm! What did he die of?"

Iona turns his whole body round to his fare, and says:

"Who can tell! It must have been from fever. . . . He lay three days in the hospital and then he died. . . . God's will."

"Turn round, you devil!" comes out of the darkness. "Have you gone cracked, you old dog? Look where you are going!"

"Drive on! drive on! . . ." says the officer. "We shan't get there till tomorrow going on like this. Hurry up!"

The sledge-driver cranes his neck again, rises in his seat, and with heavy grace swings his whip. Several times he looks round at the officer, but the latter keeps his eyes shut and is apparently disinclined to listen. Putting his fare down at Vyborgskaya, Iona stops by a restaurant, and again sits huddled up on the box. . . . Again the wet snow paints him and his horse white. One hour passes, and then another. . . .

Three young men, two tall and thin, one short and hunchbacked, come up, railing at each other and loudly stamping on the pavement with their galoshes.

"Cabby, to the Police Bridge!" the hunchback cries in a cracked voice. "The three of us, . . . twenty kopecks!"

Iona tugs at the reins and clicks to his horse. Twenty kopecks is not a fair price, but he has no thoughts for that. Whether it is a rouble or whether it is five kopecks does not matter to him now so long as he has a fare. . . . The three young men, shoving each other and using bad language, go up to the sledge, and all three try to sit down at once. The question remains to be settled: Which are to sit down and which one is to stand? After a long altercation, ill-temper, and abuse, they come to the conclusion that the hunchback must stand because he is the shortest.

"Well, drive on," says the hunchback in his cracked voice, settling himself and breathing down Iona's neck. "Cut along! What a cap you've got, my friend! You wouldn't find a worse one in all Petersburg. . . ."

"He-he! . . . he-he! . . ." laughs Iona. "It's nothing to boast of!"

"Well, then, nothing to boast of, drive on! Are you going to drive like this all the way? Eh? Shall I give you one in the neck?"

"My head aches," says one of the tall ones. "At the Dukmasovs' yesterday Vaska and I drank four bottles of brandy between us."

"I can't make out why you talk such stuff," says the other tall one angrily. "You lie like a brute."

"Strike me dead, it's the truth! . . ."

"It's about as true as that a louse coughs."

"He-he!" grins Iona. "Me-er-ry gentlemen!"

"Tfoo! the devil take you!" cries the hunchback indignantly. "Will you get on, you old plague, or won't you? Is that the way to drive? Give her one with the whip. Hang it all, give it her well."

Iona feels behind his back the jolting person and quivering voice of the hunchback. He hears abuse addressed to him, he sees people, and the feeling of loneliness begins little by little to be less heavy on his heart. The hunchback swears at him, till he chokes over some elaborately whimsical string of epithets and is overpowered by his cough. His tall companions begin talking of a certain Nadyezhda Petrovna. Iona looks round at them. Waiting till there is a brief pause, he looks round once more and says:

"This week . . . er . . . my . . . er . . . son died!"

"We shall all die, . . ." says the hunchback with a sigh, wiping his lips after coughing. "Come, drive on! drive on! My friends, I simply cannot stand crawling like this! When will he get us there?"

"Well, you give him a little encouragement . . . one in the neck!"

"Do you hear, you old plague? I'll make you smart. If one stands on ceremony with fellows like you one may as well walk. Do you hear, you old dragon? Or don't you care a hang what we say?"

And Iona hears rather than feels a slap on the back of his neck.

"He-he! . . ." he laughs. "Merry gentlemen . . . God give you health!"

"Cabman, are you married?" asks one of the tall ones.

"I? He-he! Me-er-ry gentlemen. The only wife for me now is the damp earth. . . . He-ho-ho! . . . The grave that is! . . . Here my son's dead and I am alive. . . . It's a strange thing, death has come in at the wrong door. . . . Instead of coming for me it went for my son. . . ."

And Iona turns round to tell them how his son died, but at that point the hunchback gives a faint sigh and announces that, thank God! they have arrived at last. After taking his twenty kopecks, Iona gazes for a long while after the revelers, who disappear into a dark entry. Again he is alone and again there is silence for him. . . . The misery which has been for a brief space eased comes back again and tears his heart more cruelly than ever. With a look of anxiety and suffering Iona's eyes stray restlessly among the crowds moving to and fro on both sides of the street: can he not find among those thousands someone who will listen to him? But the crowds flit by heedless of him and his misery. . . . His misery is immense, beyond all bounds. If Iona's heart were to burst and his misery to flow out, it would flood the whole world, it seems, but yet it is not seen. It has found a hiding-place in such an insignificant shell that one would not have found it with a candle by daylight. . . .

Iona sees a house-porter with a parcel and makes up his mind to address him.

"What time will it be, friend?" he asks.

"Going on for ten. . . . Why have you stopped here? Drive on!"

Iona drives a few paces away, bends himself double, and gives himself up to his misery. He feels it is no good to appeal to people. But before five minutes have passed he draws himself up, shakes his head as though he feels a sharp pain, and tugs at the reins. . . . He can bear it no longer.

"Back to the yard!" he thinks. "To the yard!"

And his little mare, as though she knew his thoughts, falls to trotting. An hour and a half later Iona is sitting by a big dirty stove. On the stove, on the floor, and on the benches are people snoring. The air is full of smells and stuffiness. Iona looks at the sleeping figures, scratches himself, and regrets that he has come home so early. . . .

"I have not earned enough to pay for the oats, even," he thinks. "That's why I am so miserable. A man who knows how to do his work, . . . who has had enough to eat, and whose horse has had enough to eat, is always at ease. . . ."

In one of the corners a young cabman gets up, clears his throat sleepily, and makes for the waterbucket.

"Want a drink?" Iona asks him.

"Seems so."

"May it do you good. . . . But my son is dead, mate. . . . Do you hear? This week in the hospital. . . . It's queer business. . . ."

Iona looks to see the effect produced by his words, but he sees nothing. The young man has covered his head over and is already asleep. The old man sighs and scratches himself. . . . Just as the young man had been thirsty for water, he thirsts for speech. His son will soon have been dead a week, and he has not really talked to anybody yet. . . . He wants to talk of it properly, with deliberation. . . . He wants to tell how his son was taken ill, how he suffered, what he said before he died, how he died. . . . He wants to describe the funeral, and how he went to the hospital to get his son's clothes. He still has his daughter Anisya in the country. . . . And he wants to talk about her too. . . . Yes, he has plenty to talk about now. His listener ought to sigh and exclaim and lament. . . . It would be even better to talk to women. Though they are silly creatures, they blubber at the first word.

"Let's go out and have a look at the mare," Iona thinks. "There is always time for sleep. . . . You'll have sleep enough, no fear. . . ."

He puts on his coat and goes into the stables where his mare is standing. He thinks about oats, about hay, about the weather. . . . He cannot think about his son when he is alone. . . . To talk about him with someone is possible, but to think of him and picture him is insufferable anguish. . . .

"Are you munching?" Iona asks his mare, seeing her shining eyes. "There, munch away, munch away. . . . Since we have not earned enough for oats, we will eat hay. . . . Yes, . . . I have grown too old to drive. . . . My son ought to be driving, not I. . . . He was a real coachman. . . . He ought to have lived. . . ."

Iona is silent for a while, and then he goes on:

"That's how it is, old girl. . . . Kuzma Ionitch is gone. . . . He said good-by to me. . . . He went and died for no reason. . . . Now, suppose you had a little colt, and you were that little colt's own mother. . . . And all at once that same little colt went and died. . . . You'd be sorry, wouldn't you? . . ."

The little mare munches, listens, and breathes on her master's hands. Iona is carried away and tells her all about it.

Ralph Ellison

KING OF THE BINGO GAME

The woman in front of him was eating roasted peanuts that smelled so good that he could barely contain his hunger. He could not even sleep and wished they'd hurry and begin the bingo game. There, on his right, two fellows were drinking wine out of a bottle wrapped in a paper bag, and he could hear soft gurgling in the dark. His stomach gave a low, gnawing growl. "If this was down South," he thought, "all I'd have to do is lean over and say, 'Lady, gimme a few of those peanuts, please ma'am,' and she'd pass me the bag and never think nothing of it." Or he could ask the fellows for a drink in the same way. Folks down South stuck together that way; they didn't even have to know you. But up here it was different. Ask somebody for something, and they'd think you were crazy. Well, I ain't crazy. I'm just broke, 'cause I got no birth certificate to get a job, and Laura 'bout to die 'cause we got no money for a doctor. But I ain't crazy. And yet a pinpoint of doubt was focused in his mind as he glanced toward the screen and saw the hero stealthily entering a dark room and sending the beam of a flashlight along a wall of bookcases. This is where he finds the trapdoor, he remembered. The man would pass abruptly through the wall and find the girl tied to a bed, her legs and arms spread wide, and her clothing torn to rags. He laughed softly to himself. He had seen the picture three times, and this was one of the best scenes.

On his right the fellow whispered wide-eyed to his companion, "Man, look a-yonder!"

"Damn!"

"Wouldn't I like to have her tied up like that . . ."

"Hey! That fool's letting her loose!"

"Aw, man, he loves her."

"Love or no love!"

The man moved impatiently beside him, and he tried to involve himself in the scene. But Laura was on his mind. Tiring quickly of watching the picture he looked back to where the white beam filtered from the projection room above the balcony. It started small and grew large, specks of dust dancing in its whiteness as it reached the screen. It was strange how the beam always landed right on the screen and didn't mess up and fall somewhere else. But they had it all fixed. Everything was fixed. Now suppose when they showed that girl with her dress torn the girl started taking off the rest of her clothes, and when the guy came in he didn't untie her but kept her there and went to taking off his own clothes? *That* would be something to see. If a picture got out of hand like that those guys up there would go nuts. Yeah, and there'd be so many folks in here you couldn't find a seat for nine months! A strange sensation played over his skin. He shuddered. Yesterday he'd seen a bedbug on a woman's neck as they walked out into the bright street. But exploring his thigh through a hole in his pocket he found only goose pimples and old scars.

The bottle gurgled again. He closed his eyes. Now a dreamy music was accompanying the film and train whistles were sounding in the distance, and he was a boy again walking along a railroad trestle down South, and seeing the train coming, and running back as fast as he could go, and hearing the whistle blowing, and getting off the trestle to solid ground just in time, with the earth trembling beneath his feet, and feeling relieved as he ran down the cinder-strewn embankment onto the highway, and looking back and seeing with terror that the train had left the track and was following him right down the middle of the street, and all the white people laughing as he ran screaming . . .

"Wake up there, buddy! What the hell do you mean hollering like that? Can't you see we trying to enjoy this here picture?"

He stared at the man with gratitude.

"I'm sorry, old man," he said. "I musta been dreaming."

"Well, here, have a drink. And don't be making no noise like that, damn!"

His hands trembled as he tilted his head. It was not wine, but whiskey. Cold rye whiskey. He took a deep swoller, decided it was better not to take another, and handed the bottle back to its owner.

"Thanks, old man," he said.

Now he felt the cold whiskey breaking a warm path straight through the middle of him, growing hotter and sharper as it moved. He had not eaten all day, and it made him light-headed. The smell of the peanuts stabbed him like a knife, and he got up and found a seat in the middle aisle. But no sooner did he sit than he saw a row of intense-faced young girls, and got up again, thinking, "You chicks musta been Lindy-hopping somewhere." He found a seat several rows ahead as the lights came on, and he saw the screen disappear behind a heavy red and gold curtain; then the curtain rising, and the man with the microphone and a uniformed attendant coming on the stage.

He felt for his bingo cards, smiling. The guy at the door wouldn't like it if he knew about his having *five* cards. Well, not everyone played the bingo game; and even with five cards he didn't have much of a chance. For Laura, though, he had to have faith. He studied the cards, each with its different numerals, punching the free center hole in each and spreading them neatly across his lap; and when the lights faded he sat slouched in his seat so that he could look from his cards to the bingo wheel with but a quick shifting of his eyes.

Ahead, at the end of the darkness, the man with the microphone was pressing a button attached to a long cord and spinning the bingo wheel and calling out the number each time the wheel came to rest. And each time the voice rang out his finger raced over the cards for the number. With five cards he had to move fast. He became nervous; there were too many cards, and the man went too fast with his grating voice. Perhaps he should just select one and throw the others away. But he was afraid. He became warm. Wonder how much Laura's doctor would cost? Damn that, watch the cards! And with despair he heard the man call three in a row which he missed on all five cards. This way he'd never win . . .

When he saw the row of holes punched across the third card, he sat paralyzed and heard the man call three more numbers before he stumbled forward, screaming.

"Bingo! Bingo!"

"Let that fool up there," someone called.

"Get up there, man!"

He stumbled down the aisle and up the steps to the stage into a light so sharp and bright that for a moment it blinded him, and he felt that he had moved into the spell of some strange, mysterious power. Yet it was as familiar as the sun, and he knew it was the perfectly familiar bingo.

The man with the microphone was saying something to the audience as he held out his card. A cold light flashed from the man's finger as the card left his hand. His knees trembled. The man stepped closer, checking the card against the numbers chalked on the board. Suppose he had made a mistake? The pomade on the man's hair made him feel faint, and he backed away. But the man was checking the card over the microphone now, and he had to stay. He stood tense, listening.

"Under the O, forty-four," the man chanted. "Under the I, seven. Under the G, three. Under the B, ninety-six. Under the N, thirteen!"

His breath came easier as the man smiled at the audience.

"Yessir, ladies and gentlemen, he's one of the chosen people!"

The audience rippled with laughter and applause.

"Step right up to the front of the stage."

He moved slowly forward, wishing that the light was not so bright.

"To win to-night's jackpot of $36.90 the wheel must stop between the double zero, understand?"

He nodded, knowing the ritual from the many days and nights he had watched the winners march across the stage to press the button that controlled the spinning wheel and receive the prizes. And now he followed the instructions as though he'd crossed the slippery stage a million prize-winning times.

The man was making some kind of a joke, and he nodded vacantly. So tense had he become that he felt a sudden desire to cry and shook it away. He felt vaguely that his whole life was determined by the bingo wheel; not only that which would happen now that he was at last before it, but all that had gone before, since his birth, and his mother's birth and the birth of his father. It had always been there, even though he had not been aware of it, handing out the unlucky cards and numbers of his days. The feeling persisted, and he started quickly away. I better get down from here before I make a fool of myself, he thought.

"Here, boy," the man called. "You haven't started yet."

Someone laughed as he went hesitantly back.

"Are you all reet?"

He grinned at the man's jive talk, but no words would come, and he knew it was not a convincing grin. For suddenly he knew that he stood on the slippery brink of some terrible embarrassment.

"Where are you from, boy?" the man asked.

"Down South."

"He's from down South, ladies and gentlemen," the man said. "Where from? Speak right into the mike."

"Rocky Mont," he said. "Rock' Mont, North Car'lina."

"So you decided to come down off that mountain to the U.S.," the man laughed. He felt that the man was making a fool of him, but then something cold was placed in his hand, and the lights were no longer behind him.

Standing before the wheel he felt alone, but that was somehow right, and he remembered his plan. He would give the wheel a short quick twirl. Just a touch of the button. He had watched it many times, and always it came close to double zero when it was short and quick. He steeled himself; the fear had left, and he felt a profound sense of promise, as though he were about to be repaid for all the things he'd suffered all his life. Trembling, he pressed the button. There was a whirl of lights, and in a second he realized with finality that though he wanted to, he could not stop. It was as though he held a high-powered line in his naked hand. His nerves tightened. As the wheel increased its speed it seemed to draw him more and more into its power, as though it held his fate; and with it came a deep need to submit, to whirl, to lose himself in its swirl of color. He could not stop it now. So let it be.

The button rested snugly in his palm where the man had placed it. And now he became aware of the man beside him, advising him through the microphone, while behind the shadowy audience hummed with noisy voices. He shifted his feet. There was still that feeling of helplessness within him, making part of him desire to turn back, even now that the jackpot was right in his hand. He squeezed the button until his fist ached. Then, like the sudden shriek of a subway whistle, a doubt tore through his head. Suppose he did not spin the wheel long enough? What could he do, and how could he tell? And then he knew, even as he wondered, that as long as he pressed the button, he could control the jackpot. He and only he could determine whether or not it was to be his. Not even the man with the microphone could do anything about it now. He felt drunk. Then, as though he had come down from a high hill into a valley of people, he heard the audience yelling.

"Come down from there, you jerk!"

"Let somebody else have a chance . . ."

"Ole Jack thinks he done found the end of the rainbow . . ."

The last voice was not unfriendly, and he turned and smiled dreamily into the yelling mouths. Then he turned his back squarely on them.

"Don't take too long, boy," a voice said.

He nodded. They were yelling behind him. Those folks did not understand what had happened to him. They had been playing the bingo game day in and night out for years, trying to win rent money or hamburger change. But not one of those wise guys had discovered this wonderful thing. He watched the wheel whirling past the numbers and experienced a burst of exaltation: This is God! This is the really truly God! He said it aloud, "This is God!"

He said it with such absolute conviction that he feared he would fall fainting into the footlights. But the crowd yelled so loud that they could not hear. Those fools, he thought. I'm here trying to tell them the most wonderful secret in the world, and they're yelling like they gone crazy. A hand fell upon his shoulder.

"You'll have to make a choice now, boy. You've taken too long."

He brushed the hand violently away.

"Leave me alone, man. I know what I'm doing!"

The man looked surprised and held on to the microphone for support. And because he did not wish to hurt the man's feelings he smiled, realizing with a sudden pang that there was no way of explaining to the man just why he had to stand there pressing the button forever.

"Come here," he called tiredly.

The man approached, rolling the heavy microphone across the stage.

"Anybody can play this bingo game, right?" he said.

"Sure, but . . ."

He smiled, feeling inclined to be patient with this slick looking white man with his blue shirt and his sharp gabardine suit.

"That's what I thought," he said. "Anybody can win the jackpot as long as they get the lucky number, right?"

"That's the rule, but after all . . ."

"That's what I thought," he said. "And the big prize goes to the man who knows how to win it?"

The man nodded speechlessly.

"Well then, go on over there and watch me win like I want to. I ain't going to hurt nobody," he said, "and I'll show you how to win. I mean to show the whole world how it's got to be done."

And because he understood, he smiled again to let the man know that he held nothing against him for being white and impatient. Then he refused to see the man any longer and stood pressing the button, the voices of the crowd reaching him like sounds in distant streets. Let them yell. All the Negroes down there were just ashamed because he was black like them. He smiled inwardly, knowing how it was. Most of the time he was ashamed of what Negroes did himself. Well, let them be ashamed for something this time. Like him. He was like a long thin black wire that was being stretched and wound upon the bingo wheel; wound until he wanted to scream; wound, but this time himself controlling the winding and the sadness and the shame, and because he did, Laura would be all right. Suddenly the lights flickered. He staggered backwards. Had something gone wrong? All this noise. Didn't they know that although he controlled the wheel, it also controlled him, and unless he pressed the button forever and forever and ever it would stop, leaving him high and dry, dry and high on this hard high slippery hill and Laura dead? There was only one chance; he had to do whatever the wheel demanded. And gripping the button in despair, he discovered with surprise that it imparted a nervous energy. His spine tingled. He felt a certain power.

Now he faced the raging crowd with defiance, its screams penetrating his eardrums like trumpets shrieking from a juke-box. The vague faces glowing in the bingo lights gave him a sense of himself that he had never known before. He was running the show, by God! They had to react to him, for he was their luck. This is *me*, he thought. Let the bastards yell. Then someone was laughing inside him, and he realized that somehow he had forgotten his own name. It was a sad, lost feeling to lose your name, and a crazy thing to do. That name had been given him by the white man who had owned his grandfather a long lost time ago down South. But maybe those wise guys knew his name.

"Who am I?" he screamed.

"Hurry up and bingo, you jerk!"

They didn't know either, he thought sadly. They didn't even know their own names, they were all poor nameless bastards. Well, he didn't need that old name; he was reborn. For as long as he pressed the button he was The-man-who-pressed-the-button-who-held-the-prize-who-was-the-King-of-Bingo. That was the way it was, and he'd have to press the button even if nobody understood, even though Laura did not understand.

"Live!" he shouted.

The audience quieted like the dying of a huge fan.

"Live, Laura, baby. I got holt of it now, sugar. Live!"

He screamed it, tears streaming down his face. "I got nobody but YOU!"

The screams tore from his very guts. He felt as though the rush of blood to his head would burst out in baseball seams of small red droplets, like a head beaten by police clubs. Bending over he saw a trickle of blood splashing the toe of his shoe. With his free hand he searched his head. It was his nose. God, suppose something has gone wrong? He felt that the whole audience had somehow entered him and was stamping its feet in his stomach and he was unable to throw them out. They wanted the prize, that was it. They wanted the secret for themselves. But they'd never get it; he would keep the bingo wheel whirling forever, and Laura would be safe in the wheel. But would she? It had to be, because if she were not safe the wheel would cease to turn; it could not go on. He had to get away, *vomit* all, and his mind formed an image of himself running with Laura in his arms down the tracks of the subway just ahead of an A train, running desperately *vomit* with people screaming for him to come out but knowing no way of leaving the tracks because to stop would bring the train crushing down upon him and to attempt to leave across the other tracks would mean to run into a hot third rail as high as his waist which threw blue sparks that blinded his eyes until he could hardly see.

He heard singing and the audience was clapping its hands.

Shoot the liquor to him, Jim, boy!
Clap-clap-clap
Well a-calla the cop
He's blowing his top!
Shoot the liquor to him, Jim, boy!

Bitter anger grew within him at the singing. They think I'm crazy. Well let 'em laugh. I'll do what I got to do.

He was standing in an attitude of intense listening when he saw that they were watching something on the stage behind him. He felt weak. But when he turned he saw no one. If only his thumb did not ache so. Now they were applauding. And for a moment he thought that the wheel had stopped. But that was impossible, his thumb still pressed the button. Then he saw them. Two men in uniform beckoned from the end of the stage. They were coming toward him, walking in step, slowly, like a tap-dance team returning for a third encore. But their shoulders shot forward, and he backed away, looking wildly about. There was nothing to fight them with. He had only the long black cord which led to a plug somewhere back stage, and he couldn't use that because it operated the bingo wheel. He backed slowly, fixing the men with his eyes as his lips stretched over his teeth in a tight, fixed grin; moved toward the end of the stage and realizing that he couldn't go much further, for suddenly the cord became taut and he couldn't afford to break the cord. But he had to do something. The audience was howling. Suddenly he stopped dead, seeing the men halt, their legs lifted as in an interrupted step of a slow-motion dance. There was nothing to do but run in the other direction and he dashed forward, slipping and sliding. The men fell back, surprised. He struck out violently going past.

"Grab him!"

He ran, but all too quickly the cord tightened, resistingly, and he turned and ran back again. This time he slipped them, and discovered by running in a circle before the wheel he could keep the cord from tightening. But this way he had to flail his arms to keep the men away. Why couldn't they leave a man alone? He ran, circling.

"Ring down the curtain," someone yelled. But they couldn't do that. If they did the wheel flashing from the projection room would be cut off. But they had him before he could tell them so, trying to pry open his fist, and he was wrestling and trying to bring his knees into the fight and holding on to the button, for it was his life. And now he was down, seeing a foot coming down, crushing his wrist cruelly, down, as he saw the wheel whirling serenely above.

"I can't give it up," he screamed. Then quietly, in a confidential tone, "Boys, I really can't give it up."

It landed hard against his head. And in the blank moment they had it away from him, completely now. He fought them trying to pull him up from the stage as he watched the wheel spin slowly to a stop. Without surprise he saw it rest at double zero.

"You see," he pointed bitterly.

"Sure, boy, sure, it's O.K.," one of the men said smiling.

And seeing the man bow his head to someone he could not see, he felt very, very happy; he would receive what all the winners received.

But as he warmed in the justice of the man's tight smile he did not see the man's slow wink, nor see the bow-legged man behind him step clear of the swiftly descending curtain and set himself for a blow. He only felt the dull pain exploding in his skull, and he knew even as it slipped out of him that his luck had run out on the stage.

Louise Erdrich

FLEUR

The first time she drowned in the cold and glassy waters of Lake Turcot, Fleur Pillager was only a girl. Two men saw the boat tip, saw her struggle in the waves. They rowed over to the place she went down, and jumped in. When they dragged her over the gunwales, she was cold to the touch and stiff, so they slapped her face, shook her by the heels, worked her arms back and forth, and pounded her back until she coughed up lake water. She shivered all over like a dog, then took a breath. But it wasn't long afterward that those two men disappeared. The first wandered off, and the other, Jean Hat, got himself run over by a cart.

It went to show, my grandma said. It figured to her, all right. By saving Fleur Pillager, those two men had lost themselves.

The next time she fell in the lake, Fleur Pillager was twenty years old and no one touched her. She washed onshore, her skin a dull dead gray, but when George Many Women bent to look closer, he saw her chest move. Then her eyes spun open, sharp black riprock, and she looked at him. "You'll take my place," she hissed. Everybody scattered and left her there, so no one knows how she dragged herself home. Soon after that we noticed Many Women changed, grew afraid, wouldn't leave his house, and would not be forced to go near water. For his caution, he lived until the day that his sons brought him a new tin bathtub. Then the first time he used the tub he slipped, got knocked out, and breathed water while his wife stood in the other room frying breakfast.

Men stayed clear of Fleur Pillager after the second drowning. Even though she was good-looking, nobody dared to court her because it was clear that Misshepeshu, the waterman, the monster, wanted her for himself. He's a devil, that one, love-hungry with desire and maddened for the touch of young girls, the strong and daring especially, the ones like Fleur.

Our mothers warn us that we'll think he's handsome, for he appears with green eyes, copper skin, a mouth tender as a child's. But if you fall into his arms, he sprouts horns, fangs, claws, fins. His feet are joined as one and his skin, brass scales, rings to the touch. You're fascinated, cannot move. He casts a shell necklace at your feet, weeps gleaming chips that harden into mica on your breasts. He holds you under. Then he takes the body of a lion or a fat brown worm. He's made of gold. He's made of beach moss. He's a thing of dry foam, a thing of death by drowning, the death a Chippewa cannot survive.

Unless you are Fleur Pillager. We all knew she couldn't swim. After the first time, we thought she'd never go back to Lake Turcot. We thought she'd keep to herself, live quiet, stop killing men off by drowning in the lake. After the first time, we thought she'd keep the good ways. But then, after the second drowning, we knew that we were dealing with something much more serious. She was haywire, out of control. She messed with evil, laughed at the old women's advice, and dressed like a man. She got herself into some half-forgotten medicine, studied ways we shouldn't talk about. Some say she kept the finger of a child in her pocket and a powder of unborn rabbits in a leather thong around her neck. She laid the heart of an owl on her tongue so she could see at night, and went out, hunting, not even in her own body. We know for sure because the next morning, in the snow or dust, we followed the tracks of her bare feet and saw where they changed, where the claws sprang out, the pad broadened and pressed into the dirt. By night we heard her chuffing cough, the bear cough. By day her silence and the wide grin she threw to bring down our guard made us frightened. Some thought that Fleur Pillager should be driven off the reservation, but not a single person who spoke like this had the nerve. And finally, when people were just about to get together and throw her out, she left on her own and didn't come back all summer. That's what this story is about.

During that summer, when she lived a few miles south in Argus, things happened. She almost destroyed that town.

When she got down to Argus in the year of 1920, it was just a small grid of six streets on either side of the railroad depot. There were two elevators, one central, the other a few miles west. Two stores competed for the trade of the three hundred citizens, and three churches quarreled with one another for their souls. There was a frame building for Lutherans, a heavy brick one for Episcopalians, and a long narrow shingled Catholic church. This last had a tall slender steeple, twice as high as any building or tree.

No doubt, across the low, flat wheat, watching from the road as she came near Argus on foot, Fleur saw that steeple rise, a shadow thin as a needle. Maybe in that raw space it drew her the way a lone tree draws lightning. Maybe, in the end, the Catholics are to blame. For if she hadn't seen that sign of pride, that slim prayer, that marker, maybe she would have kept walking.

But Fleur Pillager turned, and the first place she went once she came into town was to the back door of the priest's residence attached to the landmark church. She didn't go there for a handout, although she got that, but to ask for work. She got that too, or the town got her. It's hard to tell which came out worse, her or the men or the town, although the upshot of it all was that Fleur lived.

The four men who worked at the butcher's had carved up about a thousand carcasses between them, maybe half of that steers and the other half pigs, sheep, and game animals like deer, elk, and bear. That's not even mentioning the chickens, which were beyond counting. Pete Kozka owned the place, and employed Lily Veddar, Tor Grunewald, and my stepfather, Dutch James, who had brought my mother down from the reservation the year before she disappointed him by dying. Dutch took me out of school to take her place. I kept house half the time and worked the other in the butcher shop, sweeping floors, putting sawdust down, running a hambone across the street to a customer's bean pot or a package of sausage to the corner. I was a good one to have around because until they needed me, I was invisible. I blended into the stained brown walls, a skinny, big-nosed girl with staring eyes. Because I could fade into a corner or squeeze beneath a shelf, I knew everything, what the men said when no one was around, and what they did to Fleur.

Kozka's Meats served farmers for a fifty-mile area, both to slaughter, for it had a stock pen and chute, and to cure the meat by smoking it or spicing it in sausage. The storage locker was a marvel, made of many thicknesses of brick, earth insulation, and Minnesota timber, lined inside with sawdust and vast blocks of ice cut from Lake Turcot, hauled down from home each winter by horse and sledge.

A ramshackle board building, part slaughterhouse, part store, was fixed to the low, thick square of the lockers. That's where Fleur worked. Kozka hired her for her strength. She could lift a haunch or carry a pole of sausages without stumbling, and she soon learned cutting from Pete's wife, a string-thin blonde who chain-smoked and handled the razor-sharp knives with nerveless precision, slicing close to her stained fingers. Fleur and Fritzie Kozka worked afternoons, wrapping their cuts in paper, and Fleur hauled the packages to the lockers. The meat was left outside the heavy oak doors that were only opened at 5:00 each afternoon, before the men ate supper.

Sometimes Dutch, Tor, and Lily ate at the lockers, and when they did I stayed too, cleaned floors, restoked the fires in the front smokehouses, while the men sat around the squat cast-iron stove spearing slats of herring onto hardtack bread. They played long games of poker or cribbage on a board made from the planed end of a salt crate. They talked and I listened, although there wasn't much to hear since almost nothing ever happened in Argus. Tor was married, Dutch had lost my mother, and Lily read circulars. They mainly discussed about the auctions to come, equipment, or women.

Every so often, Pete Kozka came out front to make a whist, leaving Fritzie to smoke cigarettes and fry raised doughnuts in the back room. He sat and played a few rounds but kept his thoughts to himself. Fritzie did not tolerate him talking behind her back, and the one book he read was the New Testament. If he said something, it concerned weather or a surplus of sheep stomachs, a ham that smoked green or the markets for corn and wheat. He had a good-luck talisman, the opal-white lens of a cow's eye. Playing cards, he rubbed it between his fingers. That soft sound and the slap of cards was about the only conversation.

Fleur finally gave them a subject.

Her cheeks were wide and flat, her hands large, chapped, muscular. Fleur's shoulders were broad as beams, her hips fishlike, slippery, narrow. An old green dress clung to her waist, worn thin where she sat. Her braids were thick like the tails of animals, and swung against her when she moved, deliberately, slowly in her work, held in and half-tamed, but only half. I could tell, but the others never saw. They never looked into her sly brown eyes or noticed her teeth, strong and curved and very white. Her legs were bare, and since she padded around in beadwork moccasins they never saw that her fifth toes were missing. They never knew she'd drowned. They were blinded, they were stupid, they only saw her in the flesh.

And yet it wasn't just that she was a Chippewa, or even that she was a woman, it wasn't that she was good-looking or even that she was alone that made their brains hum. It was how she played cards.

Women didn't usually play with men, so the evening that Fleur drew a chair up to the men's table without being so much as asked, there was a shock of surprise.

"What's this," said Lily. He was fat, with a snake's cold pale eyes and precious skin, smooth and lily-white, which is how he got his name. Lily had a dog, a stumpy mean little bull of a thing with a belly drum-tight from eating pork rinds. The dog liked to play cards just like Lily, and straddled his barrel thighs through games of stud, rum poker, vingt-un. The dog snapped at Fleur's arm that first night, but cringed back, its snarl frozen, when she took her place.

"I thought," she said, her voice soft and stroking, "you might deal me in."

There was a space between the heavy bin of spiced flour and the wall where I just fit. I hunkered down there, kept my eyes open, saw her black hair swing over the chair, her feet solid on the wood floor. I couldn't see up on the table where the cards slapped down, so after they were deep in their game I raised myself up in the shadows, and crouched on a sill of wood.

I watched Fleur's hands stack and ruffle, divide the cards, spill them to each player in a blur, rake them up and shuffle again. Tor, short and scrappy, shut one eye and squinted the other at Fleur. Dutch screwed his lips around a wet cigar.

"Gotta see a man," he mumbled, getting up to go out back to the privy. The others broke, put their cards down, and Fleur sat alone in the lamplight that glowed in a sheen across the push of her breasts. I watched her closely, then she paid me a beam of notice for the first time. She turned, looked straight at me, and grinned the white wolf grin a Pillager turns on its victims, except that she wasn't after me.

"Pauline there," she said, "how much money you got?"

We'd all been paid for the week that day. Eight cents was in my pocket.

"Stake me," she said, holding out her long fingers. I put the coins in her palm and then I melted back to nothing, part of the walls and tables. It was a long time before I understood that the men would not have seen me no matter what I did, how I moved. I wasn't anything like Fleur. My dress hung loose and my back was already curved, an old woman's. Work had roughened me, reading made my eyes sore, caring for my mother before she died had hardened my face. I was not much to look at, so they never saw me.

When the men came back and sat around the table, they had drawn together. They shot each other small glances, stuck their tongues in their cheeks, burst out laughing at odd moments, to rattle Fleur. But she never minded. They played their vingt-un, staying even as Fleur slowly gained. Those pennies I had given her drew nickels and attracted dimes until there was a small pile in front of her.

Then she hooked them with five-card draw, nothing wild. She dealt, discarded, drew, and then she sighed and her cards gave a little shiver. Tor's eye gleamed, and Dutch straightened in his seat.

"I'll pay to see that hand," said Lily Veddar.

Fleur showed, and she had nothing there, nothing at all.

Tor's thin smile cracked open, and he threw his hand in too.

"Well, we know one thing," he said, leaning back in his chair, "the squaw can't bluff."

With that I lowered myself into a mound of swept sawdust and slept. I woke up during the night, but none of them had moved yet, so I couldn't either. Still later, the men must have gone out again, or Fritzie come out to break the game, because I was lifted, soothed, cradled in a woman's arms and rocked so quiet that I kept my eyes shut while Fleur rolled me into a closet of grimy ledgers, oiled paper, balls of string, and thick files that fit beneath me like a mattress.

The game went on after work the next evening. I got my eight cents back five times over, and Fleur kept the rest of the dollar she'd won for a stake. This time they didn't play so late, but they played regular, and then kept going at it night after night. They played poker now, or variations, for one week straight, and each time Fleur won exactly one dollar, no more and no less, too consistent for luck.

By this time, Lily and the other men were so lit with suspense that they got Pete to join the game with them. They concentrated, the fat dog sitting tense in Lily Veddar's lap, Tor suspicious, Dutch stroking his huge square brow, Pete steady. It wasn't that Fleur won that hooked them in so, because she lost hands too. It was rather that she never had a freak hand or even anything above a straight. She only took on her low cards, which didn't sit right. By chance, Fleur should have gotten a full or flush by now. The irritating thing was she beat with pairs and never bluffed, because she couldn't, and still she ended up each night with exactly one dollar. Lily couldn't believe, first of all, that a woman could be smart enough to play cards, but even if she was, that she would then be stupid enough to cheat for a dollar a night. By day I watched him turn the problem over, his hard white face dull, small fingers probing at his knuckles, until he finally thought he had Fleur figured out as a bit-time player, caution her game. Raising the stakes would throw her.

More than anything now, he wanted Fleur to come away with something but a dollar. Two bits less or ten more, the sum didn't matter, just so he broke her streak.

Night after night she played, won her dollar, and left to stay in a place that just Fritzie and I knew about. Fleur bathed in the slaughtering tub, then slept in the unused brick smokehouse behind the lockers, a windowless place tarred on the inside with scorched fats. When I brushed against her skin I noticed that she smelled of the walls, rich and woody, slightly burnt. Since that night she put me in the closet I was no longer afraid of her, but followed her close, stayed with her, became her moving shadow that the men never noticed, the shadow that could have saved her.

August, the month that bears fruit, closed around the shop, and Pete and Fritzie left for Minnesota to escape the heat. Night by night, running, Fleur had won thirty dollars, and only Pete's presence had kept Lily at bay. But Pete was gone now, and one payday, with the heat so bad no one could move but Fleur, the men sat and played and waited while she finished work. The cards sweat, limp in their fingers, the table slick with grease, and even the walls were warm to the touch. The air was motionless. Fleur was in the next room boiling heads.

Her green dress, drenched, wrapped her like a transparent sheet. A skin of lakeweed. Black snarls of veining clung to her arms. Her braids were loose, half-unraveled, tied behind her neck in a thick loop. She stood in steam, turning skulls through a vat with a wooden paddle. When scraps boiled to the surface, she bent with a round tin sieve and scooped them out. She'd filled two dishpans.

"Ain't that enough now?" called Lily. "We're waiting." The stump of a dog trembled in his lap, alive with rage. It never smelled me or noticed me above Fleur's smoky skin. The air was heavy in my corner, and pressed me down. Fleur sat with them.

"Now what do you say?" Lily asked the dog. It barked. That was the signal for the real game to start.

"Let's up the ante," said Lily, who had been stalking this night all month. He had a roll of money in his pocket. Fleur had five bills in her dress. The men had each saved their full pay.

"Ante a dollar then," said Fleur, and pitched hers in. She lost, but they let her scrape along, cent by cent. And then she won some. She played unevenly, as if chance was all she had. She reeled them in. The game went on. The dog was stiff now, poised on Lily's knees, a ball of vicious muscle with its yellow eyes slit in concentration. It gave advice, seemed to sniff the lay of Fleur's cards, twitched and nudged. Fleur was up, then down, saved by a scratch. Tor dealt seven cards, three down. The pot grew, round by round, until it held all the money. Nobody folded. Then it all rode on one last card and they went silent. Fleur picked hers up and blew a long breath. The heat lowered like a bell. Her card shook, but she stayed in.

Lily smiled and took the dog's head tenderly between his palms.

"Say, Fatso," he said, crooning the words, "you reckon that girl's bluffing?"

The dog whined and Lily laughed. "Me too," he said, "let's show." He swept his bills and coins into the pot and then they turned their cards over.

Lily looked once, looked again, then he squeezed the dog up like a fist of dough and slammed it on the table.

Fleur threw her arms out and drew the money over, grinning that same wolf grin that she'd used on me, the grin that had them. She jammed the bills in her dress, scooped the coins up in waxed white paper that she tied with string.

"Let's go another round," said Lily, his voice choked with burrs. But Fleur opened her mouth and yawned, then walked out back to gather slops for the one big hog that was waiting in the stock pen to be killed.

The men sat still as rocks, their hands spread on the oiled wood table. Dutch had chewed his cigar to damp shreds, Tor's eye was dull. Lily's gaze was the only one to follow Fleur. I didn't move. I felt them gathering, saw my stepfather's veins, the ones in his forehead that stood out in anger. The dog had rolled off the table and curled in a knot below the counter, where none of the men could touch it.

Lily rose and stepped out back to the closet of ledgers where Pete kept his private stock. He brought back a bottle, uncorked and tipped it between his fingers. The lump in his throat moved, then he passed it on. They drank, quickly felt the whiskey's fire, and planned with their eyes things they couldn't say out loud.

When they left, I followed. I hid out back in the clutter of broken boards and chicken crates beside the stock pen, where they waited. Fleur could not be seen at first, and then the moon broke and showed her, slipping cautiously along the rough board chute with a bucket in her hand. Her hair fell, wild and coarse, to her waist, and her dress was a floating patch in the dark. She made a pig-calling sound, rang the tin pail lightly against the wood, froze suspiciously. But too late. In the sound of the ring Lily moved, fat and nimble, stepped right behind Fleur and put out his creamy hands. At his first touch, she whirled and doused him with the bucket of sour slops. He pushed her against the big fence and the package of coins split, went clinking and jumping, winked against the wood. Fleur rolled over once and vanished in the yard.

The moon fell behind a curtain of ragged clouds, and Lily followed into the dark muck. But he tripped, pitched over the huge flank of the pig, who lay mired to the snout, heavily snoring. I sprang out of the weeds and climbed the side of the pen, stuck like glue. I saw the sow rise to her neat, knobby knees, gain her balance, and sway, curious, as Lily stumbled forward. Fleur had backed into the angle of rough wood just beyond, and when Lily tried to jostle past, the sow tipped up on her hind legs and struck, quick and hard as a snake. She plunged her head into Lily's thick side and snatched a mouthful of his shirt. She lunged again, caught him lower, so that he grunted in pained surprise. He seemed to ponder, breathing deep. Then he launched his huge body in a swimmer's dive.

The sow screamed as his body smacked over hers. She rolled, striking out with her knife-sharp hooves, and Lily gathered himself upon her, took her foot-long face by the ears and scraped her snout and cheeks against the trestles of the pen. He hurled the sow's tight skull against an iron post, but instead of knocking her dead, he merely woke her from her dream.

She reared, shrieked, drew him with her so that they posed standing upright. They bowed jerkily to each other, as if to begin. Then his arms swung and flailed. She sank her black fangs into his shoulder, clasping him, dancing him forward and backward through the pen. Their steps picked up pace, went wild. The two dipped as one, box-stepped, tripped each other. She ran her split foot through his hair. He grabbed her kinked tail. They went down and came up, the same shape and then the same color, until the men couldn't tell one from the other in that light and Fleur was able to launch herself over the gates, swing down, hit gravel.

The men saw, yelled, and chased her at a dead run to the smokehouse. And Lily too, once the sow gave up in disgust and freed him. That is where I should have gone to Fleur, saved her, thrown myself on Dutch. But I went stiff with fear and couldn't unlatch myself from the trestles or move at all. I closed my eyes and put my head in my arms, tried to hide, so there is nothing to describe but what I couldn't block out, Fleur's hoarse breath, so loud it filled me, her cry in the old language, and my name repeated over and over among the words.

The heat was still dense the next morning when I came back to work. Fleur was gone but the men were there, slack-faced, hung over. Lily was paler and softer than ever, as if his flesh had steamed on his bones. They smoked, took pulls off a bottle. It wasn't noon yet. I worked awhile, waiting shop and sharpening steel. But I was sick, I was smothered, I was sweating so hard that my hands slipped on the knives, and I wiped my fingers clean of the greasy touch of the customers' coins. Lily opened his mouth and roared once, not in anger. There was no meaning to the sound. His boxer dog, sprawled limp beside his foot, never lifted its head. Nor did the other men.

They didn't notice when I stepped outside, hoping for a clear breath. And then I forgot them because I knew that we were all balanced, ready to tip, to fly, to be crushed as soon as the weather broke. The sky was so low that I felt the weight of it like a yoke. Clouds hung down, witch teats, a tornado's green-brown cones, and as I watched one flicked out and became a delicate probing thumb. Even as I picked up my heels and ran back inside, the wind blew suddenly, cold, and then came rain.

Inside, the men had disappeared already and the whole place was trembling as if a huge hand was pinched at the rafters, shaking it. I ran straight through, screaming for Dutch or for any of them, and then I stopped at the heavy doors of the lockers, where they had surely taken shelter. I stood there a moment. Everything went still. Then I heard a cry building in the wind, faint at first, a whistle and then a shrill scream that tore through the walls and gathered around me, spoke plain so I understood that I should move, put my arms out, and slam down the great iron bar that fit across the hasp and lock.

Outside, the wind was stronger, like a hand held against me. I struggled forward. The bushes tossed, the awnings flapped off storefronts, the rails of porches rattled. The odd cloud became a fat snout that nosed along the earth and sniffed, jabbed, picked at things, sucked them up, blew them apart, rooted around as if it was following a certain scent, then stopped behind me at the butcher shop and bored down like a drill.

I went flying, landed somewhere in a ball. When I opened my eyes and looked, stranger things were happening.

A herd of cattle flew through the air like giant birds, dropping dung, their mouths opened in stunned bellows. A candle, still lighted, blew past, and tables, napkins, garden tools, a whole school of drifting eyeglasses, jackets on hangers, hams, a checkerboard, a lampshade, and at last the sow from behind the lockers, on the run, her hooves a blur, set free, swooping, diving, screaming as everything in Argus fell apart and got turned upside down, smashed, and thoroughly wrecked.

Days passed before the town went looking for the men. They were bachelors, after all, except for Tor, whose wife had suffered a blow to the head that made her forgetful. Everyone was occupied with digging out, in high relief because even though the Catholic steeple had been torn off like a peaked cap and sent across five fields, those huddled in the cellar were unhurt. Walls had fallen, windows were demolished, but the stores were intact and so were the bankers and shop owners who had taken refuge in their safes or beneath their cash registers. It was a fair-minded disaster, no one could be said to have suffered much more than the next, at least not until Fritzie and Pete came home.

Of all the businesses in Argus, Kozka's Meats had suffered worst. The boards of the front building had been split to kindling, piled in a huge pyramid, and the shop equipment was blasted far and wide. Pete paced off the distance the iron bathtub had been flung—a hundred feet. The glass candy case went fifty, and landed without so much as a cracked pane. There were other surprises as well, for the back rooms where Fritzie and Pete lived were undisturbed. Fritzie said the dust still coated her china figures, and upon her kitchen table, in the ashtray, perched the last cigarette she'd put out in haste. She lit it up and finished it, looking through the window. From there, she could see that the old smokehouse Fleur had slept in was crushed to a reddish sand and the stockpens were completely torn apart, the rails stacked helter-skelter. Fritzie asked for Fleur. People shrugged. Then she asked about the others and, suddenly, the town understood that three men were missing.

There was a rally of help, a gathering of shovels and volunteers. We passed boards from hand to hand, stacked them, uncovered what lay beneath the pile of jagged splinters. The lockers, full of the meat that was Pete and Fritzie's investment, slowly came into sight, still intact. When enough room was made for a man to stand on the roof, there were calls, a general urge to hack through and see what lay below. But Fritzie shouted that she wouldn't allow it because the meat would spoil. And so the work continued, board by board, until at last the heavy oak doors of the freezer were revealed and people pressed to the entry. Everyone wanted to be the first, but since it was my stepfather lost, I was let go in when Pete and Fritzie wedged through into the sudden icy air.

Pete scraped a match on his boot, lit the lamp Fritzie held, and then the three of us stood still in its circle. Light glared off the skinned and hanging carcasses, the crates of wrapped sausages, the bright and cloudy blocks of lake ice, pure as winter. The cold bit into us, pleasant at first, then numbing. We must have stood there a couple of minutes before we saw the men, or more rightly, the humps of fur, the iced and shaggy hides they wore, the bearskins they had taken down and wrapped around themselves. We stepped closer and tilted the lantern beneath the flaps of fur into their faces. The dog was there, perched among them, heavy as a doorstop. The three had hunched around a barrel where the game was still laid out, and a dead lantern and an empty bottle, too. But they had thrown down their last hands and hunkered tight, clutching one another, knuckles raw from beating at the door they had also attacked with hooks. Frost stars gleamed off their eyelashes and the stubble of their beards. Their faces were set in concentration, mouths open as if to speak some careful thought, some agreement they'd come to in each other's arms.

· · · ·

Power travels in the bloodlines, handed out before birth. It comes down through the hands, which in the Pillagers were strong and knotted, big, spidery, and rough, with sensitive fingertips good at dealing cards. It comes through the eyes, too, belligerent, darkest brown, the eyes of those in the bear clan, impolite as they gaze directly at a person.

In my dreams, I look straight back at Fleur, at the men. I am no longer the watcher on the dark sill, the skinny girl.

The blood draws us back, as if it runs through a vein of earth. I've come home and, except for talking to my cousins, live a quiet life. Fleur lives quiet too, down on Lake Turcot with her boat. Some say she's married to the waterman, Misshepeshu, or that she's living in shame with white men or windigos, or that she's killed them all. I'm about the only one here who ever goes to visit her. Last winter, I went to help out in her cabin when she bore the child, whose green eyes and skin the color of an old penny made more talk, as no one could decide if the child was mixed blood or what, fathered in a smoke-house, or by a man with brass scales, or by the lake. The girl is bold, smiling in her sleep, as if she knows what people wonder, as if she hears the old men talk, turning the story over. It comes up different every time and has no end-ing, no beginning. They get the middle wrong too. They only know that they don't know anything.

Zora Neale Hurston

SWEAT

I

It was eleven o'clock of a Spring night in Florida. It was Sunday. Any other night, Delia Jones would have been in bed for two hours by this time. But she was washwoman, and Monday morning meant a great deal to her. So she col-lected the soiled clothes on Saturday when she returned the clean things. Sunday night after church, she sorted and put the white things to soak. It saved her al-most a half-day's start. A great hamper in the bedroom held the clothes that she brought home. It was so much neater than a number of bundles lying around.

She squatted on the kitchen floor beside the great pile of clothes, sorting them into small heaps according to color, and humming a song in a mournful key, but wondering through it all where Sykes, her husband, had gone with her horse and buckboard.

Just then something long, round, limp, and black fell upon her shoulders and slithered to the floor beside her. A great terror took hold of her. It soft-ened her knees and dried her mouth so that it was a full minute before she could cry out or move. Then she saw that it was the big bull whip her husband liked to carry when he drove.

She lifted her eyes to the door and saw him standing there bent over with laughter at her fright. She screamed at him.

"Sykes, what you throw dat whip on me like dat? You know it would skeer me—looks just like a snake, an' you knows how skeered Ah is of snakes."

"Course Ah knowed it! That's how come Ah done it." He slapped his leg with his hand and almost rolled on the ground in his mirth. "If you such a big fool dat you got to have a fit over a earth worm or a string, Ah don't keer how bad Ah skeer you."

"You ain't got no business doing it. Gawd knows it's a sin. Some day Ah'm gointuh drop dead from some of yo' foolishness. 'Nother thing, where you been wid mah rig? Ah feeds dat pony. He ain't fuh you to be drivin' wid no bull whip."

"You sho' is one aggravatin' nigger woman!" he declared and stepped into the room. She resumed her work and did not answer him at once. "Ah done tole you time and again to keep them white folks' clothes outa dis house."

He picked up the whip and glared at her. Delia went on with her work. She went out into the yard and returned with a galvanized tub and set it on the wash-bench. She saw that Sykes had kicked all of the clothes together again, and now stood in her way truculently, his whole manner hoping, *praying*, for an argument. But she walked calmly around him and commenced to re-sort the things.

"Next time, Ah'm gointer kick 'em outdoors," he threatened as he struck a match along the leg of his corduroy breeches.

Delia never looked up from her work, and her thin, stooped shoulders sagged further.

"Ah ain't for no fuss t'night Sykes. Ah just come from taking sacrament at the church house."

He snorted scornfully. "Yeah, you just come from de church house on a Sunday night, but heah you is gone to work on them clothes. You ain't nothing but a hypocrite. One of them amen-corner Christians — sing, whoop, and shout, then come home and wash white folks' clothes on the Sabbath."

He stepped roughly upon the whitest pile of things, kicking them helter-skelter as he crossed the room. His wife gave a little scream of dismay, and quickly gathered them together again.

"Sykes, you quit grindin' dirt into these clothes! How can Ah git through by Sat'day if Ah don't start on Sunday?"

"Ah don't keer if you never git through. Anyhow, Ah done promised Gawd and a couple of other men, Ah ain't gointer have it in mah house. Don't gimme no lip neither, else Ah'll throw 'em out and put mah fist up side yo' head to boot."

Delia's habitual meekness seemed to slip from her shoulders like a blown scarf. She was on her feet; her poor little body, her bare knuckly hands bravely defying the strapping hulk before her.

"Looka heah, Sykes, you done gone too fur. Ah been married to you fur fifteen years, and Ah been takin' in washin' fur fifteen years. Sweat, sweat, sweat! Work and sweat, cry and sweat, pray and sweat!"

"What's that got to do with me?" he asked brutally.

"What's it got to do with you, Sykes? Mah tub of suds is filled yo' belly with vittles more times than yo' hands is filled it. Mah sweat is done paid for this house and Ah reckon Ah kin keep on sweatin' in it."

She seized the iron skillet from the stove and struck a defensive pose, which act surprised him greatly, coming from her. It cowed him and he did not strike her as he usually did.

"Naw you won't," she panted, "that ole snaggle-toothed black woman you runnin' with ain't comin' heah to pile up on mah sweat and blood. You ain't paid for nothin' on this place, and Ah'm gointer stay right heah till Ah'm toted out foot foremost."

"Well, you better quit gittin' me riled up, else they'll be totin' you out sooner than you expect. Ah'm so tired of you Ah don't know whut to do. Gawd! How Ah hates skinny wimmen!"

A little awed by this new Delia, he sidled out of the door and slammed the back gate after him. He did not say where he had gone, but she knew too well. She knew very well that he would not return until nearly daybreak also. Her work over, she went on to bed but not to sleep at once. Things had come to a pretty pass!

She lay awake, gazing upon the debris that cluttered their matrimonial trail. Not an image left standing along the way. Anything like flowers had long ago been drowned in the salty stream that had been pressed from her heart. Her tears, her sweat, her blood. She had brought love to the union and he had brought a longing after the flesh. Two months after the wedding, he had given her the first brutal beating. She had the memory of his numerous trips to Orlando with all of his wages when he had returned to her penniless, even before the first year had passed. She was young and soft then, but now she thought of her knotty, muscled limbs, her harsh knuckly hands, and drew herself up into an unhappy little ball in the middle of the big feather bed. Too late now to hope for love, even if it were not Bertha it would be someone else. This case differed from the others only in that she was bolder than the others. Too late for everything except her little home. She had built it for her old days, and planted one by one the trees and flowers there. It was lovely to her, lovely.

Somehow, before sleep came, she found herself saying aloud: "Oh well, whatever goes over the Devil's back, is got to come under his belly. Sometime or ruther, Sykes, like everybody else, is gointer reap his sowing." After that she was able to build a spiritual earthworks against her husband. His shells could no longer reach her. AMEN. She went to sleep and slept until he announced his presence in bed by kicking her feet and rudely snatching the covers away.

"Gimme some kivah heah, an' git yo' damn foots over on yo' own side! Ah oughter mash you in yo' mouf fuh drawing dat skillet on me."

Delia went clear to the rail without answering him. A triumphant indifference to all that he was or did.

II

The week was full of work for Delia as all other weeks, and Saturday found her behind her little pony, collecting and delivering clothes.

It was a hot, hot day near the end of July. The village men on Joe Clarke's porch even chewed cane listlessly. They did not hurl the cane-knots as usual. They let them dribble over the edge of the porch. Even conversation had collapsed under the heat.

"Heah come Delia Jones," Jim Merchant said, as the shaggy pony came 'round the bend of the road toward them. The rusty buckboard was heaped with baskets of crisp, clean laundry.

"Yep," Joe Lindsay agreed. "Hot or col', rain or shine, jes'ez reg'lar ez de weeks rool roun' Delia carries 'em en' fetches 'em on Sat'day."

"She better if she wanter eat," said Moss. "Syke Jones ain't wuth de shot an' powder hit would tek tuh kill 'em. Not to *huh* he ain't."

"He sho' ain't," Walter Thomas chimed in. "It's too bad, too, cause she wuz a right pretty li'l trick when he got huh. Ah'd uh mah'ied huh mahself if he hadnter beat me to it."

Delia nodded briefly at the men as she drove past.

"Too much knockin' will ruin *any* 'oman. He done beat huh 'nough tuh kill three women, let 'lone change they looks," said Elijah Moseley. "How Syke kin stommuck dat big black greasy Mogul he's layin' roun' wid, gits me. Ah swear dat eight-rock couldn't kiss a sardine can Ah done thowed out de back do' 'way las' yeah."

"Aw, she's fat, thass how come. He's allus been crazy 'bout fat women," put in Merchant. "He'd a' been tied up wid one long time ago if he could a' found one tuh have him. Did Ah tell yuh 'bout him come sidlin' roun' *mah* wife—bringin' her a basket uh peecans outa his yard fuh a present? Yessir, mah wife! She tol' him tuh take 'em right straight back home, 'cause Delia works so hard ovah dat washtub she reckon everything on de place taste lak sweat an' soap-suds. Ah jus' wisht Ah'd a' caught 'im 'roun' dere! Ah'd a' made his hips ketch on fiah down dat shell road."

"Ah know he done it, too. Ah sees 'im grinnin' at every 'oman dat passes," Walter Thomas said. "But even so, he useter eat some mighty big hunks uh humble pie tuh git dat li'l 'oman he got. She wuz ez pritty ez a speckled pup! Dat wuz fifteen years ago. He useter be so skeered uh losin' huh, she could make him do some parts of a husband's duty. Dey never wuz de same in de mind."

"There oughter be a law about him," said Lindsay. "He ain't fit tuh carry guts tuh a bear."

Clarke spoke for the first time. "'Tain't no law on earth dat kin make a man be decent if it ain't in 'im. There's plenty men dat takes a wife lak dey do a joint uh sugar-cane. It's round, juicy, an' sweet when dey gits it. But dey squeeze an' grind, squeeze an' grind an' wring tell dey wring every drop uh pleasure dat's in 'em out. When dey's satisfied dat dey is wrung dry, dey treats 'em jes' lak dey do a cane-chew. Dey thows 'em away. Dey knows whut dey is doin' while dey is at it, an' hates theirselves fuh it but they keeps on hangin' after huh tell she's empty. Den dey hates huh fuh bein' a cane-chew an' in de way."

"We oughter take Syke an' dat stray 'oman uh his'n down in Lake Howell swamp an' lay on de rawhide till they cain't say Lawd a' mussy. He allus wuz uh ovahbearin niggah, but since dat white 'oman from up north done teached 'im how to run a automobile, he done got too beggety to live—an' we oughter kill 'im," Old Man Anderson advised.

A grunt of approval went around the porch. But the heat was melting their civic virtue and Elijah Moseley began to bait Joe Clarke.

"Come on, Joe, git a melon outa dere an' slice it up for yo' customers. We'se all sufferin' wid de heat. De bear's done got *me!*"

"Thass right, Joe, a watermelon is jes' whut Ah needs tuh cure de eppizu-dicks," Walter Thomas joined forces with Moseley. "Come on dere, Joe. We all is steady customers an' you ain't set us up in a long time. Ah chooses dat long, bow-legged Floridy favorite."

"A god, an' be dough. You all gimme twenty cents and slice away," Clarke retorted. "Ah needs a col' slice m'self. Heah, everybody chip in. Ah'll lend y'all mah meat knife."

The money was all quickly subscribed and the huge melon brought forth. At that moment, Sykes and Bertha arrived. A determined silence fell on the porch and the melon was put away again.

Merchant snapped down the blade of his jackknife and moved toward the store door.

"Come on in, Joe, an' gimme a slab uh sow belly an' uh pound uh coffee —almost fuhgot 'twas Sat'day. Got to git on home." Most of the men left also.

Just then Delia drove past on her way home, as Sykes was ordering magnificently for Bertha. It pleased him for Delia to see.

"Git whutsoever yo' heart desires, Honey. Wait a minute, Joe. Give huh two bottles uh strawberry soda-water, uh quart parched ground-peas, an' a block uh chewin' gum."

With all this they left the store, with Sykes reminding Bertha that this was his town and she could have it if she wanted it.

The men returned soon after they left, and held their watermelon feast.

"Where did Syke Jones git da 'oman from nohow?" Lindsay asked.

"Ovah Apopka. Guess dey musta been cleanin' out de town when she lef'. She don't look lak a thing but a hunk uh liver wid hair on it."

"Well, she sho' kin squall," Dave Carter contributed. "When she gits ready tuh laff, she jes' opens huh mouf an' latches it back tuh de las' notch. No ole granpa alligator down in Lake Bell ain't got nothin' on huh."

III

Bertha had been in town three months now. Sykes was still paying her room-rent at Della Lewis'—the only house in town that would have taken her in. Sykes took her frequently to Winter Park to "stomps." He still assured her that he was the swellest man in the state.

"Sho' you kin have dat li'l ole house soon's Ah git dat 'oman outadere. Everything b'longs tuh me an' you sho' kin have it. Ah sho' 'bominates uh skinny 'oman. Lawdy, you sho' is got one portly shape on you! You kin git *anything* you wants. Dis is *mah* town an' you sho' kin have it."

Delia's work-worn knees crawled over the earth in Gethsemane and up the rocks of Calvary many, many times during these months. She avoided the villagers and meeting places in her efforts to be blind and deaf. But Bertha nullified this to a degree, by coming to Delia's house to call Sykes out to her at the gate.

Delia and Sykes fought all the time now with no peaceful interludes. They slept and ate in silence. Two or three times Delia had attempted a timid friendliness, but she was repulsed each time. It was plain that the breaches must remain agape.

The sun had burned July to August. The heat streamed down like a million hot arrows, smiting all things living upon the earth. Grass withered, leaves browned, snakes went blind in shedding, and men and dogs went mad. Dog days!

Delia came home one day and found Sykes there before her. She wondered, but started to go on into the house without speaking, even though he was standing in the kitchen door and she must either stoop under his arm or ask him to move. He made no room for her. She noticed a soap box beside the steps, but paid no particular attention to it, knowing that he must have brought it there. As she was stooping to pass under his outstretched arm, he suddenly pushed her backward, laughingly.

"Look in de box dere Delia, Ah done brung yuh somethin'!"

She nearly fell upon the box in her stumbling, and when she saw what it held, she all but fainted outright.

"Syke! Syke, mah Gawd! You take dat rattlesnake 'way from heah! You *got-tuh*. Oh, Jesus, have mussy!"

"Ah ain't got tuh do nuthin' uh de kin'—fact is Ah ain't got tuh do nothin' but die. Taint no use uh you puttin' on airs makin' out lak you skeered uh dat snake—he's gointer stay right heah tell he die. He wouldn't bite me cause Ah knows how tuh handle 'im. Nohow he wouldn't risk breakin' out his fangs 'gin yo skinny laigs."

"Naw, now Syke, don't keep dat thing 'round tryin' tuh skeer me tuh death. You knows Ah'm even feared uh earth worms. Thass de biggest snake Ah evah did see. Kill 'im Syke, please."

"Doan ast me tuh do nothin' fuh yuh. Goin' 'round tryin' tuh be so damn asterperious. Naw, Ah ain't gonna kill it. Ah think uh damn sight mo' uh him den you! Dat's a nice snake an' anybody doan lak 'im kin jes' hit de grit."

The village soon heard that Sykes had the snake, and came to see and ask questions.

"How de hen-fire did you ketch dat six-foot rattler, Syke?" Thomas asked.

"He's full uh frogs so he cain't hardly move, thass how Ah eased up on 'm. But Ah'm a snake charmer an' knows how tuh handle 'em. Shux, dat ain't nothin'. Ah could ketch one eve'y day if Ah so wanted tuh."

"Whut he needs is a heavy hick'ry club leaned real heavy on his head. Dat's de bes' way tuh charm a rattlesnake."

"Naw, Walt, y'all jes' don't understand dese diamon' backs lak Ah do," said Sykes in a superior tone of voice.

The village agreed with Walter, but the snake stayed on. His box remained by the kitchen door with its screen wire covering. Two or three days later it had digested its meal of frogs and literally came to life. It rattled at every movement in the kitchen or the yard. One day as Delia came down the kitchen steps she saw his chalky-white fangs curved like scimitars hung in the wire meshes. This time she did not run away with averted eyes as usual. She stood for a long time in the doorway in a red fury that grew bloodier for every second that she regarded the creature that was her torment.

That night she broached the subject as soon as Sykes sat down to the table.

"Syke, Ah wants you tuh take dat snake 'way fum heah. You done starved me an' Ah put up widcher, you done beat me an Ah took dat, but you done kilt all mah insides bringin' dat varmint heah."

Sykes poured out a saucer full of coffee and drank it deliberately before he answered her.

"A whole lot Ah keer 'bout how you feels inside uh out. Dat snake ain't goin' no damn wheah till Ah gits ready fuh 'im tuh go. So fur as beatin' is concerned, yuh ain't took near all dat you gointer take ef yuh stay 'round *me*."

Delia pushed back her plate and got up from the table. "Ah hates you, Sykes," she said calmly. "Ah hates you tuh de same degree dat Ah useter love yuh. Ah done took an' took till mah belly is full up tuh mah neck. Dat's de reason Ah got mah letter fum de church an' moved mah membership tuh Woodbridge—so Ah don't haftuh take no sacrament wid yuh. Ah don't wan-tuh see yuh 'round me atall. Lay 'round wid dat 'oman all yuh wants tuh, but gwan 'way fum me an' mah house. Ah hates yuh lak uh suck-egg dog."

Sykes almost let the huge wad of corn bread and collard greens he was chewing fall out of his mouth in amazement. He had a hard time whipping himself up to the proper fury to try to answer Delia.

"Well, Ah'm glad you does hate me. Ah'm sho' tiahed uh you hangin' ontuh me. Ah don't want yuh. Look at yuh stringey ole neck! Yo' rawbony laigs an' arms is enough tuh cut uh man tuh death. You looks jes' lak de devvul's doll-baby tuh *me*. You cain't hate me no worse den Ah hates you. Ah been hatin' *you* fuh years."

"Yo' ole black hide don't look lak nothin' tuh me, but uh passle uh wrinkled up rubber, wid yo' big ole eahs flappin' on each side lak uh paih uh buzzard wings. Don't think Ah'm gointuh be run 'way fum mah house neither. Ah'm goin' tuh de white folks 'bout *you*, mah young man, de very nex' time you lay yo' han's on me. Mah cup is done run ovah." Delia said this with no signs of fear and Sykes departed from the house, threatening her, but made not the slightest move to carry out any of them.

That night he did not return at all, and the next day being Sunday, Delia was glad she did not have to quarrel before she hitched up her pony and drove the four miles to Woodbridge.

She stayed to the night service—"love feast"—which was very warm and full of spirit. In the emotional winds her domestic trials were borne far and wide so that she sang as she drove homeward,

> *Jurden water, black an' col*
> *Chills de body, not de soul*
> *An' Ah wantah cross Jurden in uh calm time.*

She came from the barn to the kitchen door and stopped.

"Whut's de mattah, ol' Satan, you ain't kickin' up yo' racket?" She addressed the snake's box. Complete silence. She went on into the house with a new hope in its birth struggles. Perhaps her threat to go to the white folks had frightened Sykes! Perhaps he was sorry! Fifteen years of misery and suppression had brought Delia to the place where she would hope *anything* that looked towards a way over or through her wall of inhibitions.

She felt in the match-safe behind the stove at once for a match. There was only one there.

"Dat niggah wouldn't fetch nothin' heah tuh save his rotten neck, but he kin run thew whut Ah brings quick enough. Now he done toted off nigh on tuh haff uh box uh matches. He done had dat 'oman heah in mah house, too."

Nobody but a woman could tell how she knew this even before she struck the match. But she did and it put her into a new fury.

Presently she brought in the tubs to put the white things to soak. This time she decided she need not bring the hamper out of the bedroom; she would go in there and do the sorting. She picked up the pot-bellied lamp and went in. The room was small and the hamper stood hard by the foot of the white iron bed. She could sit and reach through the bedposts—resting as she worked.

"*Ah wantah cross Jurden in uh calm time.*" She was singing again. The mood of the "love feast" had returned. She threw back the lid of the basket almost gaily. Then, moved by both horror and terror, she sprang back toward the door. *There lay the snake in the basket!* He moved sluggishly at first, but even as she turned round and round, jumped up and down in an insanity of fear, he began to stir vigorously. She saw him pouring his awful beauty from the basket upon the bed, then she seized the lamp and ran as fast as she could to the kitchen. The wind from the open door blew out the light and the darkness added to her terror. She sped to the darkness of the yard, slamming the door after her before she thought to set down the lamp. She did not feel safe even on the ground, so she climbed up in the hay barn.

There for an hour or more she lay sprawled upon the hay a gibbering wreck.

Finally she grew quiet, and after that came coherent thought. With this stalked through her a cold, bloody rage. Hours of this. A period of introspection, a space of retrospection, then a mixture of both. Out of this an awful calm.

"Well, Ah done de bes' Ah could. If things ain't right, Gawd knows tain't mah fault."

She went to sleep—a twitch sleep—and woke up to a faint gray sky. There was a loud hollow sound below. She peered out. Sykes was at the wood-pile, demolishing a wire-covered box.

He hurried to the kitchen door, but hung outside there some minutes before he entered, and stood some minutes more inside before he closed it after him.

The gray in the sky was spreading. Delia descended without fear now, and crouched beneath the low bedroom window. The drawn shade shut out the dawn, shut in the night. But the thin walls held back no sound.

"Dat ol' scratch is woke up now!" She mused at the tremendous whirr inside, which every woodsman knows, is one of the sound illusions. The rattler is a ventriloquist. His whirr sounds to the right, to the left, straight ahead, behind, close under foot—everywhere but where it is. Woe to him who guesses wrong unless he is prepared to hold up his end of the argument! Sometimes he strikes without rattling at all.

Inside, Sykes heard nothing until he knocked a pot lid off the stove while trying to reach the match-safe in the dark. He had emptied his pockets at Bertha's.

The snake seemed to wake up under the stove and Sykes made a quick leap into the bedroom. In spite of the gin he had had, his head was clearing now.

"Mah Gawd!" he chattered, "ef Ah could on'y strack uh light!"

The rattling ceased for a moment as he stood paralyzed. He waited. It seemed that the snake waited also.

"Oh, fuh de light! Ah thought he'd be too sick"—Sykes was muttering to himself when the whirr began again, closer, right underfoot this time. Long before this, Sykes' ability to think had been flattened down to primitive instinct and he leaped—onto the bed.

Outside Delia heard a cry that might have come from a maddened chimpanzee, a stricken gorilla. All the terror, all the horror, all the rage that man possibly could express, without a recognizable human sound.

A tremendous stir inside there, another series of animal screams, the intermittent whirr of the reptile. The shade torn violently down from the window, letting in the red dawn, a huge brown hand seizing the window stick, great dull blows upon the wooden floor punctuating the gibberish of sound long after the rattle of the snake had abruptly subsided. All this Delia could see and hear from her place beneath the window, and it made her ill. She crept over to the four o'clocks and stretched herself on the cool earth to recover.

She lay there. "Delia, Delia!" She could hear Sykes calling in a most despairing tone as one who expected no answer. The sun crept on up, and he called. Delia could not move—her legs had gone flabby. She never moved, he called, and the sun kept rising.

"Mah Gawd!" She heard him moan, "Mah Gawd fum Heben!" She heard him stumbling about and got up from her flower-bed. The sun was growing warm. As she approached the door she heard him call out hopefully, "Delia, is dat you Ah heah?"

She saw him on his hands and knees as soon as she reached the door. He crept an inch or two toward her—all that he was able, and she saw his horribly swollen neck and his one open eye shining with hope. A surge of pity too strong to support bore her away from that eye that must, could not, fail to see the tubs. He would see the lamp. Orlando with its doctors was too far. She could scarcely reach the chinaberry tree, where she waited in the growing heat while inside she knew the cold river was creeping up and up to extinguish that eye which must know by now that she knew.

William Kotzwinkle

Follow the Eagle

Johnny Eagle climbed onto his 750-cubic-centimeter Arupa motorcycle and roared out of the Navaho Indian Reservation, followed by the Mexican, Domingo, on a rattling Japanese cycle stolen from a Colorado U law student.

Up the morning highway they rode toward the Colorado River, half-drunk and full-crazy in the sunlight, Eagle's slouch hat brim bent in the wind, Domingo's long black moustaches trailing in the air.

Yes, thought Eagle, wheeling easy over the flat land, yes indeed. And they came to Navaho Canyon where they shut down their bikes. Mist from the winding river far below rose up through the scarred plateau and the air was still.

Eagle and Domingo wheeled their bikes slowly to the edge of the Canyon. Domingo got off and threw a stone across the gorge. It struck the far wall, bounced, echoed, fell away in silence.

"Long way to the other side, man," he said, looking at Eagle.

Eagle said nothing, sat on his bike, staring across the gaping crack in the earth.

Domingo threw another stone, which cleared the gap, kicking up a little cloud of dust on top of the other cliff. "How fast you got to go—hunnert, hunnert twenty-five?"

Eagle spit into the canyon and tromped the starter of his bike.

"When you goin', man?" shouted Domingo over the roar.

"Tomorrow!"

That night was a party for Johnny Eagle on the Reservation. He danced with Red Wing in the long house, pressed her up against a corner. Medicine Man came by, gave Eagle a cougar tooth. "I been talkin' to it, Eagle," he said.

"Thanks, man," said Eagle and he put it around his neck and took Red Wing back to his shack, held her on the falling porch in the moonlight, looked at the moon over her shoulder.

She lay on his broken bed, hair undone on his ragged pillow, her buckskin jacket on the floor. Through the open window came music from the party, guitar strings and a drum head and Domingo singing

Uncle John have everything he need

"Don't go tomorrow," said Red Wing, unbuttoning Eagle's cowboy shirt.

"Gitchimanito is watchin' out for me, baby," said Eagle, and he mounted her, riding bareback, up the draw, slow, to the drumbeat. His eyes were closed but he saw her tears, like silver beads, and he rode faster and shot his arrow through the moon.

"Oh, Johnny," she moaned, quivering beneath him, "don't go," and he felt her falling away, down the waving darkness.

They lay, looking out through the window. He hung the cat's tooth around her neck. "Stay with me," she said, holding him till dawn, and he rose up while she was sleeping. The Reservation was grey, the shacks crouching in the dawn light.

Eagle shook Domingo out of his filthy bed. The Mexican crawled across the floor, looking for his sombrero, and they walked across the camp to the garage where the pickup truck was stowed with Eagle's bike.

Eagle pulled the cycle off the kickstand and they rolled it up a wooden ramp into the back of the truck, then slid the ramp in the truck, roped it down, and drove quietly off the Reservation.

They went down the empty highway, Domingo at the wheel, Eagle slouched in the corner by the door. "Why you doin' this, man?" asked the Mexican, not looking at Eagle.

Eagle's hat was over his eyes. He slept a little, nodding with the bounces in and out of a dream. His head dropped against the cold window. The truck was stopped.

Eagle stepped down onto the silent mesa. *My legs shakin,* he thought and went round to the back of the truck, where Domingo was letting down the ramp. Eagle touched the cold handlebars of the bike and stopped shaking. They wheeled the cycle to the ground.

"I know a chick," said Domingo. They pushed the ramp to the edge of the canyon. "—with a fantastic ass—" They faced the ramp to the misty hole, bracing it with cinder blocks. "She lives down in Ensenada, man, whattya say we go down there?"

Eagle climbed onto the bike, turned over the motor, breaking the morning stillness. He circled slowly, making bigger circles until the motor was running strong, then drove over to Domingo at the edge of the ramp.

"*Buena suerte, amigo!*" shouted the Mexican over the roaring engine.

"On the other side!" called Eagle, and drove away from the ramp, fifty, a hundred, two, three, four hundred yards. He turned, lined the bike up with the ramp. A white chicken fluttered in his stomach. Domingo waved his black hat.

In neutral, Eagle gunned the big Arupa engine, once, twice, and engaging first gear spun out toward the ramp.

The sun was rising, the speedometer climbing as he shifted into second gear, fifty, sixty, seventy, eighty miles an hour. Eagle burned across the table land toward Navaho Canyon, into third gear, ninety, a hundred, had jumped twelve cars on this bike, had no job, saw Domingo from the corner of his eye, was going one twenty-five and that was it as he hit the ramp and sailed his ass off into space.

The cycle whined above the mist, floating like a thunder clap, and Johnny Eagle in his slouch hat rode lightly as an arrow, airborne in the glory of the moment as a sunbeam struck him in his arc of triumph, then his sunset came upon him and he saw the flaw in his life story, *one fifty, man, not one twenty-five*, as the far cliff for which he hungered came no closer, seemed to mock him through the mist, was impossible, always had been, and his slouch hat blew away.

Don't go, Johnny.

He strained to lift his falling horse, to carry her above the morning, to fly with her between his legs, rupturing several muscles in his passion and then as he fell for certain just clung sadly with the morning rising up his asshole, poor balls groaning Johnny Eagle, falling down Navaho Canyon, the geological formations quite apparent as the mist was clearing from the rock.

"SO LONG, MAN!" he shouted, with quite a way to go, falling like a regular comet, smoke and fire out the tailpipe as the bike turned slowly over, plunging through the hollow entry. Jesus Christ my blood is boiling there goes the engine.

He fell quietly, hissing through the mist, dreaming it was still dawn on Red Wing's red-brown thighs.

Johnny, don't go. O.K. babe I'll stay here.

But he saw the real rocks rushing past him.

I uster dance. Neck down in the fender. She held me in my screwloose, Johnny Eagle, be my old man, babe I'm crazy and mus' go to Gitchegumee.

Down in Ensenada man

Domingo falling to the barroom laughing with his knife blade bloody, my look at that terra cotter there like faces in the Canyon, Sheriff you kin let us out now, won't do no harm. There goes my shoes man where am I.

A fantastic

Water lick rock. Thousand fist pound my brain out. Crack me, shell me, awful snot death crap death hunnert bucks that bike death cost me black death o no Colorado do not take me.

Yes I took you Johnny Eagle

Wham the arrow crossed the morning. I am shot from out my body whoooooooooooooooo the endless sunrise.

Some time later a fledgling eagle was hatched by an old white-headed fierce-beaked queen of the Canyon. She pushed the little eagle into space where he learned to soar, crying *kyreeeee*, high above the morning, turning in the mist upon the wind.

And Domingo, riding down to Ensenada, to see the girl in Ensenada, crossed the border singing

He saw Aunt Mary comin' an'
He duck back in the alley

Gabriel García Márquez

THE WOMAN WHO CAME AT SIX O'CLOCK

The swinging door opened. At that hour there was nobody in José's restaurant. It had just struck six and the man knew that the regular customers wouldn't begin to arrive until six-thirty. His clientele was so conservative and regular that the clock hadn't finished striking six when a woman entered, as on every day at that hour, and sat down on the stool without saying anything. She had an unlighted cigarette tight between her lips.

"Hello, queen," José said when he saw her sit down. Then he went to the other end of the counter, wiping the streaked surface with a dry rag. Whenever anyone came into the restaurant José did the same thing. Even with the woman, with whom he'd almost come to acquire a degree of intimacy, the fat and ruddy restaurant owner put on his daily comedy of a hard-working man. He spoke from the other end of the counter.

"What do you want today?" he said.

"First of all I want to teach you how to be a gentleman," the woman said. She was sitting at the end of the stools, her elbows on the counter, the extinguished cigarette between her lips. When she spoke, she tightened her mouth so that José would notice the unlighted cigarette.

"I didn't notice," José said.

"You still haven't learned to notice anything," said the woman.

The man left the cloth on the counter, walked to the dark cupboards which smelled of tar and dusty wood, and came back immediately with the matches. The woman leaned over to get the light that was burning in the man's rustic, hairy hands. José saw the woman's lush hair, all greased with cheap, thick Vaseline. He saw her uncovered shoulder above the flowered brassiere. He saw the beginning of her twilight breast when the woman raised her head, the lighted butt between her lips now.

"You're beautiful tonight, queen," José said.

"Stop your nonsense," the woman said. "Don't think that's going to help me pay you."

"That's not what I meant, queen," José said. "I'll bet your lunch didn't agree with you today."

The woman sucked in the first drag of thick smoke, crossed her arms, her elbows still on the counter, and remained looking at the street through the wide restaurant window. She had a melancholy expression. A bored and vulgar melancholy.

"I'll fix you a good steak," José said.

"I still haven't got any money," the woman said.

"You haven't had any money for three months and I always fix you something good," José said.

"Today's different," said the woman somberly, still looking out at the street.

"Every day's the same," José said. "Every day the clock says six, then you come in and say you're hungry as a dog and then I fix you something good. The only difference is this: today you didn't say you were as hungry as a dog but that today is different."

"And it's true," the woman said. She turned to look at the man, who was at the other end of the counter checking the refrigerator. She examined him for two or three seconds. Then she looked at the clock over the cupboard. It was three minutes after six. "It's true, José. Today is different," she said. She let the smoke out and kept on talking with crisp, impassioned words. "I didn't come at six today, that's why it's different, José."

The man looked at the clock.

"I'll cut off my arm if that clock is one minute slow," he said.

"That's not it, José. I didn't come at six o'clock today," the woman said.

"It just struck six, queen," José said. "When you came in it was just finishing."

"I've got a quarter of an hour that says I've been here," the woman said.

José went over to where she was. He put his great puffy face up to the woman while he tugged on one of his eyelids with his index finger.

"Blow on me here," he said.

The woman threw her head back. She was serious, annoyed, softened, beautified by a cloud of sadness and fatigue.

"Stop your foolishness, José. You know I haven't had a drink for six months."

"Tell it to somebody else," he said, "not to me. I'll bet you've had a pint or two at least."

"I had a couple of drinks with a friend," she said.

"Oh, now I understand," José said.

"There's nothing to understand," the woman said. "I've been here for a quarter of an hour."

The man shrugged his shoulders.

"Well, if that's the way you want it, you've got a quarter of an hour that says you've been here," he said. "After all, what difference does it make, ten minutes this way, ten minutes that way?"

"It makes a difference, José," the woman said. And she stretched her arms over the glass counter with an air of careless abandon. She said: "And it isn't that I wanted it that way; it's just that I've been here for a quarter of an hour." She looked at the clock again and corrected herself: "What am I saying — it's been twenty minutes."

"O.K., queen," the man said. "I'd give you a whole day and the night that goes with it just to see you happy."

During all this time José had been moving about behind the counter, changing things, taking something from one place and putting it in another. He was playing his role.

"I want to see you happy," he repeated. He stopped suddenly, turning to where the woman was. "Do you know that I love you very much?"

The woman looked at him coldly.

"Ye-e-es . . . ? What a discovery, José. Do you think I'd go with you even for a million pesos?"

"I didn't mean that, queen," José said. "I repeat, I bet your lunch didn't agree with you."

"That's not why I said it," the woman said. And her voice became less indolent. "No woman could stand a weight like yours, even for a million pesos."

José blushed. He turned his back to the woman and began to dust the bottles on the shelves. He spoke without turning his head.

"You're unbearable today, queen. I think the best thing is for you to eat your steak and go home to bed."

"I'm not hungry," the woman said. She stayed looking out at the street again, watching the passers-by of the dusking city. For an instant there was a murky silence in the restaurant. A peacefulness broken only by José's fiddling about in the cupboard. Suddenly the woman stopped looking out into the street and spoke with a tender, soft, different voice.

"Do you really love me, Pepillo?"

"I do," José said dryly, not looking at her.

"In spite of what I've said to you?" the woman asked.

"What did you say to me?" José asked, still without any inflection in his voice, still without looking at her.

"That business about a million pesos," the woman said.

"I'd already forgotten," José said.

"So do you love me?" the woman asked.

"Yes," said José.

There was a pause. José kept moving about, his face turned toward the cabinets, still not looking at the woman. She blew out another mouthful of smoke, rested her bust on the counter, and then, cautiously and roguishly, biting her tongue before saying it, as if speaking on tiptoe:

"Even if you didn't go to bed with me?" she asked.

And only then did José turn to look at her.

"I love you so much that I wouldn't go to bed with you," he said. Then he walked over to where she was. He stood looking into her face, his powerful arms leaning on the counter in front of her, looking into her eyes. He said: "I love you so much that every night I'd kill the man who goes with you."

At the first instant the woman seemed perplexed. Then she looked at the man attentively, with a wavering expression of compassion and mockery. Then she had a moment of brief disconcerted silence. And then she laughed noisily.

"You're jealous, José. That's wild, you're jealous!"

José blushed again with frank, almost shameful timidity, as might have happened to a child who'd revealed all his secrets all of a sudden. He said:

"This afternoon you don't seem to understand anything, queen." And he wiped himself with the rag. He said:

"This bad life is brutalizing you."

But now the woman had changed her expression.

"So, then," she said. And she looked into his eyes again, with a strange glow in her look, confused and challenging at the same time.

"So you're not jealous."

"In a way I am," José said. "But it's not the way you think."

He loosened his collar and continued wiping himself, drying his throat with the cloth.

"So?" the woman asked.

"The fact is I love you so much that I don't like your doing it," José said.

"What?" the woman asked.

"This business of going with a different man every day," José said.

"Would you really kill him to stop him from going with me?" the woman asked.

"Not to stop him from going with you, no," José said. "I'd kill him because he *went* with you."

"It's the same thing," the woman said.

The conversation had reached an exciting density. The woman was speaking in a soft, low, fascinated voice. Her face was almost stuck up against the man's healthy, peaceful face, as he stood motionless, as if bewitched by the vapor of the words.

"That's true," José said.

"So," the woman said, and reached out her hand to stroke the man's rough arm. With the other she tossed away her butt. "So you're capable of killing a man?"

"For what I told you, yes," José said. And his voice took on an almost dramatic stress.

The woman broke into convulsive laughter, with an obvious mocking intent.

"How awful, José. How awful," she said, still laughing. "José killing a man. Who would have known that behind the fat and sanctimonious man who never makes me pay, who cooks me a steak every day and has fun talking to me until I find a man, there lurks a murderer. How awful, José! You scare me!"

José was confused. Maybe he felt a little indignation. Maybe, when the woman started laughing, he felt defrauded.

"You're drunk, silly," he said. "Go get some sleep. You don't even feel like eating anything."

But the woman had stopped laughing now and was serious again, pensive, leaning on the counter. She watched the man go away. She saw him open the refrigerator and close it again without taking anything out. Then she saw him move to the other end of the counter. She watched him polish the shining glass, the same as in the beginning. Then the woman spoke again with the tender and soft tone of when she said: "Do you really love me, Pepillo?"

"José," she said.

The man didn't look at her.

"José!"

"Go home and sleep," José said. "And take a bath before you go to bed so you can sleep it off."

"Seriously, José," the woman said. "I'm not drunk."

"Then you've turned stupid," José said.

"Come here, I've got to talk to you," the woman said.

The man came over stumbling, halfway between pleasure and mistrust.

"Come closer!"

He stood in front of the woman again. She leaned forward, grabbed him by the hair, but with a gesture of obvious tenderness.

"Tell me again what you said at the start," she said.

"What do you mean?" José asked. He was trying to look at her with his head turned away, held by the hair.

"That you'd kill a man who went to bed with me," the woman said.

"I'd kill a man who went to bed with you, queen. That's right," José said.

The woman let him go.

"In that case you'd defend me if I killed him, right?" she asked affirmatively, pushing José's enormous pig head with a movement of brutal coquettishness. The man didn't answer anything. He smiled.

"Answer me, José," the woman said. "Would you defend me if I killed him?"

"That depends," José said. "You know it's not as easy as you say."

"The police wouldn't believe anyone more than you," the woman said.

José smiled, honored, satisfied. The woman leaned over toward him again, over the counter.

"It's true, José. I'm willing to bet that you've never told a lie in your life," she said.

"You won't get anywhere this way," José said.

"Just the same," the woman said. "The police know you and they'll believe anything without asking you twice."

José began pounding on the counter opposite her, not knowing what to say. The woman looked out at the street again. Then she looked at the clock and modified the tone of her voice, as if she were interested in finishing the conversation before the first customers arrived.

"Would you tell a lie for me, José?" she asked. "Seriously."

And then José looked at her again, sharply, deeply, as if a tremendous idea had come pounding up in his head. An idea that had entered through one ear, spun about for a moment, vague, confused, and gone out through the other, leaving behind only a warm vestige of terror.

"What have you got yourself into, queen?" José asked. He leaned forward, his arms folded over the counter again. The woman caught the strong and ammonia-smelling vapor of his breathing, which had become difficult because of the pressure that the counter was exercising on the man's stomach.

"This is really serious, queen. What have you got yourself into?" he asked.

The woman made her head spin in the opposite direction.

"Nothing," she said. "I was just talking to amuse myself."

Then she looked at him again.

"Do you know you may not have to kill anybody?"

"I never thought about killing anybody," José said, distressed.

"No, man," the woman said. "I mean nobody goes to bed with me."

"Oh!" José said. "Now you're talking straight out. I always thought you had no need to prowl around. I'll make a bet that if you drop all this I'll give you the biggest steak I've got every day, free."

"Thank you, José," the woman said. "But that's not why. It's because I *can't* go to bed with anyone any more."

"You're getting things all confused again," José said. He was becoming impatient.

"I'm not getting anything confused," the woman said. She stretched out on the seat and José saw her flat, sad breasts underneath her brassiere.

"Tomorrow I'm going away and I promise you I won't come back and bother you ever again. I promise you I'll never go to bed with anyone."

"Where'd you pick up that fever?" José asked.

"I decided just a minute ago," the woman said. "Just a minute ago I realized it's a dirty business."

José grabbed the cloth again and started to clean the glass in front of her. He spoke without looking at her.

He said:

"Of course, the way you do it it's a dirty business. You should have known that a long time ago."

"I was getting to know it a long time ago," the woman said, "but I was only convinced of it just a little while ago. Men disgust me."

José smiled. He raised his head to look at her, still smiling, but he saw her concentrated, perplexed, talking with her shoulders raised, twirling on the stool with a taciturn expression, her face gilded by premature autumnal grain.

"Don't you think they ought to lay off a woman who kills a man because after she's been with him she feels disgust with him and everyone who's been with her?"

"There's no reason to go that far," José said, moved, a thread of pity in his voice.

"What if the woman tells the man he disgusts her while she watches him get dressed because she remembers that she's been rolling around with him all afternoon and feels that neither soap nor sponge can get his smell off her?"

"That all goes away, queen," José said, a little indifferent now, polishing the counter. "There's no reason to kill him. Just let him go."

But the woman kept on talking, and her voice was a uniform, flowing, passionate current.

"But what if the woman tells him he disgusts her and the man stops getting dressed and runs over to her again, kisses her again, does . . . ?"

"No decent man would ever do that," José says.

"What if he does?" the woman asks, with exasperating anxiety. "What if the man isn't decent and does it and then the woman feels that he disgusts her so much that she could die, and she knows that the only way to end it all is to stick a knife in under him?"

"That's terrible," José said. "Luckily there's no man who would do what you say."

"Well," the woman said, completely exasperated now. "What if he did? Suppose he did."

"In any case it's not that bad," José said. He kept on cleaning the counter without changing position, less intent on the conversation now.

The woman pounded the counter with her knuckles. She became affirmative, emphatic.

"You're a savage, José," she said. "You don't understand anything." She grabbed him firmly by the sleeve. "Come on, tell me that the woman should kill him."

"O.K.," José said with a conciliatory bias. "It's all probably just the way you say it is."

"Isn't that self-defense?" the woman asked, grabbing him by the sleeve.

Then José gave her a lukewarm and pleasant look.

"Almost, almost," he said. And he winked at her, with an expression that was at the same time a cordial comprehension and a fearful compromise of complicity. But the woman was serious. She let go of him.

"Would you tell a lie to defend a woman who does that?" she asked.

"That depends," said José.

"Depends on what?" the woman asked.

"Depends on the woman," said José.

"Suppose it's a woman you love a lot," the woman said. "Not to be with her, but like you say, you love her a lot."

"O.K., anything you say, queen," José said, relaxed, bored.

He'd gone off again. He'd looked at the clock. He'd seen that it was going on half-past six. He'd thought that in a few minutes the restaurant would be filling up with people and maybe that was why he began to polish the glass with greater effort, looking at the street through the window. The woman stayed on her stool, silent, concentrating, watching the man's movements with an air of declining sadness. Watching him as a lamp about to go out might have looked at a man. Suddenly, without reacting, she spoke again with the unctuous voice of servitude.

"José!"

The man looked at her with a thick, sad tenderness, like a maternal ox. He didn't look at her to hear her, just to look at her, to know that she was there, waiting for a look that had no reason to be one of protection or solidarity. Just the look of a plaything.

"I told you I was leaving tomorrow and you didn't say anything," the woman said.

"Yes," José said. "You didn't tell me where."

"Out there," the woman said. "Where there aren't any men who want to sleep with somebody."

José smiled again.

"Are you really going away?" he asked, as if becoming aware of life, quickly changing the expression on his face.

"That depends on you," the woman said. "If you know enough to say what time I got here, I'll go away tomorrow and I'll never get mixed up in this again. Would you like that?"

José gave an affirmative nod, smiling and concrete. The woman leaned over to where he was.

"If I come back here someday I'll get jealous when I find another woman talking to you, at this time and on this same stool."

"If you come back here you'll have to bring me something," José said.

"I promise you that I'll look everywhere for the tame bear, bring him to you," the woman said.

José smiled and waved the cloth through the air that separated him from the woman, as if he were cleaning an invisible pane of glass. The woman smiled too, with an expression of cordiality and coquetry now. Then the man went away, polishing the glass to the other end of the counter.

"What, then?" José said without looking at her.

"Will you really tell anyone who asks you that I got here at a quarter to six?" the woman said.

"What for?" José said, still without looking at her now, as if he had barely heard her.

"That doesn't matter," the woman said. "The thing is that you do it."

José then saw the first customer come in through the swinging door and walk over to a corner table. He looked at the clock. It was six-thirty on the dot.

"O.K., queen," he said distractedly. "Anything you say. I always do whatever you want."

"Well," the woman said. "Start cooking my steak, then."

The man went to the refrigerator, took out a plate with a piece of meat on it, and left it on the table. Then he lighted the stove.

"I'm going to cook you a good farewell steak, queen," he said.

"Thank you, Pepillo," the woman said.

She remained thoughtful as if suddenly she had become sunken in a strange subworld peopled with muddy, unknown forms. Across the counter she couldn't hear the noise that the raw meat made when it fell into the burning grease. Afterward she didn't hear the dry and bubbling crackle as José turned the flank over in the frying pan and the succulent smell of the marinated meat by measured moments saturated the air of the restaurant. She remained like that, concentrated, reconcentrated, until she raised her head again, blinking as if she were coming back out of a momentary death. Then she saw the man beside the stove, lighted up by the happy, rising fire.

"Pepillo."

"What!"

"What are you thinking about?" the woman asked.

"I was wondering whether you could find the little wind-up bear someplace," José said.

"Of course I can," the woman said. "But what I want is for you to give me everything I asked for as a going-away present."

José looked at her from the stove.

"How often have I got to tell you?" he said. "Do you want something besides the best steak I've got?"

"Yes," the woman said.

"What is it?" José asked.

"I want another quarter of an hour."

José drew back and looked at the clock. Then he looked at the customer, who was still silent, waiting in the corner, and finally at the meat roasting in the pan. Only then did he speak.

"I really don't understand, queen," he said.

"Don't be foolish, José," the woman said. "Just remember that I've been here since five-thirty."

Bobbie Ann Mason

SHILOH

Leroy Moffitt's wife, Norma Jean, is working on her pectorals. She lifts three-pound dumbbells to warm up, then progresses to a twenty-pound barbell. Standing with her legs apart, she reminds Leroy of Wonder Woman.

"I'd give anything if I could just get these muscles to where they're real hard," says Norma Jean. "Feel this arm. It's not as hard as the other one."

"That's 'cause you're right-handed," says Leroy, dodging as she swings the barbell in an arc.

"Do you think so?"

"Sure."

Leroy is a truckdriver. He injured his leg in a highway accident four months ago, and his physical therapy which involves weights and a pulley, prompted Norma Jean to try building herself up. Now she is attending a body-building class. Leroy has been collecting temporary disability since his tractor-trailer jackknifed in Missouri, badly twisting his left leg in its socket. He has a steel pin in his hip. He will probably not be able to drive his rig again. It sits in the backyard, like a gigantic bird that has flown home to roost. Leroy has been home in Kentucky for three months, and his leg is almost healed, but the accident frightened him and he does not want to drive any more long hauls. He is not sure what to do next. In the meantime, he makes things from craft kits. He started by building a miniature log cabin from notched Popsicle sticks. He varnished it and placed it on the TV set, where it remains. It reminds him of a rustic Nativity scene. Then he tried string art (sailing ships on black velvet), a macrame owl kit, a snap-together B-17 Flying Fortress, and a lamp made out of a model truck, with a light fixture screwed in the top of the cab. At first the kits were diversions, something to kill time, but now he is thinking about building a full-scale log house from a kit. It would be considerably cheaper than building a regular house, and besides, Leroy has grown to appreciate how things are put together. He has begun to realize that in all the years he was on the road he never took time to examine anything. He was always flying past scenery.

"They won't let you build a log cabin in any of the new subdivisions," Norma Jean tells him.

"They will if I tell them it's for you," he says, teasing her. Ever since they were married, he has promised Norma Jean he would build her a new home one day. They have always rented, and the house they live in is small and nondescript. It does not even feel like a home, Leroy realizes now.

Norma Jean works at the Rexall drugstore, and she has acquired an amazing amount of information about cosmetics. When she explains to Leroy the three stages of complexion care, involving creams, toners, and moisturizers, he thinks happily of other petroleum products—axle grease, diesel fuel. This is a connection between him and Norma Jean. Since he has been home, he has felt unusually tender about his wife and guilty over his long absences. But he can't tell what she feels about him. Norma Jean has never complained about his traveling; she has never made hurt remarks, like calling his truck a "widow-maker." He is reasonably certain she has been faithful to him, but he wishes she would celebrate his permanent home-coming more happily. Norma Jean is often startled to find Leroy at home, and he thinks she seems a little disappointed about it. Perhaps he reminds her too much of the early days of their marriage, before he went on the road. They had a child who died as an infant, years ago. They never speak about their memories of Randy, which have almost faded, but now that Leroy is home all the time, they sometimes feel awkward around each other, and Leroy wonders if one of them should mention the child. He has the feeling that they are waking up out of a dream together—that they must create a new marriage, start afresh. They are lucky they are still married. Leroy has read that for most people losing a child destroys the marriage—or else he heard this on *Donahue*. He can't always remember where he learns things anymore.

At Christmas, Leroy bought an electric organ for Norma Jean. She used to play the piano when she was in high school. "It don't leave you," she told him once. "It's like riding a bicycle."

The new instrument had so many keys and buttons that she was bewildered by it at first. She touched the keys tentatively, pushed some buttons, then pecked out "Chopsticks." It came out in an amplified fox-trot rhythm, with marimba sounds.

"It's an orchestra!" she cried.

The organ had a pecan-look finish and eighteen preset chords, with optional flute, violin, trumpet, clarinet, and banjo accompaniments. Norma Jean mastered the organ almost immediately. At first she played Christmas songs. Then she bought *The Sixties Songbook* and learned every tune in it, adding variations to each with the rows of brightly colored buttons.

"I didn't like these old songs back then," she said. "But I have this crazy feeling I missed something."

"You didn't miss a thing," said Leroy.

Leroy likes to lie on the couch and smoke a joint and listen to Norma Jean play "Can't Take My Eyes Off You" and "I'll Be Back." He is back again. After fifteen years on the road, he is finally settling down with the woman he loves. She is still pretty. Her skin is flawless. Her frosted curls resemble pencil trimmings.

Now that Leroy has come home to stay, he notices how much the town has changed. Subdivisions are spreading across western Kentucky like an oil slick. The sign at the edge of town says "Pop: 11,500"—only seven hundred more than it said twenty years before. Leroy can't figure out who is living in all the new houses. The farmers who used to gather around the courthouse square on Saturday afternoons to play checkers and spit tobacco juice have gone. It has been years since Leroy has thought about the farmers, and they have disappeared without his noticing.

Leroy meets a kid named Stevie Hamilton in the parking lot at the new shopping center. While they pretend to be strangers meeting over a stalled car, Stevie tosses an ounce of marijuana under the front seat of Leroy's car. Stevie is wearing orange jogging shoes and a T-shirt that says CHATTAHOOCHEE SUPER RAT. His father is a prominent doctor who lives in one of the expensive subdivisions in a new white-columned brick house that looks like a funeral parlor. In the phone book under his name there is a separate number, with the listing "Teenagers."

"Where do you get this stuff?" asks Leroy. "From your pappy?"

"That's for me to know and you to find out," Stevie says. He is slit-eyed and skinny.

"What else you got?"

"What you interested in?"

"Nothing special. Just wondered."

Leroy used to take speed on the road. Now he has to go slowly. He needs to be mellow. He leans back against the car and says, "I'm aiming to build me a log house, soon as I get time. My wife, though, I don't think she likes the idea."

"Well, let me know when you want me again," Stevie says. He has a cigarette in his cupped palm, as though sheltering it from the wind. He takes a long drag, then stomps it on the asphalt and slouches away.

Stevie's father was two years ahead of Leroy in high school. Leroy is thirty-four. He married Norma Jean when they were both eighteen, and their child Randy was born a few months later, but he died at the age of four months and three days. He would be about Stevie's age now. Norma Jean and Leroy were at the drive-in, watching a double feature (*Dr. Strangelove* and *Lover Come Back*), and the baby was sleeping in the back seat. When the first movie ended, the baby was dead. It was the sudden infant death syndrome. Leroy remembers handing Randy to a nurse at the emergency room, as though he were offering her a large doll as a present. A dead baby feels like a sack of flour. "It just happens sometimes," said the doctor, in what Leroy always recalls as a nonchalant tone. Leroy can hardly remember the child anymore, but he still sees vividly a scene from *Dr. Strangelove* in which the President of the United States was talking in a folksy voice on the hot line to the Soviet premier about the bomber accidentally headed toward Russia. He was in the War Room, and the world map was lit up. Leroy remembers Norma Jean standing catatonically beside him in the hospital and himself thinking: Who is this strange girl? He had forgotten who she was. Now scientists are saying that crib death is caused by a virus. Nobody knows anything, Leroy thinks. The answers are always changing.

When Leroy gets home from the shopping center, Norma Jean's mother, Mabel Beasley, is there. Until this year, Leroy has not realized how much time she spends with Norma Jean. When she visits, she inspects the closets and then the plants, informing Norma Jean when a plant is droopy or yellow. Mabel calls the plants "flowers," although there are never any blooms. She also notices if Norma Jean's laundry is piling up. Mabel is a short, overweight woman whose tight, brown-dyed curls look more like a wig than the actual wig she sometimes wears. Today she has brought Norma Jean an off-white dust ruffle she made for the bed; Mabel works in a custom upholstery shop.

"This is the tenth one I made this year," Mabel says. "I got started and couldn't stop."

"It's real pretty," says Norma Jean.

"Now we can hide things under the bed," says Leroy, who gets along with his mother-in-law primarily by joking with her. Mabel has never really forgiven him for disgracing her by getting Norma Jean pregnant. When the baby died, she said that fate was mocking her.

"What's that thing?" Mabel says to Leroy in a loud voice, pointing to a tangle of yarn on a piece of canvas.

Leroy holds it up for Mabel to see. "It's my needlepoint," he explains. "This is a *Star Trek* pillow cover."

"That's what a woman would do," says Mabel. "Great day in the morning!"

"All the big football players on TV do it," he says.

"Why, Leroy, you're always trying to fool me. I don't believe you for one minute. You don't know what to do with yourself—that's the whole trouble. Sewing!"

"I'm aiming to build us a log house," says Leroy. "Soon as my plans come."

"Like *heck* you are," says Norma Jean. She takes Leroy's needlepoint and shoves it into a drawer. "You have to find a job first. Nobody can afford to build now anyway."

Mabel straightens her girdle and says, "I still think before you get tied down y'all ought to take a little run to Shiloh."

"One of these days, Mama," Norma Jean says impatiently.

Mabel is talking about Shiloh, Tennessee. For the past few years, she has been urging Leroy and Norma Jean to visit the Civil War battleground there. Mabel went there on her honeymoon—the only real trip she ever took. Her husband died of a perforated ulcer when Norma Jean was ten, but Mabel, who was accepted into the United Daughters of the Confederacy in 1975, is still preoccupied with going back to Shiloh.

"I've been to kingdom come and back in that truck out yonder," Leroy says to Mabel, "but we never yet set foot in that battleground. Ain't that something? How did I miss it?"

"It's not even that far," Mabel says.

After Mabel leaves, Norma Jean reads to Leroy from a list she has made. "Things you could do," she announces. "You could get a job as a guard at Union Carbide, where they'd let you set on a stool. You could get on at the lumberyard. You could do a little carpenter work, if you want to build so bad. You could—"

"I can't do something where I'd have to stand up all day."

"You ought to try standing up all day behind a cosmetics counter. It's amazing that I have strong feet, coming from two parents that never had strong feet at all." At the moment Norma Jean is holding on to the kitchen counter, raising her knees one at a time as she talks. She is wearing two-pound ankle weights.

"Don't worry," says Leroy. "I'll do something."

"You could truck calves to slaughter for somebody. You wouldn't have to drive any big old truck for that."

"I'm going to build you this house," says Leroy. "I want to make you a real home."

"I don't want to live in any log cabin."

"It's not a cabin. It's a house."

"I don't care. It looks like a cabin."

"You and me together could lift those logs. It's just like lifting weights."

Norma Jean doesn't answer. Under her breath, she is counting. Now she is marching through the kitchen. She is doing goose steps.

Before his accident, when Leroy came home he used to stay in the house with Norma Jean, watching TV in bed and playing cards. She would cook fried chicken, picnic ham, chocolate pie — all his favorites. Now he is home alone much of the time. In the mornings, Norma Jean disappears, leaving a cooling place in the bed. She eats a cereal called Body Buddies, and she leaves the bowl on the table, with the soggy tan balls floating in a milk puddle. He sees things about Norma Jean that he never realized before. When she chops onions, she stares off into a corner, as if she can't bear to look. She puts on her house slippers almost precisely at nine o'clock every evening and nudges her jogging shoes under the couch. She saves bread heels for the birds. Leroy watches the birds at the feeder. He notices the peculiar way goldfinches fly past the window. They close their wings, then fall, then spread their wings to catch and lift themselves. He wonders if they close their eyes when they fall. Norma Jean closes her eyes when they are in bed. She wants the lights turned out. Even then, he is sure she closes her eyes.

He goes for long drives around town. He tends to drive a car rather carelessly. Power steering and an automatic shift make a car feel so small and inconsequential that his body is hardly involved in the driving process. His injured leg stretches out comfortably. Once or twice he has almost hit something, but even the prospect of an accident seems minor in a car. He cruises the new subdivisions, feeling like a criminal rehearsing for a robbery. Norma Jean is probably right about a log house being inappropriate here in the new subdivision. All the houses look grand and complicated. They depress him.

One day when Leroy comes home from a drive he finds Norma Jean in tears. She is in the kitchen making a potato and mushroom-soup casserole, with grated cheese topping. She is crying because her mother caught her smoking.

"I didn't hear her coming. I was standing here puffing away pretty as you please," Norma Jean says, wiping her eyes.

"I knew it would happen sooner or later," says Leroy, putting his arm around her.

"She don't know the meaning of the word 'knock,'" says Norma Jean. "It's a wonder she hadn't caught me years ago."

"Think of it this way," Leroy says. "What if she caught me with a joint?"

"You better not let her!" Norma Jean shrieks. "I'm warning you, Leroy Moffitt!"

"I'm just kidding. Here, play me a tune. That'll help you relax."

Norma Jean puts the casserole in the oven and sets the timer. Then she plays a ragtime tune, with horns and banjo, as Leroy lights up a joint and lies on the couch, laughing to himself about Mabel's catching him at it. He thinks of Stevie Hamilton — a doctor's son pushing grass. Everything is funny. The whole town seems crazy and small. He is reminded of Virgil Mathis, a boastful policeman Leroy used to shoot pool with. Virgil recently led a drug bust in a back room at a bowling alley, where he seized ten thousand dollars' worth of marijuana. The newspaper had a picture of him holding up the bags of grass and grinning widely. Right now, Leroy can imagine Virgil breaking down the door and arresting him with a lungful of smoke. Virgil would probably have been alerted to the scene because of all the racket Norma Jean is making. Now she sounds like a hard-rock band. Norma Jean is terrific. When she switches to a Latin-rhythm version of "Sunshine Superman," Leroy hums along. Norma Jean's foot goes up and down, up and down.

"Well, what do you think?" Leroy says, when Norma Jean pauses to search through her music.

"What do I think about what?"

His mind has gone blank. Then he says, "I'll sell my rig and build us a house." That wasn't what he wanted to say. He wanted to know what she thought—what she *really* thought—about them.

"Don't start in on that again," says Norma Jean. She begins playing "Who'll Be the Next in Line?"

Leroy used to tell hitchhikers his whole life story—about his travels, his hometown, the baby. He would end with a question: "Well, what do you think?" It was just a rhetorical question. In time, he had the feeling that he'd been telling the same story over and over to the same hitchhikers. He quit talking to hitchhikers when he realized how his voice sounded—whining and self-pitying, like some teenage-tragedy song. Now Leroy has the sudden impulse to tell Norma Jean about himself, as if he had just met her. They have known each other so long they have forgotten a lot about each other. They could become reacquainted. But when the oven timer goes off and she runs to the kitchen, he forgets why he wants to do this.

The next day, Mabel drops by. It is Saturday and Norma Jean is cleaning. Leroy is studying the plans of his log house, which have finally come in the mail. He has them spread out on the table—big sheets of stiff blue paper, with diagrams and numbers printed in white. While Norma Jean runs the vacuum, Mabel drinks coffee. She sets her coffee cup on a blueprint.

"I'm just waiting for time to pass," she says to Leroy, drumming her fingers on the table.

As soon as Norma Jean switches off the vacuum, Mabel says in a loud voice, "Did you hear about the datsun dog that killed the baby?"

Norma Jean says, "The word is 'dachshund.'"

"They put the dog on trial. It chewed the baby's legs off. The mother was in the next room all the time." She raises her voice. "They thought it was neglect."

Norma Jean is holding her ears. Leroy manages to open the refrigerator and get some Diet Pepsi to offer Mabel. Mabel still has some coffee and she waves away the Pepsi.

"Datsuns are like that," Mabel says. "They're jealous dogs. They'll tear a place to pieces if you don't keep an eye on them."

"You better watch out what you're saying, Mabel," says Leroy.

"Well, facts is facts."

Leroy looks out the window at his rig. It is like a huge piece of furniture gathering dust in the backyard. Pretty soon it will be an antique. He hears the vacuum cleaner. Norma Jean seems to be cleaning the living room rug again.

Later, she says to Leroy, "She just said that about the baby because she caught me smoking. She's trying to pay me back."

"What are you talking about?" Leroy says, nervously shuffling blueprints.

"You know good and well," Norma Jean says. She is sitting in a kitchen chair with her feet up and her arms wrapped around her knees. She looks small and helpless. She says, "The very idea, her bringing up a subject like that! Saying it was neglect."

"She didn't mean that," Leroy says.

"She might not have *thought* she meant it. She always says things like that. You don't know how she goes on."

"But she didn't really mean it. She was just talking."

Leroy opens a king-sized bottle of beer and pours it into two glasses, dividing it carefully. He hands a glass to Norma Jean and she takes it from him mechanically. For a long time, they sit by the kitchen window watching the birds at the feeder.

Something is happening. Norma Jean is going to night school. She has graduated from her six-week body-building course and now she is taking an adult-education course in composition at Paducah Community College. She spends her evenings outlining paragraphs.

"First, you have a topic sentence," she explains to Leroy. "Then you divide it up. Your secondary topic has to be connected to your primary topic."

To Leroy, this sounds intimidating. "I never was any good in English," he says.

"It makes a lot of sense."

"What are you doing this for, anyhow?"

She shrugs. "It's something to do." She stands up and lifts her dumbbells a few times.

"Driving a rig, nobody cared about my English."

"I'm not criticizing your English."

Norma Jean used to say, "If I lose ten minutes' sleep, I just drag all day." Now she stays up late, writing compositions. She got a B on her first paper—a how-to theme on soup-based casseroles. Recently Norma Jean has been cooking unusual foods—tacos, lasagna, Bombay chicken. She doesn't play the organ anymore, though her second paper was called "Why Music Is Important to Me." She sits at the kitchen table, concentrating on her outlines, while Leroy plays with his log house plans, practicing with a set of Lincoln Logs. The thought of getting a truckload of notched, numbered logs scares him, and he wants to be prepared. As he and Norma Jean work together at the kitchen table, Leroy has the hopeful thought that they are sharing something, but he knows he is a fool to think this. Norma Jean is miles away. He knows he is going to lose her. Like Mabel, he is just waiting for time to pass.

One day, Mabel is there before Norma Jean gets home from work, and Leroy finds himself confiding in her. Mabel, he realizes, must know Norma Jean better than he does.

"I don't know what's got into that girl," Mabel says. "She used to go to bed with the chickens. Now you say she's up all hours. Plus her a-smoking. I like to died."

"I want to make her this beautiful home," Leroy says, indicating the Lincoln Logs. "I don't think she even wants it. Maybe she was happier with me gone."

"She don't know what to make of you, coming home like this."

"Is that it?"

Mabel takes the roof off his Lincoln Log cabin. "You couldn't get me in a log cabin," she says. "I was raised in one. It's no picnic, let me tell you."

"They're different now," says Leroy.

"I tell you what," Mabel says, smiling oddly at Leroy.

"What?"

"Take her on down to Shiloh. Y'all need to get out together, stir a little. Her brain's all balled up over them books."

Leroy can see traces of Norma Jean's features in her mother's face. Mabel's worn face has the texture of crinkled cotton, but suddenly she looks pretty. It occurs to Leroy that Mabel has been hinting all along that she wants them to take her with them to Shiloh.

"Let's all go to Shiloh," he says. "You and me and her. Come Sunday."

Mabel throws up her hand in protest. "Oh, no, not me. Young folks want to be by theirselves."

When Norma Jean comes in with groceries, Leroy says excitedly, "Your mama here's been dying to go to Shiloh for thirty-five years. It's about time we went, don't you think?"

"I'm not going to butt in on anybody's second honeymoon," Mabel says.

"Who's going on a honeymoon, for Christ's sake?" Norma Jean says loudly.

"I never raised no daughter of mine to talk that-a-way," Mabel says.

"You ain't seen nothing yet," says Norma Jean. She starts putting away boxes and cans, slamming cabinet doors.

"There's a log cabin at Shiloh," Mabel says. "It was there during the battle. There's bullet holes in it."

"When are you going to *shut up* about Shiloh, Mama?" asks Norma Jean.

"I always thought Shiloh was the prettiest place, so full of history," Mabel goes on. "I just hoped y'all could see it once before I die, so you could tell me about it." Later, she whispers to Leroy, "You do what I said. A little change is what she needs."

"Your name means 'the king,'" Norma Jean says to Leroy that evening. He is trying to get her to go to Shiloh, and she is reading a book about another century.

"Well, I reckon I ought to be right proud."

"I guess so."

"Am I still king around here?"

Norma Jean flexes her biceps and feels them for hardness. "I'm not fooling around with anybody, if that's what you mean," she says.

"Would you tell me if you were?"

"I don't know."

"What does *your* name mean?"

"It was Marilyn Monroe's real name."

"No kidding!"

"Norma comes from the Normans. They were invaders," she says. She closes her book and looks hard at Leroy. "I'll go to Shiloh with you if you'll stop staring at me."

On Sunday, Norma Jean packs a picnic and they go to Shiloh. To Leroy's relief Mabel says she does not want to come with them. Norma Jean drives, and Leroy, sitting beside her, feels like some boring hitchhiker she has picked up. He tries some conversation, but she answers him in monosyllables. At

Shiloh, she drives aimlessly through the park, past bluffs and trails and steep ravines. Shiloh is an immense place, and Leroy cannot see it as a battleground. It is not what he expected. He thought it would look like a golf course. Monuments are everywhere, showing through the thick clusters of trees. Norma Jean passes the log cabin Mabel mentioned. It is surrounded by tourists looking for bullet holes.

"That's not the kind of log house I've got in mind," says Leroy apologetically.

"I know *that*."

"This is a pretty place. Your mama was right."

"It's O.K.," says Norma Jean. "Well, we've seen it. I hope she's satisfied."

They burst out laughing together.

At the park museum, a movie on Shiloh is shown every half hour, but they decide that they don't want to see it. They buy a souvenir Confederate flag for Mabel, and then they find a picnic spot near the cemetery. Norma Jean has brought a picnic cooler, with pimiento sandwiches, soft drinks, and Yodels. Leroy eats a sandwich and then smokes a joint, hiding it behind the picnic cooler. Norma Jean has quit smoking altogether. She is picking cake crumbs from the cellophane wrapper, like a fussy bird.

Leroy says, "So the boys in gray ended up in Corinth. The Union soldiers zapped 'em finally. April 7, 1862."

They both know that he doesn't know any history. He is just talking about some of the historical plaques they have read. He feels awkward, like a boy on a date with an older girl. They are still just making conversation.

"Corinth is where Mama eloped to," says Norma Jean.

They sit in silence and stare at the cemetery for the Union dead and, beyond, at a tall cluster of trees. Campers are parked nearby, bumper to bumper, and small children in bright clothing are cavorting and squealing. Norma Jean wads up the cake wrapper and squeezes it tightly in her hand. Without looking at Leroy, she says, "I want to leave you."

Leroy takes a bottle of Coke out of the cooler and flips off the cap. He holds the bottle poised near his mouth but cannot remember to take a drink. Finally he says, "No, you don't."

"Yes, I do."

"I won't let you."

"You can't stop me."

"Don't do me that way."

Leroy knows Norma Jean will have her own way. "Didn't I promise to be home from now on?" he says.

"In some ways, a woman prefers a man who wanders," says Norma Jean. "That sounds crazy, I know."

"You're not crazy." Leroy remembers to drink from his Coke. Then he says, "Yes, you *are* crazy. You and me could start all over again. Right back at the beginning."

"We *have* started all over again," says Norma Jean. "And this is how it turned out."

"What did I do wrong?"

"Nothing."

"Is this one of those women's lib things?" Leroy asks.

"Don't be funny."

The cemetery, a green slope dotted with white markers, looks like a sub-division site. Leroy is trying to comprehend that his marriage is breaking up, but for some reason he is wondering about white slabs in a graveyard.

"Everything was fine till Mama caught me smoking," says Norma Jean, standing up. "That set something off."

"What are you talking about?"

"She won't leave me alone—*you* won't leave me alone." Norma Jean seems to be crying, but she is looking away from him. "I feel eighteen again. I can't face that all over again." She starts walking away. "No, it *wasn't* fine. I don't know what I'm saying. Forget it."

Leroy takes a lungful of smoke and closes his eyes as Norma Jean's words sink in. He tries to focus on the fact that thirty-five hundred soldiers died on the grounds around him. He can only think of that war as a board game with plastic soldiers. Leroy almost smiles, as he compares the Confederates' daring attack on the Union camps and Virgil Mathis's raid on the bowling alley. General Grant, drunk and furious, shoved the Southerners back to Corinth, where Mabel and Jet Beasley were married years later, when Mabel was still thin and good-looking. The next day, Mabel and Jet visited the battleground, and then Norma Jean was born, and then she married Leroy and they had a baby, which they lost, and now Leroy and Norma Jean are here at the same battleground. Leroy knows he is leaving out a lot. He is leaving out the insides of history. History was always just names and dates to him. It occurs to him that building a house of logs is similarly empty—too simple. And the real inner workings of a marriage, like most of history, have escaped him. Now he sees that building a log house is the dumbest idea he could have had. It was clumsy of him to think Norma Jean would want a log house. It was a crazy idea. He'll have to think of something else, quickly. He will wad the blueprints into tight balls and fling them into the lake. Then he'll get moving again. He opens his eyes. Norma Jean has moved away and is walking through the cemetery, follow-ing a serpentine brick path.

Leroy gets up to follow his wife, but his good leg is asleep and his bad leg still hurts him. Norma Jean is far away, walking rapidly toward the bluff by the river, and he tries to hobble toward her. Some children run past him, scream-ing noisily. Norma Jean has reached the bluff, and she is looking out over the Tennessee River. Now she turns toward Leroy and waves her arms. Is she beck-oning to him? She seems to be doing an exercise for her chest muscles. The sky is unusually pale—the color of the dust ruffle Mabel made for their bed.

Flannery O'Connor

A GOOD MAN IS HARD TO FIND

The grandmother didn't want to go to Florida. She wanted to visit some of her connections in east Tennessee and she was seizing at every chance to change Bailey's mind. Bailey was the son she lived with, her only boy. He was sitting on the edge of his chair at the table, bent over the orange sports section of the *Journal.* "Now look here, Bailey," she said, "see here, read this," and she stood with one hand on her thin hip and the other rattling the newspaper at his bald head. "Here this fellow that calls himself The Misfit is aloose from the Federal Pen and headed toward Florida and you read here what it says he did to these people. Just you read it. I wouldn't take my children in any direction with a criminal like that aloose in it. I couldn't answer to my conscience if I did."

Bailey didn't look up from his reading so she wheeled around then and faced the children's mother, a young woman in slacks, whose face was as broad and innocent as a cabbage and was tied around with a green head-kerchief that had two points on the top like rabbit's ears. She was sitting on the sofa, feeding the baby his apricots out of a jar. "The children have been to Florida before," the old lady said. "You all ought to take them somewhere else for a change so they would see different parts of the world and be broad. They never have been to east Tennessee."

The children's mother didn't seem to hear her but the eight-year-old boy, John Wesley, a stocky child with glasses, said, "If you don't want to go to Florida, why dontcha stay at home?" He and the little girl, June Star, were reading the funny papers on the floor.

"She wouldn't stay at home to be queen for a day," June Star said without raising her yellow head.

"Yes and what would you do if this fellow, The Misfit, caught you?" the grandmother said.

"I'd smack his face," John Wesley said.

"She wouldn't stay at home for a million bucks," June Star said. "Afraid she'd miss something. She has to go everywhere we go."

"All right, Miss," the grandmother said. "Just remember that the next time you want me to curl your hair."

June Star said her hair was naturally curly.

The next morning the grandmother was the first one in the car, ready to go. She had her big black valise that looked like the head of a hippopotamus in one corner, and underneath it she was hiding a basket with Pitty Sing, the cat, in it. She didn't intend for the cat to be left alone in the house for three days because he would miss her too much and she was afraid he might brush against one of the gas burners and accidentally asphyxiate himself. Her son, Bailey, didn't like to arrive at a motel with a cat.

She sat in the middle of the back seat with John Wesley and June Star on either side of her. Bailey and the children's mother and the baby sat in front and they left Atlanta at eight forty-five with the mileage on the car at 55890. The grandmother wrote this down because she thought it would be interesting to say how many miles they had been when they got back. It took them twenty minutes to reach the outskirts of the city.

The old lady settled herself comfortably, removing her white cotton gloves and putting them up with her purse on the shelf in front of the back window. The children's mother still had on slacks and still had her hair tied up in a green kerchief, but the grandmother had on a navy blue straw sailor hat with a bunch of white violets on the brim and a navy blue dress with a small white dot in the print. Her collars and cuffs were white organdy trimmed with lace and at her neckline she had pinned a purple spray of cloth violets containing a sachet. In case of an accident, anyone seeing her dead on the highway would know at once that she was a lady.

She said she thought it was going to be a good day for driving, neither too hot nor too cold, and she cautioned Bailey that the speed limit was fifty-five miles an hour and that the patrolmen hid themselves behind billboards and small clumps of trees and sped out after you before you had a chance to slow down. She pointed out interesting details of the scenery: Stone Mountain; the blue granite that in some places came up to both sides of the highway; the brilliant red clay banks slightly streaked with purple; and the various crops that made rows of green lace-work on the ground. The trees were full of silver-white sunlight and the meanest of them sparkled. The children were reading comic magazines and their mother had gone back to sleep.

"Let's go through Georgia fast so we won't have to look at it much," John Wesley said.

"If I were a little boy," said the grandmother, "I wouldn't talk about my native state that way. Tennessee has the mountains and Georgia has the hills."

"Tennessee is just a hillbilly dumping ground," John Wesley said, "and Georgia is a lousy state too."

"You said it," June Star said.

"In my time," said the grandmother, folding her thin veined fingers, "children were more respectful of their native states and their parents and everything else. People did right then. Oh look at the cute little pickaninny!" she said and pointed to a Negro child standing in the door of a shack. "Wouldn't that make a picture, now?" she asked and they all turned and looked at the little Negro out of the back window. He waved.

"He didn't have any britches on," June Star said.

"He probably didn't have any," the grandmother explained. "Little niggers in the country don't have things like we do. If I could paint, I'd paint that picture," she said.

The children exchanged comic books.

The grandmother offered to hold the baby and the children's mother passed him over the front seat to her. She set him on her knee and bounced him and told him about the things they were passing. She rolled her eyes and screwed up her mouth and stuck her leathery thin face into his smooth bland one. Occasionally he gave her a faraway smile. They passed a large cotton field with five or six graves fenced in the middle of it, like a small island. "Look at the graveyard!" the grandmother said, pointing it out. "That was the old family burying ground. That belonged to the plantation."

"Where's the plantation?" John Wesley asked.

"Gone With the Wind," said the grandmother. "Ha. Ha."

When the children finished all the comic books they had brought, they opened the lunch and ate it. The grandmother ate a peanut butter sandwich and an olive and would not let the children throw the box and the paper napkins out the window. When there was nothing else to do they played a game by choosing a cloud and making the other two guess what shape it suggested. John Wesley took one the shape of a cow and June Star guessed a cow and John Wesley said, no, an automobile, and June Star said he didn't play fair, and they began to slap each other over the grandmother.

The grandmother said she would tell them a story if they would keep quiet. When she told a story, she rolled her eyes and waved her head and was very dramatic. She said once when she was a maiden lady she had been courted by a Mr. Edgar Atkins Teagarden from Jasper, Georgia. She said he was a very good-looking man and a gentleman and that he brought her a watermelon every Saturday afternoon with his initials cut in it, E. A. T. Well, one Saturday, she said, Mr. Teagarden brought the watermelon and there was nobody at home and he left it on the front porch and returned in his buggy to Jasper, but she never got the watermelon, she said, because a nigger boy ate it when he saw the initials, E. A. T.!

This story tickled John Wesley's funny bone and he giggled and giggled but June Star didn't think it was any good. She said she wouldn't marry a man that just brought her a watermelon on Saturday. The grandmother said she would have done well to marry Mr. Teagarden because he was a gentleman and had bought Coca-Cola stock when it first came out and that he had died only a few years ago, a very wealthy man.

They stopped at The Tower for barbecued sandwiches. The Tower was a part stucco and part wood filling station and dance hall set in a clearing outside of Timothy. A fat man named Red Sammy Butts ran it and there were signs stuck here and there on the building and for miles up and down the highway saying, TRY RED SAMMY'S FAMOUS BARBECUE. NONE LIKE FAMOUS RED SAMMY'S! RED SAM! THE FAT BOY WITH THE HAPPY LAUGH. A VETERAN! RED SAMMY'S YOUR MAN!

Red Sammy was lying on the bare ground outside The Tower with his head under a truck while a gray monkey about a foot high, chained to a small chinaberry tree, chattered nearby. The monkey sprang back into the tree and got on the highest limb as soon as he saw the children jump out of the car and run toward him.

Inside, The Tower was a long dark room with a counter at one end and tables at the other and dancing space in the middle. They all sat down at a board table next to the nickelodeon and Red Sam's wife, a tall burnt-brown woman with hair and eyes lighter than her skin, came and took their order. The children's mother put a dime in the machine and played "The Tennessee Waltz," and the grandmother said that tune always made her want to dance. She asked Bailey if he would like to dance but he only glared at her. He didn't have a naturally sunny disposition like she did and trips made him nervous. The grandmother's brown eyes were very bright. She swayed her head from side to side and pretended she was dancing in her chair. June Star said play something she could tap to so the children's mother put in another dime and played a fast number and June Star stepped out onto the dance floor and did her tap routine.

"Ain't she cute?" Red Sam's wife said, leaning over the counter. "Would you like to come be my little girl?"

"No I certainly wouldn't," June Star said. "I wouldn't live in a broken-down place like this for a million bucks!" and she ran back to the table.

"Ain't she cute?" the woman repeated, stretching her mouth politely.

"Ain't you ashamed?" hissed the grandmother.

Red Sam came in and told his wife to quit lounging on the counter and hurry up with these people's order. His khaki trousers reached just to his hip bones and his stomach hung over them like a sack of meal swaying under his shirt. He came over and sat down at a table nearby and let out a combination sigh and yodel. "You can't win," he said. "You can't win," and he wiped his sweating red face off with a gray handkerchief. "These days you don't know who to trust," he said. "Ain't that the truth?"

"People are certainly not nice like they used to be," said the grandmother.

"Two fellers come in here last week," Red Sammy said, "driving a Chrysler. It was a old beat-up car but it was a good one and these boys looked all right to me. Said they worked at the mill and you know I let them fellers charge the gas they bought? Now why did I do that?"

"Because you're a good man!" the grandmother said at once.

"Yes'm, I suppose so," Red Sam said as if he were struck with this answer.

His wife brought the orders, carrying the five plates all at once without a tray, two in each hand and one balanced on her arm. "It isn't a soul in this green world of God's that you can trust," she said. "And I don't count nobody out of that, not nobody," she repeated, looking at Red Sammy.

"Did you read about that criminal, The Misfit, that's escaped?" asked the grandmother.

"I wouldn't be a bit surprised if he didn't attact this place right here," said the woman. "If he hears about it being here, I wouldn't be none surprised to see him. If he hears it's two cent in the cash register, I wouldn't be a-tall surprised if he . . ."

"That'll do," Red Sam said. "Go bring these people their Co'-Colas," and the woman went off to get the rest of the order.

"A good man is hard to find," Red Sammy said. "Everything is getting terrible. I remember the day you could go off and leave your screen door unlatched. Not no more."

He and the grandmother discussed better times. The old lady said that in her opinion Europe was entirely to blame for the way things were now. She said the way Europe acted you would think we were made of money and Red Sam said it was no use talking about it, she was exactly right. The children ran outside into the white sunlight and looked at the monkey in the lacy chinaberry tree. He was busy catching fleas on himself and biting each one carefully between his teeth as if it were a delicacy.

They drove off again into the hot afternoon. The grandmother took cat naps and woke up every five minutes with her own snoring. Outside of Toombsboro she woke up and recalled an old plantation that she had visited in this neighborhood once when she was a young lady. She said the house had six white columns across the front and that there was an avenue of oaks leading up to it and two little wooden trellis arbors on either side in front where you sat down with your suitor after a stroll in the garden. She recalled exactly which road to turn off to get to it. She knew that Bailey would not be willing to lose any time looking at an old house, but the more she talked about it, the more she wanted to see it once again and find out if the little twin arbors were still standing. "There was a secret panel in this house," she said craftily, not telling the truth but wishing that she were, "and the story went that all the family silver was hidden in it when Sherman came through but it was never found . . ."

"Hey!" John Wesley said. "Let's go see it! We'll find it! We'll poke all the woodwork and find it! Who lives there? Where do you turn off at? Hey, Pop, can't we turn off there?"

"We never have seen a house with a secret panel!" June Star shrieked. "Let's go to the house with the secret panel! Hey Pop, can't we go see the house with the secret panel!"

"It's not far from here, I know," the grandmother said. "It wouldn't take over twenty minutes."

Bailey was looking straight ahead. His jaw was as rigid as a horseshoe. "No," he said.

The children began to yell and scream that they wanted to see the house with the secret panel. John Wesley kicked the back of the front seat and June Star hung over her mother's shoulder and whined desperately into her ear that they never had any fun even on their vacation, that they could never do what THEY wanted to do. The baby began to scream and John Wesley kicked the back of the seat so hard that his father could feel the blows in his kidney.

"All right!" he shouted and drew the car to a stop at the side of the road. "Will you all shut up? Will you all just shut up for one second? If you don't shut up, we won't go anywhere."

"It would be very educational for them," the grandmother murmured.

"All right," Bailey said, "but get this: this is the only time we're going to stop for anything like this. This is the one and only time."

"The dirt road that you have to turn down is about a mile back," the grandmother directed. "I marked it when we passed."

"A dirt road," Bailey groaned.

After they had turned around and were headed toward the dirt road, the grandmother recalled other points about the house, the beautiful glass over the front doorway and the candle-lamp in the hall. John Wesley said that the secret panel was probably in the fireplace.

"You can't go inside this house," Bailey said. "You don't know who lives there."

"While you all talk to the people in front, I'll run around behind and get in a window," John Wesley suggested.

"We'll all stay in the car," his mother said.

They turned onto the dirt road and the car raced roughly along in a swirl of pink dust. The grandmother recalled the times when there were no paved roads and thirty miles was a day's journey. The dirt road was hilly and there were sudden washes in it and sharp curves on dangerous embankments. All at once they would be on a hill, looking down over the blue tops of trees for miles around, then the next minute, they would be in a red depression with the dust-coated trees looking down on them.

"This place had better turn up in a minute," Bailey said, "or I'm going to turn around."

The road looked as if no one had traveled on it for months.

"It's not much farther," the grandmother said and just as she said it, a horrible thought came to her. The thought was so embarrassing that she turned red in the face and her eyes dilated and her feet jumped up, upsetting her valise in the corner. The instant the valise moved, the newspaper top she had over the basket under it rose with a snarl and Pitty Sing, the cat, sprang onto Bailey's shoulder.

The children were thrown to the floor and their mother, clutching the baby, was thrown out the door onto the ground; the old lady was thrown into the front seat. The car turned over once and landed right-side-up in a gulch off the side of the road. Bailey remained in the driver's seat with the cat—gray-striped with a broad white face and an orange nose—clinging to his neck like a caterpillar.

As soon as the children saw they could move their arms and legs, they scrambled out of the car, shouting, "We've had an ACCIDENT!" The grandmother was curled up under the dashboard, hoping she was injured so that Bailey's wrath would not come down on her all at once. The horrible thought she had had before the accident was that the house she had remembered so vividly was not in Georgia but in Tennessee.

Bailey removed the cat from his neck with both hands and flung it out the window against the side of a pine tree. Then he got out of the car and started looking for the children's mother. She was sitting against the side of the red gutted ditch, holding the screaming baby, but she only had a cut down her face and a broken shoulder. "We've had an ACCIDENT!" the children screamed in a frenzy of delight.

"But nobody's killed," June Star said with disappointment as the grandmother limped out of the car, her hat still pinned to her head but the broken front brim standing up at a jaunty angle and the violet spray hanging off the side. They all sat down in the ditch, except the children, to recover from the shock. They were all shaking.

"Maybe a car will come along," said the children's mother hoarsely.

"I believe I have injured an organ," said the grandmother, pressing her side, but no one answered her. Bailey's teeth were clattering. He had on a yellow sport shirt with bright blue parrots designed in it and his face was as yellow as the shirt. The grandmother decided that she would not mention that the house was in Tennessee.

The road was about ten feet above and they could see only the tops of the trees on the other side of it. Behind the ditch they were sitting in there were more woods, tall and dark and deep. In a few minutes they saw a car some distance away on top of a hill, coming slowly as if the occupants were watching them. The grandmother stood up and waved both her arms dramatically to attract their attention. The car continued to come on slowly, disappeared around a bend and appeared again, moving even slower, on top of the hill they had gone over. It was a big black battered hearse-like automobile. There were three men in it.

It came to a stop just over them and for some minutes, the driver looked down with a steady expressionless gaze to where they were sitting, and didn't speak. Then he turned his head and muttered something to the other two and they got out. One was a fat boy in black trousers and a red sweat shirt with a silver stallion embossed on the front of it. He moved around on the right side of them and stood staring, his mouth partly open in a kind of loose grin. The other had on khaki pants and a blue striped coat and a gray hat pulled down very low, hiding most of his face. He came around slowly on the left side. Neither spoke.

The driver got out of the car and stood by the side of it, looking down at them. He was an older man than the other two. His hair was just beginning to gray and he wore silver-rimmed spectacles that gave him a scholarly look. He had a long creased face and didn't have on any shirt or undershirt. He had on blue jeans that were too tight for him and was holding a black hat and a gun. The two boys also had guns.

"We've had an ACCIDENT!" the children screamed.

The grandmother had the peculiar feeling that the bespectacled man was someone she knew. His face was as familiar to her as if she had known him all her life but she could not recall who he was. He moved away from the car and began to come down the embankment, placing his feet carefully so that he wouldn't slip. He had on tan and white shoes and no socks, and his ankles were red and thin. "Good afternoon," he said. "I see you all had you a little spill."

"We turned over twice!" said the grandmother.

"Oncet," he corrected. "We seen it happen. Try their car and see will it run, Hiram," he said quietly to the boy with the gray hat.

"What you got that gun for?" John Wesley asked. "Whatcha gonna do with that gun?"

"Lady," the man said to the children's mother, "would you mind calling them children to sit down by you? Children make me nervous. I want all you all to sit down right together there where you're at."

"What are you telling US what to do for?" June Star asked.

Behind them the line of woods gaped like a dark open mouth. "Come here," said their mother.

"Look here now," Bailey began suddenly, "we're in a predicament! We're in . . ."

The grandmother shrieked. She scrambled to her feet and stood staring. "You're The Misfit!" she said. "I recognized you at once!"

"Yes'm," the man said, smiling slightly as if he were pleased in spite of himself to be known, "but it would have been better for all of you, lady, if you hadn't of reckernized me."

Bailey turned his head sharply and said something to his mother that shocked even the children. The old lady began to cry and The Misfit reddened.

"Lady," he said, "don't you get upset. Sometimes a man says things he don't mean. I don't reckon he meant to talk to you thataway."

"You wouldn't shoot a lady, would you?" the grandmother said and removed a clean handkerchief from her cuff and began to slap at her eyes with it.

The Misfit pointed the toe of his shoe into the ground and made a little hole and then covered it up again. "I would hate to have to," he said.

"Listen," the grandmother almost screamed, "I know you're a good man. You don't look a bit like you have common blood. I know you must come from nice people!"

"Yes ma'am," he said, "finest people in the world." When he smiled he showed a row of strong white teeth. "God never made a finer woman than my mother and my daddy's heart was pure gold," he said. The boy with the red sweat shirt had come around behind them and was standing with his gun at his hip. The Misfit squatted down on the ground. "Watch them children, Bobby Lee," he said. "You know they make me nervous." He looked at the six of them huddled together in front of him and he seemed to be embarrassed as if he couldn't think of anything to say. "Ain't a cloud in the sky," he remarked, looking up at it. "Don't see no sun but don't see no cloud neither."

"Yes, it's a beautiful day," said the grandmother. "Listen," she said, "you shouldn't call yourself The Misfit because I know you're a good man at heart. I can just look at you and tell."

"Hush!" Bailey yelled. "Hush! Everybody shut up and let me handle this!" He was squatting in the position of a runner about to sprint forward but he didn't move.

"I pre-chate that, lady," The Misfit said and drew a little circle in the ground with the butt of his gun.

"It'll take a half a hour to fix this here car," Hiram called, looking over the raised hood of it.

"Well, first you and Bobby Lee get him and that little boy to step over yonder with you," The Misfit said, pointing to Bailey and John Wesley. "The boys want to ast you something," he said to Bailey. "Would you mind stepping back in them woods there with them?"

"Listen," Bailey began, "we're in a terrible predicament! Nobody realizes what this is," and his voice cracked. His eyes were as blue and intense as the parrots in his shirt and he remained perfectly still.

The grandmother reached up to adjust her hat brim as if she were going to the woods with him but it came off in her hand. She stood staring at it and after a second she let it fall on the ground. Hiram pulled Bailey up by the arm as if he were assisting an old man. John Wesley caught hold of his father's hand and Bobby Lee followed. They went off toward the woods and just as they reached the dark edge, Bailey turned and supporting himself against a gray naked pine trunk, he shouted, "I'll be back in a minute, Mamma, wait on me!"

"Come back this instant!" his mother shrilled but they all disappeared into the woods.

"Bailey Boy!" the grandmother called in a tragic voice but she found she was looking at The Misfit squatting on the ground in front of her. "I just know you're a good man," she said desperately. "You're not a bit common!"

"Nome, I ain't a good man," The Misfit said after a second as if he had considered her statement carefully, "but I ain't the worst in the world neither. My daddy said I was a different breed of dog from my brothers and sisters. 'You know,' Daddy said, 'it's some that can live their whole life out without asking about it and it's others has to know why it is, and this boy is one of the latters. He's going to be into everything!'" He put on his black hat and looked up suddenly and then away deep into the woods as if he were embarrassed again. "I'm sorry I don't have on a shirt before you ladies," he said, hunching his shoulders slightly. "We buried our clothes that we had on when we escaped and we're just making do until we can get better. We borrowed these from some folks we met," he explained.

"That's perfectly all right," the grandmother said. "Maybe Bailey has an extra shirt in his suitcase."

"I'll look and see terrectly," The Misfit said.

"Where are they taking him?" the children's mother screamed.

"Daddy was a card himself," The Misfit said. "You couldn't put anything over on him. He never got in trouble with the Authorities though. Just had the knack of handling them."

"You could be honest too if you'd only try," said the grandmother. "Think how wonderful it would be to settle down and live a comfortable life and not have to think about somebody chasing you all the time."

The Misfit kept scratching in the ground with the butt of his gun as if he were thinking about it. "Yes'm, somebody is always after you," he murmured.

The grandmother noticed how thin his shoulder blades were just behind his hat because she was standing up looking down on him. "Do you ever pray?" she asked.

He shook his head. All she saw was the black hat wiggle between his shoulder blades. "Nome," he said.

There was a pistol shot from the woods, followed closely by another. Then silence. The old lady's head jerked around. She could hear the wind move through the tree tops like a long satisfied insuck of breath. "Bailey Boy!" she called.

"I was a gospel singer for a while," The Misfit said. "I been most everything. Been in the arm service, both land and sea, at home and abroad, been twict married, been an undertaker, been with the railroads, plowed Mother Earth, been in a tornado, seen a man burnt alive oncet," and he looked up at the children's mother and the little girl who were sitting close together, their faces white and their eyes glassy; "I even seen a woman flogged," he said.

"Pray, pray," the grandmother began, "pray, pray . . ."

"I never was a bad boy that I remember of," The Misfit said in an almost dreamy voice, "but somewheres along the line I done something wrong and got sent to the penitentiary. I was buried alive," and he looked up and held her attention to him by a steady stare.

"That's when you should have started to pray," she said. "What did you do to get sent up to the penitentiary that first time?"

"Turn to the right, it was a wall," The Misfit said, looking up again at the cloudless sky. "Turn to the left, it was a wall. Look up it was a ceiling, look down it was a floor. I forget what I done, lady. I set there and set there, trying to remember what it was I done and I ain't recalled it to this day. Oncet in a while, I would think it was coming to me, but it never come."

"Maybe they put you in by mistake," the old lady said vaguely.

"Nome," he said. "It wasn't no mistake. They had the papers on me."

"You must have stolen something," she said.

The Misfit sneered slightly. "Nobody had nothing I wanted," he said. "It was a head-doctor at the penitentiary said what I had done was kill my daddy but I known that for a lie. My daddy died in nineteen ought nineteen of the epidemic flu and I never had a thing to do with it. He was buried in the Mount Hopewell Baptist churchyard and you can go there and see for yourself."

"If you would pray," the old lady said, "Jesus would help you."

"That's right," The Misfit said.

"Well then, why don't you pray?" she asked trembling with delight suddenly.

"I don't want no hep," he said. "I'm doing all right by myself."

Bobby Lee and Hiram came ambling back from the woods. Bobby Lee was dragging a yellow shirt with bright blue parrots in it.

"Thow me that shirt, Bobby Lee," The Misfit said. The shirt came flying at him and landed on his shoulder and he put it on. The grandmother couldn't name what the shirt reminded her of. "No, lady," The Misfit said while he was buttoning it up, "I found out the crime don't matter. You can do one thing or you can do another, kill a man or take a tire off his car, because sooner or later you're going to forget what it was you done and just be punished for it."

The children's mother had begun to make heaving noises as if she couldn't get her breath. "Lady," he asked, "would you and that little girl like to step off yonder with Bobby Lee and Hiram and join your husband?"

"Yes, thank you," the mother said faintly. Her left arm dangled helplessly and she was holding the baby, who had gone to sleep, in the other. "Hep that lady up, Hiram," The Misfit said as she struggled to climb out of the ditch, "and Bobby Lee, you hold onto that little girl's hand."

"I don't want to hold hands with him," June Star said. "He reminds me of a pig."

The fat boy blushed and laughed and caught her by the arm and pulled her off into the woods after Hiram and her mother.

Alone with The Misfit, the grandmother found that she had lost her voice. There was not a cloud in the sky nor any sun. There was nothing around her but woods. She wanted to tell him that he must pray. She opened and closed her mouth several times before anything came out. Finally she found herself saying, "Jesus. Jesus," meaning, Jesus will help you, but the way she was saying it, it sounded as if she might be cursing.

"Yes'm," The Misfit said as if he agreed. "Jesus thown everything off balance. It was the same case with Him as with me except He hadn't committed any crime and they could prove I had committed one because they had the papers on me. Of course," he said, "they never shown me my papers. That's why I sign myself now. I said long ago, you get you a signature and sign everything you do and keep a copy of it. Then you'll know what you done and you can hold up the crime to the punishment and see do they match and in the end you'll have something to prove you ain't been treated right. I call myself The Misfit," he said, "because I can't make what all I done wrong fit what all I gone through in punishment."

There was a piercing scream from the woods, followed closely by a pistol report. "Does it seem right to you, lady, that one is punished a heap and another ain't punished at all?"

"Jesus!" the old lady cried. "You've got good blood! I know you wouldn't shoot a lady! I know you come from nice people! Pray! Jesus, you ought not to shoot a lady. I'll give you all the money I've got!"

"Lady," The Misfit said, looking beyond her far into the woods, "there never was a body that give the undertaker a tip."

There were two more pistol reports and the grandmother raised her head like a perched old turkey hen crying for water and called, "Bailey Boy, Bailey Boy!" as if her heart would break.

"Jesus was the only One that ever raised the dead," The Misfit continued, "and He shouldn't have done it. He thown everything off balance. If He did what He said, then it's nothing for you to do but thow away everything and follow Him, and if He didn't, then it's nothing for you to do but enjoy the few minutes you got left the best way you can — by killing somebody or burning down his house or doing some other meanness to him. No pleasure but meanness," he said and his voice had become almost a snarl.

"Maybe He didn't raise the dead," the old lady mumbled, not knowing what she was saying and feeling so dizzy that she sank down in the ditch with her legs twisted under her.

"I wasn't there so I can't say He didn't," The Misfit said. "I wisht I had of been there," he said, hitting the ground with his fist. "It ain't right I wasn't there because if I had of been there I would of known. Listen lady," he said in a high voice, "if I had of been there I would of known and I wouldn't be like I am now." His voice seemed about to crack and the grandmother's head cleared for an instant. She saw the man's face twisted close to her own as if he were going to cry and she murmured, "Why you're one of my babies. You're one of my own children!" She reached out and touched him on the shoulder. The Misfit sprang back as if a snake had bitten him and shot her three times through the chest. Then he put his gun down on the ground and took off his glasses and began to clean them.

Hiram and Bobby Lee returned from the woods and stood over the ditch, looking down at the grandmother who half sat and half lay in a puddle of blood with her legs crossed under her like a child's and her face smiling up at the cloudless sky.

Without his glasses, The Misfit's eyes were red-rimmed and pale and defenseless-looking. "Take her off and thow her where you thown the others," he said, picking up the cat that was rubbing itself against his leg.

"She was a talker, wasn't she?" Bobby Lee said, sliding down the ditch with a yodel.

"She would of been a good woman," The Misfit said, "if it had been somebody there to shoot her every minute of her life."

"Some fun!" Bobby Lee said.

"Shut up, Bobby Lee," The Misfit said. "It's no real pleasure in life."

Amy Tan

Two Kinds

My mother believed you could be anything you wanted to be in America. You could open a restaurant. You could work for the government and get good retirement. You could buy a house with almost no money down. You could become rich. You could become instantly famous.

"Of course you can be prodigy, too," my mother told me when I was nine. "You can be best anything. What does Auntie Lindo know? Her daughter, she is only best tricky."

America was where all my mother's hopes lay. She had come here in 1949 after losing everything in China: her mother and father, her family home, her first husband, and two daughters, twin baby girls. But she never looked back with regret. There were so many ways for things to get better.

We didn't immediately pick the right kind of prodigy. At first my mother thought I could be a Chinese Shirley Temple. We'd watch Shirley's old movies on TV as though they were training films. My mother would poke my arm and say, "*Ni kan*"—You watch. And I would see Shirley tapping her feet, or singing a sailor song, or pursing her lips into a very round O while saying, "Oh, my goodness."

"*Ni kan*," said my mother as Shirley's eyes flooded with tears. "You already know how. Don't need talent for crying!"

Soon after my mother got this idea about Shirley Temple, she took me to a beauty training school in the Mission district and put me in the hands of a student who could barely hold the scissors without shaking. Instead of getting big fat curls, I emerged with an uneven mass of crinkly black fuzz. My mother dragged me off to the bathroom and tried to wet down my hair.

"You look like Negro Chinese," she lamented, as if I had done this on purpose.

The instructor of the beauty training school had to lop off these soggy clumps to make my hair even again. "Peter Pan is very popular these days," the instructor assured my mother. I now had hair the length of a boy's, with straight-across bangs that hung at a slant two inches above my eyebrows. I liked the haircut and it made me actually look forward to my future fame.

In fact, in the beginning, I was just as excited as my mother, maybe even more so. I pictured this prodigy part of me as many different images, trying each one on for size. I was a dainty ballerina girl standing by the curtains, waiting to hear the right music that would send me floating on my tiptoes. I was like the Christ child lifted out of the straw manger, crying with holy indignity. I was Cinderella stepping from her pumpkin carriage with sparkly cartoon music filling the air.

In all of my imaginings, I was filled with a sense that I would soon become *perfect*. My mother and father would adore me. I would be beyond reproach. I would never feel the need to sulk for anything.

But sometimes the prodigy in me became impatient. "If you don't hurry up and get me out of here, I'm disappearing for good," it warned. "And then you'll always be nothing."

Every night after dinner, my mother and I would sit at the Formica kitchen table. She would present new tests, taking her examples from stories of amazing children she had read in *Ripley's Believe It or Not*, or *Good Housekeeping*, *Reader's Digest*, and a dozen other magazines she kept in a pile in our bathroom. My mother got these magazines from people whose houses she cleaned. And since she cleaned many houses each week, we had a great assortment. She would look through them all, searching for stories about remarkable children.

The first night she brought out a story about a three-year-old boy who knew the capitals of all the states and even most of the European countries. A teacher was quoted as saying the little boy could also pronounce the names of the foreign cities correctly.

"What's the capital of Finland?" my mother asked me, looking at the magazine story.

All I knew was the capital of California, because Sacramento was the name of the street we lived on in Chinatown. "Nairobi!" I guessed, saying the most foreign word I could think of. She checked to see if that was possibly one way to pronounce "Helsinki" before showing me the answer.

The tests got harder—multiplying numbers in my head, finding the queen of hearts in a deck of cards, trying to stand on my head without using my hands, predicting the daily temperatures in Los Angeles, New York, and London.

One night I had to look at a page from the Bible for three minutes and then report everything I could remember. "Now Jehoshaphat had riches and honor in abundance and . . . that's all I remember, Ma," I said.

And after seeing my mother's disappointed face once again, something inside of me began to die. I hated the tests, the raised hopes and failed expectations. Before going to bed that night, I looked in the mirror above the bathroom sink and when I saw only my face staring back—and that it would always be this ordinary face—I began to cry. Such a sad, ugly girl! I made high-pitched noises like a crazed animal, trying to scratch out the face in the mirror.

And then I saw what seemed to be the prodigy side of me—because I had never seen that face before. I looked at my reflection, blinking so I could see more clearly. The girl staring back at me was angry, powerful. This girl and I were the same. I had new thoughts, willful thoughts, or rather thoughts filled with lots of won'ts. I won't let her change me, I promised myself. I won't be what I'm not.

So now on nights when my mother presented her tests, I performed listlessly, my head propped on one arm. I pretended to be bored. And I was. I got so bored I started counting the bellows of the foghorns out on the bay while my mother drilled me in other areas. The sound was comforting and reminded me of the cow jumping over the moon. And the next day, I played a game with myself, seeing if my mother would give up on me before eight bellows. After a while I usually counted only one, maybe two bellows at most. At last she was beginning to give up hope.

Two or three months had gone by without any mention of my being a prodigy again. And then one day my mother was watching *The Ed Sullivan Show* on TV. The TV was old and the sound kept shorting out. Every time my mother got halfway up from the sofa to adjust the set, the sound would go back on and Ed would be talking. As soon as she sat down, Ed would go silent again. She got up—the TV broke into loud piano music. She sat down—silence. Up and down, back and forth, quiet and loud. It was like a stiff embraceless dance between her and the TV set. Finally she stood by the set with her hand on the sound dial.

She seemed entranced by the music, a little frenzied piano piece with this mesmerizing quality, sort of quick passages and then teasing lilting ones before it returned to the quick playful parts.

"*Ni kan*," my mother said, calling me over with hurried hand gestures. "Look here."

I could see why my mother was fascinated by the music. It was being pounded out by a little Chinese girl, about nine years old, with a Peter Pan haircut. The girl had the sauciness of a Shirley Temple. She was proudly modest like a proper Chinese child. And she also did this fancy sweep of a curtsy, so that the fluffy skirt of her white dress cascaded slowly to the floor like the petals of a large carnation.

In spite of these warning signs, I wasn't worried. Our family had no piano and we couldn't afford to buy one, let alone reams of sheet music and piano lessons. So I could be generous in my comments when my mother bad-mouthed the little girl on TV.

"Play note right, but doesn't sound good! No singing sound," complained my mother.

"What are you picking on her for?" I said carelessly. "She's pretty good. Maybe she's not the best, but she's trying hard." I knew almost immediately I would be sorry I said that.

"Just like you," she said. "Not the best. Because you not trying." She gave a little huff as she let go of the sound dial and sat down on the sofa.

The little Chinese girl sat down also to play an encore of "Anitra's Dance" by Grieg. I remember the song, because later on I had to learn how to play it.

Three days after watching *The Ed Sullivan Show*, my mother told me what my schedule would be for piano lessons and piano practice. She had talked to Mr. Chong, who lived on the first floor of our apartment building. Mr. Chong was a retired piano teacher and my mother had traded housecleaning services for weekly lessons and a piano for me to practice on every day, two hours a day, from four until six.

When my mother told me this, I felt as though I had been sent to hell. I whined and then kicked my foot a little when I couldn't stand it anymore.

"Why don't you like me the way I am? I'm *not* a genius! I can't play the piano. And even if I could, I wouldn't go on TV if you paid me a million dollars!" I cried.

My mother slapped me. "Who ask you be genius?" she shouted. "Only ask you be your best. For you sake. You think I want you be genius? Hnnh! What for! Who ask you!"

"So ungrateful," I heard her mutter in Chinese. "If she had as much talent as she has temper, she would be famous now."

Mr. Chong, whom I secretly nicknamed Old Chong, was very strange, always tapping his fingers to the silent music of an invisible orchestra. He looked ancient in my eyes. He had lost most of the hair on top of his head and he wore thick glasses and had eyes that always looked tired and sleepy. But he must have been younger than I thought, since he lived with his mother and was not yet married.

I met Old Lady Chong once and that was enough. She had this peculiar smell like a baby that had done something in its pants. And her fingers felt like a dead person's, like an old peach I once found in the back of the refrigerator; the skin just slid off the meat when I picked it up.

I soon found out why Old Chong had retired from teaching piano. He was deaf. "Like Beethoven!" he shouted to me. "We're both listening only in our head!" And he would start to conduct his frantic silent sonatas.

Our lessons went like this. He would open the book and point to different things, explaining their purpose: "Key! Treble! Bass! No sharps or flats! So this is C major! Listen now and play after me!"

And then he would play the C scale a few times, a simple chord, and then, as if inspired by an old, unreachable itch, he gradually added more notes and running trills and a pounding bass until the music was really something quite grand.

I would play after him, the simple scale, the simple chord, and then I just played some nonsense that sounded like a cat running up and down on top of garbage cans. Old Chong smiled and applauded and then said, "Very good! But now you must learn to keep time!"

So that's how I discovered that Old Chong's eyes were too slow to keep up with the wrong notes I was playing. He went through the motions in half-time. To help me keep rhythm, he stood behind me, pushing down on my right shoulder for every beat. He balanced pennies on top of my wrists so I would keep them still as I slowly played scales and arpeggios. He had me curve my hand around an apple and keep that shape when playing chords. He marched stiffly to show me how to make each finger dance up and down, staccato like an obedient little soldier.

He taught me all these things, and that was how I also learned I could be lazy and get away with mistakes, lots of mistakes. If I hit the wrong notes because I hadn't practiced enough, I never corrected myself. I just kept playing in rhythm. And Old Chong kept conducting his own private reverie.

So maybe I never really gave myself a fair chance. I did pick up the basics pretty quickly, and I might have become a good pianist at that young age. But I was so determined not to try, not to be anybody different, that I learned to play only the most ear-splitting preludes, the most discordant hymns.

Over the next year, I practiced like this, dutifully in my own way. And then one day I heard my mother and her friend Lindo Jong both talking in a loud bragging tone of voice so others could hear. It was after church, and I was leaning against the brick wall wearing a dress with stiff white petticoats. Auntie Lindo's daughter, Waverly, who was about my age, was standing farther down the wall about five feet away. We had grown up together and shared all the closeness of two sisters squabbling over crayons and dolls. In other words, for the most part, we hated each other. I thought she was snotty. Waverly Jong had gained a certain amount of fame as "Chinatown's Littlest Chinese Chess Champion."

"She bring home too many trophy," lamented Auntie Lindo that Sunday. "All day she play chess. All day I have no time do nothing but dust off her winnings." She threw a scolding look at Waverly, who pretended not to see her.

"You lucky you don't have this problem," said Auntie Lindo with a sigh to my mother.

And my mother squared her shoulders and bragged: "Our problem worser than yours. If we ask Jing-mei wash dish, she hear nothing but music. It's like you can't stop this natural talent."

And right then, I was determined to put a stop to her foolish pride.

A few weeks later, Old Chong and my mother conspired to have me play in a talent show which would be held in the church hall. By then, my parents had saved up enough to buy me a secondhand piano, a black Wurlitzer spinet with a scarred bench. It was the showpiece of our living room.

For the talent show, I was to play a piece called "Pleading Child" from Schumann's *Scenes from Childhood.* It was a simple, moody piece that sounded more difficult than it was. I was supposed to memorize the whole thing, playing the repeat parts twice to make the piece sound longer. But I dawdled over it, playing a few bars and then cheating, looking up to see what notes followed. I never really listened to what I was playing. I daydreamed about being somewhere else, about being someone else.

The part I liked to practice best was the fancy curtsy: right foot out, touch the rose on the carpet with a pointed foot, sweep to the side, left leg bends, look up and smile.

My parents invited all the couples from the Joy Luck Club to witness my debut. Auntie Lindo and Uncle Tin were there. Waverly and her two older brothers had also come. The first two rows were filled with children both younger and older than I was. The littlest ones got to go first. They recited simple nursery rhymes, squawked out tunes on miniature violins, twirled Hula Hoops, pranced in pink ballet tutus, and when they bowed or curtsied, the audience would sigh in unison, "Awww," and then clap enthusiastically.

When my turn came, I was very confident. I remember my childish excitement. It was as if I knew, without a doubt, that the prodigy side of me really did exist. I had no fear whatsoever, no nervousness. I remember thinking to myself, This is it! This is it! I looked out over the audience, at my mother's blank face, my father's yawn, Auntie Lindo's stiff-lipped smile, Waverly's sulky expression. I had on a white dress layered with sheets of lace, and a pink bow in my Peter Pan haircut. As I sat down I envisioned people jumping to their feet and Ed Sullivan rushing up to introduce me to everyone on TV.

And I started to play. It was so beautiful. I was so caught up in how lovely I looked that at first I didn't worry how I would sound. So it was a surprise to me when I hit the first wrong note and I realized something didn't sound quite right. And then I hit another and another followed that. A chill started at the top of my head and began to trickle down. Yet I couldn't stop playing, as though my hands were bewitched. I kept thinking my fingers would adjust themselves back, like a train switching to the right track. I played this strange jumble through two repeats, the sour notes staying with me all the way to the end.

When I stood up, I discovered my legs were shaking. Maybe I had just been nervous and the audience, like Old Chong, had seen me go through the right motions and had not heard anything wrong at all. I swept my right foot out, went down on my knee, looked up and smiled. The room was quiet, except for Old Chong, who was beaming and shouting, "Bravo! Bravo! Well done!" But then I saw my mother's face, her stricken face. The audience clapped weakly, and as I walked back to my chair, with my whole face quivering as I tried not to cry, I heard a little boy whisper loudly to his mother, "That was awful," and the mother whispered back, "Well, she certainly tried."

And now I realized how many people were in the audience — the whole world it seemed. I was aware of eyes burning into my back. I felt the shame of my mother and father as they sat stiffly throughout the rest of the show.

We could have escaped during intermission. Pride and some strange sense of honor must have anchored my parents to their chairs. And so we watched it all: the eighteen-year-old boy with a fake mustache who did a magic show and juggled flaming hoops while riding a unicycle. The breasted girl with white makeup who sang from *Madama Butterfly* and got honorable mention. And the eleven-year-old boy who won first prize playing a tricky violin song that sounded like a busy bee.

After the show, the Hsus, the Jongs, and the St. Clairs from the Joy Luck Club came up to my mother and father.

"Lots of talented kids," Auntie Lindo said vaguely, smiling broadly.

"That was somethin' else," said my father, and I wondered if he was referring to me in a humorous way, or whether he even remembered what I had done.

Waverly looked at me and shrugged her shoulders. "You aren't a genius like me," she said matter-of-factly. And if I hadn't felt so bad, I would have pulled her braids and punched her stomach.

But my mother's expression was what devastated me: a quiet, blank look that said she had lost everything. I felt the same way, and it seemed as if everybody were now coming up, like gawkers at the scene of an accident, to see what parts were actually missing. When we got on the bus to go home, my father was humming the busy-bee tune and my mother was silent. I kept thinking she wanted to wait until we got home before shouting at me. But when my father unlocked the door to our apartment, my mother walked in and then went to the back, into the bedroom. No accusations. No blame. And in a way, I felt disappointed. I had been waiting for her to start shouting, so I could shout back and cry and blame her for all my misery.

I assumed my talent-show fiasco meant I never had to play the piano again. But two days later, after school, my mother came out of the kitchen and saw me watching TV.

"Four clock," she reminded me as if it were any other day. I was stunned, as though she were asking me to go through the talent-show torture again. I wedged myself more tightly in front of the TV.

"Turn off TV," she called from the kitchen five minutes later.

I didn't budge. And then I decided. I didn't have to do what my mother said anymore. I wasn't her slave. This wasn't China. I had listened to her before and look what happened. She was the stupid one.

She came out from the kitchen and stood in the arched entryway of the living room. "Four clock," she said once again, louder.

"I'm not going to play anymore," I said nonchalantly. "Why should I? I'm not a genius."

She walked over and stood in front of the TV. I saw her chest was heaving up and down in an angry way.

"No!" I said, and I now felt stronger, as if my true self had finally emerged. So this was what had been inside me all along.

"No! I won't!" I screamed.

She yanked me by the arm, pulled me off the floor, snapped off the TV. She was frighteningly strong, half pulling, half carrying me toward the piano as I kicked the throw rugs under my feet. She lifted me up and onto the hard bench. I was sobbing by now, looking at her bitterly. Her chest was heaving even more and her mouth was open, smiling crazily as if she were pleased I was crying.

"You want me to be someone that I'm not!" I sobbed. "I'll never be the kind of daughter you want me to be!"

"Only two kinds of daughters," she shouted in Chinese. "Those who are obedient and those who follow their own mind! Only one kind of daughter can live in this house. Obedient daughter!"

"Then I wish I wasn't your daughter. I wish you weren't my mother," I shouted. As I said these things I got scared. It felt like worms and toads and slimy things crawling out of my chest, but it also felt good, as if this awful side of me had surfaced, at last.

"Too late change this," said my mother shrilly.

And I could sense her anger rising to its breaking point. I wanted to see it spill over. And that's when I remembered the babies she had lost in China, the ones we never talked about. "Then I wish I'd never been born!" I shouted. "I wish I were dead! Like them."

It was as if I had said the magic words. Alakazam!—and her face went blank, her mouth closed, her arms went slack, and she backed out of the room, stunned, as if she were blowing away like a small brown leaf, thin, brittle, lifeless.

It was not the only disappointment my mother felt in me. In the years that followed, I failed her so many times, each time asserting my own will, my right to fall short of expectations. I didn't get straight As. I didn't become class president. I didn't get into Stanford. I dropped out of college.

For unlike my mother, I did not believe I could be anything I wanted to be. I could only be me.

And for all those years, we never talked about the disaster at the recital or my terrible accusations afterward at the piano bench. All that remained unchecked, like a betrayal that was now unspeakable. So I never found a way to ask her why she had hoped for something so large that failure was inevitable.

And even worse, I never asked her what frightened me the most: Why had she given up hope?

For after our struggle at the piano, she never mentioned my playing again. The lessons stopped. The lid to the piano was closed, shutting out the dust, my misery, and her dreams.

So she surprised me. A few years ago, she offered to give me the piano, for my thirtieth birthday. I had not played in all those years. I saw the offer as a sign of forgiveness, a tremendous burden removed.

"Are you sure?" I asked shyly. "I mean, won't you and Dad miss it?"

"No, this your piano," she said firmly. "Always your piano. You only one can play."

"Well, I probably can't play anymore," I said. "It's been years."

"You pick up fast," said my mother, as if she knew this was certain. "You have natural talent. You could been genius if you want to."

"No I couldn't."

"You just not trying," said my mother. And she was neither angry nor sad. She said it as if to announce a fact that could never be disproved. "Take it," she said.

But I didn't at first. It was enough that she had offered it to me. And after that, every time I saw it in my parents' living room, standing in front of the bay windows, it made me feel proud, as if it were a shiny trophy I had won back.

Last week I sent a tuner over to my parents' apartment and had the piano reconditioned, for purely sentimental reasons. My mother had died a few months before and I had been getting things in order for my father, a little bit at a time. I put the jewelry in special silk pouches. The sweaters she had knitted in yellow, pink, bright orange — all the colors I hated — I put those in moth-proof boxes. I found some old Chinese silk dresses, the kind with little slits up the sides. I rubbed the old silk against my skin, then wrapped them in tissue and decided to take them home with me.

After I had the piano tuned, I opened the lid and touched the keys. It sounded even richer than I remembered. Really, it was a very good piano. Inside the bench were the same exercise notes with handwritten scales, the same secondhand music books with their covers held together with yellow tape.

I opened up the Schumann book to the dark little piece I had played at the recital. It was on the left-hand side of the page, "Pleading Child." It looked more difficult than I remembered. I played a few bars, surprised at how easily the notes came back to me.

And for the first time, or so it seemed, I noticed the piece on the right-hand side. It was called "Perfectly Contented." I tried to play this one as well. It had a lighter melody but the same flowing rhythm and turned out to be quite easy. "Pleading Child" was shorter but slower; "Perfectly Contented" was longer, but faster. And after I played them both a few times, I realized they were two halves of the same song.

12

Writing Drama:

Constructing the Story

Writing to Warm Up

Think of a short story or memoir that you have written or that you know well and write a short summary of it. Now read over the summary and imagine adapting this story for performance as a play. Would it be feasible to dramatize this story? Why or why not? What elements of the short story could be dramatized? What elements could not be dramatized? Make a list of the changes you would need to make for the story to work as a dramatic piece. What are the similarities and differences between fiction and drama?

In chapters 8–11, you learned and practiced the art of writing fiction and literary nonfiction. Although writers use many of the same skills in writing drama as they do in writing literary prose, writing plays presents a different kind of challenge to the writer, for stories are primarily literary pieces. Even if they are read aloud for an audience, the audience must still *visualize* the action and characters in the story. In a segment of his show "Prairie Home Companion," which is performed live and broadcast over the radio, Garrison Keillor tells stories of the townspeople in Lake Wobegon, Minnesota. Even though these stories are written to be performed, the audience can only see the characters in their imaginations through Keillor's descriptions. Keillor tells us what a character is thinking, just as a narrator might do in a short story. In fiction, the audience must rely on the narrator to open up the world of the story.

The magic of the theater is that the story is enacted on stage. The audience does not need a narrator to describe the characters and recount the events that take place because they are there, in the theater, watching life unfold. Although plays are often anthologized in literature books and are studied as works of literature, their purpose transcends their literary value. They exist on paper so that they can be transformed into reality on stage.

Therefore, even though an audience can *listen* to a story being read aloud, an audience *experiences* a play. Energy exists between the actors and the audience, and the match that ignites the fire between them is found in the script, the written word transformed into spoken words and actions. No one performance of a play can be exactly like another. The script might be the same for each performance, but plays depend on the interaction between the actors and the audience as well as the chemistry that exists among the actors themselves. When you write a play, then, you enable your words to live, and although this means entrusting them to others, it also means that you have not just written words on a page; you have created something that evolves and grows from a raw script through casting and rehearsal to production. Writing a play and seeing it performed and the energy that results is as close to being Dr. Frankenstein as most of us will get.

What the playwright has the opportunity to do with this energy is to reveal to the audience a small part of life by presenting it with imaginative hindsight. The playwright mirrors an aspect of life, creating an imaginary world that reveals or comments on the mysteries of the human experience. Playwright Marsha Norman says that the playwright has the "power to take the attention of a group of people and focus it in one place. It's kind of a magnifying-glass trick. You capture sunlight and focus it and burn the hole right through." As she moves forward through the play, the playwright reflects on some aspect of life.

This doesn't mean that all playwrights depict life and time realistically. Some plays incorporate absurdity, surrealism, or other unrealistic elements, and many well-written plays propose more questions than answers. What they do have in common is that they all use the energy of the spoken word (dialogue) coupled with visual presentation (staging) to explore the complexities of the human experience.

Writing the Drama

In a narrative, a narrator possesses a direct line to the reader, and although readers' interpretations of a work of literature may vary, the line of communication is direct. In a play, a playwright creates dialogue and action, but the work is then interpreted by a director and the actors who portray the characters. You must, therefore, write precisely and clearly, for these words of yours will be heard as well as seen, and these actions you describe will be seen as well as imagined. As Edward Albee states, "I always think I'm writing a string quartet when I'm writing a play. It's the same aural experience, and you have to be as precise in your notation." As a dramatist, you don't just create action in your reader's mind; you create real action, real conversation.

To hone your skills as a playwright, you should read plays and see plays. In addition, you should associate yourself with a theater or theater group, and this is much easier than it sounds. You don't have to audition at your college or a repertory theater group and get the lead part or have your first play produced as a major production. That is probably not realistic. But you can always volunteer some time swinging a hammer or painting a set. Free labor is always in short supply around theaters, and even though you might not see the immediate benefits of taking hinges off of flats or sweeping the stage shop, you will learn about the theater. Playwright Terrence McNally worked as stage manager for the Actors Studio. "I did a lot of moving and sweeping," he states. "But I also saw how some great professionals worked, how they shaped, rehearsed, rewrote."

The more you know about the production of a play, the better equipped you are to write plays. Even if you are more interested in writing for television or film, you might have easier access to local theater than to movie soundstages. Learning to write good plays for the theater provides you with an excellent foundation for whatever kind of dramatic writing you would like to do. In the theater you will learn what makes a play's production feasible. Beginning playwrights need to have a realistic view of staging considerations and production costs. Many theaters are on shoestring budgets and cannot produce plays that require expensive casting and scenery.

Another good way to prepare yourself for writing drama is to read and study plays. There are many different kinds of plays, ranging from comedy, where the protagonist overcomes the conflicts of the play, to tragedy, which chronicles the protagonist's ruin, and every degree in between. Tragicomedy has a plot line that is patterned after tragedy, but the protagonist is victorious in the end. Black comedy uses humor to comment critically on some aspect of life. Read and see as many plays as you can, for each play you see helps you make decisions about your own work.

You might find that you want to experiment with character and form, but learning about the history of dramatic literature can provide you with a solid foundation, whether your writing is traditional or experimental. Read the great tragedies such as Sophocles's *Oedipus Rex* and Shakespeare's *Macbeth* as well as plays by Henrik Ibsen, Tennessee Williams, Terrence McNally, Sam Shepard, and Wendy Wasserstein. Reading Aristotle's advice to dramatists in the *Poetics* would also contribute to your knowledge of a dramatic model that playwrights have followed for over two thousand years. In the *Poetics*, Aristotle discusses the six essential elements of tragedy, including plot, character, diction, thought, music, and spectacle.

A portion of the *Poetics* outlines the basic structure of tragedy, emphasizing plot and character as being the most important aspects of drama, and citing diction and thought as being the cornerstones of good speech or dialogue. According to Aristotle, the plot should contain some type of significant action, and in this action the main character (hero) must experience a reversal of fortune (from good to bad, in tragedy), many times through no fault of his own. He tries to overcome his bad fortune, but fate prevails. Eventually he recognizes the inevitability of his fall, and he nobly meets his fate. The Aristotelian hero is a man who is above other men in character, so that his fall will be more significant, but human enough for the audience to empathize and identify with him. He is more than other men, for the hero lives life beyond its limitations, rising above societal norms. The intent of Greek tragedy is to shake the audience to the core and invoke a catharsis, or emotional purification.

While most playwrights today don't adhere strictly to all of Aristotle's tenets, many successful plays and films follow at least some of Aristotle's advice, although as philosophical outlooks change from age to age, the philosophical content of the drama will change as well. For example, in Arthur Miller's play *All My Sons*, the "hero," Joe Keller, knowingly sends out defective airplane parts from his manufacturing plant during World War II. When the parts are found to be defective, Keller frames his business partner, who is sent to jail. When his family finds out about his part in the crime, he tries to make them understand that he committed the crime for the good of his family, for stopping the shipment would have meant closing the plant. Although the plot structure of *All My Sons* adheres to Aristotle's model, the hero is not a nobleman or a man whose character is above all others. He does exhibit heroic characteristics, and near the end of the play he recognizes his transgressions, but he has also committed unjustifiable criminal acts. The audience pities him rather than reveres him, although they can identify with his motivation to protect his own family at all costs.

Joe Keller is not a hero by Aristotle's definition, and we don't perceive him in the same way we perceive Hamlet or Oedipus. We see him as an anti-hero, an ordinary man who has many flaws and yet, like Aristotle's hero, goes beyond the ordinary man in his actions and thought. At the end of the play he acknowledges that the pilots who lost their lives due to the defective parts were his sons, too, that his responsibility extended beyond his immediate family.

In the last century, playwrights have experimented with traditional literary patterns and forms, exploring what the protagonist of a modern play can be or become. For example, the hero in a drama does not have to be a male. Norwegian playwright Henrik Ibsen follows the basic Aristotelian pattern in his play *A Doll's House*, but his hero is a housewife and mother named Nora, not a noble king or prince. This seems radical considering that Ibsen wrote the play in the late nineteenth century. However, as Nora leaves her husband and children, she exhibits the inner characteristics of the Aristotelian hero, moving above and beyond societal norms and expectations to live a life of self-examination, and in so doing, sacrifices her comfortable and familiar lifestyle. In his essay "Tragedy and the Common Man," Arthur Miller states, "the tragic feeling is evoked in us when we are in the presence of a character who is willing to lay down his life, if need be, to secure one thing—his sense of personal dignity. From Orestes to Hamlet, Medea to Macbeth, the underlying struggle is that of the individual attempting to gain his 'rightful' position in his society." In the last act of the play, Nora explains to her husband, Torvald Helmer, why she must leave. As you read this excerpt, think about Miller's assertions about the tragic hero and see if his assertions apply to Nora:

NORA: I'm leaving you now, at once. Christine will put me up for tonight —

HELMER: You're out of your mind! You can't do this! I forbid you!

NORA: It's no use your trying to forbid me any more. I shall take with me nothing but what is mine. I don't want anything from you, now or ever.

HELMER: What kind of madness is this?

NORA: Tomorrow I shall go home—I mean, to where I was born. It'll be easiest for me to find some kind of a job there.

HELMER: But you're blind! You've no experience of the world—

NORA: I must try to get some, Torvald.

HELMER: But to leave your home, your husband, your children! Have you thought what people will say?

NORA: I can't help that. I only know that I must do this.

HELMER: But this is monstrous! Can you neglect your most sacred duties?

NORA: What do you call my most sacred duties?

HELMER: Do I have to tell you? Your duties towards your husband, and your children.

NORA: I have another duty which is equally sacred.

HELMER: You have not. What on earth could that be?

NORA: My duty towards myself.

HELMER: First and foremost you are a wife and a mother.

NORA: I don't believe that any longer. I believe that I am first and foremost a human being, like you—or anyway, that I must try to become one. I know most people think as you do, Torvald, and I know there's something of the sort to be found in books. But I'm no longer prepared to accept what people say and what's written in books. I must think things out for myself, and try to find my own answer.

A few passages later, Helmer tells her that she doesn't understand the society she lives in. Nora responds by saying "No, I don't. But I want to find out about it. I have to make up my mind who is right, society or I." At the end of *A Doll's House* the hero moves outside her domestic world, at a great personal cost, in an attempt to achieve self-actualization.

Writing for Ideas and Practice 12-1

Think of a contemporary play or film that follows the tragic model as outlined in the *Poetics,* either directly or as a derivative of the model. What heroic characteristics does the protagonist display? What happens in the story that makes you think that this work fits the pattern of classic tragedy?

No matter how common the model, not all Western theater is modeled on Greek tragedy. Familiarizing yourself with different forms of theater can provide you with a rich source of ideas. During the Middle Ages, for example, episodic miracle or mystery plays, religious in nature, were performed throughout the medieval towns in pageant, like a play acted out in parade form. Western theater tends to focus on plot and character, but you might also find inspiration in Japanese Noh or Kabuki theater, or any theatrical forms that stress spectacle and tradition over plot and characterization. Playwright Bertolt Brecht based *The Caucasian Chalk Circle* on a Chinese play written during the Yuan dynasty (1279–1368) called *The Story of the Chalk Circle* by Li Ch'ien'fu. As in any genre, the playwright can find inspiration in many different forms.

Studying the classic patterns does not mean that you should feel restricted by dramatic tradition. Really great literature of any kind expands the limits of what has been done before, but a good foundation in the classics provides you with a good indication of what works. Imitation is a good place to begin; you can then experiment with structure and form. If you want to be on the cutting edge, you need to know where the edges are.

There is no one formulaic approach to writing a play, and the work habits and procedures of playwrights vary as much as any other group of writers. David Mamet says that he may write *several thousand pages* of dialogue before he writes an outline. Christopher Durang doesn't work with an outline; instead, he begins with an idea and follows the idea where it leads him. Marsha Norman outlines her writing technique, using her play *'night Mother*, a play about a woman who decides to kill herself, as an example:

I have a great trick during that period of thinking about the play. I say, "I'm not writing until I absolutely have to, till I can no longer contain it." I build up the piece in a pressure cooker, as it were. All that time I'm writing myself notes in the form of questions. What did Daddy do? How long ago did he die? Where did he die? What did he ever do for Jessie? Those kinds of questions. Curiously enough, you'll find that just from asking the questions, you'll get all the answers during the next weeks. It's internal research into the lives of these people. From those questions will come lines of dialogue—you begin to hear the voicing, what they can talk about, what they think is funny. The first line of dialogue I wrote for *'night Mother* was Jessie's line, "We got any old towels?" As soon as I wrote it down, I understood that it was a ritual piece, that Jessie was coming in to celebrate this requiem mass, that she has these stacks of towels: here are the witnesses, the household objects. She comes in as though she is the altar boy.[1]

1 From *In Their Own Words: Contemporary American Playwrights* by David Savran. New York: Theatre Communications Group, Inc., 1988.

Although playwrights differ in their work habits and techniques, some focusing on story first, others letting the story evolve through the characters, the end result will be still be a well-developed story. This chapter discusses story and plot structure. Chapter 13 will deal with character, dialogue, the visual aspects of staging a play, and the technical aspects of writing a script. But realize that the creative process is circular: character development can lead to story development and story development can lead to character development and dialogue. Whatever your procedure might be, the end result should still be the same: a well-constructed play.

As we discussed in chapter 10, narratives focus on plot structure and characterization to tell a story, especially in writing mainstream or conventional fiction. Playwrights follow much the same pattern in constructing a mainstream or conventional play or scene. The difference is that the dramatist uses the spoken words of the characters and their actions rather than the consciousness of a narrator to communicate the story, incorporating plot elements such as exposition, conflict, rising action, climax, falling action, and denouement into their plays, in both traditional and experimental ways.

However experimental, though, most plays have some traditional plot elements in them. When they have been left out, many times they are left out intentionally in order to communicate a specific theme or idea. How much you adhere to a typical plot structure depends on your purpose and intent. Is it your intent for your audience to understand what happens in the play as it is happening? Then you will want to adhere to a logical order that the audience can follow but one that is not so formulaic that your audience jumps ahead of you and goes home after the first act. David Mamet states that "the rules of dramatic structure, redefine them how you will, are based on the rules of human perception. That's what enables deviation from them to work." It is helpful as a reader and as a writer to know the conventions and to know when they are being manipulated or omitted for a particular purpose.

Exposition

As in fiction, plays will include enough background information about setting and character to enable the audience to make sense of what is happening on stage. This information is called **exposition**. Dramatic writing differs from fiction, however, because a great deal of exposition can be presented visually. The curtain opens, and the audience *sees* the opulent living room of the mansion of Lady Ebberly, a room that would have taken four pages to describe in a novel. Therefore, the initial orientation to time and place can be instantaneous.

An orientation to time and place is just a part of exposition, however.

Events that occur outside the time and space of the play might also be crucial to audience understanding. You must decide how much background information about the story and characters the audience needs to know to understand the play.

You will also want to decide *how much* exposition you want at the beginning of the play. If you want the audience to know that your main character spent three years in a prison camp in Vietnam, you will need to decide on the best dramatic moment to communicate this part of his background. It is tempting to reveal everything in the first three pages of the play, but consider the dramatic possibilities of withholding this information until later.

You also need to decide *how* to reveal pertinent background information as well. Do you want the main character to discuss being in a POW camp in a monologue? Or can this information be hinted at and intimated by the way his wife treats him as she makes cryptic references to the reasons for his erratic and unusual behavior? Your decision probably rests on the dramatic importance of this exposition. Audiences will notice references that are repeated and references that are problematic. You don't want to confuse your audience to the point of boredom or frustration, but you don't want to give them the Cliff's Notes version of your play either. Keep them intrigued and interested by slipping them information gradually, so that they can put the pieces of the puzzle together themselves. Good audiences appreciate a good challenge.

Here is an excerpt from the beginning of A. R. Gurney's play *The Cocktail Hour*. In this conventional exposition, identify what expository information Gurney reveals about the characters and their relationships.

(The action takes place in the family living room.)

ACT I

AT RISE: The stage is empty. The light from the windows indicates early evening, early fall. After a moment, Bradley enters, carrying a silver ice bucket. He is in his seventies and very well dressed. He is followed by his son, John, who is in his early forties and more informally dressed. John carries a silver tray with several liquor bottles and glasses on it.

BRADLEY (*Turning on the light in the hall*): This is what's called bringing the mountain to Mohammed.

JOHN: Right.

BRADLEY: Otherwise we'd have to trek all the way back to the pantry whenever we needed to return to the well.

JOHN: Makes sense to me.

BRADLEY (*Setting down the ice bucket on the table behind the couch*): Of course when we had maids, it was different. You could just push the buzzer, and say bring this, bring that, and they'd bring it.

JOHN (*Setting down the tray*): I remember.

BRADLEY: Not that they could mix a drink. They couldn't make a martini to save their skin. But they could make ice, bring water, pass cheese. It was very pleasant.

JOHN: Before the war.

BRADLEY: That damn war. Those Germans have a lot to answer for. Well. Let's see . . . What are we missing? . . . Have we got the lemon for your mother's martini?

JOHN (*Taking it out of his pocket*): It's right here, Pop.

BRADLEY: Your mother likes a small twist of lemon in her martini.

JOHN: I know.

BRADLEY: And my Cutty Sark scotch.

JOHN: Oh yes.

BRADLEY (*Looking at the label*): It's a good scotch. Not a great scotch, but a good one. I always enjoy the picture on the label. The American clipper ships were the fastest in the world. Magnificent vessels. Beautifully built. Made our country great.

JOHN: The "Cutty Sark" was English, Pop.

BRADLEY: I know that. I'm speaking generally.

JOHN: Actually the clipper ships only lasted a few years.

BRADLEY: Not true.

JOHN: Only a few—before steam.

BRADLEY: Not true at all.

JOHN: I think so, Pop.

BRADLEY: I wish your brother were here. He'd know. He knows all there is to know about boats.

JOHN (*Going to the bookcase*): I'll look it up.

BRADLEY: Never mind. I said, *never mind*. We are not going to waste the evening in pedantic arguments. (*JOHN returns from the bookcase.*) Now look what I did. I brought out a whole bottle of soda water. Automatically. Thinking your brother *would* be here. Won't drink anything else. Never did.

JOHN: Smart man.

BRADLEY: I telephoned him yesterday. Tried to get him to come up. "Come on, Jigger," I said. "Join us. John's coming. Your sister will be here. We'll all have cocktails and your mother will provide an excellent dinner. You can play the piano. We'll all gather around the piano and sing. Bring Sylvia, if you want. Bring the children. I'll pay for the whole thing." But no. Wouldn't do it. Jigger's a very positive person, once he's made up his mind.

JOHN: It's a tough trip for him, Pop.

BRADLEY: I know that.

JOHN: He's working weekends now. They've put him back in sales.

BRADLEY: We all have to sell. One way or another.

JOHN: He's looking for another job.

BRADLEY: I know all that. You don't need to tell me that. I'm in touch with him all the time. (*He returns to the bar.*) What'll you have, by the way?

Notice the amount of information that this short excerpt communicates. The conversation between Bradley and his son John tells the audience about the social position of the family. The financial condition and social setting are reinforced by the stage setting, the details of which are not included here. We will discuss the visual aspects of staging in chapter 13.

More importantly, this conversation between father and son reveals a great deal about the kind of relationship they have with one another and the relationship of each of the characters to Jigger, the son who never appears in the play and is yet a presence in it. The audience is unaware of the primary conflict at this point in the play, yet this scene lays the groundwork as it provides exposition that establishes place, time, character identity, and character relationship.

Writing for Ideas and Practice 12-2

1. Read over the excerpt from *The Cocktail Hour* again and answer the following questions:
    a.   What are some of Bradley's more prominent characteristics?
    b.   What are some of John's more prominent characteristics?
    c.   What does their conversation about clipper ships reveal about the nature of their relationship?
    d.   If Jigger is not going to appear in the play, why is he mentioned at all here? How does his implied presence reveal more about the relationship between John and Bradley?
2. Write the first two pages of a play. The play should have four people in it, but only two of the characters appear on stage in these pages. At the end of your piece, the audience should know the time and place your play takes place, a little bit about all four characters, and the relationship that exists between the four.

Omitting important expository information about the characters and events can be a technique itself, one that keeps the audience from completely understanding the motives of the characters and allowing the audience to experience the action and dialogue in isolation from the events that occur before the play begins. Perhaps the technique used in fiction that most closely parallels this technique is the use of the objective point of view. Harold Pinter intentionally omits character background in *The Birthday Party*. One of the challenges an audience faces with this play (and other plays that omit detailed exposition) is discerning relationships. Although the play follows a conventional plot structure, the omission of this information, coupled with dialogue that at times is illogical, gives the piece an unsettling and disturbing touch. At the same time, however, the play is humorous.

In act 1 of *The Birthday Party*, Meg and Petey, a married couple who run a boarding house in a seaside town, are eating breakfast at their dining room table. They refer to another character, Stanley, who is sleeping upstairs. As you read, try to discern the relationship between Stanley and Meg:

PETEY: Didn't you take him up his tea?

MEG: I always take him up his cup of tea. But that was a long time ago.

PETEY: Did he drink it?

MEG: I made him. I stood there till he did. I'm going to call him. (*She goes to the door.*) Stan! Stanny! (*She listens.*) Stan! I'm coming up to fetch you if you don't come down! I'm coming up! I'm going to count three! One! Two! Three! I'm coming to get you! (*She exits and goes upstairs. In a moment, shouts from Stanley, wild laughter from Meg. Petey takes his place to the hatch. Shouts. Laughter. Petey sits at the table. Silence. She returns.*) He's coming down. (*She is panting and arranges her hair.*) I told him if he didn't hurry up he'd get no breakfast.

PETEY: That did it, eh?

MEG: I'll get his cornflakes.

> *Meg exits to the kitchen. Petey reads the paper. Stanley enters. He is unshaven, in his pyjama jacket and wears glasses. He sits at the table.*

PETEY: Morning, Stanley.

STANLEY: Morning.

> *Silence. Meg enters with the bowl of cornflakes, which she sets on the table.*

MEG: So he's come down at last, has he? He's come down at last for his breakfast. But he doesn't deserve any, does he, Petey? (*Stanley stares at the cornflakes.*) Did you sleep well?

STANLEY: I didn't sleep at all.

MEG: You didn't sleep at all? Did you hear that, Petey? Too tired to eat your breakfast, I suppose? Now you eat up those cornflakes like a good boy. Go on.
> *He begins to eat.*

STANLEY: What's it like out today?

PETEY: Very nice.

STANLEY: Warm?

PETEY: Well, there's a good breeze blowing.

STANLEY: Cold?

PETEY: No, no, I wouldn't say it was cold.

MEG: What are the cornflakes like, Stan?

STANLEY: Horrible.

MEG: Those flakes? Those lovely flakes? You're a liar, a little liar. They're refreshing. It says so. For people when they get up late.

STANLEY: The milk's off.

MEG: It's not. Petey ate his, didn't you, Petey?

PETEY: That's right.

MEG: There you are then.

STANLEY: All right, I'll go on to the second course.

MEG: He hasn't finished the first course and he wants to go on to the second course!

STANLEY: I feel like something cooked.

MEG: Well, I'm not going to give it to you.

PETEY: Give it to him.

MEG: (*sitting at the table, right*) I'm not going to.
> *Pause.*

STANLEY: No breakfast.

Pause.

All night long I've been dreaming about this breakfast.

MEG: I thought you said you didn't sleep.

STANLEY: Day-dreaming. All night long. And now she won't give me any. Not even a crust of bread on the table.

Pause.

    Well, I can see I'll have to go down to one of those smart hotels on the front.

MEG (*rising quickly*): You won't get a better breakfast there than here. (*She exits to the kitchen. Stanley yawns broadly. Meg appears at the hatch with a plate.*) Here you are. You'll like this. (*Petey rises, collects the plate, brings it to the table, puts it in front of Stanley, and sits.*)

Although the entire beginning of the play is not included in this excerpt, based on what is in the text, what kind of assertions would you make about Stanley and his relationship to Meg and Petey? Does your impression of the relationships between the three characters change in any way throughout the excerpt? Is there anything confusing or disconcerting about Stanley's place in the household? If so, what is it? How does the omission of exposition contribute to the tone or feel of the play?

In a typical dramatic plot structure, once the audience is aware of time and place, the primary conflict is presented and developed. In many plays there is an event that is the catalyst for the conflict called the **inciting incident**. If not for the inciting incident, in many cases, there would be no conflict. For example, in *Hamlet*, the inciting incident occurs when Hamlet's uncle kills his father and marries his mother. This event takes place before the play begins and is presented at the beginning of the play as exposition, when the ghost of Hamlet's father appears to him and instructs him to avenge his murder. If this murder had not occurred, there would be no conflict between Hamlet and his uncle.

On rare occasions the inciting incident occurs at the beginning of the play, but most of the time (as in *Hamlet*) the inciting incident takes place in the past and the play begins in the middle of the story, or *in medias res*. Action that occurs before the drama begins exists in all plays, just as there is action that occurs after the play ends, unless of course the entire cast dies at the end of the play.

Writing for Ideas and Practice 12-3

1. Write the first two pages of a play which contains two characters discussing a recent event. You should include no exposition except to reveal time and place.
2. Now rewrite the piece and use exposition to detail the relationship between the two characters.

So how do you decide where to begin the play? One technique some playwrights use is to map out the story on a timeline. On this timeline you note all of the important events that occur in the story, beginning with the inciting incident (or what led to the inciting incident, if that is important), conflict and crises, climax, falling action, and the ultimate resolution of the story. Consider the following as you decide where on the timeline to begin your play:

1. Would including the inciting action shift the focus away from the main conflict? The most effective beginning is one that focuses on the story you want to tell.

2. Would the inciting action have more dramatic impact if it were staged or if it were revealed through exposition? (For example, if the inciting incident in your play is the rape of the main character, revealing that event through exposition might have more dramatic impact than actually staging a rape scene. Beginning a play with a rape scene might seem like a good idea, and it might be; however, consider carefully the complexities of staging such a scene as well as the audience's perception of the conflict in the play.)

Here is a sample initial timeline:

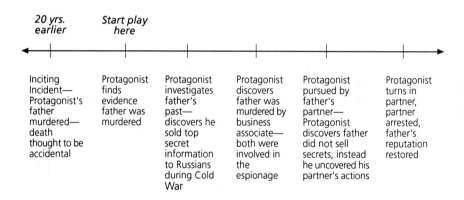

20 yrs. earlier	Start play here				
Inciting Incident— Protagonist's father murdered— death thought to be accidental	Protagonist finds evidence father was murdered	Protagonist investigates father's past— discovers he sold top secret information to Russians during Cold War	Protagonist discovers father was murdered by business associate— both were involved in the espionage	Protagonist pursued by father's partner— Protagonist discovers father did not sell secrets, instead he uncovered his partner's actions	Protagonist turns in partner, partner arrested, father's reputation restored

CONFLICT

A drama always contains a primary conflict, usually introduced or at least referred to somewhere close to the beginning to the play, and this conflict constitutes the heart of the drama. As in narration, in the play, the main character has a goal or desire but is kept from reaching that goal or getting what he desires. The conflict exists because the character wants something he cannot have. In addition to the main conflict, the play also contains a series of interwoven subconflicts involving the protagonist as well as subconflicts that occur among the other characters in the play.

Even plays which don't present life in a physical, realistic context will have some element of conflict in them. Absurdist plays such as *Waiting for Godot* by Samuel Beckett present man as he exists metaphysically rather than as he exists physically. They present man isolated in a world without meaning, disconnected from purpose. The conflict in an absurdist play is a physical portrayal on stage of man's inner search for meaning in a meaningless world. In *Waiting for Godot*, two tramps wait for someone named Godot to arrive, and even though Godot never arrives in the play, the basis of the conflict rests in the anticipation of Godot's arrival as well as in the confusion of the characters. Beckett says, "Confusion of mind and of identity is an indispensable element of the play and the effort to clear up the ensuing obscurities, which seems to have exercised most critics to the point of blinding them to the central simplicity, strikes me as quite nugatory." The confusion in *Waiting for Godot*, then, is an external reflection of an internal conflict and it contributes to the overall purpose of the work.

In prose fiction, a protagonist faces conflicts, both those within himself and those presented by antagonists and by circumstances. The same types of conflicts are presented in drama, but in drama conflict is not revealed through interior monologue (a character's thoughts) or narrative exposition. Instead, conflict is revealed through speech and action as characters who have different goals and desires encounter each other.

A writer of fiction uses narration, possibly combined with dialogue, to present conflict. The dramatist, though, depends solely on dialogue and action to develop conflict and to propel the action forward. This usually requires a precise and methodical technique. When you have determined where your play will begin and you have decided, in general terms, what the conflict is, you will want to clarify some things about your characters. Before you start, determine the character basics:

1. Who is your protagonist?
2. What does he or she want?
3. What obstacles stand in his or her way?

In addition to answering those basic questions about the protagonist, you might want to use the same questions to analyze the other main characters, paying particular attention to the antagonist. For example, in the fairy tale *Little Red Riding Hood*, the protagonist is Little Red Riding Hood. We know that she is young, naive, and kind to grandmothers. What does she want? She wants to see her aged grandmother and bring her some goodies. Nice story. But no conflict exists. What obstacles stand in her way? Enter the wolf and the *real* story begins. Ask the same questions of the wolf that you did Little Red. Who is the antagonist? The wolf. What does he want? To eat Little Red Riding Hood. What obstacles stand in his way? Although she is unaware of his intentions, Little Red does not want to be eaten by the wolf and would resist.

This list seems simplistic, especially considering the task of putting together a full-length stage play, but these three questions help you to focus. For example, in Christopher Durang's play *The Actor's Nightmare*, George, the main character, wanders into a theater and is mistakenly identified as the replacement for an actor who has been in a car accident, which acts as the inciting incident. It also might be that there is a reason George does not know where he is, but the audience is never given that expository information.

Take a moment to read the first three pages of *The Actor's Nightmare* in the Drama to Consider section of this book (pp. 372–374).

The conflict is revealed in these first few pages as George encounters the other actors in the ensemble and ends up acting in a series of plays. He has no recollection of any of the actors, does not know any of the lines, and has no idea who or where he is.

In the next segments of the play, George finds himself in the middle of *Hamlet*, *Checkmate*, and *A Man For All Seasons*. He muddles his way through the plays, alternating calling for cues, making up lines, and bemoaning the fact that he did not join the monastery as he had intended.

Even a play filled with preposterous situations such as this can be discussed using the basic three questions noted above. George is the protagonist of the play, and unfortunately for him, he has no idea who or where he is. He finds himself being cast in the lead of plays he doesn't know, and as he tries to find his way out of the mess he is in, he muddles his way through the plays, improvising and begging for lines. His last role is as Sir Thomas More, and George is executed at the end of the play. At least it appears that way, for as the stage directions indicate, the characters "*gesture for George to take his bow, but he seems to be dead. They applaud him, and then bow again, and lights out.*" George does not survive his acting debut, and he never really finds out who he is or why he is in the theater at all. In this play, clearly, the protagonist does not reach his goal.

Writing for Ideas and Practice 12-4

1. Write a short scene where two characters discuss a dramatic event which has occurred offstage.
2. Write the first four pages of a play in which the inciting incident takes place before the action of the play begins. Reveal the inciting action gradually through character dialogue and action in the exposition.
3. What is the main conflict in the following stories?
   a. Cinderella
   b. Goldilocks and the Three Bears
   c. The Three Little Pigs

Structuring the Drama

Plays are divided into units of time and place called **acts** and **scenes**. Acts and scenes are used to structure time and place and to break the play into content units. For example, a change of location or a progression of time could be indicated by a scene or act change, or a new obstacle for the protagonist to overcome could be introduced in a new scene. A wise strategy could be to leave something unresolved at the end of each scene or act (except the final act) to stimulate the audience's interest.

A full-length play will run approximately 90–130 minutes (excluding intermissions). Acts run from 20–50 minutes within the full-length play, the first act usually being longer than subsequent acts. Acts are ordinarily divided into scenes, but a play could consist of only one act without scene divisions and could run in continuous time. The structure of the play will be dictated by your content, but keep in mind that audiences are used to film and television, where scene changes provide constant visual stimulation. If you construct a play that runs in continuous time, be sure that your play is written tightly enough to sustain the attention of your audience.

The obstacles that the main characters face in full-length plays are not all presented at once on the first page. As in narration, the obstacles are introduced, resolved, and complicated in order to accelerate the audience's attention and anticipation. This part of the play is called the **rising action**. Although a **one-act play** also contains rising action, in a full-length play the obstacles are usually connected and separated by the use of **scenes**.

Scenes are smaller units of time within acts that many times indicate a change of time and/or location. Each separate scene should advance the action by complicating the main problem or obstacle the protagonist must overcome. A scene can introduce new information or a new obstacle or complication (as in a subplot or secondary plot) while presenting the character's reaction to the problem or the actions he takes to resolve the problem.

A scene might consist of the resolution of one of the obstacles facing the protagonist. The play consists of a series of high and low tension points. It is important to allow for low tension points at times, because it is difficult, if not impossible, to sustain tension indefinitely. If *nothing* is resolved until the end, the audience is likely to stop caring about the outcome. The successful dramatist will use scenes to bring the audience to a high tension point and know how and when to provide tension breaks without losing the attention of the audience.

As an example, the main character in a drama is being followed by a man as she delves into the mystery of her father's disappearance. The audience knows she is being followed, but the protagonist does not. The audience sees the man hiding behind the door, and as she enters the room, he jumps out and puts his hand across her mouth. This is a high tension point. The mysterious man tells her to keep quiet and listen, for he has information that will help her locate her missing father. Now that the audience knows that the man is not an enemy and that the main character will not be harmed, the tension is released. The main conflict, the mystery of the missing father, has not been resolved in this scene, but as the main conflict develops, other conflicts or obstacles appear to provide the high and low tension points.

A dramatist's method of scene construction can be one way of providing the high and low tension points in a drama. For example, if a character overcomes an obstacle in a scene, it is a good strategy to introduce a new obstacle or complication before moving to the next scene. Although *The Actor's Nightmare* is not divided into formal scenes, at the end of one of the plays that the actors are presenting, for instance, the Noel Coward play, the next play begins, which is *Hamlet*. Something should be left unresolved in the scene so that the audience focuses its full attention on each scene as it opens.

In each new scene, just as the protagonist seems within reach of his goal, a new complication is added. These secondary complications are intertwined as they are introduced and resolved until the main problem is resolved at or near the end of the play.

Just as in narration, **foreshadowing** can be utilized to hint at events that are to take place in future scenes. A dialogue reference to the mailbox in act 1 might hint that something important to the story will center around it in act 3. Many times the audience will not recognize the foreshadowing until after the conflict is resolved, and sometimes not even until the second time they read or see the drama, and that is probably what the playwright intends. Foreshadowing is subtle, not overt, and it should work underneath the surface of the primary story.

Another tool a dramatist can use to present and enhance conflict is **dramatic irony**, where the playwright allows the audience to know something that the character is unaware of. For example, in a typical late-night drive-in horror movie, the ingenue walks down a very long hall to her bedroom. The camera flashes to the bedroom, and the audience sees the ax murderer behind the door, silently awaiting her. The camera shot shifts back to the girl, and the audience knows that unless the girl turns around and runs, she will be killed. The audience at the drive-in yells at the girl (some honk their car horns), "warning" the celluloid image that she should run for it. The suspense comes from the audience knowing something that the character does not. Dramatic irony is used, therefore, not to replace the essential conflict, but to develop it and build audience interest and suspense.

Watch the audience when you go to see a really good play. They become physically involved in what goes on on-stage. At a pivotal entrance, they crane their necks to get a better look at the character who has just entered, because the playwright has prepared the audience to anticipate that character's entrance or has written the text so that the character's entrance is a complete surprise. And even though the director decides how the play is to be presented, the playwright is the one who creates that anticipation.

Take the time to create the ups and downs of the play, the movement and turns of the conflict and the plot.

Writing for Ideas and Practice 12-5

1. Write the end of one scene and the beginning of the next. Time should have passed between the two scenes, and your goal is to make a smooth transition from one to the other.
2. Write a scene of two to three pages that utilizes dramatic irony. You should have no more than three characters in your scene.

CLIMAX

Eventually you will reach a point in the play when your protagonist is at the point of no return, the **climax**. Either she will overcome the obstacles in her way or she will be overcome by them. Playwrights often place this moment very close to the end of the play and prepare the audience for this moment by weaving the crises so that they act in a cumulative way to build tension in the audience. The climax in a play occurs just *before* the outcome is known, and the result of the climax is what the audience came for. As you write the climax of the play, then, take the time to build to it and make it compelling.

In the play *Trifles*, two women discover why Mrs. Wright, a woman they know, murdered her husband. They find the woman's pet bird, its neck broken, in a box among the woman's things. It is obvious to the women that the wife murdered her husband because he killed her precious bird. The climax of the play occurs as the women decide whether or not to hide the bird from the sheriff and the county attorney, as detailed in these stage directions:

 (HALE *goes outside. The* SHERIFF *follows the* COUNTY ATTORNEY *into the other room. Then* MRS. HALE *rises, hands tight together, looking intensely at* MRS. PETERS, *whose eyes take a slow turn, finally meeting* MRS. HALE'S. *A moment* MRS. HALE *holds her, then her own eyes point the way to where the box is concealed. Suddenly* MRS. PETERS *throws back quilt pieces and tries to put the box in the bag she is wearing. It is too big. She opens box, starts to take the bird out, cannot touch it, goes to pieces, stands there helpless. Sound of a knob turning in the other room.* MRS. HALE *snatches the box and puts it in the pocket of her big coat. Enter* COUNTY ATTORNEY *and* SHERIFF.)

FALLING ACTION AND DENOUEMENT

After the climax of a play, the conflicts are resolved. This could mean that the protagonist is victorious, as in a mystery, adventure, or comedy; or that he falls to his demise, as in a tragedy or dark comedy. After the conflict is resolved, the resolution ties up loose ends and provides the audience with a sense of closure. Whatever the result, ultimately the drama ends, even if the ending is ambiguous.

As you write, you should resist rushing through the conflict to get to the resolution too quickly. Ibsen said that in his first draft he met his characters. In his second draft he saw what they would say and do, and in his third draft he discovered why. Be willing to go the distance here. Conflicts that are complex enough to warrant writing about usually have complex resolutions, unless the aim or goal of the piece is slapstick or sitcom humor.

Some plays cut away too soon, leaving the audience dissatisfied, and others won't let the audience out of the theater, for fear that if the play doesn't hammer the theme in the last few minutes the audience won't get it. Deciding when to end your play is an important consideration. If your protagonist is sent to death row after being convicted of a crime he didn't commit, do you end the play there, or do you show his execution? Sometimes it is difficult to know when to end the piece, but as we said earlier, your job is to consider the dramatic impact of what you might include. Would including the execution have more dramatic impact? And would the complexities of staging the execution require an extra scene to indicate location and time changes? You will want to have a clear sense of the feeling you want the audience to have as they leave the theater. What you do in the last few minutes of the play can affect how they feel about the play long after it is over. Tend to the details here and think through your ending carefully.

Writing for Ideas and Practice 12-6

1. Recall three plays (or movies) you have seen. For each drama, answer the following questions:
   a. Who is the protagonist?
   b. What does he want?
   c. What obstacles stand in his way? (In a full-length drama, there might be many obstacles—just list the ones that seem most important.)
2. Write a short scene (three pages maximum) using two characters. Reveal in the scene that one of the characters is hiding something. Before you write the dialogue, write an outline of what is to happen in this scene. Have two people in your group or class read or act out your scene so that you can hear and see your work. After you have

seen your work, make a list of the things you liked about your scene and the things that did not seem to work.

Here is a scene written by one of our students, Delisa Bice, as a response to the previous exercise:

Mirrored Past
Cy and Jo Anne
> (*After being gone fifteen years, Cy shows up to ask for an official end to the marriage that ended long ago.*)

CY: Why didn't you sign the papers?

JO ANNE: What papers?

CY: You know what papers. I want a divorce. We haven't had a marriage now for quite a while.

JO ANNE: Why do you want this now? Why not when you decided to leave—why not when you wrote me that letter fifteen years ago? Why not make a clean break then?

CY: I don't know why I didn't then. I guess I always expected you to end it.

JO ANNE: Don't lie to me. You never asked for one then 'cause you didn't need one. You could sleep with anyone you wanted to married or not 'cause chances were you wouldn't have to look them in the eye again. That worked just fine for you for fifteen years, but it won't do now will it?

CY: I don't know what you're . . .

JO ANNE: You've found someone you want to marry haven't you? But you can't get married unless you divorce me first. Isn't that right? Isn't that the reason you're here?

CY: I just thought we ought to make official what died a long time ago. That's all.

JO ANNE: No, I don't think that's all, Cy. I know you have it in mind to marry someone else. There couldn't be any other logical reason for you showing up on my porch again.

CY: Alright—alright. There is someone else. And I want to marry her.

JO ANNE: Does she know about me? About your kids?

CY: Yes. But she thinks it was over a long time ago. Not that I told her it was. . . . She just assumed.

JO ANNE: Does she know you're here?

CY: No.

JO ANNE: Have you already set the date?

CY: I haven't asked her yet. Look, I'm just trying to set things straight. Things didn't work out between us, but I did do right by the kids. I gave them a name. I sent money whenever I could for them, and I made sure you had a house to stay in. They're grown. I have a new life. I want to do things right this time. It's not like it's just in my interest. You get the same chance I get with this.

JO ANNE: What do you mean?

CY: A chance to start over. Meet someone—hell, maybe you already have.

JO ANNE: That's a laugh.

CY: I don't see anything funny about it.

JO ANNE: Do you know how old I am? Do you think I can just start over just like that?

CY: I'm older than you, Jo Anne, and I'm starting over.

JO ANNE: But you're a man. Men can start over whenever they damn well please.

CY: It's never too late . . .

JO ANNE: Don't give me that bullshit! It is too late! I'm forty years old! I don't have a teenager's figure anymore. I don't have soft skin or bright eyes. I've got bad nerves and fallen arches from fifteen years of humiliation and hard work trying to take care of two kids who for years kept asking me when Daddy was coming home. I get gray hair from imagining the women you must be with and the great time you must be having out there on the open road with no one to answer to. I've got bags and dark circles under my eyes from drinking myself to sleep those nights that I hated you and crying myself to sleep on the nights when I missed you. And you say—just start over? There's not much left that anyone would want.

3. Now write the next scene between Cy and Jo Anne, when Jo Anne meets Cy's fiance.

The plot is only one element of a play, but it is a crucial one. If you don't develop the conflicts in your characters and resolve those conflicts in a believable way, no matter how colorful or endearing your characters, no matter how opulent and magnificent the set, no matter how wonderful the music is, the play will not carry the weight and impact you intend it to. When you write a play, you create a world, a space in time when your audience enters that world and experiences life through your eyes. August Wilson says that when he was working on *Ma Rainey's Black Bottom* at the O'Neill Theatre, he "learned to respect the stage and trust that it will carry your ideas." Tell the story that matters to you, and you will make that story matter to others as well.

Writing on Your Own

1. Write a short play which contains two scenes. Complete the following steps in preparation for writing the final draft:

   a. Answer the following questions in writing:

   Who is the protagonist of this play?

   What does he or she want?

   What obstacles must he or she overcome to achieve this goal?

   b. Write an outline of the plot or story line of the play. Divide the story into two scenes.

Writing to Revise

Trade a scene you have written with a member of your group or class. Examine the turns and rising action. Use horizontal arrows to mark a turn in the action and vertical arrows to mark the acceleration of the pace of the piece through rising action or the deceleration through falling action. Mark clear stops in the action with straight vertical lines. If there is a climax, mark that with a *C*. Examine how your scene has been marked. Are your scenes marked as you wrote them?

Now rewrite the piece as you see it unfolding. Revise the piece as needed so that your play communicates your desired effect.

13

STAGING DRAMA:
CHARACTERS IN ACTION

Writing to Warm Up

1. Go to a cafe, barber shop, or other public place and eavesdrop on a conversation between two or three people. Write out the conversation in script form and have the conversation read aloud. Could this dialogue be effective on stage? What kinds of changes would you make to enhance its dramatic effectiveness? What kind of conflict could you build around this conversation?
2. Think of a historical figure whose life would make a compelling drama. Once you have decided on someone, discuss why you chose this figure.

CHARACTER

Chapter 12 focused on the elements of dramatic plot, the story itself. In order to make that story come to life, you must create characters who can, through their dialogue and action, communicate the story you want to tell. This chapter centers on creating characters and placing them in their environment, the stage.

So how do playwrights create characters in drama? The basic elements are the same in drama as in narration, but since playwrights lack the advantage of a narrator in most plays, they must communicate character more directly. Thorton Wilder's *Our Town* is an exception, for the narrator is a character in the play. The Greeks used the **chorus**, a group of characters who commented on the play as a narrator would. **Soliloquies**, speeches in which characters talk to themselves, also relate the inner thoughts of the character.

To a lesser extent, playwrights use **monologues**, long speeches by characters directed to a character who may or may not be present on stage, to communicate the thoughts of the character. A monologue should be constructed as a story within the play itself, containing a complication and resolution. Many times it is used to give the audience expository information about the character. You will be able to find other examples of narrators in plays as well, but narrators tend to be the exception rather than the rule in drama. Since your play probably won't have a narrator, you need to know your characters, know what they want and what drives them to do what they do in your drama.

In creating characters, it is important to know your characters so well that you write dialogue that is consistent with your characters' personalities. Be sensitive to your characters; know them and create them with care, even the dysfunctional ones. It is difficult to write good dialogue for a character unless your characters are well-developed, three dimensional people who are alive and believable on stage. Think of the memorable characters from classical tragedy—Willy Loman, Antigone, Nora, Oedipus, Hamlet— each of them is a fully realized human being. You encounter very few cardboard cutout characters in the great plays. Even the great villains in literature are multifaceted. Although Shylock from *The Merchant of Venice* is clearly the antagonist in the play, demanding "a pound of flesh" from Antonio for the injustices he has endured, the audience also sees his motivations. The audience does not necessarily agree with Shylock, but they are given his point of view. The dialogue is powerful because the character behind the dialogue is powerful.

However, in drama, as in fiction, not all of your characters will be three-dimensional. If you were to develop each character fully, you would have to spend too much time on exposition to develop a good story line. You might have some flat characters in your play as well as round characters. Be sure, however, to take the time to create all of the main characters with care, not just the protagonist.

To develop characters from the imagination to the page, give them lives and histories. Begin thinking of your character's existence before the beginning of the play and give your major characters a history to add texture and complexity to them. Write out a character history for the main characters, including their family backgrounds, their educational backgrounds, their socio-economic backgrounds. Let the characters evolve logically based on the history you have created for them.

A technique that some writers use as a prewriting strategy is to keep a notebook for each major character in their plays, writing down bits of information about their physical appearance, their personalities, their histories, and perhaps potential lines of dialogue as well. Keeping a notebook helps you know the characters better, so that you can write good dialogue. In addition, keeping a character notebook or journal keeps you thinking about a character, for the more you think and write about a character, the more real she becomes in your mind.

Have you ever had a friend or relative you knew so well you could finish her sentences? How does this phenomenon occur? Is it some type of psychic telepathy? Perhaps, but the only way you can communicate with someone so directly is to truly *know* that person. Attempt to get to know your characters in the same way, so that as you write dialogue, you finish their sentences the way *they* would finish them, not the way you would finish them if you were speaking. One evidence of weak writing is when a writer relies heavily on stereotypes to convey information about a character. Giving a Southern accent to a character to convey stupidity or ignorance, or a Bronx accent to a character who is boisterous and aggressive rarely works outside the realm of low comedy. If you are creating a character who has a specific dialect, it is probably better to indicate it in the character's description rather than write the dialogue in dialect. Feel free to use phrases and sentences that are indicative of that character's speech, but unless you are absolutely certain you can create dialect that rings true, let the actors add the accents.

Writing for Ideas and Practice 13-1

1. Create a character that you could use in a play or scene by answering the following ten questions about him or her:
   a. Where was this person born?
   b. How old is this character?
   c. What does this character look like?
   d. What is this character's ethnic or cultural background?
   e. What is this character's family background?
   f. What are this character's physical attributes?
   g. What is this character's educational background?
   h. What was this character's first real disappointment in life?
   i. What is this character's favorite food?
   j. How would this character define himself or herself?
   Now make up ten more "character questions" and add them to the previous list. Share your list with others in your group.
2. Create two characters who are related to each other and keep a character notebook for each one.

You want your audience to identify with your protagonist. That does not mean that the protagonist must be perfect, but the more complex the conflict, the more dramatic possibilities are afforded you. One of the strengths of the film *Crimson Tide* is that the two main characters pitted against each other are both admirable characters, both with flaws. One character is the commanding officer of a submarine, the other is the executive officer. The submarine receives orders to launch a nuclear missile aimed at Russia, but then the communication system fails. The commanding officer of the ship gives orders to fire the missile based on the order received, but the executive officer does not want to launch the missile until the orders can be confirmed.

The conflict in this film is based on the battle of wills between these two characters, and both characters elicit sympathy from the audience at different times in the film. At times it seems likely that the commanding officer has interpreted naval policy correctly, and at other times it seems likely that the executive officer is acting more wisely. Although the executive officer is the protagonist and is victorious in the end, the commanding officer is not perceived as being *evil*, as antagonists many times are. The essential conflict is not between clear good and evil, bad guys with black hats against good guys with white hats. The conflict is between two good men, each trying to do what he thinks is right.

As in narration, the way an audience perceives a character is also affected by what other characters say about and to him, as well as what they do to him both in and out of his presence. The way other characters speak about or to a character gives the audience insight into how that character is perceived in the context of the dramatic world that the character exists in. What kind of language is used to address a character? Are the other characters comfortable around a character, or do they become stiff and reserved in his presence? Does your protagonist act differently with different characters? There is an adage that acting is as much reacting as it is acting. This saying is true when you are writing a play as well. Don't create your characters in isolation; realize that they are a part of that community of characters in the play.

A **soliloquy** is a longer speech spoken by a character on stage as if to himself. An **aside** is a brief comment or speech addressed directly to the audience.

Instead of pumping the play full of monologues and soliloquies that give a character an opportunity to tell about himself, use dialogue and action between characters that give audience insight into the relationship between those characters and clarify the wants and needs of your protagonist. Although monologues and soliloquies can have an important place in drama, they shouldn't be used as shortcuts to character development or exposition.* As in fiction, the audience learns about a character not just from the character himself, but also from the relationship he has with other characters in the drama. In some dramas these insights into relationships provide the heart of the main or secondary conflict of the play.

Writing for Ideas and Practice 13-2

1. Write a short scene (one to two pages) between two characters who discuss another character at length. The scene should end with the entrance of the character being discussed.
2. Placing your protagonist at the apex of a triangle containing three characters is an effective way to communicate his characteristics. Write a short scene (one to two pages) containing three characters. The scene should reveal that two of the characters want something different from the other character.

The setting of the drama also contributes to character development just as character development contributes to the creation of a sense of place in your drama. The most obvious way to create a sense of place in a drama is to devise a setting that suggests place. But a sense of place or atmosphere is also created through the characters by the way they view and act in their surroundings. If a play's central action takes place in a kitchen, how each character fits into that environment tells a great deal about that character. For example, if a character comes home after a long absence and knows where everything is, the audience might sense that this place still seems comfortable, like home. Place and atmosphere are helpful in creating character by showing how the character acts and reacts in that environment.

In some cases, what the character owns is very important to the overall theme of the play. The character's possessions not only tell the audience obvious things about the character's social status, but they sometimes are symbolic of the character herself. In *The Glass Menagerie* by Tennessee Williams, Laura Wingfield is the protagonist of the play. Her most prized possession is her collection of glass animals, and the menagerie is symbolic of Laura herself. In the beginning stage directions, Laura is said to be isolated from the rest of the world. The directions state that "LAURA's separation increases till she is like a piece of her own glass collection, too exquisitely fragile to move from the shelf." In the play, Laura shows Jim, a potential suitor that her brother Tom has brought home for supper, her glass collection:

JIM: Now how about you? Isn't there something you take more interest in than anything else?

LAURA: Well, I do—as I said—have my—glass collection—
A peal of girlish laughter from the kitchen.

JIM: I'm not right sure I know what you're talking about. What kind of glass is it?

LAURA: Little articles of it, they're ornaments mostly! Most of them are little animals made out of glass, the tiniest little animals in the world. Mother calls them a glass menagerie! Here's an example of one, if you'd like to see it! This one is one of the oldest. It's nearly thirteen. (*He stretches out his hand.*) (**Music: "The Glass Menagerie."**) Oh, be careful—if you breathe, it breaks!

JIM: I'd better not take it. I'm pretty clumsy with things.

LAURA: Go on, I trust you with him! (*Places it in his palm.*) There now—you're holding him gently! Hold him over the light, he loves the light! You see how the light shines through him?

JIM: It sure does shine!

LAURA: I shouldn't be partial, but he is my favorite one.

JIM: What kind of a thing is this one supposed to be?

LAURA: Haven't you noticed the single horn on his forehead?

JIM: A unicorn, huh?

LAURA: Mmm-hmmm!

JIM: Unicorns, aren't they extinct in the modern world?

LAURA: I know!

JIM: Poor little fellow, he must feel sort of lonesome.

LAURA (*smiling*): Well, if he does he doesn't complain about it. He stays on a shelf with some horses that don't have horns and all of them seem to get along nicely together.

JIM: How do you know?

LAURA (*lightly*): I haven't heard any arguments among them!

JIM (*grinning*): No arguments, huh? Well, that's a pretty good sign! Where shall I set him?

LAURA: Put him on the table. They all like a change of scenery once in a while!

JIM (*stretching*): Well, well, well, well—Look how big my shadow is when I stretch!

LAURA: Oh, oh, yes—it stretches across the ceiling!

JIM (*crossing to door*): I think it's stopped raining. (*Opens fire-escape door.*) Where does the music come from?

LAURA: From the Paradise Dance Hall across the alley.

JIM: How about cutting the rug a little, Miss Wingfield?

LAURA: Oh, I—

JIM: Or is your program filled up? Let me have a look at it. (*Grasps imaginary card.*) Why, every dance is taken! I'll just have to scratch some out. (**Waltz Music: "La Golondrina."**) Ahhh, a waltz! (*He executes some sweeping turns by himself, then holds his arms toward Laura.*)

LAURA (*breathlessly*): I—can't dance!

JIM: There you go, that inferiority stuff!

LAURA: I've never danced in my life!

JIM: Come on, try!

LAURA: Oh, but I'd step on you!

JIM: I'm not made out of glass.

LAURA: How—how—how do we start?

JIM: Just leave it to me. You hold your arms out a little.

LAURA: Like this?

JIM: A little bit higher. Right. Now don't tighten up, that's the main thing about it— relax.

LAURA (*laughing breathlessly*): It's hard not to.

JIM: Okay.

LAURA: I'm afraid you can't budge me.

JIM: What do you bet I can't? (*He swings her into motion.*)

LAURA: Goodness, yes, you can!

JIM: Let yourself go, now, Laura, just let yourself go.

LAURA: I'm—

JIM: Come on!

LAURA: Trying!

JIM: Not so stiff—Easy does it!

LAURA: I know but I'm—

JIM: Loosen th' backbone! There now, that's a lot better.

LAURA: Am I?

JIM: Lots, lots better! (*He moves her about the room in a clumsy waltz.*)

LAURA: Oh, my!

JIM: Ha-ha!

LAURA: Goodness, yes you can!

JIM: Ha-ha-ha! (*They suddenly bump into the table, Jim stops.*) What did we hit on?

LAURA: Table.

JIM: Did something fall off it? I think—

LAURA: Yes.

JIM: I hope that it wasn't the little glass horse with the horn!

LAURA: Yes.

JIM: Aw, aw, aw. Is it broken?

LAURA: Now it is just like all the other horses.

JIM: It's lost its—

LAURA: Horn! It doesn't matter. Maybe it's a blessing in disguise.

JIM: You'll never forgive me. I bet that that was your favorite piece of glass.

LAURA: I don't have favorites much. It's no tragedy, Freckles. Glass breaks so easily.
No matter how careful you are. The traffic jars the shelves and things fall off them.

JIM: Still I'm awfully sorry that I was the cause.

LAURA (*smiling*): I'll just imagine he had an operation. The horn was removed to
make him feel less—freakish! (*They both laugh.*) Now he will feel more at home
with the other horses, the ones that don't have horns . . .

JIM: Ha-ha, that's very funny! (*Suddenly serious.*) I'm glad to see that you have a sense
of humor. You know—you're—well—very different! Surprisingly different from
anyone else I know! (*His voice becomes soft and hesitant with a genuine feeling.*)
Do you mind me telling you that? (*Laura is abashed beyond speech.*) You make me
feel sort of—I don't know how to put it! I'm usually pretty good at expressing
things, but—This is something that I don't know how to say! (*Laura touches her
throat and clears it — turns the broken unicorn in her hands.*) (*Even softer.*) Has
anyone ever told you that you were pretty? (**Pause: Music.**) (*Laura looks up slowly,
with wonder, and shakes her head.*) Well, you are! In a very different way from anyone else. And all the nicer because of the difference, too. (*His voice becomes low
and husky. Laura turns away, nearly faint with the novelty of her emotions.*) I wish
you were my sister. I'd teach you to have some confidence in yourself. The differ-

ent people are not like other people, but being different is nothing to be ashamed of. Because other people are not such wonderful people. They're one hundred times one thousand. You're one times one! They walk all over the earth. You just stay here. They're common as—weeds, but—you—well, you're—*Blue Roses!*

Laura treasures her glass menagerie, and at the same time the objects are symbolic of her delicate and fragile nature. This is especially true of the unicorn, which is beautiful and unique, and yet alone in its singularity. Later in the play Laura discovers that Jim is engaged to be married, thus echoing the comments she herself made about the broken unicorn, "Glass breaks so easily. No matter how careful you are." Laura loves the unicorn because Laura is the unicorn. The objects or things your characters touch, treasure, or revile can communicate meaning in a powerful yet subtle way. Not everything in a play has to be verbalized.

Playwright Horton Foote, author of such plays and screenplays as *The Trip to Bountiful, 1918,* and *Tender Mercies,* is especially adept at creating place in his work, setting forty of his plays in Harrison, Texas, a fictional name for his hometown of Wharton, Texas. Foote states, "I picked a difficult subject, a little lost Texas town no one's heard of or cares about." For Foote, place is more than just a stage setting. In many of Foote's plays, place serves as the heart of the drama, and the conflict, especially in a play like *The Trip to Bountiful,* is couched in terms of the protagonist's dream of home or what home should be.

In creating character, then, a playwright considers the following:

1. What a character says and does
2. What a character looks like
3. What other characters say about him
4. What other characters say to him (as well as how they say it)
5. How a character reacts to his environment or place

Playwrights will know all of their characters well enough to create speech that rings true as it forwards the action of the drama. As Aristotle said, the play's action unfolds in relation to the characters' journeys through the conflicts they face. Your characters should be so real that they will control the plot rather than being controlled by the plot. In this way, your plot rings true as well.

DIALOGUE

After you have created your primary characters and written down pertinent information about them, you will want to prepare to write the script. In addition to completing activities which help you develop character, you also should write an outline of each scene. While it is true that you might change things in later drafts, you will want a roadmap or guideline before you begin writing. You can work from an initial story outline or timeline as we discussed in chapter 12 to get an overview of the story. For each individual act and scene, ask yourself the basic W questions: *who, what, where, when,* and *why.*

Instead of writing dialogue as soon as an idea germinates, playwrights generally map out what they want to happen before they begin to put words into their characters' mouths. Since you will use dialogue and action to move the play forward, you will need to decide what you want to happen before you write your script in order to write dialogue that propels the drama forward.

After you are sure of what you want to happen, map out the basic action of the individual scene: what happens first, second, third? Separate each turn of the action or progression of the plot into a separate part, called a **unit** or **beat**. The beat is the *one thing* you want to happen next. It might consist of a character's entrance, it might include a character picking up an old photograph off of the mantle, or it might require that a character lie or evade something. Each beat marks a specific movement in the play's progression.

As you proceed, decide what should happen in each beat. For example, in one beat or unit, you might want to add an obstacle to place in your protagonist's way. In another beat, you might reveal something about a character that the protagonist will remain unaware of. Mapping out the beats of the play will take time, but doing it ensures that you know exactly what is to happen and when it is to happen.

After you know what you want to accomplish in each beat, then write dialogue and stage direction for that beat. It is important to be able to manipulate each detail so it contributes to the whole of the drama. As we mentioned earlier, writing rituals vary among writers, and playwrights are no exception, but dividing the story into beats and then writing dialogue for the beats is a solid way to begin.

Dialogue is not a replication of ordinary human speech, but it must *sound* like ordinary human speech on stage. In Writing to Warm Up at the beginning of this chapter, we asked you to go to a public place and write down every word of a conversation you overheard. If you go into a restaurant and write down every word of the conversation taking place in the booth beside you, you might have an accurate transcript of what was said, but you do not have an accurate record of what transpired between those people. In order to capture the essence of what happened between those two people at the restaurant, you would have to cut the superfluous speech and alter the syntax and diction to capture the characters as they should be presented on stage. As Anne Lamott says of dialogue in prose, "One line of dialogue that rings true reveals character in a way that pages of description can't."

The playwright takes ordinary speech and speech patterns and transforms them into what will appear to be natural on stage. The emotion, then, is real human emotion even if the language is not what we would expect in real life. Good dialogue seems natural, even if it is seemingly illogical or unimportant, and it constantly moves the play forward.

The characters in David Mamet's play *Oleanna* use language as a weapon to gain and brandish power, even if they are unaware of their intent. At the beginning of the play, Carol comes to John, a university professor up for tenure, in frustration because she is failing the class. John, in the process of closing on a new house, is constantly distracted by phone calls. After speaking to her and getting nowhere, he tells her that if she comes back to see him so that he can help her, she will receive an A in the class. In act 2 we find out that she has accused him of sexual harassment, and she takes her complaint to the tenure committee.

Throughout the play the power paradigm gradually shifts from John to Carol, and this shift is reflected in the language. At the beginning of the play, John often finishes Carol's sentences for her and tells her about his own fear of inadequacy in an attempt to make her feel better. In act 3, we see Carol use John's own words to accuse him, twisting them out of the context that he intended. In this excerpt from act 3, John tries to talk Carol into withdrawing her complaint:

JOHN: ALL RIGHT. ALL RIGHT. ALL RIGHT. (*He picks up the phone.*) Hello. Yes. No. I'm here. Tell Mister . . . No, I can't talk to him now . . . I'm sure he has, but I'm fff . . . I know . . . No I have no time t . . . tell Mister . . . tell Mist . . . tell Jerry that I'm *fine* and that I'll call him right aw . . . (*Pause*). My wife . . . Yes. I'm sure she has. Yes, thank you. Yes, I'll call her too. I cannot talk to you now. (*He hangs up. Pause*) All right. It was good of you to come. Thank you. I have studied. I have spent some time studying the indictment.

CAROL: You will have to explain that word to me.

JOHN: An "indictment" . . .

CAROL: Yes.

JOHN: Is a "bill of particulars." A . . .

CAROL: All right. Yes.

JOHN: In which is alleged . . .

CAROL: No. I cannot allow that. I cannot allow that. Nothing is alleged. Everything is proved . . .

JOHN: Please, wait a sec . . .

CAROL: I cannot *come* to allow . . .

JOHN: If I may . . . If I may, from whatever you feel is "established," by . . .

CAROL: The issue here is not what I "feel." It is not my "feelings," but the feelings of women. And men. Your superiors, who've been "polled," do you see? To whom *evidence* has been presented, who have ruled, do you see? Who have weighed the testimony and the evidence, and have *ruled,* do you see? That you are *negligent.* That you are *guilty,* that you are found *wanting,* and in *error;* and are *not,* for the reasons so-told, to be given tenure. That you are to be disciplined. For facts. For *facts.* Not "alleged," what is the word? But *proved.* Do you see? *By your own actions.*

     That is what the tenure committee has said. That is what my lawyer said. For what you did in class. For what you did *in this office.*

JOHN: They're going to discharge me.

CAROL: As full well they should. You don't understand? You're angry? What has *led* you to this place? Not your sex. Not your race. Not your class. YOUR OWN AC-TIONS. And you're *angry.* You *ask* me here. What *do* you want? You want to "charm" me. You want to "convince" me. You want me to recant. I will *not* re-cant. Why should I . . . ? What I say is right. You tell me, you are going to tell me that you have a wife and child. You are going to say that you have a career and that you've worked twenty years for this. Do you know what you've *worked* for? *Power.* For *power.* Do you understand? And you sit there, and you tell me *sto-ries.* About your *house,* about all the private *schools,* and about *privilege,* and how you are entitled. To *buy,* to *spend,* to *mock,* to *summon.* All your stories. All your silly weak *guilt,* it's all about *privilege;* and you won't know it. Don't you see? You worked twenty years for the right to *insult* me. And you feel entitled to be *paid* for it. Your Home. Your Wife . . . Your sweet "deposit" on your house . . .

JOHN: Don't you have feelings?

CAROL: That's my point. You see? Don't you have feelings? Your final argument. What is it that has no feelings. *Animals.* I don't take your side, you question if I'm Human.

JOHN: Don't you have feelings?

CAROL: I have a responsibility. I . . .

JOHN: . . . to . . . ?

CAROL: To? This institution. To the *students.* To my *group.*

JOHN: . . . your "group." . . .

CAROL: Because I speak, yes, not for myself. But for the group; for those who suffer what I suffer. On behalf of whom, even if I, were, inclined, to what, forgive? Forget? What? Overlook your . . .

JOHN: . . . my behavior?

CAROL: . . . it would be wrong.

JOHN: Even if you were inclined to "forgive" me.

CAROL: It would be wrong.

JOHN: And what would transpire.

CAROL: Transpire?

JOHN: Yes.

CAROL: "Happen?"

JOHN: Yes.

CAROL: Then *say* it. For Christ's sake. Who the *hell* do you think that you are? You want a post. You want unlimited power. To do and to say what you want. As it pleases you—Testing, Questioning, Flirting . . .

JOHN: I never . . .

CAROL: Excuse me, one moment, will you? (*She reads from her notes.*) The twelfth:

"Have a good day, dear." The fifteenth: "Now, don't *you* look fetching . . ." April seventeenth: "If you girls would come over here . . ." I saw you. I saw you, Professor. For two semesters sit there, stand there and exploit your, as you thought, "paternal prerogative," and what is that but rape; I swear to God. You asked me in here to explain something to me, as a child, that I did not understand. But I came to explain something to you. You Are Not God. You ask me why I came? I came here to instruct you. (*She produces his book.*) And your book? You think you're going to show me some "light"? You "*maverick.*" Outside of tradition. No, no, (*she reads from the book's liner notes*) "*of* that fine tradition of *inquiry.* Of Polite *skepticism*". . . and you say you believe in free intellectual discourse. YOU BELIEVE IN NOTHING. YOU BELIEVE IN NOTHING AT ALL.

JOHN: I believe in freedom of thought.

CAROL: Isn't that fine. *Do* you?

JOHN: Yes. I do.

CAROL: Then why do you question, for one moment, the committee's decision refusing your tenure? Why do you question your suspension? You believe in what *you call* freedom of thought. Then, fine. *You* believe in freedom-of-thought *and* a home, and, *and* prerogatives for your kid, *and* tenure. And I'm going to tell you. You believe *not* in "freedom of thought," but in an elitist, in, in a protected hierarchy which rewards you. And for whom you are the clown. And you mock and exploit the system which pays your rent. You're wrong. I'm not wrong. You're wrong. You think that I'm full of hatred. I know what you think I am.

JOHN: Do you?

CAROL: You think I'm a, of course I do. You think I am a frightened, repressed, confused, I don't know, abandoned young thing of some doubtful sexuality, who wants, power and revenge. (*Pause.*) Don't you? (*Pause.*)

JOHN: Yes. I do. (*Pause.*)

CAROL: Isn't that better? And I feel that that is the first moment which you've treated me with respect. For you told me the truth. (*Pause.*) I did not come here, as you are assured, to gloat. Why would I want to gloat? I've profited nothing from your, your, as you say, your "misfortune." I came here, as you did me the honor to *ask* me here. I came here to *tell* you something. (*Pause.*) That I think . . . that I think you've been wrong. That I think you've been terribly wrong. Do you hate me now? (*Pause.*)

JOHN: Yes.

CAROL: Why do you hate me? Because you think me wrong? No. Because I have, you think, *power* over you. Listen to me. Listen to me, Professor. (*Pause.*) It is the power that you hate. So deeply that, that any atmosphere of free discussion is impossible. It's not "unlikely." It's *impossible.* Isn't it?

JOHN: Yes.

CAROL: *Isn't* it . . . ?

JOHN: Yes. I suppose.

In this excerpt, Mamet uses dialogue that reflects the abyss between John and Carol. In act 1, John answers his own questions and pontificates about the ideas espoused in his book. In act 3, John stands accused of his own words. Carol's speeches are much longer in act 3, and she uses the language of the accuser to subjugate John just as he used words to condescend to her in act 1. Their short exchanges are verbal wrestling matches; they speak to each other, but they don't communicate. Many times the dialogue doesn't reflect real-life speech. It is artificial, but it reflects the real relationship between them. They interpret each other's language according to their own backgrounds, and this inability to communicate is the cause of the chasm between them and is also the weapon they use to wield power over each other. Ultimately, she accuses him of raping her and he beats her in a frenzied rage. When language fails, power can only be found in physical dominance.

As you try to capture veracity in speech, listen to people talk. Then transform their voices on the page. The challenge in capturing speech on paper is to translate something aural and put it into a visual form. Syntax and diction are very important here as well as inflection and dialect. One helpful source in learning how to capture speech on paper is the book *American Dreams: Lost and Found* by Studs Terkel (or any of the oral histories edited by Studs Terkel). In this book Terkel interviews Americans about their definition of the American Dream. He captures the speech patterns of the various dialects without stereotyping his subjects. Here is an excerpt from an interview with Rafael Rosa, a nineteen-year-old bellhop in New York City:

My American Dream is to be famous. Like a big boss at a big firm, sit back, relax, and just collect. Oh, I treat my employees nice, pay 'em real good, don't overwork 'em too much, not like most bosses, they fire you right away.

I really would like to have a chauffeur-driven limousine, have a bar one side, color TV on the other. The chicks, the girls, oh yeah. Instead of coming in at eight in the morning and leavin' at eight in the afternoon. Maybe I'll invent something one of these days and wind up a millionaire. As for now, I'd really like to be chief pilot at the air force.

As I ride my bike here in New York, I see all these elegant-looking people, fancy-dressed, riding around in a limousine, just looking all normal. I figured if they can do, why can't I? Why can't I just go out there and get myself driven around for a while? I haven't hit it big yet, but I'm still working on it.

As I started growing older, I figured it's a jungle out there, you better grab a vine. So I grabbed a vine, and here I landed. (Laughs.) It's really hard out there in the city; you can't get a job any more. I would just like to be on TV, a newsman or something.

Writing for Ideas and Practice 13-3

1. Answer the following questions about the Studs Terkel excerpt:
   a. List five adjectives you would use to describe Rafael Rosa.
   b. What in the text caused you to draw those conclusions about Rosa?

c.   Did Rosa reveal anything about himself that he did not state directly? How did he do this?

d.   Did you notice anything unique about his diction and/or syntax?

2. Write a short monologue for a character who explains what the American Dream means to him or her.

3. Write a sentence containing at least five words and an action. (*Example:* The man robbed a convenience store and was shot as he was trying to escape.) Then rewrite the sentence three times, each as a different character would say it.

Although the content of your dialogue develops the plot of the scene or play, much of the success of dramatic dialogue rests in pacing. How do you write dialogue that moves? Pay attention to timing. In a piece of music, the rests are scored and are as important as the notes: the silence is part of the music. The same is true of dialogue. A playwright uses the same tools as the poet to create dialogue that reads quickly or slowly. The more punctuation a speech has, the slower it will read. The longer the speeches, the slower the pace. The pace of the dialogue is determined by the length of the lines and the rests or pauses in between the words.

For example, if you want to create intensity on stage, infusing the dialogue with exclamation marks will not automatically create intensity. Yes, shouting and screaming is unsettling, but there are many other ways to achieve the effect you desire. Short, clipped fragments which are interrupted by another character can create intensity. Silence can also create intensity. Think of a woman who is calling for her husband after she hears a shot in the bedroom. She knows in her heart that he has killed himself, but she calls for him, softly and tentatively in short, hoarse whispers as she reaches for the doorknob. You can use softness and silence as well as shouting and screaming to create power and intensity in your work. Experiment with line length and silences to alter the pace of your piece until you *hear* what you want.

Pacing is important in any drama, but it is essential in writing comedic dialogue. Sometimes the humor of a scene is based on threads, ideas that are woven together as word play throughout the scene. Much of the humor in Shakespeare's comedies is based on word play, as in this scene from *Taming of the Shrew*, where Petruchio and Kate flirt, fight, and match wits:

 PETRUCHIO: Good morrow, Kate, for that's your name, I hear.
KATHARINA: Well have you heard, but something hard of hearing.
   They call me Katharine that do talk of me.
PETRUCHIO: You lie, in faith, for you are called plain Kate,
   And bonny Kate, and sometimes Kate the curst;
   But Kate, the prettiest Kate in Christendom,
   Kate of Kate Hall, my superdainty Kate,
   For dainties are all Kates, and therefore, Kate,

Take this of me, Kate of my consolation:
Hearing thy mildness praised in every town,
Thy virtues spoke of, and thy beauty sounded,
Yet not so deeply as to thee belongs,
Myself am moved to woo thee for my wife.

KATHARINA: Moved? In good time! Let him that moved you hither
Remove you hence. I knew you at the first
You were a movable.

PETRUCHIO: Why, what's a movable?

KATHARINA: A joint stool.

PETRUCHIO: Thou hast hit it. Come, sit on me.

KATHARINA: Asses are made to bear, and so are you.

PETRUCHIO: Women are made to bear,* and so are you.

KATHARINA: No such jade* as you, if me you mean.

PETRUCHIO: Alas, good Kate, I will not burden thee,
For knowing thee to be but young and light.

KATHARINA: Too light* for such a swain as you to catch,
And yet as heavy as my weight should be.

PETRUCHIO: Should be? Should—buzz!

KATHARINA: Well ta'en, and like a buzzard.

PETRUCHIO: O slow-winged turtle,* shall a buzzard take thee?

KATHARINA: Ay, for a turtle, as he takes a buzzard.

PETRUCHIO: Come, come, you wasp, i' faith, you are too angry.

KATHARINA: If I be waspish, best beware my sting.

PETRUCHIO: My remedy is then to pluck it out.

KATHARINA: Ay, if the fool could find it where it lies.

PETRUCHIO: Who knows not where a wasp does wear his sting?
In his tail.

KATHARINA: In his tongue.

PETRUCHIO: Whose tongue?

KATHARINA: Yours, if you talk of tales, and so farewell.

PETRUCHIO: What, with my tongue in your tail? Nay, come again.
Good Kate, I am a gentleman—

KATHARINA: That I'll try. (*She strikes him.*)

Bear children, but also to bear the weight of men in the sexual act

An old horse

Witty

Turtledove

The humor in this excerpt is found in the content of the dialogue, the double entendres and the quick-witted insults, a rapid-fire battle between Kate and Petruchio, and the quick pace of the piece is heightened by the short lines of dialogue and frequent alliteration.

Construct your dialogue with care, using sound and rhythm in addition to word denotation and connotation to control the pace of the scene. Sustaining a frenetic or somber pace throughout several scenes can tire or bore your audience even though the content of your dialogue might be good, so vary the pace from scene to scene or within the scenes themselves.

Writing for Ideas and Practice 13-4

1. Write a page of dialogue between two people who have recently severed their relationship. Each line of dialogue should be *at least* one sentence long.
2. Now write the same piece again. This time each line of dialogue should be *no longer* than one sentence.

As you weave dialogue and action, consider that sometimes saying less means more. The subterranean or unspoken part of dialogue is called the **subtext** of a work. As opposed to focusing all of your attention on what your characters are saying, create an undercurrent in your dialogue. Is the character holding back? Is he or she saying something that doesn't seem to connect to the thread of the action? Why? What does that communicate? A wife might say to her husband, "The kids and I waited as long as we could, but we gave up and ate without you. I kept your dinner warm for you just in case you came home hungry." What she might really be saying is "You were inconsiderate. You should have let me know if you were going to be late."

Actors identify and interpret subtext to better know how to play their characters on stage. The difficulty for the author is constructing dialogue so that actors can recognize and interpret the subtext correctly in your work without being so heavy-handed that you overwrite the dialogue or obscure the text. The best way to write what you really mean is to map out what you want to happen, unit by unit, before you start writing the dialogue. Write out what you want to say, and then find the right words to communicate the subtext. David Mamet says that "the point is not to speak the desire but to speak that which is most likely to bring about the desire."

Although not all of your text will be infused with subtext, it adds nuance and depth to your work. You can add character action and stage direction to guide actors, but you should write dialogue that is strong enough to be interpreted without excessive direction. If your dialogue is true to life, you probably already have subtext, for it is an integral part of human communication (or miscommunication). But if you wish to be more deliberate about learning subtext, beyond watching and reading plays, study people. Be a "fly on the wall" and listen in on conversations. Understand and be sensitive to the complexities of communication, and then capture the undercurrent, the meaning beyond the words of your characters.

Here is another scene by student Delisa Bice which infuses subtext into the dialogue. Notice what is said underneath the words themselves.

(As scene opens Mammaw is going through several boxes in the living room of her new home. She seems out of sorts and becomes more and more upset as she goes through more and more boxes. She is searching for something. Dennis enters through the back door in coaching shorts and shirt with a cap on. He is about 48,

but still takes his cap off upon entering house.)

DENNIS: Knock. Knock.

MAMMAW: Who is it? Oh, Dennis.

DENNIS: What are you doin' Mammaw?

MAMMAW: Dennis, I can't find Upton's scrapbook that I done him. I have looked everywhere and I just can't find it nowhere. I don't know what I'm going to do.

DENNIS: Why do you need it, Mammaw?

MAMMAW: Why do I need it? Because—I've just got to have it. It just makes me sick.

(*She starts back to the boxes.*)

DENNIS: Well, come on Mammaw. Come walk around the track while I unlock the fieldhouse for the boys. It'll pop up sooner or later as you get things settled.

MAMMAW: No . . . I don't want to go to the fieldhouse. I can't find anything here. It's just awful.

DENNIS: What's awful, Mammaw?

MAMMAW: What do you mean what's awful? You just don't know what it's like. You and them boys just grabbed everything I had and threw it in boxes and moved me here in one afternoon. I don't know where anything is.

(*At the point of tears.*)

I can't find my cookbooks, I don't know where I'm goin' to put any of my pictures, I can't find Mama's and Papa's pictures or Junior's scrapbook. It's just awful!

DENNIS: Well, Mammaw, we can't get it all unpacked in a day. We'll just do a little at a time. Now get your walking shoes and hat and come down to the track with me. It'll make you feel better.

MAMMAW: No. I just don't want to go. I can't and I'm not goin' to feel better until I find that.

DENNIS: Mammaw, it's just a book. You'll run across it sooner or later.

MAMMAW: It's not just a book either, Denny. That had Upton Junior's newsclippings from basketball and graduation and college. I just hate this. It's just awful. Sweet Jesus, I don't know why this had to happen. Everything's just awful.

DENNIS: Mother, I know it's awful. It's not just awful for you. It's hard on all of us. It's hard on me, on Joan. It's hard on the girls.

MAMMAW (*Almost in tears again*): Yeah, I know it is. They lost both Upton and Jan. And Melba—but she's at peace now. She's not hurting anymore. She just couldn't take it. Oh Lord, I know how she felt.

DENNIS: I know you know—but Mammaw, Melba just wasn't right after the stroke and all.

MAMMAW: Naw, she wasn't right. And I don't think she knew what she was doin' when she shot herself.

DENNIS: No, she probably didn't. Depression makes people do strange things. She just couldn't bear losing them.

MAMMAW (*Mammaw has pulled herself together a little.*): No, she couldn't. You know Junior and Jan took such good care of her. But I feel sorry for Joan. She was trying to get where she could take care of Melba, and she just wouldn't wait. You know . . . she always liked Jan more . . . or at least that's how she acted. That was awful what she done. And right before Mother's Day.

DENNIS: It's a mean thing for a person to do. Now come on Mammaw, get your walk-ing shoes and let's go up to the fieldhouse. You'll feel better after you walk. I'll help you with some boxes when we get through.

MAMMAW: You will? Well, I guess I'll go. You know it really helps my arthritis when I go do that.

DENNIS: That's right. That's why I want you to go . . . walking is the best thing you can do for your body right now.

MAMMAW: Yeah? Let me get my shoes and I'll go. (*She starts to the bedroom and then pauses.*) Dennis.

DENNIS: Yes, Mammaw?

MAMMAW: You think God will forgive Melba for what she done?

DENNIS: God is a forgiving God, Mammaw, and Melba wasn't herself.

MAMMAW: No, she wasn't.

DENNIS: Now get ready.

MAMMAW: Yeah, I will.

(*She exits. Dennis sits down on the couch, puts his head in his hands. He takes a few deep breaths to keep from breaking down, then looks up toward heaven. He shakes his head back to reality and wipes his eyes as he hears her approaching.*)

MAMMAW (*As she enters*): Denny, you think you can trim them branches on them trees out front?

DENNIS: I'll try, Mother. Ready? Let's go.

(*They exit out the back door.*)

In the conversation between Mammaw and Dennis, Mammaw is upset over a lost scrapbook. What does the writer try to communicate to the au-dience here without stating it directly? Dennis reacts to Mammaw's state of mind by trying to get her to go to the fieldhouse with him. Is he merely concerned about her arthritis, or does he have another, unstated reason for wanting her to go with him? In addition to subtext this scene contains other clues that hint at the relationship between Mammaw and Dennis. At certain moments Mammaw refers to Dennis as "Denny," perhaps a name Dennis was called as a child. The change in address from "Dennis" to "Denny" during the scene is a subtle hint that Mammaw, at least for that moment, sees Dennis as her child, and not as a grown man.

Writing for Ideas and Practice 13-5

1. Write part of a scene (two pages maximum) that is a conversation between two char-acters that is insignificant or trivial yet at the same time reveals the type of relation-ship that those two characters have. After you have written the outline and the dia-logue, have it read aloud.

2. Now rewrite the piece. Cut it in half yet still communicate the same information. You

might want to add some character (action) or stage direction here. Again, have the text read aloud. Compare the two. Which scene is better? Can you say less and mean more?

3. Many newer televisions have closed-caption capabilities. Watch a movie with the sound turned off and the closed captioning on. Just read the dialogue. What do you notice by just reading dialogue instead of hearing it?

As you write dialogue for the beats that you have outlined, remember that every word that is spoken needs to help elicit the content of the beat and then lead to the next point or turn. This building and turning helps pace the scene. If a scene drags, it is possible that the actors are slowing the scene by not picking up cues, but it is also possible that the dialogue simply isn't going anywhere. There is very little margin of error here. Keep your audience wanting to see the next turn.

Writing for Ideas and Practice 13-6

1. In the scene that you wrote in Writing for Ideas and Practice 12-6.2, the conflict was created by the fact that one of the characters was hiding something. Withholding and gradually revealing certain information to the audience at pivotal moments can create audience interest and suspense, especially when this information is essential to the perpetuation or resolution of the conflict. This exercise focuses on adding a character to add complexity to the essential conflict and to provide you with interesting dramatic possibilities. Write out each beat or unit of a scene in which one of the characters has a problem. The scene will focus on the revelation and/or discussion of the problem. Don't worry about resolving the problem in this scene. The scene should end with the entrance of a third character, and the third character should have no more than two lines at the end of the scene. You may incorporate the third character in any way you wish.

2. Using dialogue and stage directions, write out the scene you mapped out in the previous exercise. Have three people in your group or class read or act out the scene so you can examine your work.

THE PHYSICAL ENVIRONMENT

One of the most important things to remember about writing for the stage is that you are working within a particular physical environment. Plays are presented on a stage with an audience seated on one or more sides of the stage. The physical environment of the stage will dictate the way a play is presented, and, even more importantly, how a play should be constructed.

A great number of plays are produced on a **proscenium stage**, a stage that looks like a frame with the audience seated on only the front side of the stage, but there are other stage configurations as well. The **arena** or **circle stage** is a stage surrounded on all sides by the audience. Characters usually exit and enter from audience aisles. The **thrust** or **horseshoe stage** is surrounded on three sides by the audience, and the **open** or **end stage** is like a proscenium stage without the frame, border, or wings.

You might not know what type of stage your play might be produced on, but each of these stages have two things in common: a place upon which the action can take place, and a place for the audience. It is possible, of course, to merge the space between audience and actors. Characters could interact with the audience or could interact with each other in a theater aisle. You can experiment with the space, but keep the different stage configurations in mind as you envision your drama.

You might add other types of media to your play. Tennessee Williams incorporates slides into *The Glass Menagerie* to supplement the action and dialogue. Emily Mann also incorporates slides into her documentary play *Still Life*. The play examines the effects of the Vietnam War on both the soldier as well as those he comes home to. Mann's dialogue braids together parts of interviews with the three characters, Mark, a Vietnam veteran, his wife Cheryl, and his friend Nadine. Mark shows his slides to the audience off and on throughout the play as he speaks to them about his experiences in Vietnam and about his relationships with the other two characters. Each character speaks directly to the audience and does not interact with the other characters, and yet their stories are intertwined against the backdrop of the slide screen upstage. Here is an segment from act 3 of *Still Life*:

MARK (*snaps on slide of him and R. J.*):
    This is a picture of me and R. J.
    We look like a couple of bad-asses.
    It was hot. Shit, I miss him.
    We were so close.
    We talked about everything.
    We talked about how each of us lost our
    virginity, we talked about girls.
CHERYL (*agitated*):
    My girlfriend across the street told me
    how babies were made when I was ten years old.
    I just got sick. I hated it.
MARK:
    We talked about fights, getting back on the streets, drugs.
CHERYL:
    From that moment on,

I had a model:
I wanted kids . . .

MARK:
We talked about getting laid . . .

CHERYL:
But I didn't want the husband that went along with it.
I still feel that way.

MARK:
We talked about how we would be inseparable
when we came home.
We never would have, even if he hadn't died.
We knew too much about each other.

CHERYL:
And this spooks me because I said this
when I was ten years old.

MARK (*new slide*):
This is the place, the Alamo.
That's where the rocket came in and
killed a man . . . uh . . .
(*Indicates in the picture.*)
We got hit one night.
Some several people were sleeping, this fellow . . .
(*Picture of him.*)
A rocket came in and blew his head off.

NADINE:
I said to Mark:
"You're still pissed off because they let you go.
Even assholes stopped their kids from going.
Your good Catholic parents sent you to slaughter."

In a well-constructed play, structure reinforces content and theme. In *Still Life*, the slides are not superimposed on the play; instead, they provide powerful and disturbing visual exposition. In addition, the nature of the medium reinforces the "still life" nature of the piece as the characters tell their stories individually. As you write your play, try to see the production in your mind and be open to incorporating elements into your play that you might not normally associate with the theater.

Although the visual aspects of a play are important, because of a theater's physical construction, plays revolve around verbal encounters. Even though on-stage actions will play a pivotal role in the plot of a play, the verbal encounters between the characters are probably given more emphasis than the action in a stage play. In a stage play, the stage environment prevents the revelation of certain small details that the movie screen close-up affords. A giant movie screen allows the audience member in the last row of the balcony to see the wistful half-smile on the protagonist's face as she sees her former lover across the room. In the theater, only the people in the first three rows are able to see that expression. So, while it is true that actors can exaggerate their movements to compensate for the physical constraints of the theater, the playwright must use dialogue as the primary means of telling the story.

The stage play, therefore, is primarily verbal and consists of dialogue, with character action and stage direction supplementing the speech of the characters. A playwright must consider the theater's physical environment in developing character action and stage direction The stage setting of a play might be realistic or symbolic, and if you decide that your play will have different locations, you will want to consider pragmatic staging possibilities. A set could portray a king's palace with realistic set decorations, or the staging might merely suggest setting by the use of a few columns draped with gold material and a raised platform. The level of realism of your set will probably be determined by the level of realism in your play or your visualization of the staging, as well as the physical feasibility of changing locations from scene to scene or act to act.

Be realistic as you visualize your stage setting and scene changes. Elaborate, realistic sets with multiple scene changes are probably best left to the Broadway musical. Most smaller theaters do not have the resources to produce plays with expensive stage settings and complicated scene changes. Focus not only on the content of your work, but also ensure that your play can indeed be performed on stage, especially by a theater group with limited resources.

The playwright's stage directions supplement the play script by giving the actors and directors important information about what happens in the play, from indicating a character's entrance to giving important lighting cues.

The way you stage your play can have tremendous impact. Think about how you move your characters on and off stage, and incorporate movement which will engage the audience. If all of your characters have to enter and exit from only one place on stage, then movement will be rather static and forced. It might be that the characters are in a prison cell, and the only characters that enter and exit are the guards. In that case, there might not be any other options for staging the piece, but then try to think of some interesting possibilities for movement inside the cell.

Characters don't just stand in one place, facing the audience as they deliver their lines one at a time. Life contains movement, and drama probably contains more movement than real life in order to maximize audience interest in what happens on stage. You might also think in terms of triangles and angles as you move your characters through their space, for angular movement on stage is dramatically effective. If you want to focus attention on a character, place him in a prominent position onstage, either closer to the audience (downstage), or perhaps at the apex of a triangle of characters. Don't overdo it, though. The key to character action is to create dynamic and interesting movement without the audience being aware that you are trying hard to create interesting movement on stage. The dramatist is like a magician; if the audience knows how the magician did the trick, it isn't nearly as interesting anymore.

A misconception of writing drama is that the writing doesn't need to be polished, since so much rewriting is done in workshop and rehearsal and production. In fact, the opposite is true. Whatever writing strategies you adopt for writing drama, remember that writing drama perhaps requires the most methodical technique. The playwright writes to perfection, and only then is it good enough to workshop. As Edward Albee states, "Rehearsal is where you prove the play, not improve it."

The Script

The play script usually contains the following stage directions:

1. Character names and descriptions
2. Stage directions given at the beginning of the play
3. Stage directions given throughout the play
4. Character stage directions or actions

The character page contains a list of characters and their descriptions. List the characters' names and give a description of those characters. In your descriptions, you should be specific, but don't take this space to editorialize or delve into the character's history too much. Be brief. Here is an example of a character list:

MATTIE	In her late thirties to early forties. Attractive but often disheveled in her appearance. Political science professor.
THOMAS	Mid-thirties. Computer software engineer.
TRUDY	Thomas's grandmother. In her seventies. Chain smokes.

The opening stage directions give a brief description of the setting and indicate special lighting cues and character action that takes place before the dialogue begins. If your play begins on an empty stage, then indicate the entrances and exits of the actors. If your actors are on stage at the beginning of the play or scene, then indicate that also. Describe any action that takes place previous to the first line of dialogue, and then indicate subsequent action during the play or scene.

Most opening stage directions are short and to the point, as in the following example:

SCENE I
(*A park bench near a playground. Mattie is seated, reading a newspaper. Thomas comes up behind her.*)

On occasion, however, you might find that you have quite a bit of character action before the dialogue begins, and your opening directions might be rather complex, as in the opening stage directions for Sam Shepard's play *Suicide in B♭*.

Slightly raked stage. A plain white muslin flat represents the upstage wall. It does not run the full width of the stage but leaves empty space on either side of it. It should be made obvious that it's a flat to the audience. There are no side walls. Dead center upstage, almost flush with the flat is a black upright piano. Not a grand piano. Downstage left is a blue stuffed arm chair with a brass floor lamp set to the upstage side of it. The lamp has a pale yellow shade with small green palm trees painted all around it in a circle. These are the only objects on stage. The floor of the stage is not painted but left bare. The entire set is visible to the audience as they come in. In the center of the floor, the outline of a man's body sprawled out in an awkward position of death is painted in white. The lights begin to dim very slowly. At their half way point, the PIANO PLAYER rushes on from stage right, hiding his face from the audience with his coat, as though afraid to be photographed. He is wearing a shabby black suit. He sits quickly on the piano stool, back to audience and faces the piano. As the lights continue to dim, he raises both arms very slowly with the fingers of both hands interlaced until they are straight above his head. When he gets to the top of this stretch he cracks his knuckles loudly. The lights go to black. A loud gun shot is heard off stage, in the dark. Sound of a body falling hard to the floor. Lamp is switched on. Lights bank back up fast. PIANO PLAYER is still sitting at the bench with both arms still raised high, fingers together. Lights begin to slowly dim again. As they do, PIANO PLAYER lowers his arms slowly and sets them on the keys of the piano. He begins to play. PABLO and LOUIS, the two detectives, enter from right accompanied by the music. LOUIS is playing dead and being dragged across the floor by his heels by PABLO. PABLO is dressed in a long overcoat, baggy pants, shiny black shoes and a detective's hat. LOUIS wears striped pants, brown and white brogans, striped shirt and tie, black vest, black garters on his arms and a black detective's hat which he holds on his stomach while he's being dragged. The piano music continues as PABLO pulls him into center stage with some effort then drops both heels to the floor. Piano stops. LOUIS stays on the floor on his back. PABLO looks down at him. PIANO PLAYER just sits with back to audience. Lights stop at ½ level.

Shepard details the beginning of his play, indicating specific lighting cues and staging elements. Not all stage directions are this specific; the amount of information included depends on the playwright's visual concept of the scene. The best advice is to be as specific as you need to be without making your play so difficult to stage that it isn't possible to perform it.

Shepard uses the vocabulary of theater to indicate his directions. As you write stage directions, you will utilize the same vocabulary. Familiarize yourself with the following key terms used in stage direction:

Downstage — *the part of the stage closest to the audience*
Upstage — *the part of the stage farthest from the audience*
Stage Left — *the actor's left*
Stage Right — *the actor's right*

Stage directions found within the play itself are separated from the text and indicate character action (including entrances and exits) and lighting and/or sound cues. Ends of scenes are usually indicated by a lighting cue (Lights dim, Blackout) within the stage directions. This lighting cue is followed by the words "END OF SCENE" or "END OF ACT." Here is an example of a general stage direction.

For information on formatting scripts for submission, see pages 415–416

MATTIE: Did you think I wouldn't remember what you said last night?
(*Mattie turns her back to Thomas and continues chopping the vegetables.*)
THOMAS: Haven't we fought enough for one week?
(*Mattie is silent. Thomas takes his coat off, throws it down, stops, picks the coat back up again and storms out the door.*)
(*BLACKOUT*)

(*END OF SCENE*)

Important character actions or gestures are indicated throughout the text. It is sometimes difficult to know how much is enough or how much is too much, but gestures and character actions can be inserted to communicate something quickly and more effectively than verbalizing it. The key here is that each action should either forward the action or reveal more about the character. Separate the directions and place them in parentheses close to the dialogue.

MATTIE (*In tears*): I have looked everywhere, and I can't find the letter anywhere.

The overall guiding force behind stage direction is to give only directions crucial to staging or character action. Stage directions should support the dialogue, not supplant it.

Writing for Ideas and Practice 13-7

1. Write one page which consists solely of stage direction. This page will be the first page of a play or scene, describing the setting. Then begin either with the entrance of the main character or the beginning of the play with the main character onstage. Write stage directions which take the character through a series of actions which reveal a character's personality or main characteristics. You may have another character enter the room if you wish, but any interaction between them should be communicated through action or gesture rather than dialogue. Hint: This type of scene probably works best in comedy, since the actors have an opportunity to exaggerate a bit.

2. Write an ending to a scene that ends with a character delivering a piece of news that surprises or shocks the other characters on stage. Incorporate stage directions, including the stage directions that indicate the end of the scene.

3. Imagine a main character. List at least ten details which define or describe him or her. Which of these details could be communicated purely through dialogue? Which of these details should be included in the stage directions or character list? Which of these details should be under the control of the director or the actor?

THE ONE-ACT PLAY

As you begin to write plays, think about starting with the one-act play. If you have a full-length play in you begging to be written, by all means write it. However, one-act plays are easier to manage if you are just starting out, and many well-known plays by well-known playwrights are one-acts. One of the most prestigious play competitions in the country is a short play contest sponsored by the Actor's Theatre of Louisville. Horton Foote has written both full-length and one-acts, and he says that the one-act play "allows me to flesh out and explore facets of what has become for me an attempt to create a moral and social history of a particular idea over a period of time."

In a full-length play, as in a novel, the playwright might spend a lot of time on exposition and subplots. The one-act play is the dramatic equivalent of the short story, which develops one conflict. In a one-act play, exposition and conflict must appear very early on, and although the one-act usually has anywhere from three to seven characters in it, only one conflict or idea is developed. In the following excerpt from the beginning of Horton Foote's one-act play *Blind Date*, notice that the conflict is introduced as soon as the audience knows the who and the where of the play.

 Setting: The living room of Robert and Dolores Henry. It is empty. Robert comes in. He is a lawyer and has a briefcase, several newspapers, a package of purchases from the drugstore. He drops all these on the sofa and takes his coat off, throwing that over a chair. He calls: "Dolores." There is no answer. he kicks his shoes off and calls: "Children." Again no answer. He goes to the radio and turns it on. He gets one of the newspapers and spreads it around the room as he looks through it. He calls again: "Dolores, I am home." A voice calls back: "She's not here."

ROBERT (*Calling.*): Where is she?
SARAH NANCY (*The voice — calling.*): Yes.
ROBERT: Where?
SARAH NANCY: She took the children to a friend's to spend the night.
ROBERT: Where are you?
SARAH NANCY: In my room.
ROBERT: Did your aunt say when we were having supper?
SARAH NANCY: We've had supper. We ate with the children.
ROBERT: What did you have?

SARAH NANCY: Peanut butter and jelly sandwiches. (*He is depressed by that. He goes to the window and looks out. He goes to the radio and turns it off. He sees two college yearbooks on a table. He goes and picks them up to look at them when his wife* Dolores *comes in.*)

ROBERT: Where is my supper?

DOLORES: What?

ROBERT: Where is my supper? Do you know what time it is? I'm starved. I have been here at least half an hour.

DOLORES: Have you forgotten our conversation at breakfast?

ROBERT: What conversation?

DOLORES: Oh, Robert. I told you to eat uptown tonight.

ROBERT: I don't remember that.

DOLORES: I told you I was not going to fix supper tonight.

ROBERT: I don't remember a single word of that.

DOLORES: You were looking right at me when I told you. I said I was giving the children peanut butter and jelly sandwiches at five-thirty and at six-thirty after their baths I was taking them over to Hannah's to spend the night so they would not be running in and out of here while Sarah Nancy was entertaining her date.

ROBERT: Does Sarah Nancy have another date?

DOLORES: Yes. Thank God. I told you that too this morning.

ROBERT: If you did I don't remember.

DOLORES: Of course not. You never listen to a word I say. Oh, if I live through this I'll live through anything. (*Whispering.*) Don't you remember my telling you this morning that at last I had arranged another date for her? After trying desperately for three days?

ROBERT: No.

DOLORES: Well, I did. And I hope this one turns out better than the last time. I talked to Sister late this afternoon. She is just beside herself. "You know suppose," she said, "she takes it into her head to insult this date too." "Sister," I said, "I refuse to get discouraged. I did not get on the beauty pages of the University of Texas and the Texas A&M yearbooks on my looks alone. It was on my personality. And that can be acquired." Don't you agree?

ROBERT: I guess.

Two pages into this one-act play the audience knows that Dolores is desperately trying to seek suitors for her niece, Sarah Nancy. The audience has not yet seen Sarah Nancy, but it is apparent that she is an unwilling participant in this venture. She tells her aunt that all boys are "Dumb and stupid," and that Felix, her date, "looks just like a warthog." The main conflict is clear, and the obstacles Dolores must overcome are formidable. But Foote isn't so simplistic that he ignores other dramatic possibilities. Robert plays a part in the action as well, but at first glance he seems to be more of an observer and not a pivotal character in the play, a character who could easily be cut from the action. So why is he important? For one, Robert's presence provides the opportunity to provide expository material. In addition, the audience can see what kind of marriage Dolores has, and that insight provides a touch of irony as Dolores tries to play matchmaker for Sarah Nancy.

In constructing a one-act play, remember that although you have a multitude of possiblities for dramatic scenes and character interaction, you don't have the time to weave complicated subplots through the work. You can, however, develop relationships and create rich, fully-realized characters. Develop just a few main characters well and focus on the one main conflict of the play. Think of making the most of the short time you have to communicate your message, and make every word and move count.

Always remember in writing a play that the play, whatever the length, is written to be performed. As Tennessee Williams said, "When I write, everything is visual, as brilliantly as if it were on a lit stage." Focus on your vision, listen to your words, and be true to your heart.

Writing on Your Own

Write a one-act play for the stage that is from fifteen to thirty minutes long. Your play should contain one main conflict, introduced somewhere in the first three pages, and you should have at least three obstacles for your protagonist to overcome. Include no more than five characters.

Writing to Revise

Choose a scene that you have written in response to one of the exercises in chapters 12 or 13. Direct a performance of your scene, from casting to performance. (You should not be part of the cast.) It does not have to be a formal production. Casting classmates and reading through the play a few times will suffice. After the performance, evaluate your scene, using the following questions as a guide:

1. Did the dialogue communicate the plot and theme of the scene?
2. Was the pacing appropriate to the tone of the scene?
3. Did the action of the scene contribute to the audience's interest?
4. Were the characters' actions appropriate and consistent with their personalities?

Based on the comments you wrote down as well as comments others might have given you, revise the scene as necessary.

Internet Resources for Dramatists

E-mail lists

Screenwriters e-mail list

SCRNWRIT (listserv@tamvm1.tamu.edu)   *An e-mail list for published and aspiring screenwriters.*

Women Playwrights List

ICWP-L (listserv@ubvm.cc.buffalo.edu)   *A discussion group for women playwrights.*

Usenet discussion groups

rec.arts.theatre.plays   *Discussions of plays.*

rec.arts.theatre.misc   *Discussion of various theatre issues.*

World Wide Web Sites

The Playwriting Seminars

http://www.vcu.edu/artweb/playwriting/   *A playwriting/screenwriting course on the Net.*

Theatre Central

http://www.theatre-central.com   *A comprehensive guide to theater resources, including numerous helpful links.*

The Dramatic Exchange

http://www.dramex.org/   *A resource for publishing and reading online plays.*

Playbill On-Line

http://www.playbill.com/   *Current theater news.*

New Dramatists Home Page

http://www.itp.tsoa.nyu.edu/~diana/ndintro.html   *The home page for the New Dramatists, a professional association for playwrights.*

Screenwriters and Playwrights Home Page

http://www.teleport.com/~cdeemer/scrwriter.html   *A wealth of information for screenwriters and playwrights with a searchable database. Maintained by Charles Deemer.*

E-zines and Journals

American Drama

http://jazz.san.uc.edu/www/amdrama   *The online site for the journal* American Drama. *Contains abstracts of* American Drama *articles, interviews, and links to theater resources.*

Drama to Consider

Christopher Durang

The Actor's Nightmare

SCENE – *basically an empty stage, maybe with a few set pieces on it or around it.
George Spelvin, a young man (20 to 30), wanders in. He looks baffled and uncertain
about where he is. Enter Meg, the stage manager. In jeans and sweat shirt, perhaps,
pleasant, efficient, age 25 to 30 probably.*

GEORGE: Oh, I'm sorry. I don't know how I got in here.

MEG: Oh thank goodness you're here. I've been calling you.

GEORGE: Pardon?

MEG: An awful thing has happened. Eddie's been in a car accident, and you'll
have to go on for him.

GEORGE: Good heavens, how awful. Who's Eddie?

MEG: Eddie. (*He looks blank*) Edwin. You have to go on for him.

GEORGE: On for him.

MEG: Well he can't go on. He's been in a car accident.

GEORGE: Yes I understood that part. But what do you mean "go on for him"?

MEG: You play the part. Now I know you haven't had a chance to rehearse it
exactly, but presumably you know your lines, and you've certainly seen it
enough.

GEORGE: I don't understand. Do I know you?

MEG: George, we really don't have time for this kind of joshing. Half-hour. (*Exits*)

GEORGE: My name isn't George, it's . . . well, I don't know what it is, but it isn't George.

(*Enter Sarah Siddons, a glamorous actress, perhaps in a sweeping cape*)

SARAH: My God, did you hear about Eddie?

GEORGE: Yes I did.

SARAH: It's just too, too awful. Now good luck tonight, George darling, we're all counting on you. Of course, you're a little too young for the part, and you are shorter than Edwin so we'll cut all the lines about bumping your head on the ceiling. And don't forget when I cough three times, that's your cue to unzip the back of my dress and then I'll slap you. We changed it from last night. (*She starts to exit*)

GEORGE: Wait, please. What play are we doing exactly?

SARAH: (*Stares at him*) What?

GEORGE: What is the play please.

SARAH: Coward.

GEORGE: Pardon?

SARAH: Coward. (*Looks at him as if he's crazy*) It's the Coward. Noel Coward. (*Suddenly relaxing*) George, don't do that. For a second, I thought you were serious. Break a leg, darling. (*Exits*)

GEORGE: (*To himself*) Coward. I wonder if it's *Private Lives*. At least I've seen that one. I don't remember rehearsing it exactly. And am I an actor? I thought I was an accountant. And why does everyone call me George? (*Enter Dame Ellen Terry, younger than Sarah, a bit less grand*)

ELLEN: Hello, Stanley. I heard about Edwin. Good luck tonight. We're counting on you.

GEORGE: Wait. What play are we doing?

ELLEN: Very funny, Stanley.

GEORGE: No really. I've forgotten.

ELLEN: *Checkmate.*

GEORGE: *Checkmate?*

ELLEN: By Samuel Beckett. You know, in the garbage cans. You always play these jokes, Stanley, just don't do it onstage. Well, good luck tonight. I mean, break a leg. Did you hear? Edwin broke both legs. (*Exits*)

GEORGE: I've never heard of *Checkmate*.

(*Re-enter Meg*)

MEG: George, get into costume. We have 15 minutes. (*Exits*)

(*Enter Henry Irving, age 28–33*)

HENRY: Good God, I'm late. Hi Eddie. Oh you're not Eddie. Who are you?

GEORGE: You've never seen me before?

HENRY: Who the devil are you?

GEORGE: I don't really know. George, I think. Maybe Stanley, but probably George. I think I'm an accountant.

HENRY: Look, no one's allowed backstage before a performance. So you'll have to leave, or I'll be forced to report you to the stage manager.

GEORGE: Oh she knows I'm here already.

HENRY: Oh. Well, if Meg knows you're here it must be alright. I suppose. It's not my affair. I'm late enough already. (*Exits*)

MEG: (*Off-stage*) 10 minutes, the call is 10 minutes, everybody.

GEORGE: I better just go home. (*Takes off his pants*) Oh dear, I didn't mean to do that.

(*Enter Meg*)

MEG: George, stop that. Go into the dressing room to change. Really, you keep this up and we'll bring you up on charges.

GEORGE: But where is the dressing room?

MEG: George, you're not amusing. It's that way. And give me those. (*Takes his pants*) I'll go soak them for you.

GEORGE: Please don't soak my pants.

MEG: Don't tell me my job. Now go get changed. The call is 5 minutes. (*Pushes him of to dressing room; crosses back the other way, calling out:*) 5 minutes, everyone. 5 minutes. Places. (*Exits*)

(*A curtain closes on the stage. Darkness. Lights come up on the curtain. A voice is heard*)

VOICE: Ladies and gentlemen, may I have your attention please? At this evening's performance, the role of Elyot, normally played by Edwin Booth, will be played by George Spelvin. The role of Amanda, normally played by Sarah Bernhardt, will be played by Sarah Siddons. The role of Kitty the bar maid will be played by Mrs. Patrick Campbell. Dr. Crippin will play himself. The management wishes to remind the audience that the taking of photographs is strictly forbidden by law, and is dangerous as it may disorient the actor. Thank you.

(*The curtain opens. There is very little set, but probably a small set piece to indicate the railing of a terrace balcony. Some other set piece [a chair, a table, a cocktail bar] might be used to indicate wealth, elegance, French Riviera.*

Sarah Siddons is present when the curtain opens. She is in a glamorous evening gown, and is holding a cocktail glass and standing behind the terrace railing, staring out above the audience's head. There is the sound of applause.

After a moment George arrives onstage, fairly pushed on. He is dressed as Hamlet—black leotard and large gold medallion around his neck. [He might be missing the bottom part of the leotard and still be in his boxer shorts.] As soon as he enters, several flash photos are taken, which disorient him greatly. When he can, he looks out and sees the audience and is very taken aback.

We hear music)

SARAH: Extraordinary how potent cheap music is.

GEORGE: What?

SARAH: Extraordinary how potent cheap music is.

GEORGE: Yes, that's true. Am I supposed to be Hamlet?

SARAH: (*Alarmed; then going on*) Whose yacht do you think that is?

GEORGE: Where?

SARAH: The duke of Westminster, I expect. It always is.

GEORGE: Ah, well perhaps. To be or not to be. I don't know any more of it.

(*She looks irritated at him; then she coughs three times. He unzips her dress, she slaps him*)

SARAH: Elyot, please. We are on our honeymoons.

GEORGE: Are we?

SARAH: Yes. (*Irritated, being over-explicit*) Me with Victor, and you with Sibyl.

GEORGE: Ah.

SARAH: Tell me about Sibyl.

GEORGE: I've never met her.

SARAH: Ah, Elyot, you're so amusing. You're married to Sibyl. Tell me about her.

GEORGE: Nothing much to tell really. She's sort of nondescript, I'd say.

SARAH: I bet you were going to say that she's just like Lady Bundle, and that she has several chins, and one blue eye and one brown eye, and a third eye in the center of her forehead. Weren't you?

GEORGE: Yes. I think so.

SARAH: Victor's like that too. (*Long pause*) I bet you were just about to tell me that you traveled around the world.

GEORGE: Yes I was. I traveled around the world.

SARAH: How was it?

GEORGE: The world?

SARAH: Yes.

GEORGE: Oh, very nice.

SARAH: I always feared the Taj Mahal would look like a biscuit box. Did it?

GEORGE: Not really.

SARAH: (*She's going to give him the cue again*) I always feared the Taj Mahal would look like a biscuit box. Did it?

GEORGE: I guess it did.

SARAH: (*Again*) I always feared the Taj Mahal would look like a biscuit box. Did it?

GEORGE: Hard to say. What brand biscuit box?

SARAH: I always feared the Taj Mahal would look like a biscuit box. Did it? (*Pause*) Did it? Did it?

GEORGE: I wonder whose yacht that is out there.

SARAH: Did it? Did it? Did it? Did it?
(*Enter Meg. She's put on an apron and maid's hat and carries a duster, but is otherwise still in her stage manager's garb*)

MEG: My, this balcony looks dusty. I think I'll just clean it up a little. (*Dusts and goes to George and whispers in his ear; exits*)

GEORGE: Not only did the Taj Mahal look like a biscuit box, but women should be struck regularly like gongs.
(*Applause*)

SARAH: Extraordinary how potent cheap music is.

GEORGE: Yes. Quite extraordinary.

SARAH: How was China?

GEORGE: China?

SARAH: You traveled around the world. How was China?

GEORGE: I liked it, but I felt homesick.

SARAH: (*Again this is happening; gives him cue again*) How was China?

GEORGE: Lots of rice. The women bind their feet.

SARAH: How was China?

GEORGE: I hated it. I missed you.

SARAH: *How was China?*

GEORGE: I hated it. I missed . . . Sibyl.

SARAH: How was China?

GEORGE: I . . . miss the maid. Oh, maid!

SARAH: How was China?

GEORGE: Just wait a moment please. Oh, maid! (*Enter Meg*) Ah, there you are. I think you missed a spot here.
> (*She crosses, dusts, and whispers in his ear; exits*)

SARAH: How was China?

GEORGE: (*With authority*) Very large, China.

SARAH: And Japan?

GEORGE: (*Doesn't know, but makes a guess*) Very . . . small, Japan.

SARAH: And Ireland?

GEORGE: Very . . . green.

SARAH: And Iceland?

GEORGE: Very white.

SARAH: And Italy?

GEORGE: Very . . . Neapolitan.

SARAH: And Copenhagen?

GEORGE: Very . . . cosmopolitan.

SARAH: And Florida?

GEORGE: Very . . . condominium.

SARAH: And Perth Amboy?

GEORGE: Very . . . mobile home, I don't know.

SARAH: And Sibyl?

GEORGE: What?

SARAH: Do you love Sibyl?

GEORGE: Who's Sibyl?

SARAH: Your new wife, who you married after you and I got our divorce.

GEORGE: Oh were we married? Oh yes, I forgot that part.

SARAH: Elyot, you're so amusing. You make me laugh all the time. (*Laughs*) So, do you love Sibyl?

GEORGE: Probably. I married her.
> (*Pause. She coughs three times, he unzips her dress, she slaps him*)

SARAH: Oh, Elyot, darling, I'm sorry. We were mad to have left each other. Kiss me.
> (*They kiss. Enter Dame Ellen Terry as Sibyl, in an evening gown*)

ELLEN: Oh, how ghastly.

SARAH: Oh dear. And this must be Sibyl.

ELLEN: Oh how ghastly. What shall we do?

SARAH: We must all speak in very low voices and attempt to be civilized.

ELLEN: Is this Amanda? Oh, Elyot, I think she's simply obnoxious.

SARAH: How very rude.

ELLEN: Oh, Elyot, how can you treat me like this?

GEORGE: Hello, Sibyl.

ELLEN: Well, since you ask, I'm very upset. I was inside writing a letter to your mother and wanted to know how to spell apothecary.

SARAH: A-P-O-T-H-E-C-A-R-Y.

ELLEN: (*Icy*) Thank you. (*Writes it down; Sarah looks over her shoulder*)

SARAH: Don't scribble, Sibyl.

ELLEN: Did my eyes deceive me, or were you kissing my husband a moment ago?

SARAH: We must all speak in very low voices and attempt to be civilized.

ELLEN: I was speaking in a low voice.

SARAH: Yes, but I could still hear you.

ELLEN : Oh. Sorry. (*Speaks too low to be heard*)

SARAH: (*Speaks inaudibly also*)

ELLEN: (*Speaks inaudibly*)

SARAH: (*Speaks inaudibly*)

ELLEN: (*Speaks inaudibly*)

SARAH: I can't hear a bloody word she's saying. The woman's a nincompoop. Say something, Elyot.

GEORGE: I couldn't hear her either.

ELLEN: Elyot, you have to choose between us immediately—do you love this creature, or do you love me?

GEORGE: I wonder where the maid is.

ELLEN AND SARAH: (*Together, furious*) Forget about the maid, Elyot! (*They look embarrassed*)

ELLEN: You could never have a lasting relationship with a maid. Choose between the two of us.

GEORGE: I choose . . . oh God, I don't know my lines. I don't know how I got here. I wish I *weren't* here. I wish I had joined the monastery like I almost did right after high school. I almost joined, but then I didn't.

SARAH: (*Trying to cover*) Oh, Elyot, your malaria is acting up again and you're ranting. Come, come, who do you choose, me or that baggage over there.

ELLEN: You're the baggage, not I. Yes, Elyot, who do you choose?

GEORGE: I choose . . . (*To Sarah*) I'm sorry, what is your name?

SARAH: Amanda.

GEORGE: I choose Amanda. I think that's what he does in the play.

ELLEN: Very well. I can accept defeat gracefully. I don't think I'll send this letter to your mother. She has a loud voice and an overbearing manner and I don't like her taste in tea china. I hope, Elyot, that when you find me hanging from the hotel lobby chandelier with my eyes all bulged out and my tongue hanging out, that you'll be very, very sorry. Goodbye. (*Exits*)

SARAH: What a dreadful sport she is.

GEORGE: (*Doing his best to say something his character might*) Poor Sibyl. She's going to hang herself.

SARAH: Some women should be hung regularly like tapestries. Oh who cares? Whose yacht do you think that is?

GEORGE: (*Remembering*) The duke of Westminster, I exp . . .

SARAH: (*Furious*) How dare you mention that time in Mozambique? (*Slaps him*) Oh, darling, I'm sorry. (*Moving her cigarette grandly*) I love you madly!

GEORGE: (*Gasps*) I've inhaled your cigarette ash.

(*He coughs three times. Sarah looks confused, then unzips the front of his Hamlet doublet. He looks confused, then slaps her. She slaps him back with a vengeance. They both look confused*)

SARAH: There, we're not angry anymore, are we? Oh, Elyot, wait for me here and I'll pack my things and we'll run away together before Victor gets back. Oh, darling, isn't it extraordinary how potent cheap music can be?

(*She exits; recorded applause on her exit. George sort of follows a bit, but then turns back to face the audience. Flash photos are taken again; George blinks and is disoriented. Lights change, the sound of trumpets is heard, and Henry Irving, dressed in Shakespearean garb, enters and bows grandly to George*)

HENRY: Hail to your Lordship!

GEORGE: Oh hello. Are you Victor?

HENRY: The same, my Lord, and your poor servant ever.

GEORGE: This doesn't sound like Noel Coward.

HENRY: A truant disposition, good my Lord.

GEORGE: You're not Victor, are you?

HENRY: My Lord, I came to see your father's funeral.

GEORGE: Oh yes? And how was it?

HENRY: Indeed, my Lord, it followed hard upon.

GEORGE: Hard upon? Yes, I see. (*Enter Meg*) Oh, good, the maid. (*She whispers to him*) Thrift, thrift, Horatio. The funeral baked meats did coldly furnish forth the marriage tables. What does that mean? (*Meg exits*) Ah, she's gone already.

HENRY: My Lord, I think I saw him yesternight.

GEORGE: Did you? Who?

HENRY: My Lord, the king your father.

GEORGE: The king my father?

HENRY: Season your admiration for a while with an attent ear till I may deliver upon the witness of these gentlemen this marvel to you.

GEORGE: I see. I'm Hamlet now, right?

HENRY: Ssssh! (*Rattling this off in a very Shakespearean way:*)

> Two nights together had these gentlemen,
> Marcellus and Bernardo, on their watch
> In the dead waste and middle of the night
> Been thus encountered. A figure like your father,
> Arméd at point exactly, cap-a-pe,
> Appears before them and with solemn march
> Goes slow and stately by them. Thrice he walked
> By their oppressed and fear-surprised eyes
> Within his truncheon's length, whilst they, distilled
> Almost to jelly with the act of fear,
> Stand dumb and speak not to him. This to me
> In dreadful secrecy impart they did,
> And I with them the third night kept the watch,
> Where, as they had delivered, both in time,
> Form of the thing, each word made true and good,
> The apparition comes. I knew your father.
> These hands are not more like.

GEORGE: Oh, my turn? Most strange and wondrous tale you tell, Horatio. It doth turn my ear into a very . . . (*At a loss*) merry . . . bare bodkin.

HENRY: As I do live, my honored lord, tis true,

> and we did think it writ down in our duty
> To let you know of it.

GEORGE: Well, thank you very much. (*Pause*)

HENRY: Oh yes, my Lord. He wore his beaver up.

GEORGE: His beaver up. He wore his beaver up. And does he usually wear it down?

HENRY: A countenance more in sorrow than in anger.

GEORGE: Well I am sorry to hear that. My father was a king of much renown. A favorite amongst all in London town. (*Pause*) And in Denmark.

HENRY: I war'nt it will.

GEORGE: I war'nt it will also.

HENRY: Our duty to your honor. (*Exits*)

GEORGE: Where are you going? Don't go. (*Smiles out at audience*)
(*Enter Sarah dressed as Queen Gertrude*)
Oh, Amanda, good to see you. Whose yacht do you think that is?

SARAH: O Hamlet, speak no more.
Thou turn'st mine eyes into my very soul,
And there I see such black and grainéd spots
As will not leave their tinct.

GEORGE: I haven't seen Victor. Someone was here who I thought might have been him, but it wasn't.

SARAH: Oh speak to me no more.
These words like daggers enter in mine ears.
No more, sweet Hamlet.

GEORGE: Very well. What do you want to talk about?

SARAH: No more! (*Exits*)

GEORGE: Oh don't go. (*Pause; smiles uncomfortably at the audience*) Maybe someone else will come out in a minute. (*Pause*) Of course, sometimes people have soliloquies in Shakespeare. Let's just wait a moment more and maybe someone will come.
(*The lights suddenly change to a dim blue background and one bright, white spot center stage. George is not standing in the spot*)
Oh dear. (*He moves somewhat awkwardly into the spot, decides to do his best to live up to the requirements of the moment*)
To be or not to be, that is the question.
(*Doesn't know any more*) Oh maid! (*No response; remembers that actors call for "line"*) Line. Line! Ohhhh.
Oh, what a rogue and peasant slave am I.
Whether tis nobler in the mind's eye to kill oneself,
     or not killing oneself, to sleep a great deal.
We are such stuff as dreams are made on; and our lives
     are rounded by a little sleep.
(*The lights change. The spot goes out, and another one comes onstage right. George moves into it*)
Uh, thrift, thrift, Horatio. Neither a borrower
nor a lender be. But to thine own self be true.
There is a special providence in the fall of a sparrow.
Extraordinary how potent cheap music can be.
Out, out, damn spot! I come to wive it wealthily in
Padua; if wealthily, then happily in Padua.
     (*Sings*) Brush up your Shakespeare; start quoting him now;
     Da da . . .
(*Lights change again. That spot goes off; another one comes on, center stage, though closer to audience. George moves into that*)
I wonder whose yacht that is. How was China? Very large, China. How was Japan? Very small, Japan.
     I pledge allegiance to the flag of the United States of America and to the republic for which it stands, one nation, under God, indivisible with liberty and justice for all.

Line! Line! Oh my God. (*Gets idea*)

O my God, I am heartily sorry for having offended thee, and I detest all my sins because I dread the loss of heaven and the pains of hell. But most of all because they offend thee, my God, who art all good and deserving of all my love. And I resolve to confess my sins, to do penance, and to amend my life, Amen. (*Friendly*) That's the act of contrition that Catholic school children say in confession in order to be forgiven their sins. Catholic adults say it too, I imagine. I don't know any Catholic adults.

Line! (*Explaining*) When you call for a line, the stage manager normally gives you your next line, to refresh your memory.

Line!

The quality of mercy is not strained. It droppeth as the gentle rain upon the place below, when we have shuffled off this mortal coil.

Alas, poor Yorick. I knew him well. Get thee to a nunnery.

Line. Nunnery. As a child, I was taught by nuns, and then in high school I was taught by Benedictine priests. I really rather liked the nuns, they were sort of warm, though they were fairly crazy too.

Line.

I liked the priests also. The school was on the grounds of the monastery, and my junior and senior years I spent a few weekends joining in the daily routine of the monastery—prayers, then breakfast, then prayers, then lunch, then prayers, then dinner, then prayers, then sleep. I found the predictability quite attractive. And the food was good. And if there is a God, and an afterlife, and an inner life of the soul, then the monastery had everything in the proper order. And if there isn't all those things, it's still a very restful way to live.

I was going to join the monastery after high school, but they said I was too young and should wait. And then I just stopped believing in all those things, so I never did join the monastery. I became an accountant. I've studied logarithms, and cosine and tangent . . .

(*Irritated*) Line! (*Apologetic*) I'm sorry. This is supposed to be *Hamlet* or *Private Lives* or something, and I keep rattling on like a maniac. I really do apologize. I just don't recall attending a single rehearsal. I can't imagine what I was doing.

And also you came expecting to see Edwin Booth and you get me. I really am very embarrassed. Sorry. *Line!* It's a far, far better thing I do than I have ever done before. It's a far, far better place I go to than I have ever been before. (*Sings the alphabet song*) A, B, C, D, E, F, G; H, I, J, K, L, M, N, O, P; Q, R, S, T . . .

(*As he starts to sing, enter Ellen Terry, dragging two large garbage cans. She puts them side by side, gets in one*)

Oh, good. Are you Ophelia? Get thee to a nunnery.

(*She points to the other garbage can, indicating he should get in it*)

Get in? Okay. (*He does*) This must be one of those modern *Hamlets*.

(*Lights change abruptly to "Beckett lighting"*)

ELLEN: Nothing to be done. Pause. Pause. Wrinkle nose. (*Wrinkles nose*) Nothing to be done.

GEORGE: I guess you're not Ophelia.

ELLEN We'll just wait. Pause. Either he'll come, pause pause pause, or he won't.

GEORGE: That's a reasonable attitude. Are we, on a guess, waiting for Godot?

ELLEN: No, Willie. He came already and was an awful bore. Yesterday he came. Garlic on his breath, telling a lot of unpleasant jokes about Jews and Polacks and stewardesses. He was just dreadful, pause, rolls her eyes upward. (*She rolls her eyes*)

GEORGE: Well I am sorry to hear that. Pause. So who are we waiting for?

ELLEN: We're waiting for Lefty.

GEORGE: Ah. And is he a political organizer or something, I seem to recall?

ELLEN: Yes, dear, he is a political organizer. He's always coming around saying get involved, get off your behind and organize, fight the system, do this, do that, uh, he's exhausting, he's worse than Jane Fonda. And he has garlic breath just like Godot, I don't know which of them is worse, and I hope neither of them ever comes here again. Blinks left eye, blinks right eye, closes eyes, opens them. (*Does this*)

GEORGE: So we're really not waiting for anyone, are we?

ELLEN: No, dear, we're not. It's just another happy day, pause, smile, pause, picks nit from head. (*Picks nit from head*)

GEORGE: Do you smell something?

ELLEN: That's not your line. Willie doesn't have that many lines. (*Louder*) Oh, Willie, how talkative you are this morning!

GEORGE: There seems to be some sort of muck at the bottom of this garbage can.

ELLEN: Mustn't complain, Willie. There's muck at the bottom of everyone's garbage can. Count your blessings, Willie. I do. (*Counts to herself, eyes closed*) One. Two. Three. Are you counting, Willie?

GEORGE: I guess so.

ELLEN: I'm up to three. Three is my eyesight. (*Opens her eyes*) Oh my God, I've gone blind. I can't see, Willie. Oh my God. Oh what a terrible day. Oh dear. Oh my. (*Suddenly very cheerful again*) Oh well. Not so bad really. I only used my eyes occasionally. When I wanted to see something. But no more!

GEORGE: I really don't know this play at all.

ELLEN: Count your blessings, Willie. Let me hear you count them.

GEORGE: Alright. One. Two. Three. That's my eyesight. Four. That's my hearing. Five, that's my . . . Master Charge. Six, that's . . .

ELLEN: Did you say God, Willie?

GEORGE: No.

ELLEN: Why did you leave the monastery, Willie? Was it the same reason I left the opera?

GEORGE: I have no idea.

ELLEN: I left the opera because I couldn't sing. They were mad to have hired me. Certifiable. And they were certified shortly afterward, the entire staff. They reside now at the Rigoletto Home for the Mentally Incapacitated. In Turin. Pause. Tries to touch her nose with her tongue. (*Does this*)

VOICE: Ladies and gentlemen, may I have your attention please?

ELLEN: Oh, Willie, listen. A voice. Perhaps there is a God.

VOICE: At this evening's performance, the role of Sir Thomas More, the man for all seasons, normally played by Edwin Booth, will be played by George Spelvin. The role of Lady Alice, normally played by Sarah Bernhardt, will be played by Sarah Siddons. The role of Lady Margaret, normally played by

Eleonora Duse, will be read by the stage manager. And at this evening's performance the executioner will play himself.

GEORGE: What did he say?

ELLEN: The executioner will play himself.

GEORGE: What does he mean, the executioner will play himself?

(*Enter Sarah as Lady Alice [Sir Thomas More's wife] and Meg with a few costumed touches but otherwise in her stage manager's garb and carrying a script as Lady Margaret [Sir Thomas More's daughter]*)

MEG: Oh father, why have they locked you up in this dreadful dungeon, it's more than I can bear.

SARAH: I've brought you a custard, Thomas.

MEG: Mother's brought you a custard, father.

GEORGE: Yes, thank you.

MEG: Oh father, if you don't give in to King Henry, they're going to cut your head off.

SARAH: Aren't you going to eat the custard I brought you, Thomas?

GEORGE: I'm not hungry, thank you.

(*Sudden alarming crash of cymbals, or something similarly startling musically occurs. The Executioner appears upstage. He is dressed as the traditional headsman —the black mask, bare chest and arms, the large ax*)

GEORGE: Oh my God, I've got to get out of here.

MEG: He's over here. And he'll never give in to the King.

GEORGE: No, no, I might. Quick, is this all about Anne Boleyn and everything?

MEG: Yes, and you won't give in because you believe in the Catholic Church and the infallibility of the Pope and the everlasting life of the soul.

GEORGE: I don't necessarily believe in any of that (*To Executioner*) Oh, sir, there's been an error. I think it's fine if the King marries Anne Boleyn. I just want to wake up.

MEG: Oh don't deny God, father, just to spare our feelings. Mother and I are willing to have you dead if it's a question of principle.

SARAH: The first batch of custard didn't come out all that well, Thomas. This is the second batch. But it has a piece of hair in it, I think.

GEORGE: Oh shut up about your custard, would you? I don't think the Pope is infallible at all. I think he's a normal man with normal capabilities who wears gold slippers. I thought about joining the monastery when I was younger, but I didn't do it.

ELLEN (*Waking up from a brief doze*): Oh I was having such a pleasant dream, Willie. Go ahead, let him cut your head off, it'll be a nice change of pace. (*The Executioner, who has been motionless, now moves. In a sudden gesture, he reveals the cutting block that waits for George's head. Note: In the Playwrights Horizons production, our set designer constructed a square furniture piece that doubled as a settee and/or small cocktail table during the Private Lives section. However, when the Executioner kicked the top of it, the piece fell open, revealing itself to contain a bloodied cutting block*)

GEORGE: That blade looks very real to me. I want to wake up now. Or change plays. I wonder whose yacht that is out there. (*Sarah offers him the custard again*) No, thank you. A horse, a horse! My kingdom for a horse!

EXECUTIONER: Sir Thomas More, you have been found guilty of the charge of High Treason. The sentence of the court is that you be taken to the Tower of London, thence to the place of execution, and there your head shall be stricken from your body, and may God have mercy on your soul. *(Meg helps George out of the garbage can)*

GEORGE: All this talk about God. Alright, I'm sorry I didn't join the monastery, maybe I should have, and I'm sorry I giggled during Mass in third grade, but I see no reason to be killed for it.

ELLEN: Nothing to be done. That's what I find so wonderful.

(Meg puts George's head on the block)

GEORGE: No!

EXECUTIONER: Do I understand you right? You wish to reverse your previous stand on King Henry's marriage to Anne and to deny the Bishop of Rome?

GEORGE: Yes, yes, God, yes. I could care less. Let him marry eight wives.

EXECUTIONER: That's a terrible legacy of cowardice for Sir Thomas More to leave behind.

GEORGE: I don't care.

EXECUTIONER: I'm going to ignore what you've said and cut your head off anyway, and then we'll all pretend you went to your death nobly. The Church needs its saints, and school children have got to have heroes to look up to, don't you all agree?

ELLEN: I agree. I know I need someone to look up to. Pause smile picks her nose. *(Does this)*

GEORGE: Yes, yes, I can feel myself waking up now. The covers have fallen off the bed, and I'm cold, and I'm going to wake up so that I can reach down and pull them up again.

EXECUTIONER: Sir Thomas, prepare to meet your death.

GEORGE: Be quiet, I'm about to wake up.

EXECUTIONER: Sir Thomas, prepare to meet your death.

GEORGE: I'm awake! *(Looks around him; Sarah offers him custard again)* No, I'm not.

SARAH: He doesn't know his lines.

EXECUTIONER: Sir Thomas, prepare to meet your death.

GEORGE: Line! Line!

MEG: You turn to the executioner and say, "Friend, be not afraid of your office. You send me to God."

GEORGE: I don't like that line. Give me another.

MEG: That's the line in the script, George. Say it.

GEORGE: I don't want to.

MEG: Say it.

ELLEN: Say it, Willie. It'll mean a lot to me and to generations of school children to come.

SARAH: O Hamlet, speak the speech, I pray you, trippingly on the tongue.

EXECUTIONER: Say it!

GEORGE: Friend, be not afraid of your office. You send me . . . Extraordinary how potent cheap music is.

MEG: That's not the line.

GEORGE: Women should be struck regularly like gongs.

MEG: George, say the line right.

GEORGE: They say you can never dream your own death, so I expect I'll wake up just as soon as he starts to bring the blade down. So perhaps I should get it over with.

MEG: Say the proper line, George.

GEORGE: Friend, be not afraid of your office.

ELLEN: Goodbye, Willie.

SARAH: Goodbye, Hamlet.

MEG: Goodbye, George.

EXECUTIONER: Goodbye, Sir Thomas.

GEORGE: You send me to God.

(*Executioner raises the ax to bring it down. Blackout. Sound of the ax coming down*)

EXECUTIONER: (*In darkness*) Behold the head of Sir Thomas More.

ELLEN: (*In darkness*) Oh I wish I weren't blind and could see that, Willie. Oh well, no matter. It's still been another happy day. Pause, smile, wrinkles nose, pause, picks nit from head, pause, pause, wiggles ears, all in darkness, utterly useless, no one can see her. She stares ahead. Count two. End of play.

(*Music plays. Maybe canned applause. Lights come up for curtain calls. The four take their bows [if Henry Irving does not play the executioner, he comes out for his bow as well]. Sarah and Ellen have fairly elaborate bows, perhaps receiving flowers from the executioner. They gesture for George to take his bow, but he seems to be dead. They applaud him, and then bow again, and lights out*)

Terrence McNally

ANDRE'S MOTHER

Characters

Cal, a young man
Arthur, his father
Penny, his sister
Andre's Mother

Time: Now
Place: New York City, Central Park

Four people — Cal, Arthur, Penny, and Andre's Mother — enter. They are nicely dressed and each carries a white helium-filled balloon on a string.

CAL: You know what's really terrible? I can't think of anything terrific to say. Goodbye. I love you. I'll miss you. And I'm supposed to be so great with words!

PENNY: What's that over there?

ARTHUR: Ask your brother.

CAL: It's a theatre. An outdoor theatre. They do plays there in the summer. Shakespeare's plays. (*To Andre's Mother.*) God, how much he wanted to play Hamlet again. He would have gone to Timbuktu to have another go at that part. The summer he did it in Boston, he was so happy!

PENNY: Cal, I don't think she . . . ! It's not the time. Later.

ARTHUR: Your son was a . . . the Jews have a word for it . . .

PENNY (*quietly appalled*): Oh my God!

ARTHUR: Mensch, I believe it is, and I think I'm using it right. It means warm, solid, the real thing. Correct me if I'm wrong.

PENNY: Fine, Dad, fine. Just quit while you're ahead.

ARTHUR: I won't say he was like a son to me. Even my son isn't always like a son to me. I mean . . . ! In my clumsy way, I'm trying to say how much I liked Andre. And how much he helped me to know my own boy. Cal was always two handsful but Andre and I could talk about anything under the sun. My wife was very fond of him, too.

PENNY: Cal, I don't understand about the balloons.

CAL: They represent the soul. When you let go, it means you're letting his soul ascend to Heaven. That you're willing to let go. Breaking the last earthly ties.

PENNY: Does the Pope know about this?

ARTHUR: Penny!

PENNY: Andre loved my sense of humor. Listen, you can hear him laughing. (*She lets go of her white balloon.*) So long, you glorious, wonderful, I-know-what-Cal-means-about-words . . . man! God forgive me for wishing you were straight every time I laid eyes on you. But if any man was going to have you, I'm glad it was my brother! Look how fast it went up. I bet that means something. Something terrific.

ARTHUR (*lets his balloon go*): Goodbye. God speed.

PENNY: Cal?

CAL: I'm not ready yet.

PENNY: Okay. We'll be over there. Come on, Pop, you can buy your little girl a Good Humor.

ARTHUR: They still make Good Humor?

PENNY: Only now they're called Dove Bars and they cost twelve dollars.
(*Penny takes Arthur off. Cal and Andre's Mother stand with their balloons.*)

CAL: I wish I knew what you were thinking. I think it would help me. You know almost nothing about me and I only know what Andre told me about you. I'd always had it in my mind that one day we would be friends, you and me. But if you didn't know about Andre and me . . . If this hadn't happened, I wonder if he would have ever told you. When he was sick, if I asked him once I asked him a thousand times, tell her. She's your mother. She won't mind. But he was so afraid of hurting you and of your disapproval. I don't know which was worse. (*No response. He sighs.*) God, how many of us live it this city because we don't want to hurt our mothers and live in mortal terror of their disapproval. We lose ourselves here. Our lives aren't furtive, just our feelings toward people like you are! A city of fugitives from our parents' scorn or heartbreak. Sometimes he'd seem a little down and I'd say, "What's the matter, babe?" and this funny sweet, sad smile would cross his face and he'd say, "Just a little homesick, Cal, just a little bit." I always accused him of being a country boy just playing at being a hotshot, sophisticated New Yorker. (*He sighs.*)

It's bullshit. It's all bullshit. (*Still no response.*)

Do you remember the comic strip *Little Lulu*? Her mother had no name, she was so remote, so formidable to all the children. She was just Lulu's mother. "Hello, Lulu's Mother," Lulu's friends would say. She was almost anonymous in her remoteness. You remind me of her. Andre's mother. Let me answer the questions you can't ask and then I'll leave you alone and you won't ever have to see me again. Andre died of AIDS. I don't know how he got it. I tested negative. He died bravely. You would have been proud of him. The only thing that frightened him was you. I'll have everything that was his sent to you. I'll pay for it. There isn't much. You should have come up the summer he played Hamlet. He was magnificent. Yes, I'm bitter. I'm bitter I've lost him. I'm bitter what's happening. I'm bitter even now, after all this, I can't reach you. I'm beginning to feel your disapproval and it's making me ill. (*He looks at his balloon.*) Sorry, old friend. I blew it. (*He lets go of the balloon.*)

Good night, sweet prince, and flights of angels sing thee to thy rest! (*Beat.*)

Goodbye, Andre's mother.

(*He goes. Andre's Mother stands alone holding her white balloon. Her lips tremble. She looks on the verge of breaking down. She is about to let go of the balloon when she pulls it down to her. She looks at it awhile before she gently kisses it. She lets go of the balloon. She follows it with her eyes as it rises and rises. The lights are beginning to fade. Andre's Mother's eyes are still on the balloon. The lights fade.*)

Part Three

❖ ❖ ❖ ❖ ❖
❖ ❖ ❖
❖

REVISING, PUBLISHING,
AND THE BUSINESS OF WRITING

14

REVISION:

SEEING AND WRITING AGAIN

Writing to Warm Up

1. Is it possible to know whether what you have written is any good? How?
2. Is it possible to know whether what you have written accomplishes what you wanted it to? How?
3. Is it necessary to have clear expectations for the work when you begin writing it? when you finish writing it? Why or why not?
4. Do you feel comfortable receiving input about your writing from writers' groups, instructors, colleagues? Why or why not?

Throughout this book we have included exercises entitled "Writing to Revise." In these exercises we have asked you to look at work that you have written and to consider the ways you can improve and refine what you have written. Each exercise focuses on a different aspect of revision which applies to a specific genre or even a specific writing assignment. This chapter focuses on the overall process of revision and examines those common denominators of the revision process, regardless of genre or specific task.

As you are writing, you are going to be thinking at some point about what your ultimate aim for the work is, and what will make the work "complete." You may also be thinking about whom to show the work to, and what will happen to it, and whether it will hold together. The writer has the difficult job not only of creating, but also of refining and editing her work, and writers use a group of steps to check, evaluate, and rewrite their work so that it will be as good as it can be, and therefore, perhaps, complete (if any writing is ever complete).

The word *revision* comes from two Latin words meaning "to look at again"—literally, *re-vision*. But how does one see something again?

First, it is probably impossible, in some ways, to see something that one has created in an objective way. The difficulty lies in attempting in some clear-cut way to distinguish the components of the writing process as separate or sequential. Fifteen years ago when we began teaching, most freshman composition texts espoused a theory that writing is done in three stages: prewriting (thinking, brainstorming, note-taking, organizing), drafting, and revision (editing, proofreading, overall re-examination). The term "*prewriting*" itself suggests that said steps occur before the actual writing begins. However, our experience in the classroom and in editing sessions with students, as well as our own writing experiences, led us to the conclusion that writing, while containing all three of those components, seldom falls into three neatly defined steps. Instead, writing seems many times to be an organic, self-generating, often mysterious process. Revision and drafting and even brainstorming all occur together, sometimes simultaneously, sometimes in clearly defined steps.

Chapter 2 spoke of writing as a journey, a process involving not only the mind but also the heart, the soul, the memory, tools of craft, tools of intuition. Poet Joseph Brodsky, in his address given upon winning the 1987 Nobel Prize, noted the following:

One who writes a poem writes it because the language prompts, or simply dictates, the next line. Beginning a poem, the poet as a rule doesn't know the way it's going to end, and at times he is very surprised by the way it turns out, since often it turns out better than he expected.

Sam Shepard said of the process of writing plays, "I can remember being dazed with writing, with the discovery of finding I actually had these worlds inside me. These voices. Shapes. Currents of language. Light. All the mysterious elements that cause anyone to make a journey." The process of writing, it seems, has its own way of becoming, of causing discovery, of evolving in the mind of the writer. Writing, then, cannot be neatly categorized to say, "First you prewrite, then you compose, then you revise."

However, this is not to say that different aspects of writing do not contain different activities or require different modes of thinking and writing or recording information and ideas. The writer of a literary essay which includes a description of geese migrating had better know something about the migratory patterns of geese, and so will need to do some research in the library or on the Internet. That same essayist may begin thinking about the process of growing older, and may decide to explore that issue by spending many hours drafting about what it feels like during fall, recording memories and ideas and feelings about leaves turning bright orange and yellow, Friday evenings spent watching football games under blankets in loud stands full of fans and parents, taking children to Grandmother's house for Thanksgiving. That same essayist may also spend many hours thinking about which of these images, sounds, sights, smells, and details best communicate the truth of what the essay is about.

Each of these activities requires different thought patterns and mental tools. The essayist may perform each of the activities separately. She may, however, be in the middle of recording a paragraph describing the patterns of geese in the sky and think of a moment from high school when she spilled nacho cheese all over her boyfriend at the football game, and make a note of it. Or she may stop to record its details and feelings, to return to the research when she is finished. Or it may be that in gathering the information about the geese, she realizes that the structure of the essay doesn't allow inclusion of the two-paragraph discussion about her Grandmother's turkey and dressing, and so decides not to make it part of the essay. And she may realize as she works that the essay isn't about growing older, after all, but about lost love and lost innocence. Should she then go back and expand, delete, or rework the section about the geese, high above, honking their way south before the cold?

She is revising as she progresses, because all along she is making decisions about what to include and what works best. So revision isn't only done when composing or drafting the work has ended. But as you finish your first draft, you may want to consider some techniques for revising overall, as a way of checking the work to make sure it is what you want it to be. This may especially be true *over time*—sometimes it is helpful to let a poem or story sit a while after you have worked on it, and then come back to it with a fresh perspective. Some writers will write an initial few drafts of a work and then purposely not look at them, at all, for a week, a month, a number of months, and then read them with critical eyes.

Revision often requires thinking critically and carefully about things you may not have considered in other parts of the writing process. Sometimes a fresh perspective is necessary in order to "see" the work again. It often happens that when one is in the white heat of writing, it's difficult to tell whether a detail is worth including. Students have said to us, "Well, I don't know why I put it in there. I just did!" And then, when we've gone over the story with them or returned the poem to them with our suggestions, they've said, in amazement, "I can't believe I put that in there."

Writing for Ideas and Practice 14-1

1. Think back to—or, if possible, read again—something you wrote during childhood or during school. Make a list of things in the piece you would never write about today. Make a list of the things you like still, or might still like to write about today.

2. Look back at something you wrote at least one year ago—a short story, a poem, a letter, a dramatic scene, an essay, a memoir—and make a list of the things you would change if you wrote that same piece today.
3. Look back at something you wrote within the past month or two. Make a list of the things you would change if you wrote that same piece today.

One way to approach revision is to examine it in terms of technique, craft, nuts and bolts. Check the work with a critical eye, as if testing it to see if it will hold up once it is out of your hands. As you go back through the piece, you may read to see whether the poem works well as an example of its poetic form. You may go back to the work and check for spelling, grammar, sentence structure. You may examine the story to see whether you have included just the right words, or the right images, or the right setting details. You may reread the play to check for wooden or unrealistic dialogue. You may go back and test the essay once again to see whether its structure works well given the aim of the essay overall. This sense of revision can in some ways be called *editing*, because editing can involve everything from checking a story's overall effect to making sure the words are all spelled correctly. And things like spelling and word choice make a difference, just as large thematic questions about the work do.

So in revising for craft, genre, and technique, the writer is checking the work over with specific issues in mind, looking for whether the poem or essay works well in certain ways. This revision step involves thinking about how the reader or the audience will see the work, so the writer will need to get some distance from the work in order to evaluate it in this way. Sometimes that distance can come over a time of not working on a specific piece. Sometimes that distance comes from "changing gears," deliberately changing the thinking process from creation and inspiration to critique and examination.

Another way to revise is to examine whether the piece is successful in less tangible but nevertheless real and important ways. Questions such as *Have I dealt with a theme I wanted to address? What did I hope to accomplish by writing this? Am I satisfied with what the work has become?* and *What is most important to me as the writer about this piece?* all cross the writer's mind as he thinks about the piece's overall effect, the deepest sense of what it is about, what it is for. Sometimes it's not difficult to test a work in these terms—an essay about the loss of love or a poem capturing the wonder of light moving through a shaded room may fairly clearly focus on one specific aim. You may see the work as doing more or less what you had hoped it would; you may decide the whole thing's not worth pursuing any more, or that the work needs to take a completely different tack, or that the work really needs to be a short story instead of a one-act play. Asking these large-scale questions about the work's overall purpose or effect can help you focus on how well the piece has been constructed.

As you revise, consider the following questions: Are you revising so that the work will please and satisfy you, the writer? Are you revising so that your classmates or instructor or mother will approve of it? Are you working on it with a specific genre in mind, or letting it evolve as it will? Thinking about your overall purpose will help you in the revision process as well. Ultimately, the best judge of a work's overall purpose is the writer himself.

CRAFT AND SPECIFICS

How do you begin to go back and evaluate the technique you have used? It's a difficult task, and as we said earlier, it may be difficult to disengage your mind from the purely generative process and begin the perhaps more arduous work of examining the work's overall structure, testing the work's sentences, and worrying about genre and craft issues. John Gardner observes:

The dreaming part is angel-like; it is the writer's eternal, childlike spirit, the daydreaming being who exists (or seems to) outside time. But the part of the writer that handles the mechanics, typing or writing with pencil or pen, choosing one word instead of another, is human, fallible, vulnerable to anxiety and shame. Making mistake after mistake, the beast in the writer begins to sweat and grind its teeth, longing to be raised up once more by the redeeming angel within—but miserably unworthy, shy in the presence of the holy, and afraid of heights.

Gardner illustrates a key difference between composing and editing. One process often seems effortless, as if the writer is under a magic spell and the words just flow out, while revising for specific technical issues seems trivial and mean. And yet, as we have discussed, many times the writer cannot simply sit down and write brilliant lines—often, writers long for the process of revision in order to take more slowly and more deliberately the words which have been written and shape them, guide them, re-think them. So perhaps the generative process isn't better or easier than the revision process, but they are often different from one another.

As we said above, of course, the writer has in a sense been doing this sort of thinking and revising all along during the entire writing process. Writing is deciding what to put down and what not to put down, a constant evaluation and examining of one's ideas and how one expresses them. But, too, it is often necessary to go back, whether along the way or at the end of part of the writing process, and ask some specific questions about "one word instead of another."

Writing for Ideas and Practice 14-2

1. Pick one of the four genres we discussed in part 2—poetry, literary nonfiction, narration, drama—or a subgenre within one of the four. Make a list of the specific revi-

sion issues which the writer of that kind of work needs to keep in mind. List as many guidelines or suggestions as possible for the genre or subgenre you choose.

2. Refine the list, shortening it as necessary, to make it a checklist for the kind of writing you are doing or would like to do within that genre.

UNITY AND EXPOSITION

A work that aspires, however humbly, to the condition of art should carry its justification in every line.

— *Joseph Conrad*

Writers struggle with what they have written, wondering how effectively they have involved the reader in their stories, poems, plays, essays. It is too overwhelming, perhaps, to think of revising by tackling the whole issue of whether what you have written is any good at all. However, one specific way to revise is to examine your work for *unity*, reading it detail by detail, image by image, to see whether each component of what you have written meets two basic requirements:

1. Does this word, detail, image, or sentence contribute to information or detail in order to comprehend what I am trying to communicate?
2. Does this word, detail, image, or sentence contribute to the emotional and evocative effect the work can have?

The two questions can almost be summed up by asking, does this detail help the reader *understand*, and does this detail help the reader *feel?* We say "almost," because the distinction between understanding and feeling probably can't be clearly made in a work of literature. After all, literature is often about combining those two parts of ourselves that "real life" seems to try to separate.

Still, readers sometimes protest when encountering a great poem or story, "I just don't *get* this," implying that the work isn't worth the trouble it will take to "get" it, when the real issue is that they would be helped if they found out certain information—definitions of new words, background information about a certain culture or time period or dialect, explanation of the ideas related to a certain detail. T. S. Eliot's *The Waste Land* is an amazing poem, but if one reads it at a literal, surface level only, it can seem incomprehensible. Knowing the references Eliot is making to literature, mythology, and English culture, however, can open up the poem and make it powerful to read.

Sometimes "getting" a work isn't about acquiring more information as much as it is connecting in some emotional or even visceral way to the work. And there is no guarantee that a work, no matter how great, will necessarily communicate to the reader. Part of this possible connection depends on where the reader is emotionally, in terms of prior experience, in terms of depth of understanding or maturity or awareness.

But part of whether a reader feels anything or connects to the work does depend upon the writer. If the story is written with so much background detail — *exposition* — that the story skimps on dramatic detail, then the story will likely not engage the reader. As we discussed in chapter 3, a writer's basic tools must include the ability to choose the specific rather than the abstract term, to make the work come to life not by explaining to the reader but by *showing* the reader, *involving* the reader. If a poem makes sweeping generalizations about some aspect of love or life instead of offering concrete images and sounds and rhythms on that issue, then the poem will likely leave its readers unaffected. The revision process often presents the writer with an opportunity to look again at the details and images to see whether they can be made more dramatic or concrete and less expository.

Here is a paragraph from a short story by a student, Lucia Hawkins. It contains a good illustration of the need to balance exposition with concrete detail:

Shimmering willows festooned around Ashleigh's head as she lay dreaming on the lush banks of the lazy stream. Contemplating three carefree months at home was more than she could fathom. Life in Chicago this past year had been too hectic; an accounting degree from Harvard was a feather in her cap and lots of money in her pocket, but she had forfeited the quality of life that had always been so dear to her. She needed this extended vacation; she needed to find herself again.

Writing for Ideas and Practice 14-3

1. What information does the paragraph present? Make a list of every detail you know about Ashleigh from reading the paragraph.
2. What percentage of the information does the story *tell* the reader, and what percentage *show* the reader? Is the ratio between them appropriate?

The opening sentence works well to describe a specific moment in physical space: Ashleigh lying by a stream with willows above. And immediately, the story begins to try to give background details to the reader about what Ashleigh is feeling. By the end of the paragraph, the reader has been told that Ashleigh has decided to retreat to this place in order to balance her accounting work in Chicago—a job she got because of her degree from Harvard. All of those details may be helpful in discovering information about the progression Ashleigh will make during the story.

However, that information has not been shown to the reader through action, dialogue, other characters, or physical detail—so those details are only information; they haven't impacted the reader yet. And this might be all right, depending on what Lucia does with the rest of her story. But remember: the writer's job is to convey experience, real or imagined, so that it becomes a part of the experience of the reader.

Writing for Ideas and Practice 14-4

How could the information in Lucia's paragraph be communicated so that it becomes a part of the action, the experience, of the story? Make a suggestion about how to make each of the following details more concrete and specific, either through action, dialogue, physical detail, or other characters, by writing a few short sentences for each detail:
1. Ashleigh cannot fathom three carefree months.
2. Ashleigh's life in Chicago this past year has been too hectic.
3. Ashleigh has an accounting degree.
4. Ashleigh's accounting degree is from Harvard.
5. Ashleigh's accounting degree from Harvard gives her prestige.
6. Ashleigh's job pays well.
7. Ashleigh has a quality of life that has always been dear to her.
8. Ashleigh has forfeited that quality of life.
9. Ashleigh needs an extended vacation.

Lucia has imparted a number of details in the opening paragraph, as if she is trying to set the stage of the story before beginning it. Those details, however, as we see above, could all have been shown to the reader in more dramatic ways. The question arises: which details are worth communicating to the reader, and how? What if a detail doesn't really change the outcome of the story, and it doesn't make the story more powerful or effective? Why include it? What if the only details you were allowed to include were those you presented directly within the action of the story or in the images and rhythms of the poem, rather than stated as information?

While many writers begin with background information, as this writer has, the burden is upon the writer to communicate that information in a powerful way in order to advance the story and to make the story come to life for the reader. In the next paragraphs of the above story, the writer makes the story much more specific:

Slumbering in and out of daydreams, Ashleigh didn't hear his approaching footsteps. He gave a couple of short coughs and drew closer. She sprang to her knees and turned quickly in his direction. She thought she was still dreaming. The apparition she beheld was all male, at least 6'2" tall, blonde hair tickling his collar, pale blue eyes, Hawaiian Tropic suntan, and his clothing was 100% denim. He toted a brown leather pack nonchalantly over his right shoulder.

"I'm sorry, I didn't mean to startle you," he said. "I'm looking for Jack Bond's place—am I in the general direction?" he questioned.

"Oh, yes, he's my father. Just keep walking along the trail by the river's edge and you'll come to our house. He should be home by now—and anyway, Mother's there," she rattled on.

"Thanks a lot. Let me introduce myself. Dillon McKane," he said, outstretching his hand. She arose and took it.

"Oh, I'm Ashleigh, Ashleigh Bond," she answered. The sunlight danced on her light brown hair, her green eyes sparkled against the reflection of the rippling stream.

"Well, I had better go up and meet with your dad. I've applied for the manager's job, and I hope I'll get it. Pleased to meet you Ashleigh—see you again," he said, as he sauntered off.

"Bye," Ashleigh managed to splutter as she watched him go. She gave another sigh, long and low.

Writing for Ideas and Practice 14-5

1. What details has the writer communicated in these paragraphs? Make a list of everything you know, directly or indirectly, about the story now.
2. What details could the writer still have made less overt and communicated less directly but more powerfully? List some of them, and make brief suggestions about what you would do differently if you were the writer.
3. What details could have been left out altogether, if any?

Lucia does a better job in these paragraphs of letting the action and dialogue communicate; it makes sense that Dillon might tell the boss's daughter why he's here, and so the reader gets that piece of information without its revelation seeming too obvious. And while some of the writer's description of Dillon seems cliche—"he was all male," with a "Hawaiian Tropic suntan"—the writer gives us a number of physical details with which to see Dillon through Ashleigh's eyes, as she sees him, romantic and beautiful, without cluttering up the presentation of the character with a lot of background information. It works well, too, that instead of saying something like, "Ashleigh felt immediately that this was the man for her, the man she had been looking for," we are told that she "splutters" a good-bye and sighs as she watches him leave.

Later in the chapter we will discuss how to deal with other people's critiques of your work and how much of what they say to accept or reject. But overall, it is up to the writer not to change the work based on what others say, but to use questions such as those above to check the work to see whether it is unified, tight, concrete, and specific.

CONSISTENCY AND APPROPRIATENESS

Another related issue is whether a detail or image or word is appropriate for the kind of writing one is doing. Making decisions about what in one's work is right for a given audience, reader, or market can very often come down to a question of individual words and images to consider and revise. As we discussed in the earlier chapters dealing with poetry, plays, literary nonfiction, and narration, each genre—and each form within each genre—has its own guidelines and norms regulating how the writer is to construct the work in question. The writer should take care to work within those guidelines in order to present a piece which doesn't distract the reader because it doesn't "fit."

For instance, what if a poem takes a serious look at the pain of divorce, focusing on one image of destruction and despair after another—and then throws in an offhand reference to Bugs Bunny? Many writers use surprise or incongruent elements to bring an issue to light or heighten or relieve tension. However, a problem exists if the work includes a line or phrase that seems out of place and the writer didn't mean to do so. What if Hamlet's soliloquy went something like this:

> To be or not to be, that is the question.
> Whether 'tis nobler in the mind to suffer
> The slings, arrows, grenades, and other cruddy
> Weapons of destruction piled on by the sorry scum of the world,
> Or by opposing, end them.

A glaringly inconsistent detail or image may not always seem so obvious to the writer when it's his own work. Consistency in tone, in purpose, in word choice, and in sentence structure can mean the difference between the language working to make the piece successful and the language becoming a distraction. When is language a distraction? Different authors use different styles and patterns of language and images, of course, so to apply one overall standard with which to revise everyone's work isn't feasible or a good idea, but you should have a clear sense of the tone and voice that emanates from your piece and check that your tone is consistent throughout. Cormack McCarthy's language in *Blood Meridian* is consistent in style and tone:

They took to riding by night, silent jornadas save for the trundling of the wagons and the wheeze of the animals. Under the moonlight a strange party of elders with the white dust thick on their moustaches and their eyebrows. They moved on and the stars jostled and raced across the firmament and died beyond the inkblack mountains. They came to know the night skies well.

McCarthy's language is very different from that of Hunter S. Thompson in *The Curse of Lono*:

We were in downtown Honolulu now, cruising along the waterfront. The streets were full of joggers, fine-tuning their strides for the big race. They ignored passing traffic, which made Skinner nervous.

"This running thing is out of control," he said. "Every rich liberal in the Western world is into it. They run ten miles a day. It's a goddamn religion."

"Do *you* run?" I asked.

He laughed. "Hell yes, I run. But never with empty hands. We're *criminals*, Doc. We're not *like* these people and I think we're too old to learn."

The two samples seem wildly inconsistent if placed together, but of course they come from different styles—the heavy, symbolic fiction of McCarthy versus the "gonzo journalism" of Thompson. The language in each excerpt is consistent with the work from which it comes.

You can check your work for problems with consistency by asking some questions:

1. What word choices and sentence structures are best for this kind of writing? Is it an informal work—a memoir, a lyric poem? Is it a formal work—a three-act tragedy, a short story headed to a literary magazine? The piece's overall level of formality will determine which words are best, whether the sentence structures are too complex or too simple.
2. What will the audience reading or seeing this work expect—within the guidelines of this genre, my own stylistic guidelines, within the appropriate boundaries of the market the work is headed toward?
3. What words, phrases, images, or language patterns in this work don't really fit my overall writing pattern, or seem inconsistent with the work I am attempting to do? Why have I chosen them? In using them, will they become distracting, or do they help serve the overall pattern of the work I've created and the overall purpose of the work?

You will also want to go back over every work and check it for some basic language issues, by asking:

1. Are there any words or phrases that seem awkwardly written—that is, word choice or structures that are inconsistent or do not serve the work's overall effect?

2. Do I use any cliche or "tired" or "wooden" wording or images?
3. How can I rewrite in order to eliminate these inconsistencies or this awkwardness, so that the wording or images flow smoothly and clearly fit together as a unified whole?
4. Have I checked—or gotten someone else to help me check—for spelling errors, sentence problems, other grammatical errors, or problems with mechanics and punctuation?

All of these ways of checking back over your work can help you separate your editing mind from your creating mind, and keep you focused on one or two things to look for at a time. Then you can continue to write and create as well, because going back through the work will help you see more things you'd like to create, to add, to think about.

Audience and Purpose

I don't know if that grocer on my shoulder digs all the references, but other than him, I write pretty much for myself. If, at the close of business each evening, I myself can understand what I've written, I feel the day hasn't been totally wasted.

— S. J. Perelman

Consistency and appropriateness are important when thinking about one's audience or purpose in writing the work. In chapter 1, we discussed why writers write and suggested ways in which you might think about the purposes of your own writing and the audiences you might write for. Now, in our discussion of revision, consider again why you are writing a particular poem, story, memoir, sketch, or song.

Some writers enjoy shocking their readers. And certainly, there are genres in which the more shocking or unexpected the detail or word or image is, the better. Most great innovations in literature have come about because a writer was willing to break convention, change the rules, violate readers' expectations. Baudelaire's images were so shocking as to be revolting. One of the most significant innovations in the conventions of Greek tragic drama was the addition of a third actor—a revolutionary step at the time. Richard Pryor took standup comedy to new heights by saying things and dealing with subjects no one had dared broach before. If you feel led to do the same, do it.

However, you also need to think about what is appropriate for one audience or another. More innovative is not always better. And we suggest that your job as a writer is not to carve out new genres or forms as much as it is to write truthfully and well—with consistency and care—about your real or imagined experience so that it becomes a part of the experience of the reader. New genres may emerge as a result of your work, but they develop organically as a by-product of your telling the truth.

Writing for Ideas and Practice 14-6

1. Whom do you trust to critique your work? Why?
2. What effect do the following audiences have on writing:
   a. Teacher
   b. Literary critic
   c. Family member
   d. Pen pal
   e. Self
   f. Imaginary audience
3. How have your feelings about your writing and expressing yourself been affected by the comments of others? In what ways?
4. What do you do to deal with others' criticism of your ideas, your creativity, or your work?

One way to test your work is to try it out on an audience, to see what happens. But letting someone else read your writing and asking what they think can be dangerous. Seeking the advice of a fellow writer or teacher can help, but knowing what to listen to is sometimes difficult. If someone says he doesn't like something about the scene or poem you have written, does that mean you should listen?

It is difficult to do anything when an audience is watching. As chapter 2 suggested, everyone to a certain extent suffers from "stage fright," whether presenting in person or through writing. This is an especially acute problem for the writer, who, though alone, is onstage as she writes, expressing her ideas, her feelings, her imagination, her memories, her opinions.

Chapter 1 asked you to think about who your audience is, whom you imagine reading your work. Remember what Kurt Vonnegut, Jr., said: "Every successful creative person creates with an audience of one in mind." When you revise, you prepare a work you yourself can read and enjoy. But writing is often also written to be read by others, and so as a part of the revision process, consider what the audience will think, whether the poem communicates, whether the play will be laughed at or appreciated.

As you revise, carefully consider whom to show your work to. You won't get very far by showing your writing to someone in your family and asking, "What do you think?" If you come from families like ours, they will either display your work on the refrigerator, or say, "That's nice, dear," and send you to a therapist. Remember: just because someone knows and loves you does not mean that that person is qualified to judge or evaluate your work. Yes, it's true that your audience may be the general reading public, but a difference exists between how people see "writers" and how your family members see *you*. Your family and friends know you not as the writer of that excellent short story that spoke to their hearts, but as the person whose diaper they changed or whose secrets they know. So it's difficult for them to evaluate your work with any objectivity.

And it is also often the case that loved ones simply don't know as much about craft or technique as you do, in which case, you would do better to consult with someone who has some expertise in the area you are working in. The question then is, who has the expertise, the objectivity, and the fairness of mind to help me revise this work?

You may have been showing your work to your instructor. Teachers can offer great help to their students. We have had professors who were very able, sometimes amazingly so, to give us great insight into how to write better. Getting good advice from a good writer is very helpful. When a writing teacher critiques your story or poem, she can sometimes give you a comment which may seem small, but which can provide huge insights as you work.

You may also want to show your work to fellow students. The exercises in this text have given you many opportunities to discuss your ideas and insights and even to trade your work with your classmates. You probably have already discovered, then, both the positive and negative aspects of having other students critique your work. On the positive side, your fellow students share with you your enthusiasm for the writing process, your desire to create and revise in order to do this strange and exciting thing.

The lore of writers in history tells of many groups of writers who gathered in pubs or living rooms or salons or college classrooms to read each other's work and direct one another along the path. Ezra Pound's work on T. S. Eliot's *The Waste Land* made the poem so much better than Eliot's earlier drafts that Eliot dedicated the poem to Pound. As graduate students, we used to gather in each other's living rooms or kitchens, drinking beer, eating pretzels, and reading and critiquing each other's work. Sometimes that process can be very helpful, because fellow writers know what you are going through, and often understand what you are trying to accomplish in your writing or what ideas and issues you are struggling to write about.

But on the other hand, your colleagues may not have the insight or expertise to tell you anything helpful at all, though, like family members, they feel qualified to tell you anyway. They may in fact just be dead wrong. John Irving has remarked that he likes what Cocteau said about other people's reviews: "Listen very carefully to the first criticism of your work. Note just what it is about your work that the reviewers don't like; it may be the only thing in your work that is original and worthwhile."

Whether in a class setting or in some other exchange of one's work, your fellow writer may give you advice which sends you in a wrong direction. We have shared our work with inept or aloof teachers, or reviewers with skewed ideas about what makes good writing, or colleagues with whom we just didn't agree. How do you tell the difference between constructive criticism and destructive criticism?

It may be helpful to adopt the rule that you should never accept *anyone's* criticism of your work at *face value*, not even if John Updike, Alice Walker, and E. L. Doctorow themselves wrote you personally to comment on your poem. Always decide what that person's critical comment can contribute to your creative process, and if an idea or suggestion is helpful, adopt it, make it part of your own system of writing. Take anything that is not helpful and throw it in the garbage, ignore it, or burn it, and go on.

Woody Allen has said that he doesn't attend the Academy Awards even when he is nominated because since he refuses to listen to criticism or input when making his films, he must also refuse to listen to accolades. For him, the work is the thing, not people's reaction to it. So, does that mean that the writer doesn't really have to listen to anyone? Well, the whole purpose of getting others to critique your writing is to get help in revising *your work*. You alone can judge whether or not your work is successful, for you determine its scope, its purpose, the thing that makes it what it should be. But—the good advice of a person of fairness and expertise can transform a mediocre draft into a good work. And if you want to share your work with other people, or even publish your writing, it can be very helpful to get other people's insights about what works and what doesn't in what you've written. So don't shun people's input; solicit it, and then evaluate it and use what is helpful.

The writer must have an idea, even if not yet fully articulated, of what the work is to be. Sometimes we don't have the confidence yet to say, "I know what I want this poem to be"—but getting input can help us decide. If you disagree with what a reviewer, critic, or editor says, deciding that you disagree can help you focus more clearly on what you do want the work to be. Hemingway wrote to his editor Maxwell Perkins, in response to reviewers' comments on his novel *The Sun Also Rises*, "It's funny to write a book that seems as tragic as that and have them take it for a jazz superficial story. If you went any deeper inside they couldn't read it because they would be crying all the time." He knew what he wanted the novel to be, and what he had accomplished in writing it—and now it is considered perhaps his best work ever.

Here are some general guidelines, then, for receiving help from others in revising your writing:

1. Do not react immediately to what your reviewer or instructor tells you. Once you have read the reviewer's comments, back off, take some time, and then return to the work with the clear eye not of the com-

poser of the work but of the editor, willing to do whatever is necessary to make the piece as good as it can be.

2. Never write just one thing, send it off to a publisher or teacher for review or acceptance, and then wait for it to come back. Keep writing. Do not wait to see what someone else says. If you are writing simply to please someone else or to sell your work, it may not be very good anyway, since writing must come from the heart, the soul. Work on something else for a while until the piece comes back.

No matter what happens, as we said in chapter 2, your writing process is a journey, not a destination. The point is not to create a poem or essay, but to write, to keep writing, to keep discovering and finding out and expressing through your writing what you feel and think.

Another thing to think about as you revise is the question of *purpose*. Emily Dickinson saw only seven of her poems published during her lifetime—though she wrote over 1,700 and submitted many to publishers and magazines. When the editors suggested she cut her words, or change them, or make her rhythms smoother or her rhyme schemes more regular, she came to accept that few other people were ready to understand what she was trying to explore with her poetry. So she would write for herself, perhaps sharing a poem with a friend or confidant or family member (though not often), and when she died, she left scores of little packets of poems, numbered and tied up in bundles, for posterity to deal with as it might. It took another fifty years before the literary world was able to understand how much Dickinson had accomplished with her remarkable poetry. Dickinson remained true to her purpose even though her audience did not always appreciate her work.

What is the purpose of your work? If it is a memoir written to illustrate your concern for your grandfather dying of lung cancer after many years of smoking cigarettes, will your memoir primarily focus on your own process of grief and loss, on a loving portrait of your once vital and vibrant grandfather who is now weakened and in despair, on your anger at the tobacco companies for their negligent willingness to inflict this cancer-causing substance on the world for their own profit, or on the effects of your grandfather's death on your future emotional state? Each of these may be a part of your thinking process as you work, but in order to deal with any one of these very large issues, an essay will need particular care and work—and no essay can deal with all of them. So focusing on the purpose of what you have written as you revise is necessary in order to ensure that you end up with what you want. You will need to make decisions as you revise about what to include and what to change, in small things such as individual words or phrases, or large things such as structure and entire paragraphs or stanzas, based on your work's purpose.

Is the work for your own enjoyment or exploration? Is it for a specific market or audience? Is it for sharing with only those who understand the thing you are writing about? Or is it for anyone interested in taking a journey along with your characters? Your decisions about what you are doing will inform everything you choose to include and describe in your writing.

Writing for Ideas and Practice 14-7

1. In chapter 1 you were assigned to write a statement about why you are a writer. Rewrite that statement. What is the purpose of your writing?
2. Write down some of the comments other people have made about your work. Have they been helpful? Why or why not?

Keep in mind as you revise that with some things you write, you have to accept simply that you wrote it that way because you just did. You may want to ask as you revise, *Does this detail, image, sentence, or paragraph contribute to what I am trying to say overall, even though I may not be sure how?* While this question may seem to indicate that the writer hasn't worked the piece through, that is very often not the case at all. Many times, even after having written something and rewriting it many times, writers may not be sure why a particular word or phrase or detail seems right or appropriate. Again, the issue is your overall purpose in writing—so consider specific concerns and guidelines within the genre or form, and be aware of correctness and sentence structure and word choice, and then just keep writing.

In filmmaking, the overall process of writing, creating, and revising which the poet or fiction writer or essayist does alone is subdivided into many tasks handled by many different people or even teams of people. One person who plays a key role is the editor—or, in the language we are using in this chapter, the *reviser*. While decisions about what to include or what to cut from the film are ultimately up to the film's director or producer, the editor often has great power to decide what scenes work well and do not, and how to take the "raw" footage the director has shot and make that footage into a coherent, consistent whole that tells the story clearly and with power. How does the director know the editor will make the right choices? How does the director know the editor will stay true to the original vision for the film, for what the film at its core is about? Even if the director, rather than dictating how to cut the film, works with the editor in discovering what to do to the film to make it what it needs to be, there must always be a kind of center to come back to in order to ensure the film's integrity and consistency.

This situation is true in writing as well, though editor and director are usually the same person. How does the poem or story stay true through the revision process? It is up to the writer to know what to cut, what to rewrite, what to expand, and what to leave just as it is. And if the writer knows deep down, and continues to remember during revision, why the essay or scene or poem exists, why she wrote it, what it is really about—then the work will become what it can be. So, director, know what you are trying to do with your work; and editor, make the work the best work it can be.

Writing on Your Own

Choose a full-length work you have written: a story, poem, short play, or essay.

1. Write down your own assessment of the work's
   a. Unity and exposition
   b. Consistency and appropriateness
   c. Audience and purpose
2. Get two different people to write a critique of the work.
3. Compare the two critiques with your own assessment. Write a critique of their critiques. How helpful were they in assisting you in thinking about what you accomplished with the piece? What work can you do with the piece you have written to make it stronger, now that you have gotten their input?
4. Answer the following questions, thinking about your writing overall:
   a. What have you learned about your own writing process?
   b. What attitudes about writing and your own work have changed since beginning your work with this text ? Which ones have stayed the same or been strengthened? Why?
   c. What do you want to write more than anything else? Why?
   d. What do you NOT want to write, and why not?

15

Marketing Your Manuscript

Writing to Warm Up

1. Think about the kinds of writing or authors you enjoy reading most.
    a. What kind of publishing do these types of writing fit into—magazines, journals, books, newspapers, anthologies, song lyrics?
    b. Would you like to publish your work in these same places? Why or why not?
2. What experiences have you already had with publishing? Positive? Negative? Both? Give some specific information about what you have published, if at all, and what that experience has been like.

Throughout the text we have asked you to contemplate your purpose in pursuing the craft, the journey, and the work of creative writing. Perhaps in doing the exercises, thinking through some of the issues presented in the text, and doing your own writing, you have come to an understanding of what you like to write, what kinds of writing you do best, and where you want your writing to go from here. And all along, you may have also had in mind the idea of other people—besides your fellow writers or your instructor—reading your writing.

Different kinds of writing are appropriate for different audiences and readers. Some writings must be shared; others are best left private, or shared only with an audience of informed or focused readers or listeners who know certain things about the writer or the genre involved. A poem can be written simply as an exercise by the poet thinking through an idea or experience or feeling; the poem may or may not have to be published somewhere in order to be "successful"—that is, to fulfill its purpose in being created. On the other hand, a one-man performance art piece probably needs to be presented in front of a live audience in order to be "successful."

Also, some kinds of literature, like Stephen King novels, fit large audiences, and others, such as haiku poetry, are best appreciated by smaller groups. Some kinds of writing would be best published in book form, while some kinds are more appropriate as individual magazine articles, essays in newspapers, poems tucked between larger stories in a literary journal.

Publishing Success

Many people believe that if you sell your writing to some publishing company, all will be well, and you will have fame and fortune and happiness. Is that your idea of "success"? We define success as when the work fulfills the purpose for which it was created. If your purpose was to capture, really well, with specific images and powerful, melodious language, what it feels like on your back porch on a winter afternoon, and you're pretty convinced your poem has in fact done just that, then that poem is a success.

So should you share the poem with others? Publishing the poem so that other people can read it and feel, too, what you feel on a winter's afternoon, might be your ultimate goal, since it communicates not only with you, but also with others. So, what is *success* to you?

Writing for Ideas and Practice 15-1

1. Define *success* for any kind of writing you are doing or would like to do.
2. Would you be content to write your work and then die without anyone ever reading or appreciating it? Why or why not?

A question to consider, too, is whether you are primarily interested in publishing your work in order to make money, to advance yourself as a writer, to be noticed and recognized as a literary figure, to participate in a particular genre or kind of writing or with a certain group of writers or thinkers, or for other reasons. As we discussed in chapter 1, it is important for you to consider why you write, why you want to do this thing, and what your expectations are.

Students sometimes enter a creative writing class filled with stories of Robert James Waller writing *The Bridges of Madison County* in two weeks' time, convinced that they, too, can crank out a best-seller. After all, everyone's always told them they should "write some of this stuff down!" When they're told that John Grisham's first book was rejected by multiple publishers and at first only sold a small number of copies, these students remark, "Yeah, but look at him now!" And it's true, many writers toiled away at other jobs, sending their manuscripts out patiently for years, waiting for them to sell, only finally to break through and become millionaires. Theodore Geisel—Dr. Seuss—sent his first children's book, *And to Think That I Saw It on Mulberry Street*, to twenty-seven publishers before it was accepted, but in time he would become the author with more books in print than any other writing in the English language. However, for every phenomenal success like Dr. Seuss or John Grisham, there are dozens—hundreds—of hopeful writers who slave away forever with little or no recognition. John Kennedy O'Toole, whose first novel, *A Confederacy of Dunces*, would go on to be an award-winning best-seller, never saw his success; despondent over his languishing career and unhappy life, he committed suicide in his twenties, and his mother saw that his book was shown to editors who published his book posthumously.

One of our students a few years ago began the class by saying that all she wanted out of writing was to record her experiences as a little girl in Poland, before World War II when her family immigrated to America, and pass those stories along to her grandchildren. The woman next to her had a similarly clear, but very different, objective: she wanted more than anything to learn how to write a good, interesting, detailed story she could publish as a romance novel. She loved romance novels and had decided that she could write one, and wanted to write one so that she could make more money—and buy more romance novels!

For one woman, publishing was not important; for the other, it was the ultimate goal. For both, the basic rules of writing we have worked on in this text applied—genre questions, the need for specific details, the need for clear organization and form, the need to be authentic and "tell the truth" in one's writing. And yet, one writer saw herself as a published author already, just waiting to finish the book and mail it off, while the other had no dream at all that she might publish her memoir.

What happened, however, was that the romance writer published her work after a great deal of time, research, and diligent effort, writing and attending workshops and having her work critiqued and reviewed, and she is still writing and publishing as she hoped to do. But the woman's memoir about her childhood was published as well, when she sent it off to a small magazine which accepted it—and then it was noticed by an editor at a large publishing company who encouraged the woman to expand her memoir into a book-length manuscript for his company to publish!

And, after all, one's goals for one's writing can change over time as one evolves as a writer and a person. One writer we know wanted for years to write the definitive book of essays on woodland lore—homeopathic cures found in tree roots and nuts and berries, and recounted legends and stories from the woods of the South. He labored for what seemed like forever, with no publishing success and little satisfaction. As time went on, he discovered that what was bothering him was his great frustration with modern, industrialized society. He would rant about what was "wrong with these crazy people today," shaking his head, his huge bush of bright white hair flopping all about his denim shirt and earrings. Over time, essays not about tree sap but about his feelings about contemporary culture began to slip into his work. They weren't picked up by publishers much either—a little article here and there in a small magazine—but he seemed much happier to be writing them. He didn't seem to mind any more that no one read his stories about the woods. Writing the stories about the woods had been a way for him to work through his feelings and ideas about the world he lives in.

So, again, what you want to do with what you write may or may not have anything to do with its being published. Many people who want very desperately for their work to be published and who mail off manuscript after manuscript only find rejection and years of frustration. And there is no guarantee that a good manuscript will be published. Publishing, like any other industry, is focused on the law of supply and demand, and if someone can get a certain amount of money for a book, it is because the publishing companies are sure they can recoup their investment.

Some literary-minded writers have shunned the mainstream publishing arena, preferring to stick with smaller publishing companies, or write and publish small chapbooks of their works. The fact that many literary magazines are read by only a handful of people doesn't mean that the works in them are less successful than those in the big bookstores. The question, again, is one of what you consider success for your writing.

However, don't be fooled and think that all those who publish in literary rather than mainstream magazines and books are doing so only for the higher purposes of Art. Many writers use small magazines as a way to "move up the ladder" in publishing. Their objective is to get their work in print, and any number of appropriate periodicals will do. The more they publish their work, the more likely it is that in time, they can use this publishing history as a way to be noticed and publish not only in the smaller magazines but also in the larger. This method has worked well for many writers, and you may want to try this path. It is difficult, since many aspiring writers are trying to do the same thing. But then, there are not nearly as many people publishing in this "literary" arena as there are trying to break into mainstream, best-seller publishing.

The issue of why you are sending your manuscript off to be published, though, will be better informed by your knowing some specific things about the publishing options you face.

Finding a Publisher

Students ask, "How am I supposed to pick a place to send my work? It's overwhelming!" And they are right. But some tools exist which can cut down the amount of time you waste and focus your energies so that you can have a better sense of how to send your work out there.

Writing for Ideas and Practice 15-2

As you are thinking about various markets, ask yourself a few questions, either in general or about a specific piece of creative writing you have produced:

1. What kind of writing am I doing? What kind of publishing arena best suits its focus, length, subject matter, and style?
2. What would make an editor or decision-maker at the appropriate publishing company interested in my work?

Magazines such as *Writer* and *Writer's Digest*, as well as others, publish information about the craft of writing, but, along with *Publisher's Weekly*, they also print articles about trends in publishing and ways to understand different issues in the publishing field: what kind of children's books are popular this year, tips for dealing with agents, the going rate for rewrite services, etc. Reading these articles can help alleviate the feeling of being overwhelmed, as well as provide helpful information relative to the kinds of publishing you might want to do.

Conferences and workshops are offered all over the country, providing opportunities to learn about specific issues facing writers. These workshops appeal to every genre—mystery, western, nonfiction, romance, poetry. Some conferences offer time to meet with published authors in the field, some offer time with literary agents, editors, and publishing company representatives.

Small Press vs. Large Press

Many writers dream of seeing their short stories in *The New Yorker* or *Atlantic Monthly*, and there is certainly nothing wrong with a goal of publishing in such periodicals. If that is your goal, by all means work toward it. But realize that the journey toward the goal is important too. Some writers collect rejection slip after rejection slip from large magazine editors, still waiting for that lucky break, like trying to win the lottery. While it is true that getting published, especially by a large-press periodical, sometimes seems as random as winning the lottery, there are options you may consider, such as submitting your work to publications that you might not have previously considered.

If you want to begin publishing while you are waiting for that big break, look to smaller presses for an opportunity to publish your work. You won't get rich, but you will have the satisfaction of seeing your work in print and will be able to share your work with others. Publishing in smaller markets will also help you accumulate a portfolio of publications.

You can find publishing opportunities in your own community. Submitting an essay to the editorial editor of your local or neighborhood newspaper, or placing a poem in the newsletter of a local community group can provide you with that first break that probably won't come from *The New Yorker*.

Many colleges and universities have student literary magazines. Some of these magazines are for student and faculty work only. These magazines can provide good opportunities for you to submit your work and learn about the editing and submission processes, as well as to give your work exposure. Don't ignore opportunities that could open the door to other opportunities.

Many universities also publish literary magazines, most of them falling under the larger category of the **little magazine**, which publishes literary fiction by established and new writers. Little magazines have small distribution markets and specialized audiences. You probably will only get paid in copies of the issue in which your work appears, but the exposure level is regional or national rather than local.

If you are interested in finding a suitable little magazine for your work, an excellent source of information is *The International Directory of Little Magazines and Small Presses* edited by Len Fulton, issued yearly. It is a comprehensive guide to little magazines and small publishing houses, listed alphabetically and indexed by subject and region.

There are other publications which provide broader listings of magazines and presses that you might consider sending your work to. Writer's Digest Books publishes books which cover submission information for specific markets, such as *Poet's Market*, *Children's Writer and Illustrator's Market*, *Artist's Market*, and *Novel and Short Story Writer's Market*. These publications cover both large and small markets and describe the magazines you may be considering sending your work to. *Writer's Market* is divided into various large sections—book publishers, magazine publishers, specific kinds of magazines, syndicates, and so forth. As in *The International Directory of Little Magazines and Small Presses*, the Writer's Digest books provide submission guidelines along with the names and addresses of the editors of each magazine or publishing house. Be sure to refer to a current issue, however, so that you know you are addressing your work to the current editor and are sending your work to the correct address.

Aiming at Your Target

As you read through one of the *Market* books that give all sorts of information about the places you can publish your work, use strategies that help you pick publishers that are appropriate for your work.

Look for publishers who deal in the kind of work you want to write. If you write stories about cowboys, then look for information about a pretty restricted group of magazines and journals dealing with cowboys, the West, cowboy poetry, farm and ranch news, and so forth. Don't waste your time sending these stories to book publishers or to fashion magazines.

Look for publishers who publish works similar to yours in length and style. Most publishers will tell authors what they are looking for, and it is wise to pick potential publishers and presses that will be open to your long poem or your 1,500-word article or your short short story or your one-act play because that's the sort of thing they typically print. If you want to publish your story or poem or essay in a certain magazine, a good idea is to pick up copies of the magazine over as long a period as you can and note the kind of things that magazine publishes.

Once you have narrowed the hundreds of book publishing companies, magazines, journals, syndicates, and other resources into a manageable group which you think may suit your ideas about where you would like to publish your work and who might be open to your work, you will want to contact them. Don't just send off your manuscript, hoping for an instant sale. A series of steps to contact and approach these potential publishers will help you establish yourself as a professional writer worth considering.

MAKING CONTACT WITH PUBLISHERS

Many times the author, who may have little understanding of the workings of the publishing industry, must rely on others to explain or interpret the legalese in contracts, the way **royalties** are distributed, and how marketing operations work.

Using a literary agent can be very helpful. A literary agent is in the business of finding ways to sell and market the author's work, and negotiating contracts and rights for the author. And the agent's job is not only to negotiate contracts, but also to be aware of marketing and sales trends, of larger issues regarding clients' legal rights, and of what is happening in publishing overall. Literary agents can charge as much as ten percent of your work's sales, but having someone in your corner who knows the business makes the process much easier. However, your agent must be *your* representative first, so be willing to walk away from an agent that does not have your best interests at heart.

Vanity presses publish unpublished authors' works in anthologies that are only mailed out to the people who published in the anthology, all of whom paid a hefty price to have their poem or story published in a pretty volume to put on the shelf. There is nothing wrong with publishing in a vanity press, but it is important to realize that these volumes are not read by the general public, nor are the works in them considered legitimate literature by critics and reviewers.

Likewise, some companies call themselves literary agents and may even promise you that they will publish your work, but instead make their money off of "reading fees," money the hopeful writer pays the company to review the manuscript and market it. Sometimes these companies can give helpful reviews, and some reputable companies offer workshops and distance-mail or in-person classes which will actually help writers refine their work and publish it. But beware of those masquerading as agents only to bilk unsuspecting writers out of hundreds of dollars with no guarantee of ever sending your work out to any company.

If you want to publish shorter works such as individual short stories or poems, a literary agent will probably not be willing to represent you. In this case you will be much better off contacting publishers yourself, but there are a few guidelines you will want to follow. First, find out everything you can about the publisher and find the name of an editor who you think will handle the kind of work you are sending. You will want to address all correspondence to an editor, by name. It may be that as you go you find out that that person is not your audience, but at least your work will have been delivered to someone who can direct it to its proper place within the organization, as opposed to the slush pile.

The **slush pile** is what publishers call that huge amount of manuscripts that come into their offices every day, manuscripts from aspiring writers, some of whom have good writing to submit, and some of whose writing does not fit the publisher's standards for quality, length, or subject matter. How to keep out of the slush pile? Tailoring your work to the publisher's specifications will help.

Most publishers, both of books and of periodicals, will send you **author guidelines**, sometimes called a "style sheet." Author guidelines outline what the company wants to publish, and what form that work should take when the writer submits it.

You can get an author guidelines sheet by writing a brief **entry letter** to the editor. Simply write a very brief letter introducing yourself as a writer of a certain kind of work, and stating your interest in finding out more about the publishing company. Ask for a copy of the publisher's author guidelines. Enclose a self-addressed, stamped envelope — letter size is acceptable, but some companies mail their guidelines flat in 9" × 12" envelopes, so you may want to enclose that size to be safe. Make the entry letter very short and to the point. This is not the time to sell anyone on your ideas.

Read the author guidelines for specific information about manuscript format, the approaches the publishers like their writers to take, the kinds of things they do and do not like to publish, and any other information they think you need to know. If they say it in their author guidelines, they mean it; don't think your work is so brilliant that they will bend the rules just for you.

Some writers contact publishers initially with a **query letter**. In this case, the letter is not a simple opening of the relationship, but also a way to test the waters to see if the publisher may have an interest in what you are working on or have completed.

You will still address the editor in question by name. In the query letter, however, state in an opening paragraph your name, your background or occupation (if they are of any relevance to the writing you hope to submit), and a history of the places you have published your work before. If you have not published your work anywhere, that doesn't mean you won't be considered; but if you have published your work, even in local or small ways, mention this briefly so that the editor will have a sense of the kinds of writing you do.

In your next paragraph, say what it is you would like to submit to this publisher, and why you have chosen this publisher for your work. (You can see why the preliminary research and thinking you have done regarding where to publish your work are essential.) You may explain what need you perceive in the market for your work and why you think the work you would like to send is appropriate for this publisher. Give pertinent information about the work: number of words or pages, subject matter, audience you are writing for, and the unique angle or approach you are taking.

This entire letter must absolutely be *no longer than one page* in length. Magazines, even small and specialty magazines, receive far more manuscripts than they publish. The editors and their assistants do not have time to read your life story—they want to see, quickly, what you can offer them with your work.

Mention that you are looking forward to hearing from the publisher soon. Some writers prefer to set a date by which the publisher should respond, but it is courteous simply to leave that up to the publishers to decide. Some writers also suggest in their closing that they are going to send the manuscript unless they hear otherwise. Read the *Writer's Market* entries or the Author Guidelines you have to see if this will be acceptable. If the publishers do not accept "unsolicited manuscripts," that is, manuscripts they did not ask for or consent to look at, then you have little hope of their paying much attention to your work.

Never call the publishing company on the phone, unless you have some question about a current address. Never just "show up" on the publisher's doorstep with manuscript in hand. There are stories of authors who have tried this and gotten someone to look at their work, but such cases are more legend than fact, and such an approach may mark you as unprofessional. Be as professional as you can in dealing with publishers, and they will more likely see you as someone they will want to work with.

Submitting Your Work

If you should receive some encouragement from a publisher in a letter saying they might like to see some sample of your work or the specific piece you have described, then you are ready to submit your manuscript or some part of it.

Each genre has specific format rules you will want to follow. But in general, you will want to submit your work in 12-point type, on one side of the page only, with one-inch margins all around the page, double spaced.

Do not bind the pages or put them in any sort of folder or notebook. You may attach the sheets with a paper clip, but do not staple them. Do not include any visual elements on the pages as decoration or as a way to market the manuscript. If you are including photographs or illustrations of some kind, be sure you have guidelines from the publisher to find out how they prefer those materials submitted.

In the upper left corner of your first page, include a heading, single spaced, that states your name on the top line. If you are using a pen name, include your real name in parentheses after the pseudonym. On the second line, give your street address. On the third line, give your city, state, and zip code. You may include your phone number on a fourth line if you wish. Some authors include e-mail and fax addresses as well. In the upper right corner of your first page, include a word count, even if approximate.

Double space and then center the title of your work. Double space again and begin the text itself. On successive pages, in the upper right corner, include your name and the page number, so if the pages get out of order, the editor is able to reassemble them.

Script Format

A play in a literature book is presented in a form that is designed to help the reader. The character names are placed beside the text on the left margin and separated from the text by a colon. A play script prepared for submission has a different format, and adherence to standardized form will at least be partial insurance that your play will not end up in the trash bin before anyone has a chance to read the title page. There are a few guidelines that you will want to follow as you put together your final copy:

Typing Guidelines

1. Leave a gutter (approximately 1.5") on the left side of the page to compensate for binding.
2. Center names (about 2.5" from left margin, 4" from left side of the page).
3. Opening stage directions begin at the center and continue to the right margin.
4. Character directions go under the character's name and are left of center (approximately 1.25" from left margin, 2.75" from left side of the page).
5. Single space text, but double space between character speeches and general stage directions.*

If you are using a word processor, 1.5 spaces between lines is considered acceptable in most cases and will perhaps eventually become the standard.

Manuscript Guidelines

1. Enclose your manuscript in a three-hole folder or soft notebook (avoid bulk).
2. Include a title page which includes the title of your work (in caps), the number of acts in your play, and your name in the middle of the page. At the bottom left of the page indicate copyright information if you have secured a copyright for your play. Some experts advise against this, because you don't want your script dated. Place your name, address, and telephone number at the bottom right of the page.
3. Insert your character list after the title page.
4. Include a setting and time page after the character list. On this page, briefly describe the time and place of the play.
5. The next page begins the text of the play.
6. Begin a new page for each new act or scene.
7. Indicate page numbers in the upper right-hand corner of the page. The act should be designated by a Roman numeral; the scenes and pages are designated by Arabic numerals. Thus, page 7 of scene 3 of act 2 would look like this: II-3-7.

These basic manuscript guidelines seem overly formal, but manuscripts are standardized so that agents and directors can more accurately calculate the length of the play. If the dialogue is spaced at 1.5, the play will run at about one minute per page. This is also helpful for the playwright. An act that is seventy pages long should probably be subdivided. Structure helps you make decisions about your content here.

No matter what genre you want to publish, keep copies of everything you submit—never send your only copy. While it is rare, it does sometimes happen that the postal service, a delivery service, or the publishing company might lose your work. Having a ready copy to send again once you have discovered by checking with the publisher that this has happened can expedite their being able to consider your story.

Some authors worry that someone is going to steal their ideas. While this is not likely since you own the rights to a work as soon as you write it, you can get a copyright request form from the Library of Congress in Washington, D.C. Fill out the form and pay the fee if you are worried about someone stealing your idea.

On the top of your manuscript, enclose a **cover letter**. The cover letter should be very simple, for record-keeping and routing purposes mostly; include all of the information about your address and phone, and then briefly state what you are sending and why. If the editor to whom you are sending the manuscript has asked you to send it, then state that clearly, indicating the date of the letter from the editor or your conversation. Include a SASE large enough to handle a return of the manuscript.

You will need to indicate if this is a **multiple submission**, which means that you are sending the same work to more than this publisher at the same time. Some publishers do not mind whether a submission is going to other companies or magazines, but some publishers will not accept multiple submissions; again, you will need to check their Author Guidelines or any other information you find about their submission policies in order to find out their preference. Writers sometimes prefer to send out a manuscript to two or three potential publishers in order to more quickly get a sense of the work's potential.

Keep track of what works you have sent to what publishers, and when you sent them. And then be patient. The response time for an editor to let you know whether they will publish your manuscript varies from six weeks to six months or more.

You can begin to contact the publisher if you have not heard anything from them within the indicated response time. Send a simple letter in which you state when you sent your work, the title and type of work it is, and whom you sent it to and why. Say that you have not heard a response to your work, and that you are including another SASE. Sign off by saying that you are looking forward to hearing from the editor or publisher.

A standard **rejection letter**, a form letter or card prepared by the publisher, will simply state that at this time the publisher is not interested in accepting your work, and thank you for your submission. If your manuscript has received more serious consideration you might receive a letter from an editor, including more specific information for you about why she did not feel your work was what they are looking for. Keep all the publisher information, copies of your work, and letters you receive on file, so that you can continue submitting your writing and refine the process as you go.

NEGOTIATING WITH YOUR PUBLISHER

It is possible, of course, that you will not receive a rejection letter, but an acceptance! The editor will write and say that your manuscript has been accepted, and propose the terms under which the publisher wishes to purchase the right to print and distribute the work.

Before you actually sign the contract, be sure you understand the terms in it; you may have a lawyer look at it with you so that you understand it fully, and you can also ask your editor about things which are unclear or you want more information about. As we stated earlier, copyright law states that once you have written something, you own the copyright to it, so sending it out with your name on it ensures that you are in fact the owner of the rights to that work. But there are a number of restrictions and factors which impact who owns copyrights once a work has been published, and you will need to research this information in order to retain the kind of reprint rights you want.

You will want to keep careful records of your business dealings as a writer. First, keep all of your receipts for tax purposes. You will also want to make notes of every expense you incur because of your writing, including keeping a record of all of the long distance phone calls and postage expense, whether with the Post Office or a private company.

You will also, hopefully, need to record how much you get paid for your writing. Keep records of what you sent and what you were paid for it and when; also, keep check stubs which will verify your income. All of this information is necessary if you make over a certain amount of money from your writing, for that income will be taxed.

CONTINUING THE JOURNEY

All of the above information can help you with the specifics of publishing and working with submitting your manuscripts. But the larger issue is still what you want your writing to be. Think about what you want to acheive or explore in your writing, and stay focused on your goals for your writing, even if your goals for your writing may seem small. It is not what you *publish* so much as what you *write* that matters; Gauguin said, "The work of a man is the explanation of that man."

So, what is your work? Annie Dillard recounts in her essay "Write Till You Drop" that after Michaelangelo died, a note to his apprentice was discovered among his work, which said, "Draw, Antonio, draw, Antonio, and do not waste time." It may take time to discover what it is you want to draw, to write, to explore, to discover, but as you progress along that journey, remember that all the time, you are writing—in your head, in your heart. Keep writing. No matter what happens—if you have to quit school for a while, or quit work for a while, or quit a relationship for a while, do not stop writing. Even if you have to quit writing for a *while*, keep writing. Your writing is your story of who you are and what matters, to you and to your reader, and it is worth working on. Stay the course. And you will discover, as you go, that the writing is its own best reward, its own reason for going on, your best secret, your private record, your life.

May your work as a writer be filled with the joy of discovery, of experiencing your own work and that of other writers, sometimes in laughter, sometimes through tears, and may it be, above all, *yours*.

Writing on Your Own

Pick a piece of writing you have worked on, revised, cleaned up, and have made as good as it can be for now. Go through the steps outlined in this chapter for finding an appropriate publisher for your work, and mail it off.

Appendix

Writing Every Day:
365 Journal Prompts

1 What are your writing goals for the year?

2 What would your life be like if you were always hungry?

3 Create a character who never goes outside.

4 If you were to equate yourself with a flower, what flower best describes you? Why?

5 Write a letter to someone you went to elementary school with.

6 Write a poem using only words you see on road signs.

7 Think of a smell that evokes a memory.

8 Listen to instrumental music and write what the music tells you.

9 Describe the place you would like to live.

10 Describe a place you felt safe as a child.

11 What is hanging at the back of your closet?

12 Find a dark place and describe it.

13 Tell a joke.

14 Write about gambling.

15 Write about halves and wholes.

16 If you could tell someone something you have always wanted to say, what would you say and to whom would you say it?

17 Find someone to listen to (not to talk to), then write about it.

18 When you were little, what did you want to be when you grew up?

19 What's the hardest thing about writing?

20 Have you ever really enjoyed doing something bad? What was it?

21 Go somewhere and watch people eat. Write about eating.

22 Describe what it's like to be really, really, cold.

23 Say goodbye to someone you never got to say goodbye to.

24 What do you want?

25 Who is the most interesting person you have ever met?

26 Write about a time when you were really honest.

27 Tell a lie.

28 Write dialogue between you and someone you love.

29 What is the worst physical pain you have ever experienced?

30 Make a list of character names.

31 Don't write today—draw a picture instead.

32 Write about the sky.

33 Write about movement.

34 Tell a children's story.

35 What is it like to be old?

36 Write about fire.

37 What was your first real disappointment?

38 How far away is it?

39 If you were only allowed to speak once in your life, what would you say?

40 If you had an unlimited supply of money, what would you do with your life?

41 Go shoe shopping and try on all different kinds of shoes. Write about the way different shoes looked on you.

42 Have you ever been someplace where you really didn't think you belonged?

43 Write about the same outside scene at different times of the day.

44 Buy a box of Valentine heart candy and write what is on your heart.

45 Love someone on paper.

46 Write about your spiritual side.

47 Look under all of the furniture at your house. Gather everything you find and write about those things.

48 What was it like when you sold or gave away something you loved?

49 What was your favorite toy as a child?

50 What is it like to be embarrassed by someone?

51 Write the unspeakable.

52 Write about your obsessions and compulsions.

53 Write about a day in your life but place yourself in a different historical time period.

54 What is your first memory as a child?

55 Locate a collection or series of poems. Write down the first line of each and make a new poem.

56 Write about childhood smells

57 Write about a small town.

58 Write about leaving.

59 You are eighty-eight years old. What has happened in your lifetime?

60 Take the day off from writing.

61 What would you put on your tombstone?

62 Write about the most unusual member of your family.

63 Write about a time you were lonely.

64 Write a song and sing it.

65 Write about the smell of someone you love.

66 When was the first time you knew you were growing up?

67 Imagine that someone told you that you had no talent as a writer. Write about it.

68 Describe your encounter with the perfect stranger.

69 Write a fairy tale.

70 Write twenty fortunes to be placed in fortune cookies.

71 Tell a secret.

72 Write something that scares you.

73 Write about something artificial.

74 Write twenty first lines of stories or dialogue.

75 Take one of the lines from journal prompt 74 and complete the thought you started.

76 Write five ideas for scenes involving conflict between men and women.

77 Write about one color.

78 Write a poem or story called "How to Be a Writer."

79 Write about your writing tools.

80 If a movie were made of your life, who would play the lead and why?

81   Write about imprisonment.

82   Write in imitation of another writer's style.

83   Write some gossip.

84   Write about bubbles.

85   Gather three one dollar bills and describe each one separately.

86   Describe mannerisms in others that you find irritating.

87   Plant a seed and describe the process.

88   Write about the smell of an unfamiliar place.

89   Write what it feels like to be lovely.

90   Try to remember a dream you had recently and record it as vividly as you can.

91   If aliens exist, what do they look like?

92   Be playful with your writing today.

93   Describe the most beautiful part of a human body.

94   Write a poem about a kitchen utensil.

95   If you could ask one person in history for advice, who would it be and what would you ask?

96   Finish this thought: "It was a dark and stormy night. . . ."

97   What kind of clothes define you?

98   Create the complete wardrobe for a character from one of your stories or dramas.

99   Write the opening visual directions for a film.

100 Write about fragments.

101 Feel four different fabrics and describe their textures.

102 Describe the most impulsive thing you have ever done.

103 Someone is looking in your window. What does he or she look like behind the glass? Describe him or her.

104 Write a poem about the produce section of your grocery store.

105 What is the closest you have ever come to dying?

106 Write a poem to the IRS and mail it in with your taxes.

107 What places make you uncomfortable?

108 Write about what is in your garbage (or someone else's if you can).

109 Write about something you have lost.

110 Describe three different kinds of trees.

111 You are on an exploratory mission to another planet. Describe the planet to the mother ship.

112 You are a big-rig truck driver. Using stream-of-consciousness point of view, tell about a night of driving.

113 What are your greatest strengths as a writer?

114 Write about light.

115 Create dialogue that might occur on a school bus.

116 Do you believe there is life on other planets?

117 Write about your hometown's downtown.

118 What are your prejudices?

119 Go to a flea market, swap meet, or garage sale and make a list of the things you see that you would put in a character's house or yard.

120 Now write a character description of the character you have created from choosing his or her belongings.

121 Look at a state or U.S. map. Write down the ten most interesting town or city names that you see. Describe one of the towns.

122 Describe the changing of the seasons.

123 What is the point of no return? Describe it.

124 Describe what you admire most in the human spirit.

125 Describe what about human beings you find flawed or disappointing.

126 What happens to you after you die? Describe it.

127 Go to a neighborhood that is unfamiliar to you. Without judging anyone or anything, describe the neighborhood and the people who live there.

128 Visit a nursing home and write about it.

129 Visit a nursing home and get one of the residents to tell you his or her story.

130 Describe how the climate or weather in a particular area determines the characteristics of the people who live there.

131 Go through a family member's closet or junk room or drawer and write about the surprises you find there.

132 Describe the sound of your own voice.

133 Use water as a symbol in five different ways.

134 Create different views of the sky by using different colors to describe it.

135 Describe the sounds that terrify or trouble you.

136 Explain how much of a person's personality is determined by genetics and how much is determined by environment.

137 Assuming that the majority of a person's personality is a result of his heredity, create a character's heredity and describe how it would determine that character's personality.

138 Assuming that the majority of a person's personality is a result of his environment, create a character's environment and describe how it would determine the character's personality.

139 Try to talk someone out of something.

140 Write dialogue for someone who is drunk.

141 Describe a gospel revival.

142 Describe a funeral from the point of view of the dead person.

143 Describe a birth from the point of view of the baby.

144 Write about something that is round.

145 You are a radio sportscaster. Relay the action at some type of sporting event.

146 Describe something and distort the physical details.

147-151 Look at a newspaper and write down five headlines without reading the articles that follow them. For the next five days, use those headlines as journal prompts, writing about anything those headlines suggest.

152 Describe a naked human body in detail.

153 What if your furniture became completely fed up with serving your needs and confronted you? Write down what each piece would have to say.

154 Describe a memory associated with the smell of vanilla.

155 Write a list of words, all associated with one another and moving sequentially from A to Z.

156 Write about addiction.

157 Write down the first thing you think about when you hear the word *flat*. Fill a page.

158 Write a passage that imitates the style of any writer with an extreme style.

159 Look around the room you are in and describe what you see. Then turn that into a poem.

160 Look at something that has texture. Then look and see if you can find some interesting formations (a face, an animal). Write about what you see.

161 Write a poem which imitates the style of Dr. Seuss.

162 What were you doing ten years ago today?

163 Describe a day in the life of a department store Santa.

164 Write about a reunion.

165 Describe your favorite pajamas.

166 Describe the inside of your car, thinking of it as it is at this moment.

167 What are the sounds of the night? Describe them.

168 Pick a book at random and open to any page. Select a sentence to use as an opening or closing line, and then write.

169 What senses predominate when you encounter external stimuli?

170 You are absent one foot. Describe how you move.

171 Find duality in any five things.

172 Write down a line from a song and write about wherever it takes you.

173 Find something good in your worst experience and write about it.

174 If you were invisible, where would you go? What would you do?

175 Describe what would be the worst way to die.

176 If you could go to one specific point in time in the past, where would you go? Why?

177 Write about your morning routine.

178 How would being deaf or blind affect how you wrote?

179 You are locked in a vault with dead bodies. Record your impressions.

180 Imagine yourself as a dragon. What do you do? How do you feel?

181 What was the best lie you ever told?

182 Imagine that you are deaf and mute. Describe how you would tell someone how you feel.

183 Write a poem as soon as you wake up in the morning.

184 Write down ten reasons not to be a writer.

185 List five oxymorons and choose one to write about.

186 If you were a building, what kind of building would you be? Describe yourself.

187 If you could change your nationality or ethnic background, what would you be and why?

188 What do you believe in?

189 What is the difference between hot and cold?

190 Who is the most important person in human history (excluding religious figures)?

191 Why do we use black ink on white paper rather than white ink on black paper?

192 Who are you?

193 Create a character by listing the CDs, records, or tapes he owns.

194 If you could eliminate one thing from your life, what would it be?

195 Describe a grandfather.

196 Describe a kind act you have performed.

197 Describe the perfect meal.

198 What are the coolest shoes you have ever owned? Describe them.

199 What is more important, honesty or kindness? Explain.

200 If being a vampire were an option, would you become one? Why or why not? Explain.

201 What are the three most important things in human civilization?

202 What is the most important film in history? Why?

203 There is a plot to take over the world. Who is behind it and why?

204 If you could dedicate your life to any one of the seven deadly sins, which one would it be and why?

205 If you and your family were starving, would you make money off of the suffering of others if you had the opportunity? Why or why not?

206 Create a character by equating him or her with a flavor of ice cream.

207 If you could instantly learn another language, what would it be and why?

208 Write a short short story that has an ax and a feather in it.

209 Write a paragraph that uses wind to create setting.

210 What is the most important book in history? Why?

211 What does the word "creative" mean to you?

212 Describe the progression of a storm from its beginning to its end.

213 Write a poem of approximately ten lines with no fewer than ten "p" sounds.

214 Write a poem of approximately ten lines with no fewer than ten "m" sounds.

215 Do something today you have never done before.

216 Name the most gentle animal you know and equate it with the most gentle person you know.

217 Describe a scene that takes place under a house.

218 Describe the life of the mites that live in your carpet.

219 What is more important, justice or mercy? Explain.

220 Memorize and recite a poem.

221 Finish this thought: In spring, I . . .

222 Write from the point of view of a character who is senile.

223 Write about gestures.

224 Write about squares.

225 Which came first, the chicken or the egg?

226 What do you need?

227 If you could change your face, would you? Describe what it would be.

228 Finish this thought: If only . . .

229 Whom would you most want to be trapped in an elevator with? Explain.

230 Whom would you least want to be trapped in an elevator with? Explain.

231 Clap out a beat, then write a poem to that beat.

232 Finish this thought: When he heard the door shut behind him . . .

233 What do you think of when you think of the word "housewife"?

234 List ten reasons to be a writer.

235 Write about divorce.

236 What is more important — structure or content?

237 Can you escape your personality when you write? Explain.

238 Take a bath and write about it.

239 What goes on at the zoo after everyone leaves?

240 Describe the forces that undermine your writing

241 Write with affection about a despicable character.

242 Write a poem of four to ten lines using only internal rhyme.

243 Write your own obituary.

244 What do you want your children to remember most about you?

245 Write graffiti on paper.

246 Write about eggs in all forms.

247 Write a love letter to yourself.

248 What do you regret most about high school?

249 Write about initiation.

250 Describe something by using personification.

251 Write about going barefoot.

252 Finish this thought: The glow of the television screen illuminated . . .

253 Describe your best holiday ever.

254 Who is the most famous person you have met, and how did you meet him or her?

255 Describe your first kiss.

256 Describe your worst holiday ever.

257 Define nausea.

258 How did your grandparents meet? Tell the story, even if you don't know it.

259 Describe your childhood home.

260 Is it better to be single or married? Explain.

261 Explore the difference between men and women.

262 Write a poem of approximately ten lines. Then consult a thesaurus and change at least five words.

263 Describe your favorite season and its colors.

264 Write about a time you were surprised.

265 Is it better to be too hot or too cold? Why? Explain.

266 Write a four- to ten-line poem and rhyme every fourth word.

267 Is art ever bad?

268 Has writing ever destroyed a relationship of yours? Could it?

269 Place yourself at a corner or end of a street and describe the scene from your stationary point of view.

270 Now describe the same scene as if you were moving through it.

271 Write about numbers.

272 Should poems be punctuated? Why or why not?

273 Write something with dogs in it.

274 Write a ballad about a historical figure.

275 Finish this thought: She stood in the men's bathroom and wondered . . .

276 Write about a time you knew you were really in trouble.

277 Describe the view of the ocean from a ship out at sea.

278 Write a scene or short story that ends with something breaking.

279 Do you crave or fear solitude? Explain.

280 Create a character who is afraid to be alone.

281 Think of an annoying or irritating sound. Recreate that sound on paper.

282 Describe a crowded, cramped place.

283 Create a character in a scene or story who is an outsider.

284 Record every single thing you see for three minutes.

285 What musical instrument best describes you? Why?

286 Do you watch cartoons? Why or why not?

287 Describe your most important relationship as a mathematical equation.

288 Write about the desert using your five senses.

289 Write about the desert using your sixth sense (intuitive).

290 Write about different fabrics.

291 Describe the mouths of five different people.

292 Write the dialogue for your favorite cartoon.

293 Place a character in a bowling alley and describe the scene.

294 Describe the last time you cried and why.

295 How many hours a week do you watch television? Describe how television influences you.

296 How far is too far?

297 What are the smells of a hospital? Describe them.

298 Describe a scene at a wedding reception.

299 Write a poem containing a paradox.

300 Write a poem that dances.

301 Describe something narrow and something wide.

302 Write about your last bad haircut.

303 Write about the last time you won the game.

304 Your car breaks down in the middle of the night. What do you do? Describe it.

305 Define boredom.

306 Imagine what it would be like to trade places with your pet.

307 Write about free fall.

308 If you got a tattoo, what would you get and where would it be? Describe it.

309 Write the script for a commercial for your favorite product.

310 Describe your first date.

311 Have you ever been in trouble through no fault of your own?

312 Describe the first time you sneaked out of the house.

313 Finish this thought: The last time I . . .

314 Develop an alternative to silverware and describe it.

315 What is a hero? Explain.

316 If you could choose another lifestyle, what would it be and why?

317 Describe a sunset or sunrise.

318 Describe an altered state of mind.

319 Write about going to a fortune teller.

320   Write a short piece about a character who is not human.

321   One day you are thrown into the life of a sitcom family. Tell about your day.

322   What is your favorite junk food? Describe it.

323   You have just arrived from another planet and stop at a convenience store to ask directions. Write the scene.

324   Write a bad country song.

325   You have just won a silver medal at the Olympics. How do you feel?

326   Describe a day in the life of a Playboy centerfold.

327   You are a Greek god. Which one are you and why?

328   What disgusts you? Could you write about it? Try it.

329   Finish this thought: Out of the cave emerged . . .

330   Write your own personal ad.

331   Write about disappearing.

332   Write dialogue between two kids waiting to see the principal.

333   Write the dialogue for a short scene in a B movie.

334   You are the Statue of Liberty. Describe what you see.

335   You are in a foreign country where you don't speak the language. How do you communicate? How do you feel?

336   What's in your medicine cabinet? Describe it and explain what that says about you.

337   Define beauty.

338   What beliefs do you have that might be considered to be unusual? Explain them.

339   Write a story for the *National Enquirer* or *The Star* or another tabloid.

340   Create a fictional town and draw a map for the town.

341   You are a camera recording a bank robbery. What do you see?

342   What was your worst experience in school? Describe it.

343   Describe a priest hearing a boring confession.

344   Write about a time when you have risked something important to you.

345   Describe the items in your refrigerator.

346   Describe a scene using shades of black and white in your description.

347   What would it be like to be the tallest person in the world? Describe it.

348   Write a poem that has a waltz rhythm.

349   Tell the story of a character trapped in a crowd or mob.

350   Write a script for a scene in a TV sitcom.

351   You are trapped in a well. Write about it.

352   Write the story of a woman who decides on her wedding day that she doesn't love her husband.

353   What is the most important thing to write about? Write about it.

354   Is there such a thing as genre, or are such divisions artificial? Explain.

355   Create a character who is immoral.

356   Write a short scene between a nurse in a psychiatric ward and one of her patients.

357   What movies have made you cry? Describe what happened.

358   Write about flannel and silk.

359   What does your psychic advisor tell you about your future?

360   Describe a flower blooming.

361   Have you ever been treated unfairly?

362   Write some garbage.

363   Write your acceptance speech for your Oscar for best screenplay.

364   Write a scene with a character who is totally free, and whose freedom causes a conflict that you explore in the scene.

365   Use jewelry to describe a character.

Write ten journal prompts of your own and keep working!

Selected Bibliography

Cameron, Julia. *A Spiritual Path to Higher Creativity*. New York: Putnam, 1992.

Ciardi, John and Miller Williams. *How Does a Poem Mean?* 2d ed. Boston: Houghton Mifflin, 1975.

Dillard, Annie. *Living By Fiction*. New York: Harper & Row, 1982.

———. *The Writing Life*. New York: HarperPerennial, 1990.

Dramatist's Sourcebook. New York: Theatre Communications Group. Issued yearly.

Elbow, Peter. *Writing Without Teachers*. New York: Oxford UP, 1973.

Forster, E. M. *Aspects of the Novel*. San Diego: Harcourt Brace Jovanovich, 1955.

Frye, Northrop. *Anatomy of Criticism: Four Essays*. Princeton, NJ: Princeton UP, 1957.

Fulton, Len. *The International Directory of Little Magazines and Small Presses*. 27th ed. Paradise, CA: Dustbooks, 1991.

Gardner, John. *On Becoming a Novelist*. New York: Harper & Row, 1983.

Gioia, Dana. *Can Poetry Matter?* St. Paul, MN: Graywolf Press, 1992.

Goldberg, Natalie. *Long Quiet Highway: Waking Up in America*. New York: Bantam, 1993.

———. *Wild Mind: Living the Writer's Life*. New York: Bantam, 1990.

———. *Writing Down the Bones: Freeing the Writer Within*. Boston: Shambhala Publications, 1986.

Herman, Jeff. *Insider's Guide to Book Editors, Publishers, and Literary Agents, 1997–1998*. Rocklin, CA: Prima Publishing, 1997.

Holman, C. Hugh. *A Handbook to Literature*. 4th ed. Indianapolis, IN: Bobbs-Merrill, 1980.

Hugo, Richard. *The Triggering Town: Lectures and Essays on Poetry and Writing.* New York: Norton, 1979.

Lamott, Ann. *Bird by Bird.* New York: Anchor, 1995.

Lane, Eric and Nina Shengold. *Take Ten: New 10-Minute Plays.* New York: Vintage, 1997.

Macauley, Robie and George Lanning. *Technique in Fiction.* New York: Harper & Row, 1964.

Moyers, Bill. *The Language of Life: A Festival of Poets.* Eds. James Haba and David Grubin. New York: Doubleday, 1995.

Plimpton, George, ed. *Poets at Work: The Paris Review Interviews.* New York: Penguin, 1989.

——. *The Writer's Chapbook.* New York: Penguin, 1989.

Professional Playscript Format Guidelines and Sample. New York: Feedback Theatrebooks and Prospero P, n.d.

Ruas, Charles. *Conversations with American Writers.* New York: Knopf, 1985.

Stanzel, F. K. *A Theory of Narrative.* Rev. ed. New York: Cambridge UP, 1987.

Strunk, William, Jr., and E. B. White. *The Elements of Style.* 3rd ed. New York: Macmillan, 1979.

Talese, Gay and Barbara Lounsberry. *Writing Creative Nonfiction: The Literature of Reality.* New York: HarperCollins, 1996.

Terkel, Studs. *American Dreams: Lost & Found.* New York: Ballantine, 1981.

Thomas, James, et al., eds. *Flash Fiction.* New York: Norton, 1992.

Thornley, Wilson R. *Short Story Writing.* New York: Bantam, 1976.

Toscan, Richard. *The Playwriting Seminars.* http://www.vcu.edu/artweb/playwriting.html (10 Nov. 1996).

Trottier, David. *The Screenwriter's Bible.* Anaheim, CA: The Screenwriting Center, 1994.

ACKNOWLEDGMENTS

Still Life is subject to a royalty. It is fully protected under the copyright laws of the United States of America and of all countries covered by the International Copyright Union (including the Dominion of Canada and the rest of the British Commonwealth), the Berne Convention, the Pan-American Copyright Convention, and the Universal Copyright Convention as well as all countries with which the United States has reciprocal copyright relations. All rights, including professional/amateur stage rights, motion picture, recitation, lecturing, public reading, radio broadcasting, television, video or sound recording, all other forms of mechanical or electronic reproduction, such as CD-ROM, CD-I, information storage and retrieval systems and photocopying, and the rights of translation into foreign languages, are strictly reserved. Particular emphasis is laid upon the matter of readings, permission for which must be secured from the Author's agent in writing. Inquiries concerning rights should be addressed to: William Morris Agency Inc., 1325 Avenue of the Americas, New York, NY 10019, Attn: George Lane.

Márquez, Gabriel García. "The Woman Who Came at Six O'Clock" from *Innocent Erendira and Other Stories* by Gabriel García Márquez and Gregory Rabassa, translator. English translation © 1978 by Harper & Row, Publishers, Inc. Reprinted by permission of HarperCollins Publishers, Inc.

Mason, Bobbie Ann. "Shiloh" from *Shiloh and Other Stories* by Bobbie Ann Mason. Copyright © 1982 by Bobbie Ann Mason. Reprinted by permission of HarperCollins Publishers, Inc.

McGaughey, Carla L. Student selections. Reprinted by permission.

McNally, Terrence. *Andre's Mother*. Published by Smith & Kraus. Copyright © 1988 by Terrence McNally. Reprinted by permission of William Morris Agency, Inc. on behalf of the author. All rights reserved. Caution: Professionals and amateurs are hereby warned that *Andre's Mother* is subject to a royalty. It is fully protected under the copyright laws of the United States of America and of all countries covered by the International Copyright Union (including the Dominion of Canada and the rest of the British Commonwealth), the Berne Convention, the Pan-American Copyright Convention, and the Universal Copyright Convention as well as all countries with which the United States has reciprocal copyright relations. All rights, including professional/amateur stage rights, motion picture, recitation, lecturing, public reading, radio broadcasting, television, video or sound recording, all other forms of mechanical or electronic reproduction, such as CD-ROM, CD-I, information storage and retrieval systems and photocopying, and the rights of translation into foreign languages, are strictly reserved. Particular emphasis is laid upon the matter of readings, permission for which must be secured from the Author's agent in writing. Inquiries concerning rights should be addressed to: William Morris Agency Inc., 1325 Avenue of the Americas, New York, NY 10019, Attn: Gilbert Parker.

McPherson, Sandra. "Bad Mother Blues," from *The God of Indeterminacy*. Copyright © 1993 by Sandra McPherson. Used with the permission of the author and the University of Illinois Press.

Millay, Edna St. Vincent. "What Lips My Lips Have Kissed" by Edna St. Vincent Millay. From *Collected Poems*, HarperCollins. Copyright © 1923, 1951 by Edna St. Vincent Millay and Norma Millay Ellis. All rights reserved. Reprinted by permission of Elizabeth Barnett, literary executor.

Moody, Anne. From *Coming of Age in Mississippi* by Anne Moody. Copyright © 1968 by Anen Moody. Used by permission of Doubleday, a division of Bantam Doubleday Dell Publishing Group, Inc.

Morton, Kathryn. "The Story Telling Animal," copyright © Kathryn Morton. First appeared in *The New York Times Review of Books*, Vol. LXXXIX, No. 52, December 23, 1984. Reprinted by permission of the author.

Neruda, Pablo. "I Like for You to Be Still" from *Twenty Love Poems and a Song of Despair* by Pablo Neruda, translated by W.S. Merwin. Translation copyright © 1969 by W.S. Merwin. Used by permission of Viking Penguin, a division of Penguin Books USA Inc.

O'Connor, Flannery. "A Good Man Is Hard to Find" from *A Good Man Is Hard to Find and Other Stories*, copyright 1953 by Flannery O'Connor and renewed 1983 by Regina O'Connor, reprinted by permission of Harcourt Brace & Company.

Owen, Wilfred. "Dulce et Decorum Est," by Wilfred Owen, from *The Collected Poems of Wilfred Owen*. Copyright © 1963 by Chatto and Windus, Ltd. Reprinted by permission of New Directions Publishing Corp. "Strange Meeting," by Wilfred Owen, from *The Collected Poems of Wilfred Owen*. Copyright © 1963 by Chatto & Windus, Ltd. Reprinted by permission of New Directions Publishing Corp.

Piercy, Marge. "The Secretary Chant." From *Circles on the Water* by Marge Piercy. Copyright © 1982 by Marge Piercy. Reprinted by permission of Alfred A. Knopf Inc.

Pinter, Harold. From *The Birthday Party*. Copyright © 1959 by Harold Pinter; copyright renewed © 1987 by Harold Pinter. Used by permission of Grove/Atlantic, Inc.

Pound, Ezra. "In a Station of the Metro" by Ezra Pound, from *Personae*. Copyright © 1926 by Ezra Pound. Reprinted by permission of New Directions Publishing Corp.

Pushkin, Alexander. Excerpt from "Eugene Onegin." From *The Poems, Prose and Plays of Alexander Pushkin* by Alexander Pushkin, edited by Avrahm Yarmolinsky. Copyright © 1936 and renewed 1964 by Random House, Inc. Reprinted by permission of Random House, Inc.

Ramsey, Buck. "Anthem." From *And As I Rode Out on the Morning*. Copyright © 1993 by Buck Ramsey. Reprinted by permission of the author.

Rich, Adrienne. "Ghazals [7/16/68: II], [7/23/68], [7/24/68: II], and [7/26/68: II]," copyright © 1993 by Adrienne Rich. Copyright © 1969 by W. W. Norton & Company, Inc., from *Collected Early Poems: 1950–1970* by Adrienne Rich. Reprinted by permission of W. W. Norton & Company, Inc.

Robinson, Edwin Arlington. "Richard Cory." Reprinted with the permission of Scribner, a Division of Simon & Schuster from *Children of the Night* by Edwin Arlington Robinson (New York: Scribner, 1897).

Roethke, Theodore. "My Papa's Waltz," copyright © 1942 by Heart Magazines, Inc. from *The Collected Poems of Theodore Roethke* by Theodore Roethke. Used by permission of Doubleday, a division of Bantam Doubleday Dell Publishing Group, Inc.

Rollin, Betty. "The Best Years of My Life," *New York Times Magazine*, April 6, 1980. Copyright © 1980 by Betty Rollin. Reprinted by permission of William Morris Agency, Inc. on behalf of the author.

Ross, Dorien. "Seeking Home," from *Tikkun*, May/June, 1990. Reprinted with permission.

Sandburg, Carl. "Fog" from *Chicago Poems* by Carl Sandburg, copyright 1916 by Holt, Rinehart and Winston, Inc. and renewed 1944 by Carl Sandburg, reprinted by permission of Harcourt Brace & Company.

Sassoon, Siegfried. "Does It Matter," copyright 1918 by E. P. Dutton, copyright renewed 1946 by Siegfried Sassoon, from *Collected Poems of Siegfried Sassoon* by Siegfried Sassoon. Used by permission of Viking Penguin, a division of Penguin Books USA Inc. and George Sassoon.

Seuss, Dr. "The Fuddnuddlers." From *Oh Say, Can You Say?* by Dr. Seuss. TM and Copyright © 1979 by Dr. Seuss Enterprises, L.P. Reprinted by permission of Random House, Inc.

Shakespeare, William. Excerpts from *The Taming of the Shrew*. From *The Complete Works of Shakespeare, 4th edition*, edited by David Bevington. Copyright © 1992 by HarperCollins College Publishers. Reprinted with permission.

Shepard, Sam. From *Suicide in B*^{b}, copyright © 1978, 1979 by Sam Shepard. From *Fool For Love and Other Plays* by Sam Shepard. Used by permission of Bantam Books, a division of Bantam Doubleday Dell Publishing Group, Inc.

Sirowitz, Hal. Excerpt from "Broken Glass." From *Mother Said* by Hal Sirowitz. Copyright © 1996 by Hal Sirowitz. Reprinted by permission of Crown Publishers, Inc.

Smith, Stevie. "Mother, Among the Dustbins" by Stevie Smith, from *Collected Poems of Stevie Smith*. Copyright © 1972 by Stevie Smith. Reprinted by permission of New Directions Publishing Corp.

Soyinka, Wole. "Black Singer" from *Idanre and Other Poems* by Wole Soyinka. Copyright © 1967 by Wole Soyinka. Reprinted by permission of Hill & Wang, a division of Farrar, Straus & Giroux, Inc.

Stafford, William. "A Way of Writing," originally appeared in *Field #2*, Spring 1970. Copyright OC Press. Reprinted by permission.

Szymborska, Wislawa. "Some Like Poetry," translated, from the Polish, by Joanna Trzeciak. Originally published in *The New Yorker*, October 21 & 28, 1996. Copyright © 1996 Wislawa Szymborska. All rights reserved. Reprinted by permission.

Tan, Amy. "Two Kinds," reprinted by permission of The Putnam Publishing Group, Inc. from *The Joy Luck Club* by Amy Tan. Copyright © 1989 by Amy Tan.

Terkel, Studs. "Interview with Rafael Rosa," as it appeared in *American Dreams: Lost and Found*. New York: Ballantine Books, 1980. 138–140.

Thomas, Dylan. "Do Not Go Gentle into That Good Night" by Dylan Thomas, from *The Poems of Dylan Thomas*. Copyright © 1952 by Dylan Thomas. Reprinted by permission of New Directions Publishing Corp. and David Higham Associates Ltd.

Wakoski, Diane. "Sestina from the Home Gardener." Copyright © 1988 by Diane Wakoski. Reprinted from *Emerald Ice: Selected Poems 1962–1987* with the permission of Black Sparrow Press.

Williams, Tennessee. Excerpt from Part Two of *The Glass Menagerie* by Tennessee Williams. Copyright © 1945 by Tennessee Williams and Edwina D. Williams. Copyright renewed 1973 by Tennessee Williams. Reprinted by permission of Random House, Inc.

Williams, William Carlos. "The Dance" by William Carlos Williams, from *Collected Poems: 1939–1962, Volume II*. Copyright © 1944 by William Carlos Williams. Reprinted by permission of New Directions Publishing Corp. "This Is Just to Say" by William Carlos Williams, from *Collected Poems: 1909–1939, Volume 1*. Copyright © 1938 by New Directions Publishing Corp. Reprinted by permission of New Directions Publishing Corp.

Yamada, Mitsuye. "To The Lady." From *Camp Notes and Other Poems*. Copyright © 1976, 1980, 1986, 1992 by Mitsuye Yamada. Reprinted by permission of the author.

Yeats, W. B. "Leda and the Swan." Reprinted with the permission of Simon & Schuster from *The Collected Works of W. B. Yeats, Volume 1: The Poems*, revised and edited by Richard J. Finneran. Copyright © 1928 by Macmillan Publishing Company; copyright renewed © 1956 by Georgie Yeats.

Photo Credits
Page 19T: © Christopher Little
Page 19B: © 1997 Rick Patrick
Page 71: © Kunsthistorisches Museum, Vienna

Glossary and Index of Terms

accentual-syllabic verse (p. 107) Verse which is measured by the number and pattern of stressed and unstressed syllables as well as the number of syllables in each line.

act (p. 336) One complete section of a play, possibly containing several scenes.

alliteration (p. 95) The repetition of the initial consonant sound in two or more words in a line or phrase.

allusion (p. 74) A reference to another work of art, music, history, or literature.

alternating method (p. 175) Changing methods of narration within a work.

amphibrachic foot (p. 108) An unaccented syllable followed by an accented syllable followed by an unaccented syllable (⏑ ′ ⏑). (See *meter*)

anapestic foot (p. 108) Two unaccented syllables followed by an accented syllable (⏑ ⏑ ′). (See *meter*)

anaphora (p. 107) The repetition of the initial word or series of words in consecutive lines.

antagonist (p. 211) A character or force that opposes the central character in a narrative or drama.

apostrophe (p. 81) The direct address of someone or something clearly not present.

arena stage (p. 362) Sometimes called theater in the round; the audience surrounds the stage.

ascend (p. 97) To move from low, rich-sounding *o*'s and *u*'s to short *i*'s and long *e*'s.

aside (p. 346) A comment made directly to the audience in a play.

assonance (p. 97) The repetition of similar vowel sounds; the repetition of similar or identical vowel sounds in stressed syllables in which the consonants change.

author guidelines (p. 413) Pages which outline what a publishing company expects, in terms of a work's subject and manuscript form.

autobiography (p. 165) A story of an individual's entire life's experiences.

ballad (p. 139) A narrative poem consisting of a number of four-line stanzas rhyming *abcb*.

beat (p. 351) One small unit of action or thought in a play.

beginning rhyme (p. 100) Rhyme which occurs in the first syllable or syllables of two or more lines of poetry.

blank verse (p. 129) Unrhymed iambic pentameter.

cadence (p. 106) The natural sound pattern created by the spoken word.

caesura (p. 115) A mark of punctuation or pause that comes within the line itself.

characters (p. 190) The people whose story you tell.

chorus (p. 344) In Greek drama, a group of characters who commented on the play as a narrator would.

cinquain (p. 113) A five-line stanza. (See *stanza*)

cliches (p. 83) Overused figurative language.

climax (p. 212, 338) The point of greatest tension in a narrative or drama.

conceit (p. 80) An elaborate metaphor or comparison used throughout a poem.

conflict (p. 196) Some sort of problem to be worked out, or tension to resolve, facing the main character and coming from some external or internal source.

consonance (p. 101) Repetition of consonant sounds.

conventional symbol (p. 83) A symbol that has one universal interpretation.

couplet (p. 113) A two-line stanza. (See *stanza*)

cover letter (p. 416) A letter included with a manuscript submitted to a publisher giving the writer's personal information and stating the purpose for sending the manuscript.

dactylic foot (p. 108) An accented syllable followed by two unaccented syllables (′ ◡ ◡). (See *meter*)

denouement (p. 213) The part of a story in which the conflicts come to their conclusion or are summed up, explained, resolved.

descend (p. 97) To move from short *i*'s and long *e*'s to low, rich sounding *o*'s and *u*'s.

dialogue (p. 83) Speech that occurs between two or more characters on stage.

diction (p. 66) Word choice.

dimeter (p. 111) A line of verse with two feet. (See *scansion*)

dissonance (p. 95) Harsh sounds.

downstage (p. 366) The part of the stage closest to the audience.

dramatic irony (p. 337) When the audience or reader knows something that the character does not.

dramatic unity (p. 218) A unity of purpose in the details and theme of the story.

end rhyme (p. 98) A rhyme occuring in the last word or words in two or more lines of poetry.

end-stopped line (p. 115) A line of poetry that stops or pauses due to punctuation or the completion of a thought.

English sonnet (also known as *Shakespearean sonnet*) (p. 135) A sonnet consisting of three quatrains and a concluding couplet, the couplet summing up the poem, or providing surprise or irony. The rhythm is iambic pentameter, and the rhyme scheme is *abab cdcd efef gg.*

enjambment (p. 115) A line of poetry which continues into the next line in thought and/or structure.

entry letter (p. 413) A brief letter from a writer to a publisher introducing the writer and stating an interest in finding out more about the publisher and author guidelines.

exposition (p. 327) The part of a narrative or drama that reveals pertinent background information.

eye rhyme (p. 100) Words that appear to rhyme on paper, but do not when read aloud.

falling action (p. 212) Everything that happens as a result of a decision or realization or turning point in a story.

feminine rhyme (p. 101) The rhyming of two words which end in unstressed syllables.

fiction (p. 189) Writing invented by the imagination.

first person (p. 226) That point of view in which the narrator is one of the characters in the story and tells the story as that character, using the pronouns *I* or *we*.

flashback (p. 177) The technique of moving back in time in a narrative or drama.

flat characters (p. 215) Characters in a narrative or drama who are not fully developed.

foot (p. 108) The unit of measure in accentual-syllabic or quantitative verse. The units are various combinations of stressed and unstressed syllables. The most common feet in the English language are as follows:

iambic foot (◡ ′)
trochaic foot (′ ◡)
anapestic foot (◡ ◡ ′)
dactylic foot (′ ◡ ◡)
spondaic foot (′ ′)
pyrrhic foot (◡ ◡)

foreshadowing (p. 215, 337) Hinting at events that are to take place in future scenes.

free verse (p. 106, 121) An open form of poetry using patterns such as line patterns, stanza patterns, or even patterns of images, but not measured in metrical feet or syllables.

ghazal (p. 158) Poem with five to fifteen couplets which are not necessarily associated with each other.

haiku (p. 123) A three-line, seventeen-syllable poem.

heptameter (p. 111) A line of verse with seven feet. (See *meter*)

hexameter (p. 111) A line of verse with six feet. (See *meter*)

iambic foot (p. 108) One unaccented syllable followed by an accented syllable (◡ ′). (See *meter*)

iambic pentameter (p. 109) A line of poetry containing five iambic feet. (See *meter*)

imagery (p. 67) Word pictures relating sensory details.

inciting incident (p. 332) The action causing the drama or conflict to occur; sometimes happens before the drama begins.

internal rhyme (p. 100) Rhyme that occurs within a line or lines.

Italian sonnet (also known as *Petrarchan sonnet*) (p. 135) Sonnet consisting of two stanzas, an octave, which introduces a problem or situation, and a sestet, which completes the thought or answers the problem introduced in the octave.

linked poetry (p. 122) A poetic form composed by several different people.

literary symbol (p. 84) Symbols used in literary works; there exist in these symbols the possibility of multiple interpretations.

masculine rhyme (p. 101) The rhyme of single stressed syllables in two or more lines of poetry.

memoir (p. 165) A story form of the literary essay focusing on just a part of a life, perhaps specific to a particular occurrence in that person's life.

metaphor (p. 76) An implied comparison between two ideas or things.

meter (p. 107) An established pattern of rhythm in a poem; the most common meter used in English poetry is accentual-syllabic and is measured by the type and number of metrical feet in a line of poetry. The most common feet in English verse are as follows:

iambic foot (◡ ′)
trochaic foot (′ ◡)
anapestic foot (◡ ◡ ′)
dactylic foot (′ ◡ ◡)
spondaic foot (′ ′)
pyrrhic foot (◡ ◡)

The standard lines of poetry are as follows:

monometer: one foot
dimeter: two feet
trimeter: three feet
tetrameter: four feet
pentameter: five feet
hexameter: six feet (also called *Alexadrine*)
heptameter: seven feet
octameter: eight feet

metonymy (p. 80) Metaphorical language in which something *related* to the thing being named is used instead of the thing itself.

mimesis (p. 94) The phenomenon of words suggesting their meanings by the sounds they make.

monologue (p. 344) A long speech delivered without interruption.

monosyllabic foot (p. 109) An extra stressed syllable in a line of poetry, possibly called an imperfect foot, though an imperfect foot could be accented or unaccented.

multiple submission (p. 416) A marketing strategy in which the writer sends a manuscript out to more than one publisher at a time.

narration (p. 189) Fiction or nonfiction which relates a series of events, not necessarily in chronological order.

narrator The person, voice, or persona relating the story; the "voice" the reader hears.

nonfiction (p. 162) Any writing which deals with subjects not invented or imagined by the author, but rather based in or commenting upon the world of events, experiences, and facts.

objective point of view (p. 231) That narrative point of view exemplified by "the fly on the wall," in which the narrator notes what he sees and hears, without intrusion or interpretation.

octameter (p. 111) A line of verse with eight feet. (See *meter*)

octave (p. 113) An eight-line stanza. (See *stanza*)

omniscient point of view (p. 235) That narrative point of view in which the narrator of the story has access to and uses any information, past or present, stated or silent, enacted or thought, relative to any character in the story.

one-act play (p. 336) A short play of anywhere from ten to forty minutes.

onomatopoeia (p. 94) The creation of words that imitate their meaning by the sounds they make.

open stage (p. 362) Sometimes called **end stage**; a proscenium stage without the frame, border, or wings.

parody (p. 141) A satirical or humorous imitation of another work, usually a song or poem.

pentameter (p. 111) A line of verse with five feet. (See *meter*)

personal symbol (p. 84) Those things which mean much to an individual because of the meaning associated with them, but having no similar meaning to others.

personification (p. 82) Attribution of one or more human qualities to inanimate objects.

Petrachan sonnet (p. 135) See *Italian sonnet*.

plot (p. 202, 210) The series of events in the story which serve to move the story from its beginning through its climax or turning point and to the resolution of its conflicts, influenced by the causality of the events and the characters' motives and decisions.

point of view (p. 224) The narrator and vantage point which the author uses to tell the story to the reader.

proscenium stage (p. 362) A box set in which the audience observes the action from the imaginary fourth wall.

protagonist (p. 211) The central character in a narrative or drama.

pyrrhic foot (p. 109) Two unaccented syllables ($\cup\cup$). (See *meter*)

quatrain (p. 113) A four-line stanza. (See *stanza*)

query letter (p. 413) A letter presenting a proposal about a work the writer is interested in sending to the publisher.

renga (p. 122) A form of linked poetry composed by several different people, used historically as a court distraction among the elite or as a drinking game among the commoners.

resolution (p. 213) The part of the story in which the writer sums up or explains the story's conflicts, or brings the conflicts to their conclusion.

rhyme (p. 98) Two or more words with the same sound.

rhythm (p. 106) The movement of sound and silence in a poem.

rising action (p. 212, 336) Every detail or action in a story leading up to the story's turning point.

round characters (p. 215) Characters which are three-dimensional and complex.

royalties (p. 412) The writer's percentage of the book's sales, agreed upon in a contract.

run-on line (p. 115) A line of poetry with no punctuation at the end which urges the reader to move to the next line without pausing. (See *enjambment*)

scansion (p. 108) A way of examining a poem's metrical pattern by marking stressed/unstressed syllables and then counting the number of syllables in a line, looking for a pattern.

scene (p. 336) A part of a drama or story, taking place in a given time and space.

septet (p. 113) A seven-line stanza. (See *stanza*)

sestet (p. 113) A six-line stanza. (See *stanza*)

sestina (p. 131) A poetic form containing six stanzas and an envoy which achieves unity by repeating end words in the lines according to the following order, numbering the last words in each line as follows:

Stanza 1: 123456
Stanza 2: 615243
Stanza 3: 364125
Stanza 4: 532614
Stanza 5: 451362
Stanza 6: 246531

Envoy: Three lines which use all six end words, two per line

setting (p. 205) The place, time, and mood of a story.

Shakespearian sonnet (p. 135) See *English sonnet*.

simile (p. 76) Figurative language which equates two ideas or things through the use of "like" or "as."

slant rhyme (p. 100) Imperfect rhyme, usually achieved by slight alterations of the vowel sounds in two or more words.

slush pile (p. 413) The unread manuscripts which are sent to publishers by aspiring writers.

soliloquy (p. 344) A long speech spoken by a character to himself on stage.

sonnet (p. 135) A poetic form consisting of fourteen lines of rhyming iambic pentameter.

spondaic foot (p. 109) Two accented syllables in a foot, usually occurring when two stressed monosyllabic words are placed together.

stage left (p. 366) The actor's left.

stage right (p. 366) The actor's right.

stanza (p. 113) A certain number of lines grouped together as a unit, usually forming a pattern throughout the poem. The most common stanzaic forms are as follows:

monostich	1 line
couplet	2 lines
tercet	3 lines
quatrain	4 lines
cinquain	5 lines
sixain	6 lines
septet	7 lines
octave	8 lines

stock characters (p. 215) Flat characters so obvious and predictable that their roles and personalities can be seen as cliches.

stream of consciousness (p. 216) In narrative, an attempt to capture *all* of the narrator's thoughts as they occur to him.

subtext (p. 358) What characters don't say as well as what they say; the implications and connotations of words and themes.

symbol (p. 83) A device using a word, image, or detail which suggests something greater than the thing itself and thereby transcends itself. In addition to its function as a concrete object in the poem or story, the symbol also suggests something abstract.

synecdoche (p. 80) A special kind of metaphor in which a writer uses a part of something to stand for the whole of it.

syntax (p. 102) Word order.

tanka (p. 123) A poem consisting of five lines containing a total of thirty-one syllables.

tenor (p. 78) The literal component of the metaphor.

tercet (p. 113) A three-line stanza. (See *stanza*)

tetrameter (p. 111) A line of verse with four feet. (See *meter*)

theme (p. 166) Those ideas, patterns, and issues which a work keeps returning to and re-examining.

third person limited (p. 229) That narrative point of view in which the narrator limits the action and information the reader receives to that which centers on and/or can be known by only one character in the story.

thrust stage (p. 362) A stage surrounded by the audience on three sides.

trimeter (p. 111) A line of verse with three feet. (See *meter*)

triple rhyme (p. 102) Three syllables rhyming with the three in the next line; this technique is usually used with a comic effect.

trochaic foot (p. 108) One accented syllable followed by an unaccented syllable (′ ˘). (See *meter*)

true rhyme (p. 100) Rhyme determined by the correlation of sound in the accented syllables of the words and the syllables which follow them.

unit (p. 351) Each separate subsection or part of the action or plot of a narrative.

unreliable narrator (p. 228) A narrator or point of view which conveys slanted or untrustworthy details or observations in relating the story.

upstage (p. 366) The part of the stage farthest from the audience.

vehicle (p. 78) The figurative component of the metaphor.

verse paragraph (p. 129) Grouped ideas determined by content or thought using punctuation, rhythm, and/or spacing.

villanelle (p. 133) A poem containing five tercets and a quatrain with a rhyme pattern of *aba aba aba aba aba abaa*. Line 1 is repeated in lines 6, 12, and 18, and line 3 is repeated in lines 9, 15, and 19, thus forming a refrain.

voice (p. 183) The personality or the mood of the speaker you hear talking to you as you read a work.

Index of Authors and Titles